XVA Desks – A New Era for Risk Management

Applied Quantitative Finance series

Applied Quantitative Finance is a new series developed to bring readers the very latest market tested tools, techniques and developments in quantitative finance. Written for practitioners who need to understand how things work 'on the floor', the series will deliver the most cutting-edge applications in areas such as asset pricing, risk management and financial derivatives. Although written with practitioners in mind, this series will also appeal to researchers and students who want to see how quantitative finance is applied in practice.

Also available

Chris Kenyon, Roland Stamm
DISCOUNTING, LIBOR, CVA AND FUNDING
Interest Rate and Credit Pricing

Marc Henrard
INTEREST RATE MODELLING IN THE MULTI-CURVE FRAMEWORK
Foundations, Evolution and Implementation

Adil Reghai
QUANTITATIVE FINANCE
Back to Basic Principles

Leo Krippner
ZERO LOWER BOUND TERM STRUCTURE MODELLING
A Practitioner's Guide

XVA Desks – A New Era for Risk Management

Understanding, Building and Managing Counterparty, Funding and Capital Risk

Ignacio Ruiz
Founder and Director, iRuiz Consulting, UK

palgrave
macmillan

First published 2015 by
PALGRAVE MACMILLAN

Palgrave Macmillan in the UK is an imprint of Macmillan Publishers Limited, registered in England, company number 785998, of Houndmills, Basingstoke, Hampshire RG21 6XS.

Palgrave Macmillan in the US is a division of St Martin's Press LLC, 175 Fifth Avenue, New York, NY 10010.

Palgrave Macmillan is the global academic imprint of the above companies and has companies and representatives throughout the world.

Palgrave® and Macmillan® are registered trademarks in the United States, the United Kingdom, Europe and other countries.

ISBN: 978–1–137–44819–4

This book is printed on paper suitable for recycling and made from fully managed and sustained forest sources. Logging, pulping and manufacturing processes are expected to conform to the environmental regulations of the country of origin.

A catalogue record for this book is available from the British Library.

A catalog record for this book is available from the Library of Congress.

To Carmen Macho, for her love, wisdom and never-ending enlightenment, that I will carry with me all my life

Disclaimer

The views and opinions expressed in this book are solely those of the author, and do not necessarily reflect the official policy or position of any of his present or past employers, nor of any of this book's contributors.

Contents

List of Figures

Acknowledgements

The author would like to acknowledge and thank the following people for their contribution to this book, in the form of their insightful conversations, feedback or direct contribution.

Aliki Georgakopoulou Director, Bank of America Merril Lynch.
Chris Morris Director, Credit Suisse.
Ersel Korusoy Director, Royal Bank of Scotland.
John Ovens Managing Director and Head, Resource Management Group, CIBC Wholesale Bank.
Antonio Ruiz Director, Credit Suisse.
Olaf Springer Managing Director, Credit Suisse.
Robert Dargavel Smith Managing Director, Banco Santander.

Part I | The Context

1 The Banking Industry, OTC Derivatives and the New XVA Challenge

Before going into the details of the XVA world, we want to understand where it fits in the whole financial and banking system. In this chapter, we are going to see the basics of how banks work and operate, where the world of derivatives fits in and what is XVA to that world.

Financial institutions are extremely complicated entities these days. Because of that, the overview that is given in this chapter is, purposely, somehow over-simplistic. Otherwise the reader may get lost with details not well understood while missing the broad picture.

1.1 A simple bank's balance sheet

Balance sheets are the accounting tool used to produce a snap shot of a bank's financial position. Let's have a look at them. In order to do this, we are going to build a balance sheet from the ground up. It is going to be a very simplified picture, to ensure that the key points are not missed out.

1.1.1 The banking book

In order to understand how banks operate, let's create a "toy" bank model.

Let's say that a collection of ten investors decide to create a bank from scratch. To do this, each of them provides, say, \$1, and so the starting bank funds are \$10, and ten equal shares are given to those investors. In accounting terms, this translates into the balance sheet of the bank so that it has assets of \$10 (the money given by the investors) and equity of \$10 too (the shares).

As a first line of business, the bank can take deposits from customers and keep their money safe in a vault. It can then provide some useful basic financial services like paying bills directly, debit and credit cards, cheque books, transfer money to another account in another bank on the client's behalf, etc., for which the bank will charge a fee. Let's say that the bank has received another \$15 in deposits. Now the bank's balance sheet has \$25 in assets (the money it has in its vaults), \$15 in money owed to customers (the money deposited by clients), and \$10 in equity.

Now, here comes a second and most important line of business: the bank realises that from the \$15 it has from depositors, it only needs to have readily available, say, \$4; the other \$11 are always sitting in its vaults and nobody ever claims them in practice. So it decides to lend money out and charge for it. It can lend out the \$10 that it had originally from the bank owners, and the \$11 that are never used. In this way, it can lend out to other customers \$21. For the sake of argument, let's say that the rate at which the bank is lending out that money is 10% per year.

Going further, the managers of this toy bank realise that there are lots of potential clients wanting to borrow money at a 10% rate, so it decides to go to other financial institutions and borrow money at, say 4%, and then lend it out at 10%, hence making 6% per year on these operations. Let's say it borrowed \$20, and let's refer to these loans as "bonds".

We are going to illustrate this graphically, but before doing so let's go one step further. In practice, our toy bank faces different sorts of borrowing requirements from clients. For example, some clients want to buy a house with a loan and are happy to secure it with the house itself (a mortgage), so the bank is happy to lend at a lower rate of, say, 6%, as the potential losses it faces in mortgages is lower than in unsecured loans.[1] Also, other customers want to be able to do instantaneous purchases of small items (e.g., buy a TV set) and so they are happy to pay a high interest if the bank can help them buy those purchases whenever they want and pay back to the bank in a few months, without asking any questions, without any fuss. These are credit cards. Our toy bank decides to charge a 20% interest rate on them as the potential losses (i.e., customers not paying back the loan) from those credit card loans are greater than those from common loans.

So, to summarise, the bank is taking money from different sources. It is keeping part of it as cash, to cover the demand for money from the depositors, and it is also lending the rest of the money out to different customers in various forms. The taking of money constitute the bank liabilities (equity from bank owners, deposits, bonds) and what it has and gets with that money are the assets (cash, loans, mortgages, credit cards).

Figure 1.1 illustrates how the balance sheet of our toy bank looks. Readers should note that, always, assets are equal to liabilities.

So far, the picture of our toy bank has been static. That is, we are considering the assets and liabilities of the bank *at a given point in time*. However, the value of the assets in a bank changes over time. Let's suppose that the bank holds some cash in a foreign currency. In this case the value of that cash will change over time following the exchange rate (FX Risk). Another source of change in value can come from changes in the present value of future money[2] (Interest Rate Risk). Another source of change in value can come from the fact that, for example, we realise that the default rate of a number of loans that we have in the past is higher than originally expected and, so, the balance sheet should reflect this and decrease the present value of those

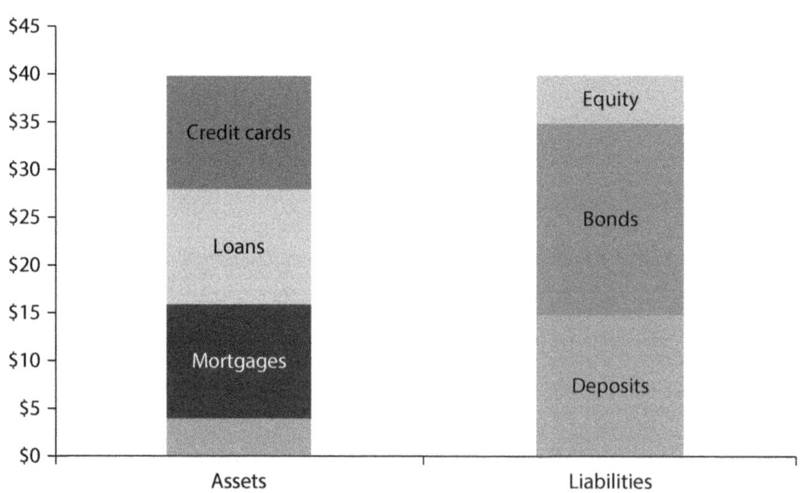

Figure 1.1 Example of a simplified banking book

loans[3] (Credit Risk). In general, a bank can have on its balance sheet other assets, like equity for example, that will change in value over time.[4]

Right now, the main point is to realise that the Asset side of the balance sheet of a bank fluctuates in value with time. The statement that reflects the changes in that value is the "Profit and Loss" statement of the bank for the period under consideration. As said, a fundamental law of accounting is that assets must be equal to liabilities. However, the liabilities that the bank has to its creditors (via deposits and bonds in this toy bank) do not change, so any profit or loss on the Asset side of the balance sheet is absorbed by the Equity: keeping the non-equity liabilities constant, when the bank balance sheet increases in value, the equity increases in value with it, and vice versa.

For the sake of completeness, in addition to the balance sheet and the profit & loss statements, a third important piece of information is the cash-flow statement, that states the cash that has gone in and out of the bank. We are not going to use it, but it is good to mention it here for completeness.

Everything seen so far in this section is called the banking book of a bank. We are going to see the different other parts of the balance sheet in the next sections.

1.1.2 The trading book

So far, every one of the assets and liabilities we have seen are "physical" in the sense that they require the transmission of relatively large amounts of money at the beginning and at the end. The bank takes deposits today and will give it back when the clients demand them, in a loan the bank gives the cash today and it will received it back in the future, etc. However, a bank can trade also financial derivatives that are less cash intense, but that can be very important for a bank and can carry a high quantity of risk. Let's give a few examples.

Our toy bank has a car manufacturer in Germany as a client; for example, BMW. BMW sells around 20% of its cars in the US.[5] Obviously, the price of the cars it sells in the US is fixed each year in US dollars. So, BMW faces foreign exchange (FX) risk in this department: it does not know how many euros it will receive for a given number of cars that it sells in the US. Companies do not like uncertainty, and even less uncertainty that is outside their core business, which is car manufacturing in this case. As a result, BMW will be happy to hedge out this FX risk: they like to know that for every car they sell, they get a fixed amount of euros; then, they will make sure they sell lots of cars, as that is their core business.

So, our toy bank steps in and offers BMW the following product: let's say that today's EURUSD exchange rate is 1.2, and that BMW wants to protect $120 million of sales, that are €100 million today. Our bank is going to sell to BMW a contract that is settled in 1 year, that is going to compensate for any loss in euros coming from changes in the FX rate. Also, they agree that any gain that BMW has in euros, should the FX rate move in its favour, will be delivered to our bank. In other words, if BMW loses euros because the FX rate goes against them, then the bank gives that loss to BMW, but if it gains euros because the FX rate moves in BMW's favour, then the bank receives that gain from BMW.

In this way, BMW is happy because it knows that if it sells its expected 4,000 cars at an average price of, say, $30,000, it will receive $120 million that, then, will transform into €100 million exactly, regardless of what happens to the EURUSD exchange rate during this year. This is, more or less, a very simple derivative called "FX forward".

However, the story does not finish here, as our toy bank may have another client in the US that has the same but symmetric problem: it sells, for example, computers in Europe, but makes its accounts in US dollars, so it likes stability in this later currency. So, our toy bank can sell the same but opposite product to that American company (Apple Computers, for example). In this way, everyone is happy: BMW has hedged out its FX risk,

Apple Computers has hedged it out too, and the bank is sitting in the middle, making a fee for this risk transfer service.

In practice, financial derivatives can be most complicated; this is a very simple and somewhat idealistic example. Banks have developed a whole range of financial derivatives that range from a simple forward to other very sophisticated contracts customised to customers' needs. With these derivatives, banks offer a channel to *transfer and mitigate risk.* Banks can offer these derivatives in all sorts of markets: FX, interest rates, equity, credit, commodities, weather, insurance, etc.

From the bank's point of view, the part of the balance sheet that deals with the value of these assets is called the trading book. As we will see, the value of the trading book can change very rapidly, as it is very sensitive to market variables, that swing around permanently. For this reason, while the banking book is typically marked (that is, it is valued) from time to time (e.g., monthly), the trading book needs to be marked daily.

A key feature of the trading book is that, ideally, a bank uses this type of trade to offer, only, financial services and so it should be, in theory, market neutral. By this it is meant that, following our example, the changes in the value of the FX forward done with BMW will be the same and opposite to the FX forward done with Apple Computers. As a result, in principle, the value of the trading book should be neutral to swings in the market variables. However, things are usually not like that, for a number of reasons. These include that a bank may choose to not be market neutral and have a directional position in some markets (e.g., to benefit if the EURUSD increases at the risk of losing money if it decreases), perhaps the nature of the market it operates does not let the bank be market neutral, perhaps the systems it has in place do not let the bank see the risks it has taken[6] ... there could be many reasons.

In practice, banks cannot become market neutral relying only on trades done with clients directly. So, in order to manage these risks, banks have access to a wholesale market of financial products that they can trade with each other to transfer risk between them. This is why this part of the book is call the "trading" book: banks trade these financial derivatives constantly with each other in order to offer the services they are required and to hedge out their risk. As a result, the number and nature of the trades sitting in the trading book is quite unstable, it can change very quickly.

To add some more complexity, the notion of the trading book is usually expanded to some products that can live both on the banking and trading book depending on the bank's intentions with respect to them. For example, a bank can decide to lend money to the US government for ten years by buying a ten-year treasury bond. If it decides to lend that money and wait for ten years to get the money back, then this bond should sit on the banking book. However, the treasury bond market is very liquid (that is, you can sell and buy these bonds very easily), and the bank may decide to buy this bond today, hold it for ten days and sell it again for whatever reason. If so, then this bond typically goes into the trading book of the balance sheet.

So, in reality, the trading book should comprise those products that are "actively" traded. The rest should go into the banking book. With this in mind, the reader may be able to see now how some financial assets go naturally to the banking book (e.g., a mortgage held to maturity) and some others go naturally to the trading book (e.g., an exotic financial derivative that is actively hedged), but there is a range of products that sit in the middle, that go into one or another book depending on the bank's intention with it and whether it is actively traded or not.[7]

The different nature of the trading versus the banking book makes the trading book more sophisticated and, hence, more difficult to risk-manage. As a result, banks need complex risk departments, with sophisticated systems, to quantify, understand and manage the risks lying in the trading book. This book will mostly cover this topic. In particular, counterparty credit and funding risk.

Figure 1.2 illustrates a simplified bank's balance sheet both with a banking and a trading book.

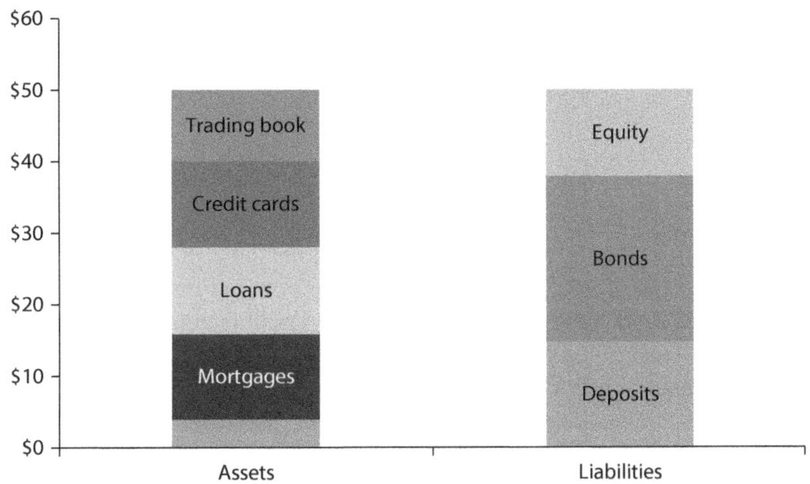

Figure 1.2 Example of a simplified bank's balance sheet

1.1.3 Off balance sheet assets

There is a last type of assets that banks can have but that do not sit on the balance sheet directly and, hence, are called "off ballance sheet" assets.

A financial institution will be holding assets on behalf of its clients, like equities or bonds, but those assets do not belong to the bank. An example is the brokerage unit of a bank. Also, a bank may "securitise" some of its debt-assets and so they will be held as off-balance sheet items. It is not the goal of this book to go into the details of what is asset securitisation in this context, so let's leave it for now saying that these are assets that the bank holds on behalf of another legal entity and, most importantly, to which it does not have direct rights.

1.2 The role of banks in the economy

Once we have understood some basics of the composition of a bank's balance sheet, we can see why banks are so important to an economy. The function that banks provide can be split into three:

1. **Money management**
   The first service they provide is what is most common to all of us: we need a place to put our money, a place that we can be assured will keep it safe, that provides us with easy access to it if we need it via check books and debit cards, and also that facilitates the transfer of money to other banks, countries, etc. This banking service, being most primary to an economy, is not the only one that is relevant.
2. **Banks facilitate the provision of credit in the economy**
   This service is also very important. We have seen how our toy bank was, in fact, a *vehicle* for savers (customers that deposit their money in the bank, and that lend money to the bank) to lend their money to borrowers that want it. This is a crucial role of banks. If banks did not exist, an individual would not have a simple way to borrow money from savers and invest it in a business, a house, etc., and hence economic development would be strongly dampened.

First of all, this is because banks facilitate a market where different ways of saving and borrowing can be accessed by individuals and companies: one individual wants to lend money for one year, another one for ten years, some want to borrow for a house, some for a TV. Banks puts them all together in an efficient way.

Secondly, banks absorb credit risk. If the bank is managed properly, a person or a collection of people defaulting on debt payments does not endanger the depositor and saver's money. This is very important too as, otherwise, very few savers will be willing to lend their money to borrowers.

In this way, banks facilitate the transfer of credit throughout the economy and, as a result, they are central to economic activity. We will stop on this topic here for now, but those interested can read more on this subject in Appendix A. The reader can see now how this credit facilitation is registered in the bank's balance sheet through the banking book.

3. **Banks transfer and mitigate economic risk**

Let's use our BMW versus Apple Computer example. One of the greatest inhibitors of investment and economic growth is uncertainty. The uncertainty that BMW has in regards to the income in Euros constitutes a real disincentive to the development of products and services in the US. This example is centred around foreign exchange risk, but the same can be said about any other asset class. For example, airlines have increasing costs if the oil price goes up, so they face a negative dependency between oil price and their business performance. However, oil extraction companies do have the opposite dependency: the value of their assets diminish when the oil price falls. As a result, financial derivatives that transfer oil price risk between them do incentivise economic development in that sector.

The list of risk-transfer examples that could be given is endless. They exist in all asset classes: interest rates, FX, equity, credit, commodities, etc. The key point here is to understand that banks facilitate the transfer and mitigation of risk so that, overall, the economic environment encourages investment and growth. The reader can see now how this risk transfer is typically done via the trading book.

Overall, these three points show how banks are central to economic activity and growth and, as a result, to social welfare, however that is understood in each society.

Most importantly, the reader can appreciate that all those services are based on one single factor: the credit worthiness of the banking system in general, and of each individual bank in particular. Banks need to be rock solid. This is because they are, in fact, the hubs of credit creation, risk transfer and risk mitigation. Otherwise, uncertainty and lack of trust can damage an economy and the social welfare it supports very deeply as we all saw in 2008. For this reason, risk management is at the core of the banking business.

1.2.1 Leverage in the balance sheet

We have just seen that the creation of money by banks through the provision of credit is crucial to the economy. From a bank's perspective, this is typically referred to, or highly linked to, "leverage": in principle, a bank could leverage from a very small amount of equity to create a very large balance sheet and, potentially, generate big amounts of revenue. Loosely speaking, leverage is the relative size of the balance sheet to the equity.

On the one hand, if the leverage in the banking system is too low, banks may not be creating the money needed in the economy. On the other hand, if leverage is too high, banks will be able to generate lots of money through the credit cycle to the point of being too much for the economy and for the bank itself.[8] It is the role of the financial regulators to ensure that the overall banking system leverage is appropriate, and the role of the senior management in each bank to ensure that the institution can withstand negative shocks in the balance sheet.

There are a number of metrics to monitor a bank's leverage. The most popular ones include:

- **Leverage Ratio:** This is obtained by dividing the value of the equity by the value of the total assets on the balance sheet. It is the most simple and straightforward measurement for leverage.
- **Capital Ratio:** The problem of the leverage ratio is that it provides no information as to the risk that the bank carries on the balance sheet. Let's imagine two banks, both with the same structure in the liability leg, but one having risky assets, like mortgages to individuals with a high risk of default, and another one with very low risk assets like loans to the US government. Obviously, the former balance sheet is riskier than the latter one, but the leverage ratio alone does not reflect this at all. A way to account for this is to assign to each asset on the balance sheet a risk weight, then multiply each asset value by its risk weight to come up with the balance sheet Risk Weighted Assets (RWA). Then we calculate the capital ratio as the size of the equity relative to the RWA.
- **Reserve Ratio:** A third ratio that is commonly used to control a bank's leverage is the reserve ratio. This controls the percentage of the deposits that the bank holds as cash on behalf of its clients.

Regulators following Basel III currently set the Leverage ratio to 3% and the Capital ratio to 8%, as explained in detail in Chapter 9. It seems there is no general consensus in the world as to the Reserve ratio, it ranges from no requirements at all in some countries to around 20% in some emerging economies.[9]

These leverage metrics are often confused with each other, but they should not be. In particular, it is important to realise that the Leverage and the Capital ratio are requirements on the balance sheet "from left to right", and the reserve ratio is a requirement "from right to left": often, the assets on a balance sheet are also referred to as the left side of the balance sheet, and liabilities as the right side. In practice, for the Leverage and Capital ratios, first we calculate the assets or the RWA on the left side, and from that we calculate what is the minimum equity needed on the right side. If the bank wants to increase those ratios it can either get more investors to put equity into the bank, or shrink the balance sheet (and hence shrink the business capability). However, the Reserve ratio works the other way: first we calculate the deposits subject to reserve requirements on the right side, and then we calculate the minimum cash needed on the left side. If the bank wants to increase this ratio it needs to sell some of its assets and keep the cash.

The reader can see how, in different ways, each ratio is a constraint from one side of the balance sheet to the other side, Leverage and Capital ratio from left to right, and Reserve ratio from right to left.

1.3 The business of finance

We have used an ultra-simple toy bank example to illustrate the key features of a bank's balance sheet and how it interlinks with the economy it operates in. Obviously, what really matters in a bank is not the balance sheet, as that is just a bunch of numbers; what really matters is the business that the balance sheet reflects.

Ideally I would like to build a map of the different financial services, but this would be mission-impossible given the complexity of this industry at present. However, I will try to somehow compartmentalise it so that the reader can get a broad idea.

The first idea that is sometimes confused is the difference between investment services and financial services. An investment service take place when a service provided manages money on behalf of its clients with the intention of making a profit for them. Examples are hedge funds, a fund of funds, pension funds, asset managers, etc. However, financial services take place when an institution facilitates money management, access to other financial vehicles and, also, provides credit. Examples are retail banks, corporate banks, brokerage houses, etc. A way to think about this is that investment service providers have a net position on behalf of their clients: they will make money or lose money depending on whether the markets go up or down. However, financial services are market neutral for their clients: in theory, their services are unaffected by market swings.[10]

Another section of financial service providers are those sometimes put in the box of "wholesale" banking. By this it is usually meant services between financial institutions. These include money market funds, that lend large amounts of money to banks for relatively little interest, stock exchanges, clearing houses and also some parts of corporate banking.

A service that should be added to this is financial advising. In the case of big multinationals and other large institutions this is a large source of business for banks and it is often referred to as Corporate Finance. In the case of smaller scale clients, they go usually together with the sale of products like, for example, loans, deposit accounts, etc.

Another approach to compartmentalising the financial industry is by looking into the type of clients. A common person has very different financial needs than a high net worth individual (a rich person), a small company or a large multinational. For example, services for most people are usually called retail banking; for to high net-worth individuals, private banking. Small companies are usually serviced via the corporate retail units, and large institutions via corporate or investment banking businesses.

As the reader may be appreciating by now, the banking industry has become a big conglomerate of small, medium and large financial institutions that operate in a web of dependencies that are very difficult, if not impossible, to unravel in detail. Often banks offer lots of these services under one brand, but each of them is very different in nature. For example, as a retail client I may have my money with, for example, Barclays Bank. Then, they may facilitate me with the possibility of investing my savings in a fund, though this fund may be a Barclays fund or not, they may offer me a credit card, but the financial institution providing me credit may or may not be Barclays.

1.3.1 Risk management

One of the objectives of this chapter is to provide the reader with some introductory background as to how the financial industry in general works, with the aim of providing some perspective for the rest of the book.

The reader can realise now how banks are central to the economy in the sense that they create money, that they facilitate the exchange of this money as it travels in parallel, but in the opposite direction, to the exchange of products and services in the real economy, and that they transfer and neutralise risk between all players in the real economy. If banks stop, the economy stops and, as a result, purchase power decreases, unemployment grows, social welfare levels go down, etc. For this reason, banks had to be rescued in 2008; otherwise, the impact to the real economy would have been devastating.

As already hinted, *the* key factor that enables banks to provide these central services is the robustness of individual banks in particular and of the banking system in general. People, companies and institutions go to banks because they are to be trusted. In the 2012 European crisis, the Swiss economy and banks did well because they were trusted by the world-wide community, the Spanish banks did badly because they lost global confidence. An economy is as robust as its banking system is, and vice versa; they feed each other.

Because of this, risk management is everything to banks and to the economies they operate in. Banks are "hubs" of risk, they are institutions that absorb and distribute it. As such, they are as good to an economy, to a society, and to their shareholders as their risk management processes and systems are. No more and no less.

Risk management is at the heart of the business of finance. Those that overlook this suffer the consequences sooner or later.

However, risk management does not mean "not taking risks", as it is sometimes mistakenly understood. Risk management means *understanding* the risk that actually exists and, then, *deciding* what to do with it.

For example, an activity that requires very fine risk management skills is extreme mountaineering.[11] Those brave people that dare to climb mountains like Everest or K2 cannot do this without a very fine talent to see the risk from low temperatures, snow avalanches, changing weather conditions, etc. They need to be able to analyse it, understand it and, then, assume risks as they see fit and make decisions accordingly, with the goal of getting to the top of the mountain and back. Similarly, banks and an economy cannot be 100% risk free, as there is always the uncertainty that someone might break into a vault, that an earthquake changes the economic landscape of a region, or that economies go into recessions or depressions because they are driven by humans and, as such, there is always a component of unpredictability. However, banks and bank regulators need to understand the risks being taken, neutralise them as much as is seen to be necessary and understand well the risks left in the business and in the economy.

Banks are very complex nowadays, and this only a reflection of the complexity of the economic environment we operate in. For this reason, they cannot be managed properly without good risk methodologies, good risk systems, and good risk processes.

1.4 The role of the trading book and OTC derivatives

As already seen with the BMW and Apple Computers example, financial derivatives are good for everyone. They are very powerful risk-transfer tools that facilitate economic development and welfare. Without derivatives a pension fund could find serious difficulties when hedging long term inflation risk, an airliner oil price risk, a car manufacturer FX risk, etc. Over-the-counter (OTC) derivatives are tailored financial derivatives so that the players in an economy have access to ad hoc products that can optimise their risk management. However, it must be said, they can be dangerous too if not dealt with using the appropriate knowledge and care.

OTC derivatives are contracts that derivative dealers (the so-called "sale side") create for their clients (the "buy side") so that the true risks that the clients have can be managed. This act of "creation" is often referred to as *hedging*. This is illustrated in Figure 1.3.

What the derivative dealer is doing in this hedging activity is to replicate the OTC derivative sold to the client. That is, the goal is to create a financial position with the market so that its Profit & Loss (P&L) is the same but with the opposite sign to the OTC derivatives with the clients. This may require frequent rebalancing of the hedging positions, the so-called dynamic hedging.

In this way, the bank, that is also called the *Derivatives Dealer* in this context, is actually *synthetically manufacturing* the OTC derivative for the client. Obviously, the dealer is going to charge a fee for this work.

Synthetic OTC derivative manufacturing: This idea of synthetic manufacture is central to the world of derivatives, so let's illustrate it with a simple example. Let's say now that we are a company in the transportation industry. One of our main sources of cost is gasoil; fluctuations in the price of gasoil are highly linked to those of oil prices. The demand for our services is seasonal, being highest in summer. We want to do some important investments during the next 2 years, but we cannot take the risk of this investment together with the risk of having fluctuations in the price of gasoil in our core business. To manage this, we can ask a derivatives dealer to sell to us the following insurance policy: a strip of 24 oil call options,[12] maturing each and every

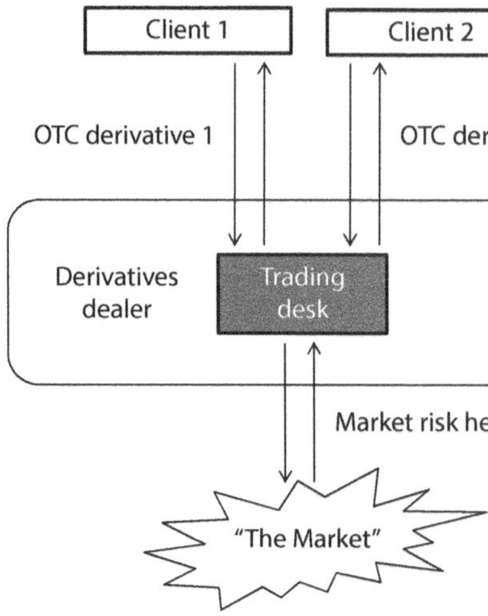

Figure 1.3 The hedging mechanism for OTC derivatives

month, and with a notional that increases in summer to reflect our gasoil consumption seasonality. We are going to have to pay for this OTC derivative a given amount of money, the insurance premium, that then we can put as a cost to the other investment opportunity in its cost–benefit analysis. In this way, we manage risk, decrease uncertainty, we can go ahead with the investment, understanding its true cost and, hopefully, create value and welfare with it.

Now on the other side of the deal, the derivatives dealer is going to hedge this contract by netting its market risk[13] with other contracts sold to other clients and, then, put a series of financial positions against the market so that the residual market risk is neutralised. With this the derivatives dealer aims to be *market risk neutral*: it does not matter where the price of oil goes, it doesn't affect its P&L.

This is a simple example around oil prices, but similar examples could be shown with interest rates, FX, equity, commodities, inflation, weather, etc. It illustrates how important OTC derivatives are to economic development and all that comes with it. These derivatives can be more or less sophisticated, but the central idea of them is to facilitate a tailored vehicle to manage risk in the real economy. The buy side of these derivatives needs derivatives dealers because either they do not have access to the global markets, or because they do not know how to create the sophisticated risk management instruments they need. Fundamentally, a dealer provides these two services in its investment bank division via OTC derivatives.

The market for these derivatives ballooned in the 1990s and early 2000s. The reason: they are excellent risk management instruments (hence there is a high demand for them) and the emergence of computers enabled the banking industry to create better tailored products.

However, there was a problem with them: they were mostly being priced and managed under the Black–Scholes–Merton theory,[14] that is based on a world in which nobody ever defaults and anyone can borrow and lend as much or as little money as wanted, whenever wanted, without any cost. Up to 2007 we lived in a world that was, arguably, fairly close to that, but the 2008/09 market events showed us that we were living in an illusion.

One of the effects of this new world we see now, where default risk is an everyday reality, is that the valuation and risk management of OTC derivatives needs to adapt accordingly. This book sets the fundamentals for this: a new way to look at valuation and risk management in the trading book for the derivatives business.

1.5 The XVA desk challenge

In particular, this book is going to deal with the counterparty credit risk from OTC derivatives that typically sits in the trading book. This is the risk of a loss that an institution has from defaults in its OTC derivative contracts.

For the sake of clarity, the term "credit risk" is normally used in the industry to refer to default risk in cash products, like loans, that typically sit in the banking book. The term "counterparty credit risk" or "counterparty risk" refers to the default risk in OTC derivatives, like a swap or an option, that typically sits in the trading book. The reason for having this distinction is that, in a cash product like a loan, the amount at risk subject to default is fairly known and stable; if we give a loan for \$1, we will roughly lose around \$1 if the other side of the deal doesn't pay. However, in a derivative product like a swap with a notional of \$1, the amount at risk (the value of the swap) subject to the default can change a lot as interest rates move. As a consequence, the way you measure and manage those risks is very different.

Black–Scholes pricing and hedging: As said, until very recently, all valuation and management of OTC derivatives was centred around this model, that is based on the following assumptions:

- **Risk-free Rate:** There are assets out there that are "risk-free"; that is, that will deliver a rate of return (r) for sure, without any uncertainty. This is the so-called *risk-free rate.*
- **Infinite Liquidity of Assets:** For every derivative product based on an underlying asset (S) (e.g., currency, bonds, equity, etc.), we can buy and sell that derivative and its underlying asset in any quantity, however big or small, and whenever we want.
- **Infinite Liquidity of Cash:** We can borrow or lend any amount of cash, whenever we want, at the risk-free rate.
- **Frictionless Markets:** We can do any of the above without any fees or costs.
- **No Arbitrage:** Any portfolio of riskless assets always returns the risk-free rate.
- **Normality of Asset Returns:** Market prices follow Brownian motion random walks.

The idea of the Black–Scholes framework is that, if we are a derivatives dealer, we can replicate the financial performance of any derivative by a combination of buying and selling the underlying asset(s) and by borrowing and lending cash at the risk-free rate. In this way, we can build a portfolio, the derivative plus its hedging positions, that does not fluctuate in value regardless of where the underlying asset goes; as such, that portfolio is a risk-less asset by itself, and hence it must return the risk-free rate. Also, the price of that derivative is the cost of creating its hedging positions as, otherwise, someone can buy it or sell it at that incorrect price, hedge it, and make a return above the risk-free rate without any risk. This is the so-called "risk-neutral" valuation framework.

There is no doubt that the Black–Scholes framework created a most important step forward in the area of financial innovation and risk transfer, with the subsequent economic development that comes with it; it constituted the pillars of the market for financial derivatives. However, given that it worked very well for several years, it also created the psychological illusion that the assumptions it is based on were true.

We know now that those assumptions can be very detached from reality, specially in stressed periods. These periods happen (by definition) rarely, but are extremely important as they can knock down otherwise-perceived strong corporates, or even governments.

In particular, it is clear now that there isn't such a thing as a default-free entity. Even the US government, generally perceived as the most financially stable and robust body in the world, was downgraded from a AAA to a AA rating in 2011. Even within the super-senior credit world, a AAA rating means that it is most unlikely that that institution will default, but nobody now is happy to say that "it is impossible for a AAA entity to default"; we have learnt our lesson.

Also, the markets have, indeed, limited liquidity. The London money market was perceived as the most active and liquid market in the world. In my early days in finance, I was told once by one of my teachers: "The London money market is the most liquid in the world, it has functioned effectively for centuries, without interruption. It will never stop". In 2008 that market froze. Again, we have learnt the lesson that the liquidity of any market can dry out; we must be ready for that event, however unlikely it may seem.

Another illusion we lived with in the early days of derivatives is that they have one unique price, and that if any derivative price diverges from it someone can make "free" money out of it. This topic is discussed extensively in Chapter 12, but let's say for now that it seems strange that if the price of anything else in the world is not unique (e.g., the price of the same shirt can change from shop to shop), why would derivatives be different? In fact, they are not.

Finally, it is well known that the prices of assets do not follow normal returns (just have a look at the historical prices of *any* asset) and that the markets are far from frictionless, very far in several cases.

All this means, amongst other things, that a Black–Scholes framework has limited value to manage derivatives.

This leads to the clear conclusion that we must move on from the Black–Scholes framework into a new way of managing derivatives. The XVA framework described in this book is the attempt that we are having at this.

1.5.1 Adjustments needed

Originally it was thought that the effect of counterparty risk stayed within the boundary of pure default risk, but the everyday reality has taught us that it doesn't: it has implications well beyond pure default risk. In particular, we must consider the following:

- **Default Risk:** This is the loss that an institution can have from *actual* defaults in its portfolio of counterparties. It is the fundamental risk that germinates into the subsequent interlinked points.
- **CVA:** The Credit Value Adjustment (CVA) is today's price of the default risk we have in our book of OTC derivatives. This price is marked in the balance sheet and creates an undesired P&L volatility that must be managed somehow, as no investor likes that volatility.

  It is important to note that this is a "paper", not a "cash", P&L: we can have a big CVA loss because the credit quality of our counterparties changes, without suffering any defaults. In fact, it was reported by the Basel Committee that two-thirds of the credit related losses in the 2008 crisis were CVA related [8].

  This CVA risk has two components: CVA_{asset} and CVA_{liab}. The first one is the price of the default risk we are facing, while the second one is the price of the default risk our counterparties are facing from us. Confusingly, they are also called "CVA" and "DVA". They are just two ways to name the same thing; in this book we are going to refer to them as the asset and liability side of CVA to avoid a confusion that often takes place: seeing them as two unrelated things. They are, indeed, two sides of the same coin; one does not make sense without the other one, in the same way one side of a coin co-exists always with the other side.
- **FVA:** As said, up to 2007 it was thought that a bank could really never default. This was a topic hardly ever discussed and the vast majority of the financial dealings were based on that assumption. However, 2008 proved that was not the case. As a consequence, the funding costs of banks increased substantially as each had now to pay a sometimes important funding spread over the risk-free rate in order to borrow cash.

We are going to see that the liability side of CVA is highly related to that funding risk, but it is not the end of the story, as CVA calculation is based in a somewhat ideal risk-neutral pricing framework, and does not truly reflect the everyday operations around OTC derivatives. The Funding Value Adjustment (FVA) is done to reflect this extra funding risk that is not captured in CVA_{liab}.

Funding risk is very linked to the liquidity of that funding. In 2008 we learnt that we can have a given expected cost of funding, but if we cannot find the depth in the market to meet our funding needs (i.e., if nobody wants to lend us the amount we need to keep alive tomorrow) we may default. Hence the problematic of funding risk is very linked to that of liquidity risk. To manage this, a Liquidity Value Adjustment (LVA) can be calculated. However, it must be treated with care, as it can lead to funding double-counting quite easily.

We could split FVA further and define a Collateral Value Adjustment (CollVA) to refer to the funding risk arising from collateral needs. It is all a matter of personal taste and naming conventions. The point to understand is that when we speak about funding risk we have to consider it globally in the organisation, with all the branches it crystallises into.

- **KVA:** On top of all this, we need to keep aside a certain amount of capital to act as a buffer against unexpected losses. In particular, the regulatory capital, which is the capital buffer that governments impose on banks, has increased very substantially since 2008. As a result, capital has become both expensive and difficult to raise.

  Consequently, a financial institution needs to account for it internally, as it must incentivise those OTC derivatives that need little capital, or even that create capital benefits, in contrast to those that are expensive from a capital standpoint. The number that captures this regulatory capital risk is KVA.

XVA is a term that comprises all these issues. At the time of this book going to press, these were the main XVAs being seriously discussed in the industry. However, this area of valuation and risk management is evolving at an outstanding speed, and so other ones may appear as time progress and we learn more about the reality of the new financial environment we are entering into.

In this book we are going to tackle one of the, arguably, biggest challenges that the banking industry has faced in recent history: accommodating the complex risk management of OTC derivatives to a realistic and practical view of the world. We are going to see that this new environment is changing fundamentally the way banks operate and, without a doubt, has created the biggest challenge this industry has ever faced from a technology standpoint: building an XVA system.

Our goal is to tackle this challenge.

Part II | Quantitative Fundamentals

2 The Roots of Counterparty Credit Risk

For many years, the main focus of risk in books on financial derivatives was Market Risk. Market Risk assesses the risk in the trading portfolio resulting from changes in the market prices. An example would be: if we were short on an equity forward, the value of that forward will decrease if the underlying equity price increases. Market risk metrics deal with short time horizons, typically ten business days, because it is perceived that we can rehedge or exit our positions in only a few days.

Up to 2008, the possibility that a counterparty would default was seen as remote or impossible. However, the cascade of defaults in that year in the so-considered super-safe financial system proved that view to be fundamentally wrong. As a result, financial institutions and regulators realised that they had to put much more emphasis in understanding, managing and controlling counterparty risk.

It is important to clarify the difference between this risk and other risks, since they are often confused. Firstly, Counterparty Credit Risk deals with the default risk embedded in financial derivatives, as opposed to Credit Risk, that is often referred to the default risk existing in cash credit products like loans, mortgages, etc. That is, credit risk refers to the default risk in products where cash is lent or borrowed; this risk typically sits in the banking book. Counterparty credit risk refers to the default risk in derivative products and, hence, it usually impacts on the trading book. They are differentiated in this way because the nature of the counterparties and the risk drivers tend to be quite different. If a bank lends a \$1 million bullet loan, the exposure the bank has is \$1 million plus any interest; but if a bank enters into an FX swap with a notional \$1 million, the exposure can change significantly during the life of the trade. Also, credit risk tends to be run against retail customers as well as small, medium and large companies, while counterparty credit risk tends to be run against financial institutions or medium to large corporates.

Sometimes the term "credit" risk is generalised and used also for default risk in financial derivatives. We are going to use this generalisation in this book, for the sake of language simplicity and because this book concentrates only on derivatives, but the reader should bear in mind the difference between them.

Another typical source of confusion is the difference between market and counterparty credit risk. It is very important to distinguish between them.

Market risk measures how much my positions can move out of the money if the market moves against me, whilst credit risk deals with how much I can lose if one (or a number) of my counterparties default and the markets moves in my favour (the corresponding positions are in the money). Hence all credit risk calculations need to be done subject to counterparties defaulting, whilst market risk calculations do not consider this.[1]

2.1 Key elements of counterparty credit risk

When dealing with default risk in books about financial derivatives, we need to deal with three major concepts.

1. **Exposure Metrics** measure how much we may be owed in the event of a counterparty defaulting.
2. **Default Probability** is an estimation of the probability that a counterparty will default at a given point in time.
3. **Loss Given Default** provides an estimate of the percentage of loss over the total exposure, in the event of default.

It is important to note that, in principle, all these three variables are time profiles, not just one number. This is especially true for the Exposure and the Default Probability. We will expand on this further when we drill down into each one of these concepts.

Another key element that we have already touched on in the introduction of this chapter is the difference between cash and paper losses when talking about credit risk. Cash losses are losses arising from actual defaults, while paper losses are balance sheet losses arising from changes in the market price of credit risk, or in the cost of hedging out credit risk, but in this case no actual defaults have happened.

In the 2008 financial crisis, the Bank for International Settlements reported that one-third of the credit losses were actual defaults, and two-thirds were paper losses. Several counterparty credit risk desks in banks and broker-dealers reported large losses during the credit crisis; those were mostly paper losses reflected in the CVA price of their balance sheet.

2.2 Exposure metrics, netting sets and collateral

Arguably, the most difficult computational part of counterparty credit risk is the calculation of the exposure. Let's illustrate this difficulty with an example, where the different components of the problem can be seen. Further to this we are going to explain how each of those problems can be solved.

Let's say that we trade with a counterparty a 1-year FX forward. The price at inception is zero and the value of that trade at any time t between inception and maturity (T) is

$$P_t = N(F_t - F_0) \tag{2.1}$$

where N is the notional, F_t is the forward exchange rate (also called the forward *price*) at time t, and F_0 is the forward value at inception. We know that the forward price can be expressed in terms of the spot exchange rate FX_t and the cross-currency yield curve[2] r_t as $F_t = FX_t e^{-r_t(T-t)}$, and then

$$P_t = N(FX_t e^{-r_t(T-t)} - F_0) \tag{2.2}$$

This equation illustrates that the value of the forward at any time in the future is going to be determined by two market variables: the value of the spot exchange rate (FX_t) and the value of the cross-currency yield curve r_t.

The task that we have is to estimate what is the exposure we may have to our counterparty if it defaults. The counterparty can default at any time between now and the trade maturity. However, it is impossible for us to know what the value of the forward will be then and, thus, all we can do is to calculate statistics about how much we can be owed in the event of default. In other words, P_t is a stochastic variable that will have a probability distribution at each future point in time. Our task is, first, to estimate that probability distribution and, second, to calculate the most relevant exposure risk metrics over the life of the trade.

2.2.1 EPE, ENE, PFE, and CESF

There are a number of risk metrics that are often used in the industry. If P is the price of the portfolio then:

1. **Current Exposure (CE):** This is, by far, the simplest metric. It is defined as

$$CE = P^{+}_{today} \tag{2.3}$$

where the function $(P)^{+} = \max(P, 0)$. It is, simply, how much we are owed today.

2. **Expected Positive Exposure (EPE):** This is how much we can be owed on average.

$$EPE_t = \int_{-\infty}^{\infty} P^{+} \cdot \Psi_t(P) \cdot dP, \tag{2.4}$$

where $\Psi_t(P)$ is our estimate of the distribution of P at time t.

It must be noted that EPE is "how much I can be owed on average", which is different to "how much I can be owed on average, when I am owed something". In the former case, we are averaging over all possible cases, but when I am not owed anything (i.e., when the exposure is negative), we replace that number by a zero. In the latter case, we average only in the cases in which I am owed something; that is, we calculate the average of the positive exposure cases.

3. **Expected Negative Exposure (ENE):** This is the symmetric metric to EPE: it is how much we can owe, on average.

$$ENE_t = \int_{-\infty}^{\infty} P^{-} \cdot \Psi_t(P) \cdot dP, \tag{2.5}$$

where the funcion $(P)^{-} = \min(P, 0)$.

4. **Potential Future Exposure (PFE):** This is a VaR-like metric. Given a confidence level X, the value of the portfolio will be lower than the PFE in X% of the cases.

$$X = \int_{-\infty}^{PFE_t^X} \Psi_t(P) \cdot dP. \tag{2.6}$$

Typical values for X are 90%, 95%, 97.5%, and 99%. Each financial institution tends to use one or two of these values. There is nothing that makes one of them better than the other ones; you just need to know what you are using, and what it means. According to the confidence level that a financial institution uses, the appropriate risk limits will need to be set to ensure consistency with the overall risk appetite of the firm. Also, it is quite normal to floor the PFE to zero, as it reflects the potential replacement cost of a transaction upon default of a counterparty, and as such it is a non-negative metric.

5. **Credit Expected Short Fall (CESF):** PFE has the same problems as VaR: it sets a frontier between large and not-so-large losses, but it says nothing about how big the losses can be when they are high. Also, it is a non-coherent measure of risk. A way to improve these shortcomings is to measure the average exposure above a given PFE point of the distribution $\Psi_t(P)$.

$$CESF_t^X = \int_{PFE_t^X}^{\infty} P \cdot \Psi_t(P) \cdot dP. \tag{2.7}$$

As with PFE, often CESF is floored at zero.

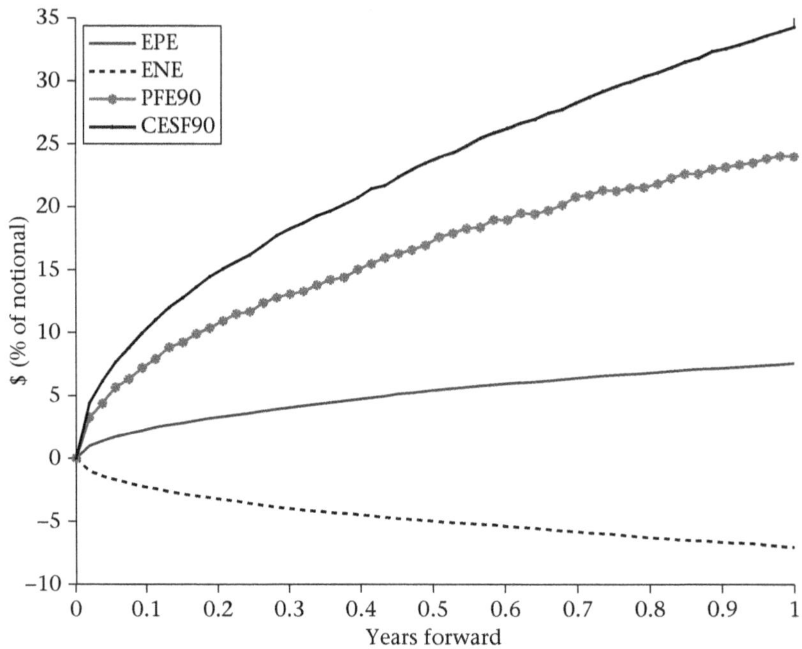

Figure 2.1 Example of EPE, ENE, PFE at 90%, and CESF at 90%, profiles for a 1-year FX forward

Figure 2.1 shows an example of all these risk metrics for one year FX forward. A number of remarks are required:

- As previously mentioned, these metrics are not just numbers, they are time profiles. We have, for example, a different EPE number for t one day from now, 1 week, 1 month, 1 year, etc., until the maturity of the trade or of the portfolio.
- EPE is not the average of all values P floored at zero, but the average of the positive values P. As a consequence, if MtM_t is the expected price of the trade at a time t in the future, then $MtM_t = EPE_t + ENE_t$:

$$
\begin{aligned}
MtM_t &= \int_{-\infty}^{\infty} P \cdot \Psi_t(P) \cdot dP \\
&= \int_{-\infty}^{\infty} (P^+ + P^-) \cdot \Psi_t(P) \cdot dP \\
&= \int_{-\infty}^{\infty} P^+ \cdot \Psi_t(P) \cdot dP + \int_{-\infty}^{\infty} P^- \cdot \Psi_t(P) \cdot dP \\
&= EPE_t + ENE_t \qquad (2.8)
\end{aligned}
$$

- As we will see as the book progresses, the ENE profiles are only used when calculating the price of credit risk in a derivative (i.e., CVA). This is because, to calculate a "fair" price, we need to account for credit risk both from my own and my counterparty's perspective. My ENE is the EPE that my counterparty calculates, and my EPE is the ENE that my counterparty calculates.

- As we will see in Chapter 9, regulatory capital calculations are based on EPE profiles. The regulatory framework for counterparty credit risk was developed for Basel II in the early 2000s. At that time, the topic of counterparty risk measurement was still immature; ENE profiles were not yet used and the term EPE was used in a different way than has been defined here; later it became the industry standard. The Basel framework refers to EPE as Expected Exposure (EE); they call EPE the time weighted average of the Expected Exposure profile over the life of the portfolio. Chapter 9 will clarify this in detail, but the reader should be aware of this now, to avoid confusion.
- When we calculate any of these profiles, the default probability of the counterparty is not taken into account. They are exposure metrics subject to counterparty default but, for now, we do not take into account whether the counterparty is a AAA or a CCC company.
- PFE tends to be calculated for high confidence levels (X). So, most often, EPE tends to be lower than PFE for a given time point. However, this is not always the case. EPE is always a positive number, by definition, but nothing stops the PFE from becoming very small or even negative (before flooring it at zero). The same applies to CESF.

Naming conventions

Unfortunately, there is quite a mix of naming conventions here, in particular with "EPE". Let's clarify them.

Currently, this "EPE" and "ENE" naming is most widely used in the industry. However, the idea behind the EPE profiles became widely spread by the Basel II accord, in around 2005. At that time, there was no need for a "negative" side for it, as Basel doesn't need it and CVA was not being priced. Consequently, Basel called an *Expected Exposure* (EE_t) profile what the industry tends to call now an EPE_t profile, and Basel called "EPE" a *number* (the average of the "EE" profile) that is never used. So, some people call a *Negative Expected Exposure* (NEE_t) profile what the industry tends to call an ENE_t profile.

This is a little mess that the reader should be aware of. The regulatory definitions can be found in Section 9.2.4.

2.2.2 Netting sets

So far, we have been discussing credit risk metrics for one single trade. However, counterparty risk is settled at netting set, hence risk metrics need to be calculated at such a level.

A netting set is a group of trades whose, in the case of default of one of the counterparties, value of the trades can be *netted off* and, under liquidation conditions, only one amount is owed.

Netting sets are defined by a legal agreement between the two counterparties that usually follows recommendations by the International Swaps and Derivatives Associations (ISDA). They are called Master Agreements or ISDA Agreements.

Two counterparties can have a number of netting sets; in fact, this is quite normal, as financial institutions often have different netting sets for different jurisdictions, for different legal entities, for different asset classes, or for any specific group of trades that needs to be treated separately.

In certain rare cases and in a few jurisdictions netting may not be allowed or there may be uncertainty as to whether it is enforceable. In these cases it is assumed that each trade is a separate netting set. Furthermore, sometimes, for regulatory reasons for example, single trades need to be treated separately and are therefore put under a single Master Agreement.

To clarify further, from a credit exposure standpoint, each netting set is a completely separate entity, even if they involve the same counterparties. If I have two netting sets with one of my counterparties, and one of them is worth, say, +\$100m (in my favour), and the other one −\$50 (against me), if the counterparty defaults

I will have to deliver the $50m and I will be owed $100. In practice, in the case of default of one counterparty or in the case of an unwinding of their portfolios the counterparties may agree to net several netting sets together, but they are not legally obliged to do so.

Netting is central to reducing counterparty credit risk. If, for example, we are long on one trade with Netting Set A and we short the same trade but with Netting Set B, we achieve a flat position from a market risk point of view, but the credit risk exposure metric will be, approximately, the sum of both exposure metrics to A and B. However, if we short the trade with Netting Set A, then they offset each other's market and credit risk. Netting reduces settlement risk when payments are made between two counterparties and the size of the potential operational risk losses.

There are two quantities that are most relevant from an exposure point of view: firstly, the credit metric (EPE, PFE, etc.) of a netting set; secondly, for a new trade, a quantity that is important is the *incremental* credit metric of this trade to the total netting set it belongs to. When a new trade is added to a portfolio of existing trades, this quantity is nearly always different to the credit metric of the trade on a stand-alone basis because it will have some netting effects with other trades in the netting set. Those quantities are always the same for gross trades (i.e., trades that cannot be netted off).

There are a number of Master Agreement features that are meant to mitigate counterparty risk:

Resetting Agreements: Counterparties can limit future exposure by agreeing, periodically, to reset a trade, to new inception conditions, and to pay or receive the value of the trade at each reset date. For example, let's say that we have a long dated forward with a given counterparty; we can agree to calculate its price every year, pay each other that quantity, and reset the forward strike to the corresponding forward price at the reset date. In this way the future exposure never exceeds the exposure of a 1 year forward, even if the trade maturity is a lot longer.

Break Clauses: In these clauses one or both counterparties agree to wind down a trade under certain conditions and pay each other its value. These triggers are sometimes negotiated at the netting set level although in most cases they are set at the trade level. There are three main type of break clauses:

1. **Mandatory, Date Based:** The trade or netting set will be wound down at a certain date. These clauses make sense when, for example, a client wants to hedge out long term interest rate risk, but for some reason the instruments that generate that risk will disappear from its book in, say, 5 years. One way to hedge this will be with a book of interest rate swaps with the same maturity as the hedged products, with a mandatory break clause in 5 years. Since these break clauses are mandatory and will take place on a specific date they are taken into account when modelling the trade's future exposure. This trade will not be contributing any exposure to the portfolio after the trigger date.
2. **Mandatory, Trigger Based:** As the future exposure that we are happy to have with a counterparty depends on its default probability, which is measured by its credit rating. To manage counterparty risk we need to ensure that we don't run sizeable risk with a counterparty that has been downgraded to a lower quality credit rating. One way to mitigate this is to add a clause in the Master Agreement by which trades are unwound if the counterparty is downgraded below a certain rating.

   This strategy does not come without dangers. Firstly, the trigger of this clause will most likely create difficulties to a firm (the counterparty) that is already in financial difficulty. In an extreme case, the clause can precisely drive the firm to default when it could be avoided by accepting less favourable but more stable conditions (from the firm standpoint). From our point of view, if that firm is systemically important, it can cause a domino effect of systemic risk that can back-fire on the firm that exercised the rating trigger in the first place.

Extra difficulties come from the fact that credit ratings cannot be implied from market data and from the fact that downgrades tend to take place quite some time after the credit of a company has deteriorated.

These triggers are not considered when modelling the risk of a portfolio since standard practice in the industry is to model counterparty risk exposure assuming default irrespective of the rating of the counterparty.

3. **Optional:** These clauses give one or both of the counterparties the option to unwind a trade, or a netting set, under certain conditions. Typical option triggers can be certain dates when the option holder can exercise the break clause if he or she wants to, because of a credit rating downgrade, MtM exceeding a certain level, etc. On top of the risks outlined for the mandatory clauses, they carry the risk that, most often, they are not executed to avoid damaging client relationships, to preserve business flow, etc.

   In practice, different institutions treat these break clauses differently from an exposure modelling perspective. Some model them similarly to mandatory break clauses, others ignore them completely whilst others choose to include them only under certain conditions. We believe that these options should be included in the risk management framework only if there is a strict culture of discipline in the organisation towards risk management.

2.2.3 Collateralised vs. uncollateralised netting sets

So far we have assumed that if a counterparty defaults, our exposure is the value of the portfolio of trades we have with this counterparty. However, this is only the case when that portfolio is uncollateralised.

In order to mitigate credit risk, financial institutions add to their Master Agreements a Credit Support Annex (CSA) by which counterparties have to post collateral when the netting set is in the money. As a simple example, if Bank A has an exposure of $1m from Bank B (i.e., the netting set under consideration has a value of $1m in favour of Bank A), then Bank B will deliver $1m to Bank A as "collateral" to mitigate the Bank A risk. If some time later the value of the netting set decreases to $0.7m, then Bank A will deliver $0.3m to Bank B, etc. In this way, institutions can significantly reduce their counterparty credit risk; the credit exposure is managed dynamically as it occurs, and the potential loss on a default is limited. We are going to see later that, as a rule of thumb, exposure can be reduced by one order of magnitude compared to its uncollateralised value.

This has very important implications. On the one hand, from a risk management point of view, the counterparty risk that I am willing to have to a given counterparty is given by its credit quality and my risk appetite; this is unrelated to the actual portfolio we have traded. Once this risk appetite is set (usually as a PFE limit), we have two options: we leave the facility uncollateralised and we are able to do, for example, around 50 trades, or we collateralise it and we are able to do around 500 trades. Collateralisation increases my capacity to trade, which implies that it also increases my capability to do business. On the other hand, we may decide to have a collateralised facility with that counterparty, but if we have only around 50 trades (as if it were uncollateralised), as a result of the decreased credit exposure we will reduce capital requirements and will be able to give more competitive prices.

CSAs were rare in the late 1990s, only 20% of the exposure in the trading book was collateralised, but during the crisis of 2008 and the years that followed there was a push for signing CSAs in order to reduce counterparty risk. CSAs are currently very common, with the collateral value nearly as big or even higher than the exposure.[3] This is depicted in Figure 2.2.

CSA documentation contains all the details and rules regarding posting and receiving of collateral. There are a number of key features that we need to keep in mind.

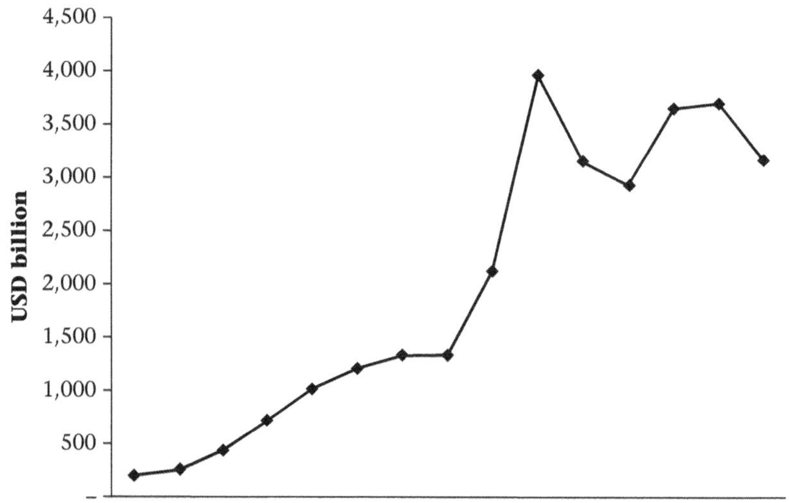

Figure 2.2 Estimated collateral in the financial system, 1999–2013
Source: ISDA Margin Survey.

CSA structure

Unilateral vs. bilateral CSA: Collateral agreements can be unilateral (or one-way) or bilateral (or two-way). If unilateral, only one party is obliged to post collateral. If bilateral, both parties post collateral. One-way agreements can be demanded by strong institutions from weaker counterparties. These agreements can make sense when the weak institution does not have the operational capability to manage collateral properly. One-way CSAs are becoming increasingly less popular is because medium and small firms are improving their management of credit risk. As a consequence, they have become more demanding from their banks as being a large institution is no longer perceived as being "default-free". It should be noted that one-way CSAs may or may not be worse than no CSA at all for a weak institution, depending on its needs. If it signs a unilateral collateral agreement, the large financial institution will be willing to trade more and offer more competitive pricing. However, the downside is that the small institution will need to run potentially large counterparty risk to the large financial institution and additionally will have to fund the collateral it needs to post.

Type of collateral: The CSA will also define what assets are eligible as collateral. The most basic and obvious one is cash, but highly rated government bonds are also common (see Figure 2.3). According to ISDA,[4] around 75% of collateral is cash, of which around 90% is equally split between USD and the Euro while GBP and JPY take around 3% each. Government bonds consist of around 15% of the total amount of collateral, with US securities being the most popular, followed by the Euro and Japanese securities. The rest is government agency securities, corporate bonds, equities, and other minor securities.

Collateral ownership: When an institution posts collateral, they remain the legal owner of the posted security. As a result, any coupons or dividends earned must be transferred to the collateral poster. Only in the event of default can the collateral receiver liquidate the securities to compensate for the credit loss.

Interest on collateral: This posting of collateral can create a funding mismatch: when the collateral is cash, the poster will have either a funding cost (if he or she needs to borrow it) or an opportunity cost (if he or she already owns it). Either way, this is usually called funding cost, or funding risk. To compensate for this, it is common that the collateral receiver pays interest to the poster on the cash delivered. The interest paid

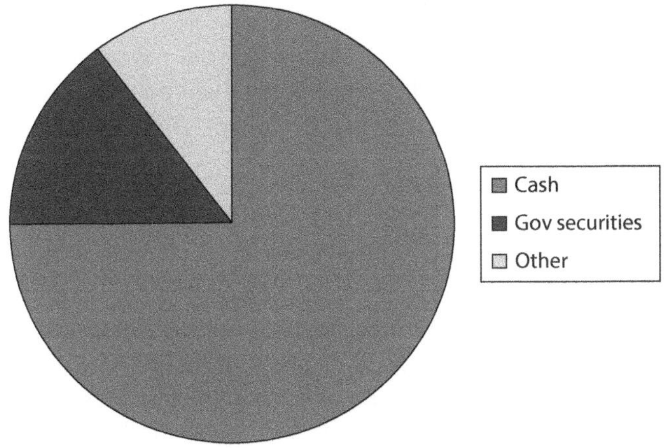

Figure 2.3 Type of collateral received
Source: ISDA Margin Survey.

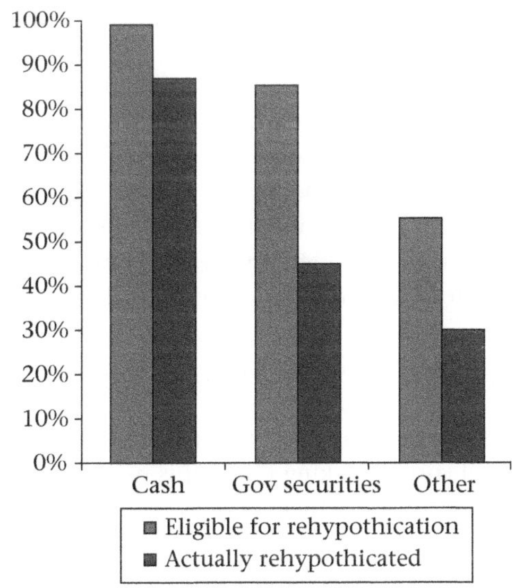

Figure 2.4 Eligible and actual posted collateral for rehypothication
Source: ISDA Margin Survey.

is agreed in the CSA, and it is typically the OIS rate, minus sometimes a spread. This funding risk will be analysed in detail in Chapter 12.

Rehypothication: It is also common practice that the collateral receiver can re-use the securities, typically by sale, repo, lending, or re-delivery. This is called rehypothication. Figure 2.4 shows ISDA figures on rehypothication.

Rehypothication can be good on the one hand as it allows the collateral receiver to earn the interest that can be delivered afterwards to the poster, as just explained; otherwise, it will be facing a funding miss-match. However, on the flip side, allowing the collateral receiver to reutilise the securities means that it will lose control of them and it may end up losing them in the event of a crisis. In fact, this is one of the sources of systemic risk that hit the financial industry in the 2008 events. For this reason, it is not uncommon that some institutions like hedge funds do not allow for rehypothication of their posted collateral.

Key CSA parameters

The CSA parameters that are key to modelling collateralised exposures are:

- **Margining Frequency:** CSAs define the frequency that collateral is called; this could be daily, weekly, monthly, etc. This is the margining frequency and the most popular frequency is daily. Frequency between large institutions is always daily, but a small counterparty on an island the middle of the Atlantic may not have the capability to handle daily margin calls, or its exposure could be so small that it does not require the daily attention of a broker dealer, and so weekly or monthly frequencies may be agreed.
- **Threshold:** This is the exposure that a financial institution is comfortable to have uncollateralised with a counterparty. This means that any exposure within the threshold will not trigger any margin call, but when it is exceeded, a margin call will be triggered to bring back the exposure to the threshold level. Higher rated counterparties will usually have a higher threshold. For example, we can have the policy with a threshold of up to $100m with a AAA counterparty, $50m with a AA, $25m with a A, $10m with a BBB, and zero threshold with the rest.[5]
- **Independent Amount (IA)** or **Initial Margin (IM):** This is an amount posted as over-collateralisation and "set aside" as an extra precaution, typically to cover potential losses from the gap risk or close out risk (to be discussed in the next section). One way to calculate this is the maximum of the PFE at a high confidence level (e.g., 99%) during the life of the trade or the netting set.

  Conceptually, both the Independent Amount and the Initial Margin are the same, but IA tends to refer to bilateral CSA with a broker-dealer, while IM tends to be used by Clearing Houses. The difference is very subtle and the industry uses either term indistinctly. From a modelling point of view, we can consider both to be equivalent.

  In contrast to the initial margin, any additional margin that is called dynamically as the value of the portfolio changes tends to be called "variation margin".
- **Minimum Transfer Amount (MTA):** Let's say that two large financial institutions agree that a call of $50 needs to be done. The operational cost of making that call is much higher than the benefit the collateral receiver will gain, so it is quite normal to agree that below a certain quantity, no transfer of collateral needs to be done.
- **Rounding:** To avoid disagreements, a CSA should mention the rounding technique to be used when calculating collateral calls.

It must be noted that the Threshold and the Independent Amount work in opposite directions: higher Threshold means higher risk, while higher Independent Amount means lower risk. The Minimum Transfer Amount works alongside the Threshold, while Rounding can go either way, so risk managers tend to put it alongside the threshold (to be conservative) but we can put it to its average, usually zero, for pricing.

So the incremental credit risk that these four parameters bring is

$$\text{Threshold} - IA + MTA + \text{Rounding}. \tag{2.9}$$

From these four parameters, the Threshold and the Independent Amount are the most important. The other two tend to be quite small.

A final note on these four parameters is that a two-way CSA can be symmetric or asymmetric in regards to these parameters: when both counterparties have the same credit profile and business, they tend to agree to the same parameters, but when one is noticeably stronger than the other one then these parameters can differ for each counterparty.

Risks inherent in a CSA

Let's discuss now the key risks that a collateral agreement brings along.

Close-out risk: Collateralising a Master Agreement does not mean it becomes risk-free; we reduce counterparty risk but may increase other types of risk like operational, funding, liquidity, or legal. One of the major sources of risk is called "close-out" risk. Let's say that we are a broker-dealer and that we have a portfolio of OTC derivative trades with a given counterparty. That portfolio should be hedged with a number of vanilla instruments so that the profit of one side (the OTC derivatives) should have an equal loss on the other side (the hedges), and vice versa, with a little spread between them, which is the fee that we make. If the counterparty defaults, the value of the portfolio of OTC derivatives crystallises, but all the hedges, that are typically vanilla products, remain as open positions. Those hedges will change in value from the time of default without any opposite profit or loss from the derivatives and, hence, we have the risk that the hedges could move against us. To minimise this risk, we need to unwind the hedges as soon as a counterparty defaults. This process will not be automatic and may take a few days, depending on the size and the complexity of the portfolio and the corresponding hedges. The potential loss that we may experience from the market moves in the hedges, from the time a default is declared until we have been able to close the hedges, is the "close-out" risk. It has been reported that in the Lehman Brother's bankruptcy, the typical close-out time was five to ten days. Hence, even if the portolio is fully collateralised, we are exposed to a few days of potential market moves against us.

Default declaration period: Another source of risk is the default declaration period. In the case of Lehman Brothers, this was only one day: on that memorable Monday everyone knew that Lehman had defaulted and started taking action. However, with several counterparties, this can take a number of days. This time has four components. First of all, it can take up to the margining frequency (one week, one month, etc.) until we make a collateral call and, hence, until we notice that a counterparty has defaulted. Secondly, there are operational reasons why a default declaration may be delayed, especially in large institutions where several different parties need to be notified (relationship manager, credit officer, legal department, etc.) or in an institution where operational processes are not running smoothly and there is no mechanism to trigger collateral payment failures. Thirdly, once we make a call and do not receive the collateral, a "grace-period" will kick-in during which a number of chase-up calls will happen, discussing whether it was a delay or an actual default, etc. Finally for relationship and reputational reasons a counterparty may not want to declare another counterparty into default unless it has absolutely exhausted all other options. At the end of the grace-period, the default will be officially declared. Typical value for the default declaration period is five working days, books of OTC derivatives with daily margining.

Gap risk: So, the actual period through which we are exposed to moves in the markets in the naked hedging positions is not only the close-out period, but also the default declaration period. This is often called the Margin Period of Risk (MPR) and is used when modelling the risk of a collateralised portfolio. The default

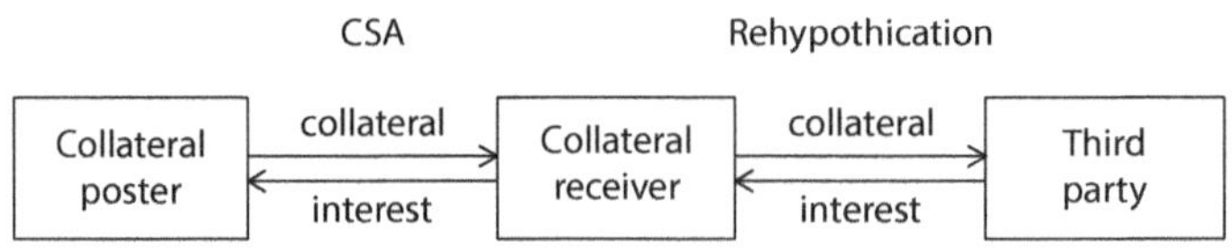

Figure 2.5 Illustration of the funding risk facing a collateralised facility

value for MPR tends to be ten days for daily margining or, in a more general form,

$$MPR(\text{days}) = 10 + \text{margining frequency (in days)} - 1 \text{ (to make MPR 10 days for daily margining)} \\ + \text{Liquidity/Concentration buffer.} \tag{2.10}$$

The liquidity or concentration buffer accounts for any extra time we may need to close down the portfolio when it contains illiquid and/or highly concentrated collateral. We explain this further below.

The risk that arises during the MPR is usually called "Gap Risk".

Funding risk: As already indicated, there are two sides to funding risk. The counterparty posting collateral faces either a funding cost or an opportunity cost. This can be mitigated by receiving an interest from the collateral receiver. From the collateral receiver perspective, the CSA may or may not allow for rehypothication. If it does, it can fund the interest it has to deliver to the collateral poster. Putting all this together, there are two typical set-ups that minimise risk: (i) if the collateral poster does not want to lose control of the cash, he or she must not allow for rehypothication, but then face an opportunity cost or (ii) if he or she wants to receive interest on the cash, he or she needs to allow for rehypothication, as otherwise the collateral receiver will face a funding mismatch. This is depicted in Figure 2.5. This funding risk leads to the Funding Value Adjustment discussed in detail in Chapter 12.

Concentration and liquidity of collateral: How long the close-out period will be depends on the complexity of the portfolio, namely its concentration and its liquidity. It is obviously faster to close out a portfolio that has only a few vanilla USD interest rate swaps as opposed to a large multi-asset class portfolio. Also, if it is too concentrated, for example if we have more than the daily average traded volume of a security, closing down the positions will either move the market against us if done quickly, or will take a long time and, hence, our gap risk will increase. Finally, the 2008 events demonstrated that even the most liquid market, the London Money Market, can dry out under the wrong conditions. Hence, liquidity must be considered as well when establishing the MPR.

Risky collateral and haircuts: In addition to the gap risk, there is another source of risk coming from market moves in a collateralised facility. Let's say that we have an exposure of \$100m to a given counterparty and that we receive \$100m worth of shares as collateral. The risk that we have during the MPR comes both from moves in the value of the portfolio *and* in the value of the collateral. Hence, to measure the exposure that we may have, we need to model both assets together. This needs to be done whenever (i) the collateral is not cash or (ii) when it is cash but in a different currency to the accounting currency of the bank, as in this case the collateral delivers FX risk.

Traditionally, banks have not had systems to measure exposure arising from risky collateral together with the risk derived from the book of trades. For this reason banks invented the notion of a "haircut" for a financial instrument. A haircut is an amount that I deduct from a security to account for how much it could decrease in value during a certain period. For example, we could say that \$100m of a two-year US government bond is worth only \$95m from a collateral standpoint, hence we are giving it a 5% haircut. The haircut value depends not only on the type of security, but also on the tenor: the haircut of a 20-year US government bond will be higher than that of a two-year one, because its price can fluctuate more dramatically. Banks usually have haircut tables for all typical collateral types and tenors that are updated periodically. For non-standard ones, an ad hoc calculation needs to be done.

From a risk-management standpoint, it must be noted that holding risky collateral is equivalent to having a repo-like[6] transaction in the collateralised facility. In the event of a counterparty defaulting, I am going to liquidate all the assets I hold as collateral, hence what I really care about is the cash-value of those assets, which is precisely the information that the repo market gives to us. In fact, if we are not comfortable with the riskiness of a security that our counterparty wants to post as collateral, we may suggest that the counterparty repos this security and posts as collateral the cash it receives. The counterparty may not always agree to this, as it can be costly.

It is often thought that the best collateral to hold is cash, but that may not be always true. To illustrate this with a simple example, let's assume that the only trade in a netting set is an equity forward, where we receive the appreciation of the underlying share. What is the best collateral I could receive? Definitely not cash, rather shares of the underlying stock in the trade! This way any move in the value of the forward will be matched with an equivalent change in the value of the shares, and the collateralised facility will be market risk flat. And what would be a second-best collateral? Shares in a stock highly correlated to the underlying value of the forward.

And this leads us naturally to the next point.

Directional way risk: The examples just given illustrate that the dependency structure between a netting set and the collateral needs to be taken into account when calculating future exposure metrics. Otherwise, the risk of the portfolio is not correctly calculated. Using the above example, if we do not have the ability to calculate the risk of the collateral together with the portfolio of trades, an immature risk system will, firstly, apply a haircut to the equity shares, asking for, say, 110% of the notional worth of the shares and, secondly, will calculate exposure metrics from a trade as if it had a constant collateral. In other words, it will "squeeze" its client unnecessarily and it will calculate exposure metrics like EPE or PFE that over-estimate the real economic risk.

Also, if in the equity forward we were receiving the potential depreciation of the share and the shares we receive as collateral is the precise counterparty's stock, holding the share as collateral will be worthless because the value of the share will depreciate precisely when our counterparty risk increases.

These examples illustrate clearly how important it is to model collateral in parallel to the book of trades. This requires us to build a dependency structure between both that is typically driven by correlation parameters. When the dependency structure decreases risk, it is said that we have Right Way Risk. When it increases it, then we have Wrong Way Risk. Right and wrong way risk are two different sides of the same coin. For this reason, we can refer to this case as Directional Way Risk.

This is one of the most difficult things to model in a counterparty credit risk system. For that reason, we will dedicate the whole of Chapter 10 to it.

Disputes: From time to time, two counterparties do not agree on the amount of collateral that needs to be transferred. Typical reasons for this include human or system errors on one of the two sides, different market data, different pricing methodologies, errors in the trade population, etc.

Traditionally, the largest financial institutions have a four-tier procedure to manage this. Firstly, they do daily portfolio reconciliations between them, and regularly with any counterparty with more than 1,000 trades. Secondly, they do monthly reconciliation performance reports as well as monthly reports on disputes greater than $20m and longer than 15 days. Thirdly, intra- and inter-firm investigations take place regularly to understand the source of disputes. Finally, if none of the above solves a problem, the existing Dealer Poll process as per the ISDA CSA kicks in. This involves asking a number of third-party market participants for their view on the collateral that should be transferred. Typical dispute times go from a few days in the simplest cases to several months in the more complicated ones.

In addition, the Basel III framework creates a strong incentive to avoid disputes: any netting set with more than two disputes within the previous two quarters will double its Margin Period of Risk for regulatory capital calculations (see Chapter 9).

2.3 Different approaches for calculating exposure

We have already seen how the exposure in a book of derivatives is a stochastic variable, and hence our metrics of counterparty credit risk need to be based on statistical values. Our job here will consist of modelling the probability distribution of possible exposure values for a given netting set ($\Psi_t(P)$) at each time point t in the future, and then calculating the relevant exposure credit metrics.

We are going to discuss a number of techniques for calculating exposure, each being the most appropriate depending on the level of accuracy needed, the time and available resources for the calculation, and the business needs for it.

- **Brownian Monte Carlo:** The most popular of all the techniques is the Brownian stochastic Monte Carlo simulation. These simulations tend to be quite expensive, both in terms of systems and computational time, but it is also the most powerful technique.
- **Historical Monte Carlo:** A less popular but very powerful technique is a Historical stochastic Monte Carlo simulation. We will see how this technique is in many cases more powerful than its Brownian counterpart.
- **Simplifications and Approximations:** There are several ad hoc techniques for individual trades or netting sets with specific properties. Some of these are quite popular as they can be very fast, using sometimes historical, analytical or semi-analytical approximations. We will review a number of them in the following chapter.

3 Exposure Measurement for Uncollateralised Portfolios

Let's start our review of exposure measurement with the most popular method: Brownian Monte Carlo.

3.1 The Brownian Monte Carlo simulation

Monte Carlo simulations reflect many possible future scenarios from which statistical values can be obtained. It is very important to understand that each scenario is a view, an instance, of how the world could develop in the future. Hence, firstly, each scenario must be calculated given today's information, and secondly, if a possible path (i.e., scenario) takes place, any other path does not occur. From a simulation point of view this means that (i) all scenarios start at the same point and that (ii) each simulation scenario must be independent of each other. We are going to refer to the number of scenarios with the letter N. Typical values for N in financial institutions for counterparty credit risk calculations range from 1,000 to 10,000.

The simulation is composed of three main steps:

1. Risk Factor Evolution
2. Pricing
3. Risk Metric Calculation

3.2 Risk factor evolution (RFE)

The first step is to diffuse stochastically a stochastic diffusion equation, all risk factors included in the existing portfolio. For example, let's say that we have a portfolio that consists of a number of USD interest rate derivatives, EUR interest rate derivatives, USDEUR FX trades, and some equity trades on a given stock. In this case we will need to simulate the USD yield curve, EUR yield curve, USDEUR FX spot price, and the equity spot price.[1] It must be noted that, sometimes, one yield curve is considered as one risk factor, but in reality it can be several risk factors, as many as may be needed to capture the necessary moves in the yield curve. Sometimes this can be one, two, three, or up to thirty points. We'll expand on this soon.

Figure 3.1 shows an example of these simulations, displaying only one point in each yield curve; for USD, for example, the 5 year swap rate may be the most important for the porfolio, but for EUR it may be the 10 year rate.

The illustrative simulations were done with the following stochastic differential equations: a Black–Karasinski process for the yield curves, and a Geometric Brownian Motion (GBM) process for the FX and

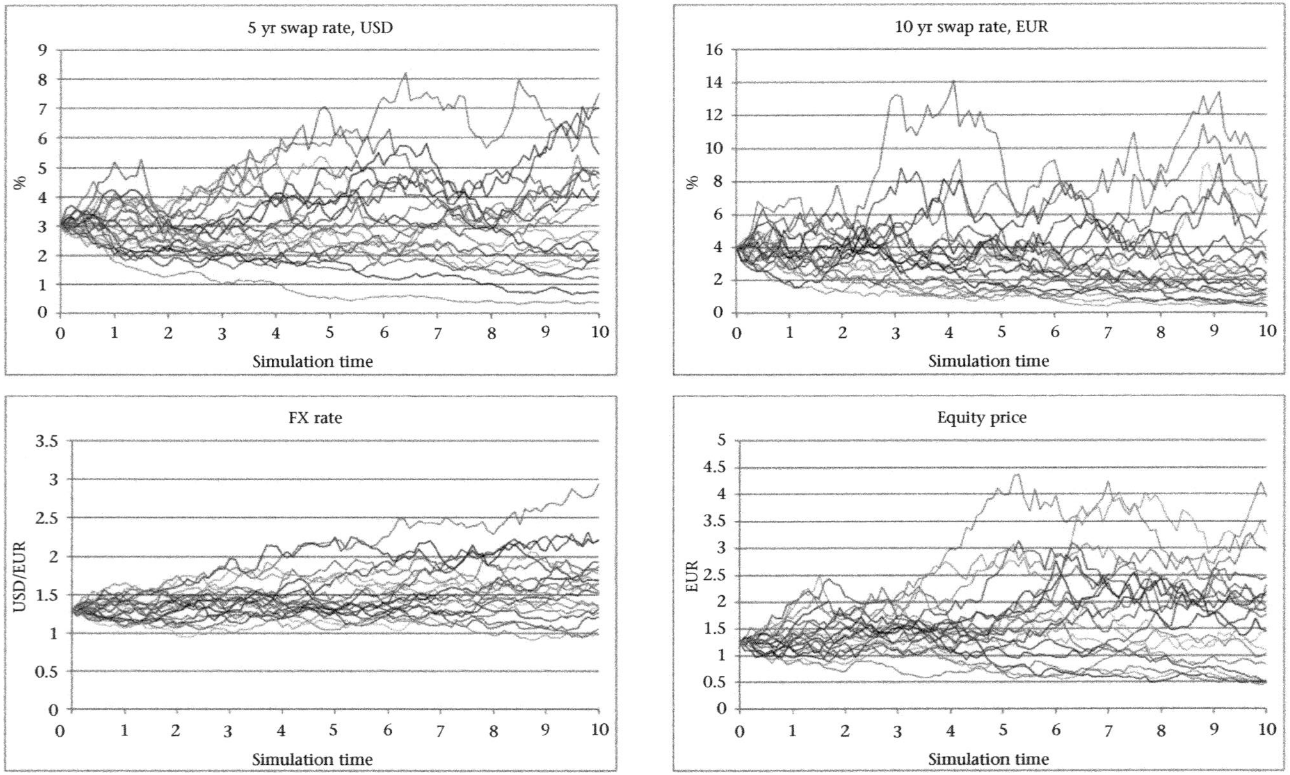

Figure 3.1 Simulated risk factors of the example, for each time point and scenario

equity spots:

$$d\ln r_t^{\text{USD}} = \theta^{\text{USD}}\left(\ln\mu^{\text{USD}} - \ln r_t^{\text{USD}}\right) dt + \sigma^{\text{USD}}\, dW_t^{\text{USD}} \tag{3.1}$$

$$d\ln r_t^{\text{EUR}} = \theta^{\text{EUR}}\left(\ln\mu^{\text{EUR}} - \ln r_t^{\text{EUR}}\right) dt + \sigma^{\text{EUR}}\, dW_t^{\text{EUR}} \tag{3.2}$$

$$dFX_t^{\text{EURUSD}} = \mu^{\text{EURUSD}}\, dt + \sigma_t^{\text{EURUSD}}\, dW_t^{\text{EURUSD}} \tag{3.3}$$

$$dS_t = \mu^{\text{S}}\, dt + \sigma_t^{\text{S}}\, dW_t^{\text{S}} \tag{3.4}$$

where σ refers to the volatility, μ to either mean reversion levels or to the drift, and θ to the mean reversion speed.

It can be seen that the starting point of each risk factor is the same for all scenarios (e.g., 3% for the USD rate, 4% for the EUR rate, etc.) as it is part of today's information, whilst the future states are derived from the simulation. The model parameters (volatilities, drifts, mean reversion levels, and mean reversion speeds in our current example) must be calibrated using all the information available.

Finally the calibration of the dependency structure needs to be taken into account. This is typically modelled with a linear correlation parameter for each pair of variables, creating a correlation matrix ρ for all the risk factors.

$$dW_t^i\, dW_t^j = \rho_{i,j}\, dt \tag{3.5}$$

Expanding on the previous comment about independence across scenarios, it must be noted that the dependency structure comes into play between risk factors. That is, the Brownian random numbers (dW) that are used for each risk factor must be generated using the given correlation matrix across risk factors, though these dW are independent across scenarios.

For how long do we need to simulate the risk factors? We must simulate as long as the maturity of the longest trade in the portfolio, but there is no need to simulate longer than that. In the simulation, we are going to divide the interval from simulation start to simulation end into M representative time buckets, and we will generate values for the risk factors in the time points at the end of each time bucket. There is no need for the time-steps to have the same frequency. In practice, most institutions use more frequent time points in the short term and less frequent ones in the longer term. Depending on computational capacity, an example of simulation time-steps would be daily for the first month, followed by weekly for the next two months, monthly for the remaining part of the first year, then quarterly for the next 4 years, etc. If there were no time nor computational constraints then it would be natural for an institution to select a daily simulation frequency over the life of the portfolio as this would be the most accurate. However, the added accuracy of a daily simulation frequency versus a frequency such as the one mentioned previously is almost always not worth its considerably high computational cost.

So, to summarise, when we finish this step we must end up with one grid of $N \times (M+1)$ numbers per risk factor, as in Figure 3.1 for the four risk factors. The "+1" comes from the first value of each risk factor, which is the starting point, today's market value, and is the same for all scenarios.

Let's see now what are typical diffusion models for the main risk factor categories. There is a wide range of books specialising in all the details of interest rate modelling, equity modelling, volatility modelling, etc. Giving those details is not the aim of this book, but we should at least understand the basics of implementing these models in a counterparty risk system for RFE modelling.

3.2.1 Interest rate models

This is the most important RFE model as this asset class is usually the one with the largest book of derivatives in financial institutions, and it also impacts on every non-interest-rate derivative via discount factors. The tenor of interest-rate derivatives typically ranges from a few months to 30 years. They can go further than that, but in practice they hardly ever trade in longer maturities.

The literature has covered the topic of interest rate modelling in great detail already. In any case, let's say that we can choose to model short rates, libor rates, bond prices, or any other rate for which we want to describe the yield curve (e.g., semi-annually compounding interest rates). Any of the typical Hull-White, Short-Rate, Libor Market Models should, in principle, do a good job for the purposes of counterparty credit risk, as long as they satisfy market arbitrage and/or backtesting requirements.[2]

In fact, given that all financial organisations already have models in place for pricing this asset class, these models should be the starting point for a counterparty risk system.

Number of independent components: It is well known that most of the yield curve changes can be described using three degrees of freedom, or three factors. When they have zero correlation between them, they are called "principal components", and they come up from diagonalising the intra-yield-curve correlation matrix. These three factors correspond roughly to parallel shifts, twists around one point, and flattening/widening anchored in two points. It must be noted that if we choose to model these principal components directly, we will most likely be generating in the future shapes of yield curves that contain arbitrage opportunities, so we may want to implement an arbitrage-check in the algorithm. However, many of the well developed interest rate models are already arbitrage-free by construction.

When modelling yield curves it is important to understand how many factors are needed for the particular portfolio.[3] For example, if the portfolio is not sensitive to yield curve rotations or flattening, then we only need one factor to model the yield curve (parallel shifts). With this in mind, a typical mistake that is sometimes made is to think along the lines of "this portfolio contains only vanilla swaps, so we only need one factor, because a swap is not very sensitive to the second or third principal components". At a portfolio level however a curve flattening may be the most significant risk factor, and hence it is therefore always important to think of the portfolio effect when deciding how to model exposure.

For example, let's say that we have a netting set composed of one 1-year vanilla payer swap and one 10-year vanilla receiver swap with approximately the same (but opposite sign) duration. During the first year of the simulation (when the 1-year swap has not matured yet), we are going to be quite (if not very) sensitive to rotations of the yield curve. Then, from year 1 to 10, the portfolio consists of only one swap, so a one factor model is sufficient. As a result, if this model is used for regulatory capital, that is based on the first year profile, we *must* have a two factor model; if we use it to calculate peak exposure (the maximum of the PFE profile), then we will get away with a one factor model quite well, as this profile will peak after 1 year. But if our model is used for both, then we need both factors.

As this example shows, if we are building an RFE model for general purposes, it should contain at least three factors.

Parametric yield curve modelling: An alternative way of modelling yield curves is via a parametrisation framework. This technique is less popular, arguably for historical reasons, but in my view it is as, or more, powerful than many classical approaches. This technique is based on the observed fact that yield curves can be described to a great precision with a range of analytical functions. For example, the Nelson-Siegel framework.

Let's say that we have a yield curve YC_t. YC_t is just a set of discount factors, or interest rates, in the future, and an interpolation scheme. Let's say that we have found a family of analytical functions $\boldsymbol{\Omega}$, such that each function is described by, for example, three parameters.[4] In other words, there is always a set of α_1, α_2, and α_3 so that

$$f_t(\alpha_1,\alpha_2,\alpha_3) \simeq YC_t, \text{where } f_t \in \Omega \tag{3.6}$$

Now we can treat the parameters α as the risk factors to be diffused. Each risk factor can be modelled by a simple Brownian motion, normal or lognormal, with a constant or mean reverting drift, and can be linearly correlated. This way we can achieve future yield curves that are realistic and that follow a simple modelling framework.

Multiple yield curves per currency: Up to 2008, counterparty risk systems would usually use one single yield curve per currency. However, that approach may not be sufficient anymore; it depends on the risks that the portfolio is sensitive to. At present we may need to consider yield spreads[5] for swaps with different payment frequency, for example. The so called risk-free yield curve is no longer given by the interbank swap market, but by the Overnight Index Swaps (OIS) market. Also, a specific cross-currency yield curve may be needed for FX forward modelling. If we are not sensitive to these spreads we can leave them as a constant number in our simulations, but if we are sensitive to them, we can model them with a mean reverting process. Ornstein-Uhlenbeck or Black-Karasinski processes are good candidates.

Calibration: Counterparty exposure systems will need to model all four major yield curves (USD, EUR, GBP, and JPY), and depending on the portfolio usually at least another 20 G10 and emerging market interest rates. If calibrated with market-implied data, these models have been traditionally fixed to Certificate of Deposits, Forward Rate Agreements, Swaps, Caps, Floors, and Swaptions. Now, we need to use also OIS, as well as the range of spreads that exist in the market. If historically calibrated, we need to create a time series of the factors that we are modelling and calculate volatilities, mean reversion, and the correlations from them.

3.2.2 Foreign exchange models

The Foreign Exchange (FX) risk factor is also very important, as cross-currency portfolios tend to be large and currency changes also affect all other trades on the books that are not in the accounting currency of the institution. FX forwards tend to have relatively short tenors, up to a few years, but it is important to model FX accurately beyond that point as well, because, as we will see, it will affect many long dated trades, as well as collateral.

In the world of FX we need to consider two parts: modelling the spot FX rate (one number), and the forward market (a whole curve). Up to 2007, the forward market was described quite nicely by the yield curves of the two currencies, but now we need to apply a spread to it, as mentioned in the previous section.

In any case, modelling of the FX forward market is based on modelling of the two yield curves.

The FX spot rate is usually modelled using a Geometric Brownian Motion (GBM) framework, that avoids negative rates. Arguably, a low mean reversion can be added to avoid the economic implications of interest rates exploding in the long run in the modelling framework.

FX jumps: A feature that can be added is a jump diffusion process, typically for emerging market currencies, to account for sudden devaluation risk. There is sufficient literature on jump diffusion processes so we won't expand on this topic further. Calibrating jump diffusion parameters (mean and standard deviation of the jump size, etc.) can be quite challenging. The most common practice is to use historical data for the calibration. It should be noted however that different historical windows can sometimes result in significantly different results, so it is advisable to perform an analysis based on different historical periods before selecting one period.

Instead of using a jump diffusion process, a simple approximation can be to use a gradual drift in the FX spot GBM process, that if calibrated consistently will, in most cases, have similar results at a risk metric level. This is because the jump will usually impact only on the tails of the FX probability distribution, and so it will not usually impact much on the EPE, because it is an average. However, it may affect the CESF, or the EPE and PFE, when our books have many exotic derivatives that contain FX gearing features.

FX rates to model: When modelling FX spot, we need to choose a base currency for all the exchange rates in our simulation. Typically a bank will choose the currency in which it bases its accounts; USD for an American bank, EUR for a European one, etc. Then it has two modelling options; if we are an American bank, we can choose to model EURUSD, JPYUSD, CHFUSD, etc., or USDEUR, USDJPY, USDCHF, etc. In principle, there is no reason why one should be better than the other, but we must be aware that the risk we measure will be slightly sensitive to that choice.

Pegged currencies can be modelled as a small spread over the currency it is pegged at. In addition, we may also want to model depegging risk. These scenarios should be treated with a jump process with a large jump size, a low probability of occurrence, and followed by a significant increase in the FX volatility.

Calibration: In our FX system, we will usually need to model at least all exchange rates for which we model a yield curve, and we may need to add on-shore and off-shore exchange rates. FX models can be calibrated to the FX forward and options market for a risk-neutral calibration, or to the time series of the spot rate if historically calibrated.

3.2.3 Equity models

Equity can also be an important risk factor, depending on the firm's portfolio. Some institutions trade heavily in equity derivatives, others hardly ever do. Equity trades tend to have a tenor up to 5 years, sometimes they might go up to 10 years, but they rarely have a maturity longer than that.

Equity modelling has some strong similarities with FX modelling. Both have a spot and a forward market. In the case of equity, there is equity spot, forward, swap and option as well as equity financing which is also called stock borrowing and lending or stock repo market, given its similarities to the bond repo market. Equity spot is usually modelled using a GBM process. We may want to use a jump diffusion process similar to FX; in general, we will only notice the difference if we measure risk with CESF, or if we have in our books exotic derivatives with gearing features that are sensitive to the tails of the equity spot distribution.

Dividends and borrowing and lending: Most institutions only model the equity spot price and use the risk-free yield curve in the currency of the stock to calculate the equity forward, via arbitrage-free arguments. However, we may want to consider dividends too. In its simplest form, future dividends can be treated as a constant yield or as a set of expected cash flows in the future. In either of these cases our Monte Carlo engine will not capture dividend risk.

To model equity derivatives accurately we need to do the following: firstly model the dividends and secondly model the equity repo rate.[6] There is a market for dividend swaps from which we can infer expected future dividends. That market has a term structure, with the typical higher volatility for the shorter tenors. Also, the equity spot price must be correlated to the dividend in that, when expected future dividends decrease, the value of the equity spot decreases. That dependency is stronger the shorter the dividend swap tenor.

The equity repo market can be described by a forward curve in the same way the FX forward market is described by a cross-currency yield curve, but we need to account for dividends too, so that $r_{\text{repo}} = r_{\text{risk-free}} - d + s_{\text{repo}}$, where d is the dividend yield and s_{repo} is the repo spread.

Equity indices: Another topic that needs attention is the modelling of equity indices. First of all, they tend to have slightly lower volatilities and softer jumps than single stocks due to the diversification effects. We can model them as a single stock itself, with its individual calibration, as long as we are not sensitive in our portfolio to its basis; i.e., a netting set that is, for example, long on one index and short on its constituents. When that is the case, we need to build the indices in the simulation adding up their single stocks and, if needed, add a small basis on top with a mean reverting process. In general, if we model an index as a single stock, we will be overestimating basis risk.[7]

One problem of modelling each stock as an individual process is that we can easily end up with a very large correlation matrix, say 1,000 × 1,000, which can be time consuming when generating correlated random numbers and manipulating such a large matrix.[8]

A practical way to get around these two problems is by modelling each country's main equity index with a GBM processes, around 20 of them, and then individual stocks with a beta to the main index of their country of risk. This way, the actual result for individual stock indices will be very similar to, if not the same as, the previous methodology, and the basis risk will be better captured and computational requirements will be considerably lower.

Calibration: The typical number of equities that a large institution needs to model ranges from a few hundred to a few thousand. Equity models can be calibrated to the market (options market and dividend swaps) for a risk-neutral RFE, or to historical time series of the spot price and dividend swaps for historical calibrations.

3.2.4 Volatility models

In all the previously mentioned models we have always considered volatility as a constant number. That is because the primary risk factor for exposure metrics tends to be the actual underlying risk factor (e.g., interest rates, FX spot, equity spot). However, a stochastic volatility model can fine-tune calculations and provide more accurate exposure profiles. It has been shown that exposure measurements can be significantly impacted on by stochastic volatility [74].

Stochastic volatility models introduce, first of all, non-normality into the diffusion processes. This is good in general as we know that real market behaviour is not normally distributed. In addition, these models are required when we have variance or volatility swaps on our books, or when we are highly sensitive to implied volatilities; for example, when we have a large book of options that are delta-hedged. However, stochastic volatility models provide better exposure profiles even for trades that do not seem to be that sensible to volatility, as with vanilla swaps, as shown in Figure 3.2.

Given the complexity of exposure systems, this risk factor has been widely neglected across the board for counterparty risk in financial institutions. Even the banks with the most advanced systems tend to have fairly basic models for volatility, if at all.

Some simplifications include introducing a time-varying volatility structure in the simulation framework, so that the same volatility will be used for all scenarios at the same time step, but a different volatility over time in the simulation. For example, we can say that the instantaneous volatility is given by

$$\sigma_t = \sigma_\infty + (\sigma_0 - \sigma_\infty)\, e^{-\gamma t}, \tag{3.7}$$

where σ_0 is today's volatility, σ_∞ is the long term volatility, and γ regulates the transition speed from one to the other. This type of model is fairly simple to implement and can be very useful in times of market stress or when a high volatility is required. Examples include uncollateralised exposures of short-term trades and collateralised exposures (see Figure 3.3).

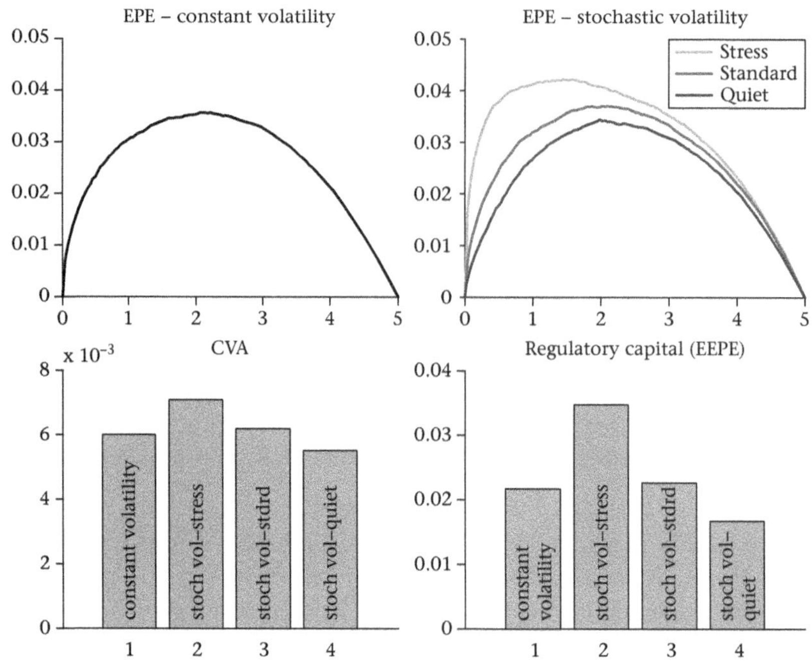

Figure 3.2 EPE uncollateralised profiles for an IR swap, modelled with a constant volatility model (top left), and a stochastic volatility model (top right). In the case of stochastic volatility, the model was calibrated to representative stress, normal, and quiet market conditions. The bottom left panel shows the CVA for each of the four cases, and the bottom right shows regulatory capital (EEPE)

Another simple alternative is the well-known local volatility models. In this case, the volatility is not stochastic, but changes, for each time step and each scenario, related to the spot (e.g., equity price or FX rate) in a deterministic way. This way of treating volatility will borrow its stochasticity from the spot simulation, but may not add the important term structure to the volatility, needed, for example, in times of market stress.

3.2.5 Credit models

Credit was *the* asset class of the 2000s. In fact, the excess money in the developed economies[9] went into this asset class to a high extent and created the well known credit bubble. The excess lending by banks was transformed into credit derivative instruments that were then traded mainly between financial institutions. The credit derivatives market is now mainly dominated by Credit Default Swaps (CDS), but there is also an important legacy market of tranched products (CDO, CLO, MBS, etc.) and Credit Default Swap Options (CDSwaptions). CDSs tend to have a tenor of up to 5 years, but they can go up to 10 years. They rarely go beyond that point.

Credit as an asset class can be quite complex to model, as there are many components that come into play.

Type of models: The behaviour of credit as a risk factor is somewhat related to equities and to interest rates. It is related to equities in that as the default probability increases, and hence the credit is spread, the equity price should decrease. This is very well described by the Merton model[10] and is widely seen in the market data.[11] It is also linked to interest rates through bond pricing, and it has a term structure that behaves very

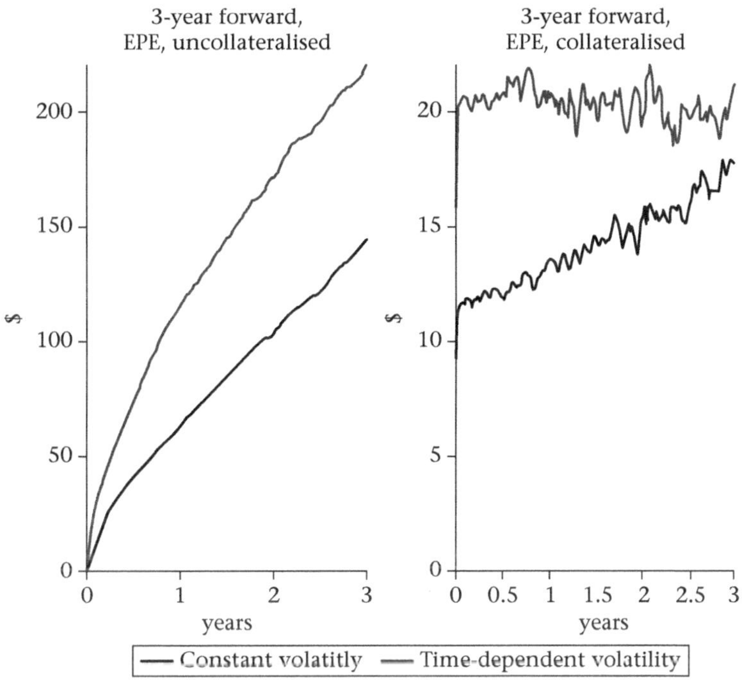

Figure 3.3 EPE profiles for a 3-year forward using a model with constant volatility ($\sigma = 30\%$) and with a time varying volatility ($\sigma_0 = 50\%$, $\sigma_\infty = 20\%$, $\gamma = 0.5$)

similarly to that of interest rates. Three factors describe it very well, which correspond to a shift, a rotation, and a flattening.

It is quite standard to split the credit spread into two stochastic sub-variables: default probability and recovery rates. However, in most cases there isn't a market large and deep enough to calibrate both stochastic variables.[12] So the recovery rate is usually left constant and it is the default probability that is stochastically modelled. The default probability is frequently modelled as an instantaneous default intensity, also called the *hazard rate*. It's quite a standard technique to model the hazard rate with a Black-Karansinsky process. Interestingly, it is widely believed that credit spreads and hazard rates are mean reverting variables, but data shows that they are not [73].

Another family of models are asset-based; they model a company's financial status with a latent asset, from which the credit standing (and the equity price) can be inferred. The Merton model is a fairly simple but relatively accurate and widely used model in this approach.

Another approach used to model credit is diffusing directly the credit spread. This is a less popular approach, but I have found it to be as good as any other modelling framework. In fact, in many cases it is my preferred choice as we are modelling something that is actually observable in the market (credit spreads) as opposed to theoretical variables.

Exposure metrics measure long term risk; and defaults can play an important role in future exposure over long time horizons. As a consequence, we most often need to simulate defaults in parallel to hazard rates, recovery rates, or credit spreads. Defaults should be simulated so that the actual default probability in each scenario is taken from the simulated default intensity. In fact, in this way the survived simulated scenarios will show a corridor effect as observed in real data.[13]

A final standard approach for credit RFE is credit-rating based models. The credit quality is bucketed into ratings, and a transition matrix with a Markov process simulates rating transitions that should include a defaulted state. Each rating can have a spread, that is stochastic, and then each name can have one idiosyncratic spread on top of the credit-rating spread.

As the reader can see, credit has a vast range of models to choose from. As a general rule, I recommend avoiding credit rating models, as what creates the exposure of a CDS is the credit spread, as opposed to the firm's credit rating. Also, credit ratings are slow to react to news compared to the CDS market; for example, Spain's government bonds reached several hundred basis points in the European Sovereign crisis while they still had high quality investment grade ratings.

In any case, any of the modelling frameworks described above offer good solutions to credit RFE as long as the model passes the arbitrage and/or backtesting requirements. We have observed that a simple GBM process for the credit spread with simulated defaults relative to the simulated default intensity behave very nicely for many purposes, and is easy to calibrate.

Dependency and correlation structures: Dependencies between credit spreads and equities can also be important when modelling counterparty exposure. Similarly to equities, a simple dependency framework with a linear correlation between each spread is computationally expensive[14] and may not capture well the regional and industry sector dependency structure between credit spreads.[15] The index and beta modelling framework described in the equity risk factor section is a good solution here too.

The Equity-Credit dependency structure, that is more complex than a simple linear correlation, may be better captured by an asset-based model or with a semi-analytical model than a simple linear correlation structure, as described in detailed in Chapter 10,[16] where the obligor hazard rate λ is given by,

$$\lambda = A s^B + \sigma \epsilon, \tag{3.8}$$

where s is the equity price, A, B, and σ are parameters, and ϵ is a normally distributed random number.

Liquidity risk: Another important topic impacting on credit is right- and wrong-way risk. I dedicate a whole chapter to it, Chapter 10, but let's say for now that the dependency between the potential default of the counterparty and that of a CDS obligor can increase or decrease substantially the exposure metric.

We may also want to capture the basis risk between bonds and CDSs. If the markets were complete, with no arbitrage, then we could (i) buy a corporate bond and (ii) buy default protection on the underlying name through a CDS, and we should end up with a default-free investment. However, in reality, the credit spread indicated by bond prices[17] can be quite different to the CDS par credit spread.[18] This is the so-called basis or credit-liquidity risk. If our portfolio is sensitive to basis risk, we should also consider modelling it.

Calibrating credit models for RFE can be challenging; data may be scarce or may be unreliable due to liquidity constraints. We will typically have a term structure of CDSs to calibrate too. If we want to calibrate both hazard rates and recovery rates, we need to have a double market of standard and digital CDSs. The standard CDSs pay $1 - RR$ (where RR is the recovery rate) at default, while a digital CDS pays 1. When that double market is not available, which is in most cases, we can only calibrate the recovery rate to historical data. There is also a limited market of CDSwaptions from which we can calibrate volatilities but, again, it is not very liquid, so often we can only refer to historical calibration even when we want to calibrate to the risk-neutral measure. Volatilities tend to be very high in this asset class.

3.2.6 Inflation models

Inflation products have been around for a long time, but have become increasingly popular since 2009, as a result of the economic crisis, the low interest rates, and the quantitative easing policies set by all major central banks; they have fuelled fear in the investor of deflation or high inflation. Typical inflation trades have very long tenors, from 30 to 50 years.

Here we need to distinguish between nominal and real inflation. Nominal is the inflation we see in the economy, real is that inflation minus the risk-free interest rates. Nominal inflation tends to be highly correlated to interest rates, so the variable that is usually modelled is real inflation as a spread over interest rates, often using a mean reverting process.

Similarly to rates, the market trades inflation swaps of different maturities that can be calibrated to inflation-linked bonds that central banks issue.

3.2.7 Commodity and utility models

Another asset class that has gathered increasing attention is commodities and utilities. All commodities tend to be discussed together, but from a modelling perspective each of them can be very different.

Oil can be modelled with a GBM process, to which we can add jumps to increase accuracy. Base metals, like copper or aluminium, and agricultural products can also be modelled using GBM. Gas, however, requires seasonality to be taken into account, that can be added with some sort of sinusoidal functions. Precious metals are often considered a currency and can be, in fact, modelled by the FX system. Power is quite a tricky variable to model, as it shows massive spikes in the price that require special modelling features. In general, all these assets have a forward (or futures) market, but it cannot be described with a yield curve as for equities or FX. This market is based in physically delivered products, and its price is given entirely by demand and supply, as opposed to no-arbitrage arguments as happens with equity or FX forwards.

For commodity markets the term structure of the forward curve is very important. The front end of the forward curve can be very volatile and the term structure can change significantly. Calibration of commodity assets with no reliable historical data is based on a proxy to a similar commodity. This should be reviewed on a regular basis to ensure it remains up to date.

Correlation between different forward contracts of an underlying and in between different commodities is also extremely important when modelling the counterparty risk of a commodity portfolio. Correlations are usually based on historical data unless there are liquid options markets available but they need to be recalibrated frequently as these can change significantly.

Finally it must be noted that a significant constraint in modelling commodity derivatives is low liquidity and insufficient price transparency.

3.2.8 Other niche risk factors

Some organisations frequently trade in other markets, and hence they will require some niche RFE modelling. These include life insurance, weather derivatives, car insurance, and natural disasters. In these cases the risk factor to model are people's life expectancy and deaths, weather behaviour, road accidents, and earthquakes.[19]

3.2.9 Dependency structures

Typically, a counterparty credit risk system simulates from a few hundred to a few thousand risk factors. The dependency structure can significantly impact on the risk of the portfolio. Hence, dependencies must be modelled with care.

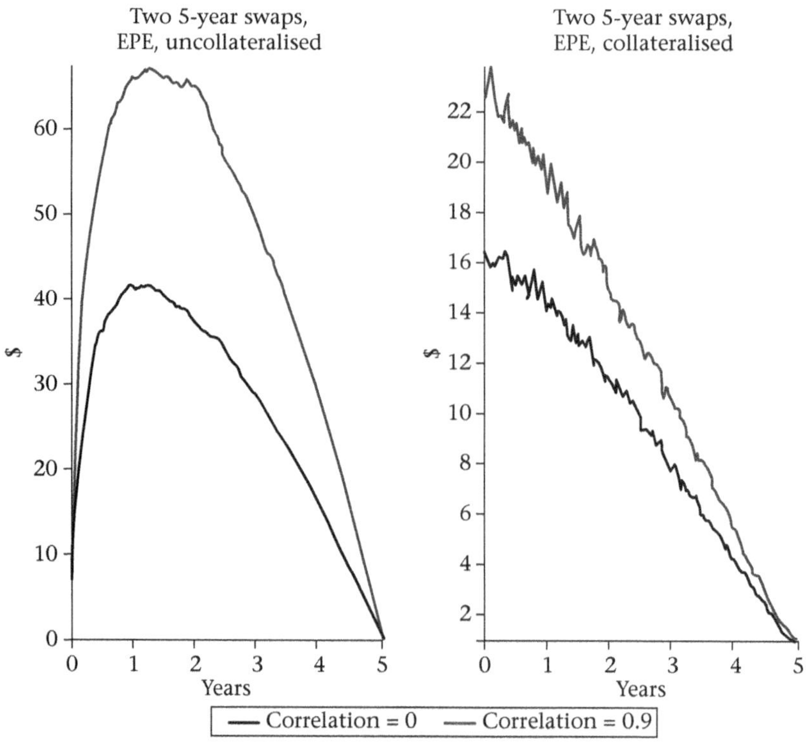

Figure 3.4 EPE profiles, uncollateralised and collateralised, of a netting set with two 5-year swaps, where the correlation between the underlyings is 0 and 0.9

This is more easily seen with an example. We need to jump a bit ahead of ourselves now and see the EPE profiles of two swaps that are netted, where the correlation between the underlyings was 0 and 0.9. Figure 3.4 shows the results. It can be clearly observed that the exposure obtained with a high correlation is noticeably higher than with zero correlation. Hence, dependency structure is very important for exposure measurement.

Dependency vs. correlation: First of all, it is very important to distinguish the difference between "dependency" and "correlation" since correlation is only one simple way to measure dependency. In fact, we can have strongly dependent variables with zero correlation. For example, two variables that follow a GBM process can have a dependency best described via a beta structure to an index (e.g., equities) but, then, when we model dependencies in this way we are changing the linear correlation parameter between them, even though *the dependency modelling is more accurate.*

Another example of the difference between correlation and dependency is that we can have two variables, with a dependency structure modelled by a correlation parameter and a copula structure. If we change the copula without changing the correlation parameter, we will be changing the dependency structure but keeping the linear correlation. Simplifying the whole dependency framework to a linear correlation number is like simplifying the distribution of a variable to a volatility number. Similarly to having the same volatility with very different skew or kurtosis, we can have the same correlation with very different dependency structures.

Methodologies and computational effort: Having said that, we must be careful of how we model dependencies. A standard way is generating Brownian random numbers from a bivariate probability distribution function, with a correlation parameter. This can be extended to n dimensions quite easily. Typically, this is implemented numerically using a Choleski or Spectral decomposition algorithm. The problem here is that the computational power of generating those random numbers becomes increasingly expensive as n grows.[20] Typical systems have an n that ranges from a few hundred to a few thousand. As a result, any savings or shortcuts that we can make to minimise the size of that matrix are highly welcome. Fortunately, the bulk of the decomposition needs to be done only once per Monte Carlo run; once it is done we can reuse it to generate correlated random numbers in each scenario and time step.

If the correlation matrix is too big so that even one decomposition is too expensive, a multi-factor technique, where single names are related to a number of indices via a beta decomposition, is a good substitute, as we have already indicated for equities and credit. Furthermore, sometimes it not only increases computational performance, but it can also describe more accurately the dependency structure.

If our portfolio contains correlation-sensitive products like credit tranched products, FX basket options, equity structured products, etc., we may want to model correlation as a stochastic variable. This however creates a big computational problem, because we are going to have to do the Cholesky or Spectral decomposition in every time step and scenario, which is a computationally expensive process. If a stochastic correlation is required, a shortcut may be to do the decomposition off-system and upload the results (or to do it once at the beginning of the Monte Carlo run) for a number of representative correlations (e.g., −0.99, −0.9, −0.8, ..., 0.8, 0.9, 0.99), and then interpolate for each time step and scenario as the stochastic correlation changes.

In conclusion, exposure metrics can be quite sensitive to dependency structures, and so they must be modelled with care; in addition, modelling dependency is a very difficult problem both from a methodology and a computational perspective.

3.3 Pricing

Let's say that we are an American bank (i.e., we measure everything in USD) and that we have a portfolio with

- Trade 1: 10-year USD interest rate (IR) receiver swap
- Trade 2: 10-year USD swaption
- Trade 3: USDEUR FX option
- Trade 4: 5-year equity swap of a EUR stock
- Trade 5: 5-year EUR IR swap, originated 3 years ago
- Trade 6: 7-year USD credit default swap, originated 1 year ago

In order to calculate exposure metrics for the portfolio, we need to price each trade at each scenario and time step of the simulation. However, before that, we need to generate the simulated risk factor scenarios for it.

Looking at that portfolio, the risk factors that we are going to need to simulate are:

- USD yield curve to price the USD swaps, swaptions, FX option, and CDS
- USD interest rate implied volatility surface (or cube) for the swaption
- USDEUR FX spot price
- USDEUR FX implied volatility surface for the FX option
- EUR yield curve for the FX option, equity swap, and EUR interest rate swap

- The equity spot price
- The CDS spread curve for the credit default swap

In addition, the share price volatility and the credit spread volatility may be simulated in order to calculate the future exposure of the equity swap and the CDS respectively. These will not be used for calculating the MtM of the trades on day 1 but for calculating the future exposure of the trades. In practice, however, given the complexity of the calculations, equity and CDS volatilities are not usually simulated, unless the portfolio includes instruments with a first order sensitivity to volatility (example, variance swaps).

Once we have all the risk factor simulations, we can price all six trades, in each scenario and time step, to end up with six price grids, each of dimension $N \times (M+1)$.

A fundamental question is what models we should use to price these trades. The best solution is to be consistent with the official daily pricing of the trades and use the same models for calculating counterparty risk. If, for example, we are considering scenario 345 in 1 year in the future, we need to price the trades as if we really are 1 year in the future, and the event of scenario 345 has actually happened, hence we need to use the actual pricing routines that the firm uses for pricing these trades. That is why we may need to simulate the rates and FX implied volatilities to price the trades, regardless of what volatility we use in the RFE simulation models.

As said, finally we end up with one $N \times (M+1)$ matrix for each trade, that consists of the trade prices in each scenario and time step. This is illustrated in Figure 3.5. It must be noted that the price of all trades at the start of the simulation is the same for all simulations (it is zero for swaps that start today and non-zero for options and for swaps that were incepted in the past) and that the price of each trade falls to zero once it has expired.

Computational effort: It is very important to realise that this pricing step, being fairly easy to explain and understand, is the most complex from a computational standpoint. In fact, I have measured that it most often takes more than 95% of the whole computational time, and sometimes in excess of 99%. This is so important that we dedicate Section 3.6 to discussing it.

3.4 Risk metric calculation

Once we have a price grid for all the trades we are interested in, we are in a position to calculate the credit risk metrics we need: typically EPE, ENE, PFE, and/or CESF.

3.4.1 Netting risk

We have already discussed the concept of a netting set: a group of trades that in the event of default can be summed up in value, so that trades with negative value offset trades with positive value, and there is only one amount owed: the sum of the value of these trades. Importantly, if a counterparty defaults, trades in different netting sets with the same counterparty cannot be netted. In other words, from a counterparty risk point of view, the concept of "single trade" is irrelevant. What makes sense is the concept of "netting set".

When trades can be netted, calculating their credit risk metrics is fairly straightforward. We are going to start with one $N \times (M+1)$ grid of prices for each trade. These prices should be calculated from the same risk factor simulations; that is, the value of the risk factors at each scenario and each time step used for each trade should be consistent.[21] Then all we have to do is sum the prices of all trades in the netting set per scenario and time step, so that we end up with one grid of dimensions $N \times (M+1)$ per netting set.

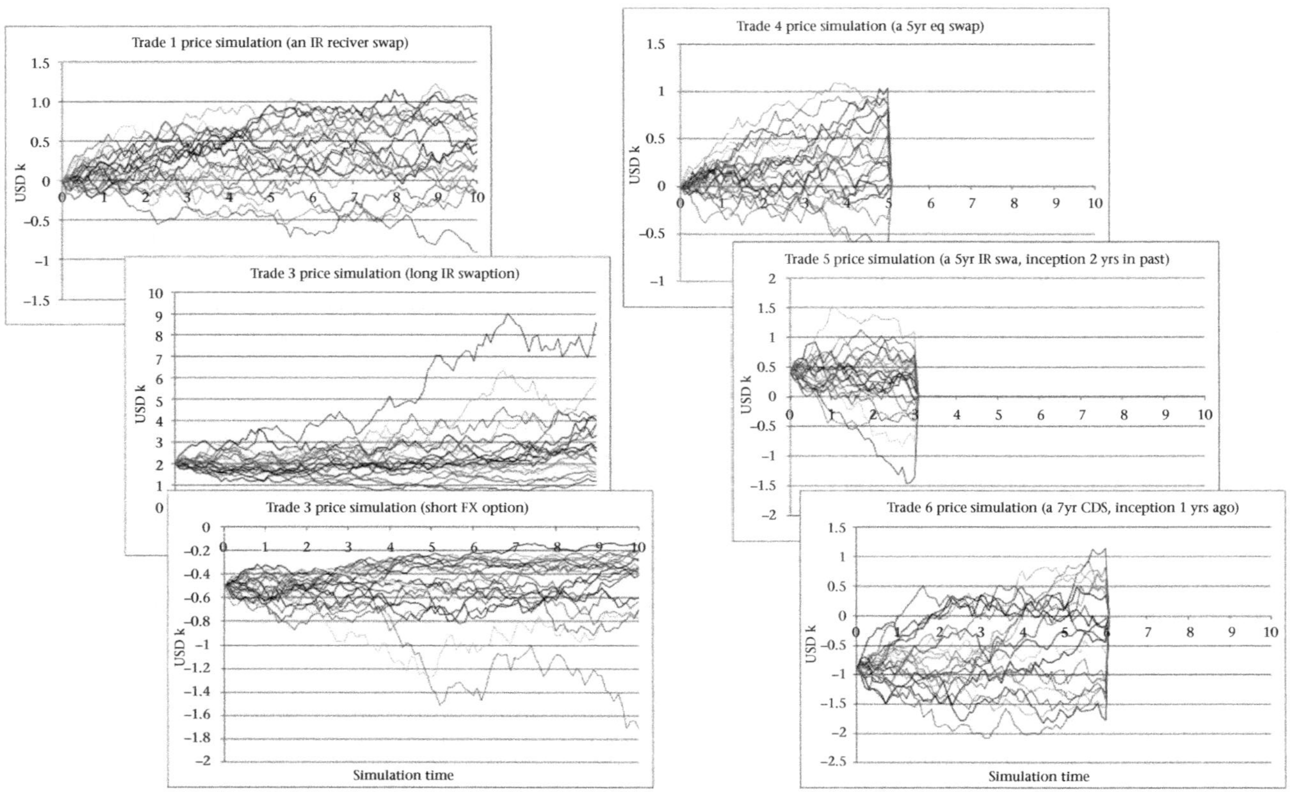

Figure 3.5 Prices of all six trades of the example, for each time point and scenario

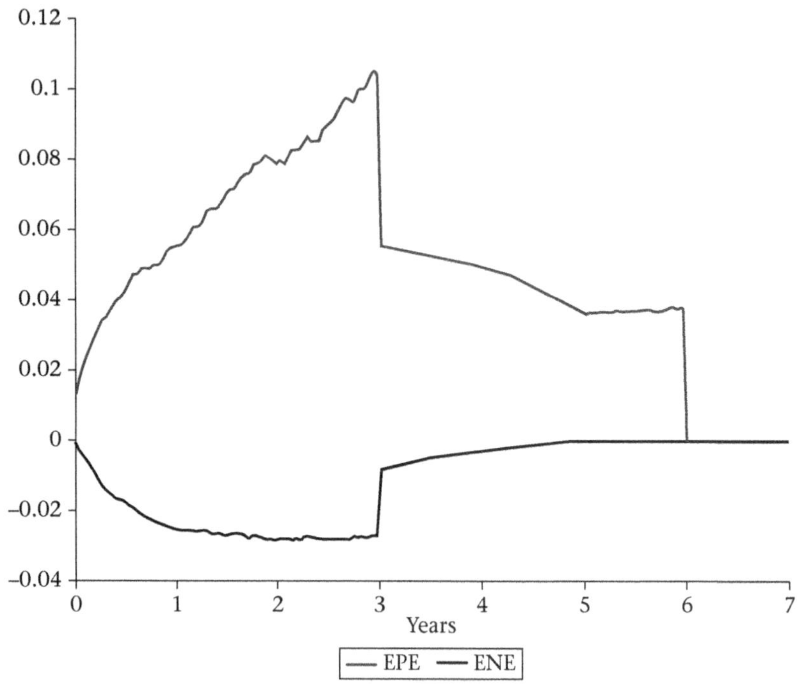

Figure 3.6 EPE and ENE profiles for a portfolio consisting of a 3-year FX forward, a 5-year interest rate swap and a 6-year equity option

Once this is done, we are in a position to do the last step of a risk profile calculation. We already mentioned that we are looking for $\Psi_t(V)$ where V is the price of the netting set. To calculate risk profiles, we can take a slice of the netting set price grid at each time point. Each of these slices will contain N prices of the netting set, from which we can measure the risk metrics: EPE will be the average of all values after flooring to zero, PFE at X% confidence level will be the $N \times X/100$ highest value, etc. If we do this calculation for each time bucket, we will obtain the risk profiles EPE_t, ENE_t, PFE_t, or $CESF_t$. An example of these profiles can be seen in Figure 3.6; an outline of all the steps needed to get to the risk profile is shown in Figure 3.7 (see page 51).

3.4.2 Adding risk

The idea behind risk adding follows quite naturally from splitting risk into netting sets. If two counterparties have two separate Master Agreements between them (i.e., two netting sets), in the event of default, the value of each netting set does not offset each other. In other words, if in netting set 1 we are owed $1m, in netting set 2 we owe $1m, and my counterparty defaults, we have to pay the $1m for netting set 1, but from the amount we are owed we will only receive a recovery rate.

Based on this idea, each netting set is a completely different entity from a credit risk point of view, and hence the exposure that we have to a counterparty is going to be the sum of the exposures of each netting set. Furthermore, the exposure profile of our portfolio across all counterparties, is the sum of the exposure profiles of all individual netting sets.

This is *Adding Risk* and it is the approach followed by lots of risk systems and by the Basel Committee for the calculation of regulatory capital.

3.4.3 Aggregating risk

However, adding risk can overestimate the true economic risk. Let's see how with an example.

Let's look at a coin tossing game: we toss a coin and arrange two bets with someone so that:

1. If Heads, we give \$1. If Tails, we receive \$1
2. If Heads, we receive \$1. If Tails, we give \$1

In this game, the coin tossing is the risk factor, the bets are the trades, and the other player is the counterparty. Each trade is the opposite of each other, so if they are booked in the same netting set, the exposure will always be zero, regardless of the outcome of the coin toss.

Let's say now that each of them constitutes a netting set by itself. Also, for illustrative purposes, let's consider that the exposure is measured as the *maximum I can be owed.* Under this risk metric (a completely valid one), the exposure of each individual trade is \$1, and hence the exposure to both trades using the risk addition rule we have seen before will be $\$1 + \$1 = \$2$.

However, in this case we only have two possible scenarios (tails and heads), so we can easily do a scenario analysis. Doing so, we can realise that if the coin toss gives tails we will have a credit exposure of \$1 from trade 1 and \$0 from trade 2, and if it gives heads we will have an exposure of \$0 from trade 1 and \$1 from trade 2. However, we also see that both events are mutually exclusive, so the maximum I can be owed is only \$1! That is, my true economic potential credit exposure to the counterparty is \$1, as we are never going to be owed more than that amount, not \$2 as calculated using the risk adding rule.

Conclusion: Adding Risk can overestimate the true economic credit exposure risk.

Now, instead of using the maximum I can be owed as a credit metric, let's use the EPE: how much I can be owed on average.

Under this metric, the exposure of each trade is \$0.5: in trade 1, we will be owed \$0 if tails and \$1 if heads, so $EPE_1 = (\$1 + \$0)/2 = \$0.5$, and a similar argument can be found for trade 2. The adding rule in this cases gives $\$0.5 + \$0.5 = \$1$, so it seems to calculate the true economic credit risk correctly.

Conclusion: Adding Risk can give the true economic credit exposure risk.

The problem is that the adding rule works for some exposure risk metrics, but it doesn't for other ones. In particular, it works for EPE and ENE, but it does not work for PFE or CESF. In these later cases, it overestimates risk. A detailed explanation can be found in Appendix B.

If we want to calculate correctly any exposure risk metric for a number of netting sets, we must:

1. Calculate all the price grids for each netting set the same way as before,
2. We must floor all $N \times (M + 1)$ prices in each grid at zero (or cap them at zero for the ENE),
3. We sum all the elements of the floored grids so we end up with one single grid for the portfolio, and
4. We calculate the exposure metrics on this final grid.

In this way we will account for the diversification effect of having trades distributed between different netting sets.

We can call this operation of "summing up floored values of trades at the scenario level" as *Aggregating* exposures, as opposed to "summing risk metrics of trades", which is *Adding* exposures.

3.5 Simulation time points

We have seen that the calculation of exposure metrics is based on grids that have $N \times (M+1)$ dimensions, where N is the number of scenarios and M is the number of time steps. Hence the computational effort is going to be roughly linear with M.[22] As mentioned in the Risk Factor Evolution section, we would ideally like to calculate the exposure daily until the portfolio maturity, but portfolios can mature 20, 30 or even in some cases 50 years in the future, so we need to make a compromise.

Financial institutions tend to have a number of pre-defined time buckets, that are close together at the beginning, but then spread out so that the calculation is feasible from a computational point of view. A typical set up could be:

- Daily calculations for 1 week
- Then, weekly calculations up to 1 month
- Then, biweekly up to 3 months
- Afer that, monthly up to 1 year
- Then, quarterly up to 5 years
- Finally, yearly up to the end time point

The calculation of the end time point has been changing over time. Arguably, any exposure calculation beyond 10 years has very limited value, as the only thing we can say fairly confidently about the financial world in 10 years, time is that it will be very different to how it is now. However, having an indication of what the risk could be in 25 years, time seems to be better than having nothing at all. Also, since counterparty credit risk became central for pricing, and banks have to compute CVA, we need to calculate expected exposures over the life of the portfolio, regardless of how long that is. For all these reasons, the calculation end point has increased from 10 to 20 years in the firstly implemented systems to 50 years and beyond at the present time. In fact, some regulators now require at least 50 years of exposure profiles. As a result, some banks reportedly calculate exposure numbers up to 100 years in the future, with 5-year time steps after 50 years.

In addition to exposure metric-reporting time points, there are other points we may want to consider:

- **Simulation Time Points:** Several exotic trades are path dependent and need the value of past risk factors to be priced on particular dates; for example, Asian options. To calculate the risk of these trades the system needs to simulate risk factors at specific time points.
- **Pricing Time Points:** If we only price the trades on the dates that the exposures are reported, we may miss important exposure peaks that could happen as a result of coupons, cash-flows or trade maturing. Hence a flexible system should be able to add these dates to the pricing time points. If we do calculate the exposure on these particular dates and we want to be consistent and report exposures always at the same time steps, the reported exposure of each time bucket could be the maximum exposure of all the time points within each bucket. Also, as we will see soon, the calculation of exposures for collateralised portfolios requires the calculation of pricing in several extra time points.

It must be noted that the simulation points must contain the pricing points, which must also contain the exposure reporting points.

Having multiple time points for different calculation layers can, in practice, increase significantly the computational requirements. For example, pricing all interest rate swaps on all their coupon dates can be very time consuming. So this multi-time-point calculation must be handled with care. In any case, a good counterparty credit risk system should ideally have this flexibility, so it can be used when required for special portfolios or counterparties.

3.6 The biggest quantitative challenge the financial industry has ever seen

We are now in a position to understand the outstanding computational requirement that the calculation of exposure brings with it. A major financial institution will have approximately:[23]

- 1,000 netting sets
- An average of 1,000 trades in each netting set
- Will try to calculate exposure metrics with 10,000 scenarios[24]
- Will have to simulate 1,000 risk factors (multi-point yield curves, FX spots, equity prices, commodity curves, credit spread curves, inflation curves, implied volatilities, etc. If fact, it can easily be up to a few thousand risk factors)
- Will report exposures in 100 time points

The complexity of this calculation is depicted in Figure 3.7. Each plane is a grid that will contain $N \times (M+1)$ calculated numbers. There will be around 1,000 of these grids with risk factor values, and around 1,000,000 of these grids with trade prices. Exposure metrics need to be calculated daily. This means that a counterparty risk system needs to compute 500,000,000 risk factor values and do 500,000,000,000 pricing jobs. Yes, that number is correct; the order of magnitude of pricing jobs required to calculate the daily CVA, exposure profiles for risk management, capital calculation, etc., is in the trillions! This is without considering the calculation of sensitivities, exposure allocations, intra-day incremental exposures, wrong way risk, and a long et cetera.

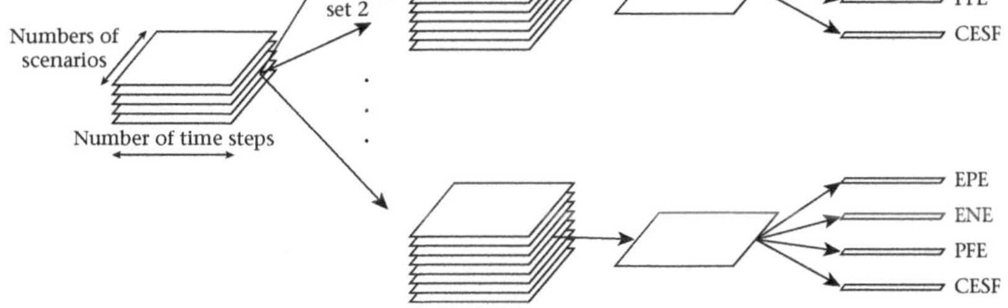

Figure 3.7 Outline of the grids during different steps of a full counterparty credit risk calculation. Each plane represents one grid, with the number of simulations in one dimension, and the number of time steps along the other dimension. The risk profiles have only one dimension, the number of time steps

Hence, the development of a counterparty credit risk system is, without a doubt, *the biggest quantitative challenge the financial industry has ever seen.* Current calculations use the most advanced computing and data storage systems the banks have, and they can barely deal with the required job. In fact, they cannot, and so shortcuts and simplifications must be used.

As a result, the complexity of building a system for credit risk of derivatives tends to be easily underestimated.

Given the complexity of these systems, having the right architecture from the beginning is very important, as well as the flexibility to allow for future changes in the system and having efficient project management procedures. We dedicate the whole of Chapter 18 to this topic.

The role of a good quant is to define methodologies that create shortcuts without too much impact on the final risk numbers. Given an ideal world with infinite computational power, anyone can build a perfect exposure measurement system, but the challenge is to do it with the very limited computing capability that we usually have. It is therefore important to understand what is necessary, what can be ignored, and what is easy to implement. Systems knowledge is therefore crucial, and intuition is key.

Where to improve the system

From the three Monte Carlo steps that we have seen (RFE, Pricing, and Risk Metric Calculation) the one that takes a vast majority of the computational time tends to be the Pricing step. It has been said already that this step can easily take in excess of 99% of the computing effort. This is because of the around 1,000,000 times that each pricing function needs to be called.

For example, a pricing function that takes 0.01 second to compute should be considered pretty fast in general. However, in counterparty risk analytics calculating the pricing grid for that trade would take around 10,000 seconds, or nearly three hours. If we have 1,000,000 of these trades, this means that the calculating all pricing grids for only one portfolio run would take many days.

As a result of this, the part of a counterparty risk analytics engine that needs most dedicated intelligence is its pricing routines.

3.7 Scenario consistency

The discussion on addition and aggregation of exposure metrics between netting sets leads to the following subtle but very important point.

We can calculate exposure metrics at many different levels. Typically we have the trade level, netting set level, counterparty level, and portfolio level. If needed, we can also calculate them for any combination of these; for example, only for the counterparties of a given country, for the counterparties that operate in a specific economic sector, for netting sets that contain trades of only one given asset class. In principle, the possibilities are endless.

These calculations are often done in a distributed computing farm of CPUs, where the computing job is split into different smaller sub-jobs, each of which is done by a different processor.

If, for example, we are calculating EPE profiles for regulatory capital purposes, following Basel rules, then there is no need to make scenarios consistent between different netting sets because, at the end, we are just going to sum the exposure metrics (EEPE) of each netting set.

Depending on how the system architecture has been designed, this may make a difference. Some systems calculate the risk factor scenarios once, then they are saved, and then they are reused whenever needed, but some other systems calculate the risk factors "on-the-fly" when needed. If we have an architecture of the latter type, this scenario consistency concept can save computing effort.

In other words, if we only need scenario consistency at the netting set level, for example, and we distribute the calculation sub-jobs so that each CPU calculates one netting set, we do not need all CPUs to have exactly the same scenarios; i.e., we don't need scenario consistency above the netting set level and, hence, between different CPUs. However, if we want to calculate exposure risk well[25] at any other level, we need scenario consistency at that level.

As a result, to reduce computational requirements, we may not require the system to go beyond the level for which scenario consistency is needed. However, the system architecture needs to be designed accordingly.

3.8 Calibration

A model is not only a set of equations, it is *also* a methodology to calibrate them. We can have the best model in the world, but it will only be as good as the quality of its calibration. For this reason, when assessing the adequacy of a model and potentially backtesting it, calibration must also be considered.

3.8.1 Market-implied vs. historical

There exist two families of calibration methodologies for any kind of financial model: market-implied and historical calibrations. Market-implied calibrations are also called "risk-neutral"; historical calibrations can also be called "real-world". Each of these two calibration types serves different purposes.

In a nutshell, the idea of risk-neutral calibration is that the profit and loss of any derivative can be *locally* replicated with vanilla products like forwards, options, simple swaps, etc. These replication products are called the "hedges", as the derivatives dealer will typically trade these positions against the original derivative that it sold to the client so that, in principle, the trading book is market neutral. In this context, the risk-neutral price of any derivative is equal to the expected cost of the hedges. For this hedging strategy to work, all derivatives must be priced using the information that the market is providing, and that is regardless of anyone's view on whether the market is right or wrong. If the market expects, for example, 3 month interest rates to be at 3% in 2 years, this is where the portfolio needs to be priced. Otherwise the price of the derivative will contain arbitrage opportunities. So, for pricing purposes, the risk-neutral valuation should be applied.

However, other functions in a financial institution may use a different approach. From a risk management point of view, the aim is to quantify potential future losses. In order to do this, we need to take a view on the market, we need to make a decision on how we expect the market to behave. That is because often markets can be erratic, and risk management must not be subject to these swings. Historical volatilities are much more stable as they are calculated over a certain period of time whilst implied volatilities can be very short lived. This is one of the reasons why if the counterparty risk metric is used for risk management or calculating capital, a historical volatility calculation may prove easier to manage. In addition, implied volatilities may be very different to actual observed historical volatilities.

For example, a piece of research that I did in early 2007 showed that the default probability that we could infer from the CDS market (i.e., the market-implied default probabilities) was well below the historical default probability implied from their credit ratings. As a result, if we are interested to hedge the credit part of a portfolio, we must use the default probability that we see in the CDS market, as that CDS spread is the actual price we have to pay to hedge our credit sensitivities. However, if we are not hedged and want to estimate the expected default losses, we must use our view on the expected default probability as the credit agencies do, which is typically done with a historical calibration.

To summarise, the difference of calibrating a model for pricing versus for risk management is that, for pricing, we must use market information irrespective of whether we agree with it, whilst for risk management we should use judgement to select the most appropriate methodology, which often leads to a historical calibration.

3.8.2 Two models to calibrate

In the calculation of exposure metrics we have two sets of models: RFE models for the market variables (step 1 in the Monte Carlo simulation), and pricing models for the derivatives (step 2).

RFE calibration: For the RFE models we have two approaches. With these models we are going to create a few thousand scenarios that could happen in the future. For risk management, we want those scenarios to contain all the information available to us, to come up with true possible future paths and assign them the right probability. As a result, these models tend to be calibrated historically for the reasons given above. However, for pricing of counterparty credit risk (i.e., for CVA), the market consensus tends to be for using market-implied calibrations in the RFE models for no-arbitrage reasons.[26]

Pricing calibration: The models to price derivatives inside the counterparty risk engine must be the same models that the institution uses for daily marking of their portfolio. As mentioned, in the Monte Carlo simulation, each scenario is a possible state of the world in the future. Hence if we are pricing our portfolio 1 year in the future in a given scenario, we must price them as if that scenario had actually happened. What models would we use to price them in that case? The answer is the standard institution's pricing models, as those are the ones we will use in reality if that scenario crystallises in the future. Therefore we must use risk neutral pricing methods in the pricing function inside the Monte Carlo engine.

3.8.3 Calibration methodologies

It is not the aim of this text to provide a detailed list of the many models available out there for RFEs and give calibration methodologies for all of them, but we should at least discuss the basic principle of model calibration.

For risk-neutral calibration, the idea is to match the current state of the market to the expected values in the models. For example, if the market implies that the three-month interest rate in 2 years is 3%, then we should reflect that in the model, so that the expected value of the three-month rate in the model in 2 years (the average across all the scenarios in the RFE process) is 3%. Regarding volatilities, we can get the options market volatilities, from where we can calculate market-implied cumulative and forward volatilities if needed using the rule

$$\sigma_{0,2}^2 = \sigma_{0,1}^2 + \sigma_{1,2}^2 \tag{3.9}$$

where $\sigma_{a,b}^2$ is the variance between t_a and t_b. For correlations, we need a market of correlation trades deep enough so that we can extract from it liquid information about correlation structures. For drifts, mean reversion speeds or mean reversion levels, we should match as closely as possible the term structure of the expected future value of the spot curve to that given by the market.

For historical calibration, we are typically going to calculate the parameters from time series of data. Volatilities and correlations can be calibrated fairly easily to those measured from the time series. Drifts, mean reversion speeds, and mean reversion levels tend to be trickier to calibrate, as they only show up in time series over a very long time horizon, often several tens of years, and most of the time that amount of data is not available.

In practice, model calibration can easily become an art more than a science. Often we have to deal with time series that are too short, have a lack of data or have data quality issues, incomplete markets, lack of liquidity, etc. As a result, often we need to use a blend of market-implied and historical calibrations to cover these problems. In any case, it is important to be consistent every time we recalibrate a model so that any changes to the exposure profile from the recalibration are due to volatility and/or correlation changes and not to methodology modifications. This is a list of some typical problems and possible solutions.

- **Calibration Tenor:** The first thing that we need to make clear is what the typical length of the exposure risk we are dealing with is. It is quite different to calibrate a model for 3-year swaps than for 20-year swaps, as short tenor volatilities are usually higher than long term ones. Then we need to think when the exposure profiles are going to peak on average; the exposure profiles of a book of 5-year interest rate swaps will peak approximately in the second or third year, but that peak will be in the fifth year if we had 5-year cash swaptions; hence if we have a simple one-factor model for interest rates, we should use the 2 or 3-year volatility for the swaps, but the 5-year volatility for the swaptions.

  Ideally, we would like to have a volatility function that can select the correct volatility from a matrix based on the tenor of the trade and the time step in the exposure profile. Also we need to consider how dispersed the tenors of the trades in the portfolio are.
- **Term Structure Calibrations:** When modelling term structures, N-factor models need N points to be calibrated. Which ones should we use? There are two considerations to take into account. First, we need to consider tenor point liquidity; the most liquid points will contain better information both for market-implied and historical calibrations. Second, we need to consider the tenor structure of the portfolio, as explained in the previous point, to decide which points of the terms structure we should calibrate our models to.
- **Lack of Liquidity:** A very common problem with market implied calibrations is that there aren't enough products, or they aren't liquid enough, to measure implied correlations. If this is the case, historical correlations should be used.
- **Length of Time Series:** For historical calibrations, a typical question is how long the time series should be.

  First of all, this is determined by how long the availability of data is: we can decide that the best length for the time series is 10 years, but then we must ensure that we have reliable data for that long. Once we have an idea of what the data length we have available is, we should consider first the typical tenor of the book of trades that we have as well as when they tend to peak the exposure profiles, as that is a key time point at which we want to reflect the exposure risk as well as possible.

  Often exposure models have a constant volatility in them. If so we have to consider how reactive we want the exposure profiles to be: on the one hand, it does not make much sense from a risk-management standpoint if an exposure profile swings around very abruptly, but on the other hand we want the exposures to reflect stressed market conditions. We need to find a balance here: the desire to capture when long-term risk must be in an equilibrium with the lack of reactivity to stressed periods in the models. A very long time series may smooth out volatile periods and it may not reflect recent volatility increases. As a rule of thumb, 5-year length for the time series tends to offer a good compromise.

  Another consideration is if we want to capture a full business cycle in the calibration; if so, data must be 7 to 10 years long. It must be noted that the Basel accord states that the minimum length of historical calibrations for capital calculations must be three years.

- **Autocorrelation:** Given the long term of the risks we are trying to measure with these counterparty exposure metrics, we may want to consider autocorrelation effects in the calibration. This is a good idea when the models do not account for autocorrelation, which is often the case. When that happens and if the models are historically calibrated, we may want to use weekly or fortnightly time steps to measure volatility and correlations (or a period that is long enough to capture the autocorrelation) instead of daily time steps.

As we can see, there are lots of considerations to account for when deciding how to calibrate RFE models. The basic idea is to be rigorous and, at the same time, be somewhat flexible and apply expert judgement as needed. As said, in reality, calibration can be more of an art than a science.

3.8.4 Recalibration frequency

Recalibration frequency of simulation models is also an important topic. Ideally we would like the models to be calibrated daily, either for market-implied or historical calibrations, but often this is not possible for practical reasons, especially in historical calibrations where the computation can be lengthy and one day of extra data hardly changes anything.

The longest frequency that is market practice for historical models is quarterly calibrations. In fact, regulators do not tend to allow longer periods. When done quarterly, historical calibrations should use long series, of several years, as otherwise the changes in the model parameters in every recalibration will be too abrupt and will surely create management problems.

Pricing models need to use current volatilities and correlations updated on a daily basis.

3.9 Right and wrong way risk

A most important feature of exposure calculation is right and wrong way risk.

Exposure calculations must be done *subject* to default of the counterparty. As a consequence, if the default of the counterparty is going to impact on the value of our portfolio we have to account for it. If default events increase exposure it is said that we have "wrong way risk"; if the other way round, we have "right way risk".

An example can be easily seen when we buy an equity option with the counterparty's own stock as the option reference variable. We know that if the counterparty defaults, its stock will be worth approximately zero. Hence, if we have a call option, we know that the exposure subject to default will be zero (right way risk), but if we have a put option, the exposure will be the whole notional of the trade (wrong way risk).

Incorporating this feature into the exposure calculation is very important, but it adds an extra degree of complexity, so we dedicate the whole of Chapter 10 to it.

3.10 Model adequacy

When we design a model for exposure measurement, we always have a number of options. It can be mean-reverting or not; normal or lognormal; a one, two, three, N-factor model; dependencies can be modelled with a copula or with other correlation structures; we can apply PCA or not; we can implement market-implied or historical calibration, with all the flavours that each of them can have. There are so many options to choose from. How should we choose which model to use?

There are a number of guidelines that should be kept in mind when designing a model.

- **Model Final Usage:** The first thing that needs to be clear is what is the final use of the model. Typically it is going to be used for CVA pricing, risk management, capital calculation, or a combination of these. This is important because, for each of these final usages, different things are more or less important. For example, having correct sensitivities is paramount for a CVA trader, while it is not as critical (even though it is still important) for risk management or capital calculation.
- **Existing Models in the Organisation:** The real challenge of counterparty credit risk analytics is not designing new complex models, but *handling the high computational requirements.* This can be easily forgotten.

  Consequently, if the organisation has a model, or a number of models, that could work for our requirements, they should be the first option. That is not only beneficial from a pure model design point of view but, in practice, it will also save a lot of work from endless discussions, from producing new documentation, and from extra testing that will be required.
- **Look at Data:** This is a fairly common mistake: design an RFE model based on a pre-idea of how the risk factor behaves, without really analysing the data.[27] It is very important to look and study the data for a fairly long period of time, even playing with it, with the aim at gaining an intuition as to how it behaves and which are its key characteristics.
- **Risks to Capture:** We must not design an RFE model without having a look at the type of risks that the book of trades is subject to. For example, if the book of trades at stake is only sensitive to parallel moves of a yield curve, a simple one-factor model will be enough to model that yield curve. However, bear in mind that while price sensitivities (delta, gamma, etc.) are additive, other risk sensitivities may not be. For example, as already mentioned, if we have a book with two interest rate swaps, one is a two-year receiver and the other one is a ten-year payer with a similar duration, each of these swaps by themselves are mainly sensitive to the first principal component of the yield curve, hence a one-factor model can capture the exposure risk accurately for each of them separately, but jointly they are mainly sensitive to rotations of the yield curve, so we need to use two principal components in our model in order to capture its real exposure risk.
- **Simplicity:** Simplicity is key. There is no need to complicate things more than necessary. Sometimes in financial markets we tend to have a brain that pays lot of attention to small details, which is very good in so many contexts, but in this case it can easily back-fire on us by doing things more complicated than is necessary. We must never forget that the exposure measurement system can be so complicated, with so many sources of uncertainty, that often fine-tuning models does not have any measurable impact. For example, any changes we do to the models that have an impact in the exposure metric of the same order of magnitude than the (usually high) numerical noise in the Monte Carlo calculation, will be in reality a waste of time.
- **Testing:** At the end of the day, any model will have to pass a testing procedure, more or less to some degree, before it is used for exposure measurement. Chapters 16 and 17 deal with this subject thoroughly, but let's highlight the main points here.

  When testing an exposure measurement model, the first thing that needs to be considered is the final use of the model. If a model is used for CVA pricing in hedgable portfolios, we typically want it to be arbitrage-free, provide good hedging sensitivities and, obviously, provide sensible prices. If used for risk management, the model must pass a back-test with real data successfully.

  One of the key challenges of CVA testing is that there isn't a liquid market to check against, which leaves big room for many models to appear to work well; some people take this one step further and call this "model arbitrage".

Regarding risk management, the main problem comes from data availability, as past exposures have not usually been saved and, even if they had been, books change over time, so it is difficult to relate "current" exposures to "past" starting points. To solve this, testing tends to split the task between the RFE and the pricing models. Regarding RFE models, the difficulty comes from the scarcity of data as, for example, we may have to test one-year forward projections of a model when we only have ten years of historical data, hence we only have ten independent points in the testing framework. Regarding pricing models, they are nearly always a simplification of the more sophisticated pricing models used for actual derivative pricing. These simplifications are needed so that the roughly one trillion pricing jobs needed every day can be done in the available time frame. The task of testing here is to make sure that the simplifications do only alter the final exposure metric in a limited way, if at all. It must be remembered that these exposure metrics are a statistical metric of a distribution of prices, so the pricing models are acceptable as long as they do not alter the exposure metrics at stake. Similarly to pricing, all these issues can easily leave a wide room for model arbitrage that may not be possible to avoid, but it must be at least recognised and managed. In large financial institutions there is a separate function within the quantitative risk organisation that deals with model risk.

3.11 MC noise

The Monte Carlo numerical noise gets reduced with $\frac{1}{\sqrt{N}}$ where N is the number of scenarios. This means that if we increase the number of simulations from 1,000 to 10,000 we are (roughly) multiplying the computing effort by a factor of ten, but reducing the noise only by a factor of around three. If we want to decrease the noise by another factor of three, we will need to increase the number of scenarios to 100,000. This non-linear function of the marginal decrease of noise per added scenario is clearly a problem.

This problem is less noticeable in CVA, as it is based on the EPE, which is an average of all the scenarios and also involves an integration of that EPE profile, so the noise gets somewhat reduced. However, the noise can be very important for risk management, which tends to be based on PFE or CESF profiles; this is shown in Figure 3.8. In spite of this "washing out" effect for CVA, Figure 3.9 illustrates that the number of scenarios needed to achieve the standard 1 basis point pricing error for the CVA of a 10 year interest rate swap is 2,000,000 scenarios.

Counterparty credit risk systems in financial institutions use between 1,000 and 10,000 scenarios. Given the technology available at the time of writing this book, investing in IT resources to increase the number of scenarios will hardly pay off after 10,000 scenarios. Hence, in practice, Monte Carlo numerical noise for counterparty credit risk analytics is something we need learn to live with: it cannot really be avoided. Consequently, development of new technologies that improve the situation in this respect can be highly valuable: anyone would agree that having a stable CVA price, as opposed to a price that changes each time we calculate it, adds value to a financial institution in many ways.

A practical solution that is sometimes used is starting the simulation always with the same random number generator seed. This technique has some dangers, as the noise is not really avoided, we only turn a blind eye to it, but it can be of some practical use when comparing profiles, so we can to some extent differentiate between changes coming from numerical noise to other ones that are genuine to the economics of the book of trades. One solution is to frequently run simulations with other random number generations in order to understand the extent of the simulation noise and to at least be aware of it.

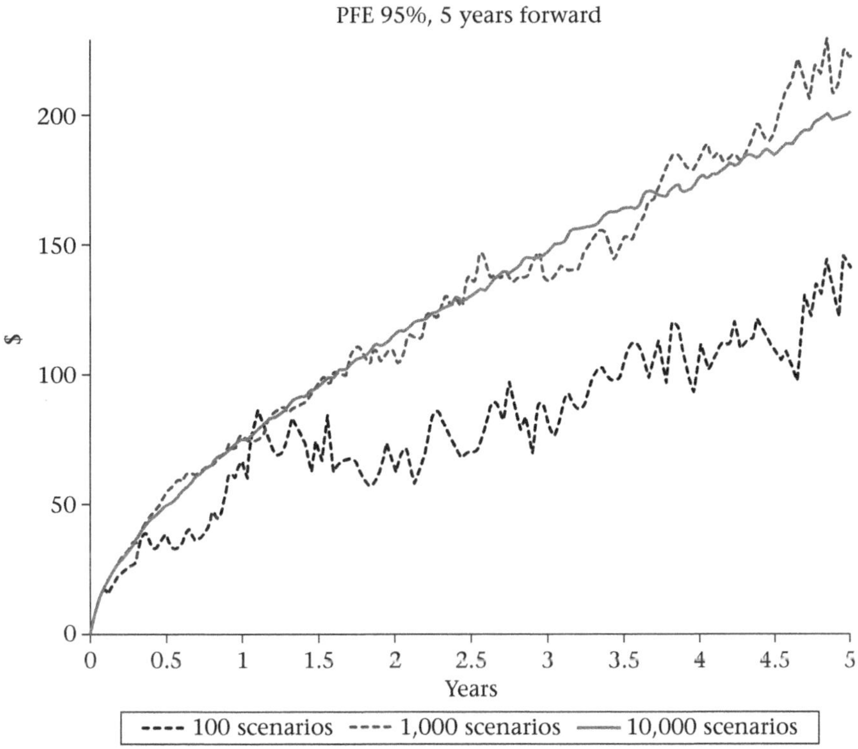

Figure 3.8 Display of the effect of numerical noise in PFE profile calculations

3.12 Examples

So far we have seen how to calculate exposure profiles. Let's run some examples now, in order to build some intuition.

First let's see the typical profile of a swap, and see how the EPE, ENE, and PFE profiles compare. This can be seen in Figure 3.10. The swap is at-the-money on the simulation start date, so all the profiles start at zero value. The profiles tend to diverge from zero during the early stages of the simulation as a result of the diffusion of the risk factor, but they start decreasing after some time because the duration of the swap decreases over time. It must be remembered that the risk factors tend to be diffused with a $\sqrt{t}$ law, while the decrease of the duration tends to be linear with time as the cashflows of a vanilla swap are paid out on a regular basis.

Now we can see in Figure 3.11 the difference in the 95% PFE profile as the trade moves from in-the-money to out-of-the-money. This shift is roughly parallel to the amount the trade is in/out of the money on the start date until the peak of the trade and then diffuses with time.

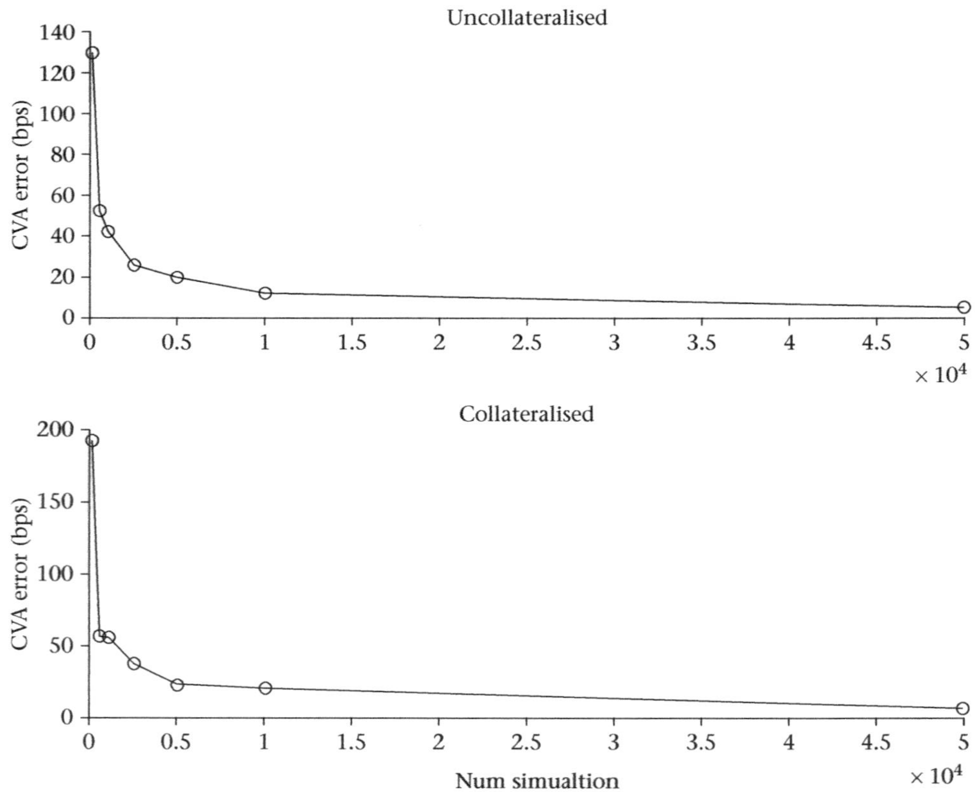

Number sims	CVA error (bps)
100	160
500	55
1,000	49
2,500	32
5,000	22
10,000	15
50,000	6

Figure 3.9 CVA pricing error (standard deviation of the price over several calculations) for a 10 year interest rate swap. We need 2,000,000 to have an accuracy of 1 basis point

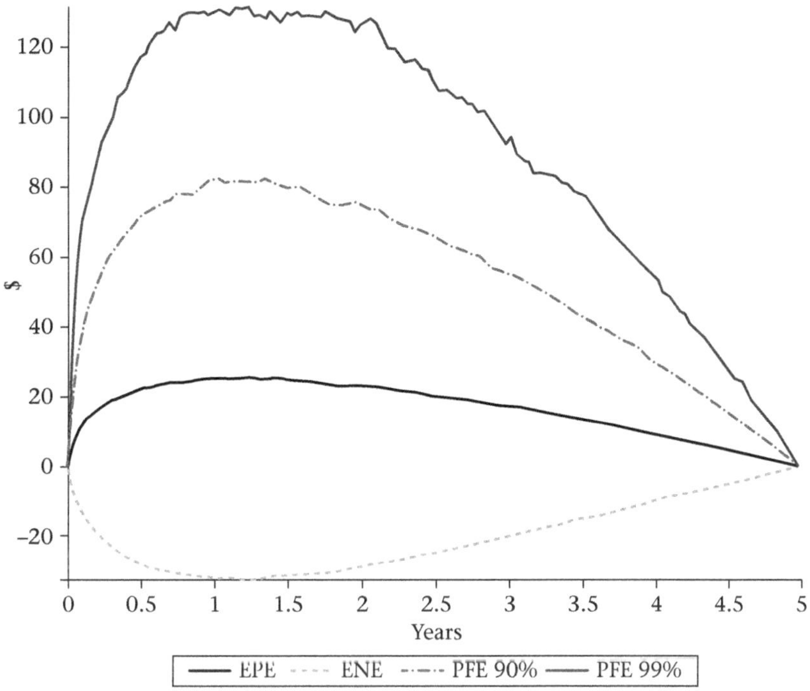

Figure 3.10 Typical profiles of a 5-year swap

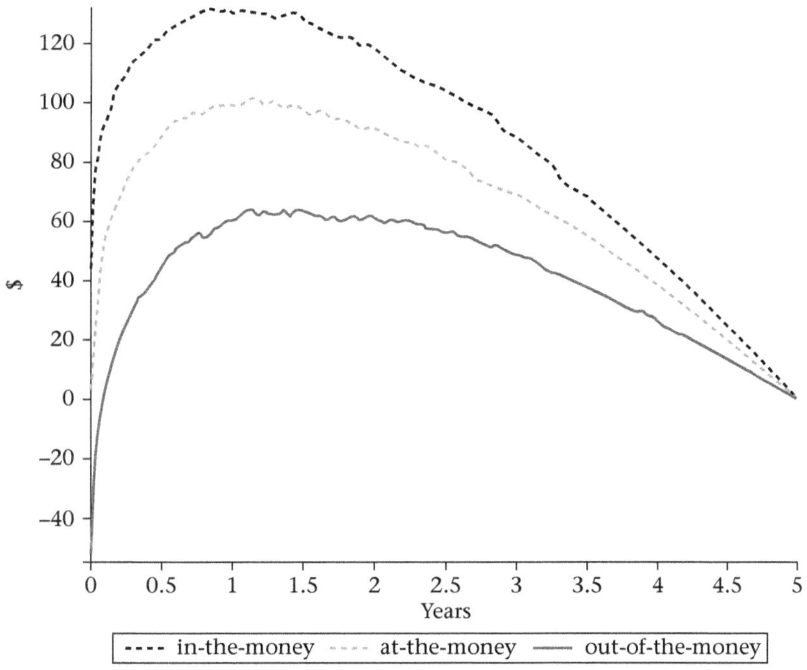

Figure 3.11 Typical PFE 95% profiles of a 5-year swap, when "in-", "at-" and "out-of-" the money

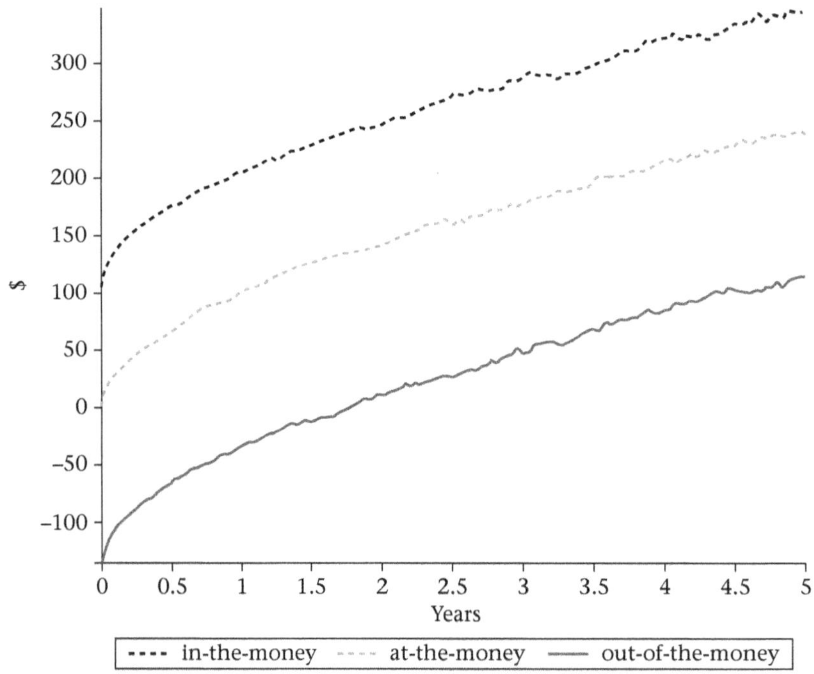

Figure 3.12 Typical PFE 95% profiles of a 5-year forward, when "in-", "at-" and "out-of-" the money

Figure 3.12 shows typical PFE profiles for a forward for different strikes. We can appreciate the $\sqrt{t}$ diffusion of the risk factor. Compared to the swap, this time we do not have any decrease in duration to reduce the profile so the peak exposure occurs at maturity.

Figure 3.13 shows PFE profiles for a call option for different moneyness. The profiles are similar to those of a forward. This is because in a long forward, as the examples show, the exposures come from those paths that have increased the value of the underlying, and those are precisely the paths that create also high values for a call option.

Figure 3.14 shows typical profiles for a put option. In this case we have used the same strikes as in the call option, and have kept the same scale in the axis for easy comparison. We can observe in the profiles that a put option has a limit to its' value whilst a call option can grow to a, theoretically, infinite price.

Both options shown were calculated when we are long with the option. The case in which we are short with the option is trivial, the exposure is zero. That is because once we have been paid the option fee, we are never going to be owed anything in the future.[28] This is based on the assumption that we do not have a collateral agreement. We will see later on that this doesn't hold if there is a CSA.

Finally, let's do a multi-trade example. Figure 3.15 shows various exposure profiles of a netting set composed of a 1-year FX forward, 3-year equity call option, and 5-year interest rate swap. It is interesting how the profile increases quite substantially from one to three years for the 99% PFE profile, but remains fairly constant for all other risk metrics. This illustrates the point that tail risk can behave in quite counter-intuitive ways.

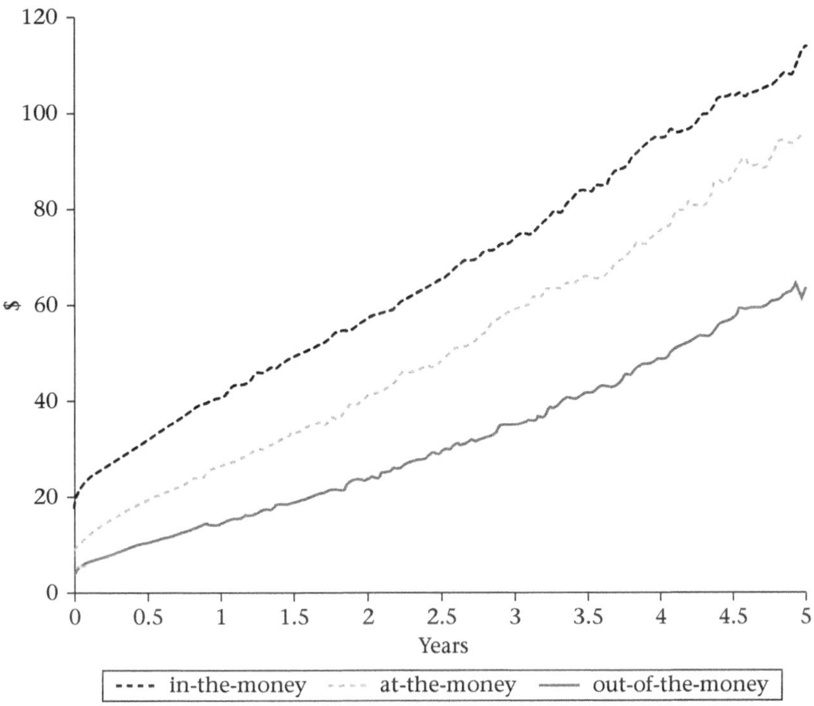

Figure 3.13 Typical PFE 95% profiles of a 5-year call option, when "in-", "at-" and "out-of-" the money

3.13 Historical Monte Carlo simulation

As explained in the previous section, the standard way to model exposure risk factors is to model each of them with a Stochastic Differential Equation, with Brownian motion, and with a dependency structure between them that follows typically a multivariate Gaussian distribution function. For example, if FX_1 and FX_2 are two exchange rates, a typical way to model them is as

$$\begin{aligned} \frac{dFX_1}{FX_1} &= \mu_1\, dt + \sigma_1 dW_1 \\ \frac{dFX_2}{FX_2} &= \mu_2\, dt + \sigma_2 dW_2 \\ dW_1\, dW_2 &= \rho\, dt \end{aligned} \tag{3.10}$$

Historical data show that neither the FX rates are log normal, nor their dependency structure is described well by a local Gaussian copula. Also, data can show autocorrelation, but the standard Brownian motion models do not capture it. We are using FX rates as an example, but this can be applied to any asset class: financial data does not generally follow Brownian motion nor the dependency structures follow analytical copulas.[29]

An alternative approach to the standard Brownian methodologies, that improves the above limitation and is fairly simple to implement, is the Historical Monte Carlo simulation.

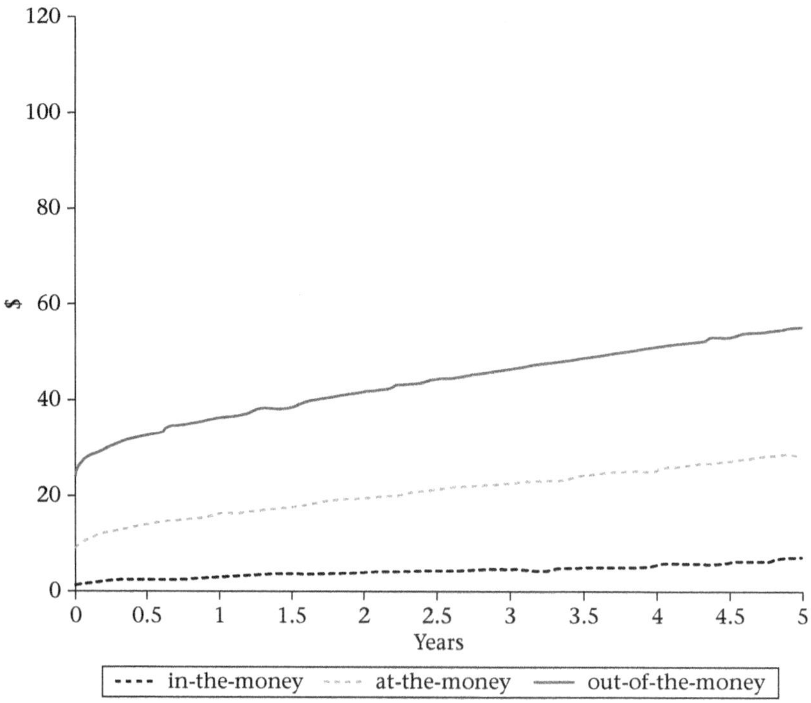

Figure 3.14 Typical PFE 95% profiles of a 5-year put option, when “in-”, “at-” and “out-of-” the money

3.13.1 Basic procedure

We are going to use FX rates as an example, but this can be applied to any asset class. Let’s get the historical daily changes of two FX rates and let’s put them in a time series indexed by time steps, as shown in Figure 3.16. The time series can be as long as deemed necessary. Let’s call the length of the time series T_h, and the number of points in it N_h. Now let’s model daily steps of FX_1 and FX_2 as

$$
\begin{aligned}
FX_{1,i+1} &= FX_{1,i}\,\Delta W_{1,i} \\
FX_{2,i+1} &= FX_{2,i}\,\Delta W_{2,i}
\end{aligned}
\tag{3.11}
$$

where $\Delta W_{1,i}$ and $\Delta W_{2,i}$ are obtained easily as follows: let’s simulate one random natural number between 1 and N_h from a uniform distribution, and let’s pick $\Delta W_{1,i}$ and $\Delta W_{2,i}$ from the time series as the change in the exchange rates on the index day given by the simulated random number.

That gives one time step of the FX rates. If we want to create a simulation path as long as T_{sim}, which contains M_{sim} daily steps, all we have to do is repeat this procedure for $i = 0, 1, 2$ up to $i = M_{sim}$. And if we want to create N Monte Carlo scenarios, all we have to do is repeat the above procedure N times.

This methodology can be more powerful than the typical Brownian method because

1. The simulated paths are going to follow the historically observed distribution, *whichever it is*. The distribution doesn’t need to fit a mathematical model; it is just taken directly from the market. If, for example, the data exhibits jumps, the simulation will have jumps of the right size and frequency.

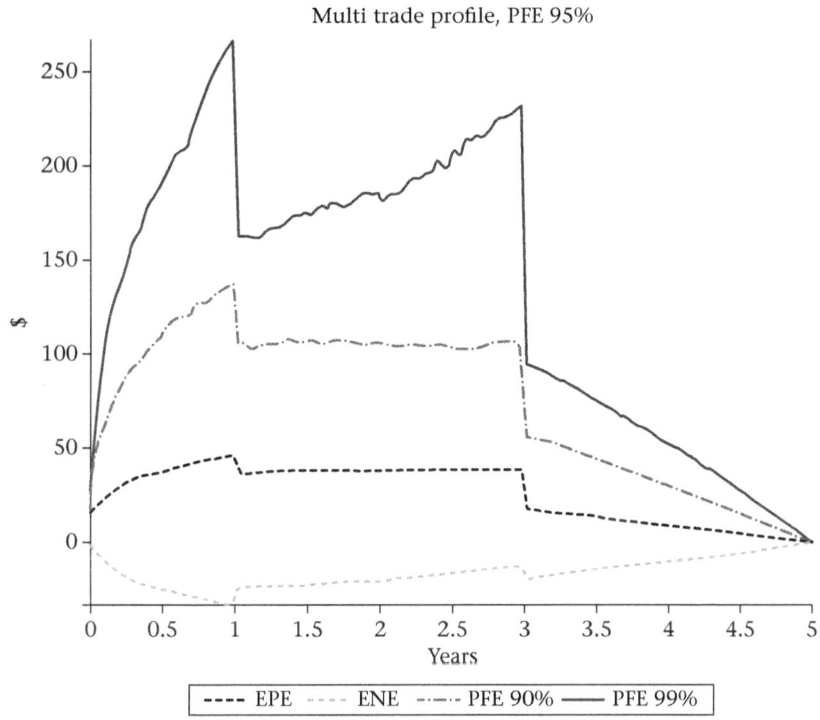

Figure 3.15 Illustration of exposure profiles of a netting set consisting of a 1-year FX forward, 3-year equity call option, and 5-year interest rate swap

2. One of the most difficult things to model in a Brownian framework is a realistic dependency structure between the risk factors. Gaussian multivariate models replicate the tails of the joint distributions very poorly, but in spite of that are widely used because they are easy to handle and mathematically robust. There are other alternative copulas, but it is always difficult, if not impossible, to find a copula that fits the data accurately. However, with this procedure the simulated paths will already have the real dependency structure automatically, *whichever it is.*
3. Computationally, the most expensive task of an RFE job is, usually, generating the correlated random numbers. That is because correlation matrices typically have dimensions of hundreds × hundreds of even thousands × thousands, and any procedure to generate correlated numbers with matrices of that size is very slow.[30] This procedure avoids that problem completely.

3.13.2 Reactive procedure

We may want to have exposure metric profiles that react quickly to current market conditions. This can be important when we apply the same RFE to short and long term trades. Let's say that we are in the middle of a market crisis. Short term volatilities (e.g., three month) will be very high, but long term volatilities (e.g., five years) may remain fairly constant. If we are calculating exposure metrics of both three-month FX forwards and five-year FX swaps, we should ideally have different volatilities for each of them. But how can we achieve that with the same RFE model?

		Daily	
Index	Time (yrs)	dFX1/FX1	dFX2/FX2
0	0	91%	34%
1	-0.004	168%	-63%
2	-0.008	138%	28%
3	-0.012	-202%	10%
4	-0.016	-47%	-20%
5	-0.02	13%	-45%
6	-0.024	-138%	-6%
7	-0.028	9%	34%
8	-0.032	-50%	26%
9	-0.036	31%	33%
10	-0.04	-105%	-218%
11	-0.044	48%	30%
12	-0.048	-49%	-6%
13	-0.052	37%	-89%
14	-0.056	-153%	105%
15	-0.06	-29%	21%
16	-0.064	93%	6%
17	-0.068	-123%	-56%
18	-0.072	-125%	24%
19	-0.076	-69%	-124%
20	-0.08	37%	-57%
21	-0.084	88%	-64%
22	-0.088	13%	-63%
23	-0.092	88%	146%
24	-0.096	-69%	-77%
25	-0.1	37%	-95%
26	-0.104	-135%	135%
27	-0.108	-134%	-157%
...	...	...	...
2488	-103%	-20%	-1%
2489	110%	-154%	94%
2490	-243%	-161%	-41%
2491	-9.964	-121%	56%
2492	-9.968	-69%	-65%
2493	-9.972	154%	51%
2494	-9.976	-37%	-133%
2495	-9.98	173%	45%
2496	-9.984	-89%	122%
2497	-9.988	-65%	-129%
2498	-9.992	-35%	38%
2499	-9.996	-38%	23%
2500	-10	129%	-70%

Figure 3.16 Illustrative example of the data of scenarios for a Historical Monte Carlo simulation

A typical Brownian way to achieve this is by having a volatility term structure in the diffusion of the FX rate:

$$\frac{dFX}{FX} = \mu\, dt + \sigma_t dW$$
$$\sigma_t = \sigma_\infty + (\sigma_0 - \sigma_\infty)\, e^{-\alpha t} \tag{3.12}$$

where σ_0 is the short term instantaneous volatility, and σ_∞ is the long term volatility. An alternative function for σ_t is to follow the forward volatility implied from the options market, for example.

The Historical Monte Carlo simulation also offers a simple way to achieve this nice effect. All we have to do is to use an appropriate alternative to the uniform distribution function when generating the random numbers in the algorithm. Let's say that we use a distribution function that follows

$$f(t_h) = \left(\frac{\beta_t}{1 - e^{-\beta_t}}\right) e^{-\beta_t t_t}$$
$$\beta_t = \beta_0 \, e^{-\gamma t} \tag{3.13}$$

where t is the Monte Carlo simulation time point, and t_h is the time stamp in the historical time series. With this function (or any other similar set of functions), the simulation will tend to pick recent events close to the end of the time series when t is small, but pick events more evenly from the historical data for longer term horizons. The strength of this non-uniform way of picking events is controlled by β, which starts as a value of β_0, but then becomes smoother towards a value of zero. As β approaches zero, we are approaching the uniform distribution in $f(t_h)$. γ controls how fast we approach that uniform distribution.

3.13.3 Autocorrelated and computationally optimised procedure

We have mentioned that the typical Brownian frameworks do not account for autocorrelations, but real market behaviour can in fact show autocorrelation. Historical Monte Carlo offers a very simple way to do RFE modelling with autocorrelation.

When storing the changes in the risk factors, we can store not only the daily changes, but also the changes seen weekly, fortnightly, monthly, etc. See Figure 3.17 for an example.

We have seen in previous sections that the RFE simulations can be performed for an unevenly spaced set of time points in the future. In this context, if the step we want to simulate is of one week, we can get the change in the risk factor value from the weekly table. This way we can substitute five daily steps by one weekly step that already contains the autocorrelation information.

In principle, we could do this for weekly, fortnightly, monthly, or even quarterly steps. From a pure autocorrelation point of view, we only need to do it with steps that are as long as the autocorrelation effect is. However, if we use monthly steps, for example, we also maximise computational speed by minimising the number of calls to the risk factor change procedure. This is a most desired effect, given how computationally demanding counterparty credit risk systems can be.

A caveat to this modelling framework is that if, for example, we have a risk factor that shows weekly autocorrelation, the RFE daily steps done at the beginning of the simulation will not contain any autocorrelation effect. It must be said that this feature will be hardly noticeable in the final credit metrics, but if we want to fine-tune the RFE simulation there are a number of ways to further optimise the methodology. For example, in the first five daily steps, we can pick a week and get the all daily moves of it. Any bias that, arguably, we are introducing, will be dissipated amongst the N scenarios. Also, we can have an average measurement of the autocorrelation and adjust the daily changes accordingly – there are lots of possibilities for fine-tuning.

3.13.4 Special features

It must be noted that for each variable modelled in this way we are going to have a number of alternatives. For example, an absolute model ($x_{i+1} = x_i + \Delta W_{abs}$) or a relative one ($x_{i+1} = x_i \, \Delta W_{rel}$). Absolute is the equivalent of a normal model in the Brownian world, and relative is the equivalent of the log normal framework. Also,

		Daily		Weekly		Fortnightly	
Index	Time (yrs)	dFX1/FX1	dFX2/FX2	dFX1/FX1	dFX2/FX2	dFX1/FX1	dFX2/FX2
0	0	91%	34%	20%	-68%	-122%	-23%
1	-0.004	168%	-63%				
2	-0.008	138%	28%				
3	-0.012	-202%	10%				
4	-0.016	-47%	-20%				
5	-0.02	13%	-45%	77%	-174%		
6	-0.024	-138%	6%				
7	-0.028	9%	34%				
8	-0.032	-50%	26%				
9	-0.036	31%	33%				
10	-0.04	-105%	-218%	131%	-30%	-109%	8%
11	-0.044	48%	30%				
12	-0.048	-49%	-6%				
13	-0.052	37%	-89%				
14	-0.056	-153%	-105%				
15	-0.06	-29%	21%	-168%	29%		
16	-0.064	93%	6%				
17	-0.068	-123%	-56%				
18	-0.072	-125%	24%				
19	-0.076	-69%	-124%				
20	-0.08	37%	-57%	-150%	-9%	6%	128%
21	-0.084	88%	-64%				
22	-0.088	13%	-63%				
23	-0.092	88%	146%				
24	-0.096	-69%	-77%				
25	-0.1	37%	-95%	-88%	24%		
26	-0.104	-135%	135%				
27	-0.108	-134%	-157%				
...	...	...	...				
2488	-103%	-20%	-1%				
2489	-103%	-154%	94%				
2490	-243%	-161%	-41%	29%	183%	2%	19%
2491	-9.964	-121%	56%				
2492	-9.968	-69%	-65%				
2493	-9.972	154%	51%				
2494	-9.976	-37%	-133%				
2495	-9.98	173%	45%	42%	119%		
2496	-9.984	-89%	122%				
2497	-9.988	-65%	-129%				
2498	-9.992	-35%	38%				
2499	-9.996	-38%	23%				
2500	-10	-129%	-70%				

Figure 3.17 Illustrative example of the data of scenarios for a Historical Monte Carlo simulation with multiple step lengths

if needed, we can incorporate other non-stochastic components to the model, like a mean reversion feature: $x_{i+1} = x_i + \theta(\mu - x_i)\,\Delta t_i + \Delta W_{abs}$.

Difficulties may arise. For example, we may want to model different points in a yield curve, each having a different distribution function. In this case, each point should have its own set of historical changes from which the changes in the rates can be taken. It's crucial that we always select the same index for each of those yield curve points, in each scenario and time step, so that we capture the correct dependency structure between them. Also, we may want to have a yield-curve arbitrage algorithm to check that the yield curves produced are plausible.

3.13.5 Conclusions

The Historical Monte Carlo method provides an alternative to the widely used Brownian method which, in my view, is better in many ways, as it is not based on unrealistic assumptions like Brownian motion, or analytical copulas for multivariate distribution functions. For this reason, RFE modelling can be more realistic in this framework, especially when we need to measure tail risk.

Of course this process is based on a strong assumption that we must not forget about: that the future distributions will be similar to the historically observed ones.

This modelling philosophy could be optimal for risk management and capital calculation, as in those contexts we want to measure true potential losses, and an accurate modelling of the tail of the loss distribution is key. However, when the arbitrage of prices is possible, the price of a derivative is given by the no-arbitrage condition and a Brownian approach is the clear market standard.

In any case, Historical Monte Carlo for RFE modelling is a clean, realistic, efficient, and quick approach to model counterparty credit risk exposures that should be definitely considered.

4 Exposure Measurement for Collateralised Portfolios

So far we have discussed how to model the exposure of a portfolio without any collateral, but we have seen that most of the netting sets these days are collateralised. In this section we will discuss how to account for collateral when calculating exposure metrics.

To summarise some of the details previously explained about collateral, we have seen that the legalities of a collateralised facility between two counterparties are typically set in a CSA agreement, that we can have one-way or two-way CSA agreements, and that collateral can consist of cash (in any currency that the CSA defines) or other securities like bonds or equities. Also, we explained that even in a perfectly collateralised facility we are exposed to a "gap risk", which represents the potential change in value of the netting set (or of the hedges) from the default time until the book is liquidated.

4.1 Simulation steps

In order to take account of the collateral in the simulation, we need to follow the subsequent steps:

1. Simulate collateral per scenario and time step
2. Calculate the gap risk per scenario and time step
3. Calculate the exposure risk metrics

4.1.1 Simulating collateral

First of all, we need to simulate the collateral posted or received under the CSA. To achieve this we need to consider all the CSA mechanics and replicate them as accurately as possible at each scenario. The key elements to consider are one-way vs. two-way CSA, margining frequency, Threshold (Thr), Initial Margin (IM), Minimum Transfer Amount (MTA), and Rounding.

At each time point in the Monte Carlo simulation we are going to look at the value of the netting set, as calculated by the Monte Carlo simulation, and we are going to simulate collateral posted and received forward in time so that we end up with a grid of collateral values.

CSA mechanics: For example, let's say that the netting set consists of a portfolio of swaps and that the CSA has the following characteristics: bilateral, daily margining, our threshold of \$5m ($Thr^{\ominus} = -5{,}000{,}000$), counterparty threshold of \$1m ($Thr^{\oplus} = 1{,}000{,}000$),[1] MTA of \$100k, and rounding of \$10.

Let's say that the netting set starts with a value of zero ($V_{NS,0} = 0$). After one day, the value of the netting set goes to $-\$2{,}478{,}397$, which is above the $-5{,}000{,}000$, so no collateral call is made. After one day the value of the netting set goes to $-\$5{,}523{,}538$, which is below our threshold $Thr^{\ominus}$, so we need to post \$523,540 as collateral, taking rounding into account. One day later the value of the netting set goes to −$836,912, within the threshold levels, so we are returned the $523,540 we had posted. One day later V_{NS} goes to +$598,509; it is again within the threshold levels, so no collateral is transferred. The next day V_{NS} goes to $1,054,209, which is above the threshold $Thr^{\oplus}$, but the collateral required, $54k, is less than the MTA, so no collateral is transferred. Then V_{NS} goes to $2,367,324, above $Thr^{\oplus} + MTA$, so we call for $1,367,320 of collateral– and we continue like this at each scenario, time step by time step, until all trades have matured.

Collateral algorithm: Basically, the algorithm needs to work as follows in each scenario, iterating through the time steps.

To start with, let's say that we can simulate on every margin call day. Let's refer to the current time step t with the index i, the value of the collateral at t_i before a collateral call has been made as $\widetilde{C}_i^{before}$, and the value of the collateral at t_i after a collateral call has been made as $\widetilde{C}_i^{after}$. We are going to denote as $\widetilde{C}$ the value in the currency of the collateral,[2] while C is the value in the base currency of the financial institution. The simulations with the prices of the netting set in each scenario and time point t_i ($V_{NS,i}$) are already in the base currency of the financial institution.

1. First we need to calculate the value of the collateral held in the CSA facility before any collateral call has been made. This is given by

$$\widetilde{C}_i^{before} = \Xi_{i-1\rightarrow i}(\widetilde{C}_{i-1}^{after}) \tag{4.1}$$

   where $\Xi_{a\rightarrow b}(\cdot)$ refers to the "time evolution" operator from time point a to time point b. It simulates the change in value of the collateral over time.[3] This operator is the Unity operator (i.e., does not do anything) when the collateral is cash. The operator does not account for changes of FX rates; that is covered in the next point.
2. Then we need to transfer the value of the collateral to the base currency used in the simulation, multiplying it by the relevant FX rate at time point i,

$$C_i^{before} = \widetilde{C}_i^{before} \cdot FX_i \tag{4.2}$$

3. Now we need to check if there is going to be any collateral call. If

$$V_{NS,i} > Threshold_{counterparty} \longrightarrow \text{We call collateral} \tag{4.3}$$

$$\Delta C_i = V_{NS,i} - C_i^{before} - Threshold_{counterparty} \tag{4.4}$$

   or if

$$V_{NS,i} > Threshold_{ours} \longrightarrow \text{We post collateral} \tag{4.5}$$

$$\Delta C_i = V_{NS,i} - C_i^{before} - Threshold_{ours} \tag{4.6}$$

   where $Threshold_{counterparty}$ is a number greater than or equal to zero and $Threshold_{ours}$ is smaller than or equal to zero.

4. Now we need to check if the collateral ΔC_i is above the minimum transfer amount (MTA). If it is smaller (in absolute value), then we reset it to zero.
5. Also, we need apply the rounding to ΔC_i.
6. At this stage, we can say what the collateral after the margin call will be:

$$C_i^{after} = C_i^{before} + \Delta C_i \tag{4.7}$$

7. And now we can add to it the initial margin:

$$C_i'^{before} = C_i^{before} + IM \tag{4.8}$$

$$C_i'^{after} = C_i^{after} + IM \tag{4.9}$$

$$IM = \widetilde{IM} \cdot FX_i \tag{4.10}$$

8. Finally, we can transform back the collateral into its currency, ready for the next iteration:

$$\tilde{C}_i^{after} = \frac{C_i^{after}}{FX_i} \tag{4.11}$$

This algorithm treats risky collateral; i.e., collateral that is not cash, or that is cash in a different currency to the accounting currency of the financial institution. This risk is calculated by the $\Xi_{a\to b}(\cdot)$ operator and by the FX_i exchange rate that changes from time point to time point, for each scenario, as per their respective implemented models.

4.1.2 Calculating gap risk

The next step is to calculate the exposure that may arise from *changes in the value of the facility* during the Margin Period of Risk (MPR). As mentioned previously MPR has two components: the default-declaration period (n_1) and the close-out period (n_2).

Strictly speaking, if we assume that a default is declared at the calculation time point, we should take the value of the CSA facility n_1 days before that calculation point, when default is first suspected, and compute the change in value it suffers to n_2 days after the calculation point *without any additional collateral exchange.* However, this subtlety complicates practical implementation very much, especially when compared to calculating those exposures from the calculation time point to MPR days afterwards ($MPR = n_1 + n_2$). The error we introduce by using this simplification is practically unnoticeable; in practice, this error will be within the numerical noise, so there is no need to make our life difficult and we should consider the gap risk from the calculation time point to MPR days after it.

We should emphasise the fact that we want to calculate the changes in the value of the *CSA facility*, as opposed to the *netting set.* By value of the netting set we mean the value of the trades, and by value of the CSA facility we mean the value of the trades plus the collateral.

The exposure gap risk is then going to be calculated from the difference in value between the netting set MPR days after the calculation and the collateral held at the calculation point:

$$\Delta V_{CSA,i} = V_{NS,i+MPR} - C_i'^{before} \tag{4.12}$$

At the end of this, we are going to have an $N \times (M+1)$ grid that will contain the gap values of the collateralised facility, for every scenario and calculation time point, ΔV_{CSA}.

4.1.3 Calculating exposure metrics

Finally, from this grid of gap values, we can compute any exposure metric like EPE or PFE in the same way we did for uncollateralised netting sets. This will give us the collateralised exposure risk.

4.2 The devil can be in the detail

In principle, this algorithm is quite mechanical, so it should be quite straightforward to implement. On one side, the bad news is that the devil is in the detail; small details of the CSA agreement, that we have skipped in this overview can, in practice, complicate the implementation somewhat. However, on the other side, the good news is that the impact that these small details will have on the final exposure profiles is, in most cases, small, and so we can make a few approximations without significantly affecting the final exposure profiles, if at all.

Non-daily margin call frequency

The algorithm described assumes that, at each time step, we can simulate the margin call of each netting set, which in most cases occurs daily, but sometimes it can be weekly or monthly, for example.[4] As shown in Equation 2.10, to take the margining frequency into account in the MPR, we can say that

$$MPR(\text{days}) = 10 + \text{margining frequency (in days)} - 1 \tag{4.13}$$

This equation is conservative as it assumes the worse case scenario: that it takes us the whole margining period to realise that the counterparty has defaulted. If we want to be less conservative, for less frequent margining periods (e.g., monthly, quarterly), we could use half of the margining period instead, for example.[5]

Different MPR per netting set

In order to perform the collateralised calculation of Equation 4.12, we need to price each netting set at each exposure calculation time point for the collateral calculation *and* at the time points MPR days after them. The difficulty comes from the fact that different netting sets are going to have different MPR values and we may need to aggregate exposure profiles of different netting sets in order to review portfolio risk (e.g., calculate the risk of a counterparty with several netting sets, aggregate different counterparties at a country level, at a legal entity level, etc.). As a result, we need to simulate the risk factors not only at all the exposure calculation time points, but at all the additional points, MPR days after each calculation time step, that each netting set requires. Then we will need to price each trade at all these time steps and calculate exposure metrics accordingly. This is, in practice, quite a challenge to implement.

Fortunately, a simple and effective way to simplify this is by pricing all netting sets only ten days after each exposure calculation time point. That is, we always use a default margin period of risk of ten days, for every netting set. We are choosing "ten" days because that is the most frequent MPR. Then, if we need to calculate exposures with an MPR of n days, we multiply all exposures in the grid given by Equation 4.12 by $\sqrt{n/MPR_{default}}$. This will generally be a good proxy of the actual exposure.

One-way CSA

The algorithm is based on a bilateral CSA. To incorporate unilateral CSAs we just need to remove one of the two "if" statements of the algorithm according to which counterparty has to post/receive collateral.

Alternatively, a common "trick" is setting the threshold of the counterparty that does not post collateral to a ridiculously large number, like $1,000 trillion. This solution, being an implementation fudge, does the job quite nicely.

Future collateral

As mentioned, CSA agreements may allow us to post as collateral cash in different currencies or bonds, equities and other securities. How can we model what mix of these will be posted/received in the future? In reality there is no perfect solution to this, as we don't know what type of collateral a Japanese bank, for example, will deliver in five years' time. To overcome this constraint, it is quite common to make one of the following three assumptions.

We can assume that the collateral mix, as a percentage of the total collateral, will be constant in the future. For example, if the collateral received in the past year by a given counterparty has been 60% in Euros, 30% in US dollars and 10% in long-term US government bonds, we can assume that that mix is going to remain the same in the future. Another alternative is to "guess" which is the cheapest-to-deliver asset(s) for the counterparty and assume that the counterparty will deliver these assets as collateral in the future. For example, most often the cheapest and most convenient currency to deliver for a US bank is USD, for a European bank EUR, for the simple fact that they tend to have better access to the money markets in their own currency. The final approach that is sometimes used for risk management purposes, where being conservative can be important, is to assume that the counterparty will post the worst type of collateral permitted under the CSA. This would usually be interpreted as the most volatile and/or less liquid collateral.

It should be noted that we would also need to make an assumption as to what type of collateral we will be posting in the future as we usually don't know this for certain. So for example, if we assume that the counterparty will post the cheapest to deliver collateral we can also make a similar assumption for ourselves.

4.3 Haircuts

We have seen that if we do not have the capability to model risky collateral, we need to apply a "haircut" to the value of the collateral to account for its potential gap risk. This gap risk does not arise from the change in value of our portfolio as we discussed in the previous section but from the change in value of the collateral. For example a 10-year German government bond may have a 5% haircut; $100 of a German government bond will be posted to cover $95 of exposure.

Now that we understand in detail how things work with collateralised facilities, we can discuss how to calculate the haircut.

With that haircut we want to be covered against moves in the value of the collateral during the MPR period, so we are going to model how much it can move over MPR days at a high level of confidence (e.g., 99%) and that is going to give us the haircut:

$$\text{Haircut} = \frac{\text{Value today} - 99\% \text{ worse value after MPR days}}{\text{Value today}} \tag{4.14}$$

However, this way of handling risky collateral can easily overestimate risk. This can be seen in Equation 4.1: if we model risky collateral with a haircut, then $\Xi_{i \to i+\delta}(\cdot)$ becomes the Unity operator and hence any dependency between the change in the value of V_{NS} and C', from i to $i+\delta$, is not taken into account in the model.

This should be clear by looking at the example explained previously. If the netting set has only one equity forward, where we receive the appreciation of the underlying shares and the counterparty posts these shares as collateral, V_{NS} and C' are going to move up and down in parallel so that $\Delta V_{CSA,i}$ in Equation 4.12 is always zero (i.e., zero exposure risk). However using a haircut approach this correlation will be ignored and therefore the risk will be overestimated. If the collateral received is highly correlated to the forward's underlying, then we will only be exposed to the residual risk:

$$\begin{aligned} &\text{if } \Delta V_{NS} = \rho\, \Delta C' + \sqrt{1-\rho^2}\,\epsilon \\ &\text{then } \Delta V_{CSA} = \sqrt{1-\rho^2}\,\epsilon \end{aligned} \tag{4.15}$$

4.4 Some important remarks

A few final comments on collateral CSA modelling.

Naming conventions: Sometimes collateralised and uncollateralised transactions are also referred to as "secured" and "unsecured".

Decrease of exposure risk with collateral: The first question we may have is how ask is: in general, the change in exposure when we change a facility from collateralised to uncollateralised? This obviously depends very much on the CSA details, like threshold or initial margins, on the trade type, on the volatility of the underlying and the maturity of the trade, though the decrease will be significant in many cases.

For example, it's been found that the decrease of exposure for some typical trades with an ideal CSA (zero threshold, zero MTA, daily margining, MPR of ten days, etc.) is 80% [39]. My experience with this corroborates that view; I have a simplified rule-of-thumb of a decrease of counterparty risk of around 10 times when collateral is considered. However, it is very important to note that this only a generalisation, and the decrease in exposure can change a lot depending on lots of factors, as indicated above. Some indicative examples of this change in exposure are shown later in the chapter; in those example we can already see a broad range of change in exposure.

Initial margin vs. threshold: We can observe in the algorithm that the initial margin and the threshold impact on the exposure in opposite directions. That is because a threshold that we "give" to a counterparty is an unsecured exposure that we are comfortable with, whilst an initial margin is an amount we require as an extra security; which is precisely the opposite.

If we perceive the counterparty as a high quality one, we are happy to give some threshold to it, as we are happy to be uncollateralised to some extent. If we perceive it as "so-so", we may choose to give a zero threshold. But if we perceive the counterparty as high risk, we should be asking for an initial margin, the reason being to cover for the gap risk that we still have when fully collateralised. We can see how threshold and initial margin work on this way in the formulae.

Risky collateral as a repo facility: We previously discussed that accepting risky collateral is, from a counterparty risk perspective, similar to having a repo-like transaction in the CSA. To clarify further, this is only the case when we use a haircut methodology for modelling risky collateral. The counterparty could, instead of pledging the risky assets as collateral, repo the risky assets out to borrow cash, and then post that cash to us as collateral. When we accept risky assets as collateral we are, de facto, being that third party too because in the event of our counterparty defaulting, we are interested in the cash value of that collateral.

However, that is the case only when either the collateral is independent of the value of the portfolio of trades, or when we don't model that dependency. That is the case because a standard repo transaction does not consider any correlation with any other asset class, while the repo-like transaction that we go into when receiving or posting risky collateral can benefit from this dependency (e.g., the already mentioned equity forward derivative that has the equity as collateral). This is why, in order to benefit from this, we must model the riskiness of the collateral.

Threshold triggers: We mentioned in previous sections threshold triggers that change the level of threshold when the credit rating of a counterparty changes. For example, we can have a threshold agreed of $10m, but which goes to zero if the counterparty's credit rating gets to BBB or worse.

The modelling framework explained here considers the threshold at constant values, which is the industry standard. In order to model threshold triggers, we will need a parallel process to simulate the credit rating of the counterparties and, then, simulate the threshold accordingly. That credit rating process should, ideally, have a dependency structure with the value of the netting set and of the collateral, but this may not always be needed. For example, if the netting set contains only FX and interest rate trades, and the counterparty is a company whose business performance is not really correlated to either, then we can model credit rating migrations as an independent process. However, if the company is an importer or exporter, or the portfolio contains many Credit Default Swaps, that dependency may be important.

Gap risk in uncollateralised facilities: As a final remark, it is the industry standard to measure the exposure of uncollateralised facilities as the value of the netting set at time of default, and of collateralised ones as the gap risk at time of default. The idea behind it is pretty simple: if the portfolio is unsecured, if a default occurs we lose the value of the netting set, while if the portfolio is collateralised we can only lose the potential change in the value of the netting set hedges until the book is liquidated (referred to as the gap risk).

The reader must note that this isn't completely accurate. In the collateralised case things are correct, but when a facility is uncollateralised and a counterparty defaults, it will also takes us MPR days to liquidate the hedges, so we also have gap risk! Hence, the exposure in an uncollateralised facility should be the value of the netting set *plus* the gap risk. The reason this is not considered in practice is because adding an extra 10 days to a 5-year FX forward may not have a material impact on the peak exposure. However, this gap risk in uncollateralised facilities shouldn't be ruled out across the board. Two examples of this are shown in Figures 4.1 and 4.2; the effect is noticeable in each of them with different intensity.

4.5 Examples

Let's now go through a few examples in order to build some intuition on CSA modelling.

4.5.1 Collateralised vs. uncollateralised profiles

Firstly let's see how the exposure profiles change when we move the master agreement from uncollateralised to an ideal CSA. What we mean by "ideal CSA" is daily margining, zero thresholds, initial margin, minimum transfer amount, and rounding. We do this for a swap, a forward, a call, and a put option, showing the EPE profiles. This is shown in Figures 4.3–4.8.

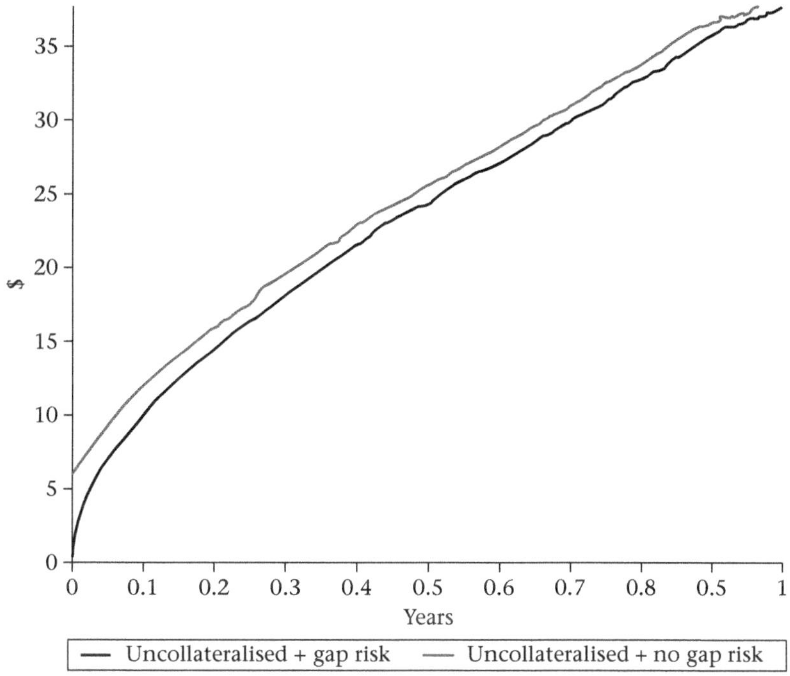

Figure 4.1 Display of the risk underestimation when considering uncollateralised risk without the gap risk. 1-year EURUSD FX forward, EPE profile

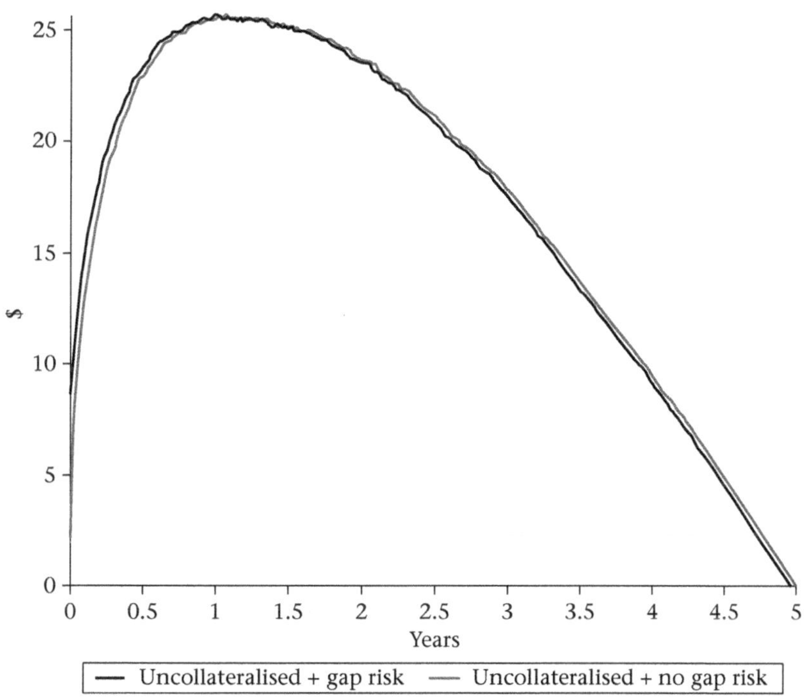

Figure 4.2 Display of the risk underestimation when considering uncollateralised risk without the gap risk. 5-year EUR interest rate swap, EPE profile

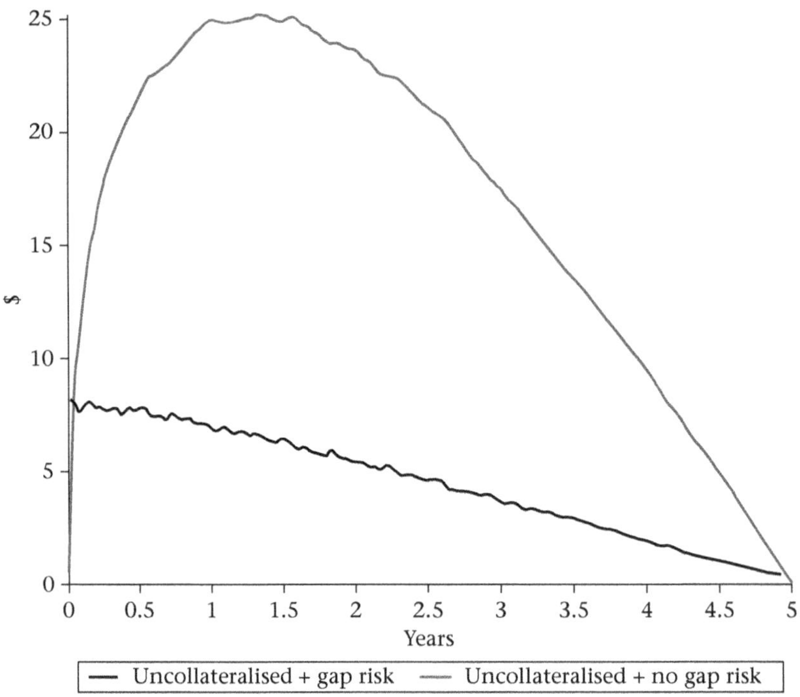

Figure 4.3 EPE profile change from collateralised to uncollateralised, for a 5-year swap

We can appreciate how the EPE profiles decrease quite substantially when moving the trade under a CSA agreement. The EPE profile of a 5-year swap under a CSA as seen in Figure 4.3 reduces with time as cashflows are paid out similarly to the unsecured case. For a 5-year forward however (Figure 4.4) the EPE is pretty flat; that is because the future 10 day move of the underlying when simulated with a constant volatility over time remains nearly the same. The decrease in exposure of long options (Figures 4.5 and 4.7) is very significant, as options are not delta-one products.[6] Also, we can appreciate how being short on an option (Figures 4.6 and 4.8) has no counterparty risk at all when uncollateralised, but it has counterparty risk when collateralised. This is because, under a collateral agreement, the seller of the option will need to post as collateral the premium he received on day 1 as it is the value of the option. The collateral required will then change as the value of the option changes during the life of the trade, and the counterparty risk to the seller will be equivalent to a 10 day potential change in value of the option.

4.5.2 Sensitivities to CSA parameters

Another set of examples can be built to see the effect of changing the CSA parameters. In these cases we depict the PFE at 90% confidence. In Figure 4.9 we can see how the profile increases with a longer margining period. Figures 4.10 and 4.11 show the impact of threshold on the exposure. When the counterparty threshold increases, the exposure approximately follows the uncollateralised profile up to the threshold level, and then is equal to the collateralised risk. Also, an increase in our own threshold has an effect on the exposure, but

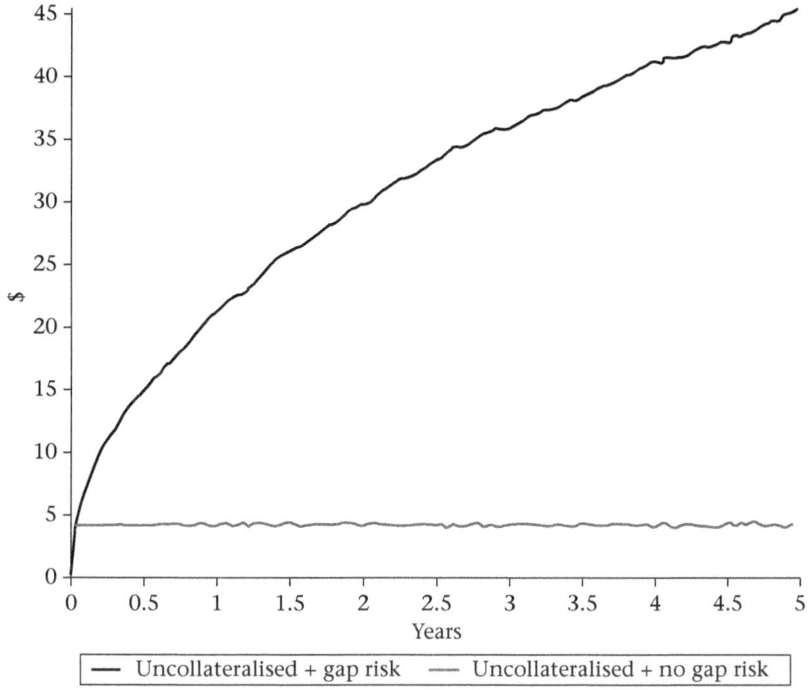

Figure 4.4 EPE profile change from collateralised to uncollateralised, for a 5-year forward

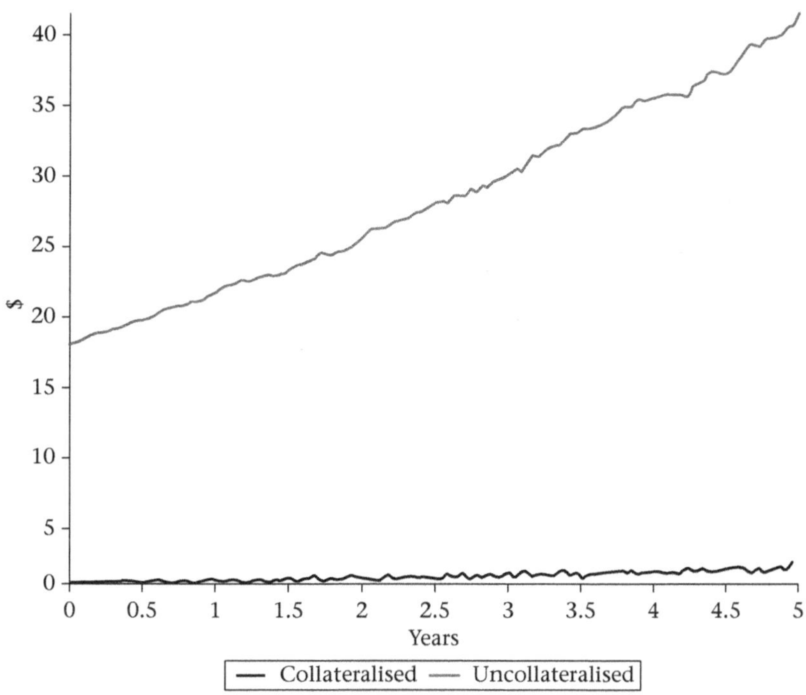

Figure 4.5 EPE profile change from collateralised to uncollateralised, for a 5-year long call option

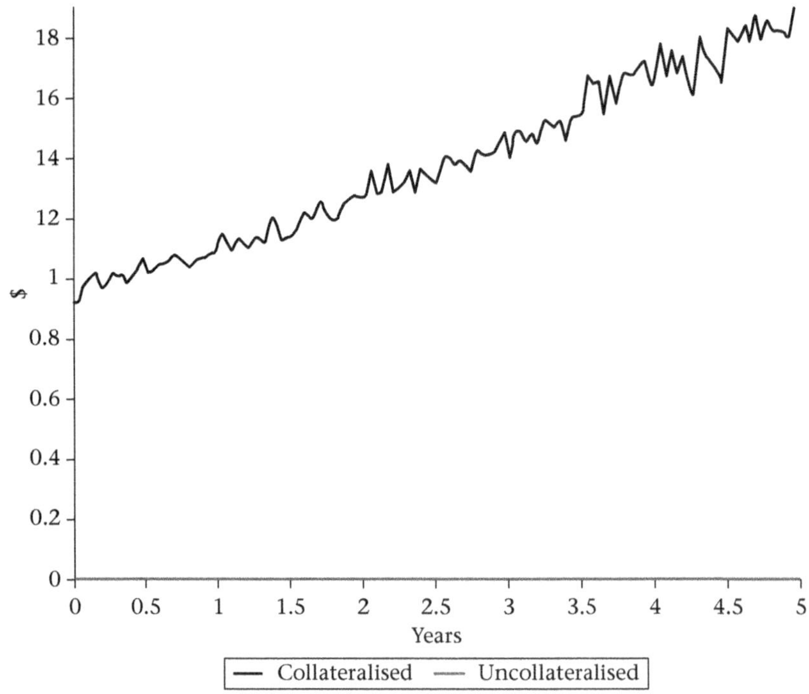

Figure 4.6 EPE profile change from collateralised to uncollateralised, for a 5-year short call option

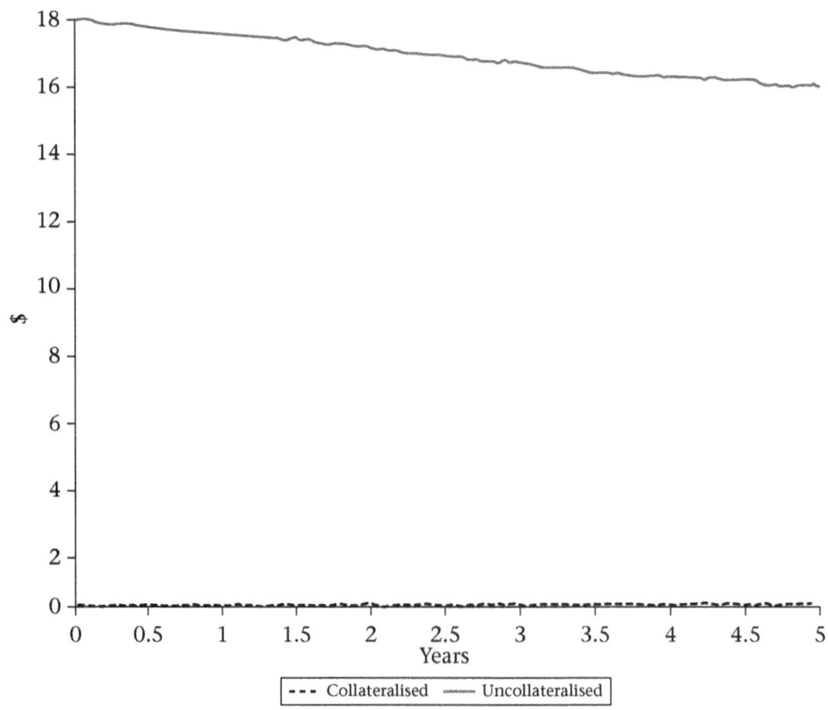

Figure 4.7 EPE profile change from collateralised to uncollateralised, for a 5-year long put option

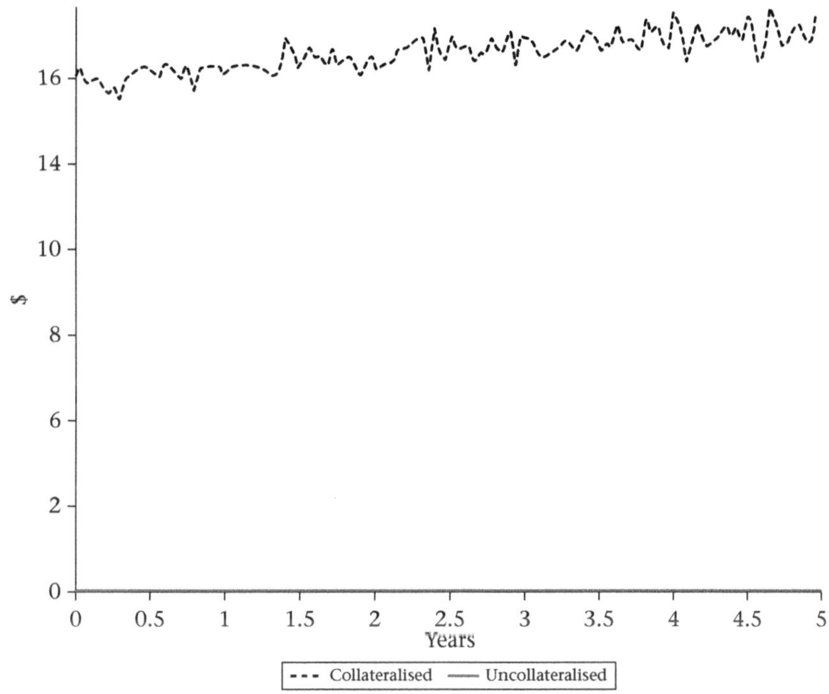

Figure 4.8 EPE profile change from collateralised to uncollateralised, for a 5-year short put option

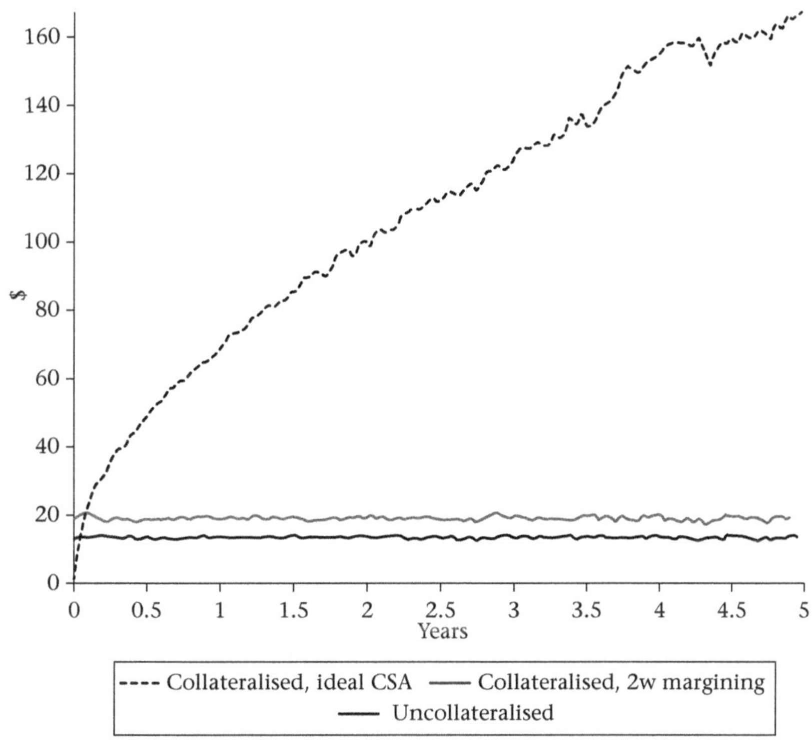

Figure 4.9 PFE 90% profile change from an ideal CSA to 2-week margining, for a 5-year forward

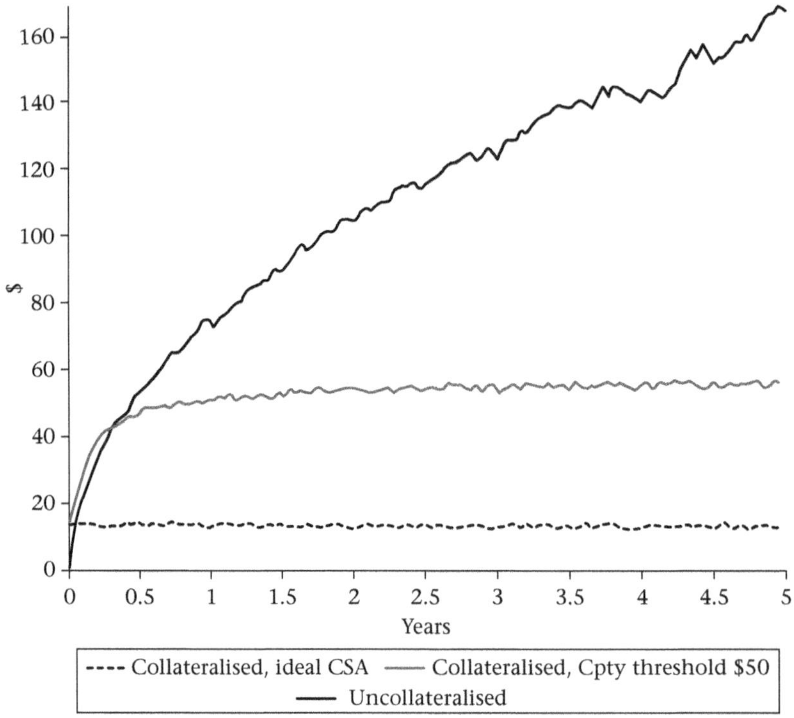

Figure 4.10 PFE 90% profile change from an ideal CSA to an increased counterparty threshold, for a 5-year forward

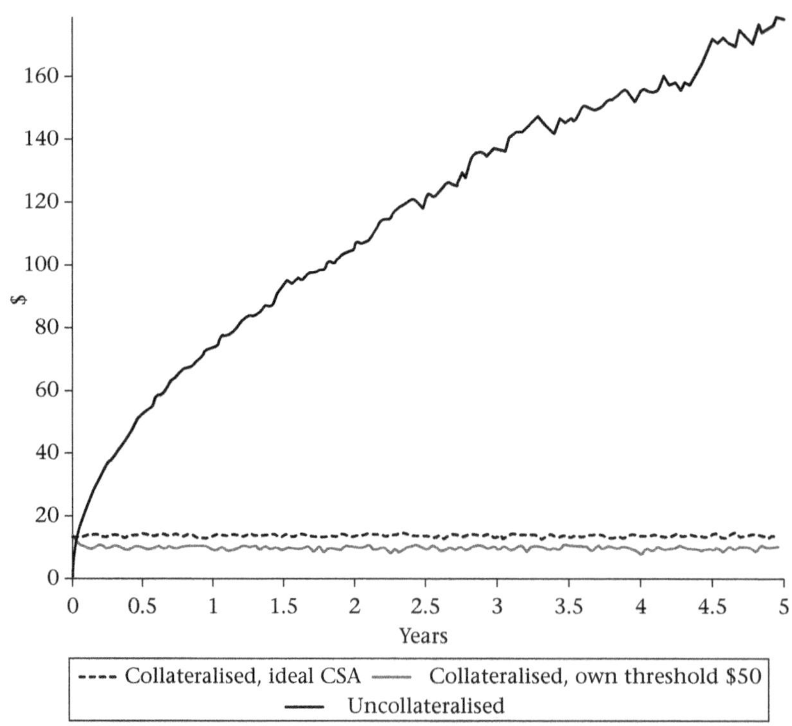

Figure 4.11 PFE 90% profile change from an ideal CSA to an increased own threshold, for a 5-year forward

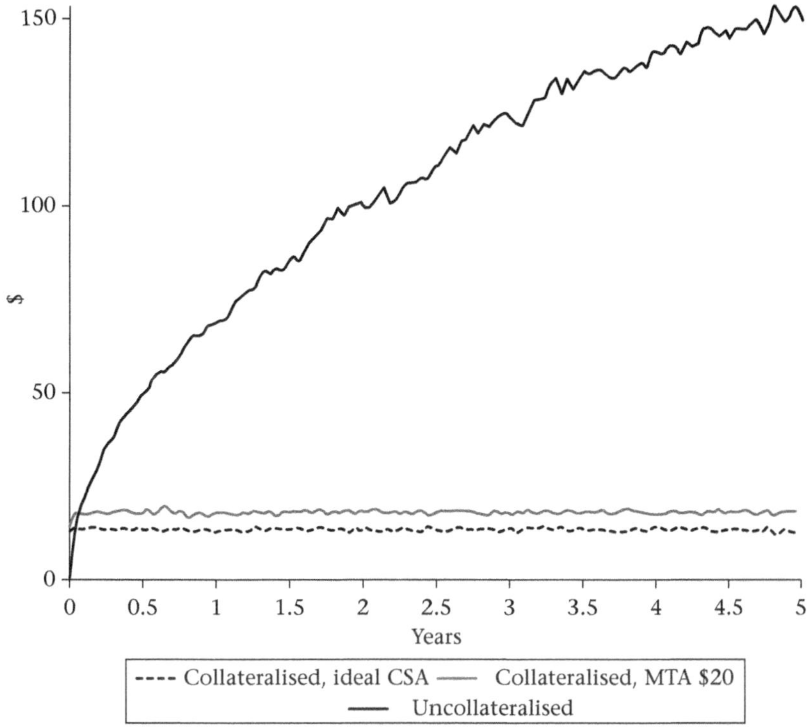

Figure 4.12 PFE 90% profile change from an ideal CSA to an increased minimum transfer amount, for a 5-year forward

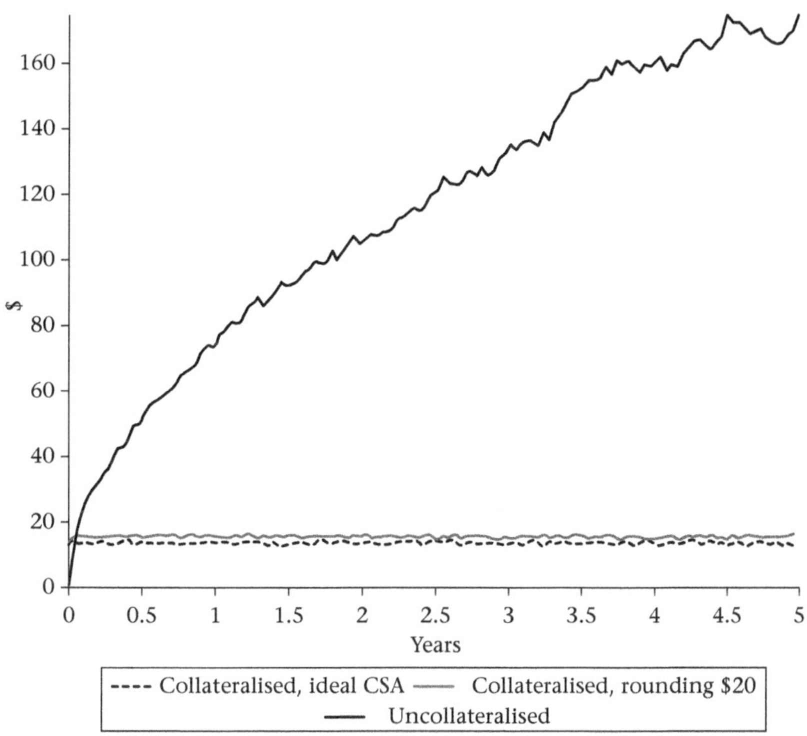

Figure 4.13 PFE 90% profile change from an ideal CSA to an increased rounding, for a 5-year forward

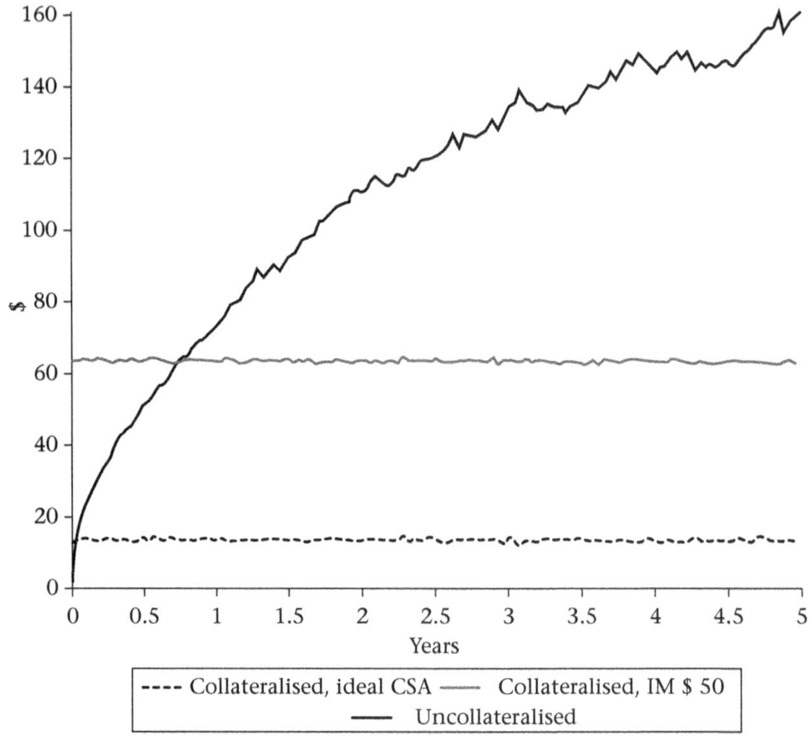

Figure 4.14 PFE 90% profile change from an ideal CSA to an increased initial margin, for a 5-year forward

quite limited. Figures 4.12 and 4.13 show the effect of minimum transfer amount and rounding. This effect is quite limited, especially in the case of rounding, as expected. Finally, Figure 4.14 displays the effect of the initial margin. In this case, the effect is a parallel shift of the exposure with an ideal CSA, so its effect depends strongly on the size of the initial margin.

5 Exposure Allocation

Up to this point, we have considered exposure calculation for a portfolio, but a question that arises very naturally is how much each trade contributes to the overall exposure.

When analysing a portfolio, a risk manager naturally wants to understand how the risk is distributed amongst its trades. A CVA desk may want to understand how much a new trade increases the CVA charge in a netting set. A trading desk may need to decrease the exposure to a counterparty because it has reached its limit, and wants to know the impact of each of its trades on the counterparty's exposure. The capital team may want to see what trades are contributing most to regulatory capital in a portfolio. The question "How much does this trade contribute to the overall exposure?" has therefore several contexts.

I wish there were a simple answer to this question; one single number, easy to calculate, per trade. But, unfortunately, there isn't. The reason is that exposure contribution of a single trade can be quite a complicated concept due to the nature of netting and aggregating. We can see this very clearly if we consider a netting set composed of two identical swaps but in opposite directions (i.e., one long and one short). The overall exposure, whichever metric we choose, is going to be zero, but if we remove one of the two trades the netting set exposure increases. In addition, one desk may be thinking of decreasing the notional of one trade by 10%, while another unit may be thinking of unwinding the trade. The meaning of "trade contribution" for each of these is going to be different.

So in order to be able to answer the question "How much does this trade contribute to the overall exposure?" we need first to define *contribution* by understanding the context of the question. If we do that, we will see that, in most cases, the question actually being asked is one of the following:

1. What happens if I book this new trade?
2. What happens if I unwind this existing trade?
3. How do I allocate exposure amongst the trades, without changing the portfolio composition?

5.1 Calculating risk contributions

In this section we are going to look at different techniques for allocating exposure amongst trades. By the term "exposure" we are referring to any exposure metric that we are interested in. In general, exposure may be a time profile (EPE, PFE, etc.) or a single number (CVA, EEPE, etc.).[1] In the equations, we are going to use E_{Port} for a portfolio exposure, and E_i for the trade's "i" contribution to the overall exposure.

5.1.1 New trade in a portfolio

Prior to a new trade being executed, it is often useful to calculate the change in the netting set exposure in order to ensure it is still within the counterparty's risk limits so as to calculate the CVA charge, etc. In that case, the incremental exposure is given by

$$\Delta E_i = E_{Port+i} - E_{Port} \tag{5.1}$$

where E_{Port+i} is the exposure with the new trade added to the portfolio.

It must be noted that this is the only way we can really assess the impact of a new trade in a portfolio. Any of the other exposure allocation methods will give only approximative numbers that could be very misleading, as netting will not be accounted for properly.

5.1.2 Unwinding an existing trade

A way to calculate the exposure contribution of each trade to the overall exposure is by removing the particular trade and leave the remaining portfolio constant:

$$\Delta E_i = E_{Port} - E_{Port-i} \tag{5.2}$$

where E_{Port-i} is the exposure of the netting set without trade i.

Again, similarly to before, this is the only way to really assess the impact in exposure of removing a trade. Any other technique will give only an approximated number, which can easily be wrong.

5.1.3 Exposure allocation in a portfolio

Often, the question asked is "What is the contribution of this or that trade to the overall exposure?". In other words, we are looking for a way to calculate an E_i, so that

$$E_{Port} = \sum_i E_i \tag{5.3}$$

where "i" sums across all trades in the portfolio, and so E_i is the contribution of trade i to the overall exposure.

There are two basic techniques for this: allocation via Notional Deltas, also called the Euler allocation, and via Expectations. The reader can find details of both techniques in Appendix C. Let's summarise them:

Contribution via notional deltas: If we define the sensitivity of the exposure to the notional of each trade (N_i) as

$$\begin{aligned} \nu_i &= \frac{\partial E_{Port}}{\partial N_i} \\ &= \frac{E_{Port}(N_i+\beta) - E_{Port}(N_i)}{\beta} \end{aligned} \tag{5.4}$$

it can be shown[2] that

$$E_{Port} = \sum_i N_i \nu_i \tag{5.5}$$

and, hence,

$$E_i = N_i \nu_i \tag{5.6}$$

This is quite a convenient technique, as if we have stored the simulated price scenarios of each trade; in order to calculate ν_i all we have to do is "bump" those prices to compute $E_{Port}(N_i + \beta)$ in Equation 5.4. That is, we don't need to run new Monte Carlo simulations.

Contribution via expectations: A different approach consists in defining each trade contribution to the exposure profile as

$$E_{i,t} = \mathbb{E}(P_{i,t} | P_{Port,t} = E_{Port,t}) \tag{5.7}$$

where $P_{i,t}$ is the price of trade i at the time point t, and $P_{Port,t}$ is the price of the portfolio. $E_{i,t}$ is the trade's contribution exposure profile to the overall exposure, from which we can calculate a trade's contribution to a single number risk metric like CVA_i or $EEPE_i$. Here, also, $E_{Port} = \sum_i E_i$.[3]

In principle, this $E_{i,t}$ profile may be difficult to compute, as we should need to run several Monte Carlo simulations in order to calculate the expectation $\mathbb{E}(\cdot)$. However, there are two shortcuts that we could take:

- We say that $\mathbb{E}(P_{i,t} | P_{Port,t} = E_{Port,t})$ is the value $P_{i,t}$ in the one simulation that we have. That is like saying that the best estimate of an average when we only have one sample is the value of that sample itself.
- Alternatively, we can get a bracket of scenarios around that one in which $P_{Port,t} = E_{Port,t}$, and take the average of those portfolio prices. For example, if we run our Monte Carlo simulation with 10,000 scenarios, we take the 100 scenarios with a portfolio price closest to the exposure, and take the average of those 100 scenarios as the expectation.[4]

Difference between both approaches: It is important to note that, in both cases,

$$E_{Port} = \sum_i E_i \tag{5.8}$$

It is understood that, in general, both approaches are going to lead to a different allocation of the exposure to each trade. Therefore a natural subsequent question is: *which of them is best?* The answer is that they are equally good (or bad).

As already said, what makes sense is the counterparty risk of a netting set, or a group of netting sets, but not of a single trade inside a netting set. In other words, from a counterparty risk standpoint, we don't have trades, we have netting sets that can be seen as one single "exotic" trade. Then we may decompose that exotic trade into several sub-trades, sub-sub-trades, etc., but that is only a way to get to the price of the netting set, which is what matters.

To give a simple parallel example, asking for the contribution of one trade to the exposure of a netting set is like asking for the contribution of one of its wheels to the price of a car. Let's say that we have a car, worth $50,000. We can find out the cost of each of its pieces if bought one by one, or the price of selling each of them as second-hand pieces, but the sum of those numbers is not going to add up to the price of the car. If we want to assign a contribution of each of its pieces to its price, that sum up to $50,000, we need to build a model for it, which is always going to have a subjective element in it. One person may say that the price contribution of one wheel is $100, another person $200; and how can we tell which is right and which is wrong? The fundamental problem here is that the question itself does not have a straight answer.

We have a similar case regarding portfolio exposure and the contribution of each trade to it. We can measure the contribution of adding or removing a trade, but we cannot really measure the contribution of each trade to the overall exposure. So, that number is no more than a theoretical number, and different models may give different contributions. Any model in which $E_{Port} = \sum_i E_i$, and that is mathematically robust, is as good as any other.

Hence, when someone asks for the contribution of a single trade to a counterparty risk metric, the first thing is to try to explain to this person why that number does not provide any barely useful information. If in spite of that, that number is still asked for (e.g., for accounting purposes, where the rules state that the marginal CVA contribution must be attributed to each single trade), then I would suggest calculating the marginal contributions with whichever sound methodology is easiest to implement.

Naive calculation: Finally, there is a somewhat popular[5] exposure allocation technique due to its simplicity, but that can very easily result in misleading numbers. We will look at it here for completeness.

Let's say that we have a portfolio with exposure metric E_{Port}. Also, each trade i in the portfolio will have an exposure on a *stand-alone basis* of E_i^{alone}. We know that due to netting,

$$E_{Port} \leq \sum_i E_i^{alone} \tag{5.9}$$

However, we can say that the contribution of each trade is given by

$$E_i = \frac{E_i^{alone}}{\sum_i E_i^{alone}} E_{Port} \tag{5.10}$$

In this methodology $E_{Port} = \sum_i E_i$, but these numbers can be very misleading for portfolios with offsetting trades. For example, we are never going to have $E_i < 0$, so we are not going to see which trades contribute by offsetting exposure risk.[6]

5.2 Charging dealing desks for risk

An interesting topic of discussion tends to be about how to charge dealing desks for the risk they generate in the organisation. Let's take CVA, the price of counterparty risk, as an example.

We have not discussed CVA yet, so for those unfamiliar with it let's say that it is an adjustment, that the price of a derivative needs, in order to reflect the counterparty risk it carries; in other words, it is the price of counterparty credit risk. Given that counterparty risk crystallises at the netting set level, the CVA must be calculated at that level. However, how can we distribute the netting set CVA amongst its trades?

Let's say that we have a netting set with 10 trades with a client, that currently has a CVA of \$10. We decide to use the Euler method to allocate CVA. This gives an allocation of approximately \$1 to each trade.

Those trades were incepted well in the past; let's say that they were interest rate trades. Now the client wants to do a new deal in the same netting set, but an FX trade this time. That new trade has, if done on a stand-alone basis, a CVA of \$5, but if done within the netting set it increases its total CVA to \$12. However, with this new trade, the Euler method gives an allocation of \$1 to the new trade, and of \$11 to the previously existing trades due to netting effects. This situation, before and after the new trade is considered, is shown in the following two tables.

Before new trade		
	Stand-alone CVA	Euler allocation
Trade 1	$2.1	$1.05
Trade 2	$1.4	$1.10
Trade 3	$1.1	$0.80
Trade 4	$2.2	$0.95
Trade 5	$2.5	$1.01
Trade 6	$1.4	$0.70
Trade 7	$0.1	$1.20
Trade 8	$0.4	$1.17
Trade 9	$1.8	$0.96
Trade 10	$0.9	$1.06
Added risk	$13.9	$10.0
Netted risk	$10.0	

After new trade		
	Stand-alone CVA	Euler allocation
Trade 1	$2.1	$1.13
Trade 2	$1.4	$1.21
Trade 3	$1.1	$0.84
Trade 4	$2.2	$1.08
Trade 5	$2.5	$1.11
Trade 6	$1.4	$0.77
Trade 7	$0.1	$1.32
Trade 8	$0.4	$1.24
Trade 9	$1.8	$1.10
Trade 10	$0.9	$1.23
New trade	$5.0	$1.0
Added risk	$15.0	$12.0
Netted risk	$12.0	

The CVA desk needs to collect $2 for the extra CVA. How shall it claim it? It has two clear candidates:

1. It uses the Euler allocation and (i) charges $1 to the FX desk for the new trade and (ii) re-charges $1 to the interest rate desk for the past trades.
2. It uses the incremental allocation and charges $2 to the FX desk.

Perhaps from a pure "fair" risk allocation standpoint, the CVA desk should use the first approach, but that will surely provide, first of all, strong management problems in the organisation, as the interest rate desk is surely going to ask "Why should we now pay as a result of a trade that the FX desk wants to do?" Also, it creates a business negative incentive, as all dealing desks will not know if, at any time in the future, the CVA desk will ask for more cash as a result of the other desk's actions.[7] The second approach, however, is cleaner and much easier to manage.

As a result of this and of the incremental nature of trading, financial institutions tend to use the second approach to charge for this risk.

5.2.1 Allocating risk in an organisation

This example was centred around CVA to make it tangible, but it can be applied to any sort of risk that individual desks create at the corporate level, like counterparty risk, funding risk, capital cost risk, etc. We will discuss all these risks in detail throughout the book.

These risk allocation techniques that we have seen should be used to allocate any XVA, and any risk metric. When doing so, the best way to do it is calculating those allocation numbers directly from the exposure metric that we are interested in, as opposed to proxies. For example, if we want to allocate CCR regulatory capital amongst trades (to be discussed in Chapter 9), that is based on a so-called EEPE exposure metric,[8] then we should calculate:

$$\nu_i^{\text{CCR}} = \frac{\partial EEPE}{\partial N_i} \tag{5.11}$$

for the Euler allocation.

This risk allocation could be a good idea for many reasons, but we must be aware of some of its limitations: it can create misleading numbers when it is "non-coherent". Let's look at that now.

5.3 Convexity of risk metric allocations

In plain language, a risk metric is said to be "coherent" when it behaves "nicely". The reader can see a more accurate definition of it in Appendix D, but one of the key characteristics of that "niceness" is that it must be homogeneous: that if we increase the notional of a trade by a factor α, its risk increases by that same α.

However, some common risk metrics are not coherent.

It will be best to illustrate this with an example. Let's say we have two netting sets with the EPE profiles as illustrated by Figure 5.1.

These two netting sets are with the same counterparty. We are interested in the risk with that counterparty, so it is typical to add up those two profiles and measure risk on that added EPE profile.

Let's pick the following two fairly common risk metrics: (i) the EEPE and (ii) the maximum of the EPE profile.[9] Figure 5.2 shows the EEPE for that counterparty as we change that notional of the first netting set, while Figure 5.3 shows also the change in the maximum of the EPE profile when we change that notional too. We can clearly see in those graphs that the allocation of EEPE and the maximum of the EPE are non-homogeneous. In other words, those risk metrics have a convexity in their allocation via the Euler method.

This can have important implications, as when we try to allocate risk with these metrics we may find that, for example, Equation 5.5 does not hold; we may need extra terms.

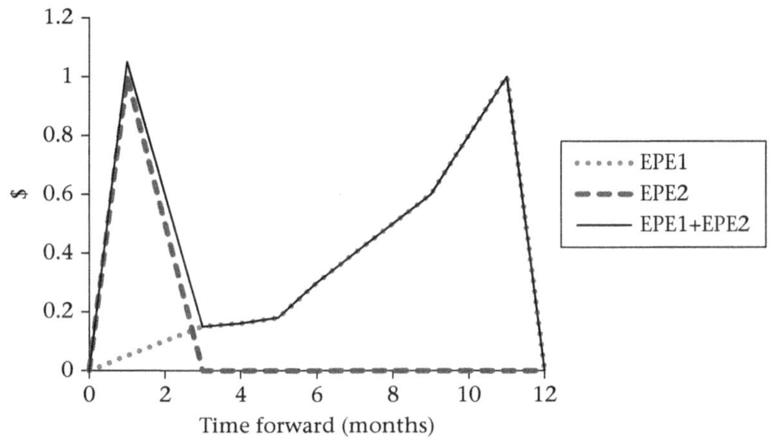

Figure 5.1 EPE profiles for two illustrative netting sets

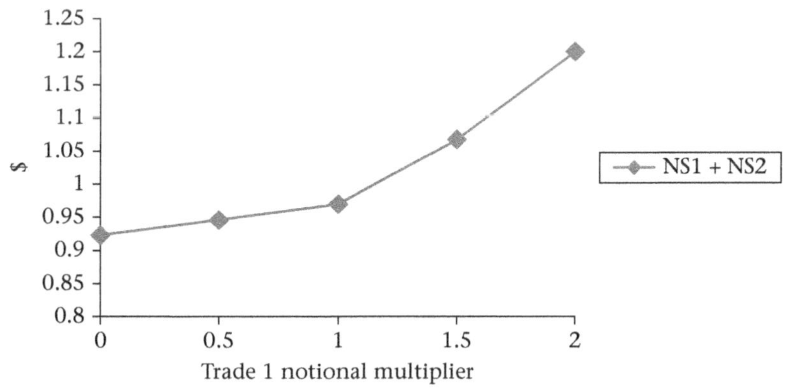

Figure 5.2 EEPE value as the notional of netting set 1 changes

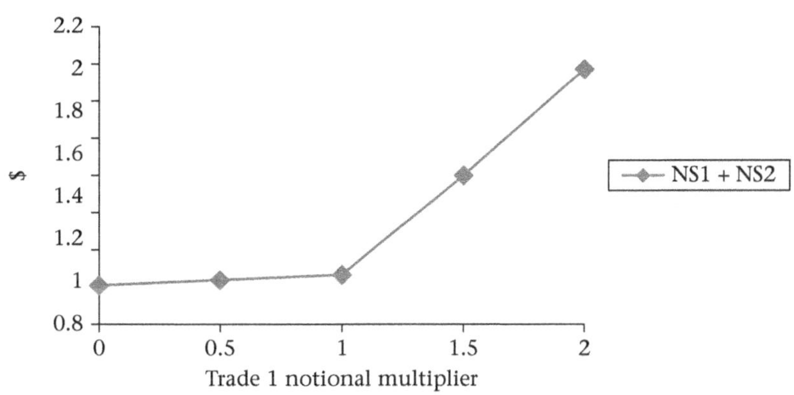

Figure 5.3 Maximum of the EPE profile value as the notional of netting set 1 changes

In this context, we could define second-order derivatives of the risk metric to the notionals as:

$$\xi_{i,j} = \frac{\partial^2 E_{Port}}{\partial N_i \partial N_j} \tag{5.12}$$

so that

$$E_{Port} \simeq \sum_i N_i \nu_i + \sum_{i,j} N_i N_j \xi_{i,j} \tag{5.13}$$

When $\xi_{i,j} = 0$ if $i \neq j$, then we could still use this method to allocate risk between the sub-parts of a portfolio, but when that is not the case, we should be careful.

6 Proxies for Exposure Measurement

So far we have seen how to calculate exposures when we have sufficient time and computational capability. However, often that is not the case. The typical problems that we may face include not having access to a Monte Carlo simulation engine, slow pricers,[1] lack of a collateral algorithm in the Monte Carlo engine, etc.

When doing simplifications and approximations, the science of quantitative analysis becomes quite an art. This is because we have to make some intuition-based assumptions to come up with a result that is reasonable. Sometimes we may not have the tools needed, and we have to be somewhat blunt with these assumptions. Needless to say, this needs to be treated with care, as it is very easy to make incorrect assumptions and simplifications. Time and practice provides the experience required to make these assumptions in a proper and informed way.

Quantiles of normal distribution: In the art of proxing, we often need to derive exposure profiles assuming normality in probability distributions. So it will be useful to see what are the quantiles of a number of typical exposure metrics in those normal conditions.

If σ is the standard deviation of the normal distribution, the following table shows the quantiles for EPE, ENE and typical PFE and CESF values:

Confidence level	PFE	CESF
90%	$1.28 \times \sigma$	$1.72 \times \sigma$
95%	$1.64 \times \sigma$	$2.03 \times \sigma$
97.5%	$1.96 \times \sigma$	$2.30 \times \sigma$
99%	$2.33 \times \sigma$	$2.63 \times \sigma$
	EPE	ENE
	$0.40 \times \sigma$	$-0.40 \times \sigma$

6.1 Mark-to-market + add-on

The most simplistic methodology to calculate exposure was in fact used by the Basel Committee in its Basel I accord in the context of regulatory capital. According to this, the exposure of a trade is given by its present value, its "Mark-to-Market" (MtM), plus an add-on number that is tabulated. Figure 6.1 shows an example of an add-on table proposed by the Basel Committee.

UNDERLYING ASSET LIFE TO MATURITY	INTEREST RATES	EXCHANGE RATES AND GOLD	STOCKS AND STOCK INDICES	PRECIOUS METALS (EXCL. GOLD)	OTHER COMMODITIES
< 1 year	0%	1%	6%	7%	10%
Between 1 and 5 years	0.5%	5%	8%	7%	12%
> 5 years	1.5%	7.5%	10%	8%	15%

Figure 6.1 Example of add-on Basel I table for calculation of PFE

These tables give the exposure add-on for single trades so that the exposure of a trade is given by:

$$\text{Exposure} = MtM + Addon \tag{6.1}$$

where *MtM* is the Mark-to-Market, the price under the typical risk-neutral assumptions, of the trade; and the *Addon* is calculated by multiplying the trade notional (N) by its percentage value ($x\%$) in the add-on table,

$$Addon = N \cdot x\% \tag{6.2}$$

When we have a netting set, netting can be partly accounted for by having a dispersion coefficient γ so that the exposure of the netting set is given by

$$\text{Exposure}_{NS} = \sum_{\text{trades}} MtM_{\text{trade}} + \gamma \sum_{\text{trades}} Addon_{\text{trade}} \tag{6.3}$$

The tables that give the add-ons can be as granular as we want. We could have, for example, one add-on number for all interest rates swaps, or one per currency, or include more granularity based on tenors, long/short, etc.; then we could have another set of tables for options, swaptions, forwards, etc. The level of granularity is endless. The choice should be based on what the institution can handle with its available resources. Obviously, in most cases, the more granular it is, the more accurate the risk is going to be.

Figure 6.2 shows an example of a netting set calculation using this method in which we can see how γ can be calculated. We start with the current value of the trades (MtM). The add-on of each trade is given by its notional multiplied by the tabulated coefficient. The dispersion coefficient can be calculated in two ways. A popular methodology is using the Net to Gross Ratio (NGR). NGR tries to measure the dispersion effect by dividing the netting set MtM by the sum of the current exposure of each trade.

This method was proposed by Basel and may provide an adequate approximation for large portfolios, but it is obviously very crude and can lead to very surprising results. For example, for two different trades that happen to have equal but opposite signs MtM will have zero exposure, as shown in Figure 6.3.

An alternative method would be to come with a more or less conservative average of this coefficient with a portfolio model, either analytically or by building a Monte Carlo simulation of an average portfolio.

Building the add-on tables: The add-on tables can be calculated with spread-sheet based models, either using simple Monte Carlo simulations or with any of the other appropriate methodologies, like the ones suggested later in this chapter. The add-on number should be based on the peak of the exposure profile given by these models for risk management, or on an average value for pricing. They should be recalibrated periodically. Those recalibrations should be done quarterly at least, with ad hoc recalibrations during periods of market stress.

	MTM ($m)	Current exposure ($m)	Notional ($m)	Add-on (%)	Add-on ($m)
Trade 1	100	100	1000	0.5%	5
Trade 2	–60	0	500	1.5%	8
Trade 3	–30	0	600	8.0%	48
Trade 4	150	150	400	7.5%	30
Trade 5	60	60	300	10.0%	30
Totals	220	310			120.5

Gamma	0.71	(NGR: Net to Gross Ratio)
Add-on	85.5	
Future exposure	305.5	

Figure 6.2 Example of exposure calculation for a netting set with the MtM + add-on methodology

	MTM ($m)	Current exposure ($m)	Notional ($m)	Add-on (%)	Add-on ($m)
Trade 1	100	100	1000	0.5%	5
Trade 2	–100	0	500	1.5%	8
Totals	0	100			12.5

Gamma	0.00	(NGR: Net to Gross Ratio)
Add-on	0.0	
Future exposure	0.0	

Figure 6.3 Example of exposure calculation for a netting set with the MtM + add-on methodology with an undesired result

We may want to take a slightly different view when calculating these add-on tables for pricing (CVA) vs. risk management (PFE, capital, etc.). As I have said, for pricing we are interested in average numbers, so if calculating an add-on for, say, five to ten years' interest rates swaps, we may want to take an average tenor for it (e.g., 7.5 years, or the weighted average of the tenor we have in our books). But when calculating these add-ons for risk management, we should take a conservative view (e.g., ten years).

Also, the add-on should be different for collateralised than for uncollateralised netting sets. When we are dealing with collateralised netting sets, we should modify Equation 6.3 with the collateral being held against this netting set and which should be adjusted with the appropriate haircuts.

$$\text{Exposure} = \sum_{\text{trades}} MtM_{\text{trade}} + \gamma \sum_{\text{trades}} Addon_{\text{trade}} - \text{Adjusted Collateral} \tag{6.4}$$

Appropriateness of add-ons: The advantages of this methodology is that, once the tables are done, exposures are very easy to calculate. On the negative side, the add-on of each trade can be quite different from its true number given the crudeness of the calculation. Also, the dispersion effects are difficult to account, the time dimension of the exposure profiles is completely lost, and there is very limited scope for gradual enhancements of the methodology. These approximations are particularly dangerous for using for pricing purposes (CVA) where accuracy is important. For risk management and/or capital purposes, where an institution may afford to be less precise and possibly more conservative, an add-on methodology can be very useful when other more sophisticated approaches are not available.

6.2 Mark-to-market + add-on with time profiles

This is a natural extension of the MtM + Add-on method and addresses the lack of time dimension in this methodology.

If we want to come up with a time exposure profile for a netting set, the simplest thing we could do is use the MtM + Add-on and then assign a flat profile for each trade up to their respective maturity. That is, when a trade matures a new exposure calculation is done for the next period, etc. An example of this method can be seen in Figures 6.4 and 6.5.

6.3 Standard approach for counterparty credit risk

The Basel Committee has published a Standard Approach for calculating exposures for Counterparty Credit Risk (SA-CCR). That approach is somewhat more risk sensitive to the real economic risk than those just described, and comes at the expense of some limited sophistication. It can be a good way of calculating exposures when nothing else is available.

Section 9.1.5 describes this approach, so we won't expand on it here.

	MTM ($m)	Current exposure ($m)	Notional ($m)	Add-on (%)	Add-on ($m)	Add-on after NGR ($m)	T (yrs)
Trade 1	100	100	1000	0.5%	5	3.55	1
Trade 2	–60	0	500	1.5%	8	5.32	2
Trade 3	–30	0	600	8.0%	48	34.06	3
Trade 4	150	150	400	7.5%	30	21.29	4
Trade 5	60	60	300	10.0%	30	21.29	5
Totals	220	310			121		

Figure 6.4 Example of exposure profile calculation for a netting set, assigning a flat exposure profile to each trade corresponding to its peak exposure

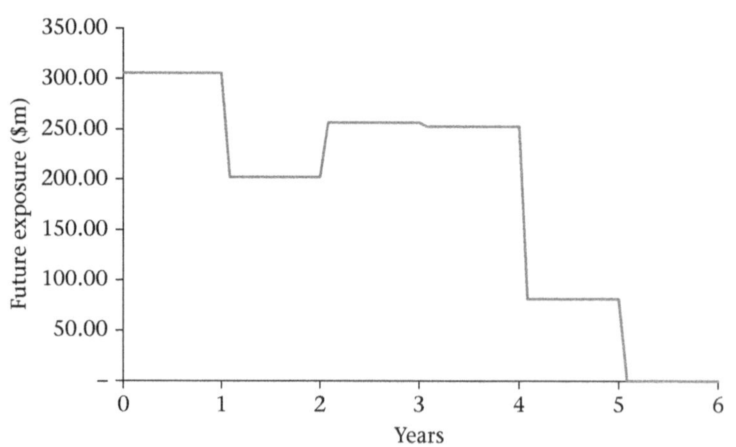

Figure 6.5 Example exposure profile for a netting set, assigning a flat line to each trade contribution

6.4 Default profile add-ons

An alternative to the previous methodology consists of assigning a predetermined shape to the profile of each trade. By doing this we take advantage of the fact that we know the typical shape of exposure profiles of some trades like swaps, options, and swaptions. These shapes can be pre-loaded in the system, either numerically with percentage-of-peak values or analytically with a fitted-to-shape formula.

6.5 When pricers are not available

A usual constraint of a Monte Carlo engine is the inability to price a number of trades. This is typically because the pricer available in the institution is too slow to be used inside the engine or it has not yet been developed for this particular engine.

In this case in which a netting set has one or more trades for which a pricer does not exist, we do not need to stop the whole calculation for that netting set. What we can do is to remove these trades from the simulation, calculate the exposure profile for the netting set without these problematic trades, and then add to it the contribution of the "unpriceable" trades, using any of the add-on methods explained above.

6.6 Simplified collateral algorithm

We have seen in Chapter 4 all the details of exposure modelling for netting sets under a collateral CSA agreement. We have seen how the main components that determine the exposure are the gap risk, margining frequency, thresholds, initial margin, minimum transfer amount and, to a lesser extent, rounding.

Fortunately, once we have a grid of prices for the uncollateralised netting set, it is quite easy to calculate the gap risk for an *ideal CSA* without a collateral algorithm.[2] In this case, if we want to calculate the gap risk over an MPR period, all we have to do is subtract, in each of the N scenarios and calculation time points, the value of the netting set MPR days after the calculation time point from the value of the netting set at the calculation time point,

$$\Delta P_{i,t_j} = P_{i,t_j+MPR} - P_{i,t_j} \tag{6.5}$$

where i counts through the Monte Carlo scenarios, and t_j is the time of the jth simulation time point. From this grid of $\Delta P_{i,t_j}$ we can calculate all the exposure metrics for the case of this ideal CSA. We will get a result that is quite close to that obtained with a sophisticated algorithm in the case of an ideal CSA; the only errors will be (i) no risky collateral is modelled and (ii) it will not account for any post or under collateralisation at the simulation start.

We have also seen in the examples that the effect of thresholds, initial margin, minimum transfer amount, and rounding is pretty close to a parallel shift of the risk profiles. Also, we have seen how when the margining frequency is not daily we can take care of it by increasing the MPR.

As a result, we can achieve a very good approximation to collateralised exposure without a collateral algorithm by following these steps:

1. Calculate the exposure profiles for an ideal CSA as per Equation 6.5.
2. Correct the MPR if we have non-daily margining.

Remember that if we can calculate Equation 6.5 only with a fixed MPR, typically 10 days, we can multiply the exposure profiles by $\sqrt{\frac{n}{10}}$, where n is the desired MPR.[3]

3. Shift up or down the profile to account for the other CSA parameters.

Hence, if we can calculate the gap risk for a fixed MPR n_{fixed}, the following quantity is a good proxy to collateralised exposure:

$$\begin{aligned}\text{Exposure Profile} = {} & \text{Gap Risk Exposure Profile}_{\text{Ideal CSA}} \cdot \sqrt{\frac{n}{n_{fixed}}} \\ & + \text{Threshold} - \text{Initial Margin} \\ & + \text{Minimum Transfer Amount} + \text{Rounding} \\ & + \sum_{\text{netting set}} MtM_{\text{trade}} - \text{Adjusted Collateral}\end{aligned} \tag{6.6}$$

6.7 Collateralised exposures from a VaR engine

In case there is no Monte Carlo simulation available for counterparty risk but there is a market risk engine that calculates VaR, we can make use of that engine to come up with a proxy for collateralised exposure.

VaR measures the market losses[4] that a financial institution may suffer over a certain time horizon and confidence level, usually ten days and at 99% confidence. This can be calculated using a number of methodologies such as historical or Monte Carlo simulation, or full or sensitivity-based pricing. In any case, whichever methodology is used, we can surely use that engine to calculate VaR at 1% confidence instead of 99%, which is precisely the PFE for today's gap risk at 99%. In fact, we can do the same for any exposure metric; we can calculate today's gap risk for any exposure metric using the VaR engine. By doing this, at the end of the day all we are doing is calculating risk metrics from the "positive" side of the 10 day[5] return distribution, instead of from the negative side as we do for the market risk's VaR.

This methodology is particularly useful when the VaR engine calculates prices based on sensitivities, that should be easily available, as we can add each trade's sensitivities to each netting set to come up with the sensitivities for the netting set.

Once we calculate the desired exposure metric, we can use the ideas already explained regarding existing collateral and CSA parameters to come up with today's exposure proxy:

$$\begin{aligned}\text{Today's Exposure} = {} & \text{Today's Gap Risk Exposure} \cdot \sqrt{\frac{n}{n_{fixed}}} \\ & + \text{Threshold} - \text{Initial Margin} \\ & + \text{Minimum Transfer Amount} + \text{Rounding} \\ & + \sum_{\text{netting set}} MtM_{\text{trade}} - \text{Adjusted Collateral}\end{aligned} \tag{6.7}$$

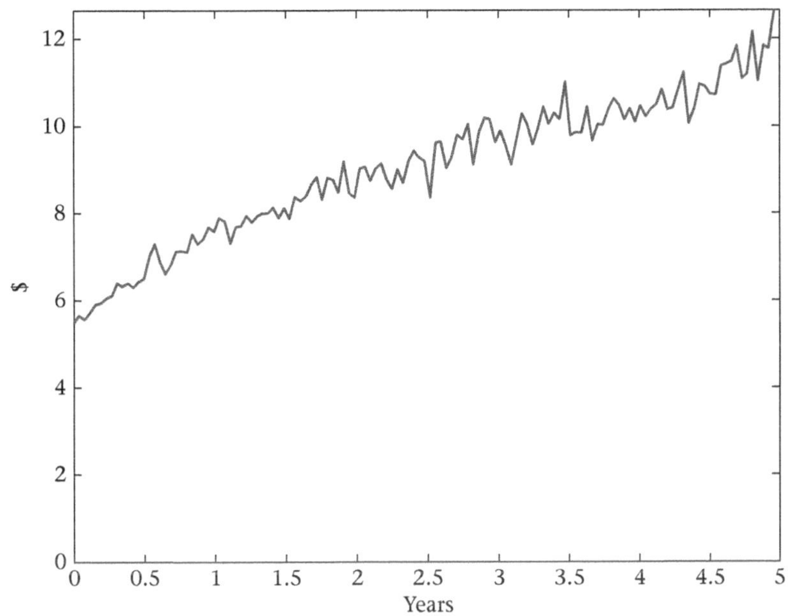

Figure 6.6 Gap risk, PFE at 95%, for an at-the-money call option

The last step is to expand today's exposure into the future so as to have an exposure profile. Given the modest tools that we have, the only thing we can do is to expand today's exposure with a flat line until the last trade of the netting set matures.

This method is, arguably, fairly good for today's exposure, but it doesn't capture two important things. Firstly, it does not account for the effect of trades rolling-off. As trades mature, the gap risk can change substantially; this is not accounted for. Secondly, it misses out the non-linearity of the gap risk. Let's say for example that the netting set is composed of only one option, that is at-the-money today. The delta of that option is going to be approximately $\frac{1}{2}$ today. However, as the trade approaches maturity, some simulation paths will be well in the money, with a delta of approximately 1, while some other paths are going to be well out of the money, with a delta of approximately 0. Near maturity the gap risk is going to be driven by those paths well in the money, with delta of ~ 1, as

$$\delta V_{i,t_j} \sim \Delta_{i,t_j} \delta S_{i,t_j} \tag{6.8}$$

where S is the option underlying and Δ_{i,t_j} is the option's delta to S. Hence the profiles will peak near maturity. This effect can be seen in Figure 6.6. This methodology will not accurately reflect the risk of option convexity.

Having said that, this methodology is much better than nothing when we do not have the means to perform full exposure simulations.

6.8 Analytical PFE exposures

This method can be applied for PFE calculations when the exposure is mainly driven by one risk factor and the relationship between the risk factor and the price of the trade (or trades) is monotonic.

It will be best to explain this with an example. If we want to calculate the uncollateralised PFE 90% of a vanilla at-the-money call option, we know that that number is going to be driven mainly by the price of the option with the underlying (S) at its 90th percentile value. That percentile value follows a path given by

$$S_t^{90} = S_0\, e^{(\mu - \frac{1}{2}\sigma^2)\, t + 1.28\sigma\, \sqrt{t}} \tag{6.9}$$

if the S follows a Geometric Brownian Motion.[6] Hence, the PFE of this trade is approximately going to be the price of the option in that S_t^{90} path

$$PFE_t^{90} = \text{Option Price } (S_t^{90}) \tag{6.10}$$

If we want the PFE at another confidence level, we can change the 1.28 in the formula by the appropriate number shown in the table at the beginning of this chapter.

In this simple way we can calculate a PFE profile pretty accurately for this type of trade. It can be applied to trades like vanilla products. They may have other risk factors that influence the price, like option implied volatilities, but this method gives a good proxy when the risk is mostly driven by one single factor, as it is generally the case for vanilla swaps or options. For trades with several risk factors, it is important to select the correct risk factor that will be the primary driver of exposure. For example for a vanilla IR swap the main risk factor will be the underlying yield curve whilst for a cross-currency swap it will be the underlying spot FX rate.

We can also apply this technique for collateralised trades, using Equation 6.7 and

$$\begin{aligned} \text{Today's Gap Risk Exposure}^{90} &= S_0\,(e^{(\mu - \frac{1}{2}\sigma^2)\, n_{fixed} + 1.28\sigma\, \sqrt{n_{fixed}}} - 1) \\ &\approx S_0\, 1.28\sigma\, \sqrt{n_{fixed}} \end{aligned} \tag{6.11}$$

where we have assumed in the approximation that a GBM process is locally normal, for a small time step.

In general, this kind of methodology is very simple and can only be applied to individual trades or simple portfolios.

6.9 Collateralised exposures from historical analysis

If we have access to a long enough history of the main risk factor (S) that drives the price of a trade, we can calculate the 10-day (or whatever MPR we need) changes in the price of the derivative historically, and take the collateralised exposure from it.

For example, if we have the time series $\{S_i\}$, we can calculate a time series of the changes in price from

$$\begin{aligned} \Delta P_i &= P(S_{i+MPR}) - P(S_i) \\ &\simeq \Delta_{S_i} \cdot \delta S_{i \to i+MPR} \end{aligned} \tag{6.12}$$

Then, from this time series $\{\Delta P_i\}$ we can calculate its 90th percentile, or any other desired risk metric.

Furthermore, if the delta of the derivative has a fairly stable value in the range of $\{S_i\}$, we can take it as a constant, calculate the 90th percentile (for example, for PFE90) of the time series of $\{\delta S_i\}$, and then

$$\begin{aligned} \text{Today's Gap Risk Exposure}^{90} &= P(S_0 + \delta S^{90}) - P(S_0) \\ &\simeq \Delta\, \delta S^{90} \end{aligned} \tag{6.13}$$

It is important to note that when doing this analysis from the time series, the series of changes in the risk factor that we build must be done from non-overlapping data, as otherwise the series will have an artificially induced autocorrelation.

This historical method can usually only be used for collateralised trades. That is because if we wanted to apply it to uncollateralised trades, we would need a very long time series (around one hundred years) so that we could have enough independent measurements of risk factor changes in the data. It must be said that even if we had that time series, the dynamics of the risk factor today may be very different to one hundred years ago, so its applicability may be questionable.

6.10 EPE and ENE as the price of an option

For simple trades, the EPE (and ENE) can be inferred from the options market. Let's see this with an example.

Let's say that we have a 10-year receiver swap, incepted today at a rate r_0, and let's say we want to calculate the EPE value one year from now. We know that at that point in time we will have a 9-year swap. EPE is the expected value of the swap at that point in time, after flooring it to zero. Well, that is precisely an option. That EPE number that we are looking for is going to be the value of a swaption, maturing in one year, with a 9-year receiver swap as underlying, with a strike of r_0. Also, by symmetry, ENE is going to be the same swaption but now as a payer swap.

Another example. Let's say we have an FX forward, maturing in one year. EPE in three months is going to be the price of a 9-month FX call option on the same rate, with strike being the price of the forward today. ENE is going to be the symmetric one: a put option instead.

Generalising the above, if we have a derivative maturing at T, EPE_t is going to be the value of an option on that product, at t, with a maturity $T - t$, and ENE its symmetric call/put option.

In this way, if we have full implied volatility data, we can estimate the EPE and ENE profiles from them.

The reader can see that this methodology can only be used for single vanilla trades. Also, implicitly, it uses a risk-neutral calibration; if we want to use a real-world calibration, we can modify the option volatility.[7]

6.11 Netting set P&L analysis

Until now, we have always tried to model the exposure of a netting set by modelling firstly each of the components that affect it (i.e., risk factor evolution and individual trade pricing) to then come up with a grid of prices for the netting set, from which we calculate all the exposure metrics like EPE, PFE, etc. Here, we are going to turn the problem around.

As already mentioned, a netting set can be seen as an exotic "super-trade" by itself. For example, a netting set that contains 200 interest rate swaps, maturing from one to twenty years, can be seen as a super-swap with a time varying notional. The same idea can be applied to a netting set with options or any other kind of financial derivatives. In fact, at the end of the day, we may decompose the exposure calculation problem into risk factor models and individual trade pricers, but what we really are looking for is *the process that the price of the netting set follows*, from which we can calculate the exposure metrics.

If things are like that, what if we go directly to the solution we are looking for, namely to model the netting set price directly?

If we do not have the capability for the sophistication of a Monte Carlo simulation with all its risk factors and trade pricers, we may have a good history of the P&L of the netting set, from which we can extrapolate information about how the netting set price may behave going forward.

6.11.1 Analytical version

The most simple way of doing this is measuring the volatility of the netting set price, perhaps a drift if we can, and then we can assume that that price will follow a normal process going forward,

$$V_{NS,t} = V_{NS,0} + \mu\, t + \sigma \sqrt{t}\epsilon. \tag{6.14}$$

If the netting set is composed of only options, all in the same direction,[8] then perhaps it is better to assume lognormality, instead of normality, for the process.

For PFE and CESF profile calculation, all we have to do is replace the normal variate ϵ by the quantile shown in the table earlier in this chapter (e.g., $\epsilon = 1.65$ for PFE at 95% confidence). For EPE and ENE, we can make use of what we have discussed in Section 6.10, as EPE_t is going to be the price of a call option, with the netting set value as underlying and strike zero, and ENE is going to be the price of the same put option; we can make use of an option pricer formula for this.

We must not forget that if we assume normality for the process, we must use the option pricer under such conditions (Black–Scholes assumes log normality).

That was for uncollaterised netting sets. For collateralised ones, we can either assume normality or log normality as appropriate, and make use of Equation 6.11 with the volatility measured in the time series, or we can do a Brownian Monte Carlo simulation of the price of the netting set and apply a full or a simplified collateral algorithm; this time we do not have to build simulations for all risk factors and price all trades, instead we only need to build one Monte Carlo simulation for the whole netting set.

It should be noted that the solution explained above (replacing ϵ by the quantile) is already the solution of a Brownian Monte Carlo simulation for the netting set, where the price follows a normal, or log normal, process.

6.11.2 Historical MC version

An alternative to this, which is a bit more sophisticated, is to use the Historical Monte Carlo methodology explained in Chapter 3, with the time series of the netting set values as the historical data for it, from which we can directly measure all uncollateralised exposure metrics.

For collateralised netting sets, we can make use of Equation 6.13, or even simulate the collateral with a full or simplified algorithm.

This historical methodology can be quite powerful given its simplicity, as once we have a full Monte Carlo price grid for the netting set, we can apply the collateral algorithm to it and measure collateralised exposure quite nicely.

Furthermore, if we do this for all the netting sets on the books, we will be able to measure very well the aggregation effects across the netting sets if we want to.[9] In this case we are replacing the massive job of simulating, typically, thousands of risk factors and pricing a few million trades in each scenario and time bucket by using only a few thousand netting set prices.

However, these techniques have some major drawbacks.

6.11.3 Some comments

The best of this methodology is that it is very clean and straightforward; it goes directly to the core of the problem, modelling directly the price of the netting set. In fact, there are some quite interesting versions of these methods in the literature [67].

It must be noted that, if using the analytical version, someone could argue that netting set prices are not going to follow a normal or log normal process for sure. We'd expect that to be true in general, but the same can be argued about normality or log normality of stock prices, FX rates, interest rates, etc.

Shortcomings: These methods are no real substitute for a good full Monte Carlo simulation. They are only useful tools when those simulations cannot be carried out, for whatever reason. We must remember some drawbacks they have.

For example, a major problem of these methods is that we are not able to model the very important trade roll-overs. A way we can somehow deal with this is by changing the netting set volatility over time, to account for the trades maturing in the netting set, though it is difficult to have any precision here.[10]

Something we have to keep in mind is that the time series we have for the netting set may contain jumps coming from cash-flow payments as well as trade roll-overs. In principle, that could be seen as "noise" in the data but, arguably, it may be good to have it there; if the trading patterns of that netting set are expected to remain the same in the future, the future netting set value will experiment similar jumps to those seen in the past. Hence, we may want our historical data to contain those jumps.

Another negative side of this method is that it will be difficult to measure any incremental effect of new trades, or of trades unwinding, in the netting set.

7 Default Probability, Loss Given Default, and Credit Portfolio Models

We have seen that counterparty credit risk calculations have, mainly, three components: first we need to estimate what the probability is of a given counterparty defaulting. This number is usually referred to as the "PD" of the counterparty. Then, we need to estimate how much we can be owed if a given counterparty defaults, the Exposure at Default (EaD). We have seen in previous chapters that there are different metrics for this, the most popular being the Expected Positive Exposure and the Potential Future Exposure.[1] Finally, we want to have a view as to how much of the whole amount that we are owed in a default we will actually be lost. This is typically called the Loss Given Default (LGD), which is expressed as a percentage of the total amount owed in a default.

In previous chapters we saw how to calculate EaD. In this chapter, we are going to see how to do so for PD and LGD.

Similarly to EaD, there are two families of models for PD and LGD: calibrating them to the market as at today, the so-called risk-neutral or market-implied calibration, or calibrating them to the past, the so-called real-world or historical calibration. We are going to see how, in reality, this distinction only exists for PD, as LGD tends to be calibrated always historically due to the lack of market information.

It must be noted that, often, the LGD is expressed in terms of its "cousin" the recovery rate (RR), where $RR = 1 - LGD$. Those two variables, LGD and RR, are completely equivalent. It's a matter of preference as to which one to use.

Later in this chapter we will introduce credit portfolio models. The calculation of EaD, PD, and LGD are done counterparty per counterparty. However, we may often be interested in the counterparty credit risk of a portfolio of counterparties. That risk should be driven, to a greater or smaller extent, by inter-counterparty dependency effects. Credit portfolio models study that.

7.1 Market implied calibrations

The credit quality of a company can be directly traded via Credit Default Swaps (CDS). These are derivatives agreed between two counterparties so that one of them (the protection seller) will pay a notional amount multiplied by a percentage number to the protection buyer, should a third entity (the obligor) go into default.[2] That percentage number is, precisely, the LGD. For this to be a business for the protection seller, the protection buyer is going to make regular payments to the protection seller up to either the CDS maturity date or the default event.

For example, let's say that Barclays sells 5-year protection to Nomura, should Alcoa default, at a price of 350 basis points (bps),[3] on a given notional. This means that Nomura will be paying to Barclays every year 3.5% of the notional, typically on a quarterly basis. If Alcoa defaults, then those payments stop and there will

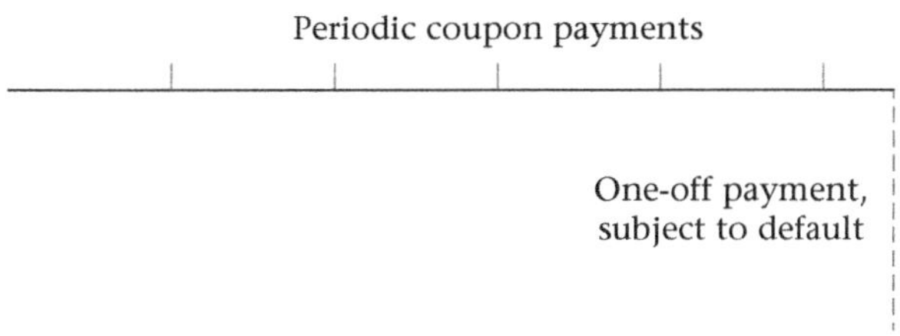

Figure 7.1 Simplifed illustration of the payments structure of a credit default swap

be a CDS auction that will determine, a few weeks later, the CDS's Loss Given Default of that credit event. If that LGD is, say, 20%, Barclays will pay Nomura 20% of the CDS notional.[4] This structure is illustrated in Figure 7.1.[5]

The basic idea of a CDS is that they offer credit protection for an entity holding a bond issued by the CDS's obligor. If that entity buys credit protection via a CDS, then it should get the risk-free rate as a return on that combined bond plus CDS. Needless to say, this will only work when there is infinite liquidity in both the bond and CDS market; the real world is not like that, since having that bond plus a CDS portfolio is not usually exactly the same as a risk-free bond (e.g., a treasury in USD). The difference between those two is usually referred to as a bond-CDS spread, or the credit "liquidity" spread.

In some contexts, this liquidity spread can be central to valuing and risk-managing OTC derivatives – but that is beyond the scope of this chapter.

CDS contracts can be quite complex agreements: there are many details that determine each of them. However, two of the very main ones are

1. The CDS credit spread; 350 bps in the example
2. The tenor; 5-year in the example

Standard CDS pricing models have two typical starting points: the probability that an obligor default happens, the PD; and how much will be paid out should that default happen, the LGD.

It is tempting to think that the credit spread will be determined by those two inputs, the PD and the LGD of the obligor: clearly the higher the PD or the LGD, the more we'll have to pay to buy credit protection. However, it is important to realise that it is, actually, the other way round. The PD and LGD are theoretical numbers, mathematical instruments. Arguably, they do not exist; i.e., they only exist in our minds. The one that really exists (i.e., that is traded, on which actual cash flows are computed) is the credit spread. What is realistic, is to see that the PD and LGD are calculated *from* the credit spreads, not the other way round. This is a subtle but important difference, that is often forgotten.

Having said that, the CDS pricing model is going to be, basically, a function

$$s = f(PD, LGD) \tag{7.1}$$

where s is the credit spread.[6]

7.1.1 PD calibration

The process of calculating the PD from CDSs is often called "bootstrapping". This is so because, typically, we are going to have a whole term structure of credit spreads. If liquid enough, we could have CDSs for 3-month, 6-month, 9-month, 1-year, 2-year, etc., tenors.

We are not going to study bootstrapping methodologies in detail, as it is very well described in many credit books, but let's have an overview of them, for those less familiar with these things.

First, we start with the shortest tenor, 3-month one in our example. We are going to fix the LGD for now (we'll deal with that later, bear with me), and we are going to invert Equation 7.1[7] to calculate the PD over the first three months, given the market 3-month credit spread. Then we are going to proceed to the next tenor, 6-month one, and we are going to invert again Equation 7.1, using this time the PD from now to 3-month's ahead that we calculated before. In this way, we are going to calculate the market implied PD for the 3-month to 6-month period. We can then proceed like this, going forward, to bootstrap a PD profile from the CDS market prices, going as far in time as the last tenor of the liquid CDSs.

It is common to express this PD in terms of the "default intensity" λ. This is defined so that the survival probability (i.e., one minus the default probability) of an obligor at time t is given by

$$S_t = exp(\int_0^t \lambda_u du) \tag{7.2}$$

S_t is obtained from the bootstrapping method just described; it is 100% equivalent to calculating the PD profile.

This is, basically, the way default probabilities are calibrated to the market. This is a fairly straightforward mechanical procedure, subject to a number of secondary caveats that we are not covering here, as it is beyond our scope.

7.1.2 LGD calibration

In the previous section we said that, for the PD calibration, we were setting the LGD of that obligor as a constant number. Let's see why.

We have seen that the CDS spread pricing function is given by something like $s = f(PD, LGD)$. In this equation, we have one fixed number[8] (s) and two variables to calibrate (PD and LGD). The reader will know that one equation with two variables has, in general, infinite solutions. So, in order to calibrate the LGD, we need a second equation.

This second equation could come from either a digital CDS,[9] or a recovery rate swap. Digital CDSs pay the full notional at default, as opposed to the standard CDSs, that pay the notional times the Loss Given Default. A recovery rate swap is a swap by which a strike is agreed, with a given notional N; if a default occurs the swap pays the actual recovery rate minus the strike (times the notional).

Either of these two instruments could potentially give a second equation, so that both the PD and LGD can be extracted from the market prices. However, the market for digital CDSs or for recovery rate swaps do not really exist. They are highly illiquid, and so, in practice, we cannot use them as a source of information.

As a consequence of all this, LGDs simply cannot be calibrated to the market in general. In reality, LGDs can only be calibrated historically.[10]

7.2 Historical calibration

Historical models for PD and LGD are needed in two contexts. Firstly, risk and capital models tend to be calibrated to historical parameters.[11] Secondly, as already said, they are the best source of information when we want a market-implied calibration but the market is not liquid enough.

Often, this job, or some parts of it, is outsourced to the credit rating agencies, as they are supposed to be the ultimate experts in this. However, several institutions feel they want to have their own view and models on this matter.

7.2.1 PD calibration

Figure 7.2 shows a time series of global real default rates. It can be seen that defaults tend to happen in time clusters, driven by the well known economic business cycles.

As a result of these cycles, it is important to understand that there are two types of PD:

1. **Point-in-time PD:** This is the default probability of an institution, or more strictly speaking, of a group of institutions, that we put into a given bucket, today. These buckets tend to be credit ratings, but they can also be segmented into industry and region, or any other classification we may find appropriate. When we say that the point-in-time default probability of a certain group of institutions is, say, 1%, what we are saying is that we expect that 1% of those institutions will have defaulted within the next 12 months.
2. **Through-the-cycle PD:** This is the time-average default probability of a group of institutions. It is the long-run average of the point-in-time default probability.

Having clarity about this distinction is very important, as otherwise we can make naive mistakes. For example, before the 2008 crisis credit products were sometimes (or often) priced as if only 1% of BB bonds[12] were ever going to default in the next year–mistake.[13]

So, when we deal with a credit rating model, we have two general approaches. In a point-in-time model, credit ratings change with the business cycle, but in a through-the-cycle model, credit ratings stay constant throughout. The typical models from credit rating agencies are through-the-cycle models and, so, when we

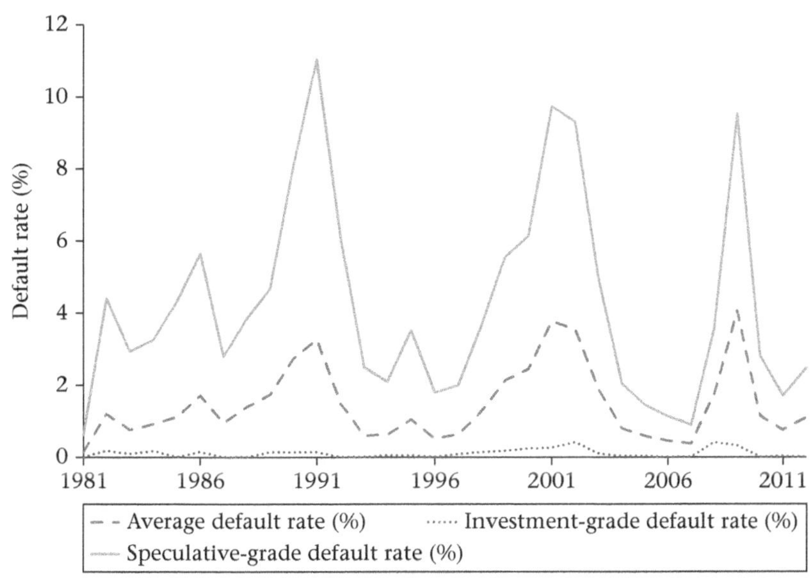

Figure 7.2 Historical default rates
Source: Standard & Poor's.

say that "the default probability of a BB company is 1%", we are usually saying that "the through-the-cycle default probability of a BB company is 1%".

In this section we are going to see the different steps we need to consider for a PD modelling framework.

A two-step process

Rating models, can, indeed, be very sophisticated. They can range from a simple model that looks at the leverage of the company, compares it to the income of the past year, and gives a credit score from it, to sophisticated models that account for the global economic situation, the business environment in which the institution operates, debt profile, past income, its volatility, future expected market growth, its volatility, future refinancing needs, liquidity constraints, share price, credit spread, their volatilities, etc. They can be based on analytical or semi-analytical formulae, Monte Carlo simulations, latent or tangible variables–the list is endless. The reader is referred to *An Introduction to Credit Risk Modeling* by C. Bluhm *et al.* for details on this [23].

As a result of this sophistication, the same credit rating can mean something different depending on the model behind it. It is easy to understand that when the model gives a credit score to a government it will be substantially different to when the model is used for a corporate. Hence, the same credit score can imply different default probabilities.

A PD modelling framework typically consist of two sub-models:

1. **Rating Models:** These models look into institutions and put a credit score to them. Sometimes it is said that "all" they do is to sort institutions by perceived default probability. They tend to be based on a combination of the current financial position together with expected future performance. Future performance tends to account for not only the individual company's performance, but also for the overall context of the industry and geographical economic environment. The output of these models is a credit score (e.g., a number from 1 to 100). Then, typically, we sort these scores and split them into groups. The most popular group terminology is the Standard & Poor's one: AAA, AA, A, BBB, BB, B, CCC, D, with their respective "+" and "−" versions (e.g., AA+).

   In a nutshell, these models can be seen as mathematical functions, with things like outstanding debt, past income, expected income growth, macro-economic performance, etc., as input, and a number x, the credit score, as the output

   $$x = f(\text{inputs}) \tag{7.3}$$

2. **PD Models:** The next step is to attach a 12-month expected default probability to each of those scores. This can be done either historically (e.g., the average default probability, over the last 20 years, of entities with a credit score between 60 and 70, for example), or with some other sort of more sophisticated approach. Having said that, if the model is not historical, it is typically going to be calibrated or backtested historically, so we can say that these models are always historical, but with different degrees of sophistication.

As a result of this split into two sub-models, there are two different kinds of PD frameworks. On the one hand you can have different PD models for different sectors, so that the same rating in different sectors has different PDs. For example, it is common to have a system in which an AA sovereign has attached to it a different default probability than a corporate AA.

On the other hand, we can have a PD framework that attaches always the same PD to each credit rating. In this framework, the rating buckets are not driven by the credit score, but by the PD.

The former modelling framework tends to be preferred by credit professionals, as the methodology tends to be more simple, easier to modify, etc. However, the former type of frameworks tend to be more popular from a final user standpoint, as it is more transparent from their perspective: a BB entity always has, say, a 1% PD, regardless of anything else.

Low default portfolio models: This general methodology described here works very nicely, with one exception: high quality credit ratings; the reason being scarcity of data. Basically, if we try to assess historically the default probability of AAA entities, we are going to have very few defaults, so any measurement that we take from it will contain a high degree of statistical uncertainty. For this case, we need the so-called "Low Default Portfolio" models.

In these models we invert the problem. We start with a PD model, that we invent, and we run T-statistics with it, assessing the probability that the PD model is compatible with the number of defaults observed. We define a threshold for the p-value of the statistic (e.g., p = 95%), and when we find a PD model that gives a p-value above that threshold, we take that model as the correct one. The reader is referred to [46, 21] for more details on this type of method.

Final smoothing: Overall, the global outcome of this modelling exercise is going to be a set of raw PD estimates. As a last step, we may want to apply some sort of smoothing technique, which can be from something as simple as an exponential adjustment (see Figure 7.3) to more sophisticated methods that account, for example, for the statistical error in each PD estimate.

7.2.2 Key features of a PD model

There are a number of features that we may want to consider when building a PD model.

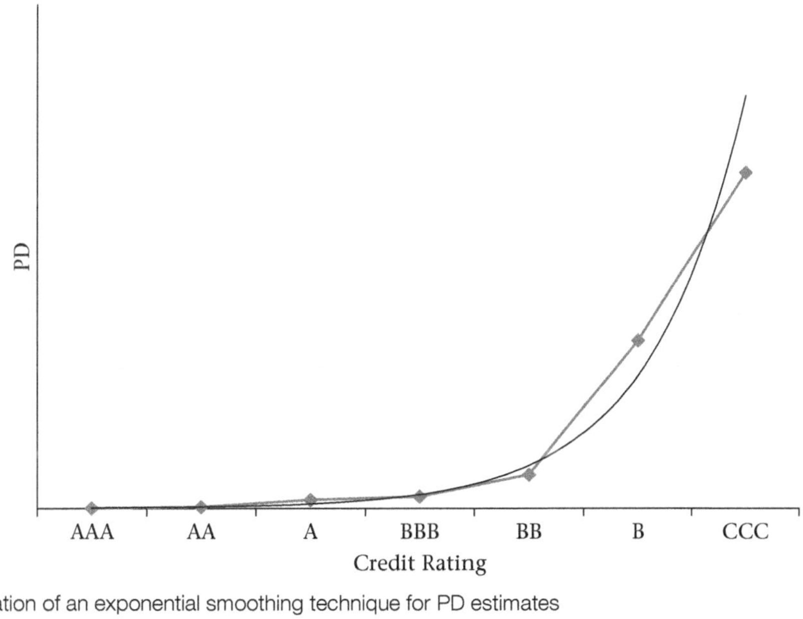

Figure 7.3 Illustration of an exponential smoothing technique for PD estimates

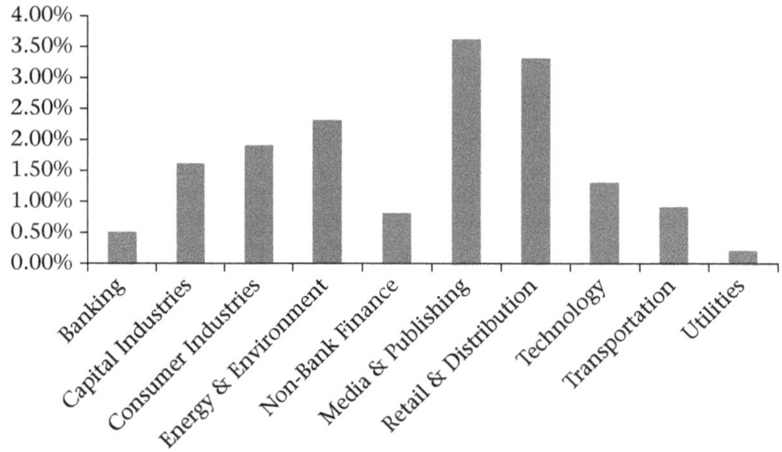

Figure 7.4 Default rates per sector in the 1920–2010 period
Source: Moody's.

Driver analysis

When we construct a PD modelling framework, the first attempt could be to have a flat model for all entities, a kind of "one size fits all" approach. However, as soon as we start digging into the problem we are going to find that there seems to be particular driving forces that create, or avoid, default scenarios. These forces are often referred to as *default drivers.* For example, Figure 7.4 shows the default rates in the 1920–2010 period by industry sector. It can be seen how some sectors tend to be more likely to default than others.

Also, another driver can be region. For example, default rates in emerging economies tend to be higher than in developed economies. Even within developed economics, default rates can change. For example, the default probabilities that Moody's gave for the 2011–12 period, to corporates in the automotive sector, was 2.5% in the US but only 0.3% in Europe. In the aerospace and defence sector, it was 1.5% in the US and 1.8% in Europe [62].

Another typical driver is the business cycle, as already shown in Figure 7.2. This driver is obviously very important to consider when we are building a model for point-in-time default rates.[14]

Choosing your drivers

What drivers to choose is very intrinsic to each institution doing the modelling exercise. The examples shown in Figure 7.4 are quite standard ones, but a bank in Spain, for example, with a large pool of small and medium corporates, may decide to build a model with drivers such as company size, region within Spain, and some very specific sectors. However, a boutique investment bank in Switzerland may decide to build the drivers around these types: family office, asset manager, large bank, small bank, and hedge fund, for example.

The main point is that this selection of drivers must be as data driven as the history of default rates that we have access to indicates, given our customer base. When this is lacking (too often the case), then market knowledge, experience, and common sense are key.

Drivers, systematic factors, and dependency structures

When we model default risk, it is common to think in terms of systematic and idiosyncratic risk. By systematic risk is understood those risks that are external to a given entity but which affect its credit quality. An obvious one is, for example, macroeconomic cycles. By idiosyncratic risk is meant those factors that are intrinsic solely to the institution. For example, the position they have in their business environment, fraud, operational risk, etc.

When we choose a set of default drivers we are, intrinsically, choosing a set of systematic factors. When we say that the credit drivers of our model are, for example, a few regions (e.g., the Americas, Europe, and Asia) and a few sectors (financial, industrial, sovereign, utilities), we are saying that the credit systemic risk is described by a combination of those 12[15] factors, and that anything else that affects the credit quality of an entity is idiosyncratic.

When we choose a model for those credit drivers, we are also implicitly choosing a dependency structure between them.[16] Let's see this with an example.

Let's consider two entities and a normal model to simulate default events.[17] Each entity's credit quality is describe by a variable, x_1 and x_2, that follow over time a log-normal process

$$\begin{aligned} dx_1 &= x_1\,\sigma_1\,dW_1 \\ dx_2 &= x_2\,\sigma_2\,dW_2 \end{aligned} \tag{7.4}$$

where dW_1 and dW_2 are normally distributed. The variables "x" could be, in principle, any variables that we deem to best describe the credit quality of the company; it can be equity prices, CDS spreads, latent variables, amongst other possibilities.

There are many ways in which we can model their dependency. For example:

1. Simply by saying that dW_1 and dW_2 have a linear correlation ρ

   $$\langle dW_1, dW_2 \rangle = \rho \tag{7.5}$$

   where ρ is calibrated from a time series of the variables x_1 and x_2.
2. Via a systematic factor Ψ (a credit CDS index, for instance) so that

   $$\begin{aligned} dW_1 &= \rho_1\,d\Psi + \sqrt{1-\rho_1^2}\,d\epsilon_1 \\ dW_2 &= \rho_2\,d\Psi + \sqrt{1-\rho_2^2}\,d\epsilon_2 \end{aligned} \tag{7.6}$$

   where Ψ and each ϵ are independent, and the correlations ρ_1 and ρ_2 are calibrated historically to the time series of x_1, x_2 and Ψ.

   If we do the maths, the linear correlation between dW_1 and dW_2 in the second model is given by

   $$\rho' = \rho_1\,\rho_2 + \sqrt{(1-\rho_1^2)(1-\rho_2^2)} \tag{7.7}$$

However, in general, we are going to find that $\rho \neq \rho'$.

Does that mean that one of the models is correct, and the other one isn't? No. What it means is that, in each of them, we are choosing a different dependency structure, and each of them may require a different linear correlation parameter. It is then the job of the quant to decide which of those two options *describe reality best.*

With this example, the reader should see that when we choose a set of drivers, and a model for them, we are implicitly choosing a dependency structure too. We must make sure that the dependency framework we choose is the best for the risk features we need to capture, and also for the computational capability we have.

PD time profile

Another variable in our modelling choice that we may want to consider is the default probability time profile.

So far, we have always been talking about PD in respect to a one-year time horizon, but the default probability of different credit ratings tends to follow a time profile that we may want to mimic. Figures 7.5 and 7.6 illustrate this. Figure 7.5 shows the cumulative default rates per credit rating. Figure 7.6 shows the marginal default rates; by marginal is meant "default subject to having survived up to the beginning of that year".

The reader can appreciate in these graphs how the time profile default probability is not linear, and how it changes depending on the starting credit quality of the institution.

This is another factor that we may want to reproduce in our PD modelling framework: a PD tenor structure.

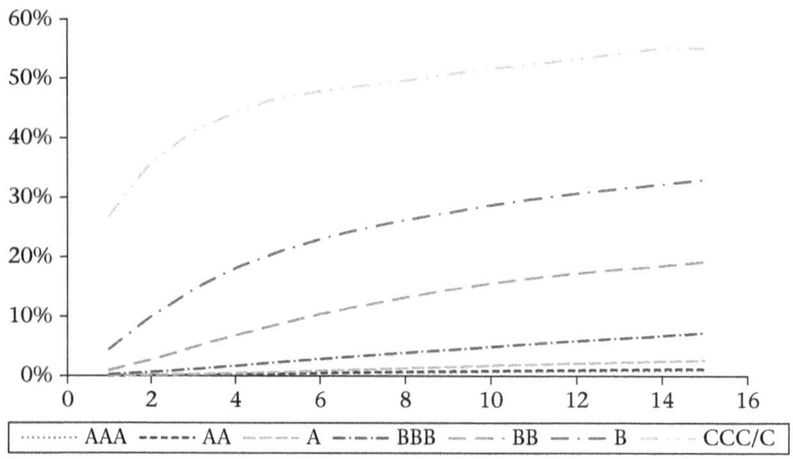

Figure 7.5 Global corporate average cumulative default rates (1981–2011)
Source: Standard & Poor's.

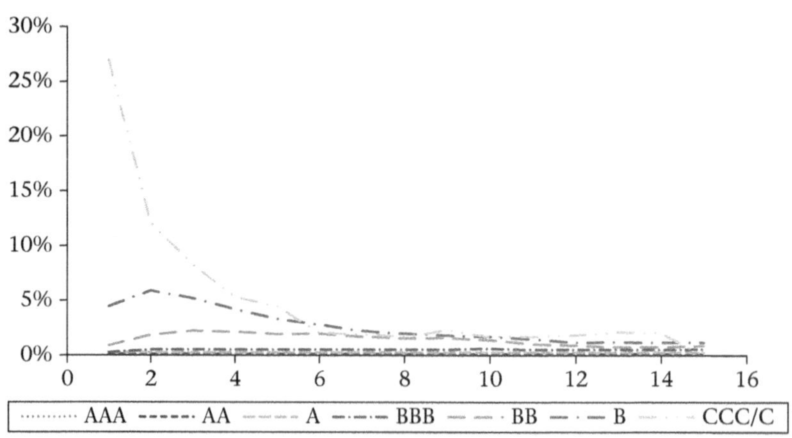

Figure 7.6 Global corporate average marginal default rates (1981–2011)
Source: Standard & Poor's.

	AAA	AA	A	BBB	BB	B	CCC/C	D
AAA	51%	0%	0%	0%	0%	0%	0%	100%
AA	49%	85%	2%	0%	0%	0%	0%	100%
A	0%	13%	91%	3%	0%	0%	0%	100%
BBB	0%	1%	7%	94%	6%	0%	0%	100%
BB	0%	0%	1%	3%	88%	7%	0%	100%
B	0%	0%	0%	0%	5%	87%	27%	100%
CCC/C	0%	0%	0%	0%	1%	4%	55%	100%
D	0%	0%	0%	0%	0%	2%	18%	100%

Figure 7.7 Sample of credit migration matrix
Source: Standard & Poor's.

Credit migration and Markov processes

A quite standard way to model credit events is with a credit rating migration matrix and a Markov process.

All credit rating agencies publish their credit migration matrix every year. Figure 7.7 shows the global corporate migration matrix from data published by Standard & Poor's as at 2011.[18]

This matrix gives the probability that a corporate, in a given rating today, will migrate to any other rating in one year. For example, companies that are AAA today will be AAA in 51% of the cases next year, and AA in 49% of them.

With this matrix we can build the following Markov process. The credit rating of a company can be described by an eight-dimensional column vector. Each component of the vector gives the probability that the company is in each of the credit ratings. For example, a company that is today a AA will be described by the vector v_0

$$\begin{bmatrix} 0 \\ 1 \\ 0 \\ 0 \\ 0 \\ 0 \\ 0 \\ 0 \end{bmatrix} \tag{7.8}$$

In one year's time, the rating profile of that company is going to be described by the vector $v_1 = M \cdot v_0$, where M is the migration matrix. Then, in two year's time, $v_2 = MMv = M^2 v$, and so on. In general, $v_t = M^t v_0$. In this way, we can simulate credit migration and default events (the state D) dynamically.

As a caveat to this, it must be noted that credit rating agencies also publish 5-year migration matrices, and it so happens that those matrices are different to M^5. The reason why they are different is that the real process that follows credit transitions has autocorrelation effects that are neglected in a Markov process. We may want to adjust the Markov process to account for these effects.

7.2.3 LGD calibration

So far, we have seen the key components for building historically calibrated models for default probabilities. Let's deal now with the other component, the Loss Given Default (LGD).

Historically based LGD models are quite important because, as we have seen, the credit market is not liquid enough to provide information for both PD and LGD, and the typical way to deal with that problem is by modelling LGD historically, and then the PD with either market-implied or historical models.

As soon as we start dealing with LGDs we encounter a major problem, scarcity of data. Information about PD has been collected for a long time, but information about LGD has usually only been collected since Basel II came onto the scene, approximately in 2006. As a result, often LGD models are, to a high extent, models of how to obtain sensible information out of only a little data. A factor that makes this data issue even more difficult to manage is that LGD information tends to be kept confidential by each counterparty. For example, in the Lehman Brother's default, the LGD for the CDS positions was publically set, but the LGD from the actual portfolio of derivatives that each counterparty had was kept secret. So each institution may have only the LGD data of the defaults they have suffered in the past.

As a consequence of this, LGD models tend to be quite simple: why should we build a complex model when the data is so scarce that we cannot tell how good (or bad) it is? In this case, we are better off with simplicity.

LGD modelling

If we have a collection of LGD data, the first thing that we need to do with it is to calculate their present value at time of default. This is necessary because the time that it takes from a default declaration, until the liquidators and the counterparties agree on the LGD and the liquidation cash-flow actually happens, can be several years. Hence, all LGD data must be brought into the present value at the moment of default.

Once we have this data, a standard way to proceed is by segregating the data into meaningful groups. Typical categories are

- **Type of Facility:** Collateralised vs. uncollateralised.
- **Seniority of the Exposure:** Senior vs. subordinated.
- **Industry Sector:** Asset rich sectors like farming or construction tend to have lower LGDs, compared to sectors with high good-will values like telecoms or services. Also, some sectors like banking tend to be highly leveraged, leading to low LGDs.
- **Region:** Emerging market defaults tend to have higher LGDs, for example. Also, the legislation that governs the liquidation process can have an impact on the final LGDs.

Once we have done this segregation, the standard way to proceed is to calculate a simple average of those numbers. This super simple model is often used because we may only have a few data points in each category, so the best we can do is to take a simple average.

Sometimes, especially for risk management and regulatory capital, where we need to be "conservative", we can put an "add-on" on top of the average LGD. This add-on can be one or two times the standard error of the LGD data. In this way, we avoid the statistical error we have in our sample.

On some occasions we are going to have hardly any data points for a given category. In that case, all we can do is extrapolate from the available data, using market know-how and common sense.

A final adjustment could be made to account for "recovery costs", such as legal costs, advisory, operational costs, etc. In complex default cases these costs can be considerable, and so they must be accounted for as a loss too.

Improvements: Later in this chapter we are going to see the *cross-section regression technique* in the context of calibrating credit spreads where there is a scarcity of data. To my knowledge, that technique has not been applied in the context of LGDs, but it seems to be a good candidate to improve on the standard "average" method described here.

LGD dependencies

A typical question is if there is any correlation between the LGD and the PD. To be more precise, the two questions that we may ask are

1. Can we see in the data any dependency between the loss given default and the default probability (i.e., the credit rating) some time (e.g., one year) before a default happens?
2. Can we see in the data any dependency between the average loss given default and the average default probability in a given year?

The answer to the first question seems to be "no". Data does not seem to show any relationship between the LGD and the credit rating of the defaulted institution some time before default.[19]

However, regarding the second question, the answer seems to be "yes". Figure 7.8 shows that there is a negative correlation between the default rate each year and the recovery rate (1-LGD). It appears that, in downturn years[20] within business cycles, defaults are not only more severe in number, but also in intensity, as the LGD is also higher in those years. Hence a sensible improvement to the simple LGD model described above would be to account for a cyclicality in it.[21]

For example, if we have a PD model with some idiosyncratic factors, that are forced to follow some oscillatory cycle like those observed in real life, then, following the data from Figure 7.8, we could model the recovery rate as

$$RR = 0.1374\, PD^{-0.293} + \sigma\, \epsilon \tag{7.9}$$

where ϵ is a random normal deviate and σ is a scaling factor.

7.2.4 Summary of steps

To summarise all we have said, in order to get a PD and LGD modelling framework, we need to go through the following steps:

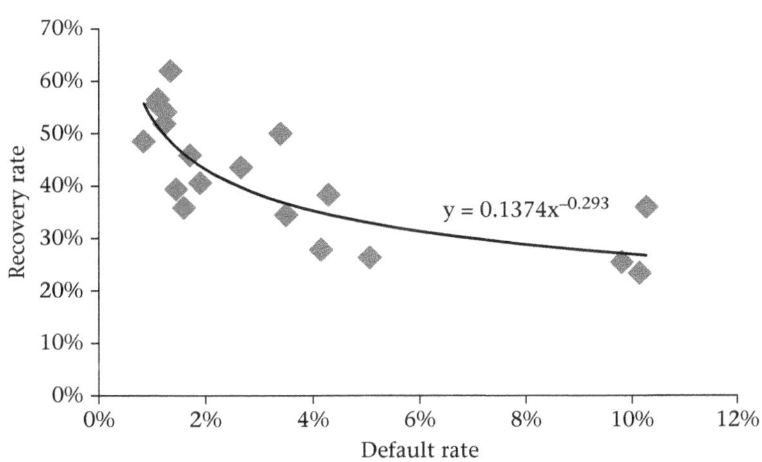

Figure 7.8 Default rate and average recovery rate (1-LGD) (1982–2001)
Source: Altman et al. [18].

PD

1. Create a credit rating model, or outsource it to an external rating agency.
2. Get historical data of credit rating migrations and defaults.
3. Find the credit drivers that best suits our portfolio.
4. Estimate annual default rates for each driver, and come up with raw estimates. For low default ratings, we will need a Low Default Portfolio model.
5. Smooth the data.

LGD

1. Calculate the present value of LGD historical data.
2. Do a driver analysis.
3. Get the long-run average LGD.
4. Implement down turn considerations.
5. Implement further calibration for internal recovery add-on, legal costs, advisory, etc.

PD-LGD dependency

1. We may want to consider the dependency structure shown in Figure 7.8.

7.3 External credit agencies

There are a number of external institutions that are expert in calculating PDs and LGDs. They are the external rating agencies that have become so important to the business world and capital markets. Indeed they provide a most valuable service to the whole investment community, together with high responsibility. The most widely known are Standard & Poor's, Moody's and Fitch.

These credit rating agencies deal only with large institutions. In addition to them, there are a number of companies that specialise in the credit rating of small and medium companies, or of individuals. They tend to be very local to each domestic market. Some of the more widely know are Experian, Equifax, and Callcredit.

In addition to all of these, we now have the PECDC. This is an association of banks that have decided to overcome the problem that each of them faces from the lack of data by creating a shared pool of historical data and research for losses from credit risk.

7.4 Calibration for pricing

We are going to see in detail in Chapter 8 that CVA can be regarded as the market price of hedging counterparty risk. In principle, calibrating PD and LGD for pricing should be quite a straightforward exercise; we just need to calibrate it to the market. However, as we are going to see, when we hit reality, things may not be that simple.

CVA needs to be calibrated to market implied PD and LGD when we see it as a hedging price, as opposed to a risk reserve. As such, it does not matter how right or wrong we think the price of that risk is, if the cost of insuring ourselves against default events via CDS is, say, 400 basis points, that is the price we need to pay and, hence, we need to calibrate our CVA pricing model to it.

7.4.1 Liquid names

When we calibrate PDs and LGDs for CVA, we are going to face the best-case scenario when the counterparty at stake CVA has a liquid CDS market. In that case, we are going to estimate its LGD from historical models,[22] and then we calibrate its PD profile, bootstrapping the default intensity profile from the CDS spreads following the method described previously in this chapter.

In fact, regarding the PD, what we are doing here is, arguably, extracting from an *average market model* the point-in-time default probability profile. We should say "arguably" because the market prices are driven also by liquidity constraints and many other factors that affect supply and demand and, consequently, market prices [51].

Regardless of this last subtlety, it is important to note that, in this framework, CVA is not very sensitive to LGD. We are going to see in the chapter dedicated to CVA that, in many cases, CVA can be approximated by

$$CVA \simeq LGD \cdot PD \cdot EPE \tag{7.10}$$

where *EPE* is the integral of the present value of the Expected Positive Exposure profile, and PD is the average default probability of the counterparty up to the netting set maturity. Also, a good approximation in many cases for the credit spread (s) is $s \simeq LGD \cdot PD$, which means that

$$CVA \simeq s \cdot EPE \tag{7.11}$$

As a result, if the LGD changes *but* the credit spread remains constant, the PD is going to change accordingly so that CVA hardly moves; in fact, it does not move at all in the approximation 7.11.

Indeed, that makes sense, because what really matters regarding the price of hedging counterparty risk is the price of buying the credit insurance, and that number is the CDS credit spreads. As said, PD and LGD are no more than two theoretical numbers.

7.4.2 Illiquid names

The problems with CVA calibration arrive when we have counterparties for which credit default swaps are highly illiquid, or completely non-existent. In fact, I have been offering consulting services to several banks that are very retail based, and so the client base that they have for OTC derivatives is highly dominated by small companies that do not have anything close to a liquid CDS market.

Illiquid names with credit rating

When we have a credit rating for the counterparty, but there is no liquid CDS market for it, a typical way to proceed is to use CDS index spread profiles, per credit rating, to price CVA. We saw in Figure 7.6 typical credit spread tenor profiles as a function of the credit quality of the name behind it. In this approach we assign a spread value, and shape of the curve, to a company of a given rating, sector, and region, based on the average values that can be extracted from the existing market data.

Further to this, a more granular model can be used by considering also industry sector, region, and/or credit seniority when building the index CDS profiles. In fact, this is the approach proposed by Basel for the calibration of the regulatory CVA price.[23]

The problem of this averaging technique is that it can have problems of statistical significance due to a lack of data. As of 2013, Markit reported around 1,700 liquid credit spreads, for eleven sectors, seven regions, seven credit ratings, and two seniorities. This creates 1,078 buckets, with an average of 1.7 data points in each of them. The data points tend to be concentrated in a few buckets: the financial sector, the US and Europe, medium credit ratings, and senior debt. As a result, the average credit spread in each bucket suffers abrupt jumps over time (e.g., as a credit rating changes and a bucket with three data points loses one of those points) or, in the worst case, some buckets do not have any data points at all.

However, there seems to be a solution for this.

The cross-section regression technique: In this technique, the proxy spread of the bucket i is not given by the average spread. Instead, it is given by

$$s_i^{proxy} = M_{global} M_{sector_i} M_{region_i} M_{rating_i} M_{seniority_i} \tag{7.12}$$

Index i runs through the index buckets.

Now, let's say that an index j runs through each of the bucket definitions plus one global extra bucket. For instance, using the example above, i runs from 1 to 1,078, while j runs from 1 to 11+7+7+2+1 = 28. Note that "1" comes from the global bucket we are adding. Now, let's define

$$y_i = log(s_i^{proxy}) \tag{7.13}$$

and

$$x_j = \log(M_j) \tag{7.14}$$

We are going to say that

$$y_i = \sum_j \delta_{i,j} x_j \tag{7.15}$$

where delta is a 1 or a 0, depending if that name is or isn't in that respective bucket. For example, Rabobank subordinated CDSs will have $\delta_{i,j} = 1$ when j refers to sector = financials, region = Europe, rating = A, seniority = subordinated and Global (this one is always 1). The rest of the deltas are zero.

The only thing that is still undetermined here is each of the M_j. We can calibrate those numbers with a simple least square regression technique that minimises the "distance" between the proxy spreads s_i^{proxy} and those seen in the market in each bucket.

This technique is described in depth by Chourdakis *et al.* [34], where it is shown quite nicely how it gives considerably smoother and more realistic results than an average technique.

Illiquid names with no credit rating

Having said that, the real problem comes when we have counterparties for which we do not even have a credit rating. This can happen when the institution doing this analysis is too small, or when it hasn't made a good risk-management job in the past.

There are a number of ways to mark the CVA for these counterparties:

- The first blunt approach would be to assign to it a default credit rating, which tends to be conservative; something like a B, for example.
- If we want a better model, we need to do a credit assessment of the counterparty (which is what we may have wanted to do in the first place). For this, we have to build a credit model, however simple or sophisticated that may be, to calculate a credit score, so as to then calculate with a credit rating its

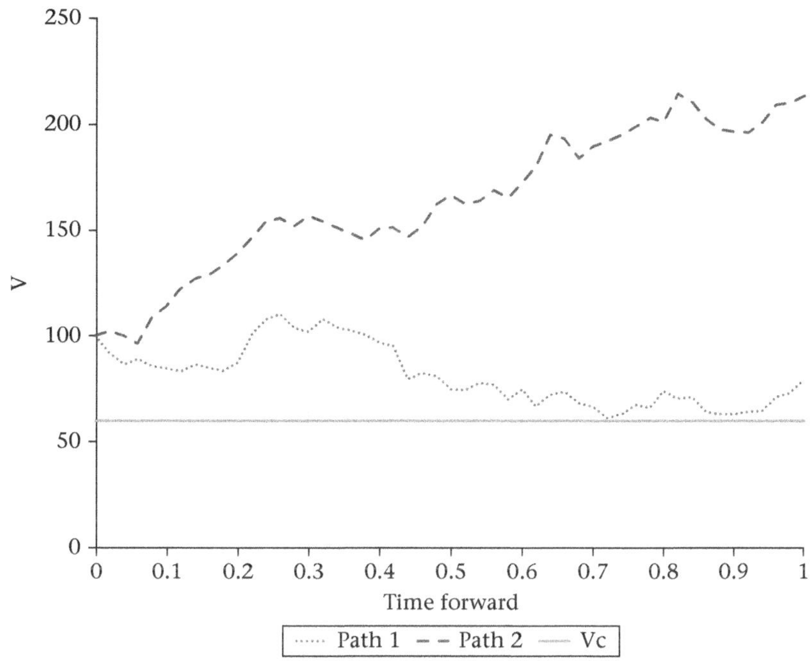

Figure 7.9 Illustration of a Merton model simulation, one path is a defaulting one, while the other under the other one the company has survived after 1 year

estimation of the counterparty default probability. For example, a simple credit model could take into account the current debt position the institution has, compare it to its income over the past few years, account for the volatility of that income, and assess the default likelihood from that.

If we don't have the resources or capability for this, we may want to outsource it to a small credit rating agency.

- If it is a private corporate for which we have a reasonable model to value its equity price, or if there is some market information that can provide us with that equity price, then we can apply the Merton model described below. This model, being very simple in nature, seems to yield quite good results.

The Merton model: In this model, an institution credit worthiness is given by the value of a latent asset (V), that is considered to follow over time a normal process,

$$V_t = V_0 + \sigma_V \sqrt{t}\epsilon \tag{7.16}$$

where σ_V is the volatility of the latent asset V, and ϵ is a standard-normally distributed random number. Default is going to occur when that asset V goes below a critical level V_c. Figure 7.9 illustrates this model with two paths, one of a surviving scenario and one a defaulting one.

This model can be fairly easily calibrated to the equity price of the company:

- If we think of a representative time horizon T, typically one year, the equity share price is the price of a call option, expiring at time T, with the asset V as the option underlying, and with V_c as the strike.

$$E_T = \max(V_T - V_c, 0) \tag{7.17}$$

As a result, the Black–Scholes option pricing formula tells us that the price of the equity today is

$$E_0 = V_0\, N(d_1) - V_c\, e^{-rT}\, N(d_2)$$
$$d_1 = \frac{\ln \frac{V_0\, e^{rT}}{V_c}}{\sigma_V\, T} + 0.5\sigma_V \sqrt{T} \tag{7.18}$$
$$d_2 = d_1 - \sigma_V \sqrt{T}$$

- A second equation comes from the volatilities σ_V and the volatility of the equity share price σ_E. From Ito's lemma we know that

$$\sigma_E\, E_0 = \frac{\partial E}{\partial V} \sigma_V\, V_0 \tag{7.19}$$

and we also know from the Black–Scholes option pricer that $\frac{\partial E}{\partial V} = N(d_1)$. Hence,

$$\sigma_E\, E_0 = N(d_1)\sigma_V\, V_0 \tag{7.20}$$

This leaves two Equations (7.19 and 7.20) and two variables (V_c and σ_V) to calibrate. Note that the initial value of V, V_0, is irrelevant, as it will only be a scaling factor for the latent asset.

Once we have solved these equations, the default probability that the company has is the probability of the asset variable being below V_c at T, which given by

$$PD_T = N(-d_2) \tag{7.21}$$

When we already have this default probability, we can use a historical estimate of its LGD to calculate the company's credit spread. If we do not have a granular model for LGD, it is market practice to use a default value of around 40%.

This model could be perhaps enhanced by using a barrier option, instead of a vanilla Black–Scholes option, as the company could default at any time in which the asset value V_t crosses V_c. However, given this is, at the end of the day, an estimate for the PD, perhaps there is no need to make life too complicated, as the final result should not change much.

The biggest problem of this model can be its calibration; we need to estimate the equity volatility, but it's precisely those corporates that may lack that information that we may be interested in. Hence we may have to do a benchmarking exercise with similar companies in order to calibrate σ_E.

In spite of the simplicity of this model, it delivers quite good measurable results. From Equations 7.18 and 7.21 we can plot the default probability as a function of the equity price. An example of that is shown in Figure 7.10. It is remarkable how such a simple model delivers results that are quite close to empirical data.[24]

7.5 Calibration for risk management and regulatory capital

In contrast to pricing, PD and LGD models for risk management and regulatory purposes tend to be calibrated historically. This is the case because indeed we now care whether the market price is right or wrong; that is, whether its price is economically sound.

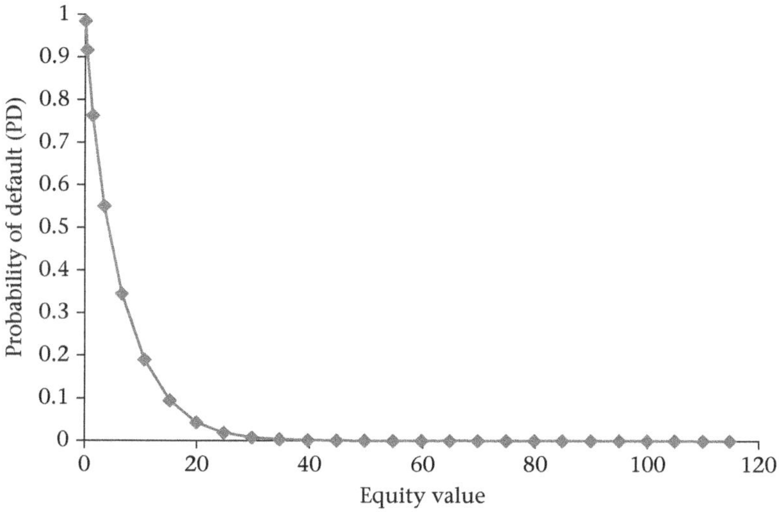

Figure 7.10 Dependency of the equity value and default probability under the Merton model

For example, let's say that the market points at a PD for a corporate at, say, 1%. However, we believe that we have better models than the average market practitioner, or that we have better information than the average market practitioner, and so we think that that PD should be 5%. In this case, we will want to set limits, build reserves, etc., for that 5% level.[25]

The models for PD and LGD used for risk management purposes are highly shaped by directives provided in the Basel II accord, because those models tend to be the same as regulatory capital ones, and the latter need to comply to Basel standards. Basel III hardly had any impact on PD and LGD modelling.

Basel does not explicitly say how banks must model PD and LGD; instead it provides some guidelines:

- **PD:** Rating models need to have at least seven buckets and PD models need to be based on long-run average annual default rates. The historical period from which the data is extracted needs to contain a least one full business cycle, or be at least five years long.
- **LGD:** Loss given default needs to be calibrated from stress periods; this is the so-called "down turn" LGD. It must use at least seven years of historical data, and it must be based on empirical data. Also, sometimes, regulators impose a floor for the discount factor to apply when calculating the present value of LGDs, and also a minimum number of data points to avoid a regulatory LGD floor of 45%.

The reason why PD is calibrated to through-the-cycle PD, while LGD is calibrated to down turn values, is because the Vasicek ASRF model, used to calculate regulatory capital, stresses the PD, but not the LGD. We will see this in the next section.

For risk management and regulatory capital, LGD is a most important number. The reason is that all formulae are proportional to the LGD, while PD tends to have a smaller effect as it is embedded in non-linear equations. As a result, a change of 5% in LGD increases or decreases capital by 5%, while a change of 5% in PD changes capital by less than 5%.

7.6 A primer on credit portfolio models

In previous chapters we have seen how to calculate the Exposure at Default for portfolios of OTC derivatives. In this chapter, we have seen how to calculate the default probability and loss given default for the counterparties we deal with. In this last section we are going to look at counterparty risk from a portfolio standpoint. This subject is very well covered by the literature, so we are not going to look at it in great detail. However, it makes sense to gain a basic understanding of how it works, so we can put lots of things into perspective.

The questions that we want to tackle with credit portfolio models are:

- How much could we lose in our portfolio of OTC derivatives from defaults?
- What reserves should we put aside to account for these losses?

7.6.1 Expected and unexpected loss

When we have a portfolio of financial instruments, we should always expect some future losses from defaults. If we have a portfolio of, say, 1,000 counterparties, in some years we are going to suffer one default, in some years five defaults, in some years ten defaults, etc. We never know how many defaults we are going to have during the next year, but we can have an idea of the probability of having one, five, ten, or any given number of defaults. If we multiply each default probability by the potential severity of each loss, we can come up with a probability distribution of default losses. The time horizon typically picked for this is one year. An illustration of this distribution is shown in Figure 7.11.

That distribution is going to be a function that is outputted by a credit portfolio model. In it, we are going to have default probability and loss severity as inputs, together with a dependency (correlation) structure. Once we obtain that function, there are two widely used quantities:

- **Expected Loss (EL):** This is the mean of the loss distribution.
- **Unexpected Loss (UL):** This is, given a confidence level (e.g., 99.9%), the loss that corresponds to that level.

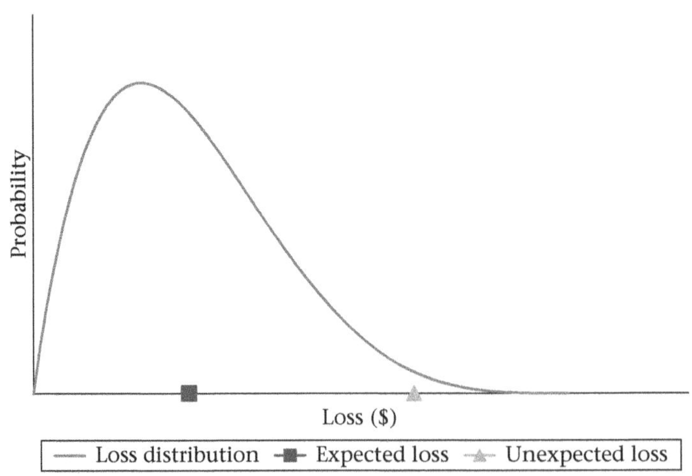

Figure 7.11 Illustrative example of a loss distribution, the expected loss and the unexpected loss

7.6.2 Economic capital

A typical definition of Economic Capital (EC) is the difference between those two numbers,

$$EC = UL - EL \tag{7.22}$$

This EC is understood as the amount of capital an institution must "set aside" as reserve, to make sure it is able to withstand financial distress to the given confidence level (e.g., 99.9%). In this section, we are going to deal only with EC that refers to default risk, but complete EC models deal with all risks a financial institution is facing.

The idea behind defining economic capital like that is that, in principle, the price of financial instruments should account for the expected loss; a low rated institution has to pay a lot more for a loan than a high quality one, precisely to compensate for the average default risk the lender is exposed to. However, the price of those loans does not account for "tail risk".[26] As a consequence, this tail risk needs to be managed with provisions and other risk management tools.

In the context of OTC derivatives, it is the same; a low rated counterparty should pay more for the same derivative than a high quality one. This is indeed reflected in the CVA price of the deal, as we will see in detail in Chapter 8. To calculate the expected loss in a book of OTC derivatives all we have to do is sum up the (unilateral) CVA of each counterparty. However, we know that defaults tend to happen in clusters. Because of that, dependencies in default events can easily create strong tail risk that we need to take into account when calculating risk reserves; CVA does not consider any of that.

Hence, to calculate the economic capital of a portfolio of derivatives we need to have a default portfolio model.

The basic idea behind those EC models is the following: the loss from a defaulted counterparty "i" is going to be given by

$$Loss_i = LGD_i \times EaD_i \tag{7.23}$$

where EaD is the Exposure at Default. Hence, the expected loss is going to be given by

$$EL_i = LGD_i \times EaD_i \times PD_i \tag{7.24}$$

In principle, if we calibrate CVA historically, the expected loss for a given counterparty should be its unilateral CVA. However, when we have a portfolio of counterparties, the portofolio expected loss is *not* going to be the sum of all EL_i due to the dependency between them; rather, generally speaking

$$EL_i = \int LGD_i \cdot EaD \cdot \Psi(LGD, EaD, \varsigma)\, d\varsigma \tag{7.25}$$

where ς refers to default events and $\Psi(LGD, EaD, \varsigma)$ is the joint probability distribution of all counterparty default events, EaDs and LGDs. Now, in order to calculate the Unexpected Loss (UL), we need to stress our multi-counterparty default model to account for, for example, 99.9% worst case scenario.

There are a number of well known methodologies to estimate the loss distribution function. Some of the most popular ones include CreditMetrics^{TM}, CreditRisk+, KMV, and the Vasicek ASRF model.

As I have said, we are not going to see the details of each of them here. The reader is referred to the excellent book on this subject by C. Bluhm *et al.* that we have already mentioned in previous sections [23]. However, in order to provide a flavour for how they work, we are going to look at one of those models: the Vasicek ASRF.

In this way we kill two birds with one stone; we are going to see an illustrative example of how those models operate and, also, gain an idea of the model behind the now-so-important regulatory capital calculation, as this is the model used by Basel for its Counterparty Credit Risk charge.

7.6.3 The Vasicek ASRF model

Let's say that each counterparty default event is governed by a latent asset (V) whose dynamic follows a Merton model. Let's say now that those dynamics can be decomposed in two factors, one systematic (X) that represents the general state of the economy, and one idiosyncratic (ε) that represents the peculiarities of the company,

$$V = \rho X + \sqrt{1-\rho^2}\,\varepsilon \tag{7.26}$$

where $X \sim N(0,1)$, $\varepsilon \sim N(0,1)$, and $\rho \in [-1,1]$ is a correlation factor.

If V_c is the critical value of V that triggers a default event, the probability that a company defaults is given by

$$PD = \Phi(V_c) \tag{7.27}$$

as V follows a normal process. In other words, a default happens if $V_c < \Phi^{-1}(PD)$ or, equivalently, if

$$\rho X + \sqrt{1-\rho^2}\,\varepsilon < \Phi^{-1}(PD), \tag{7.28}$$

that leads to a critical value for ε

$$\varepsilon_c < \frac{\Phi^{-1}(PD) - \rho X}{\sqrt{1-\rho^2}}. \tag{7.29}$$

That is, given a "through-the-cycle" default probability (PD), a state of the economy (X), and a correlation between the state of the economy and the state of the company ρ, a company will default when $\varepsilon < \varepsilon_c$.

Another way of expressing this framework is saying that the "point-in-time" default probability of the institution depends on the state of the economy, which in this model is represented by the variable X. So, given a value of X,

$$PD_t = \text{Prob}(\varepsilon < \varepsilon_c \mid X) \tag{7.30}$$

and so,

$$PD_t = \phi\left(\frac{\Phi^{-1}(PD) - \rho X}{\sqrt{1-\rho^2}}\right) \tag{7.31}$$

With this in mind, what we want to calculate is the portfolio credit loss that an institution could have in a really bad state of the economy. By "really bad" we mean a 99.9% worst case. The variable X represents the state of the economy, and a bad economy state means negative values for X, so what we need in these equations is $X = \phi^{-1}(0.1\%)$. Given that X is normally distributed, then this is equivalent to saying $X = -\phi^{-1}(99.9\%)$. If we plug this into Equation 7.31, and we multiply the default probability by the severity of the loss ($LGD \times EaD$), then the expected loss conditional in a bad state of the economy at 99.9% confidence level is given by

$$\mathrm{EL}_{99.9\%} = \phi\left(\frac{\Phi^{-1}(PD) + \rho\,\Phi^{-1}(0.999)}{\sqrt{1-\rho^2}}\right) \cdot LGD \cdot EaD. \tag{7.32}$$

As a result, the Regulatory Capital (RC)[27] coming from default events is given by

$$\begin{aligned} RC &= \mathrm{EL}_{99.9\%} - \mathrm{EL} \\ &= \left(\phi\left(\frac{\Phi^{-1}(PD) + \rho\,\Phi^{-1}(0.999)}{\sqrt{1-\rho^2}}\right) - PD\right) \cdot LGD \cdot EaD \end{aligned} \tag{7.33}$$

Now the reader can see that the Basel Committee is asking banks to keep capital that accounts for potential future losses coming from defaults in a 99.9% worst state of the economy.

So, to summarise, this model stresses portfolio default scenarios to a 99.9% worst case, leaving constant the LGD and the EaD. That is why LGD must be representative of a down turn, and EaD must be calculated subject to default.

Given that EaD is typically calculated not subject to default (i.e., without right or wrong way risk considerations), and also that this theory is based on an infinitely granular portfolio,[28] Basel decided to bump up this RC number in the Counterpaty Credit Risk charge by a factor α, which has a default value of 1.4.

8 Pricing Counterparty Credit Risk

Until 2008, counterparty credit risk in books of OTC derivatives was seen as a secondary risk. This was for a number of reasons. Most counterparties had strong credit ratings and the world economy was going through a phase of low defaults. As a result, the risk of counterparties defaulting was seen as negligible. Also, the complexity of pricing, managing, and hedging counterparty credit risk was unparalleled to any other task that financial institutions had faced until then; the farm-computing technology needed for the calculations was only starting to flourish. In parallel to this, banks were facing a very competitive market environment, where innovation in the OTC world was seen as key to success. Putting all this together, financial institutions had little incentive to invest very large amounts into a risk that was seen as small, difficult to compute, and expensive to manage.

Figure 8.1 illustrates the history of counterparty credit risk and its pricing component (CVA) in financial institutions. In the 1990s the derivatives market was still relatively small. As its size grew exponentially in the late 1990s and 2000s, regulators realised its increasing relevance and Basel II introduced a capital charge for the counterparty risk in the trading book. Also, from the pricing stand point, new accounting rules in 2006 required that the price of counterparty risk was considered in balance sheet valuations. Banks now had the incentive to invest in counterparty credit risk systems. However, in practice, only large institutions did so and with limited scope: counterparty risk was still managed at PFE level only and CVA teams were fairly small.

In 2008 Lehman Brothers defaulted, and the world changed. The financial industry came to face the fact that any firm can default and realised how important credit risk in OTC derivatives was. As a result, the resources dedicated to this topic ballooned; as anecdotal evidence, one of the tier-one institutions that I have worked in multiplied by around ten the headcount to counterparty credit risk from 2007 to 2012.

Previous chapters have given an integral perspective of how to compute all elements of counterparty risk in a financial institution. Now we are going to integrate all those chapters to incorporate counterparty risk into the price of an OTC derivative, the so-called Credit Value Adjustment (CVA). When quantitative analysts talk about the "risk-neutral" or "risk-free" price of a derivative, what is usually meant is "credit-risk-free". In other words, the derivative is priced as if none of the counterparties could default during the life of the trade and, hence, all the cash-flows will happen as the contract says. However, we now know that such assumption can be quite unrealistic and, so, we need to adjust the risk-free price by an amount that provides the market price of the counterparty risk embedded in the contract.

CVA is now very important for financial institutions. It has been reported that during the 2008/09 financial crisis, two-thirds of the credit related losses that banks suffered were CVA related, as opposed to actual default losses [8].[1] For example, Citi reported a \$4.8 billion CVA loss in 2008, that number was \$6.2 billion for

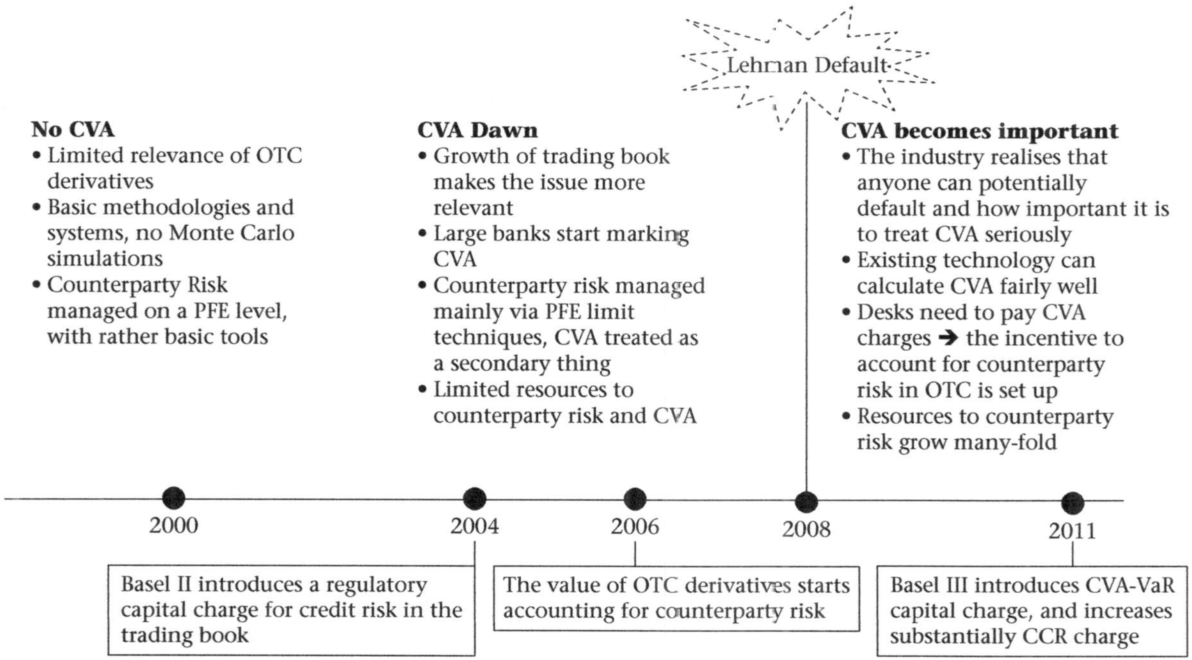

Figure 8.1 Illustration of the history of counterparty credit risk in financial institutions

Merril Lynch. For this reason, banks need to price the counterparty credit risk embedded in their book of derivatives (i.e., calculate CVA) daily, with good models. Once this is done, the bank then can decide whether to carry that risk and, hence, cash in its value (as long as defaults do not hit too hard), or hedge it out. Given that the bank's business purpose of its OTC derivatives is not to take on credit risk, most banks choose to hedge it.

8.1 CVA demystified

As said, CVA is an adjustment that we do to the "risk-free" price of a derivative contract to account for its counterparty risk. With this in mind, the price (P) of a derivative should now be given by

$$P = P_{\text{CreditRiskFree}} - CVA \tag{8.1}$$

where $P_{\text{CreditRiskFree}}$ is the price of the derivative without counterparty risk, and CVA is the counterparty credit risk adjustment.

In a risk-neutral valuation framework, the price of a risk is given by how much it costs to hedge it out. For that reason, CVA is defined as the price of hedging out the counterparty credit risk. Given that the available instruments to hedge out credit risk are CDSs, CVA should be highly related to the credit spread of the counterparties at stake. Let's expand on this.

8.1.1 CVA made simple

A good way to understand the fundamental concept of CVA is with a couple of simple examples.

Let's say that we have two institutions, A and B. For some reason, they decide to enter into a trade by which someone is going to toss a coin in one year and, at the end, A will pay B $1 if the coin toss is heads, and B will pay A $1 if it is tails. The quants of both institutions put all their thinking into this problem, and decide that the price of this trade, apart from counterparty risk, is zero.[2]

Now they want to price in the counterparty risk in this deal. There are two components here: (i) how much each counterparty can owe each other and (ii) how much it will cost to hedge it out. To tackle the first problem, initially quants establish that the potential exposure that each institution has is $0.5, as the coin is fair. This is calculated by multiplying the potential positive cash flow ($1) by the probability of it happening (0.5).[3] To tackle the second problem, they look at the CDS market and they see that, let's say, the credit spread of counterparty A is 100 bps, and that of counterparty B is 900 bps.[4] As many readers will know, that means that it will cost 1% and 9% per year, respectively, to ensure a given amount against those counterparties defaulting.

So, if counterparty A wants to hedge out the credit risk of this trade, they need to enter into a CDS contract paying $0.5 times 900 bps, and, on the other side, B will have to pay $0.5 times 100 bps. The trading desks of both institutions talk to each other and they agree to a $0.5 times 800 bps cash flow in favour of counterparty A, at trade inception, to compensate for the difference in price of hedging out the credit risk. That is, the price of the trade accounting for counterparty risk is $0.5*800bps in favour of counterparty A.

Let's summarise these trade cash flows, including the cost of hedging out the counterparty risk. Calling "X" the result of the coin toss event:

	Counterparty A	Counterparty B
Price excluding credit risk	0	0
Price of credit risk	\$1/2 800bps	−\$1/2 800bps
Spent on credit risk hedge	−\$1/2 900bps	−\$1/2 100bps
Trade pay off	X	$-X$
Total	$X-$ \$1/2 100bps	$-X-$ \$1/2 900bps

If we look at these numbers with care it appears that, apart from the coin tossing result "X", each counterparty is paying its own credit spread, which is, at this stage, their own funding cost! In other words, after netting out all payments, each company is, in addition to X, paying the expected funding cost of the trade.[5] Interesting.

The numbers in that trade worked out very well because the coin toss (the underlying market risk) was done on a fair coin (that is, it had a symmetric distribution of returns). To be a bit more realistic in terms of what usually happens in financial trades, let's say that the distribution of returns of the underlying risk factor is not symmetric; that is, the coin is not fair and it has a 1/3 chance of giving heads, and a 2/3 chance of giving tails. In that case, the exposure that A has to B is \$2/3, and the exposure that B has to A is \$1/3, and the trade price excluding credit risk is \$1/3. Now both counterparties need to agree how to price the counterparty risk. In order to hedge out counterparty risk, A needs to enter into a CDS and pay \$2/3 * 900 bps, and counterparty B needs to pay \$1/3 * 100 bps. So, the net cash flow that is necessary to make this trade fair is \$2/3 * 900 bps − \$1/3 * 100 bps = \$ 17/3 * 100 bps. Plugging these numbers into the calculation sketched previously, we get

	Counterparty A	Counterparty B
Price excluding credit risk	−\$1/3	\$1/3
Price of credit risk	−\$17/3 100bps	−\$17/3 100bps
Spent on credit risk hedge	−\$2/3 900bps	−\$1/3 100bps
Trade pay off	X	$-X$
Total	$-\$1/3+X-$ − \$1/3 100bps	$\$1/3-X-$ − \$2/3 900bps

So, again, each counterparty is paying its expected funding cost!

That is, *in expectation* or *in average*, Institution A will have to pay \$1/3 to B, which is Institution A's Expected Negative Exposure (ENE), and the cost of this trade for A (\$1/3 x 100bps) is the average cost of borrowing (the funding cost) that A needs to pay in order to meet its expected payments. And a mirror argument applies to Institution B.

With these two examples, we have illustrated the following general law: let's say that counterparty A has a potential positive exposure to B of EPE_A and a potential negative exposure to B of ENE_A, and that counterparty B has potential positive and negative exposures to A given by EPE_B and ENE_B. Also, let's say that the credit spread of counterparty A is s_A, and that of counterparty B is s_B. Also, the reader should realise that, if P is the trade price without considering counterparty risk, then

$$P = EPE_A + ENE_A = EPE_B + ENE_B \tag{8.2}$$

$$EPE_A = ENE_B \tag{8.3}$$

$$ENE_A = EPE_B \tag{8.4}$$

With this in mind, then

	Counterparty A	Counterparty B
Price excluding credit risk	P	$-P$
Price of credit risk	$EPE_A \cdot s_B -$	$-(EPE_A \cdot s_B -$
	$-EPE_B \cdot s_A$	$-EPE_B \cdot s_A)$
Spent on credit risk hedge	$-EPE_A \cdot s_B$	$-EPE_B \cdot s_A$
Trade pay off	X	$-X$
Total	$P+X-$	$-P-X-$
	$-ENE_A \cdot s_A$	$-ENE_B \cdot s_B$

Therefore, if CVA is accounted into this trade in this way and each counterparty hedges out the credit risk, then each counterparty has a trade that is, on average, credit-risk-free, and its P&L is going to be, in addition to "P" and "X", its own expected funding cost.

In this way, if things are correctly understood and managed, all institutions have an incentive to strengthen their credit quality, and trading desks have an incentive to trade with good counterparties in credit terms, for which CVA is low.

Finally, to add some jargon, let's say that the cost of hedging the credit risk is the "asset" side of CVA (CVA_{asset}), and that the expected funding cost is the "liability" side of CVA (CVA_{liab}), as it represents a liability benefit in the balance sheet.

Different ways to call CVA: Unfortunately, there are a number of ways that have been adopted to refer to this. Sometimes the asset side of CVA is called unilateral CVA, one-way CVA, or just CVA. Also, the liability side of CVA is often called DVA (Debit Value Adjustment).

For this reason, when the reader hears someone talking about CVA, the first thing that needs to be asked is what they mean by "CVA": sometimes it refers only to CVA_{asset}, sometimes to $CVA_{asset} - CVA_{liab}$.

8.1.2 CVA has been in the banking industry since their beginnings

Now that we have formulated CVA in a way that is intuitive, and it is clear how it accounts for credit risk, we should relate it all to what banks have been doing since their beginnings: borrowing and lending money.

Let's say that the trade at stake now is a loan; that is, most of the risk in the trade is credit risk. Counterparty B will borrow from A, by paying counterparty A 900 bps, and counterparty A will be financing the loan by paying 100 bps to some other lenders (e.g., its retail cash depositors); in this way, counterparty A will be making 800 bps as profit–which is the CVA of this transaction. If counterparty A wants to offload the credit risk of this loan without getting rid of the loan, it can enter into a 900 bps CDS transaction with counterparty B as obligor. By doing so, counterparty A will only be paying 100 bps (the funding cost) net. This is just a simple case of what we have discussed before.

However, if it is not necessary for counterparty A to fund this loan as the money is already available in their vaults, they will not be paying those 100 bps and therefore will not be making any 100bps loss. Hence, CVA_{liab} is "hedged out" too; that is, institution A makes sure that they will not default on this transaction.

These examples illustrate that CVA is no more than the centuries old credit risk pricing system applied to modern financial derivatives. It isn't new to banks.

8.1.3 CVA monetisation

We have seen that CVA accounts for the counterparty credit risk that a trade has embedded within it. Until recently banks had assumed default risk as negligible in derivative pricing, and as such an unnecessary adjustment. However, default risk is far from negligible these days.

CVA is a price assigned to a credit risk. So, if we assume that risk, we should be making that money somewhere (as long as the risk does not materialise into a default). How does this happen?

As already illustrated, there are two factors that contribute to CVA: credit risk and funding.

There are two common different uses of the word "monetisation", and which we are going to call *cash* monetisation and *paper* monetisation. The first one is achieved when a cash flow actually happens, and the second one only with respect to balance sheet accounting. They are related, but not the same. Let's clarify this further.

Cash monetisation of the CVA can be achieved by hedging or not hedging the trade credit risk. If the bank decides to hedge the credit risk, it can do so by buying protection against its counterparties via the CDS market. However, if it decides not to do so, the trades are exposed to default risk and the bank will have a credit-related cash profit, coming from the lack of payments that it would have to make for the CDS, as long as defaults do not occur. In this way, CVA_{asset} can be cash-monetised.

The other side of CVA monetisation comes from CVA_{liab}. Hedging it out means ensuring that we do not default. The only way we can ensure that is by having our expected potential liabilities already in our vaults, segregated, so we know we will be able to meet those liabilities in the future. However, modern banks are all leveraged; none of them has the expected funding costs in their vaults already[6] and, as a result, CVA_{liab} cannot be cash-monetised in practice.

Regarding paper monetisation, financial institutions prefer stable balance sheets and low volatility in their P&L, which means that the CVA volatility needs to be neutralised. CVA volatility comes from the fact that, like any other price, CVA value fluctuates as a result of changes in the market prices of CDS spreads and other instruments like interest rate swaps, FX forwards, equity forwards, etc. (we'll expand on this later in the text).

In order to hedge out CVA P&L volatility, banks will trade financial derivatives (CDS, IR swaps, FX forwards, EQ forwards, etc.) to delta-hedge the P&L fluctuations coming from CVA. This can be done more or less easily with CVA_{asset}, but not that easily with its liability counterpart, as in order to neutralise that side of the P&L volatility the bank will need to sell protection on itself, which cannot be done. However, a bank can partially neutralise this CVA_{liab} component of the P&L volatility by selling protection on other banks whose credit quality move similarly to his own credit, or on credit indices or baskets of CDSs that also move closely to his own CDSs. In this way, a bank can hedge out the systemic component of the CVA_{liab} P&L volatility. We will also expand on this later.

So, to summarise, it is important to understand that CVA can be monetised, and that there are two kinds of "monetisation": cash and balance sheet related. As we will see, both are very related, but not exactly the same.

8.1.4 Monetising via my own downgrade: the "perversity" of accounting rules?

Further to our previous discussion, a paradox appears around CVA: if my own rating gets downgraded, then the CVA_{liab} of my trades increases and, as a result, the value of my trade increases!

For now, let's consider the following approximation for CVA:

$$CVA \simeq EPE \cdot s_{cpty} + ENE \cdot s_{our} \tag{8.5}$$

where s_{cpty} and s_{our} are the credit spread of the counterparty and of ourselves, *EPE* is the exposure that we have to the counterparty, and *ENE* is the exposure that the counterparty has to us (a negative number in that equation). Then,

$$\begin{aligned} P &= P_{CreditRiskFree} - \text{CVA} \\ &\simeq P_{CreditRiskFree} - \left(EPE \cdot s_{cpty} + ENE \cdot s_{our}\right) \end{aligned} \tag{8.6}$$

That is, given that *ENE* is negative, if s_{our} increases, then the *P*, the value of the trade (or book of trades), increases too on my balance sheet. This is paradoxical, as it means that we book a profit in our balance sheet when our credit rating deteriorates. This can lead to easy misunderstanding of accounting and potential financial mismanagement, so it must be well understood.

This liability benefit in CVA_{liab} is equivalent to what would happen if we buy a house today with a 25-year mortgage at a fixed rate of 5% and the day after we sign the mortgage the bank decides to increase the rate for our type of mortgage to 10%. If a friend bought that same mortgage one day later than us, we will will be better off than him by having signed the mortgage at 5%, and that should be reflected in our personal balance sheet somewhere: as a liability gain.

In fact, the root of the paradox comes when we mistake a balance sheet profit with what makes us default. If we cannot pay our electricity bill in the future, our power supplier will not care at all for that "paper" liability gain, and they will cut off the power to our house.

In my view, the paradox comes from a wrong interpretation of the Profit & Loss statements. Following from the mortgage example, a company can have a very strong balance sheet, be a profitable company on paper, but default, because what makes you default is not paper profitability, but lack of cash.

The lesson from this is that P&L is an indication of the performance of a company, but the analyst needs to look into it and understand its details in order to assess the credit quality of a company.

8.1.5 Negative CVA. What does it mean?

Another confusing result of this Credit Value Adjustment is that a trade can have, in theory, negative CVA.

If we are a strong solid financial institution, CVA should be in general positive for us. If we have negative CVA it means that, on average, we will be borrowing money in the future via the book of OTC derivatives. In principle, that can well happen, but if we are supposed to be a solid financial institution, it is an *indicator* that something may be wrong in that book of trades.

In simple terms, being a solid institution (i.e., a bank) and having a permanent negative CVA is like me borrowing money every day from my 15-year-old nephew to pay for dinner. It is no problem if one day I am short of cash and he lends me a bit, so I do not starve that day, but everyone would agree that it is an indicator that something is wrong in our finances if we have to do that every day.

In fact, in a Credit Summit that I attended in London, a participant talked to us about a piece of work that he had done with a given bank before the crisis, regarding negative CVA in their books. That bank run into major difficulties in the hype of the 2008 crisis; we should not be surprised, as it seems they did not understand the actual credit risk they were carrying in their books.

8.1.6 CVA and netting sets

We have seen previously that, from a risk-free point of view, the price of a book of trades is the sum of the prices of each trade individually. In other words

$$P_{\text{Portfolio, CreditRiskFree}} = \sum_i P_{i,\text{CreditRiskFree}} \tag{8.7}$$

where i counts through the trades in the portfolio. Also, we have seen in previous chapters that counterparty risk needs to be computed at each counterparty's netting set level. That is because in the case of a counterparty defaulting, the trades within a netting set will be betted off for the liquidation of the portfolio. As a result, CVA is not a quantity intrinsic to a trade, but to a netting set. Hence, CVA for a netting set should be defined as

$$P_{NS} = \sum_i P_{i,\text{CreditRiskFree}} - CVA_{NS} \tag{8.8}$$

where NS refers to the Netting Set. For this reason, when a desk is booking a new trade, the CVA quantity that matters is the incremental CVA that that trade brings to its netting set. We will see later on how to compute this.

8.1.7 Summarising

We have seen that CVA is the adaptation to modern derivatives of what banks have been doing since their beginnings: making money through the spread of their lending and borrowing costs with different market players, called "counterparties" in the context of credit risk.

In particular, this can be applied to modern derivatives by considering the cost of hedging out the credit risk in them (CVA_{asset}) and the cost of funding the expected liabilities (CVA_{liab}). The difference between both is the CVA price, which represents a financial compensation that the counterparty carrying more credit risk should receive. That is because in this ideal world our cost of funding expected liabilities is the same as the cost of hedging out the credit risk for the other side of the deal, and vice versa.

CVA_{asset} can be cash-monetised by not hedging the counterparty risk embedded in the book of trades at stake; that is, by assuming its credit risk. But this monetisation is only crystallised if the counterparty does not default. Regarding CVA_{liab}, in practice, since all banks leverage, it cannot be cash-monetised. However, financial institutions are also very interested in balance sheet stability, also called paper-monetisation. This can be achieved to a great extent via delta hedging so that the CVA volatility can be neutralised.

After this intuitive introduction, let's see all this in more detail.

8.2 CVA definition

Let's represent the risk-neutral price of a book of trades that form a netting set as P. Today's price is represented by P_0, the price at a future time t is given by P_t. Let's define CVA as the adjustment we do to the risk-neutral price of a netting set to account for the credit risk embedded in it,

$$P_{risky,t} = P_t - CVA_t. \tag{8.9}$$

Let's see how we can compute this adjustment.

Typically, an institution should already have a pricing system that can tell us what P is today (P_0), but we cannot know with certainty the value of P in the future. All we can say about it is that P_t is a stochastic variable, with a probability density function $\Psi_t(P)$. This $\Psi_t(P)$ can be calculated as explained in detail in previous chapters. We also saw previously that from $\Psi_t(P)$ we can compute a number of risk profiles that include EPE_t and ENE_t.[7] The EPE profiles represent how much, on average, we will be owed if our counterparty defaults and the ENE profile has a symmetric meaning from my counterparty's standpoint.

As seen throughout this book, in the event of a counterparty defaulting, the actual loss will not be the exposure, but a percentage of the exposure, called the Loss Given Default (LGD), which can also be expressed in terms of the Recovery Rate (RR) as $LGD = 1 - RR$.

With all this, we can say that the present value of the credit risk that we have in a netting set with a counterparty is given by

$$CVA_{asset,0} = \int_0^T (1 - RR_{cpty,u})\, EPE_u\, DF_{0,u}\, S_{our,u}\, S_{cpty,u}\, PD_{cpty,u}\, du, \tag{8.10}$$

where $DF_{0,u}$ is the risk-neutral discount factor for time u as seen at time zero, $S_{our,u}$ is our survival probability at time u, $S_{cpty,u}$ is the counterparty survival probability at u, $PD_{cpty,u}$ is the *marginal* default probability of the counterparty related to the netting set,[8] at time u, and T is the maturity of the last trade in the portfolio.

Equivalently, we can define a symmetric quantity, taking the point of view of the counterparty:

$$CVA_{liab,0} = \int_0^T (1 - RR_{our,u})\, ENE_u\, DF_{0,u}\, S_{cpty,u}\, S_{our,u}\, PD_{our,u}\, du. \tag{8.11}$$

So, based on the findings of the previous section, which showed how CVA has two components, each accounting for the credit risk that each counterparty has to each other, CVA is

$$CVA_0 = CVA_{asset,0} + CVA_{liab,0}. \tag{8.12}$$

It must be noted that $EPE_u \geq 0$, but $ENE_u \leq 0$ and, hence, $CVA_{asset} \geq 0$ and $CVA_{liab} \leq 0$.

A derivation of this formula from first principles is shown in Appendix H.

In practice, the recovery rates are usually considered not to be stochastic and do not follow any time term structure, so that

$$CVA_{asset,0} = (1 - RR_{cpty}) \int_0^T EPE_u\, DF_{0,u}\, S_{our,u}\, S_{cpty,u}\, PD_{cpty,u}\, du, \tag{8.13}$$

and equivalently for $CVA_{liab,0}$.

We have seen that a standard way to represent PD_u is with the hazard rate λ_u. If we assume a flat credit spread (s) curve and constant recovery rate, then $\lambda \simeq s/(1-RR)$. Based on this, as typically used, the approximation consists of

$$CVA_{asset,0} \simeq \widehat{EPE}_0 \cdot s_{cpty,0}, \tag{8.14}$$

where $\widehat{EPE}_0$ is the integral of the risky discounted EPE_t profile from $t=0$ to $t=T$,

$$\widehat{EPE}_0 = \int_0^T EPE_u\, DF_{0,u}\, S_{our,u}\, S_{cpty,u}\, du. \tag{8.15}$$

To avoid confusion, we should emphasise that $\widehat{EPE}_0$ is a number, while EPE_t is a time-profile. This simplification can also be made for the liability side.

Finally, this formula can be generalised for any point in time so that CVA is not just a value "today", but will change over time so that, in its general form,

$$CVA_t = \int_t^T (1-RR_{cpty,u})\, EPE_u\, DF^*_{t,u}\, PD_{cpty,u}\, du + \int_t^T (1-RR_{our,u})\, ENE_u\, DF^*_{t,u}\, PD_{our,u}\, du \tag{8.16}$$

$$\simeq (1-RR_{cpty}) \int_t^T EPE_u\, DF^*_{t,u}\, PD_{cpty,u}\, du + (1-RR_{our}) \int_t^T ENE_u\, DF^*_{t,u}\, PD_{our,u}\, du \tag{8.17}$$

$$\simeq \widehat{EPE}_t \cdot s_{cpty,t} + \widehat{ENE}_t \cdot s_{our,t} \tag{8.18}$$

where we have used the notation referring to the risky discount factor $DF^*_{t,u} = DF_{t,u}\, S_{our,u}\, S_{cpty,u}$.

From these formulas, Equation 8.17 is the most popular one for accurate calculations, and Equation 8.18 for fast (but frequently quite good) approximations.

The reader must note that, sometimes, the formulas are relaxed and the survival terms $S_{our,t}$ and $S_{cpty,t}$ are approximated by 1 for any point in time t; i.e., $DF^*_{t,u} \simeq DF_{t,u}$. In particular, this is often done when calculating CVA in a pure risk-management context, as opposed to pricing, as here it is the market norm to always assume our own survival in the calculations.

8.2.1 Unilateral vs. bilateral CVA

This definition of CVA given is sometimes called bilateral CVA. That is because it accounts "bilaterally" for both sides of the price of counterparty risk. However, perhaps we are interested only in one side of the credit risk: a metric for how much we may lose in the future from default risk losses, not paying any attention to the fact that we may have defaulted before our counterparty defaults. This is the typical stand of a risk management function. In this case, we can then define *unilateral* CVA (uCVA) and *bilateral* CVA (bCVA) as

$$uCVA_t = (1-RR_{cpty}) \int_t^T EPE_u\, DF^*_{t,u}\, PD_{cpty,u}\, du, \tag{8.19}$$

$$bCVA_t = CVA_{asset,t} + CVA_{liab,t}. \tag{8.20}$$

Unfortunately, these two versions of CVA coexist in the market, and we must learn to live with both of them. Some professionals call bCVA the "true" CVA, others do so with uCVA. In this text, bCVA is the fundamental definition of Credit Value Adjustment,

$$CVA \doteq bCVA, \tag{8.21}$$

because we tend to see CVA as a price. As said, the reciprocal of uCVA (CVA_{liab} with $S_{cpty,t} = 1$) is often called the Debit Value Adjustment (DVA).

8.2.2 Some details of the computation

The computation of CVA is anything but straightforward. The first and more costly step is the computation of the EPE and ENE profiles. We have dedicated a number of chapters to explain how it can be done. Once we have those profiles, we need to calculate the integral in Equation 8.17. In principle, this step is fairly simple, but let's see now a number of points that are important regarding practical modelling and implementation of a CVA engine.

Independence of exposures and default probabilities: Sometimes the value of the netting set under consideration (P_t) is not independent of the default probabilities of one or both counterparties on both sides of the netting set. When this is the case, it is very important to consider that dependency structure as we want to price potential losses due to defaults, hence both EPE and ENE profiles must be calculated *subject* to default. This effect is called right-way-risk or wrong-way-risk, depending on whether default events tend to decrease (right) or increase (wrong) exposures.

This is a very important effect that must be accounted for in both its "right" and "wrong" versions.[9] Unfortunately, it adds an important level of difficulty to the computation, and hence it is often neglected.

CVA for individual trades, netting sets, counterparties, and the whole portfolio: CVA can be calculated for an individual trade by computing the EPE and ENE profiles of that trade, though the quantity we are really looking for is the CVA of a netting set. The reason is that, in the case of a default, the Master Agreements between counterparties (that define the netting sets) will legally put together trades that can be netted off for the liquidation of the portfolio and drive the subsequent payments to and from the defaulted firm. This is important because the price of counterparty credit risk needs to mimic what will happen if a counterparty defaults.

Hence the CVA of an individual trade only really makes sense when that trade is a netting set by itself, which happens quite rarely. It is very important to have it clear that CVA is a price adjustment *to a netting set.*

Two counterparties can have more than one Master Agreement (e.g., between different legal entities). The hierarchy of the CVA calculation is displayed in Figure 8.2. As a result of the effect that netting, addition, and aggregation of risk have on the EPE and ENE (see Section 3.4), the CVA adds up for any level above the netting set. That is, the CVA of a counterparty is the sum of the CVA of each of its netting sets, and similarly for a whole portfolio of trades with several counterparties.

Having said that, what really makes sense for an individual trade is its CVA contribution to the total CVA of the netting set it belongs to. Section 11.10 will cover how that CVA contribution can be calculated.

The reader should note that CVA adds up above the netting set level, but not all risk metrics do. For example, PFE doesn't. The PFE profile of a counterparty will not be the sum of the PFE profiles of each netting set due to the counterparty risk aggregation effects. See Section 3.4 for details.

CVA integration: For practical calculations, the integral of Equations 8.17 and 8.18 are transformed into their discrete forms,

$$CVA_t \simeq (1 - RR_{cpty}) \sum_{i=1}^{N} EPE_i \, DF_i^* \, PD_{cpty,t_{i-1},t_i} \, \Delta t_i + (1 - RR_{our}) \sum_{i=1}^{N} ENE_i \, DF_i^* \, PD_{our,t_{i-1},t_i} \, \Delta t_i. \tag{8.22}$$

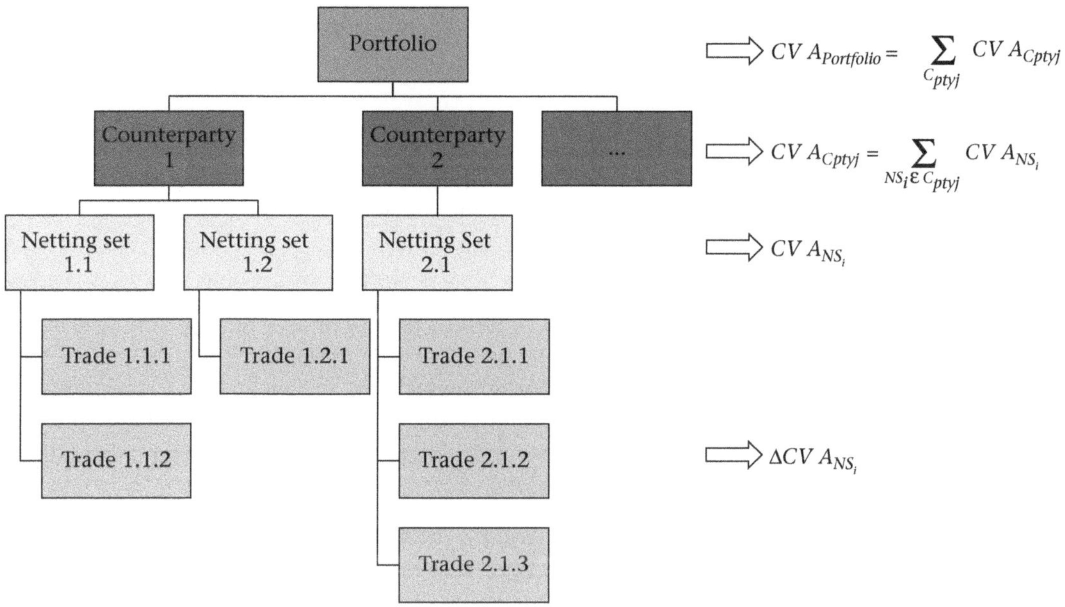

Figure 8.2 Illustration of the hierarchy of the CVA calculation

and

$$\widehat{EPE}_t \simeq \sum_{i=1}^{N} EPE_i\, DF_i^* \tag{8.23}$$

$$\widehat{ENE}_t \simeq \sum_{i=1}^{N} ENE_i\, DF_i^* \tag{8.24}$$

and also, for low credit spreads,

$$DF_i^* \simeq DF_i\, e^{-\frac{s_{cpty}}{RR_{cpty}} t_i}\, e^{-\frac{s_{our}}{RR_{our}} t_i} \tag{8.25}$$

where $i = 0$ refers to "today", i refers to the time points in the EPE and ENE calculation, PD_{a,t_{i-1},t_i} is the annualised default probability for institution a at t_i conditional on survival at t_{i-1}, and Δt_i is the size of each time bucket. Also, s_a and RR_a refer to the credit spread and recovery rate of institution a.

There are two typical ways to come up with EPE_i and DF_i^*, either the rectangle rule where $EPE_i = EPE_{t_i}$ and $DF_i = DF_{t,t_i}$, or the trapezoidal rule where $EPE_i = \frac{EPE_{t_{i-1}} + EPE_{t_i}}{2}$ and $DF_i = DF_{t,(t_{i-1}+t_i)/2}$.

CVA as a running spread: CVA is most often calculated as a one-off value. Dealing desks in a financial institution pass this cost to the clients or discount it from their own profit.[10] However, many OTC products are incepted at zero value (e.g., an interest rate swap) and any cost is charged as a running premium, also called a *spread*. Hence it is useful to calculate the spread version of a CVA amount.

The spread (s_{cva}) needs its present value to be equal to the CVA value. In other words,

$$CVA_0 = \sum_i s_{cva} \, DF^*_{t_0,t_i} \tag{8.26}$$

where i now runs through the coupon dates of the underlying derivative,[11] typically a swap. The reader may know that $\sum_i DF_{t_0,t_i}$ is the duration of the swap D_0. Hence, the spread is given by

$$s_{cva} \simeq \frac{CVA}{D}. \tag{8.27}$$

While it makes perfect sense to calculate CVA as a spread, it has an important caveat: if charged to the final client, then the CVA is also at risk of default, and so it must be included in P_t when CVA is computed. This creates a recursive problem. If done in a Monte Carlo simulation, we would calculate the CVA spread in an iterative manner until it converges. However, this can be quite costly to run. Vrins and Gregory have discussed this and come up with analytical proxies for them [77].

Close-out amounts: In the definition of CVA we have used P_t, the risk-neutral value of the netting set under consideration, to calculate the exposure metrics EPE and ENE. We must emphasise here that P_t should really represent the value of the netting set when the counterparty has defaulted.

For OTC derivatives, when one counterparty defaults, the sequence of events that follows is typically governed by an ISDA contract. The 2009 ISDA protocol for the determination of a close amount states that

> In determining a close-out amount, the determining party may consider any relevant information, including, without limitation, one or more of the following types of information: (i) quotations (either firm or indicative) for replacement transactions supplied by one or more third parties that *may take into account the creditworthiness of the determining party* [italics added] at the time the quotation is provided and the terms of any relevant documentation, including credit support documentation, between the determining party and the third party providing the quotation.

Also, in 2010 ISDA reiterated this point by saying that "upon default close-out, valuations will in many circumstances reflect the replacement cost of transactions calculated at the terminating party's bid or offer side of the market, and will often *take into account the creditworthiness of the terminating party* [italics added]" [7, 9].

In other words, we should consider the risky value of the netting set, which includes CVA, for the calculation of the exposures.[12] When calculated in a Monte Carlo engine, this creates an even more difficult iterative problem than that of the running spread because, ideally, each time we price the portfolio and calculate P_t we should also have to calculate CVA_t. The reader should be reminded that, typically, this pricing is done 1,000,000 times for each CVA calculation. This creates a Monte Carlo within a Monte Carlo problem that cannot be solved in practice; we can barely calculate CVA, given the complexity of the EPE and ENE calculation, and so a CVA calculation within each scenario and time step of the CVA calculation is simply not doable.

For this reason, this fine-tuning of the calculation is left aside, arguably because its impact should be small.

In any case, if for some reason this is seen as an important adjustment, a way to tackle it that can be manageable to some degree is calculating CVA for a number of representative lattice points in the future in the space formed by the exposure and the future time, as shown in Figure 8.3.

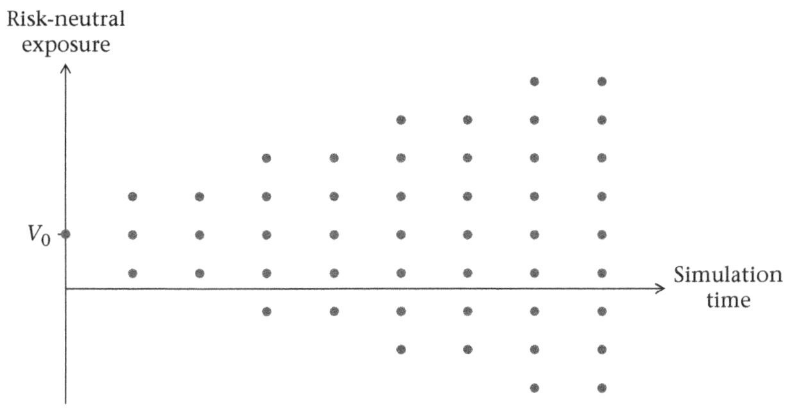

Figure 8.3 Illustration of the lattice points for a recursive CVA calculation

We could proceed as follows: first we calculate CVA in those lattice points, using the risk-neutral valuation for the EPE (and ENE). Then we do a second run, where the EPE (ENE) profiles in each lattice point is calculated with the CVA adjustment of the previous run, and we continue like this in an iterative way until the convergence of the CVA value in the "today" point,[13] the one that we are interested in, is good enough.

To make it even more tricky, exposures must be calculated subject to default, and so the CVA adjustment to the close-out amount must only consider the credit worthiness of the surviving counterparty.[14] This means that it should only take the liability side of CVA for the EPE profile calculations in the lattice points after "today", and the asset side of CVA for the ENE profile calculation. The reader can refer to Brigo and Morini (2011) for a detailed discussion on this [25].

I think it will not be too difficult to see that this fine-tuning of the calculation adds a massive level of complexity, though most likely only for a small adjustment. So we can neglect it in most cases.

The need to give sufficient care to this becomes even more clear when we see that, in reality, CVA pricing has a visible error due to numerical noise in the calculation. In plain words, we can forget about this fine-tuning because, most likely, the noise (the error) will not let us see it.

Numerical noise: Section 3.11 discussed the effect of numerical noise in a Monte Carlo simulation for counterparty risk calculations. As a reminder, the typical number of scenarios that an EPE system will have ranges from 1,000 to 10,000. Figure 8.4 shows how the CVA error changes as we increase the number of simulations. Extrapolating from it, it appears we would need 2,000,000 scenarios to achieve a one basis point error in CVA for a 10 year swap.

This means that, in practice, we will have to cope with a large error in our CVA calculations unless new technology appears. As a quant, it is very important to keep this in mind at all times, as any model or system enhancement that lies within the CVA error bars will not be seen at all, hence the effort will be fruitless.

CVA simplified formula: We have seen that CVA_{asset} can be simplified by

$$\begin{aligned} CVA_{asset,t} &\approx \widehat{EPE}_t \cdot s_{cpty,t} \\ \widehat{EPE}_t &= \int_t^T EPE_u \, DF^*_{t,u} \, du \\ DF^*_{t,u} &\simeq DF_{t,u} \, e^{-\frac{s_{cpty,u}}{RR_{cpty}}(u-t)} \, e^{-\frac{s_{our,u}}{RR_{our}}(u-t)} \end{aligned} \tag{8.28}$$

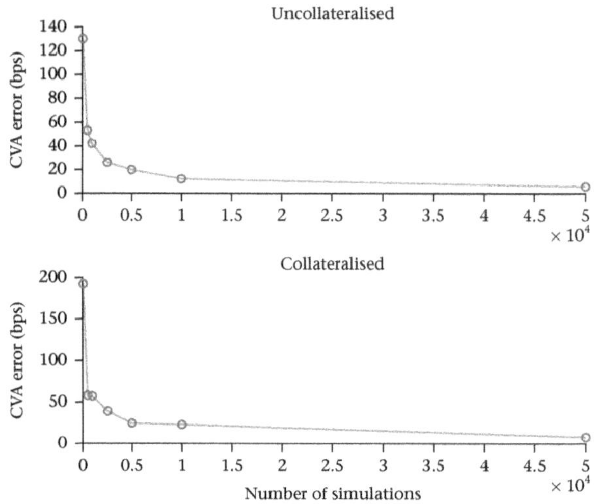

Number Sims	CVA error (bps)
100	160
500	55
1,000	49
2,500	32
5,000	22
10,000	15
50,000	6

Figure 8.4 CVA pricing error (standard deviation of the price over several calculations) for a 10-year interest rate swap. We need 2,000,000 to have an accuracy of 1 basis point

and equivalently for CVA_{liab}. Let's see now the context in which this approximation makes sense. We need the following conditions:

- Firstly, we need $s = \frac{\lambda}{1-RR}$ to be a good proxy for the credit spread s. That is the case when the default intensity λ is small because, then, non-linear components in the price of a CDS are negligible.[15]
- Secondly, in this approximation we are simplifying a whole term structure of credit spreads into a single spread value and a flat term structure. Hence we need that original term structure to be fairly flat. Again, that tends to happen when the default intensities are low, as shown in Figure 8.5.
- Finally, in order to get the credit spread out of the integral, we need $EPE_t\,DF^*_{0,t}$ to not change too much for different values of t. This is the part that is more difficult to achieve, but in many practical cases EPE_t is upward sloping, while $DF^*_{0,t}$ is downward sloping, so they can compensate each other.

In practice, most of the time we are not going to do a detailed analysis of these three points, as it may defeat the purpose of the proxy (i.e., speedy calculation). In reality the practitioner needs to pick a credit spread value representative of the whole term structure, taking into account the weight given by $EPE_t\,DF^*_{0,t}$ and the shape of the credit spread curve. A rule-of-thumb is to pick the credit spread of the tenor point near where the EPE profile peaks. In several cases, this approximation is a quite good back-of-the-envelope calculation, as an error in one place often compensate errors in another place. However, it must never be forgotten that it is a proxy, and no more than that.

Complexity of CVA computation: Calculating CVA on a trade or on a portfolio is quite a complex task. In fact, it can be seen as the most difficult pricing task ever done. If anyone disagrees with that, just think of a derivative product–which will price than CVA. Now, calculate the CVA on that product–which will be much more difficult than the risk-neutral pricing of the product itself.

To see the added degree of difficulty that we have in front of us, we recall that each point in the EPE profiles is the price of an option, with the product under consideration as the underlying (see

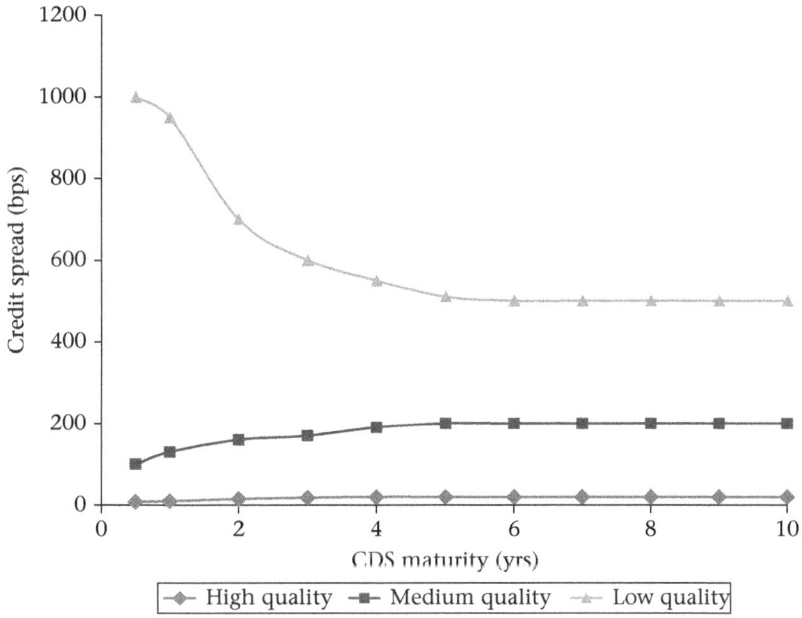

Figure 8.5 Illustrative term structures of credit spreads

Section 6.10). So pricing CVA on a product is like pricing as strip of options on that product. For example, to price CVA on a swap we have to price a strip of swaptions, to price CVA on a swaption we have to price a strip of options on swaptions, etc. This shows how the degree of difficulty gets multiplied by several orders of magnitude compared to pricing the product (or the portfolio) itself.

The most difficult part of pricing CVA is obtaining the EPE and ENE profiles. And within those taks, the around 1,000,000 times that the pricing of the underlying portfolio needs to be done is the most costly calculation (see Section 3.3). In fact, if the underlying trades in the portfolio contain exotic derivatives, which need Monte Carlo simulations for pricing, the task can become quasi-impossible. As a result, the functionality of counterparty risk calculations that we need to improve most is the pricing step. If that is not possible, very rough approximations need to be taken that can induce CVA wrong pricing and risk management.[16]

Fast pricing of exotic derivatives in the context of counterparty credit risk systems is an area open to much needed research and development.

DVA: to be or not to be: We have defined CVA as having two components: the asset side and the liability side, each reflecting the credit risk that each side of the bilateral deal is exposed to. The liability side is often referred to as DVA.

Some practitioners regard this DVA (or CVA_{liab}) as a number that should not be considered in pricing, as it provides a benefit in the balance sheet when a bank runs into financial difficulty and because it cannot be cash-hedged.

I disagree with that view. We will expand on this matter later in the text, once we have all the toolbox that is needed for the discussion.

8.3 CVA approximations

The reader can by now appreciate that calculating CVA is anything but simple. Because of that, a very reasonable questions is whether there are ways to estimate CVA in an approximated way.

If we manage to estimate the EPE and ENE profiles of a netting set in a simple way, then we can make use of Equation 8.18, choosing a representative credit spread and interest rate to calculate $\widehat{EPE}$, $\widehat{ENE}$ and, then, CVA.

Having said that, the most difficult part in CVA computation is calculating the EPE (and ENE) profile of the netting set. For that calculation, we'd like to have a full-blown Monte Carlo system for the risk factor evolution, and we need to price each trade hundred of thousands, if not a few million, times. Chapter 6 is dedicated to simplifications for exposure calculations. Let's tackle now this problem in the specific context of CVA.

Mark-to-Market + add-on methods: The MtM + add-on methods described in Sections 6.1 and 6.2 can be used for CVA calculations. They are better than nothing, but it must be noted they are *very* crude proxies, so our CVA numbers could be quite dirty.

If we use the method without a time profile component (Section 6.1), we can assume the EPE profile is a flat line up to portfolio maturity. The example of Figure 6.4 is done for EPE, but this method can easily be extended to ENE calculations by doing it as if we were the counterparty.

Once we have these profiles we can calculate $\widehat{EPE}$ and $\widehat{ENE}$ following Equation 8.15, with a representative rate and an exponential discounting.

SA-CCR: The regulatory Standardised Approach for Calculation of Exposures (SA-CCR), explained in Chapter 9, could also be used if nothing else is available. However, similarly to the add-on method, the quality of CVA pricing should suffer strongly as a result of the crudeness of the method.

No collateral algorithm: When our problem is that we do not have a collateral algorithm, we can make use of the methods described in Sections 6.6, 6.7, and 6.9 to approximate EPE and ENE profiles, taking the positive side of the distributions for EPE, and the negative one for ENE. Then we need to cap/floor the profiles by zero, and subsequently calculate $\widehat{EPE}$ and $\widehat{ENE}$.

As the price of an option: Section 6.10 described how EPE and ENE profiles can be calculated as the price of an option on the underlying product, with the option strike being the market value that make the product worth zero. This is a very good way to quickly calculate EPE and ENE, for simple products. For example, Brigo and Masetti applied it to interest rate swaps [24]. Unfortunately the limitation of this method is that it is only going to work for standalone trades and for vanilla products for which there is a liquid options market.

Netting set P&L analysis: Section 6.11 describes a very good method to obtain approximated EPE and ENE profiles if we have the history of the value of a netting set. What we basically do in that method is to price a series of options with the netting set as the option underlying and strike zero. We can use the past history of the netting set value to estimate its volatility, drift, and any other parameter we need.

9 Regulatory Capital

In the aftermath of the 2008 market events, governments changed quite deeply the way they see and regulate financial institutions. Until then, the general idea was that of "light touch" regulation, which means that the governments and regulatory bodies effectively let banks self-regulate and their function was, in practice, little more than a supervision of that self-regulation. In 2008/09 the interbank money market dried out, nearly all important banks approached a dangerous cliff, and some fell. Governments had to step in as, otherwise, the risk-hedging and deposit-credit cycle that lubricate and feed the global economy would have collapsed, with unthinkable consequences to everyone's life. Those events made it clear to governments that there were a number of financial institutions that were too big to fail. If they (governments) were, *de facto*, the last loss absorbers in the financial system, if they were in charge of running the economy and if they wanted to protect the tax payer's money, many thought that they should have an important input into how financial institutions are risk-managed. As a result, a new era of "tight" regulation started.

In 2011, the Financial Stability Board, that comprises the G-20 economies and the European Commission, released a first list of banks that were seen as "too big to fail". They were called SIFIs or G-SIFIs (Global Systematically Important Financial Institutions).[1] Membership of this list is driven not only by size, but also by other factors like complexity and interconnectedness, international reach, etc. This list is updated regularly. Those banks will have tighter regulatory requirements than other banks.

One of the most important bodies in the area of banking regulation is the Basel Committee on Banking Supervision, which lies within the Bank for International Settlements, and which is an intergovernmental organisation of central banks. This Committee provides broad standards, guidelines, and recommendations for banks and regulators. It does not have any legal power over any bank in any jurisdiction: that is left to the governments and their regulatory bodies, though, in practice, regulators follow very closely the Committee's guidelines. The Basel Committee is in constant dialogue with those governmental regulatory bodies and with banks. There are a number of "accords" that have set the regulatory standard over time. At the time of writing this book, there have been three (and a half) major accords: Basel I, II, II.5 and III, as well as some other initiatives that are either in working progress or in implementation phase [5, 8, 59, 61, 60, 15]. We will be going through them in this chapter. In particular, we are going to focus on the quantitative side of those regulatory frameworks.

One of the key elements of banking regulation is how much capital a bank must hold to withstand future losses. That capital must be a reflection not of the size of the bank's balance sheet, but of the risk in it. The capital that banks must hold is set at 8% of the "Risk Weighted Assets" (RWA):

$$\text{Capital} = 8\% \times RWA \tag{9.1}$$

The Basel accords set the rules that banks must follow to calculate RWA. This will be explained in detail later.

In this chapter we are going to see the key features of how regulators in general, and the Basel Committee in particular, approach banking supervision. We are only going to be able to skim through the subject so that the reader understands the basics of it; a proper review would comprise a whole book with a number of volumes that change constantly, which is quite beyond the scope of this book.

It is widely known that the accords have contradictions, double counting and could be improved. In this chapter we are not going to judge them; rather, we are going to focus on what they say, as that is what we most often have to deal with when working in a financial institution. Having said that, we have to recognise the very difficult task that the Basel Committee has: to provide a set of rules for bank regulation that can be applied to any bank in the world, and in some cases this has had to be done quite promptly. Limitations and mistakes are hard to avoid in that environment.

9.1 A brief history of regulatory frameworks

In 1988 the Basel Committee proposed the first methodology for capital calculation for banks. Since its first version, Basel I, the accord has evolved in form and complexity, sometimes proactively, foreseeing future problems, and sometimes reactively, as a result of problems having crystallised. This section offers a summary of that evolution.

9.1.1 Basel I

The first version of the Accord was done in 1988 and it came into effect in 1992. Firstly, it introduced the requirement that banks must hold capital for at least 8% of RWA. In the calculation of RWA, it mainly focused on the credit risk of cash products in the banking book. The RWA calculation was very simple:

$$RWA_{BI,cash} = \text{Principal} \times \text{Risk Weight}. \tag{9.2}$$

The Risk Weight is assigned for each debt product, depending on the type of counterparty at the other side of the asset. For example, it gave a risk weight of 0% for the sovereign debt of most developed countries, 20% for OECD banks, 50% on mortgages, etc. The risk weight went up to 100%.

The trading book calculation was mainly driven by repo transactions, possibly because the derivatives market was in its infancy at the time. Repo RWA was given by

$$RWA_{BI,repo} = (C_{mv} - S_{mv}) \times \text{Risk Weight}, \tag{9.3}$$

floored at zero, where C_{mv} is the value of cash proceedings, S_{mv} is the market value of the securities, and the Risk Weight is also given by the type of counterparty.

Basel I also established how this capital must be allocated. It defined three levels of capital (Tier 1, Upper Tier 2, and Lower Tier 2) and stated the minimum levels for them. Tier 1 capital ratio must be 4% at least. Further details can be found in Choudhry [33].

9.1.2 Basel II

In 2004 the Basel Committee published the first version of the Basel II accord. This accord aimed at solving a number of weakness that had been highlighted in the previous Basel I. The capital allocation remained unchanged with respect to Basel I, but the capital calculation changed, becoming more granular, as it was now based on a finer calculation for credit risk capital, and on new calculations for market and operational risk. Full details can be found in the Basel document *International Convergence of Capital Measurements and Capital Standards* [5].

The accord is based on three "pilars" that are basically sets of rules in different categories.

Pillar 1: capital

Credit risk: Firstly, for credit risk, the accord provides three approaches:

1. **Standardised Approach:** This is a development from the Basel I calculation, in which risk weights are given depending on the counterparty type: economic sector (sovereign, financial, or corporate) and external credit rating. It adds to the Basel I classification a 150% for low rated borrowers.
2. **Foundation Internal Ratings Based (FIRB) Approach:** Capital is based on the Probability of Default for each counterparty (PD), Loss given default of the counterparty (LGD), the Exposure at Default of the counterparty (EaD), and the Maturity of the netting set (M). A bank using this approach can use its own internal models for PD, but it must use the Basel prescribed LGD, EaD, and M.
3. **Advanced Internal Ratings Based (AIRB) Approach:** In this case, the bank can use its internal models for LGD, EaD, and M.

The fundamental idea is that the less sophisticated the approach, the higher the capital requirement. The idea behind capital is to make sure that the bank can resist market and economic shocks. In this sense, a proper capital level is essential for the long-term survival of any financial institution and, hence, it adds value to the balance sheet. However, in the short term, it can be seen as highly stable assets that are sitting in the balance sheet, providing a very low return if at all, hence having an important opportunity cost. As a result, with this framework banks have a regulatory-driven economic incentive to create good methodologies, systems, and process to decrease the regulatory capital requirement and manage risk. Banks need regulatory approval to qualify for any of the IRB approaches.

Regarding the EaD calculation, Basel II splits the calculation into two: "Issuer" Credit Risk (ICR) and Counterparty Credit Risk (CCR). By ICR is understood the default risk in cash intense debt products like loans, while by CCR is meant the default risk embedded in financial derivatives (e.g., swaps, options).

EaD in cash debt products is not too difficult to calculate; it is basically the amount owed in the debt product. However, we have already seen quite extensively that the amount at risk is subject to default in a derivative that is stochastic, hence Basel has a number of approaches for it: the Current Exposure Method (CEM) and the Standardised Method (SM) as the basic ones, driven by a set of mechanical rules, and the Internal Models Method (IMM) as the advanced one, in which the institutions can develop their own models to measure EaD. Those models need to be approved by the local regulators.

It must be noted that the CEM and SM method expire on 1 January 2017, and a new Standardized Approach for measuring Counterparty Credit Risk exposures (SA-CCR) replaces it.

Market risk: Secondly, for market risk, the capital calculation can be based on either a basic Standardised Measurement Method (SMM) or a more sophisticated Internal Models Approach (IMA). The SMM approach bases the calculation on a number of tables that provide risk numbers per trade type and on the underlying risk factor. However, under the IMA framework, the capital calculation is based on the ten-day VaR at 99% confidence. Banks using the IMA framework must have the VaR model approved by the local regulators. This approval is highly driven by the model backtest (see Chapter 17).

In general, the SMM approach should be capital penalising with respect to the IMA framework. In addition to the VaR capital charge, banks are also required to set up "rigorous and comprehensive" stress testing, though it does not lead to a capital charge as such.

Also, the reader should note that the advanced market risk framework is expected to be soon updated under the Fundamental Review of the Trading Book.

Operational risk: Thirdly, by operational risk is meant "the risk of loss resulting from inadequate or failed internal processes, people and systems, or from external events". It basically refers to events like fraud, systems failures, process failures, damage to property, etc. Basel II also required banks to hold capital to account for future losses coming from crystalised operational risks.

Pillar 2: Supervision

This pillar comprises a set of tools for regulators to deal with financial institutions. It also provides a framework to deal with "residual" risk that includes systemic, pension, concentration, strategic, reputational, liquidity, and legal risk.

Pillar 3: discipline

In this pillar, the Basel Committee stated how risk information must be made public for external assessment of financial institutions.

9.1.3 Basel II.5

Since the first version of the Basel II accord, the Committee revised it a number of times. From those revisions, one was so important that the industry gave it an actual name: the Basel II.5 accord. It was published by the Committee in 2009 [8].

The financial crisis of 2007/08 exposed some weaknesses in the Basel II framework, and more specifically in the trading book capital calculation. Under this accord, capital was based on a 99% ten-day VaR. This II.5 supplements the calculation for the IMA framework as follows:

1. **Stress VaR:** A new Stress VaR number must be *added* to the Basel II VaR in the capital calculation. This Stress VaR must use the same model used for VaR but calibrated to a period of significant stress that is relevant to the bank's portfolio. The stress period used must be approved by the local regulator.
2. **Incremental Risk Charge (IRC):** Basel noted that the typical ten-day VaR at 99% confidence did not capture the credit-related losses that banks had in the 2007/08 market crisis. Those losses came from the decrease in value of (typically) illiquid positions in the trading books, coming from rating migrations and defaults. As a result, it required banks to estimate a 99.9% confidence loss with a one-year time horizon coming from those risks. Also, Basel recognised that the IRC needed a special calculation for correlation-sensitive securities like CDOs or credit baskets. This calculation is generically called Comprehensive Risk Measure (CRM). Further details on the idea behind these new requirements will be provided in the next sections.

So, in a nutshell, this II.5 accord expanded the coverage of the market risk capital charge for the trading book.

9.1.4 Basel III

In December 2010, the Basel Committee published *Basel III: A Global Regulatory Framework for More Resilient Banks and Banking Systems* in response to further weakness that had been perceived in Basel II and Basel II.5 [59]. The newly proposed regulatory framework changed, mainly, at the following levels:

- **Capital RWA Calculation:** On the one hand, to the existing Market Risk capital calculation, a new CVA market-risk charge was added for the trading book. This is the price adjustment needed to account for the counterparty credit risk in a book of derivatives. On the other hand, in the Counterparty Credit Risk charge, a few changes were imposed: (i) a new methodology for the margin period of risk, (ii) the calculation of a Stress EEPE, (iii) the Monte Carlo simulation for EPE profiles must go up to portfolio maturity, and (iv) a new formula for the EEPE in the shortcut method. Those changes will be explained in more detailed in Section 9.2.
- **New Capital Buffers:** The Basel Committee noted that, after the 2008/09 events, a number of banks continued capital distributions (e.g., dividends, employee bonuses) even when the financial conditions were quite stretched. In many cases this was done because banks could not send any sign of weakness to the capital markets as, if so, it could have deteriorated their own stand. To overcome this problem in the future, two new capital charges are imposed by the Basel Committee, which are unrelated to the risk in the bank balance sheet, so no extra calculation is needed. A flat Capital Conservation Buffer of 2.5% and Countercyclical Capital Buffer that ranges from 0% to 2.5%, and which is adjusted within this range during the economic cycles. The local regulators will dictate the level required in the Countercyclical Buffer at each point in time. Any bank that does not meet these two buffers will not be allowed to do any further capital distribution.
- **Liquidity:** In the 2008 events, liquidity dried out in the interbank money markets, which is what brought the whole banking system and, thus, the whole economy very close to a major collapse. This highlighted the fact that a strong capital base is not enough to ensure stability in the banking system. As a response, Basel III created two ratios. The Liquidity Coverage Ratio (LCR) ensures a sufficiently high quality liquid resources of cash, for at least one month, in the case of a stress scenario, and the Net Stable Funding Ratio (NSFR) aims to limit over-reliance on short-term funding during times of buoyant markets, and requires a minimum amount of stable sources of funding over a one-year time horizon.
- **Leverage Ratio:** The provision of credit is central to modern societies, and it is delivered to the real economy by banks via the Money Multiplier (see Appendix A). The Committee argued that one of the underlying features of the credit crisis was the build up of excessive leverage in the banking system, and the reduction of the leverage in a way that amplified the downward pressure on asset prices. As a result, the Committee introduced a minimum Leverage Ratio of 3% that aimed at constraining the leverage that banks are allowed to have.[2]
- **Capital Allocation:** The distribution of capital between Tier 1 and Tier 2 has been modified to increase the quality of capital. For example, Tier 1 capital ratio increases, from the Basel II, from 4% to 6%.

The reader must note that the impact of this new regulation in the banking industry was very strong. It demonstrates the fact that the era of loose banking regulation, which lasted up to 2008, was over. For example, this regulatory framework increased substantially the pressure on Capital Ratios. Those ratios are defined as

$$\text{Tier 1 Capital Ratio} = \frac{\text{Tier 1 Elegible Capital}}{RWA}. \tag{9.4}$$

The new RWA calculation increases RWA substantially, and the new capital allocation rules decrease the eligible capital. As a result, the Tier 1 Capital Ratio got a double "whack": an important reduction in the numerator and an important increase in the denominator.

As a final remark, the introduction of this new regulatory framework was phased in by the Committee so that implementation started in 2013 and finishes in 2019. All major financial jurisdictions have decided to implement the accord.

9.1.5 Further developments

At the time of this book going to press, the Basel Committee has the following main modifications to the regulatory environment in progress.

Standardised Approach for the measurement of Counterparty Credit Risk exposures (SA-CCR)

As already said, the CEM and SM approaches for the calculation of EaD are set to expire on 1 January 2017. By then, banks must have replaced those calculations by the new SA-CCR approach. It should be noted that this framework is also known as the the Non-Internal Model Method (NIMM) for capitalising counterparty credit risk exposures.

This approach will be explained in the following sections.

The fundamental review of the trading book

This new framework revises the existing regulations at two main levels.

Firstly, it addresses the gaps in "regulatory arbitrage" between the trading and banking books. The idea is that, on one side, the banking book is supposed to have positions held to maturity; typically loan-like products, but it can also have derivatives that hedge some of the risks existing in those loans. On the other side, the trading book should contain positions that are actively traded; typically financial derivatives, but also loans that are actively traded in a secondary market, for example.

The split between banking vs. trading book qualifying products was somewhat unclear in previous accords. These boundaries are intended to become more clear with this regulatory reform.

Secondly, it revisits the market risk capital charge, of which details will be given in the next sections.

This new regulatory framework was still in a consultative stage at the time of this text going to press, so the final shape of the new regulation and the implementation dates were still unclear.

Margin requirements for non-centrally cleared derivatives

Starting on 1 December 2015, and with a four-year phased rolling out plan, all financial institutions and the systematically important non-financial institutions, will have to collateralise their bilaterally traded derivative transactions, with the exception of physically settled FX swaps, options, and cross-currency swaps.[3]

As a summary, let's say that it is left to the national regulators to define the types of eligible collateral, but it is suggested that only cash, high quality government and corporate bonds, equities of major indices and gold should be used as such. Also, the riskiness of collateral should be subject to the appropriate haircuts.

Initial margin is only required if the notional of the bilaterally traded derivatives is greater than € 8 billion.[4]

The initial margin cannot be re-hypothicated except in some limited circumstances. Variation margin may be re-hypothicated.

Initial margin and haircuts can be calculated either by a model approved by the regulator, or by the standarised schedules provided by the Basel Committee. Initial margin should be based on a VaR model at 99% confidence level and a 10-day margin period of risk.[5]

The framework also sets a limit to the initial margin threshold of € 50 million, and a limit to the Minimum Transfer Amount of € 500,000.

9.2 The regulatory capital calculation

This book has quite a quantitative focus, so we are going to dedicate this section to the most quantitative side of the banking regulation: the calculation of capital. As a reminder, capital is set at 8% of Risk Weighted Assets

$$\text{Capital} = 8\% \times RWA \tag{9.5}$$

The different Basel accords establish how to calculate RWA.

This section is going to cover the latest approach available at the time of this book going to press, Basel III with some later amendments. However, sometimes we will also make the progressive distinction between Basel II and III, as it will help in the explanation.

9.2.1 An overall perspective

At a high level, the capital calculation can be split into two risk types: financial and non-financial risk. The financial risk can then be decomposed into Market Risk (MR) and Credit Risk (CR).

The market risk calculation can be further decomposed into three components: VaR,[6] Incremental Risk Charge (IRC), and CVA-VaR. The credit risk calculation can be split into two components: Issuer Credit Risk (ICR) for debt products like loans or bonds, and Counterparty Credit Risk (CCR) for financial derivatives. The non-financial risk part is known as Operational Risk (OR). This decomposition is illustrated in Figure 9.1.

So, at the end, we have

$$RWA = RWA_{VaR} + RWA_{IRC} + RWA_{CVA} + RWA_{ICR} + RWA_{CCR} + RWA_{OR} \tag{9.6}$$

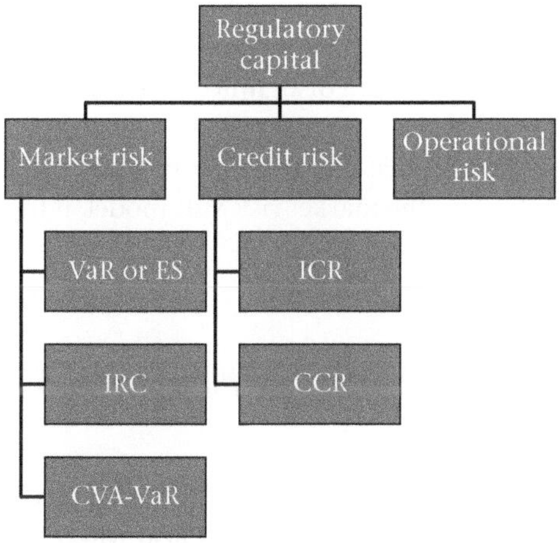

Figure 9.1 Illustration of regulatory capital charge calculation

There is sometimes confusion as to the nature of the IRC and CVA capital charge, as they are easily mistaken as credit risk charges. The reason is that they are charges imposed on the market risk (i.e., on the change of the price) of credit-related products, but it is important to realise that they are, indeed, market risk charges. We will see this in more detail in the explanation of each of them.

In this section we are going to explain to a varying level of depth each of them, with special focus on those that relate to OTC derivatives. As said, a full explanation of all of them will require a whole book by itself, and is beyond the scope of this chapter.

In general, Basel tends to set up at least two levels of rules for each of the charges: the "standard" rules and the "advanced" ones. The idea is that banks that have good models to measure risk should use the advanced frameworks. Those banks that do not have this capability can use the standard rules, which can have different versions and are intended to be easy and mechanical in nature. Standard rules are supposed to be conservative, and hence should always deliver higher capital requirements compared to the advanced ones. In this way, banks are supposed to have a regulatory-driven incentive to build good risk models. For a model to be part of an advanced calculator, it needs to be approved by its regulator.

9.2.2 VaR (or ES)

As said, the VaR capital charge is expected to be replaced soon. Let's look first into the existing calculation at the time of this book being written, and let's go through the expected changes.

VaR

Under the advanced IMA framework, the RWA from the VaR calculation is given by

$$RWA_{VaR} = 12.5 \cdot (3 + x + y) \cdot (\mathrm{VaR}^{bank}_{99\%,10d} + \mathrm{sVaR}^{bank}_{99\%,10d}) \tag{9.7}$$

where x is given by the model backtest and ranges from 0 to 1, depending on the performance[7] (see Chapter 17), y is an add-on that national regulators can impose at their discretion, VaR is the bank's 10-day 99% Value-at-Risk metric, and sVaR is the stress VaR, the VaR calculation under a stressed model calibration. Also, some regulators add an additional component called Risks-not-in-VaR (RniV), which aims at accounting for the market risks which are not captured in the VaR models, because of either inherent limitations in the models (e.g., approximations in the methodology) or because the systems cannot deal with the methodology requirements (e.g., certain sensitivities are not being fed into the system for some reason).

The calibration of sVaR will be done to a period of significant stress to the bank's trading book, and will be supervised by the national regulators.

The VaR model used for this calculation must use, at least, one year of historical data.

If a bank does not have IMA approval for the market risk VaR model, it must use the tabulated standardised rules to calculate RWA_{VaR}.

Expected changes

Subject to the final decision in this area by the Basel Committee [15], the following changes may happen to the market risk VaR capital calculation.

- **New Risk Metric:** The VaR risk metric at 99% confidence level is replaced by the Expected Shortfall (ES)[8] at 97.5%. This will provide a measure of the tail risk, and also will make the risk metric coherent.[9] Both numbers should provide a similar number for the level of risk in the absence of high or low tail risk.

- **Only Stressed Calibration:** The sum of the standard plus stress VaR is replaced by only one ES number that must be calibrated to stressed market conditions.
- **Several Liquidity Horizons:** The 10-day time horizon of the VaR calculation is supposed to represent the time it would take an institutions to rehedge or exit an existing position. Basel estimates this "10-day" assumption to be unrealistic as during the 2008 market stress it was considerably longer in many cases. Consequently it creates five categories of liquidity horizons: 10, 20, 60, 120, and 250 days. The risk factors are split into 24 categories so that each of them is linked to one of those liquidity horizons for the ES calculation. This mapping is provided by the Committee.
- **Revised Standardized Method:** The calculation still has two versions, the standardised and the advanced IMA. However, the standardised method is revised and becomes more risk sensitive compared to the previous one.
- **Mandatory Standardised Calculation:** IMA approved institutions will also have to do the standardised calculation in parallel with the advanced one. Should the IMA models fall into the "red" category,[10] the bank must switch off its IMA capital calculation and swap it to the standardised calculation.
- **Mandatory Disclosure:** Public disclosure of the standardised ES risk charge is mandatory, on a desk-by-desk level.
- **IMA Approval:** The IMA approval process becomes more rigorous. Hedging and diversification benefits must be based on empirical evidence during periods of stress.

9.2.3 IRC

As explained in Section 9.1.3, the Incremental Risk Charge (IRC) aims at capturing the credit related losses, both for general products and for securitisation correlation-based products,[11] with a 99.9% confidence and a one-year time horizon. Once that number is computed, then the IRC's RWA number is:[12]

$$RWA_{IRC} = 12.5 \cdot (\mathrm{VaR}^{irc}_{99.9\%,1yr} + \mathrm{VaR}^{crm}_{99.9\%,1yr}), \tag{9.8}$$

with an 8% floor in the CRM part of the calculation.

As previously indicated, the first thing to be noted is that IRC is credit related, but that it is a market risk charge. Credit risk refers to the potential loss that a bank may have as a result of one of its *direct* counterparties defaulting; in other words, the risk of a counterparty going into financial liquidation when it owes money to the bank. By contrast, market risk deals with the potential loss that a bank's position may incur as a result of the *market prices moving* against the bank's book, without considering defaults from direct counterparties. Often this is expressed by saying that IRC captures the rating migration risk a bank has. This credit migration includes both deterioration of the credit quality of individual names and defaults.

The Basel Committee decided to add this risk number to the capital calculation in 2009 saying that

> in light of the recent credit market turmoil where a number of major banking organizations have experienced large losses, most of which were sustained in the bank's trading books. Most of those losses were not captured in the 99% 10-day VaR. Since the losses have not arisen from actual defaults, but rather from credit migrations combined with widening of credit spreads and the loss of liquidity, applying an incremental risk charge covering default risk only would not appear adequate [6].

There are a number of reasons why those risks do not appear in the typical market risk models. First of all, the current market risk models emphasise the modelling of short-term (10-day) P&L volatility and use relatively short time series (as short as 1 year) for this. In addition to this, these models are often 1-day

VaR models that are then extrapolated to a 10-day time horizon. As a result, these models are not built to capture large cumulative price moves over periods of several weeks or months. Also, those models have survival information bias in them; by this is meant that, should a company default, that information is usually removed from the historical data and so the historical information in which market risk models are based tends to be skewed. Finally, current VaR techniques do not account for the potential liquidity problems that can appear in stressed markets.

So, on top of the credit events modelling and the impact on the value of a bank's trading book, the guidelines provided by Basel make a lot of emphasis on the liquidity risk. They say, referring to the 2008 events, that:

> Banks experienced significant illiquidity in a wide range of credit products held in the trading book... Under these circumstances, liquidity in many parts of the securitization markets dried up, forcing banks to retain exposures in securitization pipelines for prolonged periods of time. The Committee therefore expects firms to pay particular attention to the appropriate liquidity horizon assumptions within their IRC models [6].

The Committee recognises that an extra component of credit risk comes from the default correlation, and so it also makes specific mention of correlation based products like CDOs or credit baskets, saying that "a bank may incorporate its correlation trading portfolio in an internally developed approach that adequately captures not only incremental default and migration risks, but all price risks" [8]. This is the Comprehensive Risk Measure (CRM).

Banks under the advanced IMA framework for market risk calculations are required to develop internal models both for IRC and CRM and are subject to approval by the local regulators. Those models can assume a constant balance of risk: "banks are assumed to rebalance their trading positions over the 1-year time horizon in a manner that maintains the initial risk level" [6].

9.2.4 Counterparty credit risk

The Counterparty Credit Risk (CCR) capital charge tries to capture the default risk embedded in portfolios of financial derivatives. It is first calculated per netting set (NS), and then it is added for the whole portfolio

$$RWA_{CCR} = \sum_{NS} RW_{NS} \times EaD_{NS} \tag{9.9}$$

where RW is the "Risk Weight" and EaD is the "Exposure at Default".

This is, arguably, the charge that is most complex to compute.[13] Basel has a long and elaborate set of rules that provide an RW and EaD for each type of product, netting set, and counterparty, as we are going to see here.

Wrong Way Risk (WWR)[14] can be central to the estimation of Counterparty Credit Risk for derivatives. Basel recognises that measuring WWR is not easy and, in fact, when Basel II was enforced, there was very little clarity as to how to model it. For this reason, Basel assumes that the exposure calculations contain no right or wrong way risk in them and so the exposure is increased, post-calculation, with a multiplier that accounts for that WWR (typically referred to as α). In parallel to this, banks are asked to have a specific process to control wrong way risk.

Similarly to other regulatory capital charges, CCR has a standard approach that needs to be used when the bank does not have the capability to measure the different components of CCR with the complexity it needs.

This approach is based on a number of standard rules that are intendedly capital penalising, and so banks should have an economic incentive to model risk properly.

The CCR charge is based on the following components:

- **Exposure at Default (EaD):** A measurement of the amount that a bank will be exposed to lose in the event of a counterparty defaulting.
- **Probability of Default (PD):** The well known measure of the probability that a counterparty has to default in the next 12 months.
- **Loss Given Default (LGD):** The percentage of the exposure that is lost (i.e., not recovered) in a default event.
- **Maturity Adjustment (MA):** An adjustment to the perceived riskiness when considering the time to maturity of the netting set.

To avoid the standardised CCR calculation, banks must comply with the Internal Ratings Approach (IRB). In the advanced version of it, the calculation is based on the bank's own estimations of EaD, PD, and LGD. Then the maturity adjustment (MA) is added to the calculation as prescribed. As with any other advanced capital framework, those models are subject to regulatory approval.

The different frameworks in operation are shown in the following table.

Regulatory status	PD	LGD	EaD
Standardised	External rating	n/a	SA-CCR
Foundation IRB	Internal models	Prescribed	SA-CCR
Advanced IRB, no IMM	Internal models	Internal models	SA-CCR
Advanced IRB, IMM	Internal models	Internal models	IMM

In Chapter 7 we saw quite extensively how to calculate PDs and LGDs. Hence here we are going to focus only on how to calculate the regulatory EaDs.

The landscape of the EaD calculation changed only a few months before this book went to press. Before, we had three available methods: the Current Exposure Method (CEM), the Standarised Method (SM), and the most advanced Internal Models Method (IMM). The CEM and SM are now disappearing, being replaced by a single Standardised Approach for measuring Counterparty Credit Risk exposures (SA-CCR).[15] This SA-CCR tries to overcome some of the shortcomings of the CEM and SM approaches. The new SA-CCR is scheduled to take effect on 1 January 2017. An existing hybrid "IMM shortcut" method also disappears on that date.

SA-CCR

For each netting set, the Standardised Approach for measuring Counterparty Credit Risk exposures is based on

$$EaD_{NS} = \alpha(RC_{NS} + PFE_{NS}) \tag{9.10}$$

where

- $\alpha = 1.4$.
- RC, the Replacement Cost, represents the loss that a bank would suffer if a counterparty defaults "today".

- *PFE* represents the Potential Future Exposure that a counterparty may have during the next one-year period.

RC: The Replacement Cost is calculated differently for margined and unmargined netting sets.[16]

For *unmargined* netting sets,

$$RC = \max(V - C, 0) \tag{9.11}$$

where V is today's price of the netting set and C is the value of the collateral held (as initial margin) after haircut adjustments. In this case, the haircut reflects the change in value that the collateral may suffer during a one-year period.

For *margined* netting sets,

$$RC = \max(V - C, Th + MTA - NICA, 0) \tag{9.12}$$

where V and C are the same as before but with a haircut that reflects the MPR[17] of the netting set, Th is the netting set threshold, MTA is the minimum transfer amount of the netting set, and $NICA$ represents any collateral, segregated or unsegregated, that has been received, less the unsegregated collateral that has been posted.

PFE: To calculate the *PFE* term in Equation 9.10, the netting set is split into asset classes (a), so that

$$PFE = mult \cdot AddOn^{Aggr} \tag{9.13}$$

$$AddOn^{Aggr} = \sum_a AddOn^a \tag{9.14}$$

The asset classes are Interest Rates (IR), Foreign Exchange (FX), Equity (Eq) & Credit (Cr), and Commodities (Co). Additionally, "basis"[18] and volatility trades are treated as a separate asset class. The *mult* term is a number that follows a prescribed formula, that depends on V, C, and $AddOn^{Aggr}$, and that takes into account over-collateralisation.

It can be already appreciated that this approach does not allow for any offsetting between asset classes.

The calculation of each $AddOn^a$ is further decomposed into groups of "Hedging Sets". There is full risk offsetting within each hedging set, and sometimes there is some offsetting between them, within an asset class.

In the case of IR, each currency is a hedging set. In the case of FX, each currency par is also a hedging set. Equity and Credit each forms a hedging set too. Finally, in the commodity space, energy, metals, agricultural and other each form a hedging set. Within each hedging set, long and short positions offset risk with each other perfectly.

The IR calculation is divided into three tenor buckets, defined by the trade maturity being < 1 year, between 1 and 5 years and > 5 years.

Each asset class has its own furmulae for the calculation. Going into the details of each of them is beyond the scope of this chapter, but let's say that, *loosely* speaking for general illustrative purposes, the add-on in each hedging set is given by a formula along the lines of

$$AddOn^a \sim SF^a \cdot EN^a \tag{9.15}$$

The Supervisory Factor *SF* is a number attached to each hedging set type, tabulated by Basel, and that tries to assess the general overall risk size of each asset class and hedging set (e.g., different riskiness of a AAA credit derivative vs. a BBB one, of an electricity one vs. an agricultural one).

The Effective Notional *EN* is given by a specific formula in each asset class, which depends on a regulatory-prescribed delta (δ), a maturity-adjusted notional of each trade (d), a maturity factor (MF) that accounts for either the MPR in margined transactions or the netting set's maturity in unmargined ones, and a correlation factor (ρ) that allows for some inter-hedging set offsetting.

Very loosely speaking, so the reader can have a sense of how those parameters work, the Effective Notional follows a formula along the lines of

$$EN \sim \sum_i \delta_i \cdot d_i \cdot MF_i \tag{9.16}$$

where the index i runs through the trades of each hedging set. The δ_i changes in sign to reflect the direction (i.e., long vs. short) of the trade. In the case of IR, Equation 9.16 is calculated per time bucket and then aggregated using a prescribed formula. In the case of Eq & Cr and Co, Equation 9.16 is also further decomposed with another prescribed formula to account for some inter-hedging set risk offsetting, via the correlation ρ.

The following table summarises some key features of the SA-CCR approach.

Asset class	**Hedging sets**	**Risk offsetting**
IR	Each currency	Partial between time buckets in each currency
FX	Each currency pair	
Eq & Cr	Eq, Cr	Partial between hedging sets
Co	Energy, metals, agricultural, other	Partial between hedging sets

Internal models methods

For each netting set, the RWA for CCR is given by

$$RWA_{CCR} = 12.5 \times EaD \times K(PD, LGD, MA) \tag{9.17}$$

Or, in other words, relating this to Equation 9.9, the Risk Weight is given by

$$RW = 12.5 \times K(PD, LGD, MA) \tag{9.18}$$

For illustrative purposes, things become somewhat simpler if we decomposed K so that

$$K(PD, LGD, MA) = f_{PD} \times LGD \times MA \tag{9.19}$$

or

$$RWA_{CCR} = 12.5 \times EaD \times f_{PD} \times LGD \times MA \tag{9.20}$$

In this equation, f_{PD} is a function that contains the information of the default probability of the counterparty, explained in more detail later. The units of this are

- EaD in \$ (in general, the reporting currency of the bank)
- f_{PD} in years^{-1}
- LGD is unit-less
- MA in years

The Exposure at Default (EaD): The Exposure at Default tries to measure how much a bank can be owed in the case of a default by the counterparty at stake. Basel mainly focusses on

1. Long Settlement Transactions, commonly known as Over-the-Counter derivatives, or OTCs,
2. Securities Financing Transactions (SFTs), commonly known as repos, equity borrowing and lending.

We now need to learn a few new concepts and terminologies that Basel introduces. This is because Basel bases the calculation of EaD on what the industry usually calls *EPE profiles*, but we need to do some transformations on them to come up with a number of regulatory exposure metrics.

- **Expected Exposure** ($EE_{reg,t}$): is what we have called in this book EPE. We are renaming it now to use the same regulatory terminology Basel uses. As the reader knows, this is a time profile.
- **Effective Expected Exposure** ($EEE_{reg,t}$): is the non-decreasing EE_{reg}. This is also a profile.
- **Effective Expected Positive Exposure** ($EEPE_{reg}$): is the weighted average over time of EEE over the first year.[19] This is a number.
- **Expected Positive Exposure** (EPE_{reg}): is the weighted average of (EE_{reg}).[20]

An example that illustrates these four definitions can be seen in Figure 9.2.

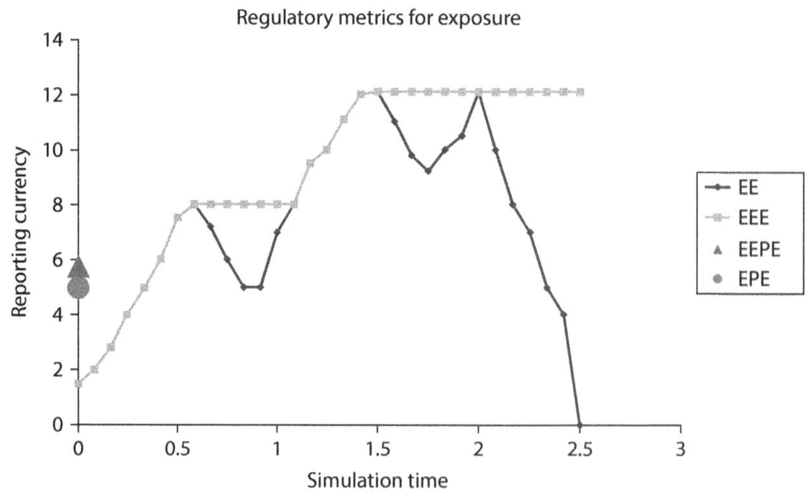

Figure 9.2 Illustration of the Basel definitions of EE_{reg}, EEE_{reg}, $EEPE_{reg}$ and EPE_{reg}

With those definitions in mind, EaD is defined as

$$EaD = \alpha \times EEPE_{reg}, \tag{9.21}$$

where the default value for α is 1.4.

A few comments are needed at this stage.

- The financial reason to "*effectivise*" the EE_{reg} into a EEE_{reg} profile is to account for roll-over risk. The idea is that exposures tend to decrease because trades approach maturity or expiry. The trading book is managed on a constant basis and, so, we could expect that as trades approach maturity or expiry other trades will be added to the books. As a result, actual exposures in the future may not decrease over time as the models predict "today". The way Basel decided to account for this is by considering, for capital calculations, that the exposure measurement over time cannot decrease.
- The sense of using a one-year time average of EEE_{reg} to come up with $EEPE_{reg}$ is that we are trying to measure default risk at one-year, and we need a single dollar-number for EaD, so a time-weighted average over one year is taken.
- The idea behind α is to capture missing risk components in the models behind these calculations. For example, the default model behind this CCR charge does not account for low granularity of counterparties.[21] Also, the models do not generally account for wrong way risk or institution-specific risks. As a result, $EEPE_{reg}$ is "bumped up" by α. This number can be increased from 1.4 by regulators if it is found appropriate and, according to Basel's text, banks can apply for a lower α, with a floor at 1.2. A bank can do this if it builds an appropriate model to measure α.
- $EEPE_{reg}$ must be calculated at the netting set level. Importantly, those trades that do not belong to any netting set will constitute a netting set by themselves in regards to this calculation. Often, these trades are called *gross* trades.
- For collateralised counterparties, the collateral must be modelled dynamically in the calculation of EE_{reg}. This model must include asymmetry in the margin agreements, frequency of margin calls, minimum transfer amount, thresholds, and margin period of risk.
- EE_{reg} must be backtested historically using data relevant for one business cycle.
- If EE_{reg} are historically calibrated, they must use at least three years of data.
- The calculation of EE_{reg} must be independent of any discounts.

The Default Probability Function f_{PD}: The idea behind the PD function is that it should capture the unexpected loss that the bank can have at a 99.9% macroeconomic confidence level. Let's expand on this.

The IRB approach is based on attaching each counterparty to a rating band (e.g., AAA, AA, A, BBB, BB, etc.), where each band has an expected one-year probability of default (PD).

Expected and unexpected loss: The starting point is a known one-year through-the-cycle PD for a rating band. By "through-the-cycle" is meant an average long-run PD. This is what we usually mean when we say "a BB company has a default probability of 1%": it is a time-averaged, expected, PD. However, the actual PD on a given year, the so-called "point-in-time" PD, will be different each year, oscillating around the through-the-cycle PD, typically driven by economic conditions.[22] Let's refer to the through-the-cycle probability of default as $\overline{PD}$ and to the "point-in-time" probability of default as PD_t.

When a default occurs, the loss may or may not be 100% of what it is owed. As already said, the percentage of the loss is the Loss Given Default (LGD). Often, this is also referred to as the recovery rate RR, where $RR = LGD - 1$.

Given a netting set with a counterparty in a rating band, we can define Expected Loss (EL) per unit of exposure as

$$EL = \overline{PD} \cdot LGD, \tag{9.22}$$

and the Unexpected Loss as the difference between the point-in-time loss and the EL:[23]

$$UL_t = PD_t \cdot LGD - \overline{PD} \cdot LGD. \tag{9.23}$$

So, the function that we are looking for is

$$f_{PD} = PD_t - \overline{PD}. \tag{9.24}$$

Figure 9.3 illustrates how this UL can change over time. Figure 9.4 illustrates the EL and the UL, in a given point in time, in an illustrative density probability function of losses.

The Basel Committee decided to use the ASRF model to calculate PD_t. We have said in Section 7.6.3 that, in this framework, PD_t is given by

$$PD_t = \phi\left(\frac{\Phi^{-1}(\overline{PD}) - \rho X}{\sqrt{1-\rho^2}}\right) \tag{9.25}$$

and f_{PD} is given by

$$f_{PD} = \phi\left(\frac{\Phi^{-1}(\overline{PD}) + \rho\Phi^{-1}(0.999)}{\sqrt{1-\rho^2}}\right) - \overline{PD}. \tag{9.26}$$

In this way, the problem is now reduced to how to estimate $\overline{PD}$ and LGD for a counterparty. The Basel Committee gives directions as to how to model them, as was explained in Chapter 7.

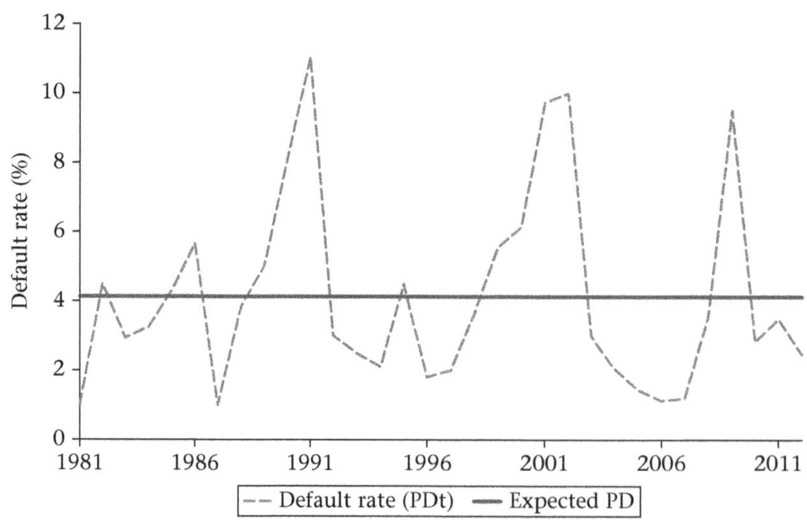

Figure 9.3 Illustrative default rate profile and expected PD. The UL is the difference between them

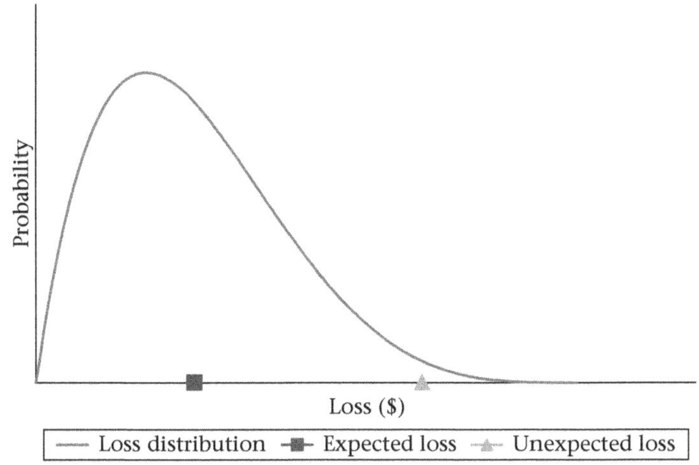

Figure 9.4 Illustration of expected and unexpected loss in a probability density graph of losses

For illustrative purposes, let's see what the size is of f_{PD}. That is, for a given counterparty with a given $\overline{PD}$, what is the capital that banks are required to hold to account for unexpected losses?

The following table shows how both $\overline{PD}$ and PD_t compare with each other using this regulatory model.[24] The "Multiplier" column shows how much PD_t increases over $\overline{PD}$. It can be seen how this multiplier goes to up to 50 for AAA rated counterparties, that is, for a trade with a AAA counterparty, banks are required to keep "aside" 50 times its expected loss as capital.

Credit rating	$\overline{PD}$	PD_t	Multiplier
AAA	0.02%	1.00%	50
AA	0.03%	1.38%	46
A	0.06%	2.35%	39
BBB	0.22%	5.90%	27
BB	1.10%	14.67%	13
B	5.58%	30.06%	5
CCC	28.23%	70.09%	2.5

Correlation fine tuning: The Basel Committee decided to give an explicit dependency between the correlation factor in Equation 9.26 and the counterparty $\overline{PD}$ and size. The Committee highlighted that, "based on both empirical evidence and intuition", asset correlations decrease with increasing PDs, and increase with firm size. So, the Committee proposed the following formulas for the correlation factor:[25]

$$\rho^2(PD) = 0.12\frac{1-e^{-50PD}}{1-e^{-50}} + 0.24\left(1-\frac{1-e^{-50PD}}{1-e^{-50}}\right) - Adj(S) \tag{9.27}$$

$$Adj(S) = 0.04\left(1-\frac{S-5}{45}\right) \tag{9.28}$$

where S is the company annual sales in million of Euros, floored at zero and capped at 0.04.

The idea behind this is that, loosely speaking, the credit standing of sound companies (low PD) tend to be more correlated to the economic environment than that of weak companies (high PD).

Default probabilities: We have seen how one of the key inputs in the calculation of regulatory capital is $\overline{PD}$. One of the bases of the IRB approach is that counterparties are assigned to a credit rating band, each of which has attached a $\overline{PD}$, and that banks can estimate these default probabilities themselves. It states that these default probabilities must be "long-run" default probabilities. Basel specifies three generic methods to estimate $\overline{PD}$, or a combination of them:

1. A bank can use internal data on the history of defaults for the estimation of long-run default probabilities, and calculate statistics on it. Given the limited default information available, institutions can use pooled data across institutions.
2. Banks can use external credit rating institutions (typically Standard & Poor's, Fitch or Moody's) for the estimations of $\overline{PD}$. The criteria must be oriented to the risk of the borrower and not reflect transaction characteristics.
3. Institutions can use default prediction models, where details of each company are used to some level, and then average default probability estimates. These models need to meet certain minimum standards.

The minimum length of underlying data for this analysis is five years, but if more relevant data is available, it must be used. Also, $\overline{PD}$ is floored at 0.03% for banks and corporates.[26] Finally, the pool of data used in the analysis must be representative of the bank's portfolio.

In practice, approaches 1 and 2, or a combination of both, are most popular, as they tend to be the easiest and, arguably, the effort required by default prediction models may not be worth the added value they deliver in this context.

As already indicated in Chapter 7, one of the most important challenges of computing $\overline{PD}$ is the lack of available data, as defaults are scarce, especially for high credit rating bands. For example, it is hard to find any example of a company that was AAA or AA and defaulted within one year. For this reason, statistical models for the low rating bands are fairly easy (e.g., the average of defaults over a long period of time is usually accepted by regulators), but those models for high rating are more difficult. A standard set of models for this later problem are the so-called "Low Default Portfolio" models. They were explained in Section 7.2.

The Loss Given Default: In Basel's regulatory CCR model, the counterparty PD is stressed to a 99.9% worst case confidence level, but it does not stress the LGD. Banks can build internal models for LGDs with the only requirement being that the LGD used for the capital calculation must be a representative LGD during down-phases in the economic business cycles.

As a summary of the explanations on LGD in Chapter 7, let's remember that

- LGD is strongly dependent on the business cycle; LGD tends to be higher in economic downturns.
- LGD for senior debt tends to be lower than for junior debt.
- There seems to be a dependency between LGD and the sector in which the corporate operates. Some sectors tend to default with very tangible assets that maintain their value after default, like telecommunications, while other sectors tend to default with strong intangible assets like goodwill, and so LGD tends to be higher.
- Another dependency in LGD comes from legal jurisdictions, as regulatory frameworks in the event of default can influence the final LGD.

- There is no evidence of dependency of LGD on the credit rating of a defaulting name some time before the default.[27]

The reader can find details on this topic in references [3, 11, 16, 17, 36, 37, 41].

The maturity adjustment: The calculations of EaD, f_{PD} and LGD are all based on a one-year time horizon, but the Basel Committee thought that netting sets with longer maturities carry more risk due to ratings migration and other effects, so they came up with a maturity adjustment term MA. That adjustment is

$$MA = \frac{1 + (M - 2.5) \cdot b(\overline{PD})}{1 - 1.5 \cdot b(\overline{PD})} \tag{9.29}$$

$$b(\overline{PD}) = \left[0.11852 - 0.05478 \ln(\overline{PD})\right]^2 \tag{9.30}$$

where M is the netting set maturity in years. MA is capped at 5 and floored at 1.

The idea behind this formula was somehow not really explained in detail by the Committee. It is the outcome of the application of a "specific... credit risk model... in a Basel consistent way". The idea behind it is that "both intuition and empirical evidence indicate that long-term credits are riskier than short-term credits.... Maturity adjustments can be interpreted as anticipations of additional capital requirements due to downgrades". The Committee says that "intuition tells that low PD borrowers have, so to speak, more potential and more room for [credit rating] down-gradings than high PD borrowers. Consistent with this consideration, the Basel maturity adjustments are a function of both maturity and PD, and they are higher (in relative terms) for low than for high PD borrowers" [4].

Basel II

In order to be IMM Basel II compliant with regard to Counterparty Credit Risk, on top of these calculations banks need to meet some procedural minimum requirements. This includes two processes that can be highly quantitative, so they will be mentioned in this book: stress testing and wrong way risk.

Stress testing: According to Basel II, banks must have in place stress and scenario testing frameworks to identify possible future events that could have a negative impact on the credit exposures to counterparties, and assess the bank's ability to withstand such stresses. Examples of these scenarios are economic or industry downturns, market place events, or decreased liquidity conditions.

Wrong way risk: Basel differentiates between two types of wrong way risk (WWR): specific and generic. Specific WWR exists when a trade's underlying is completely dependent on the trade's counterparty. An example is when a bank sells put options on its own stock, or in a subsidiary's stock: when the bank defaults, the value of the stock will be zero, and so the value of the option will be the maximum possible. However, general WWR appears when the default probability of the counterparty is related to the trade exposure but only statistically, not absolutely. An example is when a banks sells a put option on the stock of another bank that shares its macroeconomic environment; for example, if Bank of America sells a put option on Morgan Stanley stock, the stock prices of Morgan Stanley will be highly influenced by the event of Bank of America defaulting, though the dependency is not absolute. In quantitative terms, we can say that specific WWR means that the correlation between the counterparty and the exposures are 100%, but in general WWR that correlation is smaller than 100%.

Basel does not require banks to model general WWR as the parameter α is supposed to account for it, but it requires that trades with specific WWR are "identified, monitored and controlled".

Basel III

Basel III brought some extra quantitative requirements to the calculation of the CCR capital charge. Those include:

Stress testing: The requirements for the Basel II Stress Testing framework become much more granular regarding the nature of the scenarios, factors to consider, risk aggregation, and internal procedures.

Wrong way risk: Trades with specific WWR, which now specifically include trades where there is a legal connection between the counterparty and the trade's reference entity, will not be included in the same netting set as other transactions with the same counterparty. The EE_{reg} will be set to the full loss that the trade will have in the event of a jump-to-default by the counterparty and an $\alpha = 1$. That is, EaD is equal to 100% of notional. Furthermore, for the RWA calculation, LGD will be set to 100%.

Stress EEPE: In parallel to the stress testing just explained, a stress EEPE calculation needs to be done: every $EE_{reg,t}$ profile must be calculated twice: the standard calculation and another calculation where the diffusion models have been calibrated to the most relevant credit-stressed period. By this is meant that the bank must determine a three-year period in the past with stressed credit default spreads for its counterparties and calibrate *all* the models in that period. The EEPE that feeds into the EaD calculation will be the one that delivers the highest EaD on a total portfolio level.[28]

Correlation factor: Basel III decided to increase the correlation factor ρ^2 in Equation 9.27 by a factor of 1.25, for regulated financial institutions with total assets greater than US$100 billion, and to all unregulated financial institutions.

Margin Period of Risk: Under Basel II, the floors for the Margin Period of Risk (MPR) are ten days for OTCs and five days for SFTs. These floors are now increased subject to the following criteria:

- For daily remargining, the MPR for OTCs and repos remains at ten and five days respectively.
- The floor is doubled for any netting set with more than 5,000 trades.
- The floor is also doubled for a netting set that contains illiquid collateral or "hard to replace" OTCs.[29]
- Banks must consider "whether trades or securities it holds as collateral are concentrated".
- If there has been any margin dispute in the last two quarters that have lasted longer than the MPR, then the MPR is multiplied by two.[30]
- The floors are thought for daily remargining. If remargining happens every N days, and if the corresponding floor for daily remargining is F days, then $\text{MPR} = F + N - 1$.

Central counterparties: In Basel II, transactions that went through a Central Counterparty (CCP) had no CCR capital charge. That is not the case with Basel III. EaD should be calculated using the methodologies as if they were not cleared through a CCP, leaving a risk weight of 2% for its RWA calculation.

9.2.5 CVA VaR

The CVA capital charge aims at capturing the VaR coming from CVA at 99% confidence and a ten-day time horizon.

There are two versions of this charge, the standardised and the advanced approach. For a bank to calculate this charge with the advanced approach, it must have IMM and IMA approved models for counterparty credit risk and market risk, respectively.

Standardised CVA-VaR

The standard RWA for CVA is given by

$$RWA_{CVA}^{stnrd} = 12.5 \cdot 2.33 \cdot \sqrt{h} \cdot \sqrt{A+B}$$

$$A = \left(\sum_i 0.5\, w_i \left(M_i \cdot EaD_i^{tot} - M_i^{hedge} \cdot B_i\right) - \sum_{ind} w_{ind} \cdot M_{ind} \cdot B_{ind} \right)^2$$

$$B = \sum_i 0.75\, w_i^2 \left(M_i \cdot EaD_i^{tot} - M_i^{hedge} \cdot B_i\right)^2 \tag{9.31}$$

where

- $h = 1$ (1 year).
- w_i is a default probability weight, given by the counterparty credit rating and tabulated values. w_i ranges from 0.7% for AAA entities to 10% for CCC.
- EaD_i^{tot} is the exposure of counterpaty i, summing across all netting sets and including collateral, as per the exposure model used in the CCR charge.[31]
- B_i is the notional of purchased CDS referencing the counterparty i, used to hedge CVA.
- B_{ind} is the notional of the credit protection bought through credit indices.
- w_{ind} is the weight applicable to index hedges as per a mapping table.
- M_i is the effective maturity of the book of trades with counterparty i.
- M_i^{hedge} is the maturity of the hedging instrument with notional B_i.
- M^{ind} is the maturity of the index hedge "*ind*".

This calculation is very mechanical: we just have to apply Equation 9.31. More details of this calculation can be found in the Basel III document [59].

Advanced CVA-VaR

Even though this is called an "advanced" approach, the Basel Committee has come up with a very prescriptive formula to compute capital with it, in contrast to other parts of the advanced capital calculation where it gives some degree of freedom to the bank, subject to regulatory approval.

First, the Committee defines regulatory CVA as

$$CVA_{reg} = LGD_{mkt} \cdot \sum_{i=1}^{N} (S_i^{marg})^+ \cdot DEE_i^{av} \tag{9.32}$$

where

- LGD_{mkt} is the market implied LGD.[32]
- The index i counts through the time buckets used in the CVA calculation and where $i = 0$ represents the calculation day.
- $(S_i^{marg})^+$ is a market-implied simplified marginal survival probability for time bucket i, floored at zero,[33] given by[34]

$$(S_i^{marg})^+ = \left(\exp\left(-\frac{s_{i-1} \cdot t_{i-1}}{LGD_{mkt}}\right) - \exp\left(-\frac{s_i \cdot t_i}{LGD_{mkt}}\right) \right)^+ \tag{9.33}$$

where s_i is the credit spread at t_i.

- DEE_i^{av} is the average of the discounted Expected Exposure between t_{i-1} and t_i:

$$DEE_i^{av} = \frac{EE_{i-1} \cdot D_{i-1} + EE_i \cdot D_i}{2} \tag{9.34}$$

where EE_i is the regulatory Expected Exposure[35] and D_i is the default risk-free discount factor, for time point t_i.

Banks must calculate the ten-day 99% VaR following the CVA_{reg} definition in Equation 9.32. If the bank's IMA VaR model uses a full revaluation model, then Equation 9.32 must be used for it. If it uses credit spread sensitivities, then those sensitivities must be calculated from that equation. That is, the VaR model must use Equation 9.32 for any CVA market risk calculation.

The Basel III document provides formulas for the credit spread sensitivities for specific tenors t_i and for parallel shifts [59], and banks are required to calculate from Equation 9.32 any other sensitivity needed for their approved VaR models. For example, if the bank uses a one-factor model for credit spreads, then the regulatory CS01 to be applied to CVA is

$$CS01_{reg} = 0.0001 \cdot \sum_i \left(t_i \cdot \exp\left(-\frac{s_i \cdot t_i}{LGD_{mkt}}\right) - t_{i-1} \cdot \exp\left(-\frac{s_{i-1} \cdot t_{i-1}}{LGD_{mkt}}\right)\right) \cdot DEE_i^{av} \tag{9.35}$$

Similarly to the VaR charge, banks are also required to compute a stress VaR for CVA using the stress VaR computation environment *and*, in Equation 9.34, the stress EE as described in Section 9.2.4.

So, putting all this together, the RWA calculation is

$$RWA_{CVA} = 12.5 \cdot (3 + x + y) \cdot (\text{VaR}^{cva}_{99\%,10d} + \text{sVaR}^{cva}_{99\%,10d}). \tag{9.36}$$

These VaR calculations will be applied to netting sets with CVA, for all OTC derivatives in the bank's book with the *eligible* CVA hedges. Those eligible hedges are CDSs traded and managed with the only intent to hedge CVA.[36]

Eligible hedges

It is important to note that, in the Basel accord, only credit related hedges are recognised in the CVA regulatory capital calculation. That is, market risk hedges, like interest rate swaps or FX forwards, that neutralise the non-credit side of the CVA volatility and do not provoke any capital offsetting. In fact, they could be increasing capital as they will be seen as "naked" positions in the Market Risk VaR calculation. For example, Deutsche Bank reported a € 94 million loss in 2013 as a result of this hedging mismatch [30].

Also, not all credit hedging instruments are eligible for CVA capital relief. The accord states that only "single-name CDSs, single-name contingent CDSs, other equivalent hedging instruments referencing the counterparty directly, and index CDSs" are eligible.

EU vs. US interpretations

There has been some interesting differences in the interpretation of this capital charge in the European Union and the United States.

In the EU, the CVA-VaR capital has some exceptions (i.e., does not need to be calculated) that relate to counterparties that are sovereign, pension funds, and corporates [56].

The US did not follow with those exemptions [20]. Also, it corrected the CVA's market risk hedges limitation of the Basel approach by allowing the non-credit CVA hedging position to not have any market risk capital charge. Other countries like Canada followed the US version [27].

9.2.6 Issuer credit risk

This book is focused on financial derivatives, but let's overview the credit capital calculation for actual debt products like loans, bonds, credit revolver facilities, etc., the so-called Issuer Credit Risk (ICR), for the sake of completeness.

Similarly to CCR, the ICR charge is based on

$$RWA_{ICR} = \sum_i RW_i \times EaD_i \tag{9.37}$$

where i goes through all the positions with issuer risk that the bank has. The Risk Weight (RW) part of the calculation is computed in the same way as the CCR case, already explained. But the EaD is calculated following the equation

$$EaD = \text{Current Exposure} + \text{Accrued Interests} + \text{Undrawn Amount} \times CCF \tag{9.38}$$

The Current Exposure is the principal owed to us at the time of the calculation. For example, if the position at stake is a loan that had an original principal of, say, \$1 million, but \$200,000 have been paid, then the Current Exposure is \$800,000.

The Accrued Interest is the maximum interest, coupon payments, and principal that could be lost in the event of a default during one coupon period plus the time it could take to declare an exposure at default. For example, if we have monthly coupons in a loan, and if our internal policy sets a record as non-accrual, or includes it in a watch list, as soon as a payment has been missed for more than 30 days, then we would calculate the accrued interests during $30 + 30 = 60$ days.

In revolving facilities, the Undrawn Amount is the maximum amount that a client could withdraw from the credit facility in the run to default. The Credit Conversion Factor CCF is a number that typically ranges from 30 to 75%, the latter being the foundation approach for revolving facilities. In loans and bonds, this term is zero.

9.2.7 Operational risk

Basel defines operation risk as "the risk of loss resulting from inadequate or failed internal processes, people and systems or from external events. This definition includes legal risk but excludes strategic and reputational risk". Examples of materialisation of this risk are internal or external fraud (deliberately mismarking of positions, rogue trading, theft), employee litigations, damage to physical assets, business disruptions, systems failures and data errors.

Basel has defined three approaches to calculating this capital charge. The Basic Indicator Approach and the Standarised Approach are very simple and set the charge as a percentage of the positive annual gross income, averaged over the last three years. In the case of the Basic Indicator Approach that percentage is 15%, in the case of the Standarised Approach it is calculated per business line with a different percentage number in each line, that range from 12% to 18%.

The third Advanced Measurement Approach (AMA) requires firms to build models to calculate the charge and to need to have sound operational risk processes. As in any other charge, these models need to be approved by regulators. These models should capture the tail events from operational risks at 99.9% confidence and a one-year time horizon. They must make use of all these four elements: (i) internal loss data, (ii) external data, (iii) scenario analysis, and (iv) business environment and internal control factors. The Committee does not provide any more details as to the form or shape of those models.

The reader should note that the above calculations refer to capital, so in order to get an equivalent RWA we have to multiply them by 12.5. This can be useful as internal management usually measures capital in RWA terms, so in this way capital requirements coming from operational risk can be compared to financial-driven charges.

Using the framework introduced before, the operational risk capital charge is intended to represent the Unexpected Loss coming from operational risks, at 99.9% confidence level and at a one-year time horizon. So, in the case of the AMA approach,

$$RWA_{OR} = 12.5 \times UL^{OR}_{99.9\%,1yr} \tag{9.39}$$

10 Right and Wrong Way Risk

Right and wrong way risk can be an important source of counterparty risk in financial institutions. In spite of that, it must be said that this risk tends to be poorly managed in many financial institutions. One of the reasons being that it has been regarded as very intense both from a methodology and systems point of view.

As a result, this chapter is going to be the most technical of this quantitative part of the book. Here we are going to understand what is right and wrong way risk, see how to model it, and, finally, understand with real numbers the impact it can have.

As indicated, right and wrong way risk has been seen, for years, as a risk too difficult to model, both because of its methodological difficulties and the often impossible calibration to the market. However, that is not the case any more; we are going to see in this chapter a number of available methodologies and, in particular, one of them that is both fairly easy to implement and to calibrate [72].

10.1 What is right and wrong way risk?

When calculating any credit exposure metric, like the EPE_t or PFE_t profiles, we need to measure exposure *at* default. The "at" is a subtle but crucial concept. When we say, for example, that PFE at 90% confidence in one year is \$1m, we are saying that "in 90% of the potential future scenarios *in which the counterparty defaults* in one year, our exposure to it will be lower than \$1m", as opposed to "in 90% of the potential future scenarios in one year, our exposure to it will be lower than \$1m". From a mathematical standpoint, to model the former case we need to build a dependency structure between potential counterparty default events and the portfolio value. When this dependency is non-negligible, it is often said that there exists a "market-credit" dependency.[1]

When this dependency is such that the exposure increases with the probability of default, it is said that we have positive dependency. In these cases, the structure of the trade "exacerbates" the credit risk embedded in it, and hence it is said that we have wrong-way risk (WWR). However, when it works the other way round, that is when the exposure decreases as the default probability increases, it is usually said that we have negative dependency, and this effect is called right-way risk (RWR), since the size of the credit risk decreases as the counterparty approaches a potential default.

For a number of historical reasons it is common to focus on wrong-way risk only. The "other side of the coin", right-way risk, is often somewhat forgotten. It is however important to realise that both exist, and a financial institution should have a set-up that encourages the creation of RWR. We are going to see in later examples how both effects are equally important. For simplification, we shall refer to the joint effect of market-credit dependency that creates either RWR and WWR as "directional-way risk" (DWR), as they are only two sides of the same coin.

This DWR effect appears mainly in four asset classes: equity, foreign exchange (FX), commodities, and credit. This is best explained with a number of examples:

- **Equity:** As an example of WWR, let's say we buy a put option from a counterparty with its own stock as the option reference entity. In the event of the counterparty defaulting, we know that the value of the stock will be zero (or very close to zero) and hence the option value will be maximum. An example of RWR would be its complementary call option, as in the event of default we know that the value of the option would be zero.
- **Foreign Exchange:** Suppose that we are a solid institution in a mature economy and we enter a cross-currency agreement with an institution in an emerging economy; this could be the central bank, a commercial bank, or other commercial firm. In this agreement, we receive the "mature economy" currency and pay the "developing economy" currency. In the event that the counterparty is under credit distress, chances are that its currency will be suffering a devaluation and thus the value of the transaction for the solid institution should increase substantially. As a result, we shall observe that as the counterparty's default probability increases, it may owe more and more to us. This is WWR.
- **Commodities:** There are lots of companies whose financial performance depends on the price of some commodities. This includes commodity producers as well as businesses where an important source of cost are commodities. For example, an oil producer may decide to synthetically sell in advance part of its production by shorting oil futures. As a result, the dealer at the other side of the transaction will be long on those futures. In the event of a strong collapse in the price of oil, the oil producer may enter into financial stress and its default probability may increase, but from the dealer's perspective of counterparty credit risk this is good, as in this case the oil producer will not owe anything to the bank. This is an example of RWR.
- **Credit:** The credit asset class offers very good examples of WWR. Suppose that we buy protection on Bank A, via a Credit Default Swap (CDS) contract.[2] We buy this protection from a Bank B that shares a common business and economic environment with Bank A. It is quite likely that if the counterparty (Bank B) approaches default or goes into liquidation, the CDS originally bought will be well in-the-money and so my potential loss from this CDS can be very high.

10.1.1 Specific and general DWR

There is another important concept that is widely used when dealing with this topic: "specific" vs. "general" DWR. A transaction is said to have *specific* DWR when the dependency between a default event and the transaction value is absolute. An example can be seen when we buy a put option from a counterparty on its own stock. In the event of the counterparty defaulting, we know *for sure* that the value of the option will be its full nominal amount. However, when the dependency comes through general economic factors, then we have *general* DWR. An example can be when we buy a put option from a counterparty with a stock as reference entity that is highly dependent on the counterparty's stock price. In that case, it is *likely* that the value of the option will be high if the counterparty defaults, though it is not guaranteed, and the value of the option in that event is not certain in advance.

The reader should note that, in the case of specific DWR, we do not require any model. This is because, as previously stated, when we measure exposure, we always measure it *subject* to default and, in the case of specfic DWR, we know with certainty the value of the exposure in the event of counterparty default.[3]

However, in the case of general DWR, a model is needed because the exposure value subject to default cannot be predetermined; it is a stochastic variable.

A very special case that is a hybrid between those two can be seen in collateralised FX transactions when the counterparty is either a sovereign or a very big counterparty (e.g., a state-owned company that runs a monopoly) in an emerging economy, as in those cases the counterparty default will trigger a special dislocation of the market. We can see it as a hybrid between the specific and the general DWR cases as we do not know for sure the potential credit loss, but we can have a priori a good idea of what to expect in the event of default.[4]

10.1.2 Key elements of an optimal DWR model

There are a number of characteristics that an optimal DWR framework should have:

Model adequacy: Models are mathematical tools that aim to describe some aspect of reality. As a consequence, models must be driven by real data as much as possible, as opposed to pre-conceptions as to how things should behave. In this way our models will be more likely to describe the actuality of things, and hence will capture better the true economic risks.

These models must also be as simple as possible. By designing simple models, implementation and maintenance become easier, faster, and more economical, and model risk is minimised. In this way we may increase the ease of communication of model details in the organisation, as well as subsequent model usage.

Data driven calibration: A model is not only a set of equations, but also a calibrating methodology. This is quite important, since a "good" model that is not easy to calibrate, which has a large calibration error or uncertainty, or that has a strong degree of subjectivity in the calibration, has limited value.

Minimal impact on existing systems: All financial institutions already have in place a calculation framework for counterparty credit risk metrics. The approach considered to be the most advanced is the Monte Carlo simulation. An optimal DWR model should leverage as much as possible from an existing platform, so that a transition to a framework with DWR is straightforward to manage and, also, economical.

Easy understanding by non-technical users: At the end of the day, in practice, most people concerned with counterparty credit risk in a financial institution have an intuitive understanding of the models, but none of their details. For this reason, if we want a DWR to have a positive and strong impact on an organisation, it must be easy to explain to a non-technical audience and avoid overly abstract concepts as much as possible. All inputs to a model must be simple to understand by any user, and changes in results must be tractable relative to changes in the input. In my opinion, this is a central characteristic that models should possess in a commercial environment.

10.1.3 What if we do not have a DWR model?

Correct modelling of both RWR and WWR is of paramount importance to a financial institution. First of all, without such a model the exposure estimates in the counterparty credit risk framework will not be correct and hence the institution will be incapable of understanding the true extent of the risks that it is actually carrying. As a result, the pricing and management of counterparty credit risk will contain faults. Secondly, without a DWR model, the institution will not have any tool to encourage trading desks to create RWR when possible and to discourage the creation of WWR; this should be a fundamental risk management policy.

For these reasons, a good DWR model is crucial to a good management of the credit risk that a financial institution carries in its book of derivatives.

10.1.4 In this chapter

Given how important DWR is, in this chapter we are going to ask:

1. What is the optimal way to model DWR?
2. What is the actual extent of DWR in a financial institution?
3. What happens if DWR is not properly modelled?
4. Do we need to consider both right-way and wrong-way risk?

10.2 Review of existing methodologies

To my knowledge, the following are the existing fundamental methodologies for DWR modelling.

10.2.1 Basel framework

This is the simplest approach, and it is the one used by the Basel Committee for the calculation of regulatory capital [5, 59].

In this set-up, RWR is not considered; rather, only WWR is taken into consideration. WWR is accounted for by increasing the exposure metric by a constant factor α across the board, for all counterparties and nettings sets without any particular considerations. By default, $\alpha = 1.4$. In theory, financial institutions can apply for a lower α, but it can never be below 1.2 according to the Basel Accord. Reportedly some institutions have had an α greater than 1.4. The drivers of the value of α are "low granularity of counterparties, particularly high exposures to WWR, particularly high correlation of market values[5] across counterparties and other institution-specific chararteristics" [5]. Estimates of α reported by banks range from 1.07 to 1.10 [42].

Further to this, banks must have operational procedures for the identification of WWR [5]. The Basel II Accord does not give much detail as to how to do this. Financial institutions and local regulators have typically interpreted this by setting up a stress testing framework to monitor the WWR carried in their portfolios.

However, in Basel III it is given much more attention. To further address the matter, the Committee provides (i) a more detailed description of the operational procedures of stress testing, (ii) indicates how to treat trades where specific WWR is identified, and (iii) asks financial institutions to calibrate the exposure models both as normally done and to stress credit conditions for the portfolio of counterparties, so that the calibration to be used for the capital calculation should be the one that delivers the highest capital number [59].

10.2.2 Change of risk measure in RFE model

Cesari *et al.* [31] and Iacono [45] propose to change the risk measure in the Risk Factor Evolution (RFE)[6] models that drive the exposure calculations. In a risk-neutral framework, a change in a risk measure can be translated to a change in the drift of the RFE models.[7] Hence, using the example of the oil producer discussed above, if we know that the exposure subject to default is lower than that with no RWR, we can adjust the drift of the oil price in its RFE model to obtain the desired effect at the exposure metric.

10.2.3 Brute force approach

Suppose that we have a default stochastic model in our suite of RFE models that can be used to simulate defaults in our counterparties. Also, let's say that that model has some sort of dependency structure with all other market factors (e.g., equity prices, FX rates, commodity prices, credit spreads).

Suppose also that in our Monte Carlo (MC) engine for the calculation of the exposure metrics profiles (EPE_t, PFE_t) we use N scenarios. In that MC engine, what we want to measure are exposure metrics *subject* to default; hence we are interested only in those market scenarios where the counterparty at stake has defaulted. Given that we need N of those scenarios,[8] we can run the RFE models iteratively many times, more than N times for sure; we can then disregard those scenarios where the counterparty has not defaulted; and pick, for the calculation, those where a default has occurred. We can do this iteratively until we obtain the desired N scenarios of risk factors where a default has occurred. If we use these scenarios for the exposure profiles, we are measuring exposure metrics subject to counterparty default, as desired.

An alternative to this method, which is more computationally efficient, is to generate first a set of market factors, N scenarios, without considering any counterparty defaults. Then we can carry out in each scenario a stream of M default simulations *conditional* on the market factors of each particular scenario. In this way, in each MC time step, we will have N market scenarios *and* M default simulations per market scenario. Essentially, we are adding a new "counterparty default" dimension to each scenario. Then, if scenario i has m_i defaults, we can give a default weight w_i to each scenario that will be taken into account when calculating the exposure metrics. The limit when N and M are large gives the same result as the methodology of the previous paragraph.

For example, if $V_{t,i}$ is the exposure at each MC time point t and scenario i, we calculate the Expected Positive Exposure as[9]

$$EPE_t = \frac{\sum_{i=1}^{N} V_{t,i} w_{t,i}}{\sum_{i=1}^{N} w_{t,i}} \tag{10.1}$$

$$w_{t,i} = \frac{m_{t,i}}{M} \tag{10.2}$$

10.2.4 Change of risk measure in exposure metric calculation

Equations 10.1 and 10.2 provide a numerical way to perform a change in the risk weight of each scenario in an MC simulation, in order to account for DWR. However, if we had an analytical expression for the default probability subject to a given set of market factors, there would be no need to perform the M default simulations. Instead, a fast analytical operation could calculate each $w_{t,i}$ and we would only need the N market factor scenarios per MC time point.

The reader should note that this methodology is no more than a change in risk measure, implemented when the exposure metric calculations are performed. That is, we start with a distribution of exposures where no default information exists $\Psi(V)$ and we transform it to another distribution $\Psi'(V)$ where default is accounted for. In this sense, the operator that transforms $\Psi(V)$ into $\Psi'(V)$ can be seen as a Radon-Nikodym derivative [31].

There are three ways that have been proposed to do this.

Merton model approach: Cespedes *et al.* [32], Rosen & Saunders [69], and Cesari *et al.* [31] propose a Merton model for this change of risk measure, using an Asymptotic Single Risk Factor (ASRF) model for the dependency structure. This model has the following key components.

- Firstly, in this framework we say that the credit worthiness of a counterparty is dictated by a latent variable Y. This variable is then decomposed into a systematic (Z) and idiosyncratic (ϵ) components with a correlation ρ as follows:

$$Y = \rho Z + \sqrt{1-\rho^2}\,\epsilon \tag{10.3}$$

Both Z and ϵ are considered to be normally distributed (and thus also Y), as well as independent. The counterparty modelled by this framework is said to default when $Y < \tilde{Y}$. This $\tilde{Y}$ is defined by $\tilde{Y} = \Phi^{-1}(PD_t)$, where PD_t is the counterparty default probability at time t. Altogether, the probability that the counterparty defaults at time t conditional in a value Z for the systematic component is

$$PD_t(Z) = \Phi\left(\frac{\Phi^{-1}(PD_t) - \rho Z}{\sqrt{1-\rho^2}}\right) \tag{10.4}$$

- Secondly, at a given future time point t, the exposure values (V) to a given counterparty will follow a certain empirical distribution density $f(V)$ and a corresponding cumulative density function $F(V)$. By constrution, $F(V)$ is a uniform distribution, and can be mapped to a "market" factor X that is normally distributed as

$$X = \Phi^{-1}\left(F(V)\right). \tag{10.5}$$

- Thirdly, in this modelling framework X represents the market variable, and Y the credit variable of the counterparty; we need to state the dependency structure between them. Typically, we are going to link the market variable X and the default latent variable Y with a joint normal distribution function with a given correlation r.

If the reader is interested, more technical details can be seen in Appendix D.

Empirical analysis approach: The second version of this type of model has been proposed by Ruiz [70] and Hull & White [42]. In this modelling framework, the functional form that determines the dependency between the market factors and the default events is given by empirical data, as opposed to latent non-observable variables.

Suppose that we find a market factor "x" so that the default probability of a counterparty can be expressed in the form

$$PD = g(x) + \sigma\,\epsilon, \tag{10.6}$$

where ϵ is a normalised random number that can follow, in principle, any distribution. We use the variable "x" to denote the *DWR driving market factor*. This factor could be an equity price, an FX rate, a commodity price, or any market variable in which we observe a relationship as described by Equation 10.6. If the MC simulation that is used to compute the counterparty credit risk metrics already contains a simulation for x, with a given dependency structure to all other market factors, then we can use those values of x in each scenario to obtain the necessary information for the default probability for that counterparty in that scenario and time point, and hence of the weight $w_{t,i}$. In other words, we can say that

$$w_{t,i} = g(x_{t,i}) + \sigma\,\epsilon. \tag{10.7}$$

In this framework, the task of the researcher is to discover the best DWR driving factor and optimal functional form for Equation 10.6.

For example, it has been observed that an equity price could be used as the market factor x, and Equation 10.6 could be calibrated using the default information embedded in the credit spreads; Ruiz [70] showed with one illustrative example (Ford) how a functional form $g(x) = Ax^B$ could be an optimal candidate for this purpose.

Portfolio value approach: The third and final version has been proposed by Hull & White [42]. In it, the researcher estimates the default probability, and hence the scenario weight $w_{t,i}$ using a functional form like

$$w_{t,i} = h(P_{t,i}) + \sigma\,\epsilon, \tag{10.8}$$

where $P_{t,i}$ is the price of the portfolio of OTC derivatives with the counterparty at stake. In this case, the market factor that drives the dependency structure with the default probability is not an actual market risk factor, but the price of a portfolio of trades. Hull & White show a number of numerical results in this framework in the context of CVA pricing [42].

10.2.5 Stressed scenario

Finally, Mihail Turlakov [76] has proposed a model that is based on a market stressed scenario of the counterparty's government default, so that the EPE profile with DWR is a combination of the stressed and unstressed EPE profiles. Further details can be seen in Appendix E.

10.2.6 Critique and preferred model

Let's carry out a critical analysis of the models seen, highlighting my view regarding the strengths and weaknesses for each of them from a practitioner standpoint.

Basel framework: The first methodology, which is based on a constant multiplier α, stress testing, and stress calibration, can be seen as the most simple approach, as it provides the same constant shock to the capital calculation regardless of the counterparty and the actual book of trades in its portfolio. The most positive side of this method is that it is very simple to implement and understand. On the negative side, first of all, it does not provide any insight into the true DWR that an institution is carrying. Secondly, it does not provide any incentive to the dealing desks in a financial institution to create RWR, or to avoid WWR, which should be one of the key elements for an optimal DWR strategy.

Change of risk measure in RFE model: The positive aspect of this methodology is the ease with which it can be implemented: all that is required is to change the drifts in the calibration and run the calculations as usual. On the other hand, the practitioner will have to face the question: how much should I change the drift? There is no way to answer that question properly. The practitioner will have to assess externally, in a qualitative and subjective way, whether the book of trades has RWR or WWR. This may be doable for a single trade, but it can become quite difficult, if not impossible, when the book contains a few hundred or thousand trades. Also, even if that is achieved, it is not clear how much change in the drift is needed.

Brute force approach: Provided that we have a good model for the market-credit dependency, the "brute force approach" seems to offer, in principle, a good framework to measure and manage DWR. However, it unfortunately requires so much computing power that it becomes highly impractical.[10]

Change of risk measure in exposure metric calculations: From the modelling adequacy stand point, none of the explained versions is too complicated from a mathematical perspective. Mostly, all that they add to the existing algorithms is a routine to calculate the risk weight of each scenario. The difference between them is how exactly that routine works and, most importantly, how they can be calibrated. The empirical analysis approach is the only one that can be calibrated to actual market data.

Stressed scenario: In my view, the best characteristic of this method is its simplicity, that it should be quite straight-forward to implement, and that it is easy to understand for non-technical users. The negatives seem to come, again, from its calibration, as we will have to "guesstimate" the impact of a sovereign default on the markets, amongst other things.

Conclusion: In my view, the optimal modelling framework for DWR is the Empirical Analysis. I consider the following characteristics key to its success:

1. The mathematical framework is simple and corresponds best to *observed* market behaviour.
2. Its calibration is robust, based on empirical data, and is independent of the book of trades with a given counterparty.
3. Its implementation will leverage strongly from an already existing MC engine for counterparty credit risk calculations; it does not need to generate new market scenarios or derivative prices.
4. Given that it is based on empirical data, and that it does not use abstract unobservable variables or parameters, it is easy to illustrate its fundamentals to non-technical users.

10.3 Some illustrative examples of the market-credit dependency

One of the major problems of studying historical default events is that they happen quite rarely and hence it can be very difficult to obtain data that is statistically significant. This problem is even more acute when trying to find data on defaults with a DWR component in it. For this reason, in order to obtain relevant information for our purposes, it may be best to use the market available information about default probabilities that is embedded in the CDS prices, which are daily traded. In particular, we can take advantage of a widely used approximation for the instantaneous default intensity (λ), given by [42]

$$\lambda = \frac{s}{1 - RR}, \tag{10.9}$$

where s is the credit spread and RR is the expected recovery rate in the event of default. In particular, we will use data from the one-year par credit spread as this tenor should provide a good proxy for the market's view of the short-term default probability and, most impotantly, it is amongst the most liquid tenor points in the CDS market; hence we should be able to find reasonably good quality data.

Equity–credit

We want to understand the real (i.e., empirically measured) dependency between a corporate equity price and its probability of default PD.

The scatter plots in Figure 10.1 show a few examples of the equity–credit dependency structure measured in the market.

This inverse relationship between equity and credit is well known to the industry, but often in a qualitative way. In fact, it can be quite nicely extracted from the perhaps simplest equity–credit model: the Merton model. Details of this model can be seen in Appendix F.

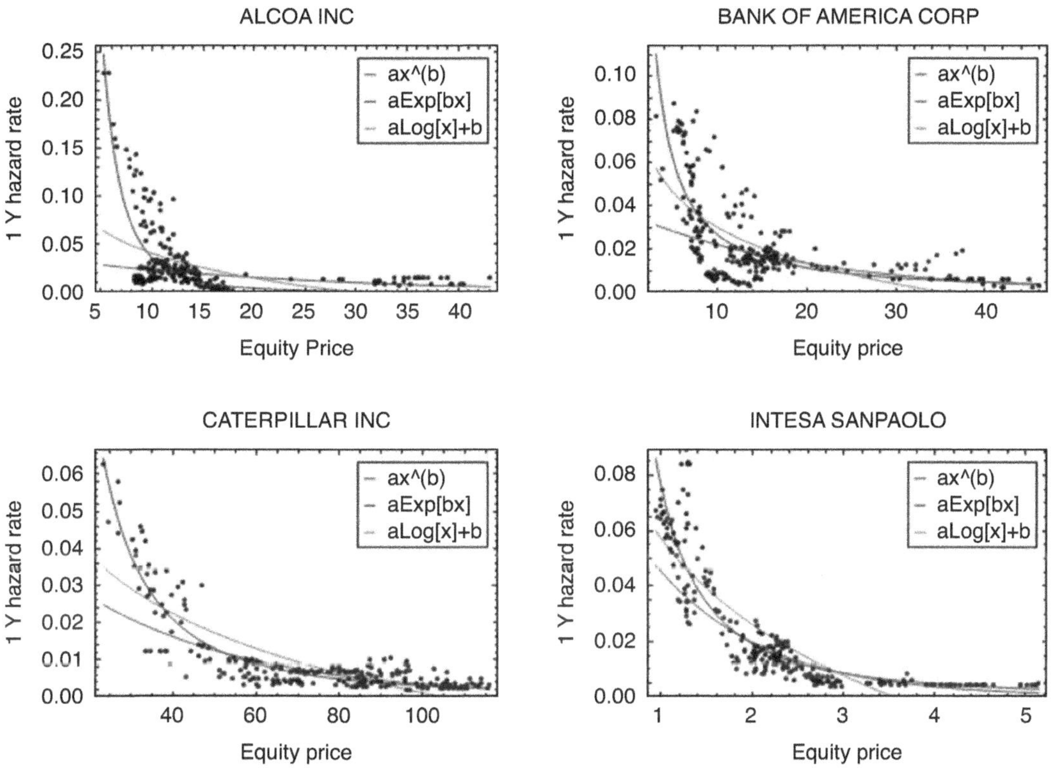

Figure 10.1 Illustration of the empirical dependency between equity and credit
Source: Bloomberg.

The best $g(x)$ for equity–credit dependency: In general, if we want to calculate a functional form for $g(x)$ in Equation 10.6 from empirical data, we should try candidates for $g(x)$ like exponential, power or logarithmic functions, as well as more complex ones if found appropriate, and try to find a $g(x)$ that delivers either the highest least-squared R^2, or the lowest noise component σ in Equation 10.6. This work has been done for many equities [75], and it was found that a power law seems to be quite good for $g(x)$ in this context.

FX–credit

We have seen that there can be a dependency between foreign exchange rates and the credit quality of counterparties, either sovereign or corporates. Let's have a look at some illustrative data in Figure 10.2. That dependency seems to appear in data when the markets are not intervened in, as in the example of China.

It must be noted that in this case the functional form for $g(x)$ should be upward sloping, but there is nothing to stop a practitioner using the inverse exchange rate, and hence using a downward sloping form for $g(x)$. Published studies of this dependency pointed at an exponential or power law as good for $g(x)$ [75].

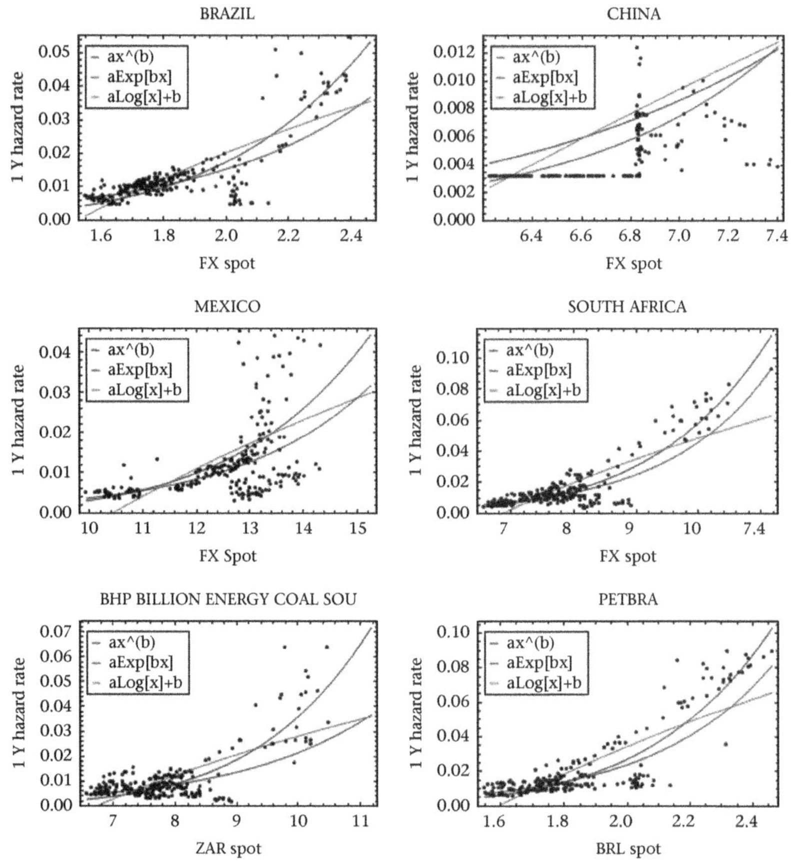

Figure 10.2 Illustration of the empirical dependency between FX (with USD as the reference currency) and credit
Source: Bloomberg.

Commodities–credit

Commodities can also be a good DWR driving asset. This is the case for those firms whose business is highly dependent on a given commodity. In some cases, the performances of those companies strengthen when the commodity prices increase (e.g., oil and gas extraction, mining, agriculture), and in some other cases the performance will be at risk when prices increase (e.g., airlines, construction). Figure 10.3 demonstrates this with some empirical data.

Credit–credit

We should also mention the case of the credit asset class here, for the sake of completeness, though DWR models in this class are quiet trivial, since if we already have a credit model in our system that has a dependency structure with all other asset classes, we may use it to estimate $w_{t,i}$ in Equation 10.7 as

$$w_{t,i} = \hat{\lambda}_{t,i}, \tag{10.10}$$

where $\hat{\lambda}_{t,i}$ represents the model's short-term default intensity for scenario i at the simulation time t.

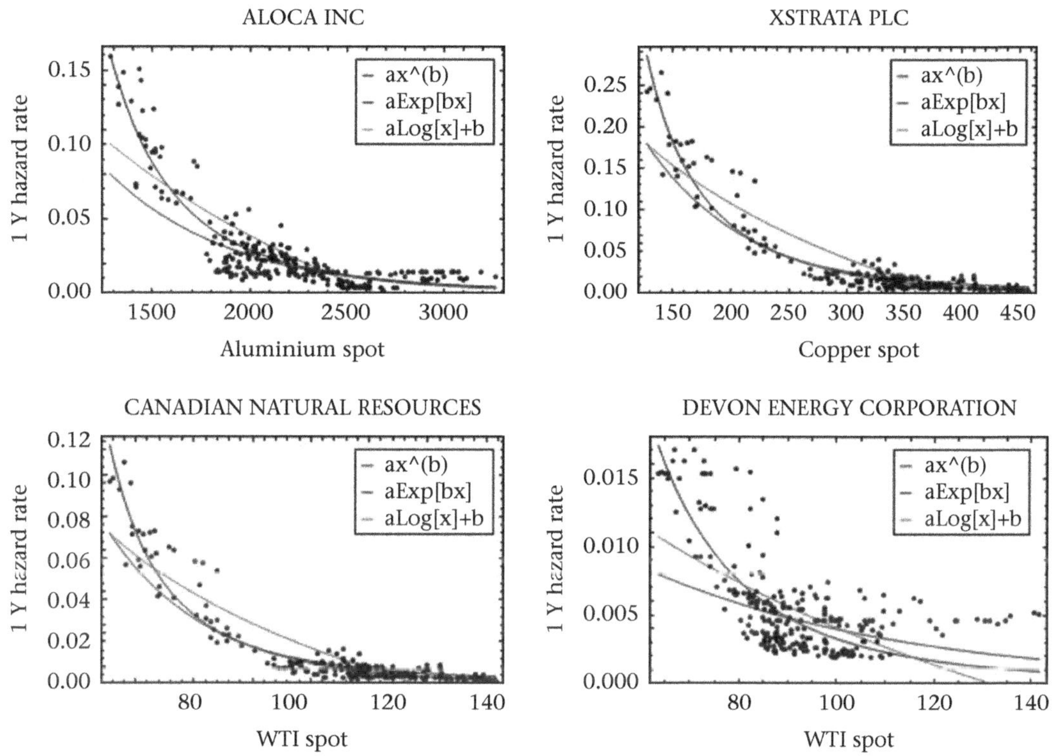

Figure 10.3 Illustration of the empirical dependency between commodities and credit
Source: Bloomberg.

10.4 A stochastic correlation model

It must be noted that the information extracted from empirical data can also be used outside of the DWR scope. The empirical data shows clear market–credit dependency structures between asset classes (equity–credit, FX–credit, commodity–credit, equity–FX–commodity–credit in emerging market firms, etc.) that go beyond the typical linear correlation models, and hence they can (arguably, they should) be used to model those dependencies in a general framework, even outside of the DWR environment.

10.4.1 Correlation implied by the empirical analysis

Let's say that the default probability of a company is given by

$$\lambda = g(x) + \sigma \, \epsilon \tag{10.11}$$

where x is a market driving factor. A change in that default probability is approximately given by

$$\Delta\lambda = g'(x)\Delta x + \sigma \, \Delta\epsilon \tag{10.12}$$

The correlation between a change in the default probability and a change in the driving factor is given by

$$\rho(x) = \frac{\sigma_{\lambda,x}}{\sigma_\lambda \sigma_x} \tag{10.13}$$

where $\sigma_{\lambda,x}$ is the covariance between $\Delta\lambda$ and Δx, and σ_λ and σ_x are the square root of the variance of $\Delta\lambda$ and Δx respectively. Making use of Equation 10.13 we can see that

$$\rho(x) = \frac{g'(x)\sigma_x}{\sqrt{g'(x)^2\sigma_x^2 + \sigma^2}} \tag{10.14}$$

It should be noted that this correlation is a function of the market driving factor x, which is a quite natural result given the data observed. For example, in the case of equities, when the equity price is very high, a change in the equity value tends to influence minimally its credit standing, hence correlation should be low. On the other hand, when the equity price is very low, a small change in the equity value tends to be highly linked to strong changes in its credit worthiness, hence correlation should be high. This observation is indeed embedded in $g'(x)$, as seen in the formula obtained.

10.4.2 A stochastic correlation model

All this has major implications in terms of risk modelling. The empirical data, that drives the functional form of $g(x)$, shows how a constant correlation model may be far from good to describe the observed market–credit correlations.

In fact, the empirical analysis modelling framework builds quite naturally a stochastic correlation model. If we have a stochastic model for the variable x, we are implicitly having a stochastic model for the correlation via Equation 10.14. Given that $g(x)$ is obtained by empirical data, this framework is going to offer, in my view, an optimal way to model the market–credit dependency structures.

For example, price and risk metrics of portfolios of securities (e.g., CDOs and other exotic derivatives, portfolios of derivatives) can be highly driven by dependency structures. Indeed, this is especially true in risk management, as risk metrics that measure tail risk are nearly always quite sensitive to correlations, and so risk management in a financial institution is always interested in the correlation between credit risk and market risk. This "driving market factor approach" might be an appropriate way of proceeding for risk metrics like, for example, the initial margin asked by central clearing houses, as they are based on highly conservative risk metrics that are very sensitive to correlations.

10.5 Impact of DWR

Let's see the impact of DWR on the real world.

To do this, we can run the preferred modelling framework through a number of sample trades (options, forwards, and swaps), with and without a DWR model, and compare the outcomes.

We are going to study the impact of DWR on four typical counterparty risk metrics: CVA, initial margin, potential future exposure, and regulatory capital calculations,[11] calibrated to real market data.[12] All calibrations are extracted from Ruiz *et al.* [75].

In this chapter we are going to see a few results, but more of them can be seen in Appendix G.

10.5.1 An FX forward in an emerging market economy

As said, a source of DWR lies in transactions that are sensitive to FX rates in emerging economies. This is due to the business nature of firms in these regions, often having export based economies, which tend to be very sensitive to their FX rates. Thus the performance of such an economy as a whole, and of individual companies in those economies, is highly linked to the FX market.

In this example we shall study an FX forward. We are going to see that we can have either right-way or wrong-way risk in the uncollateralised case, depending on whether we are long or short on the trade, but that we will always have wrong-way risk when collateralised.

Long FX forward

Suppose that we sell to Petrobras, a major oil company in Brazil, a one-year FX forward on the USD/BRL exhange rate. Data shows a clear dependency between the FX level and the default intensity of this company best fitted by $g(x) = 3.1481 \cdot 10^{-4}\, x^{6.4313}$, where x is the USDBRL exchange rate. Figures 10.4 and 10.5 show the impact of DWR on the counterparty risk metrics, both if the trade is uncollateralised (Figure 10.4) and collateralised (Figure 10.5).

In this transaction, we are long on the USD/BRL rate. Thus the DWR that we have in the uncollateralised case is such that when the BRL devalues, the default probability of Petrobras increases and the forward is in-the-money for us; so we have wrong-way risk. This is clearly shown in the PFE-90% profile in Figure 10.4. As

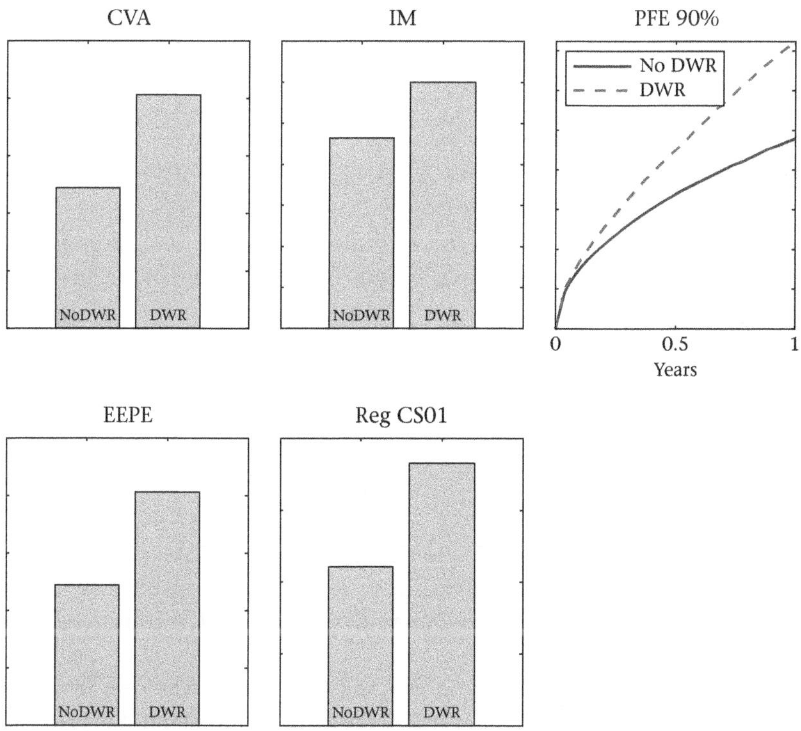

Figure 10.4 Impact of DWR modelling in counterparty credit risk metrics in an uncollateralised long FX forward. The left bar is without DWR modelling, the right bar with DWR modelling

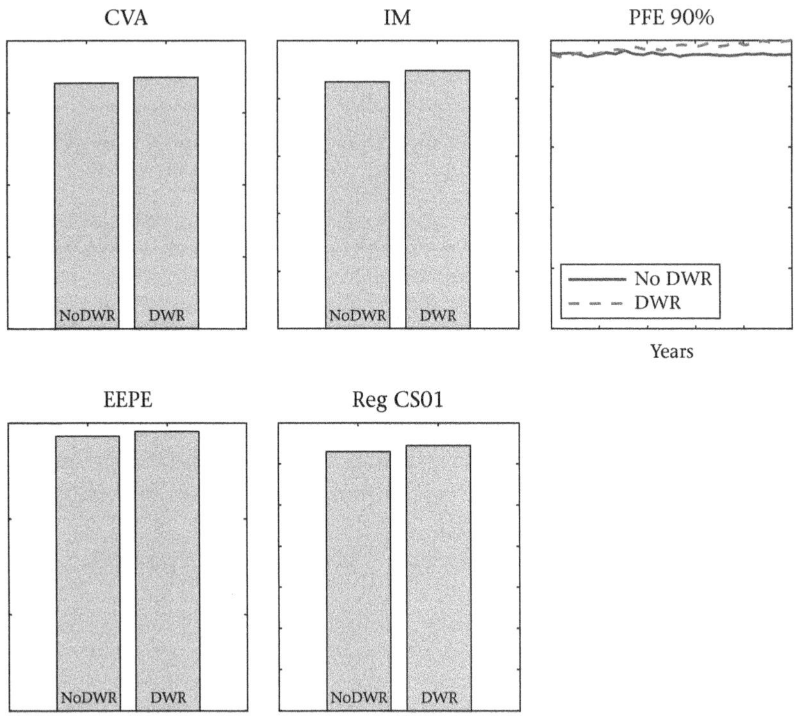

Figure 10.5 Impact of DWR modelling on counterparty credit risk metrics in a collateralised long FX forward. The left bar is without DWR modelling, the right bar with DWR modelling

a result, all CVA, initial margin (IM) and regulatory capital increase most notably compared to its non-DWR value.

In the collateralised case, the DWR effect we observe is also wrong-way risk, although smaller this time. This is because (i) the MC paths that carry the most weight w are those in which USD/BRL is high and (ii) the ten-day changes of the forward, which is a delta-one product, are bigger on those paths with high w (as a result of the geometric nature of the FX rate moves). As a consequence, we have a wrong-way risk effect. This effect is small, compared to the uncollateralised case, because exposure is only sensitive to ten-day moves in the FX rate.

Short FX forward

Suppose that we now short the same forward. If the transaction is uncollateralised (Figure 10.6), then the forward will be out-of-the-money for us when the BRL devaluates, and so we see right-way risk. CVA and capital calculations yield nearly half of their previous values when DWR is considered. IM also decreases substantially.

However, in the collateralised case, we see wrong-way risk the same as when we were long on this trade. This is because an FX forward's delta is always one, and so the distribution of ten-day price changes are nearly the same if we are short or long on the trade as per Equation 10.15 below. Hence, we always see a small wrong-way risk in this collateralised forward, regardless of whether we are long or short.

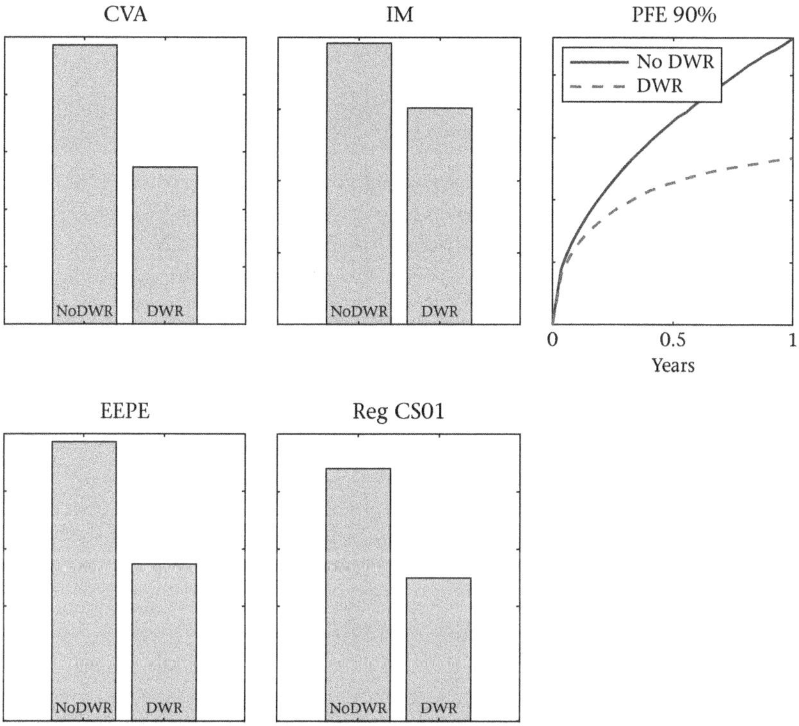

Figure 10.6 Impact of DWR modelling on counterparty credit risk metrics in an uncollateralised short FX forward. The left bar is without DWR modelling, the right bar with DWR modelling

10.5.2 Commodities

Let's see an example of how DWR can affect commodity trades. Derivative products in this asset class are often traded both by commodity producers (e.g., an oil extraction company) as well as oil consumers (e.g., an airline), typically to hedge volatility of future income and expenses.

In this commodity example we shall study the behaviour of swaps. We are going to see how we have both right-way and wrong-way risk when the trade is uncollateralised, depending on whether we are receiving or paying the fixed leg, and always right-way risk when the trade is on a collateralised basis.

Receiver swap

Suppose that we trade with Canadian Natural Resources a two-year WTI swap in which we pay floating and receive fixed. The CDS market of this counterparty links quite clearly the level of the WTI oil spot price to its default probability (Figure 10.3). A power law seems to be best for that dependency $g(x) = 2.296 \cdot 10^{-11} x^{-6.811}$, where x is the WTI price. The counterparty credit risk metrics with and without DWR are shown in Figures 10.8 and 10.9.

In the uncollateralised case (Figure 10.8), as the price of WTI decreases, the swap will become more valuable for us and hence the credit exposure will increase, but at the same time the counterparty default probability will increase, and so this trade shows wrong-way risk. The effect is very strong: CVA nearly triples, IM increases by about 20%, the PFE risk profiles moves up significantly CCR regulatory capital more than doubles, and CVA regulatory capital triples. These severe changes are a consequence of the sensitivity of this

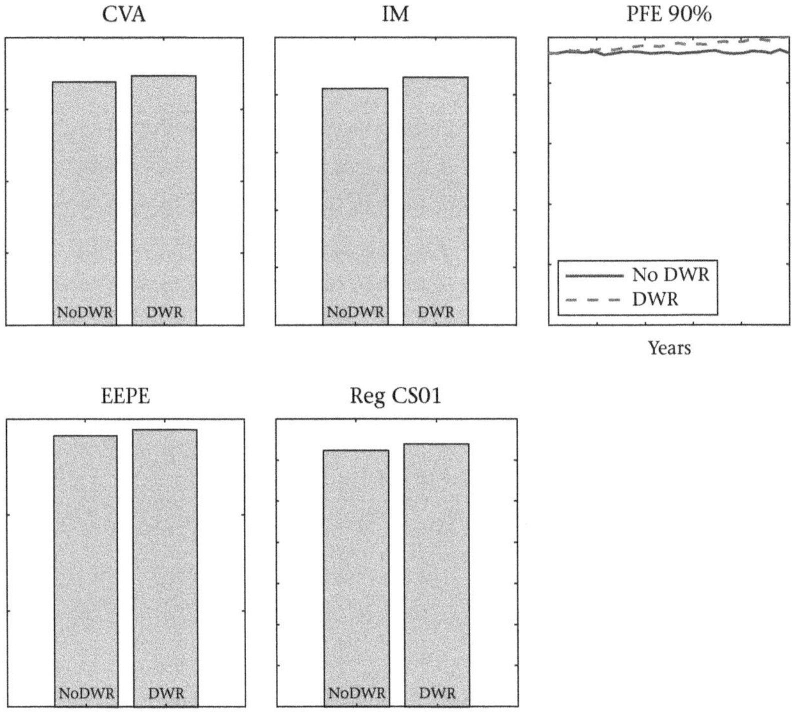

Figure 10.7 Impact of DWR modelling on counterparty credit risk metrics in a collateralised short FX forward. The left bar is without DWR modelling, the right bar with DWR modelling

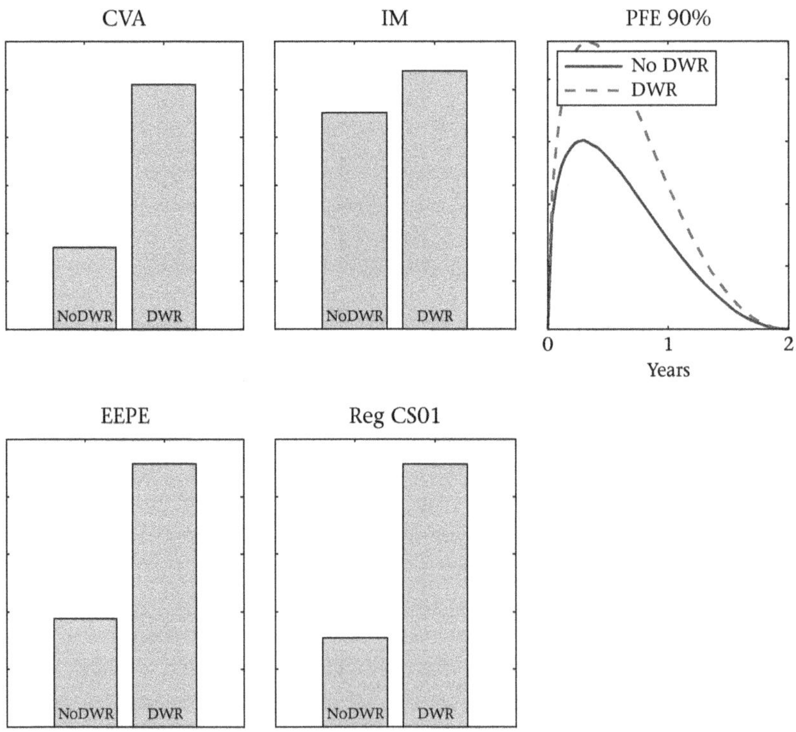

Figure 10.8 Impact of DWR modelling on counterparty credit risk metrics in a uncollateralised receiver oil swap. The left bar is without DWR modelling, the right bar with DWR modelling

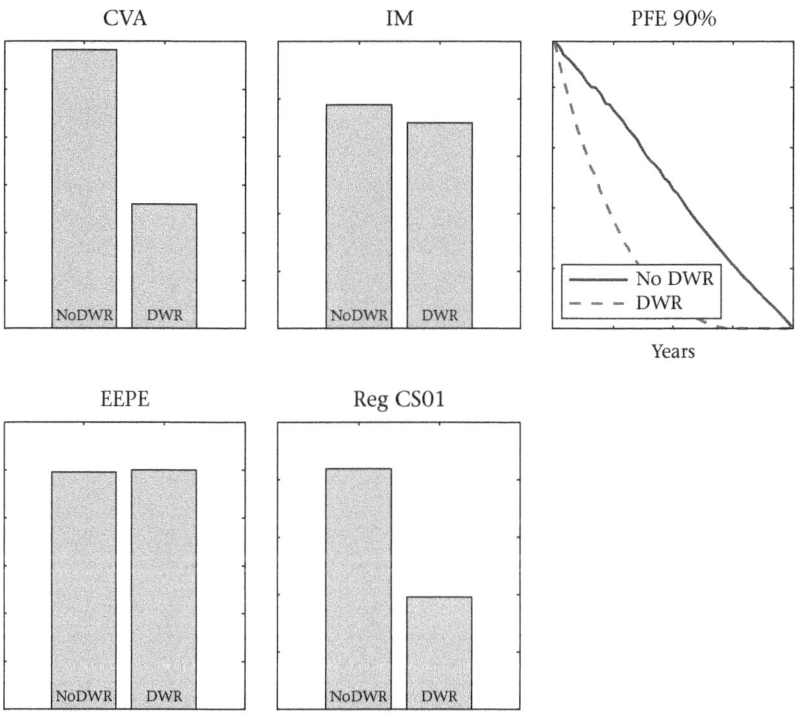

Figure 10.9 Impact of DWR modelling on counterparty credit risk metrics in a collateralised receiver oil swap. The left bar is without DWR modelling, the right bar with DWR modelling

counterparty default probability to WTI: the default probability is around 0.2% when WTI is \$110, but goes to 4% when WTI value is around \$60.[13]

When the trade is collateralised, we appear to experience right-way risk. This is because of the two effects that we previously saw in the case of the forward, which comes as no surprise as a swap can be seen as a strip of forwards.[14] This effect is especially strong in CVA and its capital charge; it more than halves when DWR is considered.

Payer swap

The symmetric case, a WTI swap where we pay fix and receive floating, shows right-way risk in the uncollateralised case, and again right-way risk in the collateralised one. The results can be seen in Figures 10.10 and 10.11.

When the trade is uncollateralised (Figure 10.10), as the price of WTI increases, the swap will become more valuable for us and hence the credit exposure increases, but at the same time the counterparty default probability will decrease, and hence this trade shows right-way risk. This effect is again dramatic as a result of the strength of the market–credit dependency captured by $g(x)$: CVA gets divided by around 6, IM more than halves, the exposure profile is strongly reduced, and both CCR and CVA capital also decrease most heavily.

In the collateralised case we have a similar effect as described in the receiver swap, as expected.[15] This effect seems to be smoother this time, though.

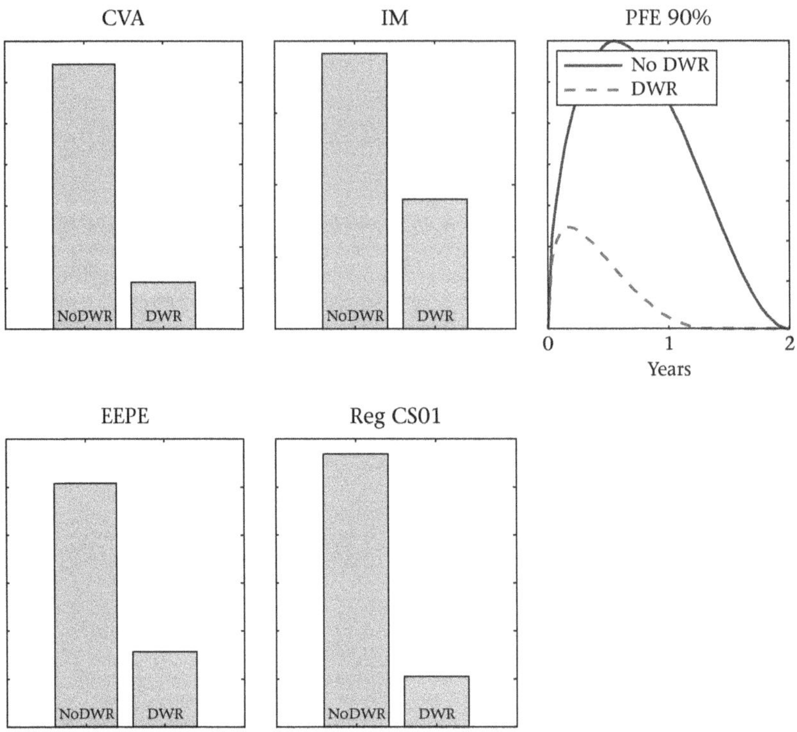

Figure 10.10 Impact of DWR modelling on counterparty credit risk metrics in a uncollateralised payer oil swap. The left bar is without DWR modelling, the right bar with DWR modelling

A remark on this example

I would like to draw the reader's attention to this example, as it demonstrates the strength of the DWR model used.

We are calibrating the Empirical Analysis approach to model DWR to real data as of January 2013. As a result we are easily able to incorporate into our DWR model the *empirically measured* dependency structure between the credit quality of the counterparty and the market factors. As a consequence, we are actually matching the intensity of the DWR effect to that indicated by the market. In this example we observe a very significant reduction in several credit risk metrics when DWR effects are considered. Such a reduction would, in my experience of working for many years in financial institutions, be very difficult to justify to a regulator, for example, without a data-driven modelling framework like this one. Also, it reduces model risk as it removes subjective judgement by the research team.

10.5.3 Sensitivities

So far we have seen how the main counterparty credit risk metrics (CVA, Initial Margin, PFE exposure, and Regulatory Capital) can vary notably in options, forwards, and swaps when considering DRW effects. We have reviewed examples where the source of DWR comes from the FX, commodity, and equity[16] markets. In addition to this, the *sensitivities* of these metrics can also be importantly affected by DWR.

We have seen already some of this by studying the impact of the DWR model in the regulatory CVA-CS01. To illustrate this case further, let's make use of the payer WTI swap from before, and observe how the CVA

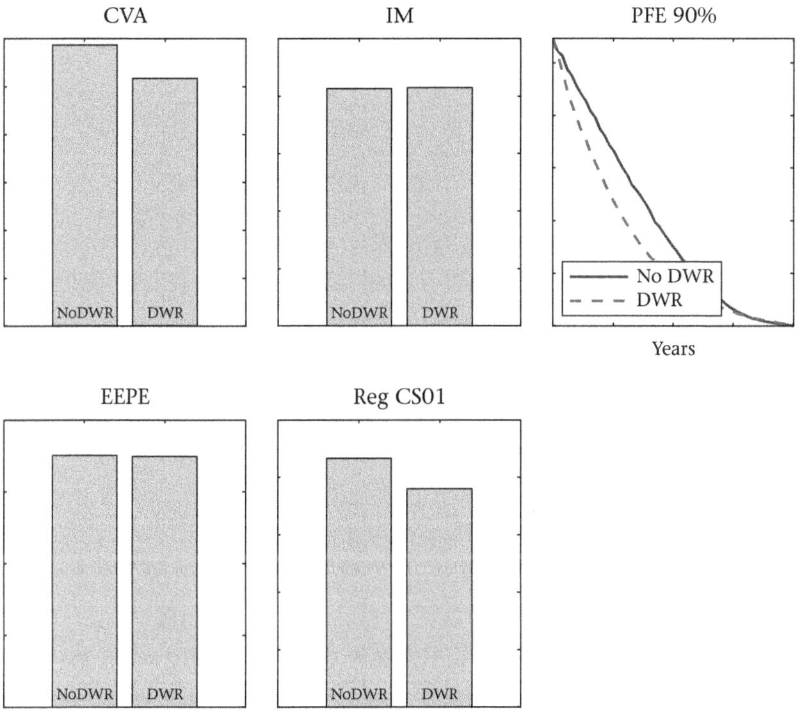

Figure 10.11 Impact of DWR modelling on counterparty credit risk metrics in a collateralised payer oil swap. The left bar is without DWR modelling, the right bar with DWR modelling

changes as the WTI volatility varies. We illustrate this here by plotting the CVA price and the CVA vega for different values of the WTI volatility, all else remaining constant. The results are shown in Figure 10.12, both on an uncollateralised and collateralised basis.

The effect is quite remarkable in both cases. In the uncollateralised case, DWR effects change the vega most strongly; in fact its sign even changes. In the collateralised case the effect is also remarkable: the vega with DWR goes to zero quite rapidly as the volatility increases, while it increases in the case without DWR.[17]

This example highlights the point that DWR is important not only for the calculation of counterparty credit risk metrics, but also for its sensitivities.

10.5.4 Some insight into the problem

We said before that right-way risk can be as important as wrong-way risk and hence our preferred term "directional-way risk" (DWR). We hope this is clear now, after the illustrative examples.

However, the results also show something else that might be somewhat unexpected. When a trade is uncollateralised, the direction of the DWR effect (i.e., right vs. wrong) flips when we change the direction of the trade (i.e., long vs. short). However, when the trade is collateralised, the direction of the DWR does not change when we change the direction of the trade. Let's see why.

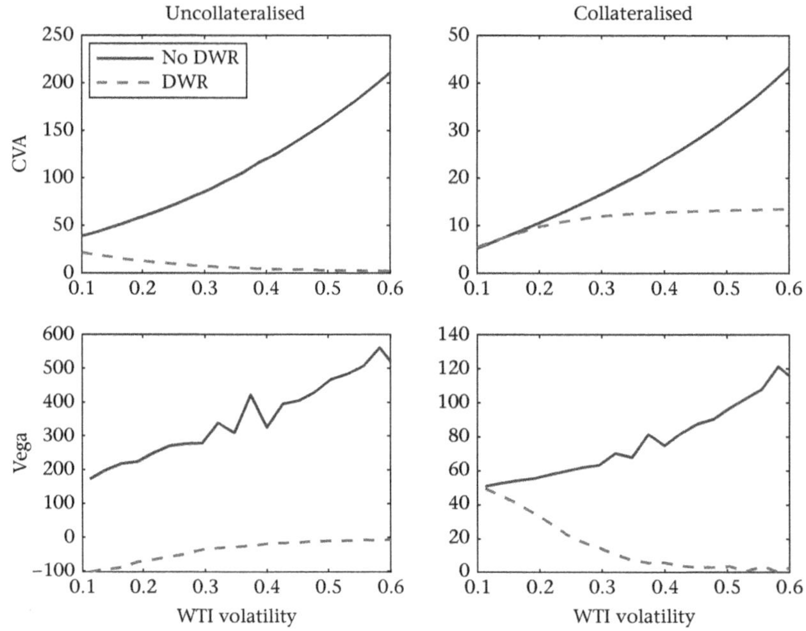

Figure 10.12 CVA price and vega as a function of WTI volatility for a payer WTI swap with Canadian natural resources as counterparty

DWR without collateral agreement

The uncollateralised case is the one that tends to be more popular, and easier to understand, because the exposure that an institution has to a given netting set is taken as the value of the trades with that netting set. If that value increases as the default probability of the counterparty increases, we have wrong-way risk, and the exposure profiles considering this effect should be higher than without it. When the value of the trade decreases as the default probability of the counterparty increases, then we have right-way risk and the exposure profiles should be below those without considering DWR. The intensity of this effect will be given by the function $g(x)$, as it sets the dependency structure between the counterparty default probability and the DWR driving factor.[18]

DWR with collateral agreement

The collateralised case is somewhat more subtle. In this case, the credit risk profiles will be mostly measured from the distribution of changes in the ten-day forward price of the trade (or portfolio of trades);[19] that is, the PFE and EPE profiles will be calculated from the distribution, at each point in time, of *changes* in the portfolio value over a rolling time horizon of ten days, as opposed to the actual *value* of the portfolio.

As a result, if P is the value of the netting set under consideration, $P = f(x)$, and if x follows geometric Brownian motion, we approximately have

$$\delta P \simeq \Delta(x) \cdot \delta x,$$

$$\delta x \simeq x \cdot \sigma \cdot \sqrt{\frac{10}{260}} \cdot \epsilon,$$

where $\Delta = \frac{\partial f}{\partial x}$, σ is the volatility of x, and ϵ is a standard normal deviate. Joining those two equations, we can say that

$$\delta P \simeq \Delta(x) \cdot x \cdot \sigma \cdot \sqrt{\frac{10}{260}} \cdot \epsilon. \tag{10.15}$$

This equation provides us with a distribution of δP at a given time point in the future, from which we calculate credit risk profiles like EPE or PFE. In other words, if we are running an MC simulation with 10,000 scenarios, at each MC calculation time point we will have 10,000 values of δP that come from 10,000 values of x_t and 10,000 values of ϵ.

So far, this does not consider any DWR modelling. When we apply our DWR model to this distribution, we need to assign a weight to each δP in each scenario. That weight will come from $w = g(x)$.

In the collateralised case, the exposure measured by the MC simulation in each scenario and time step is not the value of the portfolio (as it was in the uncollateralised instance), but a realisation of δP as given by Equation 10.15. Hence, the direction of the DWR (either "right" or "wrong") will be now determined by something different to the uncollateralised case: it will be given by a balance between (i) $g(x)$, (ii) $\Delta(x)$, and (iii) the geometric nature of δx (i.e., that δP is approximately proportional to x).

For example, suppose that we have a call option, where $\Delta(x)$ is increasingly monotonic, and suppose that $g(x)$ is decreasingly monotonic. Then, the smaller x is before a ten-day move, the greater its weight w will be on the one hand, but on the other hand its $\Delta(x)$ will tend to be smaller, and hence δP will tend to be smaller (in absolute value) with it. In this way, we could have either right-way or wrong-way risk depending on the *balance* of $g(x)$ and $\Delta(x)$.

This shows that the direction of the DWR in uncollateralised trades can be different when considered as collateralised, since the drivers of the DWR direction are quite different to those in the collateralised case.

Therefore, as a consequence of Equation 10.15 and that the weights w are a function of the level of x, if we are long on a trade and we have, for example, RWR, we will tend also to observe RWR when we are short on the same trade.

10.5.5 A few practical points

We have seen that the impact of DWR on counterparty credit risk metrics can be important. We have studied cases in which the source of the DWR lies in the FX, commodity and equity[20] markets.

The choice of the market factor: It must be noted that, for some counterparties, two or three of these models may be applicable. For example, in the case of a major oil company in an emerging economy, we may be able to use as the DWR driving asset its equity price, an FX rate, or a commodity price. Which to use best will depend on the nature of those dependencies and may also be driven by practical considerations like the models and infrastructure that a financial institution already has in place.

In some other cases only one of the models may be applicable; for example, when the counterparty is a small oil company, whose balance sheet is not very sensitive to swings in the FX market, and without a traded equity. In this case, it is sensible to use the oil price as the DWR driving asset.

Calibration: We have seen that the Empirical Analysis approach for modelling DWR is optimal from a calibration standpoint compared to the other ones. However, this does not mean that calibration will always be a trivial exercise. This is because data can be limited; for example, in the previous case of a small oil company, we may have to estimate its $g(x)$ using a variety of techniques, which may include benchmarking its $g(x)$

function to other similar companies for which data exists. However, in any case, this methodology maximises the utilisation of the available data when it is limited, which is, in my view, one of its key strengths.

Risk weights for bilateral CVA: For those readers already familiar with CVA, the examples shown in this Section 10.5 were based on the unilateral version of CVA. It must be noted that when we calculate the liability side of CVA (i.e., CVA_{liab} or DVA) we need to consider the dependency between *our own* default and changes in the value of the portfolio. As a result, the weights w that we need to apply in this case are different to those applied for the asset side of CVA or for all other typical risk metrics of counterparty risk.

In other words, we need to counstruct a self-DWR model to price the liability side of CVA. As a consequence, Equation 2.8 does not hold any more when DWR exists in the book of trades.

Implementation effort: Finally, it should be noted that the examples have shown the effect of DWR on single trades. In practice, most often we will have a portfolio of trades (as opposed to a single trade) with a given counterparty in the same netting set. In that case we will have to choose the best DWR driving asset in the same way we have done for one trade, and then we need a dependency structure between that asset "x" and all other risk factors that drive the valuation of the portfolio.

10.6 Conclusions

We are now in a position to answer the questions raised at the beginning of this chapter.

What is the optimal way to model DWR? In my opinion, the Empirical Analysis methodology is optimal for modelling DWR.[21] This is because it is the only one that achieves all the following goals.

1. It has a robust modelling framework, and it uses the *observed* market-credit dependency structure, as opposed to a guess of how that dependency structure could be.
2. It can be directly and easily calibrated to data.
3. Its implementation requires minimal work, as it makes uses of existing Monte Carlo simulations without DWR.
4. Its impact in the every day work of a financial institution can be high, as it is based on an intuitive methodology that is data-driven, and it does not make use of latent non-observable abstract variables.

What is the actual extent of DWR in a financial institution? We have seen from a number of real examples that DWR can be highly relevant. The realistic examples calibrated as of January 2013 show that CVA, Initial Margin, exposure profiles, and capital can change significantly; indeed, we have observed a case in which CVA decreased around six times. Those tests had to be done with single trades as each financial institution will have a different book of trades and, hence, it will be difficult to obtain results that can be applicable to all institutions, though those tests show that DWR can be quite important, and that it must be dealt with carefully.

What happens if this DWR is not properly modelled? The data analysed suggests that the market–credit dependency structure that provokes DWR can be modelled by linking the default probabilities to *levels* of a market risk factor. We have also seen that the correlation in the changes between those factors and credit drivers is not constant, but in fact depends on the level of the market factor. In my view, a good model for DWR should reflect this.

We have also seen how DWR can change the credit exposure metrics of a book of trades noticeably, both for collateralised and uncollateralised facilities. Moreover, the drivers of DWR effects are very different in each of those cases. If uncollateralised, the direction of the DWR effect tends to get inverted when we change the long/short direction. If collateralised, a long/short transformation tends to keep the same DWR effect.

If a good DWR model is not considered, the counterparty credit risk calculation and risk allocation within an organisation will not adequately reflect the true economic risks that the institution is carrying. As a result, management will not be aware of some actual risks, and it will be bound to make wrong decisions, while incentives will be inappropriately allocated in the organisation and the institution will be exposed to negative events, that are not known to the organisation, and that could have been anticipated and managed pre-emptively with a good DWR model.

A good DWR model will not only reverse those problems, but could also allow a bank to decrease its regulatory capital. This is because, firstly, it may apply to its regulators for a reduction in its α multiplier for capital calculation and, secondly, the EEPE and regulatory CVA-CS01 that drive the capital calculation will be reduced in those netting sets that carry right-way risk. Regulators should be open to these changes as, in this way, they will create the incentives for banks to manage DWR properly. Within the current Basel framework and regulatory policy at the time of this text going to press, risk assessment and allocation is not correct, and incentives to improve the risk management set-up regarding DWR are quite non-existent. I believe this is an important regulatory mistake.

Do we need to consider both right-way and wrong-way risk? We should indeed consider both these factors. Currently, DWR is mainly focused on wrong-way risk in the industry; the term "right-way risk" is hardly ever mentioned, while "wrong-way risk" very often. However, this study shows that right-way risk is as important as wrong-way risk for the proper understanding of the economic risks that an institution carries, and so both ought to be considered in parallel.

This modelling framework can (and arguably should) be used beyond DWR: Indeed, we have seen how data show that a constant correlation model for the market–credit dependency structure seems to be quite removed from reality. This should have strong implication in pricing and risk management of complex structures, via either a single trade (e.g., an exotic product) or a number of trades (e.g., a portfolio of OTC derivatives). This modelling framework could be a good way to proceed to calculate risk metrics highly sensitive to correlations.

Special acknowledgements: The author would like to thank Ricardo Pachón and Piero del Boca for their contribution to the research that led to some of the results shown in this chapter.

Part III The XVA Challenge

11 CVA Desk, a Bilateral Dance

We have seen that CVA is the present value of the default risk embedded in OTC derivatives. The role of the CVA desk is to manage that risk.

We have seen previously that hedging (or monetising) default risk has two related but differentiated components:

1. **Cash Hedging:** By this is meant the hedging of actual default events. That is, do something so that when one of our counterparties defaults, we do not suffer any loss, or at least losses are limited.
2. **Paper Hedging:** CVA is a price to a risk. As such, like any other price that is marked periodically, it will fluctuate and have a P&L. These fluctuations can be quite dramatic: during the credit crisis, two-thirds of the credit risk losses were balance sheet CVA related, as opposed to actual default losses [59].

In other words, when we hedge credit risk in OTC derivatives, we can hedge actual default events, and we can hedge the market price of potential future default events. These two things, being obviously highly related, are not the same.

11.1 The mechanics of a CVA desk

Let's say that we are a standard desk in a derivatives dealer; by standard is meant a typical interest rate desk, an FX desk, an equity desk, etc., that sells and synthetically creates (i.e., hedges) OTC derivatives. In order to manage the counterparty risk in our book of derivatives, the dealer can set up a specialised desk. This (CVA) desk will provide a credit insurance to us, the standard desk, against losses from our counterparties defaulting. As a result, this desk is going to charge us for this insurance service. That charge is, precisely, the CVA. Once the CVA charge is received by the CVA desk, it will go out to the market and hedge out the credit risk it has absorbed from us. In this way, CVA should be seen as a "credit insurance fee". This is illustrated in Figure 11.2.

In principle, the mandate of a CVA desk is to have a zero-flat P&L: it takes responsibility for the credit risk in the book of OTC derivatives in the organisation, and it hedges it out, so that any losses from CVA are profits from the hedges, and vice versa. However, as we will see in subsequent chapters, things are not as simple as that in reality, as a CVA desk can generate profit or loss coming from hedging friction costs and from risks that are not possible to hedge. Taking this one step further, a CVA desk may have a mandate to make money out of the credit risk it trades, hence being a profit centre for the institution.

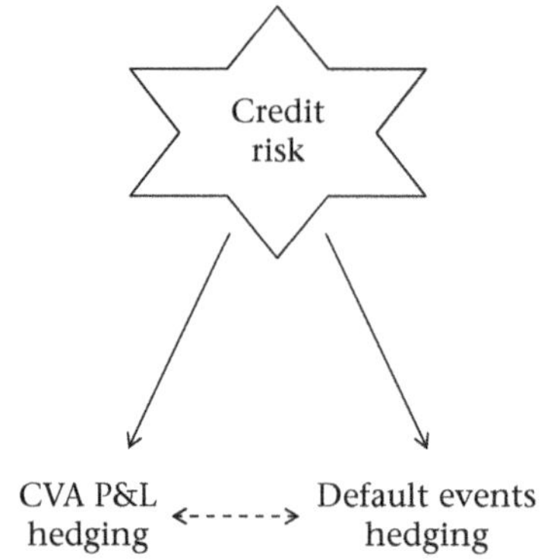

Figure 11.1 Types of counterparty credit risk hedging

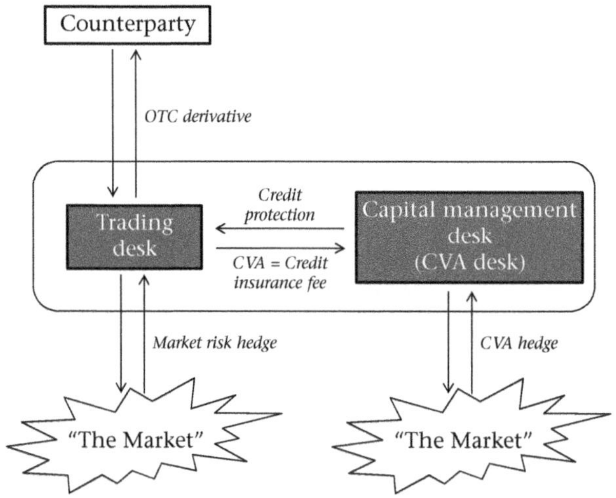

Figure 11.2 Illustration of the role of a CVA for a standard trading desk

If fact, the real problem that a CVA desk tries to handle is: *how can we minimise the counterparty risk VaR in the book of OTC derivatives in the firm, given (i) the hedging constraint that the market offers and (ii) the limited amount of cash to spend on hedging that we have*?

In less sophisticated firms, CVA hedging is done by the dealing desks directly. This is a good approach when the organisation does not have the capability to set up a group specialised in credit risk hedging, though it could easily be a suboptimal set-up given the high degree of complexity around CVA hedging.

In addition to all that has been said, a CVA desk has a key role in managing conterparty risk and, in fact, a centralised and well managed desk has the capability to generate profits via a number of mechanisms that include analysing, restructuring, or terminating trades that generate high credit risk or changing netting, or by suggesting changes in collateral agreements to decrease credit risk.

11.2 CVA interpretation

We have seen CVA as a credit insurance fee sold by the CVA desk to the dealing desks. There are a number of ways we can understand this.

CVA as the price of a CCDS: We can regard the credit insurance that the CVA desks sell internally to the dealing desks as a credit product by itself, in its own right. It is actually a credit default swap (CDS), with the given counterparty as the underlying entity, but with a notional payment in the case of default that is unknown and stochastic, as it is the value of the underlying portfolio with that counterparty at the time of default.

The CVA desk is typically going to charge for this insurance at trade inception but, as explained, the value of that insurance is going to fluctuate in value over time, as market conditions change. Consequently, it is going to have sensitivities to the underlying market factors (credit spreads, interest rates, etc.)– like any other derivative.

Hence, in that sense, the credit insurance that the CVA desk sells to the dealing deks is a credit derivative by itself. It is usually referred to as a Contingent Credit Default Swap (CCDS), because the payment to be made in the case of a default is "contingent" on the value of the portfolio of trades.

Another important difference with a standard CDS is that, typically, the credit insurance fee is paid upfront,[1] while in a standard CDS some can be paid upfront, but some is also paid as a running coupon during the life of the insurance.

CVA as the price of an option: In fact, because of this difference, some authors like referring to this credit product as an option [54]. It can be seen as a call option, with the value of the netting set (V_t) as the reference price, with strike zero, which is only paid contingent on the counterparty defaulting.

In fact, the interpretation of EPE as a strip of options on the underlying portfolio (Section 6.10) somehow reinforces this view.

CVA as a reserve amount: Another way to look at CVA is as a reserve amount. This makes special sense when the institution does not actively hedge counterparty risk. In that case, CVA is the expected loss arising from future counterparty defaults in a portfolio of OTC derivatives.

This different way of looking at CVA has an impact on its calculation. As we will see later, when CVA is seen as the price of hedging, we typically use bilateral CVA formulae, calibrated to market-implied parameters, while when seeing it as a reserve, we are going to use unilateral CVA formulae, and we may want to calibrate the models to the real world, usually via historical calibration.

CVA as the cost of clearing: A final way of looking at CVA is within the clearing space. We will see in Chapter 19 that by clearing a portfolio of trades through a central counterparty (CCP) we are minimising its credit risk, as the CCP is supposed to be a default-remote entity. In that sense, the difference in the value of a trade if it is agreed bilaterally vs. if it is cleared, should be the CVA.

This approach is not very popular as it is somewhat complicated to calculate, because the way the CCP builds the credit insurance[2] is via the assets it collects as collateral and a reserve fund. From the point of view of the counterparties, this will be related to the funding cost they face when delivering those assets.

In this text, unless otherwise stated, we are going to look at CVA as the price of a CCDS.

11.3 Calibration

We have seen that counterparty credit risk models have two classes of calibration methodologies: market implied (the risk-neutral measure) or historical (the real-world measure). In principle, the same applies to CVA.

If CVA is seen as the market price of counterparty credit risk, then CVA is typically calibrated to market implied parameters. That is because, in this case, we are not interested in how much we expect to lose from the default risk that we carry in my book of OTC derivatives, but rather how much it will cost me to hedge out that risk. The answer to those two viewpoints should be the same in an ideal world, but it isn't in reality.

However, if CVA is seen as a reserve for future losses, then it must be calibrated to the real measure, typically via historical parameters, as that measure reflects *our view* as to how the markets will behave in the future and, hence, will drive our expected future losses. It could happen that we have the opinion that the market's view on the future is the best estimate for it, in which case both measures will be the same, but it does not need to be necessarily like that.

There isn't real consensus in the market as to when to use each approach [10, 14].

Procedure: For a full calibration of the CVA models to the risk-neutral measure, we must take the default probabilities and recovery rates from the CDS market; and all drifts, volatilities, mean reverting parameters, jump parameters, etc., used in the calculation of EPE, must be taken also from the prices of vanilla derivative products in each of those asset classes. Ideally, the correlations should be too. On the other hand, for a calibration of the models to the real-world measure, we are typically going to use historical time series to calculate all the model parameters.

However, if we want to calibrate the models to the real world, we are going to find it hard to find good-quality time series for many names in the CDS market, for interest and FX rates in some emerging market currencies, for some equity prices, etc.

In practice, most calibration frameworks use a blend of both, but institutions tend of favour one or another depending on how CVA is viewed and on the modelling policy.

For example, if we want to calibrate counterparty default probabilities and recovery rates to the market, we must have a liquid market both for standard and digital CDSs,[3] as otherwise we have two variables (default intensity λ and recovery rate) to extract from one variable (the credit spread), which does not have a unique solution. So, in reality, recovery rates are nearly always calibrated using historical analysis. The same happens with correlation; generally speaking, there aren't products out there from which we can extract implied-correlation values.

11.4 CVA sensitivities

We have seen that CVA can be seen as the price of a credit trade, a CCDS, between the dealing desks in a bank and the CVA desk. As such, that product will have sensitivities to market variables like any other derivative. If x is a generic market variable (e.g., an interest rate, an FX rate, etc.),

$$\begin{aligned}\Delta CVA = & \frac{\partial CVA}{\partial s_{cpty}} \Delta s_{cpty} + \frac{\partial CVA}{\partial s_{own}} \Delta s_{own} + \frac{\partial CVA}{\partial x} \Delta x \\ & + \frac{1}{2} \frac{\partial^2 CVA}{\partial s_{cpty}^2} (\Delta s_{cpty})^2 + \frac{1}{2} \frac{\partial^2 CVA}{\partial s_{own}^2} (\Delta s_{own})^2 + \frac{1}{2} \frac{\partial^2 CVA}{\partial x^2} (\Delta x)^2\end{aligned}$$

$$+\frac{\partial^2 CVA}{\partial s_{cpty}\,\partial s_{own}}\Delta s_{cpty}\,\Delta s_{own}+\frac{\partial^2 CVA}{\partial s_{cpty}\,\partial x}\Delta s_{cpty}\,\Delta x+\frac{\partial^2 CVA}{\partial s_{own}\,\partial x}\Delta s_{own}\,\Delta x+\ldots \tag{11.1}$$

The first three terms represent delta terms, the next three gamma terms, and the last three cross-gamma terms.

As a remark, we must note that the above formula is a simplification as, in reality, we generally are going to have a term structure of credit spreads, and also of the market variable x, which must be taken into account too.

Let's forget about those terms structures for now and let's introduce the approximation of Equation 8.18, as in this way the explanation becomes more clear. If we do that, and saying for now that (i) $\frac{\partial s_{cpty}}{\partial s_{own}}=0$, (ii) the survival term in Equation 8.15 can be neglected ($S_u \simeq 1$), (iii) $\frac{\partial EPE_t}{\partial s}=0$, $\frac{\partial ENE_t}{\partial s}=0$, (iv) $\frac{\partial s}{\partial x}=0$, where s represents any credit spread (either s_{cpty} or s_{own}), we obtain

$$\Delta CVA=\widehat{EPE}\,\Delta s_{cpty}+\widehat{ENE}\,\Delta s_{own}+\left(\frac{\partial\widehat{EPE}}{\partial x}s_{cpty}+\frac{\partial\widehat{ENE}}{\partial x}s_{own}\right)\Delta x$$

$$+\frac{1}{2}\left(\frac{\partial^2\widehat{EPE}}{\partial x^2}s_{cpty}+\frac{\partial^2\widehat{ENE}}{\partial x^2}s_{own}\right)(\Delta x)^2+\frac{\partial\widehat{EPE}}{\partial x}\Delta s_{cpty}\,\Delta x+\frac{\partial\widehat{ENE}}{\partial x}\Delta s_{own}\,\Delta x+\ldots \tag{11.2}$$

From the above formula, we can observe the following interesting features:

- The credit delta to s_{cpty} is $\widehat{EPE}$, and to s_{own} is $\widehat{ENE}$.
  This means that to delta-hedge the credit component, the CDS positions that we need to build are proportional to $\widehat{EPE}$ and $\widehat{ENE}$. As the market changes, we need to rebalance the CDS positions to make them again proportional to the new $\widehat{EPE}$ and $\widehat{ENE}$.
- The market delta to x is proportional to the *level* of s_{cpty} and s_{own}.
  This implies that as the counterparty and our own credit spread changes in value, we need to rebalance the hedges, even if the market (x) has hardly moved. In particular, it must be noted that as the counterparty or our own credit standing deteriorates (i.e., when the spreads widen), CVA becomes more and more volatile, just the opposite of what we'd like to have when there is a credit crisis.
- There isn't any credit gamma.
  Within the assumptions made, we do not have to worry about credit gamma. We will relax those assumptions in a minute and analyse what happens.
- The market gamma is also proportional to the *level* of s_{cpty} and s_{own}.
  This amplifies further the problem just described: CVA becomes more and more volatile in a credit crisis, just when we need it to be most manageable.
- The market-credit cross-gamma is non-zero in general, even when $\frac{\partial\widehat{EPE}}{\partial s}=0$, $\frac{\partial\widehat{ENE}}{\partial s}=0$, and $\frac{\partial s}{\partial x}=0$.
  Even when the EPE and ENE profiles are not sensitive to the credit spreads, we can have a credit-market cross-gamma.

Those are the characteristics of the CCDS trade that make the task of hedging CVA quite a tricky one.

Credit–credit correlation: Often, both counterparties in a bilateral OTC derivative agreement are financial institutions. It is well known that credit spreads tend to be highly correlated between firms, especially when they operate in the same industry or region. When that is the case, the assumption $\frac{\partial s_{cpty}}{\partial s_{own}}=0$ made before does not hold and needs to be relaxed.

When this happens, the following additional terms apply to the sensitivities:

- The credit deltas need an extra term. For example, in the case of Δs_{cpty}, that term is

$$\widehat{ENE}\frac{\partial s_{own}}{\partial s_{cpty}} \tag{11.3}$$

- Now a credit gamma appears. In the case of $(\Delta s_{cpty})^2$, those terms are

$$\frac{1}{2}\widehat{ENE}\frac{\partial^2 s_{cpty}}{(\partial s_{own})^2} \tag{11.4}$$

- Finally, the market-credit cross-gammas also need two new terms. In the case of the $\Delta s_{cpty}\,\Delta x$ cross-gamma,

$$\frac{\partial \widehat{ENE}}{\partial x}\frac{\partial s_{own}}{\partial s_{cpty}} + \widehat{ENE}\frac{\partial s_{own}^2}{\partial s_{cpty}\,\partial x} \tag{11.5}$$

This assumption that we are relaxing here is no more than the sensitivity display of credit correlation. In fact, in later sections we will see in a more intuitive way that the CCDS insurance that the CVA desk sells internally is, in fact, a strong correlation trade.

The survival term: Another assumption done for the calculation of the sensitivities is that the survival term in Equation 8.15 can be neglected ($S_u \simeq 1$). This approximation is often done, but if we calculate CVA without it, then $\frac{\partial \widehat{EPE}}{\partial s_{own}} \neq 0$ and $\frac{\partial \widehat{ENE}}{\partial s_{cpty}} \neq 0$. In those cases, the CVA sensitivities have these additional terms:

- Credit deltas have a new term. For example, the term relative to Δs_{cpty} will now have,

$$s_{own}\frac{\partial \widehat{ENE}}{\partial s_{cpty}}. \tag{11.6}$$

- The credit gammas will also have two new terms. For example, the term with $(\Delta s_{cpty})^2$ will now have,

$$\frac{1}{2}\left(2\frac{\partial s_{own}}{\partial s_{cpty}}\frac{\partial \widehat{ENE}}{\partial s_{cpty}} + s_{own}\frac{\partial^2 \widehat{ENE}}{(\partial s_{cpty})^2}\right) \tag{11.7}$$

- The credit–credit cross-gammas $\Delta s_{cpty}\,\Delta s_{own}$ have now two new terms,

$$\frac{\partial \widehat{EPE}}{\partial s_{own}} + \frac{\partial \widehat{ENE}}{\partial s_{cpty}}. \tag{11.8}$$

Later in the chapter we will discuss the model risk that this assumption can generate.

The other two assumptions $(\frac{\partial \widehat{EPE}}{\partial s}) = 0$ and $\frac{\partial s}{\partial x} = 0$ are related to right and wrong-way risk, so they will be relaxed in Section 11.8.

Sensitivities calculation

There are two basic procedures to calculate sensitivities.

Brute force: We can calculate the sensitivities by bumping the risk factor at $t = 0$ to which the sensitivity is needed, and recalculating the CVA of the netting set so that, for example,

$$\Delta_x^{cva} \simeq \frac{CVA(x+\Delta x) - CVA(x)}{\Delta x} \tag{11.9}$$

This approach has two major problems. Firstly, it is highly computationally demanding, as we need to do a new full CVA calculation for each sensitivity. Secondly, we have seen that CVA has quite a high numerical noise, which can affect the quality of the calculation substantially. A typical trick to manage this is keeping the random numbers in the calculation the same in all CVA computations; strictly speaking this should be avoided, but in practice it may be the best we can do with the available resources.

Adjoint Algorithmic Differentiation (AAD): An alternative approach is taking advantage of the mathematical properties that the Implicit Function Theorem brings to the Monte Carlo simulations. In a nut shell, with this technique we calculate the sensitivity backwards in the Monte Carlo simulation using some nice mathematical properties in an "adjoint" space that is created via the implicit function theorem.

The nice thing of this approach is that we can compute as many sensitivities as wanted at a computational cost that is lower than four times the original CVA price cost [29]. This is quite an achievement as a CVA desk in a large organisation may need to have several hundred sensitivities computed. On the negative side, even though the theoretical idea is not too complicated, its implementation can be quite cumbersome.

A few remarks

We need to point out a few remarks.

Theta: We have not mentioned the sensitivity to time, θ, at all. That has been done to simplify things, but CVA should, in general, decrease over time, so θ is a negative number. The reason for that is easy to see if we regard CVA as the price of an option. As we approach maturity, it is going to be less likely that a default happens, simply because there is less time for it to happen, and so the present value of that optionality should decrease over time. This is a sensitivity hardly ever mentioned, because it is typically very small and is not usually hedged, but we must keep it present in our mind.

A term structure of sensitivities: In our example we are using the simplified formula for CVA, Equation 8.18 instead of 8.17. However, we must remember that, in reality, we are going to have a number of term structures of credit spreads, several market factors that are "x"-like interest rates, FX rates, equity prices, commodity prices, inflation, etc., and so in reality we are going to have a term structure of sensitivities. We have neglected that dimension to make the explanation more clear, but it must not be forgotten.

Combined sensitivities to the market: Sometimes we discuss the sensitivities of CVA_{asset} and CVA_{liab} to the market x in a separate way. We must realise that we may not need to differentiate between them. CVA sensitivity to an FX rate, for example, is what it is and will be hedged as one thing, regardless of whether it comes from the asset or the liability side of CVA.

11.5 Hedging counterparty credit risk

Hedging the default risks in a book of OTC derivatives is anything but simple. We face two main problems. Firstly, measuring well that risk, with all its sensitivities, is quite a task by itself. Secondly, even if we manage to have a super state-of-the-art machinery to measure it, building a good hedge for it is typically prohibitively expensive, or impossible all-in-all, due to a lack of the necessary hedging products or, when they exist, due to high transaction costs. In this section we are going to see how hedging can be done.

We have seen that we can hedge default risk in two different ways. Firstly, we may want to hedge the losses that we may have from actual default events. Secondly, we may also want to hedge out the volatility that the balance sheet suffers from the present value of the default risk that lies in the book of derivatives; that is, hedge out CVA volatility. These two aims should obviously be related, but they are not the same.

11.5.1 Hedging defaults

If all we want is to hedge the default risk in a book of OTC derivatives, all we have to do is buy CDS protection with a very short tenor (e.g., three months) and with a notional equal to the average EPE during the tenor of the CDS. Then, we can roll this hedge over when we approach the CDS maturity, so we are always protected against a potential counterparty default.

In this approach, the institution will put the CVA that dealing desks are charged at each trade inception as a reserve, to fund this hedging strategy. When measuring CVA for this approach, we are interested only in the liability side of it, as we should not account for the possibility that we may default in the future. As a result we should use unilateral CVA to calculate the reserve needed.

This would work quite nicely in an ideal world, and by this it is meant a world in which (i) we can find short-term CDSs for all our counterparties, (ii) the markets are such that the future exposures follow the EPE profiles, and (iii) our portfolio is large enough so that granular exposure effects are melted away. However, unfortunately the world is far from ideal.

A way to get around these idealistic conditions is to price CVA with a more conservative exposure metric like PFE or CESF, instead of EPE. In this way, the reserve will always be on the safe side, having an extra safety cushion. This is not correct from a pure pricing standpoint, but it may make sense from a risk management point of view.

In practice, an institution following this approach should typically focus on hedging only on the main exposures, the ones that are too large to be supported by the institution without an important P&L spike. Those should typically be large clients for which CDSs may be liquid enough. Then, the rest of the book is left unhedged, with CVA acting as a reserve against potential losses.

11.5.2 Hedging CVA

We have seen how CVA can be seen as the market price of hedging the default risk embedded in a book of OTC derivatives. We like that way of looking at it as it relates easily to the very act of hedging and the Black–Scholes–Merton risk-neutral valuation framework. We have also seen that the accounting standards require financial institution to account for that risk in their balance sheet calculations, including both the asset and liability sides of CVA. As a result, the balance sheet can fluctuate in value from changes in the CVA. Investors like stable balance sheets, so it is very important for a financial institution to control P&L fluctuations coming from CVA.

The above strategy, hedging default events, will be able, at most, to reduce the losses coming from actual defaults, but it does very little (or nothing) to control the potential paper losses coming from CVA changes in the balance sheet. Doing so is one of the key roles on a CVA desk.

The *ideal* role of a CVA desk is to create, with simple products, a position against the "market", whose P&L is equal and with opposite sign to the CCDS it internally sells to the dealing desks. This is typically done by delta-hedging the CCDS. In other words, the CVA desk tries to synthetically manufacture in the market the CCDS it has sold internally.

In this way, we can kill two birds with one stone. We can

1. Hedge out the actual default risk book of derivatives, and
2. Hedge out the P&L volatility. In this way, in principle, the CVA desk has a flat P&L; any gains from the CCDS on one side are losses from the hedging side, and vice versa.

Some CVA desks have a mandate to "run" the credit risk in the portfolio of derivatives, and hence try to make a profit out of it. However, more often their goal is to have a flat P&L. We can anticipate that this ideal goal will be very difficult to achieve in reality, and so the *real* goal of a CVA desk is to be as close as possible to that ideal state. As we are going to see, it gets to a point that this becomes more of an art than a science.

Let's see how this can be done.

11.5.3 Sources of CVA volatility

First of all, let's recall that CVA is measured at netting set level, as that mimics the process that would happen in the event of a default. In order to calculate CVA for a counterparty, we can add up the EPE profiles of its netting sets and compute Equation 8.17 to come up with the CVA of that counterparty.

Now let's forget for the moment about new trades coming into a counterparty's netting sets. Even if we keep a portfolio closed to new trades, its CVA value is going to change from day to day as a result of changes in the value of its counterparty risk. This can be seen clearly in Equation 8.18, as all of $\widehat{EPE}_t$, $\widehat{ENE}_t$, $s_{cpty,t}$ and $s_{own,t}$ will change daily. Let's base the rest of the explanation on this approximated CVA equation, for illustrative reasons; anything said can be extrapolated to the full CVA definition.

In particular, the sources of CVA volatility are going to be:

- **Credit Spreads:** The market's view in the credit quality of both counterparties in a netting set is going to change constantly. As such, the value of their credit spreads is going to change accordingly and, hence, the CVA with it. The CCDS being a credit product, this is going to be the most important of the sources of volatility.
- **Interest Rates:** The calculation of CVA has a sensitivity to the risk-free interest rates in a number of ways. Firstly, via interest rate derivatives that may exist in the portfolio of trades; those trades will change in value daily as the interest rates move. Secondly, even if we did not have any such derivatives, CVA will move via the discount factors that are applied across the board. Finally, we could have bonds or other interest-rate-sensitive risky collateral in the CSA facility that is going to affect the gap risk, hence the exposure in a collateralised portfolio.
- **FX Rates:** Here we also have a few sources of FX sensitivity. Firstly, we could just have FX trades in the portfolio. Secondly, we are going to be indirectly sensitive to FX if we have trades that pay in a currency different to that in which we do for the accounting in our firm; for example, an American bank that has FTSE 100 options. Finally, we could have collateral in currencies different to those used in the firm's accounting.

- **Volatilities:** CVA is sensible to market volatilities at two levels. On the one hand, we are typically going to have option trades in our portfolio. As such, those trades are going to be sensitive to changes in the implied volatilities. However, on the other hand, we have seen how a CCDS can be seen as an option with the underlying book of trades as the reference price, and a strike of zero. As such, we are going to be sensitive to the market volatilities even when we do not have any options on our books. This can also be seen in the calculation of the EPE and ENE profiles. They involve a diffusion process of risk factors (RFE models) that are driven by volatilities. As a result, a change in those volatilities will change the EPE and ENE profiles.
- **Correlations:** Similarly to the just mentioned volatility effect, we can be sensitive to correlations because the trades in our portfolio are sensitive to correlation as a pricing factor. For example, options on basket of currencies, CDOs, etc. But also, even if we do not have any such trades in the portfolio, EPE profiles are going to change if the correlations in the diffusion RFE processes change. That will drive a correlation sensitivity even if we do not have any correlation trades as such. That is because the CCDS is, by itself, a correlation product. In fact we are going to see later how it is generally very strongly sensitive to the credit correlation.
- **Other Market Variables:** In general, any market variable that the book of trades is sensitive too will drive changes in the CVA. This includes equities, commodities, and inflation, credit spreads.[4]
- **Time Decay:** As mentioned when we discussed the CVA sensitivities, as a book of trades matures and we approach maturity, CVA will naturally decay as the amount of time left for potential defaults decreases.

11.5.4 How the hedging process works

We have said that from the different sources of P&L volatility that a CCDS has the most important in most cases is the credit spreads. Let's see first how to hedge credit risk, and then let's move to other market factors like interest rates, FX rates, etc.

Hedging credit risk

Let's focus on the asset side of CVA for now. In order to hedge its credit sensitivity we can do the following: we build an array of forward CDSs, buying protection on the counterparty at stake, in which the notional of each forward CDS is the average $\widehat{EPE}$ for that time bucket.

Let's explain this with an example, illustrated in Figure 11.3. Let's say that we want to hedge the CVA for a counterparty. Typically we will be able to buy credit protection on them with a number of CDS tenors; let's say that in our case it is 1 year, 3 years, 5 years, 7 years, 10 years and 12 years. For a reminder of how CDS contracts work, the reader can refer to Section 7.1.

We are going to proceed as follows:

- First, we need to buy protection on the CDS with the longest tenor, 12 years. The notional to the 12 year CDS must be the average discounted EPE between year 10 and year 12. Let's say that value is $9 million.
- Then we calculate the average discounted EPE between year 7 and 10; let's say that value is $20 million. We already have $9 million of protection between years 10 and 12, that come from the 12 year CDS that we have bought, so we need to buy 10 years CDS protection with a notional of $11 million.
- Now we want to cover the time bucket between years 5 and 7. We find that the average discounted EPE is $25 million, and so we need to buy protection with a notional of $5 million.
- And we proceed like this until we cover the whole discounted EPE profile with forward "synthetically created" CDSs.

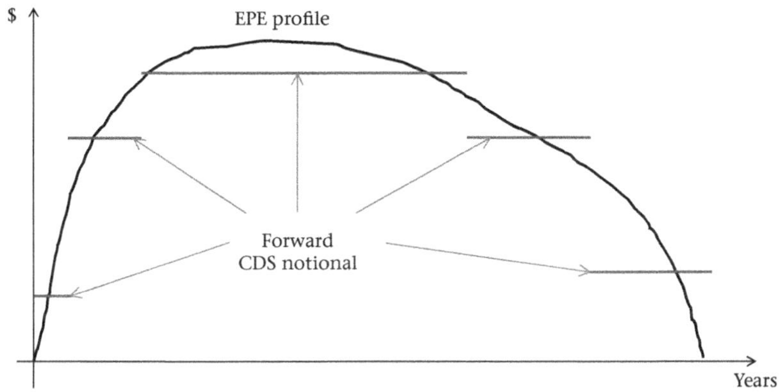

Figure 11.3 Illustration of a credit hedging position for a CCDS

This process is illustrated in Figure 11.3. It must be noted that, for some time buckets, we will have to sell protection in order to build the right forward CDS profile. In the example in the figure, that will happen for the first and second time bucket.

We can now see that with this hedging strategy, we are going to kill two birds with one stone: on the one hand, by building this array of synthetic CDSs we are mimicking the paper profit or losses, but with the opposite sign that the CCDS delivers to our balance sheet, hence neutralising its volatility. On the other hand, we are going to have a short-term CDS protection position equal to the average EPE in the first time bucket. As such, we are also going to be protected against an actual default by the counterparty at stake. In other words, we neutralise CVA volatility and losses from real defaults.

Some trading desks a decide, perhaps naively, not to put in place this hedge when the counterparty has very good credit standing, as it is very unlikely to default. However, when bad news about a counterparty hits public knowledge, there is an increased demand for credit protection, which pushes its price higher, which can create even more demand for credit protection, which can push its price even higher, etc. When a process like this starts, the credit spread gets into a self-feeding loop that takes the price of credit protection to unreasonable levels. If a CVA desk has its CDS hedging positions set before the cycle starts, this effect should only have a very limited impact in its CVA P&L,[5] but if not, the financial cost can be pretty high. This can get to the point that some CVA desks may decide not to enter into any hedging at all, as the price is prohibitive.

Hedging market risk

We have seen that in addition to credit sensitivities we also have sensitivities to other market risk factors like interest rates, FX rates, equity prices, commodities, inflation, etc., and their volatilities. In order to hedge these risks, we are going to calculate the sensitivities that CVA has to each of them, and then buy and sell in the market vanilla products like swaps, forwards, and options to hedge those risks in the standard way, like any other derivative product.

In principle, what we want to achieve is, firstly, to hedge either the volatility or the gamma sensitivity with options. Then, the combination of those options with my CCDS is typically going to leave a delta that is unhedged; then we are going to hedge that residual delta with products like swaps or forwards.

In reality, hedging all the sensitivities perfectly is going to be mission-impossible, and the task of a good CVA desk is to understand which are the important ones, hedge them in a cost-effective way, and understand which are the naked risks so nobody gets surprised when we get hit by them.

Also, it is important that these hedges are done with vanilla exchange-based products, as otherwise we would also be creating a default risk with these hedges. An exchange, similarly to a CCP, is supposed to be a default-remote entity, hence counterparty risk is minimised.

Rebalancing the hedges

As the markets move, the sensitivities that the CCDS has to all the market factors are going to change, and so we need to rebalance the hedges periodically. This is typically done weekly for important and liquid counterparties,[6] or monthly for not-so-liquid ones.

In fact, the capacity that we may or may not have to rebalance the hedges in an easy and cost-effective manner should have an important impact on the best hedging strategy.

11.5.5 What happens if we do not hedge CVA?

We saw in Chapter 1 that one of the cores of the banking business is to absorb credit risk, and charge for it. Typically a bank will borrow money at a given interbank rate and lend it out at a higher rate to riskier clients, cashing in on the rate difference.

Also, we now understand that CVA is the market price of the credit risk that a bank has in its book of OTC derivatives. So, if this is the case, why do they want to hedge out this risk?

On the one hand, if a bank decides not to hedge CVA, it actually means that it is assuming the counterparty risk embedded in its book of OTC derivatives, hoping to make money out of it. This money is made mainly by not paying the premium needed to buy credit protection via the CDS market.[7] However, if managed in this way, the bank is then exposed to being hit by large losses from counterparties defaulting.

On the other hand, if it hedges CVA it means the bank does not want to be exposed to that default risk. This makes sense in principle as OTC derivatives are not built to make money out of credit risk, and that risk is quite "hidden" in them, so perhaps it is best to set up a specialised unit for it, the CVA desk, that then gets rid of it as appropriate.

In other words, the difference between OTC derivatives and other typical credit products (i.e., loans, mortgages, credit cards) is that the core of the OTC derivative business is not assuming credit risk, but providing a financial tailored risk-hedging or investment vehicle, while credit risk-taking is the core business of other credit products. In them, the credit risk is very well under control but, in an OTC derivative, it is highly stochastic, as it is *contingent* on the value of some market parameters. As a result, banks tend to choose to hedge it out of its trading book's balance sheet as much as possible.

Having said that, nothing is stopping a bank from having a CVA desk with a mandate to make a profit. In fact, some do.

The limits of credit risk hedging: It must be noted that credit risk does not totally disappear with the described hedging strategy, even if there were no liquidity or market constraints. The reason being that the CDS positions created as hedges are set up with another institution that could default too. As such, if the credit side of CVA is unhedged we are at risk of losses from the counterparty defaulting; but if it is hedged, then we are at risk of losses from a double default: from the counterparty of the portfolio *and* of the hedges. By hedging we make the default loss probability much smaller, but not zero.

CVA hedging and CCPs: Arguably, this is one of the reasons for the push from policy-makers to clear CDS contracts via central counterparties as a first priority in the overall drive towards clearing. When done in this way, the credit hedging for bilateral OTC derivatives that have not been cleared is done by a default-remote entity, and does not suffer from the dangerous contagion effects. Hence CCPs absorb default risk from dealers by either having the derivatives themselves cleared or by having the credit hedges cleared.

11.5.6 Friction costs

So far, the hedging mechanism we have explained has been quite idealistic. In practice, there are a number of limitations that are central to the act of hedging CVA risk, typically referred to as "friction" costs. These include:

- **Limited Liquidity:** The CDS market can be highly illiquid. In many cases, there is hardly any liquidity, if at all, for some counterparties. Or, if there is, only for the five-year tenor, and hardly ever for anything beyond a ten-year tenor. These are very common conditions in which a CVA trader needs to operate.

  How affected a bank is by this problem is very particular to each institution, depending on the kind of clients it has, but all banks face it to some degree. Some banks are very focused on not-too-large companies, for which the CDS market is totally non-existent, while others have more of a large-multinational client base, hence are less affected by this problem.

  There are a number of ways to manage this. For example, if the CDS market exists, but it is quite limited in depth, the bank can buy from time to time a large CDS on that name that should in all likelihood cover for potential default losses, and manage the "P&L" CVA volatility by buying or selling protection on a highly liquid index, bringing down in this way the notional of the forward CDSs to the desired level. This is illustrated in Figure 11.4.

  If we have a portfolio that matures in, say, 20 years, but we only have reasonable liquidity in the five-year CDS tenor, then we can buy five-year CDS in excess, and hope that the shape at the end of the credit curve for that counterparty does not change much, or we can manage the CVA volatility coming from the end of the curve with index CDSs.

  In the case where there is no CDS market whatsoever to buy protection on a given counterparty, all the institution can do is manage its P&L CVA balance sheet volatility using credit indices that are highly correlated to the counterparty, though in this case there will be no protection at all for default events, and this should be then managed via traditional PFE exposure monitoring techniques.
- **Bid-offer Spread:** A problem related to the one just described is the bid-offer spread that the market offers. It is related because, in general, low liquidity crystallises in the market with a high bid-offer spread.

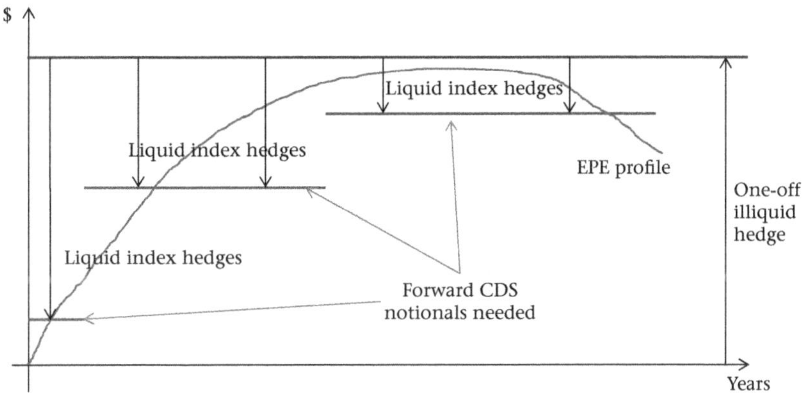

Figure 11.4 Illustration of a hedging of counterparties with low liquidity

In this context, there is a competing balance between very frequent hedging that minimises the lack of precision in the hedging position and the bid-offer spread, that can create a significant cost if rebalancing is too frequent.

In the case of CVA, this friction cost comes to a high degree from the CDS market. The bid-offer spread when liquidity is high is around one or two basis points, but it can easily go to ten or twenty basis points when liquidity is low.

Often, many of the counterparties that banks trade with have high bid-offer spreads, which cause high CCDS hedging costs. Typically, the frequency at which the CVA are rebalanced is around weekly for counterparties with a highly liquid CDS market, or monthly for low liquid counterparties.

Also, another problem related to this is the minimum size of CDS notionals. CDSs tend to trade in "clips" of USD5 million. This also puts a limit on the optimal frequency of rebalancing the hedges.

- **Non-existent Market Risk Products:** On top of the problems around credit risk hedging, market risk hedging (e.g., interest rates, FX) can be tricky too because the market lacks the required products.

  The good news is that the markets are usually quite liquid in all major currencies for vanilla products like interest rate swaps, swaptions, FX forwards, FX options, commodities futures, commodity options, inflation and equity.

  However, the bad news is that it is going to be prohibitively expensive to hedge, for example, a whole volatility smile in a CCDS, or the complete ladder of delta, gamma, and vega over all the tenors in an interest rate yield curve. In this case, the CVA trader needs to see which are the main factors driving the risk in the CVA book, and hedge them in a cost-effective way.

  On top of that, sometimes it is not only a matter of cost but also of a matter of availability. For example, there aren't products out there that can be used to hedge cross-gamma (correlation) in general (e.g., equity spot-volatility cross-gamma). A CVA desk needs to measure that risk and keep it under control in a traditional VaR-like risk management style.

As a result of these limitations, the real challenge that we face as a CVA desk is, as said before, how we can minimise the counterparty risk VaR in the book of OTC derivatives in the firm, given (i) the hedging constraint that the market offers and (ii) the limited amount of cash to spend that we have.

A good CVA desk is one that is good at this difficult task.

11.5.7 Index hedging

As already said, often we need to use credit indices to hedge CVA. This is necessary when a counterparty's CDS market lacks depth.

If we need to proceed in this way, first we need to find a credit index that is highly correlated to the counterparty's credit spread. In general, this should not be too difficult as credit spreads tend to move together, as is depicted in Figure 11.5.

Obvious generic candidates are iTraxx and CDX indices, but we could also build our own index. Let's say, for example, that we are a Canadian bank that is exposed to a number of medium or small sized commodity companies that have very limited depth in the CDS market. In that case, we could build an index with a few representatives, large commodity companies, and use that index to hedge our CVA against them.

Because of this, large institutions, when dealing with many clients with limited or no CDS depth, sometimes have a number of default credit indices readily available for this purpose. Typically, we can build those indices based on these three parameters: region, business sector, and credit rating. In this way, every company that

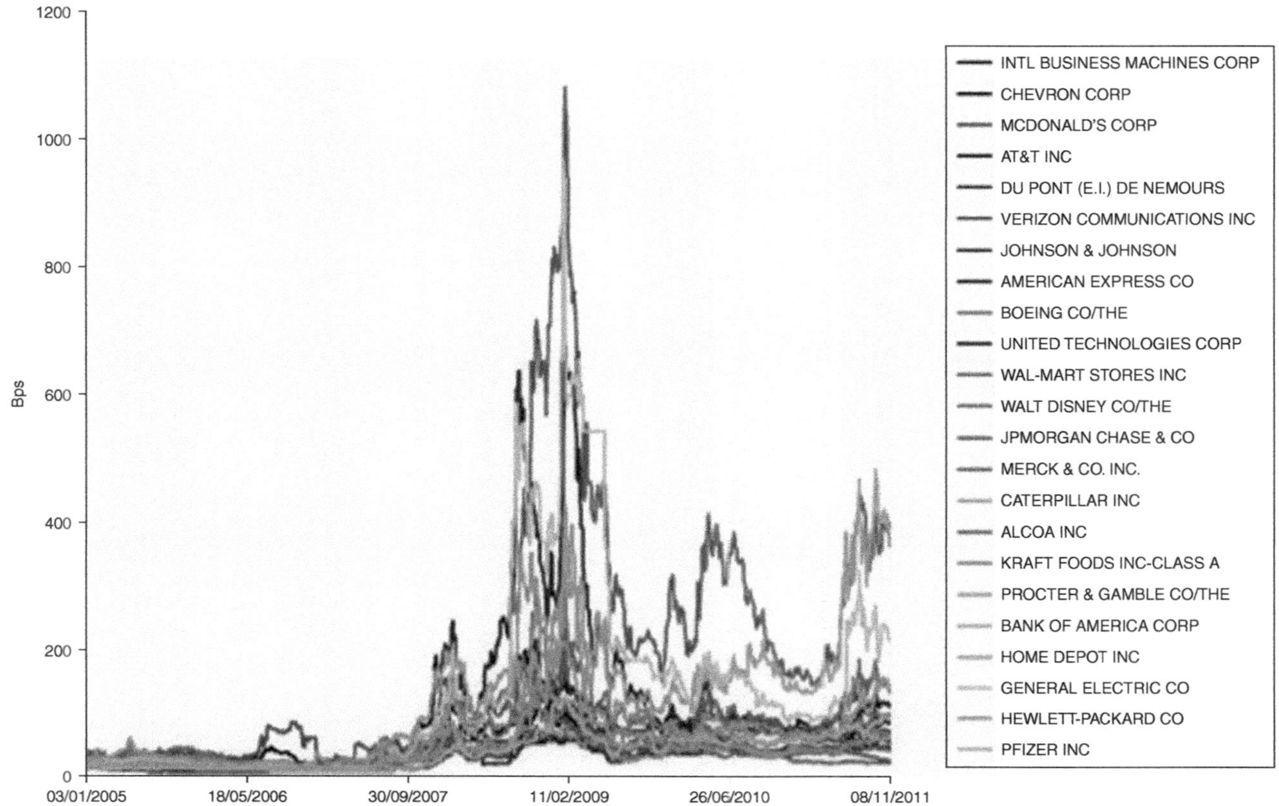

Figure 11.5 Time series of some randomly selected credit spreads
Source: Bloomberg.

has limited CDS depth can be automatically mapped on to one of these indices. The financial institution should then revise this mapping on a regular basis to adapt to changing market conditions.

In fact, as we saw in Chapter 9, the Basel III accord permits this mapping technique when calculating regulatory capital for CVA, and this is also becoming a standard for accounting purposes.

Most importantly, we must emphasise that these credit indices allow for the marking and management of the bank's CCDS position, but does not hedge the bank against default events at all, and so this existing risk must be managed in more traditional ways, typically by (i) limiting the current and potential future exposure to these counterparties and (ii) building default reserves according to the bank's policy.

Also, an additional unintended effect of this credit-index hedging is the basis risk that we become exposed to: if a component of the index defaults, we will be hit by a profit (if we are buying protection in the index) or loss (if we are selling protection) when nothing has actually happened to the counterparty they intend to hedge. This must be kept in mind too.

11.5.8 Hedging the liability side of CVA

So far, when discussing how to hedge the credit component of CVA, we have referred only to its asset side. Let's deal now with the liability side.

The asset side as a natural hedge of the liability side: We have seen in Equation 8.18 that CVA can be approximately expressed as $\widehat{EPE} \cdot s_{cpty} + \widehat{ENE} \cdot s_{own}$. We are going to see that CVA_{asset} is a natural hedge for CVA_{liab}, as a consequence of the strong dependency that credit spreads of different counterparties have (Figure 11.5).

The idea behind it is that, following Equation 8.18, the most important sensitivity in CVA is that to credit spreads. Hence

$$\Delta CVA \simeq \widehat{EPE}\, \Delta s_{cpty} + \widehat{ENE}\, \Delta s_{own} \tag{11.10}$$

If both our own credit spread and that of the counterparty move approximately in parallel, something quite common, and if the portfolio of trades is balanced so that $\widehat{EPE} \approx -\widehat{ENE}$, then changes in CVA_{asset} coming from changes in s_{cpty} will be approximately the same with the opposite sign than the changes in CVA_{liab} coming from changes in s_{own}. As a result, the net change in CVA will be approximately zero.

Elaborating a bit further, given the generally strong correlation between spread, we can say that

$$\Delta s_{cpty} = \rho\, \Delta s_{own} + \sqrt{1-\rho^2}\, \epsilon, \tag{11.11}$$

and then

$$\Delta CVA \approx (\widehat{EPE}\, \rho + \widehat{ENE})\, \Delta s_{own} + \widehat{EPE}\, \sqrt{1-\rho^2}\, \epsilon. \tag{11.12}$$

For a given netting set, we can always express $\widehat{ENE}$ as a multiple of $\widehat{EPE}$,

$$\widehat{ENE} = -\gamma\, \widehat{EPE}, \tag{11.13}$$

and so, the change in CVA can be expressed as

$$\Delta CVA \approx \widehat{EPE}\, (\rho - \gamma)\, \Delta s_{own} + \widehat{EPE}\, \sqrt{1-\rho^2}\, \epsilon. \tag{11.14}$$

We can see in this equation that when the credit spreads of both counterparties are highly correlated ($\rho \approx 1$) and when the book of trades have approximately symmetric EPE and ENE profiles ($\gamma \approx 1$), then $\Delta CVA \approx 0$.

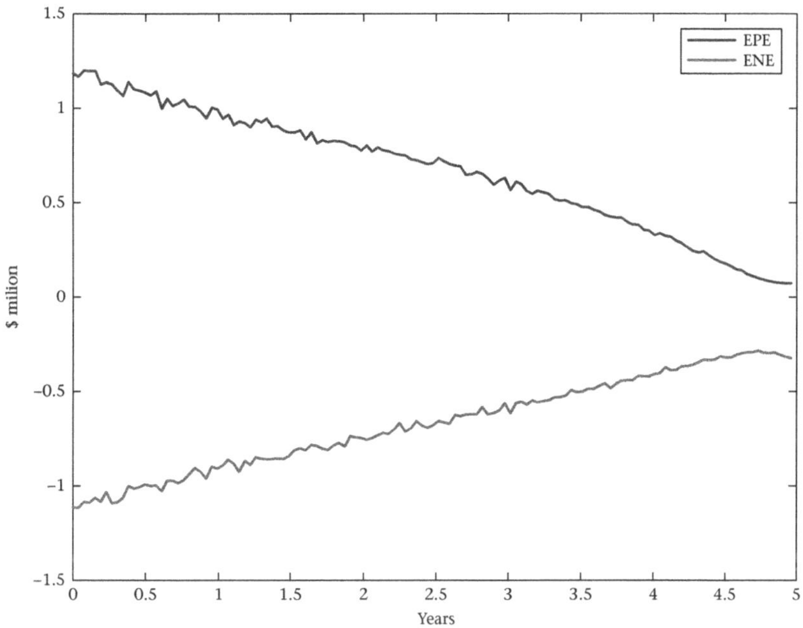

Figure 11.6 EPE and ENE profile of a $100m IR swap

As a simple illustrative example, let's say that we are a bank with a credit spread of 50 bps, and that we enter a simple interest rate swap agreement, a notional of $100m, with a counterparty that has a credit spread of 250 bps. The trade is subject to an ideal collateral agreement.[8] Figure 11.6 shows the EPE and ENE profiles of the trade with an MPR of ten days. With a constant yield curve of 5%, the CVA model run, with 5,000 scenarios, gives an $\widehat{EPE}$ of $1.692m, and an $\widehat{ENE}$ of −$1.687m, a CVA_{asset} of $42.3k, and a CVA_{liab} of $8.4k, delivering a total CVA of $33.9k. Let's say that one day has passed, in which interest rates have hardly moved (i.e., the EPE and ENE profiles are approximately the same), but the spreads have moved up 40 bps for us and 50 bps for the counterparty. In that case, we will have a CVA_{asset} of $50.8k and a CVA_{liab} of $15.2k, both have changed substantially, but the new net CVA is still $35.6k, nearly the same as the day before.

Direct hedging of the liability side: Consequently, the asset side of CVA may be a natural hedge to its sister, the liability side, but that does not mean that we do not need to do any direct hedging of it. We may still want to hedge the part of it that is not well protected by CVA_{asset}, as γ or ρ could be far from 1.

The ideal hedge for it would be to enter a CDS agreement with a third party in which we sell protection on our own default. Unfortunately, nobody in his right mind is going to buy that as he will by paying the protection premium regularly during the live of the CDS, but will never get the actual CDS notional if we default– precisely because we have defaulted.

However, that does not mean that CVA_{liab} needs to be completely naked. We can use an index strategy, in the same way we used it for CVA_{asset} when the market was lacking liquidity. What we can do is sell protection in a credit index that is highly correlated to us, or in an index that we can build for this purpose. In the former case, a typical index is the Markit iTraxx Senior Financials. In the latter case we can build the index with a number of institutions with whom we share regional reach and a business model.

In this way we can neutralise the *systematic* component of CVA_{liab}, leaving naked only the specific component. This is reportedly done by a number of tier-one investment banks. This does not hedge CVA_{liab} completely, but it can do a nice job if we build the index with care.

A drawback of this method is that we can be strongly exposed to basis risk. For example, let's say that we are Morgan Stanley, the American bank. Surely a credit index composed of Goldman Sachs, Citi, and Bank of America will move with very high correlation to us, leaving a very small specific component unhedged. However, if one of those banks defaults, for which we have sold protection, we will have a massive loss coming from the hedging positions. If we want to minimise this risk, we can build a more generic index, or use standard market indices, but then the unhedged specific component will be larger.

The reader must note that this idiosyncratic component tends to be strongest when we are under financial distress, which is precisely when we most needed a good hedge for it. A good hedging strategy should understand this basis risk well, so it is properly managed. Given that it mainly appears in distressed scenarios, stress testing is a key tool to be used here.

We cannot cash-hedge the liability side of CVA: In the way that we have described it so far we can only paper-hedge CVA_{liab}, as all we do is control the CVA P&L fluctuations. If we want to cash-hedge the liability side of counterparty risk, we need to make sure that we will not default. This is obviously not possible, as explained in Section 8.1.3, as we would need to have in our vaults, in a segregated manner, all expected future liabilities. Modern banks are all leveraged, leaving in cash only a small proportion of their future commitments.

In fact, if is often said that CVA_{liab} could be hedged by buying back our own bonds. That is the case because in practice (i) we would be selling protection on our default by removing our default risk from the market and (ii) we would be deleveraging, which moves precisely in the direction of the way to cash-hedge CVA_{liab}, as just explained. Obviously, the degree of leverage that a bank has via its bond market is not driven by CVA hedging requirements, but by funding needs and corporate strategy, so this hedging strategy is not really used in practice either.

As a result, CVA_{liab}, also called DVA, can only be partially hedged. The only part of if that we can hedge is the systematic component of the CVA fluctuations coming from it, but we cannot hedge the idiosyncratic component nor our own actual default risk.

11.6 CCDS as a correlation trade

We are now in a good position to understand that CCDSs are strong correlation derivatives.

We have seen how, if our credit spread is highly correlated to the market, and if our portfolio is sufficiently balanced so that $\widehat{EPE} \approx -\widehat{ENE}$, then CVA has a relatively low volatility, even when it is unhedged. However, if negative financial news about us spread out in the market place, we will not only be in a difficult business position, but the high credit correlation between ourselves and our counterparties will break and CVA volatility will rocket, adding problems to our market credibility precisely when we need it more.

That is what happened in 2008 in the financial industry, and why it is so important to understand CVA properly.

CCDS is a correlation product. The correlation that matters here is the credit correlation between ourselves and our clients. For most financial institutions, that correlation is pretty high in normal market conditions, as many of the most important counterparties are other financial institutions or institutions in the same region. However, when that correlation moves towards zero CVA management becomes a double challenge.

Given that the described correlation breakage tends to happen in distressed markets, stress testing is a basic tool to understand how much it can affect us.

11.7 Recovery rate risk

Up to know, we have mentioned the Recovery Rate (RR)[9] as the percentage of the value that is recovered upon a counterparty default, and we have implicitly made two key assumptions: that the recovery rate in a portfolio of derivatives is the same as the recovery rate in a CDS contract, and that both sides of the position (portfolio and CDSs) get liquidated at the same time. Unfortunately, neither is correct. Let's skim through a liquidation process to understand the basics of it.

When a company defaults there is an auction by which the holders of CDS protection receive the recovery rate on the outstanding notional in the CDSs. This action process takes, typically, a few weeks. For example, in the case of Lehman Brothers, the company filed for bankruptcy on 15 September 2008, and their CDSs recovery rate was agreed on 10 October 2008 (with a recovery of 8.625%).

However, the liquidation process of a book of OTC derivatives can be quite lengthy, as it is quite complex and comes with a large degree of legal uncertainty [57]. For example, in the case of Lehman Brothers, final agreement on liquidation of the book of OTC derivatives was reached in mid-2011, nearly three years after the bankruptcy was declared. In fact, it must be said that even the mere concept of recovery rate is difficult to measure in that context, as each part of the liquidation process is going to see the value of the portfolio differently. Using the Lehman's example again, its derivatives creditors filed \$22 billion, while Lehman's estimate was only \$10 billion. The recovery rate agreed with its derivatives creditors hasn't been made public, but it was surely different to that 8.625%.

Recovery rate management: As a result of this, CCDS is exposed to a recovery rate missmatch, both in terms of quantity and timing, which cannot be hedged, as there aren't really any products out there to do so. The only way this can be managed is by taking a view on our expectation of the future missmatch, and use one of the following two products to deal with it.

There exist Recovery Default Swaps (RDS). These are derivative contracts by which two firms agree to exchange a predetermined recovery rate against the actual CDS auctioned recovery rate, upon default of the reference entity. These swaps are typically traded at zero price, so the fixed recovery rate agreed "today" is the expected CDS recovery rate in the future. The strike of that RDS will be different to the one from the book of OTC derivatives upon default, and so the notional that we want in the RDS could be different to that of the CDS, reflecting our view on the expected recovery rate in the book of derivatives.

An equivalent way to manage this risk is with digital CDSs. These contracts are like a standard CDS, but they pay the full notional upon default. Hence the recovery rate risk is completely washed out. These contracts can also be managed to control the recovery rate we obtain the the CVA hedging positions upon default.

However, in the real world, these two derivatives are quite rare and highly illiquid, so this risk cannot be easily managed. Consequently this recovery rate risk is one of those typically left naked by the CVA desk.

CVA recovery rate sensitivity: It must be noted that CVA is hardly sensitive to the recovery rate. Let's expand a bit on this.

The price of a CDS can be quoted as a par credit spread: 10 bps, 100 bps, 500 bps, etc. The spread (s) is what is actually traded, what really exists. As explained previously, typical models then split this stochastic variable into (i) a default probability via the hazard rate λ and (ii) a recovery rate RR. Thus, calibrating a pricing model means extracting λ and RR from the market price s.

Typically, there is only one credit product liquid enough to be used for calibration, the standard CDS. So, calibrating a credit model is a problem with "infinite" solutions: one pricing equation with two variables $P(\lambda, RR)$ and only one price. In other words, if we want to extract both λ and RR from the market prices, we need in addition to the standard CDS another contract, like digital CDSs, to be liquid. This is very rarely the case.

As a result, in practice, the quantity that really matters to CVA is the credit spread, as any change in the recovery rate that happens in the *theoretical* λ-RR world that operates behind the scenes will be compensated with a change in λ so that the price of the CDS (s) is left unchanged.

Because of all this, if we change the recovery rate when pricing a CDS, we are going to change the default probability accordingly so that the CDS price is kept constant, to that number seen in the market. As a result, CVA prices, that are typically calibrated to CDS market-implied parameters, are not very sensitive to recovery rates, as any change in it will drive a change in the counterparty default probability, leaving CVA mostly unchanged overall.

11.8 CVA with right and wrong-way risk

Chapter 10 was dedicated to the non-simple task of calculating exposure profiles when the value of the underlying portfolio has a dependency structure with default events in any of the counterparties. As explained in that chapter, when that dependency decreases exposure when the default probability increases, it is said that we have right-way risk; when it operates other way round we have wrong-way risk. Typical examples can be:

- We buy an equity call option from a firm with the firm's stock price as the option underlying. In the case of the firm defaulting, we know that stock price will be worth zero,[10] hence the option will be worth close to zero too, and so the exposure will be very small, if at all. This is an example of right-way risk.
- We buy from a US derivatives dealer (Dealer 1) default protection on another US dealer (Dealer 2), via a CDS. We know that if the counterparty (Dealer 1) defaults, Dealer 2 credit spread will be very wide, so the value of the CDS should be very high. This is an example of wrong-way risk.

When we have this kind of effect in our portfolio, then the assumptions that we made in Section 11.4, $\frac{\partial EPE_t}{\partial s} = 0$ (or equivalently for ENE) and $\frac{\partial s}{\partial x} = 0$, do not hold any more. Let's discuss how the CVA sensitivities change in those cases.

Changes in EPE and ENE: The first assumption that we are going to relax is $\frac{\partial EPE_t}{\partial s} = 0$ and $\frac{\partial ENE_t}{\partial s} = 0$. When we do so, we are saying that the value of the exposures will change as the credit spreads of either (or both) counterparties move. That is, that we have right or wrong-way risk in the portfolio. When we are in that situation, the following terms need to be considered for the CVA sensitivities:

- Credit deltas that have two new terms. For example, the term relative to Δs_{cpty} will now have

$$s_{cpty} \frac{\partial \widehat{EPE}}{\partial s_{cpty}} + s_{own} \frac{\partial \widehat{ENE}}{\partial s_{cpty}} \tag{11.15}$$

- Credit gammas, that were zero, now have additional terms. For example, in the case of $(\Delta s_{cpty})^2$, we will now have

$$\frac{1}{2}\left(2\frac{\partial \widehat{EPE}}{\partial s_{cpty}} + s_{cpty}\frac{\partial^2 \widehat{EPE}}{\partial s_{cpty}^2} + s_{own}\frac{\partial^2 \widehat{ENE}}{\partial s_{cpty}^2}\right) \tag{11.16}$$

- Also, the credit–credit cross-gammas $\Delta s_{cpty}\,\Delta s_{own}$ have now two new terms,

$$\frac{\partial \widehat{EPE}}{\partial s_{own}} + \frac{\partial \widehat{ENE}}{\partial s_{cpty}} \tag{11.17}$$

- And the market–credit cross-gammas are also affected. For example, the term that goes with $\Delta s_{cpty}\,\Delta x$ now has, also,

$$s_{cpty}\frac{\partial^2 \widehat{EPE}}{\partial s_{cpty}\,\partial x} + s_{own}\frac{\partial^2 \widehat{ENE}}{\partial s_{cpty}\,\partial x} \tag{11.18}$$

It is important to note that these sensitivities will manifest in different ways depending on whether our EPE and ENE models already account for DWR in them or not. If they do, the EPE and ENE profiles are computed subject to default, hence those profiles will tend to change in a limited manner as the spread changes. That is because the default events are already accounted for in the profiles and, so, the only changes in them will come from today's changes in the value of the portfolio. However, if the EPE and ENE models do not account for DWR, then the profiles will move very strongly with changes in credit spreads, especially when the spreads widen and counterparties approach a potential default.

Unfortunately, these extra sensitivities cannot really be well hedged unless we have a good DWR model. The reason is that, if we do not have it, we will see the effects of these sensitivities in the CVA P&L, but we cannot measure them a priori because, precisely, we are lacking the model to do so. As a result, the CVA desk will be defenceless against them.

This clearly shows how important it is to have a good DWR model in an EPE Monte Carlo engine.

Market–credit correlation: Generally speaking, a netting set has right and wrong-way risk when (i) there is a market variable x that has an influence in the price of the netting set *and* (ii) $\frac{\partial s}{\partial x} \neq 0$. Let's say that we have an excellent EPE and ENE model that can calculate exposure metrics subject to default, and it so happens that the changes in the EPE and ENE profiles as a counterparty approaches default are very small ($\frac{\partial \widehat{EPE}_t}{\partial s} \approx 0$ and $\frac{\partial \widehat{ENE}_t}{\partial s} \approx 0$). Even in that case, our CVA sensitivities could change in value because $\frac{\partial s}{\partial x} \neq 0$. For example,

- The market deltas are going to have an additional term like

$$EPE\frac{\partial s_{cpty}}{\partial x} + ENE\frac{\partial s_{own}}{\partial x} \tag{11.19}$$

- The market gammas are going to have four new terms

$$\frac{1}{2}\left(2\frac{\partial \widehat{EPE}}{\partial x}\frac{\partial s_{cpty}}{\partial x} + \widehat{EPE}\frac{\partial^2 s_{cpty}}{\partial x^2} + 2\frac{\partial \widehat{ENE}}{\partial x}\frac{\partial s_{own}}{\partial x} + \widehat{ENE}\frac{\partial^2 s_{own}}{\partial x^2}\right) \tag{11.20}$$

- And the market–credit cross-gammas are going to have two more terms too. Using the $\Delta s_{cpty}\,\Delta x$ as an example, those new terms are

$$\frac{\partial s_{cpty}}{\partial x}\frac{\partial \widehat{EPE}}{\partial s_{cpty}} + \frac{\partial s_{own}}{\partial x}\frac{\partial \widehat{ENE}}{\partial s_{cpty}} \tag{11.21}$$

It must be noted that these new terms are only going to appear when we do not have a right or wrong-way risk model (when $\frac{\partial \widehat{EPE}}{\partial s} \neq 0$, and equivalently for ENE).

11.9 CVA of collateralised portfolios

Some institutions may feel tempted to not calculate CVA for collateralised counterparties because it "should be small". That is a mistake.

Up to now we have not made any CVA distinction between collateralised and uncollateralised portfolios. The reason being that, in principle, there isn't much difference between them. How we get to the EPE profile has some important differences, but once we have it, the CVA calculation is the same. The only CVA distinction is that when a bilateral master agreement is collateralised, exposures on the same portfolio tend to decrease, although that may not be always the case (e.g., short option positions). There are a few remarks that should be noted, though.

"Collateralised" does not necesarily mean lower risk: As said in Chapter 4, a rough rule of thumb is that the reduction of exposure in a portfolio when traded under a typical CSA, compared to uncollateralised, is one order of magnitude. A naive conclusion from this is that the risk of CSA facilities is lower than of non-CSA ones.

The credit exposure risk to a counterparty is mainly driven by the risk appetite we have to it. That appetite is typically measured by the risk-management department from PFE metrics. If we move a portfolio from uncollateralised to collateralised, we are reducing the exposure that the portfolio has, but if the risk appetite remains unchanged (i.e., the exposure limits do not move), what we are actually doing is creating more "exposure room" for more trades.

The credit risk appetite that we have with a counterparty is given by our perception of its default probability and our willingness to do business with it. Based on this, we are going to set an exposure limit that we are happy to tolerate. Loosely speaking, risk is how much we could lose multiplied by the probability of the loss, so the default probability multiplied by the exposure limit should be roughly constant throughout all the counterparties we have. Then we can modify this equation slightly to reflect our counterparty preferences, business strategy, etc.

As a result, moving a portfolio to a collateralised agreement means that we are reducing the exposure in that portfolio, but if we do not decrease the exposure limit too, all we are doing is leaving space for more trading, more business, etc., that could (and, arguably, should) be filled up with new trades.

The main sensitivies of CSA facilities are vega, MPR, and CSA terms: However, what we are indeed doing when we move a portfolio to a collateralised framework is to reshape the risk drivers.

Under a tight CSA (i.e., very low threshold, very low minimum transfer amounts, daily margining, fully symmetric, etc.) the most important risk factor tends to be the volatility. That is because we are assuming that the porfolio will be always fully collateralised, and hence the exposure will be driven very much by the gap risk over, typically, a margin period of risk (MPR) of ten days (see Section 2.2). The market risk factor that has the potential to influence most this gap risk is, often, the volatility, as it tends to drive the size of short-term price moves.

Further to this, changing the MPR can also have a dramatic impact on the exposure. A rule of thumb is that the gap risk increases as $\sqrt{MPR}$. Hence, doubling MPR from 10 to 20 days increases risk by around 40%.

Also, the details of the CSA terms are very important drivers of risk. Amongst them, we saw in Chapter 4 with a number of examples that the main driver of exposure in a CSA is the threshold, as it represents the amount of exposure each firm is willing to leave uncollateralised.

CVA to central counterparties: CCPs are supposed to be default-remote entities. As such, it is quite tempting to say that they cannot default and, hence, CVA is zero with them. This is a very dangerous statement. The big lesson that we have learnt from the 2008 financial events is that there is not such a thing as an institution that is never going to default. As a consequence, counterparty risk metrics in general, and CVA in particular, should also be calculated for trades cleared through CCPs.

If we are a CCP member, we could perhaps think that CVA will be negative because their default probability (hence credit spread) should be much lower than ours. However, our exposure to them is going to be relatively high given our contributions to the default fund and the margin we are asked to post, while their exposure to us should be quasi-zero (that is the point of a CCP). Hence, we are going to have a CVA, albeit small, that should be accounted for.

In fact, regulatory capital under Basel III gives a risk weight of 2% to CCPs, effectively treating them as super-AAA entities, but not "default-impossible" ones.

11.10 Risk allocation and charging for CVA

We have seen that CVA is the price of a credit insurance that the CVA desk sells to the rest of the dealing desks in a bank. That price is calculated per netting set to reflect the mechanics of a bank's portfolio liquidation in the event of a default.

Two of the key aims of a CVA desk are (i) to price default risk correctly and (ii) to incentivise dealing desks and business units properly. However, we know that the risk of a portfolio does not need to be the sum of the individual risks of its components. Hence, two natural question to ask would be:

1. How much is the whole portfolio CVA in a firm?
2. How much is the contribution of each trade to a netting set CVA?

The answer to the first question is quite straightforward. CVA is the price assigned to a default risk. If two counterparties default, the losses will be the same as the sum of the losses if each of them defaulted separately. In other words, CVA is additive above netting set level.[11]

In fact, I show in Appendix B that if we have a portfolio with a number of netting sets, the EPE of the counterparty equals the sum of the netting sets individual EPE. Interesingly, this rule does not hold for PFE (exposure management) or EEPE (regulatory capital), but it does for EPE.

Regarding the second question, that topic was already discussed in Chapter 5 in a general manner, but let's discuss it now in the context of CVA.[12]

Obviously we want to have a solid methodology to allocate CVA amongst trades, desks, etc. We could use the Euler algorithm to distribute CVA in a fair way, as it is a mathematically robust method to allocate risk. However, when we face reality, things may be a bit more complicated.

Let's say that we are a derivatives dealer and we have a fresh new client, for which we do two new trades, one done by the interest rates desk and the other one by the FX desk. The CVA on these two trades is, say, \$10k. We use Euler and we see that the algorithm gives \$4k to the rates desk, and \$6k to the FX desk, and so we (the CVA desk) charge accordingly to each desk. In this way we can fund the CVA hedges that we are going to put in place during the life of those two trades. Now, one year later the counterparty wants to do a new FX trade. The CVA of the netting set before the new trade has changed to \$9k. If we book the new trade, CVA goes to \$15k, and the Euler algorithm now allocates \$6k to the rates trade, \$2k to the old FX trade, and \$7k to the new FX trade. The question is, how much do we charge the FX desk for the new trade? Shall we recharge the rates desk for a trade that was done one year ago, because its CVA has increased, even if nothing has changed from their perspective, and only because the new FX trade modifies netting effects against the interest rate desk now?

As the reader can imagine, any solution based on the Euler algorithm will bring lots of problems and discussions in an organisation. The best practical way to manage this is by charging each desk for the incremental CVA they bring to the netting set when a new trade is booked (or removed). In the example above, the FX desk would be charged \$6k.

In this way each desk can forget about CVA once a trade is booked and the charge is done, and they are also incentivised to minimise counterparty risk: if they increase the bank's CVA, they pay for it; if they decrease it, they receive a benefit from it.

The Euler algorithm may be used by the CVA desk to distribute CVA charges amongst trades made at the same time, and also by the financial accounting unit to allocate CVA to each trade, as sometimes required in an accounting context.

CVA_{liab} attribution: Typically, the CVA desks are going to charge the following quantity to the dealing desks:

$$CVA_{charge} = CVA_{asset} + \gamma \; CVA_{liab} \tag{11.22}$$

with γ a number between 0 and 1. Different organisations choose different values for γ.

It must be noted that for an organisation seen as a global entity, this γ is irrelevant, as all it does is distribute CVA_{liab} internally. This is the case because CVA_{liab} is actually charged by the counterparties in each trade. Then, if $\gamma = 0$, what we are saying is that that charge is absorbed by the dealing desks, while if we use a $\gamma = 1$ then it is the CVA desk which takes on that credit cost. Each of these solutions has a business case behind it.

- We should put γ to zero if we want the front line of the business (the dealing desks) to be sensitive to the organisation's credit standing. In this way they have an incentive to contribute to increasing the institution's credit rating with their trading activity.
- It can also make sense to set γ to one, as the CVA desk is the ultimate expert in credit in the organisation, hence they can be seen as the natural place to absorb and manage that risk.
- Given that CVA_{liab} can only be partially hedged on the balance sheet, it may make sense to set that γ to an intermediate number, particularly to the correlation of the CVA_{liab} hedging indices with CVA_{liab} itself. In this way the CVA desk absorbs the systematic component of that risk, while the dealing desks absorb the specific one, that cannot be hedged.

In principle, any of these solutions are correct as long as the budgets, P&L attributions, and hedging strategies are managed accordingly.

A few remarks

- Under this incremental CVA charge system, the CVA charge that a set of new trades will get depends on the order they are traded. This does seem unfair, but arguably it is better to be a bit unfair than make CVA charging an unmanageable task.
- To compute the incremental CVA, all we need to calculate is the incremental EPE and ENE profiles and apply the CVA formula with those incremental profiles.
- Due to netting, incremental uCVA will always be smaller than stand-alone, but that does not necessarily need to be the case for bilateral CVA.
- As a transaction size increases, netting effects tend to disappear and, hence, the netting set CVA tends to the stand-alone CVA.

11.11 CVA in your organisation

CVA is the valuation of counterparty credit risk, but we cannot understand CVA well if we do not understand how counterparty credit risk affects the whole organisation, as CVA is only a part of it.

Figure 11.7 shows the functions that are influenced by counterparty risk in a financial company. These include

1. **Valuation:** Strictly speaking, this is CVA. It plays a central role in pricing a derivative to charge the right amount to clients, sensitivity analysis for CVA hedging, and balance sheet calculation.
2. **Risk Management:** Firms have traditionally kept counterparty risk under control by setting a limit to the exposure that it is willing to have to each individual counterparty. This is usually done with a PFE or CESF metric of exposure by the risk management unit.

   Also, initial margins need to be calculated. They are often based in PFE or CESF metrics at a high confidence level.

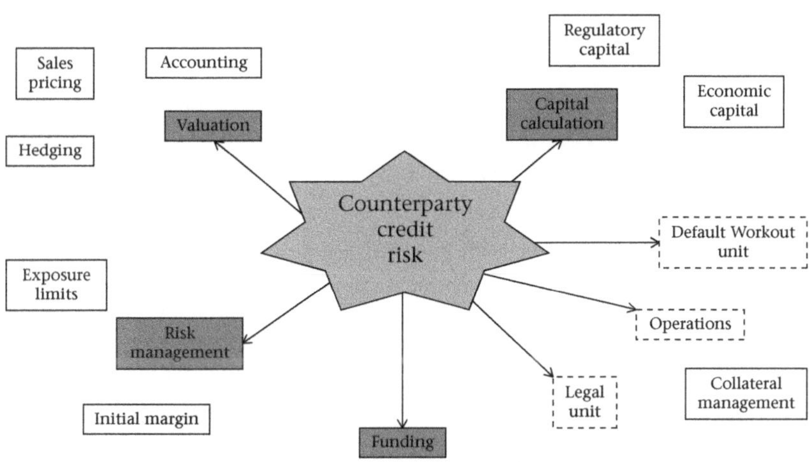

Figure 11.7 Illustration of the impact of counterparty credit risk in an organisation. The solid grey boxes indicate highly quantitative functions

3. **Capital Calculation:** Regulatory capital has become central to financial institutions as a result of the Basel II and Basel III capital rules that have continuously increased the capital banks need to have against potential credit losses in their book of derivatives. Several financial institutions now have specific groups solely dedicated to optimise the regulatory capital. Economic capital is the firms's internal calculation of the capital it needs to hold, given a desired credit standing. This is obviously also highly influenced by the counterparty risk the bank holds.
4. **Funding:** This has become a very important topic to the banking industry, as their funding costs have increased substantially since the 2008 events. I dedicate Chapters 12 and 13 to this, but the reader can anticipate that given the strong connection between funding and the liability side of CVA, this topic should be highly connected to counterparty risk.
5. **Legal Unit:** The Lehman Brothers default showed to the world the large degree of uncertainty around the liquidation of portfolios of derivative contracts, given all its accounting and jurisdictional caveats. The legal department will be central at making sure that legal risk is minimised in the event of a default, by designing good Master Agreements and CSAs and keeping information tidy and clear. There seems to be a tendency in the market to move towards standardised agreements, but even then these groups will be important to capture peculiarities that may still be needed.
6. **Operations, Collateral Management:** Collateral management used to be a secondary back-office role, but it has now become central to counterparty risk and, hence, to financial institutions. This is specially the case given the optionality that CSAs have, and hence the need to choose the optimal "cheapest-to-deliver" collateral posting strategy.
7. **Default Workout Unit:** This is the group in the bank that deals with defaults. We have seen that when a counterparty defaults there will generally be a missmatch between reserves and hedges in place and the amount actually recovered from the defaulted company. This group is typically in charge of leading this process.

The central role that counterparty risk now plays in firms has created a strong incentive to improve the interaction between the different units in a firm that handle all these functions. In the past, they were fairly split, and interaction used to be limited. Firms, especially large organisations, cannot afford that any more, and need to find ways to optimise the management of counterparty credit risk in the organisation.

Type of organisations

The way CVA is calculated, hedged, and managed can differ very strongly between firms, depending on their size, operational history, and working culture. Somewhat simplifying things, we can broadly split firms into the following categories, depending on how CVA is handled.

- **Passive Management:** These are firms with a relatively small book of OTC derivatives. They are typical clients of the wholesale banking industry that may not have the capability to measure and hedge CVA. Historically, they would have typically had negative CVA, as the banks they interact with had nearly always better credit standing than them, though that is not necessarily the case any more.

  These companies usually take CVA prices from their derivatives dealers and leave counterparty risk with relatively little management. They may decide to hedge counterparty risk, but usually only when exposures are highly concentrated around a few names. They are not going to hedge paper-CVA, but only default events with simple CDS contracts.

Given that they do not have the resources to build a full CVA pricing system, if they want to have some pricing capability themselves they can use some of the simple approximative methods explained previously, or seek help from a third party.

- **Partial Active Management:** In this bracket we should include firms with a medium to large book of OTC derivatives. These firms have a stronger incentive to be more active with counterparty risk management. They should definitely have some sort of semi-sophisticated system to price, monitor, and manage CVA, which should use the more sophisticated approximation methodologies, or even a simple Monte Carlo engine.

  In banks, CVA management will typically lie within the dealing desks, so hedging will most often be fairly simple. For example, they could only hedge the credit component of CVA. Then, an independent risk management function will supervise exposures and set limits, to ensure the bank has a well balanced book regarding counterparty risk.
- **Full Active Management:** These are, typically, large financial institutions and broker-dealers who have OTC derivatives as an important business line. They can have up to a few million OTC derivatives on their books.

  Counterparty credit risk is central to these firms. They should have a state-of-the-art Monte Carlo engine to quantify this risk, and a sophisticated system to attribute and manage it. They will typically have a specialised CVA desk to manage and hedge it. These firms may be member of CCPs, so they also have an important role as intermediaries for other smaller firms in the derivatives clearing space.

It is important to note that the optimal CVA set up by each firm is the one that is appropriate to the size of the derivatives book. It doesn't make much sense for a relatively small corporate, with a small book of derivatives, to build a full-blown CVA system, in the same way it does not make sense for a derivatives dealer to have a basic CVA system. Each organisation needs to understand well what is counterparty credit risk and CVA, what is specifically important to it and what is not, and what are the different ways to quantify and manage it. In this way, it can decide, in an informed way, what is the best approach to be taken, what systems to build, what teams to create, what training to provide, etc.

11.12 Regulatory capital

Regulatory capital is the capital that governments make financial institutions hold, to ensure their financial stability. We are going to review in this section how that capital relates to counterparty credit risk. I have dedicated the whole of Chapter 9 to regulatory capital, so we will not go into great detail here, but just enough to give an elementary understanding for those that have not read that chapter.

Regulatory capital calculations follow the recommendations given by the Basel Committee on Banking Supervision that lives within the Bank for International Settlements. Those recommendations are given through a number of "Basel Accords": Basel I (1988), Basel II (2004), Basel II.5 (2009), and Basel III (2010). This committee has no enforcing capacity on any bank, but governments and regulatory bodies follow quite closely their recommendations round the world.

The regulatory capital is divided on a number of "charges", each of them trying to capture different risks in financial institutions. It is well known that those charges overlap and often do not reflect accurately the true economic risks that banks face. However, it must be calculated in every regulated bank.

11.12.1 Basel's philosophy

Basel's capital charges always follow a tier approach. There is always a basic approach, with a calculation that is very simple, but which tends to be overly conservative.[13] This approach is meant to be used by unsophisticated institutions. However, those that are willing to invest in accurate models can use the advanced approach. In it, banks can apply for an Internal Model waiver both for counterparty credit risk (IMM) and for market risk (IMA) so that, if approved by the regulators, the capital charge can be calculated, with the risk given by the internal models developed by the institutions, and the charge formula can be closer to the real economic risks, though still conservative.

This tier approach is good, given the wide range of institutions under the Basel accords. Regulators will never be able to build a capital framework that is accurate for every institution in the world, so this tier approach is quite good in principle, as the message is sent that if a bank invests in good models, capital will be a better reflection of its true risk. Having said that, the negative side of it has been that regulators now have to approve and supervise all internal models out there, which is not an easy task.

11.12.2 Capital charges from counterparty risk

We have mentioned several times that counterparty risk can be monetised (and hedged) in two ways: cash and paper. "Cash" relates to actual default losses, while "paper" relates to balance sheet P&L, when no defaults have occurred. Basel charges follow that structure too. Let's see how they work in their advanced approach.

1. **CCR Charge:** Basel II introduced the Counterparty Credit Risk (CCR) capital charge to account for the potential losses, in books of OTC derivatives, arising from actual defaults. It uses an ASRF credit portfolio model (see Section 7.6.3) at 99.9% confidence, for which the exposure metric is the EEPE:[14] the average of the non-decreasing EPE profile during the first year. EEPE is calculated per netting set. Then it is multiplied by a number of factors that take into account several other risks, including the counterparty credit worthiness, netting set maturity, wrong-way risk and portfolio granularity effects.

   Further to it, Basel III introduced some modifications to the calculation that increased the CCR charge considerably. The main ones were that EPE needs to be calculated under stressed market conditions and that the margin period of risk in collateralised portfolios can be increased substantially if a number of conditions are met.
2. **CVA-VaR Charge:** Sometimes this is also called the "CVA charge", but it is important to emphasise the *VaR* in it, to make clear that it is, indeed, a market-risk charge. This is often not well understood.

   The way it works is that you have to calculate CVA following a prescribed regulatory CVA formula that is based on the EPE profile of each netting set,[15] and the credit spread and recovery rate for each counterparty. Basel also states which CVA hedges are eligible for the regulatory capital calculation, and which are not. With this, the risk is then treated as any other market risk charge; capital is proportional to its 10-day VaR at 99% confidence.[16]

   This framework has been widely criticised because it is based on unilateral CVA, while the bank's P&L must be calculated on bilateral CVA. Also, not all the positions that a bank can genuinely use to hedge (unilateral) CVA are eligible for the calculation. So banks are in a situation in which if they want to minimise balance sheet volatility, hence reducing risk, they increase capital requirements, and vice versa. In fact, Deutsche Bank reported a € 94 million loss in 2013 because of this [30]. Also, another area of concern has been that the advanced approach can be more punitive than the basic one [12].

11.13 Credit risk accounting

Financial institutions need to calculate the value of their balance sheet periodically. They tended to follow either the FAS 157 (US) or the IAS 39 (Europe) standards, but on 1 January 2013 both standards were superseded by a unifying IFRS 13. Regarding credit risk for OTC derivatives, they are broadly similar.

The calculation of a balance sheet under these standards is based on "fair value accounting". FAS 157 defined it as the amount at which the asset could be bought or sold in a current transaction between willing parties, or transferred to an equivalent party, other than in a liquidation sale.

Regarding credit risk, our task at hand here, these standards state that the default risk embedded in OTC derivative transactions has to be accounted for when calculating their fair value. In particular:

- FAS 157 states that "a fair value measurement should include a risk premium reflecting the amount market participants would demand because of the risk (uncertainty) in the cash flows. Otherwise, the measurement would not faithfully represent fair value. In some cases, determining the appropriate risk premium might be difficult. However, the degree of difficulty alone is not a sufficient basis on which to exclude a risk adjustment".
- IFRS 13 states that "the entity shall include the effect of the entity's net exposure to the credit risk of that counterparty or the counterparty's net exposure to the credit risk of the entity in the fair value measurement when market participants would take into account any existing arrangements that mitigate credit risk exposure in the event of default".
- FAS 157 says that "the reporting entity shall consider the effect of its credit risk (credit standing) on the fair value of the liability in al periods in which the liability is measured at fair value".
- IFRS 13 says that "the fair value of a liability reflects the effect of non-performance risk. Non-performance risk includes, but may not be limited to, an entity's own credit risk".

It is clear then: in fair value accounting we must consider both the asset and liability side of CVA.

Also, it must be noted that, traditionally, some institutions have not marked the CVA of collateralised trades or of trades cleared through a central counterparty. However, the accounting rules make no exception in those cases: CVA must be marked in the balance sheet in those cases too.

11.14 DVA, to be or not to be

One of the most interesting debates in the CVA space tends to happen around the adequacy of accounting for its liability side. We have already touched on this topic. Let's look into it again, with a bit more depth, now that we have the necessary took kit.

In my view, there is no doubt we should account for DVA, but not everyone agrees with this. The main reasons given against it are along the lines of "DVA does not make sense because it makes an institution book a profit when its credit standing deteriorates", or "we cannot cash-monetise DVA, as we will only get a benefit from it if we default".

11.14.1 DVA is a real quantity

Let's imagine now for a second that we are a corporate, and that we have a book of OTC derivatives that is quite important for our business. We have those derivatives arranged with a number of dealers. One of them is XYZ Bank. The book of trades we have with XYZ is worth, today Friday, say, $10 million in our favour.

During the weekend there has been some very bad news for XYZ Bank; for example, some political events in its home country that makes XYZ quite likely to default within the next 12 months. As a result, its credit spread has jumped up to the ceiling.

We are worried. We have a number of meetings and decide to try to close the book of trades with XYZ and open the same trades with other high-quality dealers. On Tuesday, we arrange a conference call with XYZ, proposing to them to close the portfolio of derivatives. They say that they are happy to do that, but at a 20% discount; that is, they will give us "only" $8 million for the liquidation. We look at each other, discuss internally, and decide to accept.

Everyone in his or her right mind will understand the rationale of that decision: we prefer losing 20% now to the risk of losing everything during the next 12 months. However, as a result of this, XYZ has booked a $2 million *cash*-profit, which was a consequence of its deteriorating credit quality.

Going back to our discussion, everyone should agree that the above example makes sense. Hence, XYZ booking a paper-profit on Monday, as a result of a bank's credit quality deterioration, is the correct thing to do. The example given is no more than the cash realisation on Tuesday of the paper-profit that XYZ bank actually had on Monday. In other words, if XYZ had not booked a DVA profit on its balance sheet on Monday, on Tuesday it would have made a "miraculous" $2 million profit.

This example illustrates that DVA is cash-monetisable.[17]

In fact, the haircut (20% in the example) that we, as the corporate in the example, would accept will not be higher than the cost of hedging the counterparty risk that we have. In other words, that haircut is our CVA_{asset}, which is XYZ's CVA_{liab}, or DVA.

This example shows that booking a positive DVA on a balance sheet when our credit standing deteriorates is no more than reflecting the cash-profit we would get if we liquidated the portfolio now.

Acknowledgements

The author would like to thank Harry Lo for useful discussions on this topic.

12 FVA Desk, the Effect of Funding

In 2012, Hull and White published a paper in Risk Magazine [43] that shook the quantitative community in investment banks. Since 2008, banks have suffered a notable increase in their funding costs, and hence derivative dealers have been calculating this cost and subtracting it from valuations of derivatives. However, the theorists (i.e., Hull and White and those that share their view) refute this approach, since "it can create arbitrage opportunities", and insist that funding should not be accounted for when pricing a derivative. Furthermore, they say, a Funding Value Adjustment (FVA) carries double-counting with DVA, the "funding" side of CVA, and as a result the valuation of a bank's balance sheet with bilateral CVA already accounts for the funding risk the firm has. The practitioners have responded by asserting that they must account for the actual costs when valuing a trade, and funding is an important cost not fully captured in the ideal assumptions of bilateral CVA calculations.

There is far from consensus regarding FVA in the industry and academia. Just to illustrate this, in addition to the sometimes agitated debate on whether we should or shouldn't account for FVA, those that think we should do not agree on how to do it. In 2014 eight investment banks had been reporting FVA in their accounts, but none of them were agreed in the methodology [28]. To make things somewhat more complex, the divide between the "yes" and "no" for FVA is not merely academics vs. practitioners: some banks believe FVA should not be accounted for [28], although they seem to be a minority.

Let's discuss this important topic in this chapter.

12.1 A healthy disclaimer

We would like to be able to say that we know everything about FVA, and that we understand it perfectly. However, we must admit that is not the case. FVA is a complex matter that is still under discussion in the industry and academia at the time of this book going to press. As a result, I need to be humble and accept that all I can do in this chapter is explain my view, which is the result of lots of research, conversations, and thinking, but no more than that.

In the same way this topic is still evolving in the industry, my opinion on this matter is also evolving at the time of writing this chapter. The pace of change in my view is decreasing over time, but I must admit it is still changing. As a result, it may be that if the reader talks to me some time after this book is writren, or attends one of my talks, it may be that my standpoint has matured further from what is said in this chapter.

I think this is the most reasonable approach to this convoluted topic.

12.2 A primer on CVA

In this section we will have an introduction to CVA for those readers jumping into this chapter directly, as without clarity of those concepts the FVA discussion becomes fruitless. However, those readers that have been reading this book up to this chapter, or those that are already familiar with the concept of Credit Value Adjustment, both in its asset and liability side, may want to skip this section.

It is best to explain the idea behind CVA with a simple example. Let us say that we are a corporate, and we want to enter into an OTC derivative to hedge some of our risks. We have two potential dealer banks to do this with, one that is AAA rated and one that is BBB rated. The derivatives that the two dealers offer to us are identical; the only difference between them is the dealer (i.e., our counterparty). If we leave aside subjective matters like business relationships, personal preferences, etc., and if both dealers offer us the same price, we are obviously going to prefer the transaction with the AAA counterparty, as the deal has less default risk. With this in mind, if the BBB dealer wants to be competitive and have a chance of winning the deal, they need to decrease the price. If they keep on reducing it, there will be a point at which we may consider doing the deal with the BBB bank instead. The difference between the price given by the AAA bank and that given by the BBB bank, which makes us see the two potential deals as "even", is CVA.

With this in mind, CVA is then defined as the difference between the price of a derivative with and without counterparty risk.

$$P = P_{CreditRiskFree} - CVA \tag{12.1}$$

The CVA number is driven by how much it costs to hedge out the default risk. In fact, CVA in the example above is the difference between these hedging costs for the AAA and BBB counterparty.[1]

In other words, for the BBB bank to make its price competitive, it must decrease it as much as the cost of hedging out the credit risk.

As a result of this, we can see that CVA has two components: on the one hand, the "asset" side of CVA represents the credit risk we are facing, and its value reflects our cost of hedging out that risk; on the other hand, the "liability" side of CVA represents the credit risk that our counterparty faces from us and, similarly, its value reflects their cost of hedging out that risk.

The terminology for these different sides of CVA has become somewhat convoluted. Indeed, CVA can refer either to the sum of both of these quantities, or to the asset side only; sometimes the asset side is called *unilateral* CVA (uCVA); sometimes the combined sum is called *bilateral* CVA (bCVA), which can be quite confusing. Also, the liability side is known as Debit Value Adjustment (DVA).

In this book we are considering CVA in a bilateral way by default (unless otherwise stated); that is, with two sides, asset and liability.

A CVA approximation: A sound and widely used approximation for each side of CVA is the following decomposition into two terms: one that accounts for the future exposure each counterparty may give to the other (Expected Positive Exposure, EPE, Expected Negative Exposure, ENE), and one for the credit quality of each counterparty.

$$\begin{aligned} CVA &= CVA_{asset} + CVA_{liab} \\ CVA_{asset} &\simeq \widehat{EPE} \cdot s_{cpty} \\ CVA_{liab} &\simeq \widehat{ENE} \cdot s_{our} \end{aligned} \tag{12.2}$$

where $\widehat{EPE}$ represents how much, on average, we can be owed;[2] ENE is how much, on average, we can owe;[3] and s_{cpty} and s_{our} are the counterparty and our own average credit spreads respectively.

An important feature of CVA is that it is symmetric: our asset side is our counterparty's liability side, and vice versa. In this way, the two counterparties have the same CVA but with different signs, leading to a unique derivative price, a key feature of a no-arbitrage framework.

12.2.1 The liability side of CVA as its funding component

One idea underlying the confusion between CVA and FVA is that CVA's liability side can be seen as the price of funding.

In a perfect and ideal world, with infinite information, infinite liquidity, instantaneous price updates reflecting all available information, and so on, the CDS credit spread of each company will be the same as its funding spread. By funding spread we mean the spread over the risk-free rate[4] at which an organisation can borrow cash in an unsecured way.

This leads to another way of looking at the liability side of CVA: the cost of ensuring we do not default. In other words, if we want to make sure that we do not default, we can borrow today our expected future cash liabilities, put that money aside and pay the interest for it; i.e., our funding cost. In the ideal world that we have mentioned before, that cost is going to be the same as the cost to our counterparty to hedge the credit risk it is facing from us.

As a result of this, we see the liability side of CVA is related to the funding cost in the contract we are pricing. However, we must not forget that what it really does is account for the cost of hedging default risk for our counterparty.

The reader can find a more detailed discussion of this in Chapter 8, and implications on derivative valuation and funding double-counting in Section 12.8.

12.3 The origin of the funding value adjustment

Many derivatives dealers and derivatives users now feel the need for a Funding Value Adjustment to account for the additional funding costs they are facing, especially since 2008. Funding risk arises wherever there is a cash flow in institutions. In financial institutions, if there is an outflow, it needs to be funded; if there is an inflow, it can either reduce funding needs or, even, be lent out. In non-financial corporates it can work either way depending on their cash position, but cash requirements coming from derivatives will certainly have a funding impact.

Let's focus on financial institutions for now.

In the business of OTC derivatives, there are a number distinguishable sources of funding risk.

1. **CollVA: FVA from Collateral Asymmetry:** One of the main sources of funding risk is illustrated in Figure 12.1 for an uncollateralised netting set. To start with, the derivatives dealer agrees to an OTC derivative contract (or a group of them that form a netting set) with a counterparty. Then, it is going to hedge that contract so that any profit on one side (the derivative) is a loss on the other side (the hedges), and vice versa. In this way, the derivatives dealer is market-risk neutral, and cashes in an extra spread, over the cost of hedges, that it puts to the derivative price. In other words, the dealer is synthetically recreating the (perhaps complex) derivative contract with vanilla products, typically in an exchange, and makes its fee from that synthetic manufacturing of the derivative.

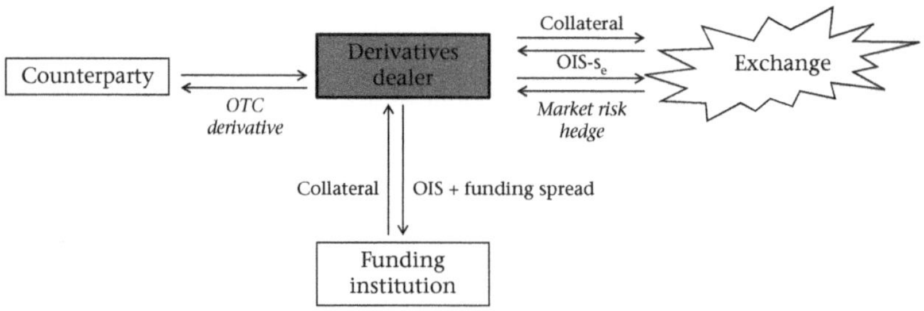

Figure 12.1 Illustration of the source of funding cost for an uncollateralised OTC derivative

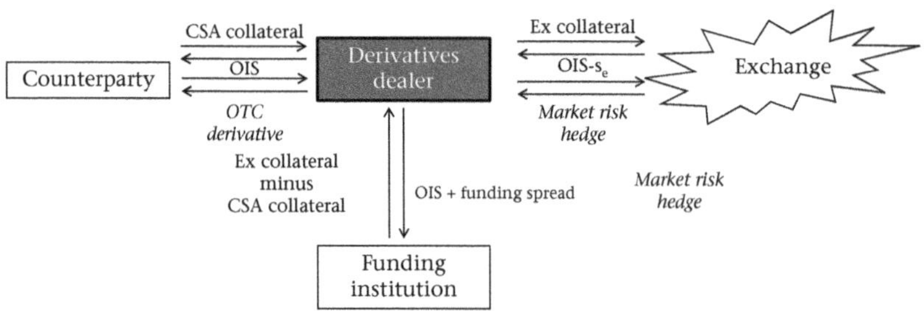

Figure 12.2 Illustration of the source of funding cost for a collateralised OTC derivative

The key here is to realise that the hedging side of the operation is going to be fully collateralised while, in this example, the OTC derivative side is not. Any collateral that needs to be posted to the exchange will need to be borrowed from a funding institution. When doing so, the dealer is going to receive the so-considered risk-free rate, typically the "OIS" rate,[5] minus maybe a spread (s_e), for the collateral posted, but it needs to pay OIS plus its own funding spread for it. As a result, the dealer is going to lose its own funding spread plus the exchange spread on the collateral borrowed in this transaction.

Let's say now that we have a collateral CSA agreed with the counterparty. That situation is illustrated in Figure 12.2. The exchange side of the collateral (ex collateral) is typically fully collateralised, with an initial margin. However, the CSA side may or may not be fully collateralised; it could have daily, weekly, etc., margin calls, collateral thresholds, and so on. As a result of the lack of symmetry between both collateral arrangements, the dealer is also going to face a funding risk from its own collateral needs.

In other words, *a derivatives dealer is going to have a funding cost coming from (i) the lack of perfect symmetry in collateral needs between the OTC derivatives and the hedging sides in its book of trades and (ii) from the spread s_e it may be charged by the exchange.* Because of this, dealers feel they need to account for it, and put it as an adjustment to the value of a derivative. We are going to call this adjustment Collateral Value Adjustment (CollVA).

2. **HVA: FVA from Derivative Cashflows:** Regardless of any collateral arrangement, a second source of funding risk comes from ideal assumptions in the standard Black–Scholes derivative pricing model. That model assumes that a dealer can borrow and lend, in unlimited amount, at a risk-free rate. However, firstly, all the cashflows that take place in a derivative must be funding at a non-risk-free rate and, secondly, they can be netted off against other cashflows with other counterparties, or even outside of the derivatives business. The risk-neutral valuation, even with a CVA component in them, do not contemplate any of these cases.

For example, if we sell an option, we will have the option premium as a positive cashflow (in our favour) at the beginning of the deal. This cash flow will somehow decrease the funding needs the organisation has overall. Another example: if the market has an upward slopping yield curve, if we agree to a payer interest rate swap, the swap rate is going to be roughly the average of the interest rate in the yield curve up to the swap maturity. As a result, at the beginning of the swap we are going to be net paying in each coupon period, but at the end we are going to be net receiving (provided the yield curve does not move much). This is going to create funding needs with an impact that go beyond a mere netting set. A third example could be if we have a semi-annual 10-year swap hedged with a quarterly 10-year swap; every three months we are going to have a cashflow in the hedge that does not correspont to a cashflow in the OTC derivative. These funding needs tend to be stronger the more exotic a derivative is. For example, we may be an energy provider that agrees to deliver power only from 4 a.m to 6 a.m every Monday to Thursday, paid quarterly. This contract can only be hedged with standard products that are quite far away from this tailored timetable, hence the hedging position will be quite far off the actual product, with the subsequent funding risk.

In general, all these outgoing and incoming cashflows are going to have an impact on our global cashflow needs, hence on our funding needs.

This divergence between reality and the typical risk-neutral framework has been already studied theoretically [26, 38, 44, 63, 65]. New modified Black–Scholes pricing frameworks are developed in those works. We do not want to enter into details for now, for clarity purposes, but we will go into it later in the chapter, though the reader should bear in mind that apart from any collateral arrangements, we may also face funding needs from the derivative cashflows themselves.

This source of funding risk comes from the lack of perfect hedging. As a result, we are going to call this adjustment a Hedging Value Adjustment (HVA).

3. **LVA: FVA from our Credit Liquidity Premium:** A third source of funding requirements comes from the bond-CDS spread basis.

   Let's say for a second that we have no collateral to fund at all (i.e., $CollVA = 0$) and that all our hedging positions perfectly match the OTC derivatives (i.e., HVA = 0). We have seen in Chapter 8 that CVA_{liab}, or DVA, accounts for our own survival (i.e., funding) cost. However, CVA_{liab} is calculated with our CDS credit spread while we fund ourselves with another rate: our funding spread.

   The difference between these two means that the cost to our counterparties to insure themselves against our default is going to be different to our cost to survive, hence we may want to introduce another funding-related adjustment to reflect our standpoint. We are going to call it the Liquidity Value Adjustment (LVA), as its root is at the liquidity premium that our real debt products have over CDSs.

Where the market stands: I am an independent consultant in the area of quantitative risk. One of the nice things of that role is being constantly in touch with a wide range of points of view in the financial industry. Interestingly, I have found two very opposing views in regard to these sources of funding risk.

Nearly everyone agrees that CollVA is important.

Regarding HVA, when discussing this topic with the global head quant of a tier-1 universal bank, I said that for him HVA was of great importance, the reason being that in his bank there are some business lines that are very cash intense, and so funding risk is not only about collateral, but also quite crucially about the timing of actual cash flows that the actual products produce. A senior manager on an energy company shared that view. However, when I exposed this idea to the head of FVA of another global tier-1 universal bank, he said that for him this source of FVA was negligible, because most often "every trade we face with a counterparty is hedged with a like-for-like trade, so the cashflows tend to match perfectly".

Finally, regarding LVA, we should see this adjustment as sensible in theory, though as we will see later, most often we can neglect it.

In any case, most financial institutions now feel the need to adjust the price of a deal with an FVA component that goes beyond CVA:

$$V = P_{CreditRiskFree} - CVA - FVA. \tag{12.3}$$

12.4 Why the controversy around FVA?

The problem is the following: we have seen that the liability side of CVA can be viewed as a funding component. So, many wonder why we need to account for it again. If we do that further funding adjustment to the price, are we not doing some sort of double-counting? Because of this, the theorists oppose this adjustment to the price of a derivative, as they say that it is double-counting, which is particular to each organisation and that as a result creates arbitrage opportunities in derivative pricing.

On the other hand, practitioners argue that they cannot price a deal without accounting for the real costs they will be facing, and funding is a true and important cost, one that is not properly covered by the ideal assumptions of the Black–Scholes risk-neutral derivative pricing framework. Hence, FVA is needed.

12.4.1 A construction company

Let's draw a parallel example that will help us understand. Let's imagine that we are a small construction company. We are assessing the value of a construction project. Given that we are small, we do not have the purchasing power of other large companies, and so the cost to us for each brick that we buy is \$0.10, while for a large company it is \$0.08. Question: when we value a project, which of those prices should we use?

I think the answer is trivial: *our* cost of the bricks. I think everyone would agree on that.

One of the core functions of a financial institution is to provide funding. That provision has a (funding) cost, which is intrinsic to each institution. So why should a bank be different to a construction company, in the sense that, to value its business, why should it not use its own intrinsic sources of cost?

Expanding a bit more on this, let's say that we (the construction company) have bought a piece of land on which to build a block of flats. We have two options: building basic or luxury apartments. In order to decide which way to go, we do the following comparative analysis:

	Basic apartments	**Luxury apartments**
Market price	\$1.0m	\$1.5m
Cost of building	\$0.6m	\$1.2m
Value to me	\$0.4m	\$0.3m

As shown in this table, let's say that the sale price of the apartments is \$1.0m if basic and \$1.5m if luxury. However, the cost of building those apartments is \$0.6m for basic or \$1.2m for luxury. As a result, the project is worth \$0.4m to me if we construct basic apartments, or \$0.3m if we build luxury ones. Which of those two possibilities is therefore the most economically sound? Obviously, the one that yields the highest value: basic apartments.

12.5 The root of the problem

Now we can get to the root of the problem: the difference between *Market Price* and *Value to Me.*

Prices are driven by supply and demand forces: If we live for a moment in a world in which there are lots of transactions and high liquidity, we have to understand that *the price of a deal is given by the market's supply and demand.* That price is set externally to each institution. This is key.

Last month I went to New York from London. I found that if I went from Monday to Thursday, a return ticket price was $1,400, but if I went from Friday to Thursday, the return ticket was $600! Why are the airlines putting the price of a trip during business days much higher than that of a personal trip with a weekend in the middle? Quite simply, because they can.

If the market price of airline tickets, flats, cars, computers, etc., are driven by supply and demand, why should OTC derivatives be different?

The "Law of One Price" does not hold: The market that we have described above, with lots of transactions and high liquidity, is quite idealistic. In reality buying and selling is also influenced by many other factors.[6] We can buy an airfare for one price on one web site, and for another price on another website. That is, things do not have a unique price in reality. If that is the case for any product you can buy or sell, why should it be different for OTC derivatives?

Having said that, prices are always governed by the laws of supply and demand. A market may become "distorted" because of its strategic value to a player; for example, it someone temporarily pushes the price down to a loss level to push competition out. However, if that happens, prices are being moved by some "special" circumstances, though the fundamentals of supply and demand still prevail; if fact, it is because of them that a player can push the price of a product down.

The problem here is that, up to 2008, all banks were more or less perceived as very similar, but since that year they are not seen as default-free any more, and each of them has a different funding and credit profile. As a result, the concept of "fair" price or "exit" price is being profoundly challenged, because the price that different institutions are willing to pay for the same product can range quite widely, as a result of their different circumstances.

The key point to realise here is that, in real life, derivatives do not have a "unique" price, in the same way that any other product in the economy does not always cost the same. Prices are driven by a supply and demand, but special circumstance also play a role. When we calculate a "fair" price, we try to estimate an "exit" price, but that is all we can do, an estimation.

And this is what some readers may find surprising. What I am saying is that one of the fundamental pillars of derivative pricing, the Law of One Price, does not hold anymore. Now we know that any institution in the world can default, one of the market real consequences of that is that derivatives do not have a unique price, in the same way that any item in the economy does not have a unique price.

Those that believe in the idea of a unique price for derivatives will argue that, after some transition period, arbitrage opportunities will drive prices to their unique "fair" price. I believe that is not correct, that there is not such a thing as a unique fair price, and that that unique price we seemed to have before 2008 was only an illusion. Anecdotal evidence in this direction is provided in Section 19.3.

12.5.1 The difference between price and value

Let's crack onto the core of the problem now.

At trade inception, and during the life of a trade, each institution involved in the derivatives business is going to calculate different values and prices. Let's explore some of them:

1. **Risk-Neutral Price** ($P_{RiskNeutral}$): This is the price that theorists consider as the "true" price. It is the price obtained from the market, typically from vanilla products, under the no-arbitrage condition. If the market had infinite liquidity, full symmetric information, if all institutions could lend and borrow as much and as little as they wanted, with no default premium in them (i.e., at the "risk-free" rate), and if all these activities involved no trading costs, then this would be the price at which a derivative should be traded.

   In this world of ideal market conditions, arbitrageurs would force the price of derivatives to be this risk-neutral price: if an institution offered to buy or sell a derivative for a price different to $P_{RiskNeutral}$, the offer and demand forces would push the traded price towards its risk-neutral level. Through this arbitrage process, some institutions will be able to make money at no risk from those institutions that are not pricing the derivatives correctly.

   This number must reflect the cost of hedging the derivative in the "risk-neutral" world that we see. As a result it is given by two components: (i) the cost of hedging without default considerations ($P_{CreditRiskFree}$) plus (ii) the cost of hedging defaults (CVA), where CVA must be in its bilateral version so that the credit-risk hedging of both institutions in the trade is accounted for.

$$P_{RiskNeutral} = P_{CreditRiskFree} - CVA \tag{12.4}$$

   The reason why we split this calculation into two components, with and without default risk, is because $P_{CreditRiskFree}$ tends to be calculated at trade level,[7] while CVA must be calculated at netting set level because that is the level at which defaults crystallise. As a result, the price of a netting set of trades is given by

$$P_{RiskNeutral,NettingSet} = \sum_i P_{CreditRiskFree,i} - CVA_{NettingSet} \tag{12.5}$$

   where i counts over trades in the netting set. Then, the price of a portfolio of netting sets is given by the sum of the price of each netting set:

$$P_{RiskNeutral,Portfolio} = \sum_{NettingSets} P_{RiskNeutral,NettingSet} \tag{12.6}$$

   This is basically what we have seen in Chapter 8.

2. **Sale Price** (P_{sale}): This is the price at which we will sell (or buy) a trade at the inception date. Let's not get into too much detail for now, and let's just say that if we are a seller we will try to push that number up as much as we can, and if we are a buyer we will try to push it down as much as we can.[8]

   Bear with me and let's say for now that this price P_{sale} is somehow a free variable. We will put some rationality into it quite soon.

3. **Exit Price** (P_{exit}): After the trade is agreed, it goes live on our systems. From this moment onwards, what we need is its "exit" price: the cash we would *actually* get if we sold the derivative in the real world to a third party.

   Up to 2008, the market was mostly trading and marking trades at the risk-neutral level. Divergences from this rule were seen as anomalies. However, the market events in 2008 made most people realise that if it traded and marked at that level, it would make a constant loss. As a result, that number can be quite detached from the market reality. As well expressed by a managing director of a tier-1 bank in a workshop I ran, "you will never *ever* get that money (the risk-neutral price) if you try to sell a trade in the real market".

Indeed, one of the major sources of cost that a derivatives institution faces now is funding. In other words, what that managing director was saying is that the counterparty buying the trade from us will also put into its valuation framework their own real funding cost, so we may need to add an FVA component to the risk-neutral price if we want to obtain a somewhat realistic exit price.

$$P_{exit} = P_{RiskNeutral} - FVA_{exit} \tag{12.7}$$

We will discuss later how to calculate that FVA_{exit}.

4. **Value to Me** (VtM): As seen previously with the construction company, in order to calculate how much we expect to make out of a project, we need to calculate how much the deal is worth to us. For that, we must account for the project's "manufacturing" cost that we will incur.

In our case, a project is an OTC derivative (or a portfolio of them). Up to now, the cost of manufacturing a derivative has typically two components: hedging and funding.[9] The cost of hedging has also two components itself: the cost of hedging its market risk plus the cost of hedging its credit risk.

In order to understand how much a trade is worth to us, we need to subtract its costs of manufacturing from its expected income. If P_{sale} is the expected present value of its future cashflows, and $P_{manufacturing}$ is the expected present value of its manufacturing cashflows, the "value to me" of that transaction is

$$VtM = P_{sale} - P_{manufacturing} \tag{12.8}$$

For example, let's say that we are the dealer, and we are asked by a corporate client for a ten-year swap. The quote we get in the market for this swap rate is 5%, so we are going to buy that swap and sell to our client an OTC derivative for, say, 5.1%. Before 2008 we would have said that we were making a ten basis point spread on the deal. However, in present times, in addition to buying the 5% swap in the market, we are going to:

a. Try to buy credit protection on this counterparty to hedge the counterparty risk of this deal.
b. Perhaps, sell credit protection somehow, so we may get some income when hedging the liability side of CVA.
c. Typically borrow cash to make sure that we can meet the cash obligations this trade creates in us.[10]

In this context, P_{sale} refers to the price we agreed with the client at inception (5.1% in our example). It is a free variable before we make the deal, and a fixed number afterwards. By this is meant that its 5.1% swap rate, for example, is fixed, but obviously the present value of that derivative will change over time. Then, $P_{manufacturing}$ has the following components,

$$P_{manufacturing} = P_{hedging} + CVA_{internal} + FVA_{internal} \tag{12.9}$$

$P_{hedging}$ is the price of market-risk hedging the product sold to the client (5% in our example). A dealer is typically going to hedge (i.e., to syntactically manufacture) an OTC derivative via vanilla exchange-traded derivatives. This market is highly collateralised, it has minimum credit risk. In fact, we could say that it is the best proxy we can have for a credit-risk-free derivative. As a result, we can say that $P_{hedging} \simeq P_{CreditRiskFree}$

$CVA_{internal}$ is the expected price of hedging the counterparty risk this trade brings with it. So, it has, in principle, two components:

$$CVA_{internal} = CVA_{asset} - \gamma\ CVA_{liab} \tag{12.10}$$

As seen, CVA_{asset} reflects the price of the counterparty risk we are assuming, while CVA_{liab} reflects the price of the counterparty risk our counterparty is assuming. If we cannot buy credit protection on the counterparty, then CVA_{asset} could be seen as a risk reserve.

Regarding CVA_{liab}, from our point of view, once the trade is transacted, we may think that we do not need to care about the credit risk that our counterparty is assuming. However, we should care about CVA_{liab} while we are alive because it introduces volatility in our balance sheet; no investor likes that. Hence, we may decide to try to hedge that volatility, and then the benefit coming from CVA_{liab} may or may not be passed on to the trading desks. Given that the volatility of CVA_{liab} cannot be fully hedged, we may want to introduce a scaling factor γ so that we do not pass benefits we are not really getting through the hedges. This γ factor can range from 0 to 1 in financial institutions, depending on internal policies.[11]

Finally, $FVA_{internal}$ is a number that reflects the funding cost that the trade carries, and which is not accounted for in any other part of the equation. We will see how to calculate this number soon.

So, to summarise, the value to me of a trade is given by

$$VtM = P_{sale} - P_{CreditRiskFree} - CVA_{internal} - FVA_{internal} \tag{12.11}$$

And so, VtM is a most important number, as it will provide the rationality of the decision-making: if $VtM > 0$ we expect to make money, but if $VtM < 0$ the trade is uneconomical for us.

We can generalise Equation 12.11 and say that

$$VtM_t = P_{sale,t} - P_{CreditRiskFree,t} - CVA_{internal,t} - FVA_{internal,t} \tag{12.12}$$

At trade inception ($t = 0$); we can use this equation to set the price we should charge to our client to break even by setting VtM_0 to a number we feel comfortable with. Later on, when the OTC derivative is set, we can use this equation to assess the money we expect to make from this trade in the future.

FVA creates a risk-neutral trade: Another way of looking into this is that if we set VtM to zero and we say that

$$P_{sale,t} + CVA_{internal,t} + FVA_{internal,t} = P_{CreditRiskFree,t} \tag{12.13}$$

it is shown that what we are doing here is creating a risk-neutral trade for the dealing desk: if an external desk deals with the credit issues on their behalf (the CVA desk), and another desk with the funding issues (the FVA desk), what the dealing desk sees is a risk-neutral trade, and they are experts in hedging and managing.

I hope it is now clear that a funding adjustment to calculate the prices and values of a trade is most important. Indeed, without it, the dealing desks will not account for the institution's real "manufacturing" costs and, hence, will not make correct business decisions. Without this FVA correction an institution is looking for trouble, as its estimation of value will not account for the costs it is actually facing. It is like the construction company not accounting for the cost of manufacturing when valuing its projects.

P_{sale} at trade inception should be highly driven by VtM. If we are a derivative dealer, P_{sale} must be set to a level that makes VtM higher than the minimum accepted profit.

If we are a derivatives user, like a corporate client that is hedging true tangible risks with the derivative, then typically VtM is going to be a negative number, and it must be agreed to a level that we feel is worth paying for the risks it is actually hedging.

FVA for internal management: Calculating the value of a trade with an FVA component in it is most important, as it is a fundamental business management policy that each business unit suffers (or enjoys) the marginal cost they create in the organisation with their activities. It is quite standard to see costs like salaries and general management as a fixed cost, but undoubtedly the incremental funding cost or benefit a trade brings should be considered in the marginal cost calculation.

It is also important that sales desks get their budgets and targets adjusted accordingly. If they now need to account for FVA, the way their performance is measured should be changed too.

FVA for balance sheet accounting: However, when marking the price of a deal to the market, things are slightly different. Now we are interested in the exit price of the deal. If we could, we would go around all the potential buyers of our trades, asking them to give us their P_{sale} or their $FVA_{internal}$. However, that is obviously not possible, so the best we can do is to *estimate* it. That is FVA_{exit}.

And here is when the real problem arrives. Accounting rules say that we must account for our own credit quality when pricing a book of derivatives, hence the CVA_{liab} component in it. However, if we sell it to someone else, they are going to do their internal FVA calculation. So which funding curve shall we use? Our funding curve to reflect our own credit quality, or someone else's curve? If the later, which one?

At the time of writing this book, there is far from market consensus in this regard. Each of the institutions that have reported FVA in their balance sheet has used a different approach [28]. Even some of them think FVA should not be used for balance sheet reporting; though this is a minority.

In addition to this, to make this problem more tricky, even if we agreed on which funding curve to use, the funding netting benefits that each institution will have, should they buy some of our trades, is going to be different, and nobody is going to tell us what other trades they have, so a proper calculation of FVA_{exit} is, in reality, impossible. In fact, it is not a number that exists, and by this is meant that it cannot be measured. All we do with it is, really, "guesstimate" it.

This is why the theorists oppose it sometimes so vigorously. It is not a clear number that can be measured with mathematically sound risk-neutral methods or that is given by the market; it is only a guesstimation of what someone may be willing to pay for our trades.

As said, at the time of writing this there is no market consensus. Should we decide to calculate FVA_{exit}, in my opinion a sensible approach would be to use the same netting that we have in our portfolio, as that is the only netting information we really have, and to use an estimation of an average funding curve, some sort of a blended curve from the potential buyers we may have, should we try to sell our trades.

12.5.2 The dependency between price and value

A source of confusion comes from the fact that market price and value are related.

Using the "block of apartments" example as an illustration, if the construction cost of luxury apartments is higher than those of basic ones, its market price should be higher in general, but that does not mean that it is *always* going to be higher. That price is driven by supply and demand, and hence also driven by many other factors, like saturation of the market, new buyers and sellers entering the market, change in the needs of market players, regulations, etc.

Similarly, the funding cost is going to be an important component in the final price of a deal, but we must not forget that this price is set by supply and demand in the market.

Sometimes we hear professionals in derivative dealers asking the question "Should we or should we not pass the FVA as a cost to the customer?". That question has no answer because it is the wrong question to ask. Quite frankly, we are going to ask for as much as we think we can get away with, in the same way as in the example before when an airline asks for the highest price they feel they can obtain. The right questions to ask from a derivative dealer viewpoint are (i) what is the maximum price I can charge for this deal, without making the customer run away? and (ii) will I make money at that price? To answer the first question sales people need to know their customers and the competitive environment they operate in. To answer the second one they need to calculate the *value to me* of the deal, with FVA in it.

Similarly, if we are a client of a derivatives dealer, a question that is often heard and yet is wrong is "Why do I have to pay for the funding cost of these guys?". The right questions are (i) what is the minimum price I can get in the market? and (ii) am I willing to pay that price to hedge my risks? The sources of the costs that the dealer puts on the table are irrelevant to us. We only care about the price (that includes the credit quality of the dealer and our own) and possibly other intangible matters like business relationships, accessibility to other dealers, etc.

The construction and airline examples clearly show how the price of things is driven by supply and demand, with the addition of "special circumstances" as explained. As said, there is no reason why OTC derivatives should be different.

12.6 The dawn of XVA desks

With all this in mind, a possible framework for counterparty and funding risk management in a financial institution is shown in Figure 12.3. The organisation could set up two specialised desks: the CVA and the FVA desk. Each of them takes on the default and funding risk the dealing desks create, so they (the dealing desks) can forget about default and funding matters and concentrate on what they know best: generating risk-neutral derivatives, selling them, and hedging their market risk.

The CVA desk will charge a default insurance fee at trade inception to the dealing desks, which should be the incremental CVA that each trades brings to the bank. Then, it will manage default risk and CVA volatility in the balance sheet, and any profit and loss coming from it will be attributed to the CVA desk.[12]

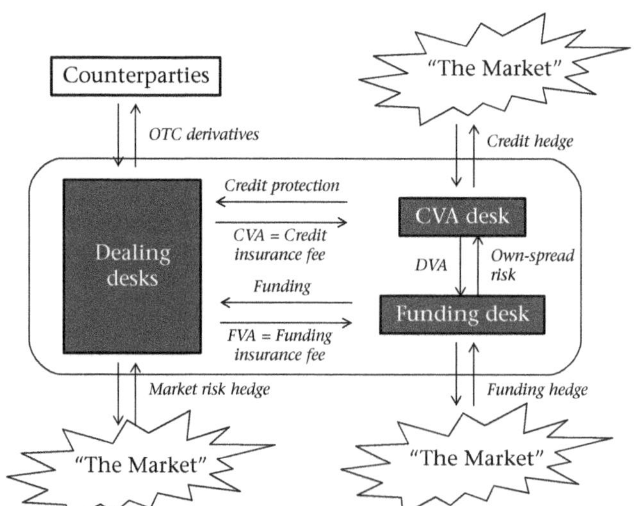

Figure 12.3 Illustration of a proposed counterparty and funding risk management framework in a large financial institution

Similarly, the FVA desk will charge a funding insurance fee at trade inception to the dealing desks, which should be the incremental FVA that each trade brings to the institution. Then, it will manage all funding risks and it will be in charge of all the funding needs that the dealing desks might have in the future.[13] In the case of the FVA desk, the "market" that it uses to source the needed funding could be external investors, or an internal treasury desk, depending on the internal operational arrangement. In other words, the FVA calculation and management strategy should reflect the set-up the institution operates under.

Hedging FVA: Each CVA and FVA desk will have the option of hedging their respective risks, or not. The CVA desk will be theoretically able to hedge its risk mainly by setting up long-term default protection positions with the market. Similarly, the FVA desk will be theoretically able to hedge its risk mainly by setting up long-term funding protection positions. However, these desks may decide (or be obliged) not to hedge their risk, or to hedge them only partially, given the market restrictions. This last option is the most common. There is no right or wrong solution as to which hedging strategy is best, as long as each desk knows what it is doing.

In reality, most often the FVA desk is going to face an internal treasury desk to borrow and lend from. Ideally, that treasury unit should offer a full funding yield curve to the FVA desk, but most often it only offers a short-term rate.

Consequently, hedging FVA is more of an art than a science right now. Similarly to CVA, the FVA hedging restrictions can be so important that the best we can hope for in many cases is to somehow control this funding risk.

Synergies with CVA: Depending on how the bilateral balance sheet CVA is managed by the organisation, and given that changes in the liability side of CVA and FVA are highly related, the funding desk may be able to help hedge some part of the CVA_{liab} component of the volatility in the balance sheet, via internal CVA-FVA desks transactions. And here this is where XVA desks are born: they can make sense of joining CVA and FVA into one single unit, the XVA desk.

With this set-up, each desk attends to what it knows best: the dealing desk sees and manages risk-neutral derivatives; the CVA desk manages and hedges credit risk, and the FVA desk does the same with funding risk.

FVA as the price of an internal derivative: The reader should realise that in the same way that we can see CVA as the price of an internal credit derivative, a CCDS, we can also see FVA as the price of another internal derivative, a Contingent Funding Swap (CFS), that is sold by the FVA desk to the dealing desk, and whose P&L is managed by the FVA desk.

12.7 The interaction between CVA_{asset}, CVA_{liab} and FVA: rehypothication, netting, and hedging

There are a few examples that help to illustrate further the interaction between CVA and FVA.

The role of rehypothication: When collateral is received we can do two things with it: we can reuse it for our benefit, or we can put it aside. As many will know, the act of reusing collateral is also called *rehypothication*.

From a CVA point of view, rehypothication makes little difference, but from a collateral FVA viewpoint, it can have a major impact.

Let's say that we are a dealer. We have a collateralised portfolio, where rehypothication is permitted. As we have seen, any collateral that we receive can be passed onto the exchange where the hedges lie, and so our funding requirements are minimal. However, if rehypothication is not permitted, the counterparty risk will remain unchanged when we receive collateral, but our funding requirements will increase substantially, as we now need to borrow the collateral that we need to post to the exchange.

Because of this, typically, a fully collateralised trading facility where rehypothication is not permitted has minimal CVA, but it has maximum collateral FVA. That is, forbidding rehypothication in a CSA has a very limited impact on CVA, though the netting set becomes "uncollateralised-like" from an FVA viewpoint.

The role of netting: CVA is calculated at netting set level, because if a counterparty defaults, trade prices can be summed up at that level for the portfolio liquidation. Because of this, trades in different netting sets cannot be netted off to compute CVA, and the CVA of a portfolio is the sum of the CVA of its netting sets.

However, the funding requirements that an institution faces crystallise at portfolio level[14] or, at least, at a "funding set" level.[15] Let's say that we have two derivative contracts, identical except that we are long in one and short in the other. Each of them constitutes a netting set by itself, and both netting sets are uncollateralised. In this case, CVA will be maximal, because each trade is a netting set in which there is no collateral to mitigate counterparty risk, but FVA will be zero, because any cashflow in one trade can be passed onto the other one.

If we only had one of those trades in the portfolio, FVA will be high, as we'd need to fund all collateral needs with the hedging institution, but in this case of two opposite trades, they hedge each other, so we do not have any collateral funding needs with any exchange.

This example illustrates that FVA must be calculated at portfolio level, while CVA must be calculated at netting set level.

Naked positions: Let's say that we have a portfolio of trades. Regarding hedging, we have two options: we can either delta-hedge the portfolio P&L with vanilla positions in an exchange or, in principle, we may decide not to do so, perhaps because we can't for whatever reason. That decision is going to drive the collateral funding requirements and hence FVA for that portfolio. However, CVA remains the same whichever decision we make about hedging, because it reflects the default risk of our counterparty and ourselves, which is in principle independent of our hedging strategy.

The following table summarises the outcome of the different options we have regarding the existence of CSAs in the portfolio (i.e., if it is collateralised or not) versus the hedging options, with the implications to CVA and FVA.

	Portfolio CSA	Market risk hedging	CVA	HVA	CollVA
1	yes	yes	min	min	min
2	yes	no	min	max	max
3	no	yes	max	min	max
4	no	no	max	max	min

If we have a fully collateralised CSA (1 & 2), CVA becomes minimal. If we can hedge its market risk well (1), then HVA will be very small, if anything at all. Also, in this case there is a lot of symmetry between the collateral requirements in the CSA versus the hedging positions, hence CollVA is small. However, if we don't hedge the position (2) for whatever reason, HVA will be high and then there could be a high asymmetry between the collateral requirements and hence CollVA is high too. However, if we do not have a CSA in the portfolio (3 & 4), CVA becomes maximum, HVA is maximal only when we don't hedge the position well (4), and CollVA can be high too (3), when there isn't collateral symmetry between the portfolio and the hedging positions.

Changing the hedging strategy does not change the future cashflows coming from the derivatives, hence the risk-neutral price of the derivative remains the same. However, the *value to me* is going to be different in each case.

12.8 Funding double-counting

A fundamental source of confusion between CVA and FVA is the sense that, if we fully account for both to value a trade, we may be double-counting our default probability. That comes from the fact that the liability side of CVA can be understood as the funding part of CVA, as explained in Section 12.2.1.

This concern is understandable. Let's expand on it.

12.8.1 The meaning of *FVA* and CVA_{liab}

We have seen in detail that CVA reflects the price of the credit risk embedded in a portfolio of derivatives. That portfolio is split into netting sets. From a credit risk standpoint, each netting set can be seen as an independent complex derivative that is at risk subject to default. We say the word "independent" because in the case of default, netting sets cannot be netted off with each other even with the same counterparty, but trades within a netting set can.

If we hedge our counterparty risk in a portfolio of trades, typically via CDS contracts, we are going to hedge it netting set by netting set. The expected cost of that hedging is CVA_{asset}; it reflects the expected true credit-hedging costs that we will have.[16]

Symmetrically, CVA_{liab} is the aggregated cost, incurred by our counterparties, of hedging the counterparty risk they are facing from us. This could be seen as our funding cost, because if we want to make sure that we do not default in our potential future liabilities in a netting set, we can borrow today those expected future liabilities, put them aside in a "pot", and use that cash for our payments as the netting sets matures. In this way, we are "hedging" our own default on average at least. Credit theory says that the expected cost of that is going to be CVA_{liab}; it is our replication of the CDS hedging activities that our counterparties do.

This way of looking at our own default, although to some degree theoretically correct, does not reflect everyday reality. That analysis is correct if (i) there were no credit liquidity spread, (ii) we only had one netting set, (iii) if banks were not highly geared institutions, and (iv) if we did not hedge at all.

The first problem can be easily dealt with: we can put an LVA adjustment to account for the credit liquidity risk.

However, the other problems show a core weakness of the CVA framework, if it is not properly interpreted. As said, in that described framework, CVA_{liab} is the cost of hedging our default *by our counterparties*. That cost should be our own funding cost if we managed our own default by *borrowing today all our expected future liabilities*; i.e., via building those "pots" of cash. However, nobody does that, that is not a real cost that we have.

If we want to account for our default risk in our valuation, we need to reflect what we *actually* do to manage it, as opposed to what our counterparties do to hedge our default, or what we might do in an imaginary world.

Firstly, $CVA_{liab} + LVA$ reflects the expected funding cost of building that "pot" described below, netting set by netting set, but it does not take into account any inter-netting set funding benefits, that we do actually see in our everyday operations.

Further to this, in order to manage our own default, no bank borrows and puts in a pot its future liabilities, as banks are, nearly by definition, highly geared institutions. Instead, we cover our potential future liabilities, and hence our default, via hedging and collateral posting. We hedge our book of derivatives so that its cash flows in one direction are compensated with cash flows in the opposite direction. We provide extra reassurance of our survival via initial margin posting. In this way we manage our own risks and, hence, our own default. This act of hedging and collateral posting has a cost. The present value of that cost is FVA.

As a result, when we say that CVA_{liab}[17] is our cost of funding, really, we are being far from accurate. That number is the cost of managing, or hedging, our default risk by all of our counterparties, which is by nature very different to *our* cost of managing our own default. Our counterparties hedge that risk via CDS contracts,[18] but we hedge it via market risk hedging and collateral posting.

So, if when valuing a book of trades, we account for CVA_{liab} and *all* FVAs, we will be valuing the trades as if, on top of hedging and posting collateral, we also build those "pots" of cash for future liabilities, netting set by netting set. Nobody does that.

When calculating the *value to me* of a portfolio of derivatives, we want to calculate the real costs that we will be facing. In my view, the correct way to calculate it is by throwing away its CVA_{liab} and *LVA*, and computing the true, tangible, real cost of hedging our own default via *CollVA* and *HVA*, so that we compute what actually happens in real life: we take advantage of inter-netting set funding benefits, we account for strategies that create funding surpluses, and we account for the specifics of our real daily "survival" costs, like for example the initial margins that we need to post and rehypothication.

This is qualitatively illustrated in Figure 12.4. The liability side of CVA takes a limited view of funding, as it only looks at each netting set individually, and it assumes that we are going to borrow today each netting set's future liabilities as a substitute to buying protection on our own default. By contrast, FVA takes a holistic view of funding, reflecting real netting funding benefits and the operations that we actually do to manage our own default.

Opportunity costs: It must be noted that if we decide to include CVA_{liab} and *LVA* also in a derivative valuation, what we are effectively doing is accounting for the opportunity cost of not building the "pots" of cash for each netting set to finance the future expected cash outgoings.

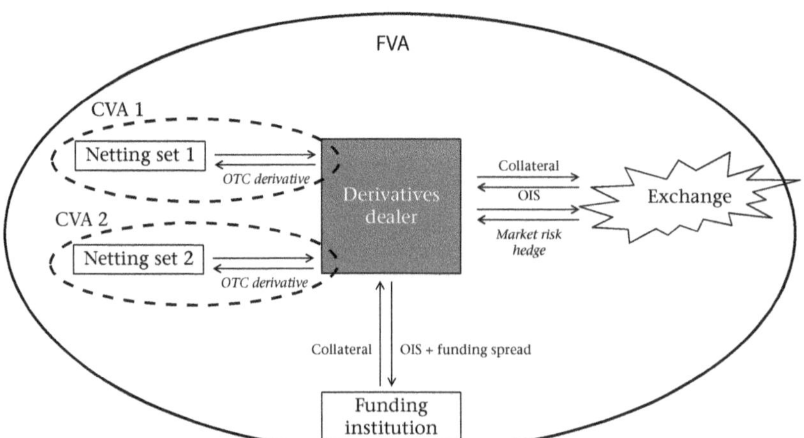

Figure 12.4 Qualitative illustration of the area that relates to CVA and to FVA

12.8.2 CVA_{liab} internal distribution

We have seen in Equation 12.10 that with a factor γ the CVA desk may pass only some of the CVA_{liab} benefit to the dealing desks. This must be well understood.

CVA_{liab} is embedded in the price of a trade when we initiate it, as in principle, our counterparties should be accounting for our credit risk in it. This price is an overall cost to an institution, reflected in worse prices it will be able to trade at its worst credit standing. With this in mind, what γ does is *allocate* CVA_{liab} internally. If $\gamma = 1$, the CVA desk absorbs this CVA_{liab} on its books with its daily P&L; if $\gamma = 0$, it is the dealing desk that takes that cost or benefit.

This can be most important, as one of the key tasks of these XVA adjustments is allocating P&L internally in an organisation in order to provide incentives as seen appropriate.

12.8.3 Arbitrage

It must be noted that some people oppose this way of looking at derivative valuation, mainly arguing that it creates arbitrage opportunities. This is the case because different institutions will value the same trades differently.

In my view, this valuation framework is correct. In the same way that two construction companies will value the same project differently, because they have a different cost base, so two financial institutions should value the same book of trades differently, because they have a different funding cost base, different netting benefits, etc.

Regarding the theoretical arbitrage opportunities that may arise, the problem there is thinking that we can always execute them. The incremental cost of trading via cost of funding, cost of capital (see Chapter 14), liquidity constraints, bid/offer spread, etc., make those theoretical arbitrage strategies impossible to execute. Indeed, a number of hedge funds that used to operate in that space have reportedly abandoned that arbitrage market.

This obviously does not mean that any price is OK. If a swap trades in an exchange at a rate of say 5%, we will definitely not be able to find a buyer at a rate of 25%, or if we find a seller at a rate of 25% we'd better buy it, hedge it, and make quasi-free money out of it. What we are saying here is that the brackets in which arbitrage is executable have become very wide as a result of the increasing trading costs. Consequently, the concept of a risk-neutral price does not hold any more as it used to.

Arguably, we could say that this has always been the case, but before 2008 we lived in an illusion: the illusion that liquidity is infinite and defaults don't exist.

12.9 Summary

The main point to understand so far is that FVA is driven by the *asymmetries* we have between a portfolio of derivatives and its hedging, and that the funding risk that we want to account for can come from the actual derivatives cashflows (LVA), hedging cashflows (HVA), or the collateral needs (CollVA). Different institutions will see each of them as more or less important, depending on their trading conditions.

CVA is related to the counterparty risk that a book of derivatives has, assuming ideal frictionless hedging. In addition, different collateral and hedging strategies for market risk employed by a derivatives dealer are going to yield different funding requirements, though these should not be seen as changing the "fair" market price of a deal, but rather as changing the price point at which a deal is economical for an institution. That point is different for each company.

Market reality indicates that we will never be able to sell a derivative for its risk-neutral price, even if it includes bilateral CVA, so we may want to introduce a funding adjustment to pricing for balance sheet purposes, so it better reflects a potential realistic "exit" price. We have called this the FVA_{exit}. The problem, though, is that this number, being arguably a sensible adjustment is, in reality, very difficult (if not impossible) to calculate. All we can do is produce an estimation of it.

Acknowledgements

The author would like to thank Tim Dun for useful discussions on this topic.

13 Calculating and Managing FVA

In Chapter 12 we have seen the idea behind Funding Value Adjustments: its sources, why and when it should be used. Let's see now how we can compute FVA.

Obviously, the disclaimer of Section 12.1 also applies here.

13.1 Analytical Black–Scholes pricing with collateral and funding

There have been a number of attempts to calculate the price of a derivative when it is collateralised and faces non-risk-free funding costs, from a theoretical standpoint. This has been done by modifying the Black–Scholes risk-neutral pricing framework to account (i) for borrowing and lending rates that are different to the risk-free rate and (ii) for collateral that is posted and received under the bilateral CSA agreements [26, 38, 44, 63, 65].

In a nutshell, the standard Black–Scholes framework defines the operator

$$\mathcal{L} = \frac{\partial}{\partial t} + \frac{\sigma^2 S^2}{2} \frac{\partial^2}{\partial S^2}, \tag{13.1}$$

where S is the underlying risk factor, and states that the change in value P over time for a risk-free derivative is given by the differential equation

$$\mathcal{L} \cdot P_t = r\,P_t - r\,S \frac{\partial P_t}{\partial S}, \tag{13.2}$$

where r is the "risk-free" rate at which the dealer can borrow, and lend in unlimited quantity, as often as needed, without trading costs. Also, the dealer can buy, sell, borrow, and lend the underlying risk factor S in unlimited amounts, as often as needed, without trading costs as well.

Importantly, by "risk-free" is meant that the resulting portfolio of the derivative, plus any cash borrowed or lent, plus any asset S bought or sold, is market-risk-free for the dealer. Another important assumption is that defaults do not exist: all parties will honour their financial commitments, with certainty.

Using Peterbarg's version of the Black–Scholes expansion for collateral and funding [65], the new equation that sets the evolution of P is

$$\mathcal{L} \cdot P_t = r_c\,C_t + r_f\,(P_t - C_t) + (r_d - r_r)\,S \frac{\partial P_t}{\partial S} \tag{13.3}$$

where r_c is the rate returned on collateral under the CSA agreement, r_f is the unsecured funding rate for the derivative dealer, r_r is the secured (repo) funding rate, and r_d is the rate of return on asset S.

These approaches tend to also make the usual assumptions; that the posting and receiving of collateral is continuous and free, and that borrowing, lending, buying, and selling are possible continuously and free of any cost.

13.2 Key elements of an FVA calculation

The analytical pricing efforts described above deal with the case when, under the Black–Scholes framework, an institution can only borrow cash at a risky rate, which is different to a market's "risk-free" rate. Also, it deals with the collateral from the bilateral agreement with the counterparty. In that sense, this modified Black–Scholes framework is an important step forward in quantitative finance.

However, we may not be able to use it to calculate FVA. That is because there are a number of important key features that need to be accounted for.

- **Bilateral CSA agreements can be quite complicated**
  The modified Black–Scholes framework still relies on some highly idealistic assumptions regarding collateral arrangements with the counterparty. Those equations usually can only be solved for the special cases when a portfolio is either fully collateralised ($C_t = P_t$), or with no collateral at all ($C_t = 0$). However, bilateral CSA agreements can be quite complicated, with thresholds, lack of symmetry, multi-currency features, break clauses, etc.
- **A particularly important source of FVA is in the collateral misalignment with the hedging institution**
  Also, the modified Black–Scholes framework does not touch on the effect of collateral non-alignment between the bilateral CSA and (typically) the exchange where the hedging positions lie. In fact, this is one of the most important sources of funding risk. This was depicted in Figure 12.2, where it can be seen that the dealer has a net loss (or gain) coming from the funding requirements for the difference in collateral needs on each side of the deal. FVA in this context is the expected present value of that loss or gain.
- **Institutions' borrowing and lending rates are not symmetric**
  Another idealistic assumption can be that financial institutions borrowing and lending rates are the same. This is not the case in real life.
- **FVA must be calculated at portfolio level, while CVA is a netting set level number**
  Figure 13.1 illustrates the point that FVA must be calculated at portfolio level. Let's say that we have two different counterparties, and we have the same trade with both of them, but we are long in one and short in the other one. Each trade is a netting set by itself, and both netting sets have the same CSA agreement, which is symmetric between the dealer and each counterparty.

  In this case, each netting set will have its own collateral calculation, but any collateral that needs to be posted by one counterparty will be equal to that needed, in the opposite direction, by the other counterparty. So, as long as rehypothication is allowed, this set-up has no funding requirements at all; i.e., $FVA = 0$.

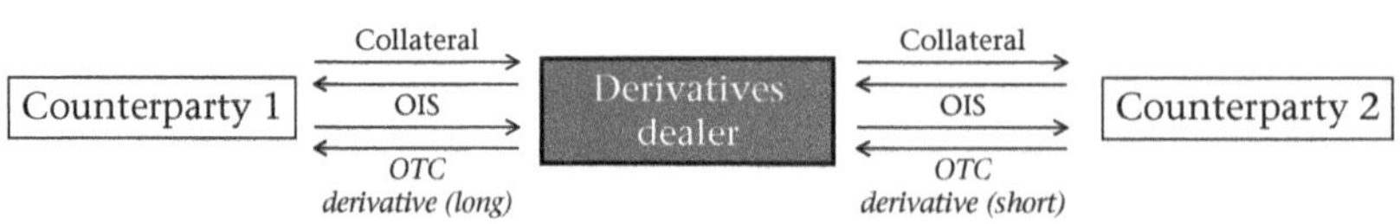

Figure 13.1 Illustration of portfolio netting effects for FVA

The only way to compute a zero FVA in this case is if we calculate that number at portfolio level. By portfolio we mean the whole book of derivatives that a financial institution has or, going even further, all the financial positions the institution has, if applicable.

13.3 The FVA calculation: a Monte Carlo simulation

It appears that the only way we can compute FVA in a realistic way is via a complete Monte Carlo simulation. This is the case because analytical attempts at FVA tend to be too idealistic.

13.3.1 A practical solution

A full and perfect FVA calculation seems to be quite close to mission-impossible: there are too many factors to account for. To be realistic, we need to compromise and find good proxies to make the FVA calculation feasible. We are going to see how we can compute FVA in stages.

The two sides of FVA

In principle, FVA has two components, one that accounts for the cost of borrowing collateral, the Funding Cost Adjustment (FCA), and one accounting for the benefit of lending excess collateral, the Funding Benefit Adjustment (FBA).

$$FVA = FCA + FBA \tag{13.4}$$

Let's say that s_t^{borrow} and s_t^{lend} are the borrowing and lending spreads over risk-free rate that an institution faces.[1] Let's define

$$EPE_t^{cash} = \mathbb{E}\left(\max\left(C_t, 0\right)\right) \tag{13.5}$$

$$ENE_t^{cash} = \mathbb{E}\left(\min\left(C_t, 0\right)\right) \tag{13.6}$$

where C_t represents an institution's cash needs at time t. FCA should reflect the present value of the expected cost of our borrowing needs, in order to meet our cash obligations; FBA should be the same, but from a lending standpoint. Hence, we define FCA and FBA at time zero (today) as

$$FCA_0 = \int_0^T EPE_t^{cash} \cdot DF_t^* \cdot s_t^{borrow}\, dt \tag{13.7}$$

$$FBA_0 = \int_0^T ENE_t^{cash} \cdot DF_t^* \cdot s_t^{lend}\, dt \tag{13.8}$$

where DF_t^* is the risky discount factor at time t, and T is the maturity of the last trade in the portfolio. A more detailed derivation can be found in Appendix H.

We will see later in the chapter that, in several cases, the *FBA* component can be neglected.

13.3.2 The Monte Carlo simulation

In order to calculate FVA, we need to compute Equations 13.7 and 13.8. We are going to focus the explanation on Equation 13.7 for simplicity, but all that is said can be extrapolated to Equation 13.8 quite easily.

In Equation 13.7, DF_t^* and s_t are given in principle by the market,[2] so the only computation needed is EPE_t^{cash}, through Equation 13.5. Let's do that now.

The problem of calculating FVA is now reduced to three problems: (i) simulating the collateral needs for the counterparties with whom we have the collateral agreements, (ii) simulating the collateral needs for the exchanges where the hedging positions sit, and (iii) simulating the cash flow needs that each derivative carries.[3]

In this calculation, we are going to assume that all collateral is cash, and in the same currency. Later we will see how to deal with those other risky collateral cases.

Let's build this calculation step by step.

13.3.3 Recycling the CVA calculation for FVA

Collateral with counterparties: In order to simulate the collateral with all counterparties, we need to do the following. To start with, we need to fix a number of time points in the future where we want to calculate the collateral, and we are going to decide on a number of scenarios for our Monte Carlo simulation. Typically, we are going to use the same set up as for the CVA calculation: around 100 time points and around 10,000 scenarios. Then:

1. **Risk Factor Evolution:** First we need to evolve all risk factors that affect the value of the trades. By risk factors we mean yield curves, FX spot rates, equity prices, credit spreads, commodity prices, inflation curves, etc. We might easily have more than 1,000 risk factors, which means that we need to generate around 1 billion risk factor numbers!
2. **Derivative Pricing:** Once we have all the risk factor values, we need to price each derivative contract in all the 1,000,000 time points and scenarios. A large institution is going to have around 1,000,000 contracts, which means they need to generate around 1 trillion prices!! The reader can imagine the demanding computing effort this step can take if there are exotic, or even semi-exotic, contracts in the portfolio.
3. **Derivative Pricing Netting:** Once we have all 1,000,000 prices per derivative, they are netted per netting set. This means that the prices of each derivative are grouped by scenario and time step. In this way, we end up with one price grid[4] per netting set.
4. **Collateral Simulation:** Now collateral also needs to be simulated. This is done in each of those netting set grids, as the CSA collateral agreements apply for each netting set. We need to simulate it while considering remargining frequency, thresholds, minimum transfer amounts, rounding, haircuts in non-cash collateral, multi-currency options, initial margin, etc. When this step is done, we are going to end up with one grid of collateral per netting set.
5. **Collateral Netting:** We have seen that FVA crystallises at the portfolio level, so we need to allow for this in our calculation. This can be done by summarising all collateral grids to come up with one overall portfolio collateral grid. This should contain the collateral that the institution will need in the future, in each scenario and time point.

The bad news is that it is terribly complicated to derive this portfolio collateral grid. However, the good news is that, if we have a good CVA system, most of these steps have already been done for CVA. Steps 1, 2, 3, and 4 can be recycled from the CVA system, so that only step 5 needs to be done now. And this step is very simple: just summing up all collateral values per scenario and time step.

If we denote by i each scenario, and by t_j each calculation time point,[5] the collateral posted/received with the counterparties is

$$C_{i,t_j}^{CSA} = \sum_k C_{i,t_j}^{CSA,k} \tag{13.9}$$

where k counts through all the netting sets.

It must be noted that, in this method, any netting set that is not collateralised is accounted for automatically, as in those cases all we have to do is set $C_{i,t_j}^{CSA,k} = 0$.

However, we need to make a special distinction regarding rehypothication. We have said before that when a CSA does not allow for rehypothication, it has no practical effect on CVA, but it does have effect on FVA, as the collateral received by the dealer cannot be posted to the exchange where the hedging sits. This can be implemented in the calculation quite simply by setting $C_{i,t_j}^{CSA,k} = 0$, for FVA calculation purposes, in those netting sets where rehypothication is not allowed.

Collateral with exchanges: The other aspect we need to consider is the collateral posted (or received) to the exchanges where the hedging positions are. This collateral typically comprises two parts: initial margin (IM) and variation margin (VM).

$$C_t^{hedge} = IM_t^{hedge} + VM_t^{hedge} \tag{13.10}$$

Let's start with the easier of them: variation margin. Exchanges operate under fully collateralised conditions, so the collateral that needs to be posted is going to be the value of the whole portfolio of derivatives.

If we denote by P_{i,t_j}^l the simulated price[6] of trade l in scenario i and time step t_j, then the grid of variation margin values will be given by

$$VM_{i,t_j}^{hedge} = \sum_l P_{i,t_j}^l \tag{13.11}$$

Again, the good news here is that those P_{i,t_j}^l grids have already been calculated in the "derivative pricing" step of the CVA calculation, hence calculating the variation margin grid is quite a trivial computation: all we have to do is sum up all the price grids.[7]

Having done that, now we are left with the calculation of the IM requested by the exchanges. This bit is somewhat more tricky, as the CVA calculation does not consider how the portfolios are hedged, and hence we cannot recycle any existing computation. There are a number of approaches that we could take here.

1. The first approach consists in trying to replicate the IM calculation that the exchanges do. They may publish some high-level details of those calculations, but trying to copy them accurately seems to be quite difficult. Also, there is no reason preventing an exchange from altering that calculation at any time, so perhaps it is best to implement some fairly simple models.

   For example, assuming that exchanges base the initial margin on ten-day 99% VaR, under normal conditions, quite a typical metric, in each time step we can say that

$$IM_{i,t_j}^{hedge} = 2.33\sqrt{\frac{10}{260}}\,\Omega \tag{13.12}$$

where Ω is the annual volatility of the portfolio in our simulation.

Calculating Ω may turn out to be difficult, but not impossible. We'd need to know the delta of each trade to each risk factor, in each scenario, then sum all the deltas of all trades, multiply them by the volatility of each risk factor and then add the variances of each of those sensitivities to derive the final portfolio volatility.

In this way, we will come up with a grid of initial margin IM_{i,t_j}^{hedge}.

However, this could be quite problematic given its calculative difficulty, and also because, at the end of the day, we are guessing the methodology used by the exchanges for the IM calculation.

2. Another approach could be to do a historical analysis and find patterns that could be easily implemented. The reader must be warned that this approach does not follow any economic or financial fundamentals, rather it just takes advantage of statistical laws we may find, without asking how we find them.

   For example, if we are a large dealer, with lots of positions in exchanges, and we do a scatter plot of the initial margin we have been asked vs. the value of the portfolio that we hold with the exchange, we may find that it follows something like a line with a noise term. If so, a relationship along the lines of $IM_t^{hedge} = \alpha \cdot P_t + \epsilon$, where P is the value of the positions we hold with the exchange, α is a constant to calibrate historically, and ϵ is a noise term, could be used. Also, we could test other more sophisticated hypotheses along the lines of $IM_t^{hedge} = \beta \cdot \Omega_t^{\gamma} + \epsilon$, where Ω is the volatility of the portfolio and β and γ are constants to be calibrated historically, or $IM_t^{hedge} = \alpha \cdot P_t + \gamma \cdot P_t^2 + \epsilon$, or any other law that we find to be suitable and practical.

   The key idea here is to do a historical analysis to find a (hopefully) easy statistical relationship $IM_t^{hedge} = f(X_t)$, where X_t is something we already simulate in the calculation.

It would be really good if we found that, regardless of the noise term,

$$IM_t^{hedge} = \alpha \cdot P_t, \tag{13.13}$$

because the equations simplify nicely. When this is the case, the collateral held with the exchanges is quite simple to calculate. It is given by

$$C_{i,t_j}^{hedge} = (1+\alpha)\sum_l P_{i,t_j}^l \tag{13.14}$$

where l ranges across all the trades in the portfolio. The "1" in this equation accounts for the variation margin, and the "α" for the initial margin.

The combinations of C^{hedge} and C^{CSA} are going to lead to CollVA.

Cashflows from derivatives: This part of the calculation comes from the actual cash needs of the derivative, regardless of any collateral arrangements. By this we mean option premiums, coupon payments, etc.[8]

Obviously, there are going to be some cases where the cashflows from derivatives will provide a funding benefit, but some other times they will create a funding cost. How important this funding risk is depends very much on the organisation. As said before, the market seems to be quite divided in this regard, some institutions see it as important, some as negligible. At the time of this book going to press, this part of the calculation seems to be mostly ignored by practitioners, but it is not clear if this is the case because it can be genuinely ignored, or because it is so difficult that efforts are focused elsewhere. In any case, if these cashflow asymmetries are intense enough in an institution, then it may be advisable to study their funding impact, as they could create a competitive advantage, or disadvantage, for the institution.

As said, this calculation can be quite tricky. What we need to do is calculate, in each time step and scenario of the Monte Carlo simulation, (i) the actual cash flows that each derivative has experienced during the previous time step, together with (ii) the cashflows from its hedging side and, then (iii) subtract one from the other, and calculate in this way the cash excess or shortage. Doing steps (i) and (ii) can be quite difficult, especially for exotic derivatives, as we will have to do both a cash flow and a hedging simulation; standard pricing functionality may not be readily available for this and may need to be modified.

Having said that, apart from the important technical difficulties, what we are going to generate now is a portfolio *cash account*, to which each derivative adds or subtracts as cash needs take place. If we do this, we are going to come up with a simulated portfolio of derivatives account $C_{i,t_j}^{portfolio}$, where

$$C_{i,t_j}^{portfolio} = \sum_l C_{i,t_j}^l \tag{13.15}$$

This cash account is going to be the sum of all *past* cashflows coming from the derivatives and their hedging positions, regardless of any collateral arrangements. It should be noted that, in general, that account will not start with a zero value.

In practice, the source of a funding cost that is usually most important is CollVA, so we are going to mostly focus on it subsequently.

Liquidity considerations: We saw that LVA comes from the ideal assumption that the CDS spread is the same as the actual funding spread in the CVA_{liab} calculation. We also saw that it could lead to funding miscomputation via what can be seen as funding double-counting, so it must be treated with care. If it needs to be computed, this LVA is going to be equal to the difference between CVA_{liab} when we calculate it with the CDS credit spread and our funding spread.

13.3.4 Calculating FVA

Now we have all the components needed to calculate FVA.

As just noted, we can say that

$$LVA = CVA_{liab}(s^{funding}) - CVA_{liab}(s^{CDS}) \tag{13.16}$$

For the calculation of value of a derivative (as opposed to the price), this LVA adjustment is equivalent to simply replacing $CVA_{liab}(s^{CDS})$ by $CVA_{liab}(s^{funding})$ in the calculation. This is why sometimes the reader may have heard other practitioners saying that when we need to make an FVA adjustment we need to remove DVA (i.e., CVA_{liab}) from the valuation.

Regarding HVA, this adjustment may be important if an institution has a business line that is highly cash intense, with strong shifts in its inflows, outflows, and fee income. However, most often this is not the case and hedging mimics sold derivatives fairly accurately and, so, any difference between the fee income from derivatives and the hedges is, precisely, the profit we are trying to make. For this reason, institutions may choose to leave this HVA calculation aside and do it only on a case-by-case basis when needed: we'd need to simulate all cashflows in a portfolio with its hedges, which is not an easy task at all.

If we put together Equations 13.5, 13.9, and 13.14 we obtain

$$EPE_t^{cash} = \mathbb{E}\left(\max\left((1+\alpha)\sum_l P_t^l - \sum_k C_t^{CSA,k}, 0\right)\right) \tag{13.17}$$

where P_t^l and $C_t^{CSA,k}$ have already been calculated by the CVA engine, and α is calibrated historically.[9] With this EPE profile, we can now calculate Equation 13.7 quite easily:

$$FCA_0 = \int_0^T EPE_t^{cash} \cdot DF_t^* \cdot s_t^{borrow}\, dt$$

It must be noted that this methodology accounts for the desired features we discussed before, since:

- It computes the expected funding cost of the collateral misalignment between the derivatives and the hedging side of the portfolio of trades.
- It nets trades and collateral at the right level for FVA: at portfolio level.

However, if for some reason we want to be more precise, or we have a portfolio of derivatives that is very cash demanding and we want to account for HVA, then we need to consider Equation 13.15 in the calculation by computing

$$EPE_t^{cash} = \mathbb{E}\left(\max\left((1+\alpha)\sum_l P_t^l - \sum_k C_t^{CSA,k} + \sum_l C_{i,t_j}^l, 0\right)\right). \tag{13.18}$$

Also, it must be remembered that the α term could be a very crude approximation to reality, that should be cross-checked and perhaps changed after a good time series analysis.

For the remainder of the text, we will stick to Equation 13.17 for illustrative purposes.

13.3.5 A few simplified cases

Let's consider now a few special cases, so we can gain some intuition as to what we are doing here and how we can put things in context.

Fully collateralised portfolio: Let's say that our portfolio of trades is fully collateralised, with an ideal CSA.[10] In this case, the collateral needed in the CSA side equals the value of the book of trades

$$\sum_k C_t^{CSA,k} = \sum_l P_t^l \tag{13.19}$$

and so, Equation 13.17 gets reduced to

$$EPE_t^{cash} = \mathbb{E}\left(\max\left(\alpha\sum_l P_t^l, 0\right)\right) \tag{13.20}$$

or, given that α is a constant number,

$$EPE_t^{cash} = \alpha\,\mathbb{E}\left(\max\left(\sum_l P_t^l, 0\right)\right) \tag{13.21}$$

It must be noted that the last term of that equation is precisely the EPE profile of the whole portfolio of trades when considered to be uncollateralised,

$$EPE_t^{portfolio,uncollateraised} = \mathbb{E}\left(\max\left(\sum_l P_t^l, 0\right)\right). \tag{13.22}$$

As a result,

$$EPE_t^{collateral} = \alpha\, EPE_t^{portfolio,uncollateraised} \tag{13.23}$$

In other words, the EPE of the collateral needed in a fully collateralised portfolio is the expected value of the initial margin posted to the exchanges, which we are approximating by α times the EPE of the portfolio when considered uncollateralised.

With this, FVA should be then quite a straightforward calculation

$$FCA_0 = \alpha \int_0^T EPE_t^{portfolio,uncollateraised} \cdot DF_t^* \cdot s_t^{borrow}\, dt \tag{13.24}$$

which rounds off the result nicely.

For simplification of notation, let's define

$$FCA_0^{\dagger} = \int_0^T EPE_t^{portfolio,uncollateraised} \cdot DF_t^* \cdot s_t^{borrow}\, dt \tag{13.25}$$

which represents the FVA of a book of trades that is fully uncollateralised, and that is hedged with full collateralisation but zero initial margin. In this case,

$$FCA_0 = \alpha\, FCA_0^{\dagger} \tag{13.26}$$

as α accounts precisely for the initial margin.

Fully uncollateralised portfolio: Let's say now that we are in the opposite case, where our portfolio of trades is fully uncollateralised. In that case,

$$\sum_k C_t^{CSA,k} = 0 \tag{13.27}$$

and, then,

$$EPE_t^{collateral} = \mathbb{E}\left(\max\left((1+\alpha)\sum_l P_t^l, 0\right)\right) \tag{13.28}$$

$$= (1+\alpha)\mathbb{E}\left(\max\left(\sum_l P_t^l, 0\right)\right) \tag{13.29}$$

$$= (1+\alpha)\, EPE_t^{portfolio,uncollateraised} \tag{13.30}$$

As a result,

$$FCA_0 = (1+\alpha)\, FCA_0^{\dagger}. \tag{13.31}$$

Partially collateralised portfolio: In reality, some of the trades will be subject to CSA agreements, and some will not. If a ζ proportion of the portfolio is collateralised, then

$$FCA_0 = (1 + \alpha - \zeta)\, FCA_0^{\dagger} \tag{13.32}$$

This can be a nice approximation for quick calculations.

The case of a CCP: There is a strong regulatory push to clear as many OTC derivative trades through central counterparties as much as possible. When that happens, counterparty risk is supposed to be reduced. However, this is not obtained for free, as the counterparties now face the funding cost of setting this up.

For example, let's say that we are a dealer. We have seen that if the whole portfolio of trades is under bilateral agreements, and fully collateralised, then FVA may be simplified to $FVA_0 = \alpha\, FVA_0^{\dagger}$. If we novate trades to a CCP, then the *variation* margin asked by one side (i.e., the hedging side) should be the same as that delivered by the other side (i.e., the CCP) so there is no funding risk coming from variation margin requirements. However, now we have to post *initial* margins on both sides, and so we have funding requirements from both sides of the trades. If the initial margin posted to the CCP can be expressed as $IM_t^{CCP} = \beta \cdot P_t$, then the FVA of this set-up may be approximated by

$$FCA_0 = (\alpha + \beta)\, FCA_0^{\dagger}. \tag{13.33}$$

13.4 Personalising FVA

A most important source of differentiation in the way we must calculate FVA comes from the way FVA desks actually operate internally. This is going to influence FVA because, as said, this number is not a price coming from a classic risk-neutral no-arbitrage pricing framework, but rather from a risk adjustment made to either account for our internal cost of manufacturing the trade ($FVA_{internal}$) or to match our perception of prices in the market (FVA_{exit}).

There are two typical cases, that we are going to review here.

13.4.1 Asymmetric FVA

Sometimes, the desk that deals with FVA and that provides funding to the dealing desks may be the same desk that goes out in the market to borrow from investors, and also to lend out any excess in cash. That desk is going to face an asymmetric funding spread. It is going to borrow at a given credit spread s^{borrow}, but any cash excess cannot be lent out without risk at any rate other than the risk-free rate, which means that its lending spread s_t^{lend} will generally be zero.[11]

This leads to the fact that, in practice, in this case, FBA could be ignored, as the funding benefit cannot be practically exercised without generating other risks.

Consequently, we can say that, in this case,

$$\begin{aligned} FBA &\simeq 0 \\ FVA &\simeq FCA \end{aligned} \tag{13.34}$$

and we can ignore the funding benefit side of the problem.

13.4.2 Symmetric FVA

A universal bank or a commodities house, for example, may be right in the opposite case. Taking the universal bank for illustrative purposes, they have, typically, three business lines: investment banking, retail banking, and private banking. The derivatives business lies within the investment banking unit.

Typically, this type of organisation is going to have a central treasury desk, in charge of borrowing funds from external investors to, subsequently, lending them out internally to its business units. From a derivatives standpoint, the investment bank unit of the bank is going to have an FVA desk that provides funding to all the dealing desks. This FVA desk is going to borrow from the treasury desk and, also, it is going to lend excess cash to the treasury, so other parts of the organisation are benefited by this. In order to set this up correctly, with the right incentives, treasury should pay the FVA desk a lending rate for the cash it is borrowing from it. Generally, that lending rate is the same as the borrowing rate it charges. In this way, the derivatives business is going to enjoy the benefits of good funding management, and the lack of symmetry referred to before is left to the treasury to deal with, at a global corporate level.

This has consequences for the FVA calculation as, now, $s_t^{borrow} = s_t^{lend} = s_t$, and given that

$$MtM_t = EPE_t + ENE_t \tag{13.35}$$

then,

$$FVA_0 = \int_0^T MtM_t^{cash} \cdot DF_t^* \cdot s_t \, dt \tag{13.36}$$

Sometimes the treasury may not offer the same rate to borrow and lend, in which case we need to calculate FCA and FBA separately.

As we are going to see later, which of these two cases (symmetric vs. asymmetric FVA) an organisation operates in is also going to determine how to manage funding risk.

13.5 Fine-tuning the calculation

There are a few other considerations that we may want to take into account too.

13.5.1 Risky collateral

So far, we have assumed that all collateral is cash, and in the same currency as the portfolio of trades. There is a push in the industry to have most CSA agreements under the ISDA's standard CSA, as this problem is mostly avoided with them.[12] However, there will surely still be cases in which bespoke CSAs are used, amongst other reasons because cash collateral is not always the least risky option.

Typical non-cash collateral is highly rated sovereign bonds, but other securities like corporate bonds, gold, or equities could be posted as well. Also, when cash is posted as collateral, but in a different currency to that of the portfolio of trades, then the whole CSA facility (i.e., portfolio of trades plus the collateral) has FX risk, hence this cash also constitutes risky collateral.

A typical way to deal with this is by applying a haircut to the collateral so that, for example, \$100 of collateral nets only, say, \$95 of exposure (a 5% haircut). This haircut is supposed to account for a typically ten day move in the price of the collateral, should the counterparty default. The higher the risk of the collateral, the higher the haircut.

However, this overestimates collateral needs and will lead to a miscalculation of FVA. This is because the dependence between the value of the portfolio and the value of the collateral is not considered. A good illustrative example of this is if we have a netting set composed of one long equity forward. In this case, the least risky collateral that we can receive is, precisely, the stock that the forward is referring to. This is so because, in that case, the value of the trade will move in parallel with the value of the collateral, hence showing quasi-zero risk in the CSA facility.[13] Because of this, in order to assess the riskiness of a collateral we must also have a look at the trades in the netting set it is attached to.[14]

The optimal way to calculate FVA when risky collateral exists in the netting set is by simulating the collateral in the Monte Carlo simulation. In this way, Equation 13.9 will contain that simulation, and this dependency we are referring to will be captured naturally in Equation 13.5.[15]

13.5.2 Secured vs. unsecured borrowing

Receiving risky collateral should, generally, decrease FVA by comparison with not receiving any collateral at all. This is true because, if we can rehypothicate that collateral, then we can always borrow cash in a secured transaction, via the repo (if securities) or the forward FX market (if cash is in a currency different to the base currency of our institution).

Indeed, the repo and FX spreads of this secured lending will generally be very small compared to our unsecured funding spread. This is illustrated in Figure 13.2.

In this case, the calculation of Equations 13.7 and 13.8 need to be split into two, one that accounts for secured and another for unsecured borrowing.

It must be noted that in many cases, like for AAA government bonds, the repo spread is so small that we may want to ignore it in the calculation if it complicates things more than the benefit we gain. Also, those bonds can generally be posted as an initial margin, so no repo transaction may be needed for them.

Spread on collateral posted

We have seen that exchanges may pay OIS minus a spread (s_e) on collateral posted to them. Consequently, we should account for this extra spread in the calculation by making

$$s^{borrow} = s_{UnsecuredFundingSpread} + s_e \tag{13.37}$$

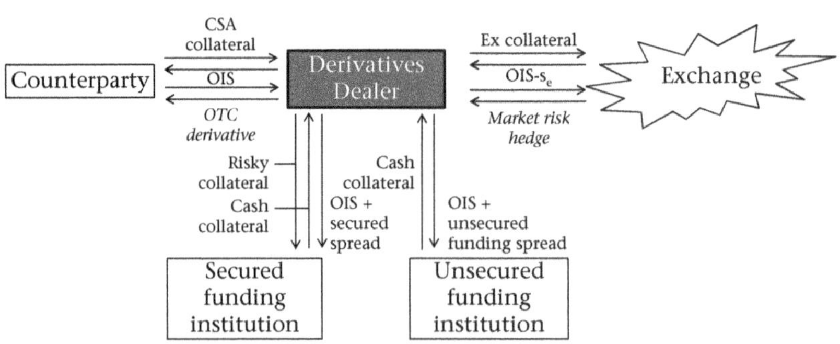

Figure 13.2 Illustration of the source of funding costs when secured and unsecured borrowing takes place

13.5.3 Settlement risk

So far the whole discussion is based on the fact that any collateral we receive can be posted as collateral "instantaneously". This is obviously not the case. In reality, we are typically going to have a one day settlement lag in this process. As a result, we may have to fund, for one day, all the collateral needed to be posted and that we have not actually received yet.

A finer calculation should also account for this. In order to do so, the collateral algorithm will have to consider the collateral that is on the way to us but has not arrived yet, and discount it from today's net theoretical collateral position, to come up with the true collateral that we need to fund.

It must be said that in some business lines, such as when a CCP member offers clearing services to clients, the effect of this settlement lag can be relevant.

13.5.4 Funding with right and wrong-way risk

Also, up to now we have implicitly assumed that the portfolio of trades under consideration does not have any right or wrong-way risk. However, sometimes we may have this kind of risk in funding. This is typically going to happen when we have credit trades in the portfolio with obligors that are highly related to us. For example, if we are UBS, and we have in our portfolio CDSs with Credit Suisse as the obligor, then there is going to be a dependency between the value of that CDS and our funding spread.

Having said that, given that FVA is a global portfolio calculation, this effect should be generally small.

In any case, when we have relevant right or wrong-way risk, we have to take one step back in the calculation and solve

$$FCA_0 = \mathbb{E}\left(\int_0^T \max(C_t, 0) \cdot DF_t^* \cdot s_t^{borrow}\, dt\right) \tag{13.38}$$

and similarly for FBA_0.

13.6 Managing funding risk

So far we have seen what is FVA and how to calculate it, but not how to manage its associated risk. Let's discuss that now.

Most financial institutions have or are setting up specialised FVA desks, often attached to their CVA function, forming the so-called XVA function. From the funding point of view, this desk will be in charge of providing all funding the dealing desks need, so they (the dealing desks) can forget about that problem. For this service, the FVA desk is going to charge, to each dealing desk, at trade inception, how much it is expected to spend (or gain) in funding as a result of every new trade. The same method is applied if a trade is unwound.

This has a number of important consequences:

- In the counterparty risk world, the CVA desks are in charge of hedging both (i) default events and (ii) undesired CVA fluctuations in the balance sheet, as much as possible given hedging market restrictions. Within the real trading constraints, a CVA desk could hedge default events by rolling short-term CDS positions with a notional equal to the current exposure, but this leaves CVA volatility naked. Also, it can choose to hedge only CVA volatility by setting a number of CDS positions in credit indices, for example, that will minimise CVA volatility, but offer no protection at all to actual counterparty default events. In practice, CVA desks tend to use a blend of those two strategies.

FVA hedging should focus at least to ensure that all funding needs will be met in the near future (the equivalent to hedging default events in the CVA world). However, in those institutions that report FVA in their balance sheet, the FVA desk should also be in charge of managing FVA volatility; not an easy task.

- So far we have discussed how to calculate FVA, but the reader must note that the number that is also most relevant is the *incremental* FVA that a new trade generates, or that the unwinding of an existing trade brings along. That is the amount that should be charged (if positive) or given (if negative) to a dealing desk for each operation they do. In this way, the dealing desks will be directly sensitive to the marginal funding cost/benefit they create with their activity, and so their incentives are aligned with the institutional ones.
- Given that FVA is not a proper risk-neutral price, but a risk metric, the FVA number should reflect the actual funding risk management strategy that the organisation has, or wants to have. For example, given the funding liquidity tightness that banks have suffered in the past, a bank may decide to be "conservative" when calculating FVA and define it as, say,

$$FCA_0 = \int_0^T \max(EPE_t^{cash}, PFE60_t^{cash}) \cdot DF_t^* \cdot s_t^{borrow} \, dt \tag{13.39}$$

where *PFE*60 refers to the Potential Future Exposure profile at 60% confidence level. With this kind of FVA metric, the FVA desk will be overcharging with respect to the typical FVA calculation, though it could make sense to account for the extra funding *liquidity* risk that the funding desk actually faces, as opposed to some quasi-ideal assumptions taken in the standard FVA calculation. More on this funding liquidity risk very soon.

Another way of doing this could be, for example, with

$$FCA_0 = \int_0^T EPE_t^{cash} \cdot DF_t^* \cdot (s_t^{borrow} + \delta s) \, dt \tag{13.40}$$

where δs is an extra spread applied to account for the mismatch between the ideal FVA assumptions and the reality of managing the funding risk.

By using this kind of approach, the institution will be constricting business development for the benefit of decreased funding risk.

13.6.1 FVA calibration and funding liquidity risk

As just indicated, one of the key challenges of financial institutions is how to manage funding risk. In particular, how to manage its liquidity, given the major constraints they faced in the aftermath of 2008.

There are two theoretical fundamental ways we can manage funding liquidity risk:

1. On the one hand, theoretically, to be fully hedged from a funding perspective, an institution should borrow forward its expected funding needs, with a notional profile that follows the EPE_t^{cash} or the MtM_t^{cash} profile, depending on whether it is facing symmetric or asymmetric FVA. This is shown in Figure 13.3. Also, it should hedge the sensitivities of the chosen profile to market risk factors like interest rates, FX rates, equity prices, commodity prices, etc. In this way, any P&L that comes from these hedging positions will theoretically fund any extra funding needs coming as a result of movements in the market.

   Unfortunately, when we face reality, things may not be as simple as that. Borrowing forward, in any amount, whenever needed, is not that simple. Reportedly, only very few treasury departments of tier-1 investment banks offer this.

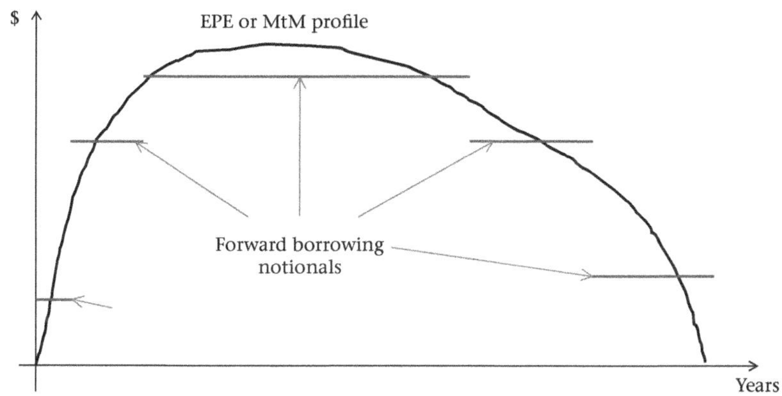

Figure 13.3 Illustration of the notional profile needed to hedge funding risk

2. On the other hand, an alternative option would be simply not to worry at all about future forward funding needs, and try to survive always with short term borrowing. An extreme case of this strategy would be to borrow, every night, all the funding required for that day. Obviously, this is very risky, as if one day the market does not have enough liquidity, we could easily run into trouble and, eventually, default. Also, our real funding cost will be highly exposed to movements in our funding rate. For these reasons, this type of on-the-fly funding strategy carries funding liquidity risk with it.

Calibrating FVA

This naturally leads to one of the most tricky points of FVA: how to calibrate the funding spread.

As said, hardly any treasury unit offers to its FVA desk a full borrow and lend yield curve, a Cost of Funding (CoF) curve. Ideally, we'd like to have a CoF "cube" that covers three dimensions: when the borrow/lend starts, when it finishes, and the amount to borrow/lend. In practice, nobody offers this and the best we can hope for is a CoF curve from which today's spot, as well as forward borrowing and lending rates, can be extracted.

Currently, most often treasury departments only offer a short-term rate. When this is so, the FVA desk cannot hedge future funding costs as shown in Figure 13.3, and hence it carries the risk that the FVA that is being charged at trade inception may be different to the actual funding cost it faces in the future. In the worst case, it could happen that liquidity dries out and it wants to borrow or lend but it is not possible, as happened to a high extent in the 2008 events. Given the experience of those years, the financial industry has become very sensitive to that risk.

If the treasury offers a full CoF curve, then this funding liquidity risk is absorbed and managed by them. This should be seen as best practice as they are the institution's expert in that risk; they are the ones facing the institution's outside world of funding.

Funding liquidity risk

From the treasury point of view, it is very important for an institution that short term cash reserves[16] are enough to withstand the market liquidity squeeze as designed in the funding strategy. In fact, as a result of the 2007 funding squeeze, Basel III created two funding ratios: the Liquidity Coverage Ratio (LCR) and the Net Stable Funding Ratio (NSFR). The LCR requires a bank to hold sufficient high-quality liquid assets to cover its total net cash outflows over 30 days. The NSFR seeks to provide enough funding liquidity over a one-year period.

FVA subject to counterparty

We have seen here that FVA is a number that must be calculated at the portfolio level, not at the netting set or counterparty level. However, I know of at least one tier-1 bank that has an FVA calculation ($FVA_{internal}$) that penalises trading with low credit quality counterparties.

Their argument is the following: My funding spread is a reflection of the market's view in my credit quality. That credit quality is given by the quality of my balance sheet. If I have a given book of trades only with AA counterparties, for example, I will see a given funding spread in the market for me. But if I have the same book of trades with BB counterparties, for example, I will see a much higher funding spread in the market. As a result, I am going to see a funding impact from the quality of my counterparties, and so I want to incentivise trading with high quality counterparties in order to decrease future funding costs. Therefore the FVA desk is going to charge, say, $0.75 \times FVA$ if the counterparty is a AA, or $1.5 \times FVA$ if the counterparty is a BB.[17]

13.7 Summary

In this chapter we have seen the calculation practicalities and risk management issues around FVA, as well as how it interconnects with both the asset and liability sides of CVA.

We have seen that, in practice, we need a Monte Carlo simulation to calculate FVA. Fortunately, most of the simulation done for the purposes of CVA can be recycled to FVA. We have seen how, with a few simplification assumptions, we can calculate the different components of FVA (CollVA, HVA, and LVA).

Finally we have seen how one of the key challenges of an FVA desk is not only to calculate it, but to manage it. This risk is obviously very linked to the funding liquidity risk all organisations face, especially since the 2008 market near-freeze.

14 KVA Desk, Capital Management, and RAROC

In this book we have discussed many functions of financial institutions that have changed profoundly as a consequence of the 2008 market events. Capital calculation and management is another of those areas that is undergoing a deep transformation.

Financial stability and robustness is at the core of the banking business. A central tool to achieve that stability is the bank's own capital. Roughly, this capital is an amount of liquid assets that an institution holds to act as a cushion against negative future scenarios.

In Chapter 7 we have seen an introduction to the concept of unexpected loss and of economic capital, and in Chapter 9 we have discussed the calculation of a specific version of an economic capital model: the regulatory version of it for financial institutions. In this chapter we are going to review how the existing capital in an organisation, as well as the management of that capital, should affect trading decisions and strategies for OTC derivatives. Also, we are going to see how this idea can be extended to non-regulated trading houses via an economic capital model, to account for unexpected losses too.

In particular, we are going to see a framework that is based on the definition of a "Capital Value Adjustment" (KVA) that can be used to create the desired management framework and internal incentives in an organisation from a capital perspective.

14.1 Another healthy disclaimer

Chapter 12 started with the following note: *We would like to be able to say that we know everything about FVA, and that we understand it perfectly. However, we must admit that is not the case. FVA is a complex matter that is still under discussion in the industry and academia at the time of this book going to press. As a result, I need to be humble and accept that all I can do in this chapter is explain my view, which is the result of lots of research, conversation, and thinking, but no more than that.*

If that note applies to FVA, it does so even more to KVA, the reason being that, at the time of this book going to press, FVA has been a topic for discussion for some time in the banking and academic circles. However, the idea of KVA is very new. There are very few publications and talks on this matter, and discussions tend to be "off the record" in conferences. For this reason, this chapter again explains my view on this topic, which is the result of a lot of research and thinking. However, that view will surely mature further over time.

14.2 An economic capital model

In Section 7.6 we introduced the concept of expected and unexpected loss in a financial institution from a credit point of view. In a general framework, a financial institution should have an economic capital model to set the amount of capital it needs to hold, given a desired credit standing and a set of business activities.

The thinking process starts with a goal for a default probability, or a credit rating. The core of the business of banking lies in financial stability; a bank must be rock solid from a credit point of view, so it should always aim for a very high rating. The following table shows the Standard & Poors credit rating for one year default rates:

S&P credit rating	One year default rate
AAA	0.00%
AA	0.02%
A	0.08%
BBB	0.24%
BB	0.90%
B	4.49%
CCC	24.16%
CC	55.68%
C	66.67%

Once a desired rating is set, the next question is: how much capital should we hold to make sure our default probability is the desired one?

In order to answer this question we need to build a model of the potential portfolio returns we may have in a chosen time horizon, typically one year. That model is going to deliver a distribution like that illustrated in Figure 14.1.

With that model we want to understand what is the return the institution is going to have under every possible scenario going forward. The model aims to include all sorts of risk factors, both external and internal

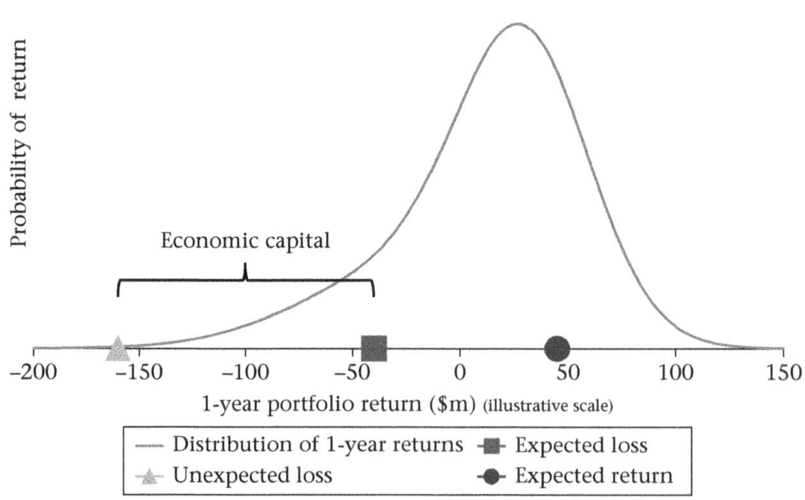

Figure 14.1 Qualitative illustration of the calculation of economic capital

to the institutions, including macro- and micro-economic events, market events, defaults, genuine errors in the organisation, and fraud. A general economic capital model will have a number of components, including market risk capital, credit risk capital (both for the banking and trading book), operational risk capital, model risk capital, regulatory risk capital, liquidity risk capital, reputational risk capital, and strategic risk capital.

14.2.1 Expected and unexpected loss

In that economic capital model, we are going to focus on two points for the determination of the capital: expected and unexpected loss.

When we sell a product as a financial institution, what we basically do is calculate how much we expect to lose from that product (an average loss), then we look at the market price of the product and if we see that we can make a profit from it, we sell it. In other words, the expected loss from that product is already accounted for when we price the product. For example, if we are selling a one year loan, and we estimate that the probability of default of that loan is 5%, then the spread we are going to require from that loan is, at least, 5%, as otherwise we are going to lose money on average, if we have a large portfolio of these type of loans.

However, in reality, the realised default rate of those type of loans is going to be 2% in some years, 9% in other years, etc., depending on a number of factors (e.g., macro-economic environment). The average may be 5%, but there is always a definite probability that we lose more than that average during the next year. If we call that average the Expected Loss (EL), then we can call the Unexpected Loss (UL) to the loss value above that EL for a given confidence level.

Going one step further, we can do this type of calculation at the portfolio level, as correlation effects within our portfolio can be important. For example, we know that default events in an economy tend to happen in clusters; that is, default correlations can be substantial. That will have an important effect on the tails of the total return distribution, for example.

An economic capital model is going to take all things into account and deliver a distribution of losses from which we can calculate the economic capital for a given confidence level. If we want to be, say, a AA entity, we are going to set that confidence level at 0.02% to determine the UL. Once we set this number, the economic capital (EC) is going to be given by the difference between the UL and the EL:

$$EC = UL - EL \tag{14.1}$$

The reason why we subtract the UL from the EL to calculate the capital we need to withstand losses, at the desired confidence level, is because, as said, the valuation of our products already contains the expected loss in them, so we only need to keep aside as a "cushion" the difference between the unexpected and the expected losses.[1]

14.3 RAROC

The Risk Adjusted Return on Capital (RAROC) is defined as

$$RAROC = \frac{\text{Expected Profit}}{\text{Capital}} \tag{14.2}$$

This metric was first introduced in the 1970s. In the 1990s a number of banks tried to introduce it in their management processes but with relatively low success as a result of a lack of data, systems limitations, imperfect methodologies, and other business pressures [19].

One of the main goals of management in a financial institution consists in maximising the shareholder's value. This requires promoting the most profitable business lines *relative* to the resources they consume. RAROC is a metric that helps in this regard. If the profitability of business activities does not consider their capital consumption, we are going to easily find ourselves promoting businesses that may bring high profits in absolute terms, though at the expense of other ones that may bring smaller absolute profits but with very little capital consumption, or even with capital benefits. As a result, if we want to maximise the utilisation of the resources (capital) that a bank has, we need to consider RAROC both when making business decisions (*ex ante*) and when measuring performance (*ex post*).

One of the fundamental ideas behind RAROC is that all transactions in a financial institution should have the same profit in a risk-adjusted basis. In other words, there is no reason why some business lines should consume more capital than others relative to the profit they generate. For this reason, RAROC should be fairly constant across an organisation.

RAROC should be used not only to allocate capital between transactions, but also to set a minimum acceptable return in risk-adjusted terms. Best practices should ensure that valuation reflects not only economic risk, but that a deal is also rejected if the price does not meet the minimum acceptable RAROC.

In this context, an organisation should have two separate key numbers: RAROC targets and RAROC hurdles. A RAROC target is the goal that the institution aims at in terms of return on capital. A RAROC hurdle is the minimum acceptable return on capital. Incentives, bonuses, etc., should be based on targets. Decisions should be based on minimum hurdles.

The retail business has vast experience in something similar to this. Retailers know that there are some products that attract customers more than others. For this reason they tend to decrease the margins on those products, sometimes to ridiculous levels, at the expense of other products, so that they can overall meet a better margin. I remember that when I first arrived in the UK I could buy a loaf of bread for only a few pence (quite a nice thing when you are a student!). That was clearly a strategy by the retailer to attract customers. Having said that, it doesn't make much sense to sell a product below its wholesale cost on an ongoing basis except when that price creates strategic value. In other words, a shop should never sell anything below cost except when there is a clear business reason for it, and this should be properly managed. Similarly, a financial institution should never sell a product below its RAROC hurdle, unless bundled with other profitable products.

Indeed, management can use RAROC to drive internal subsidies that may make sense for strategic reasons. For example, a bank may want to start a business in a new country or with a new client. This can be managed by accepting negative RAROC, temporarily, in these strategic transactions at the expense of other ones. Also it can use RAROC hurdles to set the minimum acceptable profit in a deal, with exceptions only when there is a strong strategic business case for it. Also, it can use RAROC targets to measure business performance, as opposed to absolute profit.[2]

14.3.1 The cost of capital

The natural question following this explanation is what should we use as target and hurdle for RAROC. Regarding the target, this number sets the RAROC *goal* in the organisation. This is very intrinsic to the organisation, with its history and culture, so we are not going to enter that area. However, regarding the hurdle, things are different.

We have seen in the analogy with the retail business that, with only some exceptions that create strategic value, it does not make sense to enter a deal below its wholesale cost. If we do that, we are destroying long-term value, however profitable the deal may look, and the share price of the financial institution will reflect this at some point. Banks are highly geared organisations: as seen in Chapter 1 they leverage from a relatively small amount of equity by holding a considerable amount of debt that funds their business and creates money in the economy.

Assuming that the most fundamental type of capital is cash, if we want to generate a new deal, we are going to have to borrow the capital needed to support that deal and, as a result, if we enter a deal with a RAROC below our cost of borrowing capital we will be destroying value, as we will be selling that product below our "cost of manufacturing".

Weighted average cost of capital

One of the central questions here is: what is the cost we should attach to the capital that a transaction needs? A clear candidate is the Weighted Average Cost of Capital (WACC).

Companies can raise capital (i.e., cash in its most fundamental form) in a number of ways: common or preferred equity, secured or unsecured debt, convertible debt, exchangeable debt, warrants, options, etc. If a company has a value V_i of the security i (e.g., equity, debt, etc.) in its capital structure, and the required rate of return on it is r_i, then WACC is usually defined as

$$r_{wacc} = \frac{\sum_i r_i V_i}{\sum_i V_i} \tag{14.3}$$

That is, r_{wacc} is the required averaged return on capital given today's capital structure. Any investment with a return lower than r_{wacc} will be uneconomical from a capital standpoint.

14.4 The case for a KVA charge

Not all financial institutions use RAROC as a tool to maximise value. Also, when used, it is mostly done *ex post* in order to allocate capital to business units, but hardly ever *ex ante* to incentivise the most profitable business lines on a risk-adjusted basis [19]. In my view this is a fundamental mistake. We are going to see how, by introducing a capital charge (KVA) into the derivative valuation, we can manage RAROC quite effectively both *ex ante* and *ex post*, in a natural way.

In any business sector, not only in banking, it is best practice to make each unit at the front line face the marginal costs they generate with their business activities. Similarly, the goal of such a KVA charge is to make dealing desks face the marginal costs they generate with their trading activities from a capital perspective.

14.4.1 KVA as the price of unexpected losses

When we value a deal, this is done always as the present value of expected (i.e., the average) future cash flows. However, if done just like that, we face a fundamental problem.

A simple example of KVA

Let's look into KVA through a very simple example, another coin tossing game: a *fair* coin is going to be tossed one million times; then,

1. Whenever "heads" come out, we are paid \$1.1, and whenever "tails" come out we pay \$1.0.[3] We are told that we can play this game for free. It appears this is our lucky day, as we are going to make on average \$0.1 per toss, which leads to an expected profit of \$100,000!

2. However there is a second rule. All payments ($1.1 or $1.0 respectively) must be made immediately after each toss. If someone is not able to honour that immediate payment, that person goes to jail for 25 years. Also, we cannot go away and ask for money once the game has started. Well, it appears there is some risk here now.

We have very little money, so the question that we have now is: what is the probability that we have of going to jail, given the money that we have available?

We can invert this question. If I am happy to accept a probability of X% of going to jail, how much money do I need to have to support that level of risk? And going one step forward, what is the cost of borrowing that money that I need to have to support that level of risk? The answer to this question leads to KVA.

In this example, we can solve these questions very easily with a computer. We can (i) simulate all the possible events that could happen in the game, (ii) calculate how much money we need to subsist in each of those future paths, (iii) make a probability distribution of the possible capital[4] requirements of the game, (iv) observe what the maximum capital is that we should have given the confidence level we are happy to accept, and (v) borrow, before the game starts, enough money so I know I will not go to jail with that accepted level of uncertainty.

If we are happy to accept a risk of going to jail of 0.01%, for example, in this game KVA is going to be the difference between the expected funding cost (FVA, that I already take into account when I give a value in this game) and the level of capital we need to ensure we do not go to jail with that 0.01% probability.

KVA in derivatives

The above was a simple example to illustrate the concept behind KVA. Let's say now that we have two possible derivative deals, each with the same price, the same expected profits, the same expected funding costs, etc. That is, everything stays the same *on average*. However, one has a higher UL than the other; for example, one can provide a lot of profit in some future scenarios but high losses too in other scenarios, while the second one is more balanced in that respect. If one of the core business attributes we deliver to our customers is the solidity of our balance sheet and our high credit rating (as it is for banks), which of those two deals has more value to us? Clearly, the one that has the lower UL, as it is less risky.

However, none of the standard pricing and valuation techniques, which are based on "averages", considers the price of UL when valuing a deal. This is fundamentally wrong as the uncertainty (i.e., the UL) of income and costs also has a value, as seen in the simple coin-tossing game. This is where KVA comes into play.

Let's define KVA as

$$KVA_0 = \int_0^T EK_t \cdot DF_t^* \cdot r_c \cdot dt \tag{14.4}$$

Where 0 is "now", the valuation time point; T is the portfolio maturity; EK_t is the expected capital at time t; DF_t^* is the risky discount factor; and r_c is the cost of the capital rate from t to $t + dt$. It must be noted that, in practice, this is evaluated over a set of discrete time buckets, similarly to Equation 8.22.

Further to this, Equation 12.3 which gives the value of a portfolio of derivatives is now transformed into

$$V = P_{CreditRiskFree} - CVA - FVA - KVA \tag{14.5}$$

where KVA is the cost of capital created when manufacturing a portfolio of derivatives.

In Appendix H the reader can find a more detailed derivation of this KVA within an XVA context.[5]

14.4.2 KVA as the cost of manufacturing

In this context, it is important to notice that KVA is not an adjustment to account for some risk in a loose manner. It is an actual cost that every financial institution faces: the cost of raising the capital needed to stay in business.

Consequently, similarly to FVA, KVA is not a pricing adjustment to come up to a risk-neutral price; rather it is an adjustment to come up to the *value* of a portfolio of derivatives. KVA reflects a *real* cost not considered in the classical Black–Scholes theory of pricing.[6]

In other words, KVA must not be seen as a way to find the risk-neutral price of a derivative, *but* as the minimum price at which we will make money out of it, given a level of risk we are willing to take in the organisation. It can be seen as a way to calculate the margin we get from a book of derivatives, as it reflects the true cost of "manufacturing" it.

14.4.3 *KVA* and CVA_{liab}

Similarly to FVA, one could easily say that KVA may be double counting our own default risk that is already captured in CVA_{liab}; however, this is not correct in my view.

CVA_{liab} reflects the price of hedging our default risk *by an entity that is external to us.* That is very different to the price that *we* have to pay to ensure we do not default, with a given confidence level. The average of this latter price is FVA. KVA reflects that extra cash we need to be a solid institution.

Similarly to FVA, if we lived in the Black–Scholes world of perfect symmetric information, frictionless markets, infinite liquidity, etc., then we may not need any KVA because the price of our own default risk would be marked in CVA_{liab}, and so our balance sheet would reflect that risk already. However, the world we live in can be quite far from the Black–Scholes ideal assumptions. Our equity holders and creditors are not going to look at our balance sheet as if we operated in a Black–Scholes world, because we don't. As a result, we know that we need to have some level of capital put aside to be able to survive during the difficult times. This capital is going to have a cost, which is KVA.

The confidence level at which we calculate capital and KVA is going to have an impact on our credit quality, hence on our own credit spread, hence on the CVA_{liab} that we need to pay to our counterparty's to trade with them. So, in that sense, they are not fully independent. However, given that the markets are imperfect, taking a long time to react to good news but quickly overreacting to bad news, given that there isn't symmetry of information in the markets, etc., and given that CVA_{liab} is our counterparty's standpoint in regards to our own default risk, which is very different to our own standpoint to it, we must account for a KVA adjustment if we are to calculate the "value to me" of a portfolio of trades.

14.4.4 KVA allocation

Similarly to CVA and FVA, we can allocate KVA in two ways: we can distribute the whole portfolio KVA by trades using the Euler algorithm (Equation 5.5), or we can calculate the *incremental* KVA that trading activity brings (Equations 5.1 and 5.2).

The same discussion we had for CVA and FVA applies here: to make it properly "fair", a dealing desk should be charged the KVA from the Euler algorithm, though this will make capital allocation impossible to manage, as the KVA that each desk will have could change as a result of trading activities far from them, due to netting effects. As a result, it is better in practice to charge incremental KVA to dealing desks for each new trade that comes in, or for trades that are unwound or restructured.

If KVA is charged to every new trading activity, the trading decision will automatically consider the risk it generates, calculated through the economic capital model. This is why KVA is good: it aligns trading decisions with the risk and credit stability objectives of the institution.

14.5 Calculation of the expected capital

When calculating EK_t, the first thing we need to realise is that this is a portfolio calculation. This is because, as said previously, the capital has many components that include market risk, credit risk, operational risk, model risk, etc. Hence, in general, the calculation of EK_t does not relate to a single trade, netting set, or counterparty, but to the whole portfolio.

Something also to realise is that the capital calculation that banks currently do only calculates today's spot capital. However, this KVA charge should account not only for the spot capital, but for all the capital that a portfolio will require up to its maturity.

We are going to see how, in this way, a KVA desk is able to hedge the balance sheet impact that changes in capital may have, and in this way to produce a risk-neutral world for the dealing desks.

14.5.1 Economic vs. regulatory capital

Financial institutions can have two capital calculations: the so-called Economic Capital (EC) and Regulatory Capital (RC).

Fundamentally, EC is an institution's internal view as to how much capital it needs to hold to ensure the desired credit standing. However, RC is the minimum capital that governments make financial institutions have; it constitutes a floor to the capital a bank must hold. So, in practice, the capital that a bank holds is the maximum of both EC and RC:

$$K_t = \max(EC_t, RC_t) \tag{14.6}$$

One of the after-effects of the 2008 market events is that governments have been imposing increasing levels of capital on banks. The goal of increasing capital as such is understandable, given that governments had to step up to rescue the banking system from a complete collapse. The argument is something along the lines of "given that I (a government) am the effective last resort of capital, I am going to tell you how much capital you must hold so you do not need me in the future".

However, one the problems is that regulatory capital is based on a number of flat rules, mostly set by the Basel Committee, to be applied to every bank in the world. As a result, quite naturally, those rules are not sensitive to the true economic risks each specific bank has; it is impossible to set a good economic capital model for every bank in the world from Switzerland.

There is empirical evidence of how suboptimal this is. Moody's Analytics presented in IACPM 2011 a study showing that "Economic Capital is more predictive regarding bank failure risk than reported Regulatory Capital" [78]. This is quite a natural result, as economic capital is more tailored to each institution's risk profile than the flat-model-based regulatory version of it.

In my view, the current focus on regulatory capital will have negative consequences: given that it does not create the risk incentives in line with the true economic risks an institution has, risk mismanagement will surely occur.

A very clear example of this is Right and Wrong Way Risk (RWWR) in the context of counterparty credit risk. Banks tend to have very poor models for it, and those models tend to focus only on Wrong Way Risk.

However, it has been empirically shown that this risk can be most important [75]. In spite of that, the dialogue that I have had as a consultant with the management of financial institutions has gone along the lines of me saying "I can show you a good, relatively easy to implement and easy to calibrate model for RWWR if you want." To which the banking manager replied "Interesting. How much regulatory capital relief would I get from it?"I then replied "Not sure right now, as I am not sure how it will affect your risk profiles. Basel says that you can apply for a lower α for your CCR capital if you can measure WWR but, quite frankly, I do not see a regulator decreasing the α to any bank these days, given the political agenda. However, you will be able to measure and manage your true economic risk in a much better way!" The manager replies "I see. Given that it is unlikely I will have any regulatory capital benefit, thanks but I am not interested right now, am too busy keeping my regulator happy, and trying to decrease regulatory capital." In other words: banks are being so stressed by regulators that they have little time, resources, and incentive to think of the true risks they face.[7]

In contrast, best practices for capital calculation should follow this process: first the bank decides on its target credit rating, then generates an economic capital model that reflects its true economic risk, as well as possible, and calculates the economic capital based on that. Then, it calculates in parallel the regulatory capital as dictated by the regulator, however high or low this is. If the regulatory capital is lower than the economic capital, it sets capital in the balance sheet to the economic capital. Otherwise, if regulatory capital is greater than economic capital, it sets capital in the balance sheet to the regulatory version of it (as mandated by governments) and, then, it *recalibrates up* the unexpected loss confidence level used in the economic capital model to the point at which $EC = RC$. Finally, it calculates KVAs and incremental KVAs based on its economic capital model.

In this way, it achieves two key goals:

1. Capital is always at or above the regulatory requirements.
2. Incentives in the organisation are driven by the economic capital costs which should be a good reflection of the true economic risks.[8]

However, at the time of this book being written, banks seem to be quite far away from this approach. In practice, capital calculation for the balance sheet tends to be solely driven by the regulatory version of it, without any adjustments to reflect the true risks the institution is carrying.[9]

14.5.2 KVA based on regulatory capital

Given that lots of institutions are effectively using the regulatory capital model as their economic capital model too, let's see how to calculate KVA with it.

Regulatory capital has five components: market risk (MR), credit risk (CR), CVA market risk (CVA), incremental risk charge (IRC), and operational risk (OR):

$$EK_{reg,t} = EK_{MR,t} + EK_{CR,t} + EK_{CVA,t} + EK_{IRC,t} + EK_{OR,t} \tag{14.7}$$

Most often, the number that is more important is the incremental KVA that trading activity brings with it. In this context we can neglect K_{OR} is marginal trading activities should have a very limited effect on this risk. Also, from a derivatives standpoint, we are interested in the counterparty credit risk (CCR): the version of credit risk that applies to the derivatives business.

$$EK_{reg,t} \simeq EK_{MR,t} + EK_{CCR,t} + EK_{CVA,t} + EK_{IRC,t} \tag{14.8}$$

Also, the Incremental Risk Charge tends to apply mostly to a limited amount of trades. So this is another source of capital that could be left out in many cases.

This leaves incremental capital coming, mainly, from three sources:

$$EK_{reg,t} \simeq EK_{MR,t} + EK_{CCR,t} + EK_{CVA,t} \tag{14.9}$$

The first thing that can be noted here is that EK_{CCR} and EK_{CVA} are calculated per netting set and then added up, but EK_{MR} is calculated at portfolio level. So it is clear now that KVA is a portfolio risk metric.

Also, KVA will depend not only on the portfolio of trades, but on the regulatory status and the bank's intentions. This is the case because the same portfolio of trades will have different regulatory capital treatment if the institution is Internal-Models approved or not, for example. Also, the same trade could have a different regulatory capital associated with it depending on whether it is a "buy-and-hold" trade (banking book) or "available-for-sale" (trading book).[10]

It must be noted that when a bank does not use the advanced approaches to measure regulatory capital, the KVA that each trade brings to the bank can be substantially the same when measured via the Euler or incremental method, specifically when the method to calculate regulatory capital does not contemplate any netting effects. That is because, in those cases, regulatory capital is constructed trade by trade, and then added up.

Calculating EK_t

The big difference between the standard capital calculation and this other $EK_{reg,t}$ is that, now, we need a time profile for the capital, whereas before we only needed the spot capital value.

We are going to see how to tackle that for the regulatory advanced approaches; this calculation should be considered easier for non-advanced regulatory capital calculations, so we won't cover this latter case here.[11]

Market risk capital: For $EK_{MR,t}$ we need to perform a forward market risk calculation. This calculation is made out of the 99% 10-day VaR.[12] However, market risk engines tend to be ready to do only spot VaR calculations.

Ideally we'd like to extend the market risk engine for forward looking risk metrics, but if this is not possible, we can reuse our existing CVA/FVA engine (i.e., XVA engine) to obtain a proxy for it.

In our XVA engine we should already have a future simulation of the price of all our OTC derivatives. From this, we can calculate the 99% 10-day VaR[13] by subtracting, in each scenario, the price of the derivative 10 days after each measurement point, and then calculating the 99th % worst price in those scenarios. If we do this in every time step, we can obtain a forward VaR_t profile.

It must be noted that this is the same as measuring the PFE at the 1% confidence level, without zero-flooring, for a perfectly collateralised portfolio.

Then we need to recalculate this for a stress calibration of the XVA as per Equation 9.36 and, finally,

$$EK_{MR,t} = (3 + x + y) \cdot (\mathrm{VaR}^{MR}_{(99\%,10d),t} + \mathrm{sVaR}^{MR}_{(99\%,10d),t}). \tag{14.10}$$

where we can leave x and y constant as given by the current regulatory status of the institution.

Counterparty credit risk capital: If we are an IMM approved bank, with advanced models for capital calculation, following Equation 9.20, we need to calculate a profile for each of the CCR charge components, and then calculate the capital in each time point in the future. In particular, for each netting set:

- **EEPE:** At each point in time, we need to get the regulatory Expected Exposure profile EE_{reg} looking forward for one year and calculate from it its time-weighted average, to calculate the $EEPE_t$ profile. Then, $EAD_t = \alpha \cdot EEPE_t$.
- **PD:** As a first approximation, we may want to keep constant the PD of the counterparty for f_{PD}, but ideally we should model its evolution over time too. The easiest way to do this is using a rating transition matrix and simulate a Markov process with it.

  However, if we have right or wrong way risk in the book of trades with that counterparty, we should try to model the dependency between those rating transitions and the price of the portfolio with that counterparty. Given that most likely we already have simulated values for all the risk factors and portfolio values, we can expand the right and wrong way risk model described in Section 10.4 to a rating transition model. Given that in that model we are simulating the one year default probability of the counterparty, from it we can either infer its credit rating, or use the simulated PD directly in f_{PD}.
- **LGD:** The Loss Given Default of counterparties usually depends only on region and industry sector, which will not change over time, so we can keep this constant in the simulation.
- **MA:** We are going to have to simulate the maturity adjustment in each time step following Equations 9.29 and 9.30. To make things a bit easier, we only need to do this once per time step (as opposed to in every scenario).

Once we have all these components:

$$EK_{t,CCR} = \sum_i EAD_{i,t} \cdot f_{\mathrm{PD}_{i,t}} \cdot LGD_i \cdot MA_{i,t} \tag{14.11}$$

where i covers all netting sets.

CVA-VaR Capital: Under the advanced approach, to calculate $EK_{t,CVA}$ as per Equation 9.32, we need two components:

- **Credit Spread:** For Equation 9.33 we need to simulate the credit spread of the counterparty. The first proxy for this would be the obvious solution: it stays constant. If we want to go one step further, and the portfolio does not have any right or wrong way risk, we can simulate the credit spread via the credit rating migration Markov process used in the CCR charge, assigning a typical credit spread per credit rating.[14] [15] If we have right and wrong way risk, we can use the model described for the CCR charge to simulate the credit spread of the counterparty.
- **Exposure Profiles:** We also need the exposure profiles for Equation 9.34. This can be obtained directly for the exposure profiles (EE_{reg}) from the standard spot capital calculation, but starting at the relevant time point t and taking its future profile from that point only.

With all these components, we can now calculate a CVA capital profile $EK_{CVA,t}$ at each future time step by doing a forward market risk calculation for it. Given that most likely our market risk engine is not ready for it, a good proxy could be using the regulatory CS01 for single factor credit spread models (Equation 9.35) and then multiply it by either the 99th worst historical spread shock over ten days ($\Delta s^{\mathrm{hist}}_{99\%,10\mathrm{d}}$), or assume that the spread follows a normal distribution so that $\Delta s_{99\%,10\mathrm{d}} = 2.33 \cdot \sqrt{\frac{10}{260}} \cdot \sigma_s$. So,

$$\mathrm{VaR}^{cva}_{99\%,10d} = CS01_{reg} \cdot \Delta s_{99\%,10\mathrm{d}}. \tag{14.12}$$

Finally, we must not forget that in order to calculate the CVA capital charge we must do this both in a standard and stressed calibration.

With all this, we can now calculate a $EK_{t,CVA}$ profile following Equation 9.36, as

$$EK_{t,CVA} = (3+x+y)\cdot(\text{VaR}^{cva}_{(99\%,10d),t} + \text{sVaR}^{cva}_{(99\%,10d),t}). \tag{14.13}$$

where we can keep both x and y constant.

These three components (MR, CCR, and CVA) will constitute, in most cases, the source of the incremental capital that the new trading activity brings along, from where we can calculate ΔKVA.

14.5.3 KVA beyond financial institutions

One could naively think that KVA is a concept that applies only to banks, as they are the ones that tend to have capital requirements, but nothing is further away from reality.

This point was very nicely expressed by one of my consulting clients. This is a European corporate, which asked me for help in implementing an XVA function in its trading unit. A very important source of cost in this corporate was coming from the funding of collateral. In the preliminary discussions, a senior manager in the risk department expressed the problem very clearly:

> We are a (relatively) small institution, and so we do not have the capability to implement an effective hedging strategy for our funding needs. As a result, FVA for us will be kept as a risk reserve. A big problem that we have is that we can charge a desk for FVA at trade inception, but a couple of years down the line the actual funding needs may be much higher than anticipated, and so the FVA charge itself does not cover our real funding requirements. We have to manage this. We need to incentivise trades that lower future funding volatility, and discourage those that increase that volatility.

This is, precisely, the idea behind KVA.

What this manager is saying is that, for them, future funding has a high degree of uncertainty (i.e., risk). Consequently, they need a funding capital charge to cover unexpected costs from funding.

In the same way that a bank defines the confidence level for UL from their credit rating goals, so this corporate can define a UL confidence level for funding at the number they feel comfortable with; for example, 95%. Then, following Equation 13.7, a Funding Risk (FR) capital charge can be defined as

$$KVA_{FR} = \int_0^T \max(PFE95^{cash}_t - EPE^{cash}_t, 0)\cdot DF_t \cdot s^{borrow}_t \, dt \tag{14.14}$$

where $PFE95^{cash}_t$ is the 95th percentile of the cash needs at time t. In other words, we are defining capital as the cash we need to leave aside to make sure that we have enough funds for our collateral needs in 95% of the cases.

14.6 The KVA desk

Capital is not a constant number for a given portfolio, even if the portfolio remains unchanged. For example, let's think of a portfolio of swaps that is roughly at-the-money today.[16] Tonight the Fed makes a surprise announcement that moves the interest rates abruptly, so that that portfolio becomes well in-the-money.[17]

This is good news for us, as our swaps are now worth a lot more than they were yesterday. However, given that our exposure has increased substantially, the regulatory CCR charge has also increased a lot. As a result, the bank needs to collect the extra capital needed to support that portfolio with its associated costs.

A central question here is: who should pay for this extra capital cost in the organisation?

14.6.1 Hedging capital risk

The natural answer to that question is "the dealing desk that runs that portfolio". It does not make sense that someone else in the organisation, which runs a business totally unrelated to that portfolio, has to pay for this extra cost.

However, dealing desks know about selling and hedging OTC derivatives in a risk-neutral world; they do not know about regulatory capital costs, changes in them, etc.

A solution to this is setting up a specialised KVA desk. This desk is going to sell an internal insurance to the dealing desks to cover the impact of capital costs in the future, so that any change in that cost is absorbed by this KVA desk. The premium of this insurance is going to be, precisely, KVA, because that number is, basically, the present value of the expected cost of capital during the life of our portfolio.

Once the KVA desk receives this premium, it is going to:

1. Assume the cost of capital from the dealing desks.
2. Manage any change in the cost of capital.

This can be done in the following way. The expected cost of capital is going to be taken directly from the KVA charge. Then, the KVA desk is going to set up market hedges against changes in the cost of capital. This can be done because KVA is going to have sensitivities to market factors like interest rates, FX rates, etc., in the same way CVA or FVA has.

Regulatory risk

It must be noted that not all KVA risks are hedge-able. The one that is most obvious is "regulatory risk". By this is meant the risk that the rules of the regulatory capital calculation may change.

Regulatory bodies have a long history of changing those rules: Basel I, Basel II, Basel II.5, Basel III, exemptions for CVA regulatory capital charge in Europe, SA-CCR, Fundamental Review of the Trading Book, Basel IV?

These are risks that cannot be properly hedged, but a specialised desk (i.e., the KVA desk) would be on top of upcoming changes, try to assess their impact, and foresee them in the calculations as far as possible.

14.6.2 KVA as the price of a contingent capital swap derivative

KVA can be seen as the price of an internal derivative, a Contingent Capital Swap (CKS) in the same way that CVA is the price of a Contingent Credit Default Swap (CCDS); and the FVA of a Contingent Funding Swap (CFS).

As seen, the KVA desk can place a number of hedges in the market to become P&L neutral, as far as possible given the market trading environment. In the case of the example above, the KVA desk could have in place a number of interest rate hedges with the same sensitivities as those from KVA (but with the opposite sign), so that the increase in the capital cost going forward as a result of the Fed announcement is subsidised by the profit from those hedges.

The role of the KVA desk is illustrated in Figure 14.2.

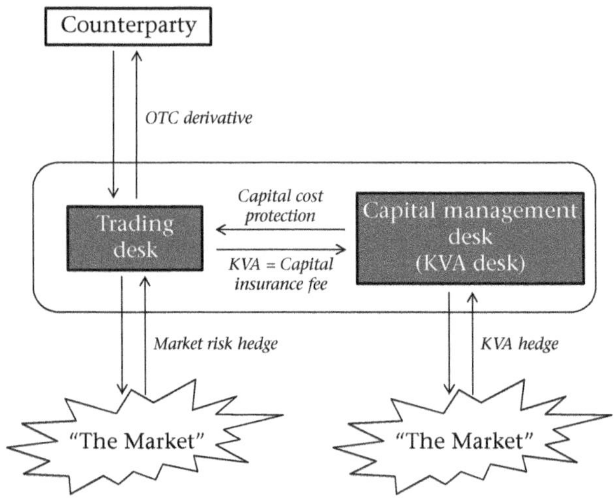

Figure 14.2 Illustration of the role of a KVA desk

14.6.3 KVA as a tool to manage risk

If we set up this KVA desk, which is going to charge to the dealing desks the incremental KVA charge they generate, they are naturally going to include this in the calculation of the minimum price to deal at, profit margins, etc. In this way the dealing desks are paying for the actual marginal cost they provoke in the organisation with their trading activities, as corporate management best practices indicate.

Needless to say, if a trade brings to the bank a capital benefit, typically due to netting, the dealing desk will be paid for this by the KVA desk, hence increasing the profit they can make from the deal.

14.6.4 KVA and RAROC

And now we are in a position to hook up the KVA activities with RAROC. With this KVA charge, we are effectively imposing a RAROC hurdle on every trade, that hurdle being the "cost of manufacturing capital". In this way, quite naturally, every trade in the organisation will be above the RAROC hurdle and, if it is not, it is because the dealing desk appreciates other strategic values (e.g., via bundling a RAROC that is losing trade with other ones that make an aggregated profit, via winning a new customer, etc.).

With this KVA charge, the organisation is making sure that trading activities are sensitive to profitability on a risk-adjusted basis. Now, in this environment, two trades with the same price and expected profits are not seen as equal in the valuation process: the one with the lower tail risk has more value as it has a lower KVA charge.

In this way, RAROC is automatically managed.

14.6.5 KVA on the balance sheet

So far we have seen KVA internally in an organisation. However, there is no reason why those who believe that FVA should be marked on the balance sheet should think otherwise for KVA.

The rationale behind marking KVA on the balance sheet is that, in that calculation, we are aiming at the exit price of our trades. Surely any potential buyer of our trades will consider in its calculation the capital impact it will have internally, and so marking KVA on the balance sheet makes sense in that context.

Similarly to FVA, this leads to two KVA compuations: one internal ($KVA_{internal}$) for our capital management, and one external (KVA_{exit}) to adjust the potential sale price of our OTC derivatives. So far in this chapter we have focused on $KVA_{internal}$.

The calculation of KVA_{exit} presents real challenges, both conceptually and methodologically. First of all, similarly to FVA, we do not know the capital netting that potential buyers may have as we do not know their portfolio of trades, nor it is clear at all the cost of capital rate that we should use.

Similarly to FVA, we could use our own capital netting as a "best guess" (actually, the only guess we can possibly make) and an "estimated average" market funding cost of capital.

However, KVA brings an other challenge, as this capital calculation is sensitive to the regulatory status of the organisation too. What is the "average" regulatory status in the market? Perhaps here the only way we can manage this is, again, assuming that everyone else has the same regulatory status as we do, which is quite a strong assumption, though.[18]

Having said all this, the rationale behind not having a KVA_{exit} at all on the balance sheet also applies here: it is not a risk-neutral pricing calculation, highly dependent on the organisation, so it shouldn't be used at all on the balance sheet.

The solution to this problem is, once again, down to opinion. In my view, if we are going to sell a derivative in the market the potential buyer is going to account for its capital impact, so a KVA_{exit} adjustment makes sense on the balance sheet if we are aiming at estimating the exit price of our deals. However, we must keep in mind that this KVA_{exit} adjustment is, in reality, no more than a "guesstimate", a kind of a "shot in the air and in the dark" at best.

14.7 Key KVA challenges

A KVA desk is quite a novel idea. We have seen how it can create true value in a financial institution by setting up a price to the actual cost of capital (i.e., the cost of uncertainty) that trading activities create. However, it doesn't come without some important challenges.

Education: The first problem that a KVA desk is going to face is making everyone understand what it is doing, and why it is doing it. Dealing desks are going to complain saying "yet a new cost charge?", clients are going to complain along the lines of "now you have found a new way to increase the price", systems people will have to extend capital calculations beyond today's value into the future, risk managers may feel their role is being duplicated if things are not well understood, etc.

For the right uptake of a KVA desk, education is critical. All parts in the organisation must understand that capital is a true cost and that we must include that cost in derivative valuation to reflect the true economics of it.

Systems: Like CVA and FVA, KVA does not come without significant challenges from the technology point of view. Up to now we only needed to calculate today's spot capital. Now we need to calculate forward capital up to the portfolio maturity.

Again, quite a challenge, but well worth the effort as, with it, we will be able to have a crystal clear view of the future capital costs we are facing. Without it, we are navigating blindly in that space.

Changing regulatory position: To add further difficulty, the regulatory calculation changes over time following the regulatory status of the institution (e.g., IMM vs non-IMM) as well as following the changing regulatory landscape. Hence the KVA desk must always be alert of what is going on in the changing regulatory space, and adapt to it swiftly.

Calibration: Calibrating KVA models can be another problem. The good side of the problem is that we do not need to think about the calibration of the (typically regulatory) capital models, as we must take them as they are: even if we think that the regulatory calibration of a VaR model, for example, is suboptimal, if that is what the regulatory calculation takes, that is the one we must take for KVA, as the future costs will be driven by it. We don't need to challenge it.

The more difficult side of the problem is how to calibrate the rate of cost of capital. We have said here that WACC is a clear candidate, but this topic is so novel that it is not clear yet which is the optimal cost of capital we should use.

As said, WACC is a clear candidate, but by using that number we are assuming that the corporate capital structure (i.e., relative size of debt, equity, etc.) will remain constant over time. Reality may not be like that in the future.

Therefore a subsequent challenge is how to calibrate forward cost of capital. In the same way as we saw in the FVA chapters that, ideally, the treasury unit should provide the FVA desk with a forward Cost of Funding (CoF) curve, the KVA desk will need the capital unit to set up for them a forward Cost of Capital (CoC) curve. How can this be done? Can it be hedged?

Management: All this environment creates a number of interesting challenges for management, including:

- Who calibrates the CoC curve? How?
- Who owns the KVA charges? The front office, the risk department?
- What synergies should we see with the CVA and FVA desks?
- What are the accounting implications of a KVA desk?
- What P&L target should the KVA desk have? A flat one? Or should it be a profit centre?

KVA charge allocation: Figure 14.2 shows how the KVA charge should be paid by the dealing desks, so they value their trading activity with the capital cost it generates. However, from the three capital charges we have seen (MR, CCR, and CVA), two of them (CCR and CVA) are managed (i.e., hedged) by the CVA desk.

So we have two models for these two credit-related charges: on the one hand, these charges could be paid directly by the sales or dealing desks to the KVA desk as shown in Figure 14.2. On the other hand, it may make sense for them to be paid by the CVA desk to the KVA desk, as it is they who manage that risk in the organisation.[19] Then, the CVA desk will naturally pass it on to the sales or dealing desks.

The second set-up makes sense because it is the CVA desk which is the one in charge of hedging default risk, so they are the ones in the best position to minimise the capital related to that risk.

Hence a key challenge that setting up a KVA desk brings is: how should the KVA charge be allocated in the organisation?

14.8 Conclusions

In this chapter we have introduced the concept of capital with OTC derivative valuation. We have seen that capital is a true tangible cost to financial institutions that are regulated, but it could also be a risk management instrument for non-regulated organisations that deal with derivatives.

Best practices suggest the usage of a risk-sensitive metric in the valuation of OTC derivatives, in addition to average metrics like CVA and FVA. RAROC offers a good way of doing this, as it ensures that tail risk is considered when valuing OTC derivatives. This is the case because capital calculation is based on the Unexpected Loss that a book of derivatives faces, which is a measurement of tail risk. Also, capital is highly linked to the aim the organisation has from a credit standing point of view and to the risk profile it aims to achieve.

We have seen how KVA is the price of an internal trade that a KVA desk can sell to the dealing desks. In this framework, the KVA desk absorbs any P&L impact coming from varying capital costs. The KVA desk can hedge this P&L volatility as far as the market permits. By imposing a KVA charge at trade inception, the dealing desk is buying an insurance policy from the KVA desk, so they can forget about future capital impact and can focus on what they know best: hedging in the risk-neutral world.

With a KVA desk an organisation can manage capital optimisation both *ex ante* and *ex post*, as best practices indicate.

The market events of 2008 can be seen as a clear example of a tail event in the financial world. Capital was not managed properly before 2008; RAROC was not well implemented and KVA was a completely unknown concept at that time. It is difficult to guess how 2008 would have unfolded had all banks had a good functional KVA desk; perhaps saying that the banking crisis would have been avoided is going too far, but it is clear to me that it would have been more contained at least. If tail risk is considered at trade inception and valuation, its effects can be subsequently managed.

15 XVA Desks: A New Era for Risk Management

In Chapter 1 we saw how risk management is at the very core of the financial industry. The past is full of examples of many years of value creation being destroyed in very short periods of time as a result of poor risk management standards. The most clear example of such events happened in 2008, when the whole financial industry was brought down to its knees. Governments had to intervene to prevent the major collapse of the economy that would have followed a collapse of the interbank financial system.

Indeed, 2008 was a major slap in the face of the banking sector. An enlightenment took place when, after the initial scare had passed away, the industry started to realise that the Black–Scholes framework may not be enough to manage the risks of derivatives.

Needless to say, this Black–Scholes framework provoked a major step forward in the ability that banks have to offer good quality financial services; the derivatives market grew as a consequence of it. In this book we have seen examples of how derivatives are an excellent tool to transfer and manage risk between the different players in a mature economy.

However, 2008 showed to everyone that the Black–Scholes "risk-neutral" model has its shortcomings. This, which was somewhat a nearly taboo topic in the past, is now openly discussed.

So far in this text we have seen three price adjustments, CVA, FVA, and KVA, which come up with the value of a book of derivatives. Which Black–Scholes based on this, we are going to see a method for best practice of valuation and risk management of OTC derivatives. We are going to see how the set-up of an XVA desk offers an optimal framework for the management of the risks that come with derivative products.

We will put together lots of points already expressed throughout the previous chapters of this book. In that sense, we will condense those ideas into a single concept: XVA. We will see that XVA has transformed the way we understand risk. It has created a new world in which business development and risk management, two units that have historically shown friction, can work in a positive, collaborative, and harmonious manner.

15.1 Moving on from Black–Scholes pricing

Let's recap on the assumptions of the Black–Scholes "risk-neutral" model that has guided the pricing of derivatives for decades:

- **Risk-free Rate:** There are assets out there that are "risk-free"; that is, they will deliver a rate of return (r) for sure, without any uncertainty. This is the so-called *risk-free rate.*

- **Infinite Liquidity of Assets:** For every derivative product based on an underlying asset (S) (e.g., currency, bonds, equity), we can buy and sell that derivative and its underlying asset in any quantity, however big or small, and whenever we want.
- **Infinite Liquidity of Cash:** We can borrow or lend any amount of cash, whenever we want, at the risk-free rate.
- **Frictionless Markets:** We can do any of the above without any fees or costs.
- **No Arbitrage:** Any portfolio of riskless assets always returns the risk-free rate.
- **Normality of Asset Returns:** Market prices follow Brownian motion random walks.

Quite frankly, if we look at the markets now and compare our observations with this list, the first reaction is to smile and think "that list is so detached from reality".

To start with, most importantly, there isn't such a thing as one unique price for a derivative. Our everyday life shows to us that nothing around us has a unique price: the real true price of anything (i.e., the cash for which I can buy or sell that thing, today) of a computer, a car, an airline ticket, a mortgage, a credit card, anything, depends on a number of factors, often quite arbitrarily. If that is the case with any product in the economy, why should derivatives be different? In fact, everyday trading reality points in that direction: derivative dealers can offer a different price for the same derivative to two customers depending on the history of their relationship, hedging strategy, operational arrangements, the "value to me" that each side of the deal has, the perceived value to the other side, their future strategy, etc. This is quite a natural thing, as it is what happens to any other product in the economy.

A purist would say that "that leads to arbitrage opportunities", to which we could respond "great, so go and exploit them, and good luck!" That purist will first face the problem that he or she needs cash for it, and that cash is a limited resource (not infinite as Black–Scholes says), has a non-risk-free cost, and markets do have friction. He or she is also going to find that we cannot buy as much or as little as we want of anything out there, as there are real liquidity constraints in the market. He or she is also going to find that real prices do not follow Brownian motion.

As a result of all this, we need to adjust the Black–Scholes pricing framework to make it useful to the reality we face on a daily basis. That is what the XVA framework does for us.

In fact, we can argue that it is precisely if we don't perform that adjustment that arbitrage opportunities arise: if we price and manage derivatives contracts within the naivity of Black–Scholes we are going to fail to run an economically self-sustaining business, and hence that failure will create the conditions arbitrageurs exploit.

It must be noted that this idea is not new. For example, Christopher James stated in 1996 that

> No self-respecting banker would accept the proposition that capital markets operate without friction. Indeed, banks and other financial intermediaries add value precisely through their ability to reduce market frictions... This role implies that a large proportion of bank assets are likely to be difficult for outside investors to value, which in turn may create information and agency problems for banks themselves when they have to raise capital externally [as we saw, precisely, in 2008] [47].

The only difference between now and the 1990s is that now we have been hit by this reality harder than ever, so very few people dare to deny it today.

Having said that, this obviously does not mean that any price for a derivative is OK. Similarly to any other item we can buy or sell, what we find in the derivatives market is that there is a bracket of prices within which arbitrage cannot be exploited due to the cost of the operational arrangements needed, the liquidity constraints, and the market friction that we would face. Black–Scholes worked more or less well up to 2008 because it was thought by most players that that bracket was very small, and so the ideal Black–Scholes assumptions were seen as quite close to reality. The aftermath of 2008 has demonstrated that that bracket is larger that it appeared to be.

XVA as a new pricing framework: In that context, XVA is a new pricing framework to fix the detachment from reality of the risk-neutral world. Given that that Black–Scholes world has proven to be very good and useful in many ways, XVA can be seen as the adjustment that we need to do to it to account for the reality of everyday trading life.

Further to that, we are going to see that we may start with what seems to be only a new pricing framework, but this then natually evolves into a fundamentally novel way to manage risk: XVA desks.

15.1.1 A history of XVAs

Figure 15.1 illustrates the history of XVA adjustments since the early 2000s.

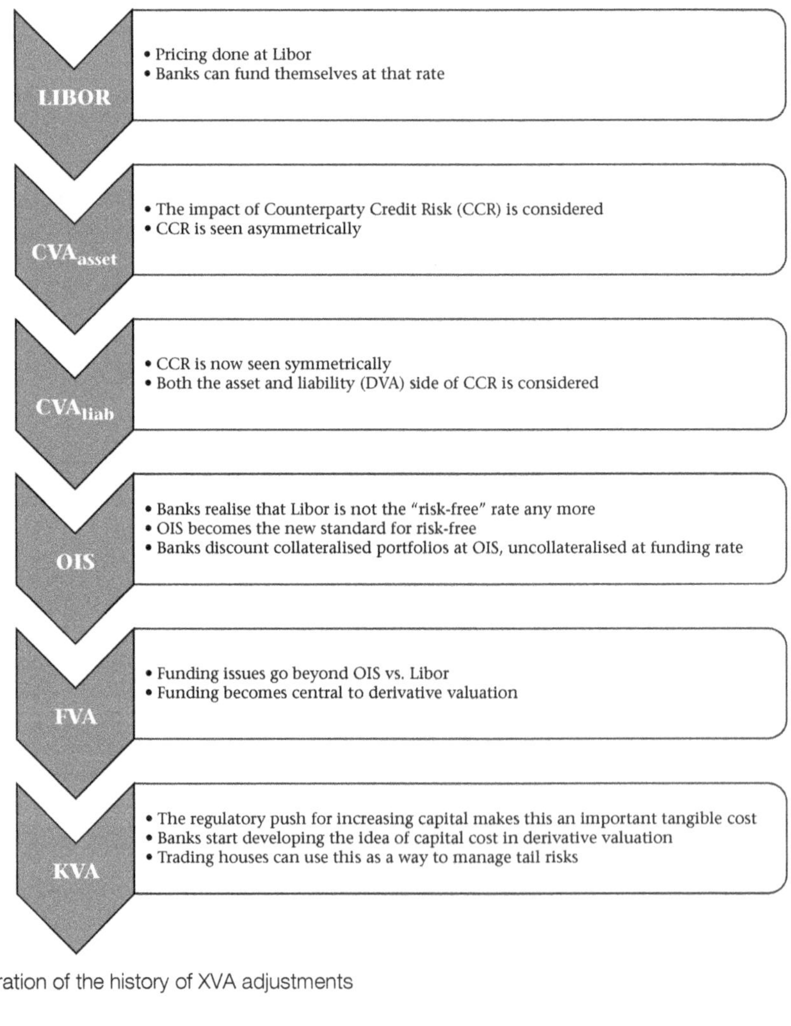

Figure 15.1 Illustration of the history of XVA adjustments

In the late 1990s and early 2000s, derivative pricing was fairly simple. Libor, the average rate at which banks can borrow cash, was considered a risk-free rate, so the discount factors were based on it. This made the pricing of a simple Libor swap quite a trivial task, as the discount rate was the same as the coupon rates.

In the early 2000s, the most sophisticated banks started to realise that OTC derivatives were carrying credit risk, so they started to account for this, but only in an asymmetric way. The only risk that was being considered was the default risk of the counterparties (CVA_{asset}). The Counterparty Credit Risk regulatory charge of Basel II was also asymmetric in that regard.

In around 2006, the new accounting standards (IAS39, FAS157) introduced symmetric CVA (CVA_{asset} and CVA_{liab}). Some banks started to set up specialised CVA desks for this, but which were quite basic in general during the first few years.

One of the effects of the 2008 events was that banks, funding rates went all over the place. Those rates were not seen as the "default-free" rates anymore. The new standard for "risk-free" rate became the Overnight Index Swap (OIS) rate. Banks started to price collateralised trades discounted at OIS, while uncollateralised at their own funding rate. The pricing of simple Libor swaps was not a trivial task anymore, as collateral considerations were important now.

In 2012 banks started to set up specialised funding desks and developed an FVA charge. Funding was not just a basis-risk derivative valuation issue. Rather, it required some extra features and skills that needed to be handled separately.

Further to this, the ever-increasing requirements for regulatory capital made banks realise that this is a true tangible cost that needs to be accounted for when valuing derivatives. The idea of a KVA charge and a KVA desk to manage it starts to emerge.

15.2 Derivative valuation

In Section 12.5.1 we discussed the difference between price and value. It all boils down to the idea that the value that a project has to me is the price for which I can sell it minus its "manufacturing" cost. In that sense, value is very similar to expected profit.

When we manufacture a derivative (or a book of them), we can distinguish two types of cost: the hedging cost of the Black–Scholes trade and the additional costs that are not covered in that framework, XVA. In that sense, the "value to me" is

$$VtM = P_{sale} - P_{BlackScholes} - XVA \tag{15.1}$$

If we set $VtM_{RiskNeutral} = P_{sale} - P_{BlackScholes}$, then

$$VtM = VtM_{RiskNeutral} - XVA \tag{15.2}$$

XVA accounts for the costs that are "hidden" to the Black–Scholes world as a result of its limiting theoretical assumptions.

In this context, if $VtM > 0$, then we should make money in the deal, but if $VtM < 0$ we expect to make a loss in it.

In the Black–Scholes world $XVA = 0$, and given that the markets are ideally "perfect", VtM must be zero as otherwise arbitrage appears. As a result, in that world, $P_{sale} = P_{Black-Scholes}$.

In this book we have seen three sources of XVA, so that

$$XVA = CVA + FVA + KVA \tag{15.3}$$

where

- **CVA:** This adjustment accounts for the counterparty credit risk of the derivative. That is, it assumes that counterparties can default along the way, and using the risk-neutral hedging-replication argument, the price of that risk is calculated as the cost of constructing the credit hedges. This adjustment has two sides: CVA_{asset} (also called only "CVA") accounts for our counterparty risk; and CVA_{liab} (also called "DVA") accounts for the counterparty's counterparty risk from us.

  This works quite nicely, except for three things. Firstly, in practice, only a few of the counterparty's credit risk is hedge-able, as there isn't any Credit Default Swap (CDS) trading depth for the majority of the derivatives users. Furthermore, in the majority of the cases where there is a CDS, there is a strong lack of liquidity that leads to important hedging constraints and trading friction costs. Secondly, the CVA framework assumes that the funding spread at which we can borrow cash is the same as the credit spread at which someone can buy credit insurance against our potential default; this is not true in real markets. Thirdly, we cannot borrow and lend as much as we want, and wherever we place our hedges, of any kind, we are going to be asked for an insurance against our own default that goes beyond CVA; for example, via an Initial Margin.

  The CVA framework does not contemplate any of those market realities. As a result, we need to adjust it if we are to build a sustainable trading business.
- **FVA:** The sources of FVA are three-fold.

  1. **CollVA:** The act of trading and hedging is going to require from us the funding of collateral that we need to post. CollVA is going to account for the funding cost of this collateral.
  2. **HVA:** There could be a mismatch between the cash flows in an OTC derivative and the cash flows in its hedging positions. This isn't contemplated in the Black–Scholes framework. HVA accounts for the funding cost subsequent to this hedging mismatch.
  3. **LVA:** As said, the CVA calculation is based on the ideal assumption that our funding spread is the same as our credit spread, when this is not true. This LVA accounts for the lack of liquidity that the funding market that we see (our bonds market) has in contrast to the credit market (our CDS) that our counterparties see (in which CVA is based).

  To simplify somehow the management of all these VAs, we can coalesce them into one single FVA that accounts for all these funding risk adjustments; the sum of the three of them.

  $$FVA = CollVA + HVA + LVA \tag{15.4}$$

  Importantly, as we saw in Section 12.8, in order to reflect well our actual own-default management, it could be wise to neglect CVA_{liab} and *LVA*. In this way we somehow get rid of what sometimes is seen as funding double-counting.

  Also, sometimes one of those sources of FVA is notably more important than the rest, and hence we can focus our computing efforts on it; often this is the case with *CollVA*. Which of those is most important depends very much on the book of trades and the characteristics of each trading house.
- **KVA:** Further to CVA and FVA, financial institutions need to hold capital to ensure their high credit rating, one of the pillars of the banking business. For this reason an extra cost for a book of trades is the cost of

that capital, which reflects the cost of ensuring ourselves against our own Unexpected Losses. This is KVA. It is important to understand the "value to me" of a book of derivatives, as that value goes beyond its expected (i.e., averaged) cash flows. KVA gives a value to the tail risk we are facing.

It must be noted that KVA does not apply only to banks, but to any trading institution. The trading unit of a corporate may decide to incorporate a KVA in the valuation of their trades to limit the probability of having to go to its company's treasury department crying for extra cash, for example.

XVA and risk-neutral pricing: It is important to note that CVA can still be seen as a risk-neutral pricing adjustment, while FVA and KVA cannot be seen like that.

For the calculation of CVA, on top of the standard Black–Scholes assumptions, we are implicitly assuming that there is an infinity of market depth for credit products (for bonds and CDSs), as well as that the entity selling credit protection cannot default. In that context, CVA still lives within the idealised Black–Scholes risk-neutral framework.

However, in contrast, FVA and KVA are not risk-neutral price metrics, as they are dependent on how each organisation is managed, how trades are hedged, netting effects beyond each counterparty and each netting set, regulatory status, etc. Because of that, two organisations with identical credit spreads and identical portfolios of OTC derivatives may have different FVA and KVA because, for example, they may have different hedging strategies and different regulators.

As a result of this, some people are opposed to FVA and KVA [43, 28], the reason being that they are not risk-neutral pricing metrics and, subsequently, they "lead to arbitrage opportunities", so they say. In other words, FVA and KVA contradict one of the deepest fundamental laws of risk-neutral pricing, that there exists one single price for a derivative, for which some people feel that any pricing framework that contradicts that law is fundamentally wrong.

I do not agree with that because, as extensively explained, the markets show that the risk-neutral assumptions do not hold in the reality of daily trading activities. As a result, the range of FVA and KVA values that market players see create a *bracket of prices* in which arbitrage is not possible, in practice. Similarly to the price of anything in the real economy, the price of financial derivatives is not unique. Market reality creates a range of prices that are sensible, outside of which trading is very difficult and, if done, admittedly, can lead to arbitrage. However, that range of sensible prices is wider that mostly thought for decades, and definitely wider than assumed in the Black–Scholes framework, which is zero.

Furthermore, I believe that if everyone in the market valued all derivatives under the risk-neutral world, blindly, this would create the market dislocations that lead to arbitrage opportunities, as market players will not be accounting properly for the true costs they create with their trading activities. In that sense, it is precisely Black–Scholes risk-neutral pricing that creates arbitrage opportunities. In fact, I believe this happened in 2008.

15.2.1 Relative size of CVA, FVA, and KVA

A natural subsequent question could be: how big are these adjustments, and how relatively important are they?

The actual size of each of them depends very much on lots of factors like netting, hedging strategy, CSA conditions, capital position of the institution, etc. However, to give an indication we can refer to a published piece of analysis that shows relative sizes of CVA, FVA, and KVA for a ten year GBP interest rate swap with semi-annual payment schedules, quite a typical trade, under certain standard conditions [40]. In this case study, the order of magnitude of each XVA component was comparable, ranging from a few basis points to a few tens of basis points.[1]

This highlights how all of them, credit, funding and capital, are important adjustments, and with relatively similar weight. Without them derivative valuation will be misleading.

15.2.2 XVA and price competitiveness

When the concept of XVA charges is first introduced to the departments at the front of the business, typically traders and sales people, there tends to be strong opposition. The following sample conversation, that I have been involved repeatedly, illustrates the issue. A risk manager says to a trader "From now on you are going to be charged by an XVA amount for every trade that you do." To which a trader or salesman replies "If you do that, I am losing competitiveness in pricing compared to my peers, which does not account for XVA, so that is crazy!" Then, the risk manager says "But you need to be charged by that amount, to account for the cost of managing the risk of that trade." To which the trader replies "If you charge me that XVA, I will be making a loss, while I wasn't making that loss before, hence I will not be able to trade." Finally the risk manager says "That is *precisely* my point! You should never enter a trade that is not economical with an XVA adjustment, as you will be thinking that you will make a profit, but you will not."

The first point to understand is that the price at which a derivative is agreed is given by market forces, as opposed to models. In other words, the price of a derivative (and anything you buy and sell in a free economy) is given by the true market forces, cost and benefit, offer and demand, not by someone's opinion (reflected in a model). Basically, a seller is going to charge as much as he or she can and a buyer is going to reduce the price as much as he or she can too. Once the price is "agreed", perceived, or sensed by the market players, then the XVA framework is going to determine the expected profit and loss in the deal.[2]

Consequently, coming back to the sample conversation from above, the problem that it highlighted is that if a financial institution moves from a classic "old school" valuation framework to an advanced one with XVA, budges and incentives need to be also changed accordingly to reflect the new world that sales people and traders see now. This is very important.

Typically, if we are a dealer in the sale side of the derivatives business, $VtM = VtM_{RiskNeutral} - XVA$ is going to determine the *minimum level* at which it is economically sound for us to trade. It could be seen as a way to calculate the margin we expect to make in the deal.

If we are now on the other side of the deal, a corporate client for example, for which $VtM = VtM_{risk-neutral} - XVA$ could easily be a negative number, this VtM is going to determine the cost of hedging the physical risk we are dealing with (e.g., changes in the cost of fuel for an airliner). If we use VtM in our trade valuation we can do a cost–benefit analysis by comparing that VtM number to the benefit that that trade brings to our organisation. Consequently, we can decide on the optimal hedging strategy to be carried out with a complete picture of the situation.

Being competitive: In other words, valuing a trade without an XVA adjustment is, quite simply, lying to ourselves. Those that think they have better pricing because they do not use XVA are only fooling themselves: they will find along the life of the trade that they are not making the money they expected, or are even making losses.

Furthermore, those institutions that value XVA accurately will, indeed, have a competitive advantage in the long run, as derivative valuation will account for *all* real costs, while those valuing without XVA will not.

Second-order effects: It must be noted that, strictly speaking, the XVA hedging positions (e.g., the credit hedges bought against counterparty risk) will themselves move the XVA charge in the organisation. For example, the collateral needed for those hedges, their funding, their capital, etc., will interact with those of the book of trades in the institution. In other words, the total CVA, FVA, and KVA moves with those new XVA hedging positions. This creates an XVA self-feeding loop and, consequently, the incremental XVA charge of a new trade will be influenced as well by the XVA hedges themselves.

Having said that, this value iterative loop is generally going to be a second-order effect, so that it can be neglected in the first calculation. It will appear naturally in subsequent calculations when the XVA hedges have been put in place.

XVA, model risk, and incentives: Chapter 16 is dedicated to model risk, but we should say now that this XVA framework can easily carry a considerable amount of model risk.

For example, in the case of credit risk, if our models to calculate CVA are fundamentally flawed, we may be able to "successfully" appear to hedge CVA volatility in our balance sheet, as it is calculated by those wrong models, but given that our estimated cost of hedging credit risk, or our estimation of future default losses, is wrong, we may find ourselves in difficulties when actual defaults hit. If we underestimated CVA, we will not be able to cover the default losses well. If we overestimated it, we will have unnecessarily constrained our competitiveness in the past.

It must be said that this creates a perverse incentive that has fed bonuses for many years and that has been (rightly) criticised. Given that bonuses have traditionally looked at one-year performance, but XVA risks crystallise many years after trade inception, there is a perverse economic incentive to underestimate XVA.[3]

However, it should be noted that up to 2008, XVA was underestimated to its maximum, as most institutions assumed it to be equal to zero.

15.3 Optimal XVA management

We have seen in each respective chapter that the CVA, FVA, and KVA desks will manage the risks associated with each of those sources of uncertainty. The CVA desk will absorb all credit related P&L, the FVA desk all funding related P&L, and the KVA desk all capital related P&L. However, they all share a number of common features. So, an optimal strategy can be to blend them together.

For example, CVA has a sensitivity to our own credit spread (via CVA_{liab}) that can be put together with the sensitivity to that spread that FVA has, in order to optimise our own credit management and hedging strategy. Also, all CVA, FVA, and KVA have market risk sensitivities (e.g., to interest rates, to FX rates) that could be blended too into one single framework of sensitivities, so they can be optimally managed too.

Furthermore, in principle trading desks may not care too much if a CVA charge is "this" number or a KVA charge is "that" number. What they really care about is the total XVA, the sum of all of them. Also, operationally, it is suboptimal that every dealing desk has to call all individual XVA desks to come up themselves with the total XVA charge.

As a result of all this, it seems that best practice consists in having one single XVA desk that centralises all XVA related internal communication and risk management of all XVA related matters. This is illustrated in Figure 15.2.

In this set-up, when a new trading activity is considered, the dealing desk will ask the XVA desk how much the XVA charge is they are facing, which will be the incremental XVA that the new trading activity brings along. The dealing desks will incorporate this single number into its trade valuation to decide on its execution strategy. Then, if that trading activity is carried out, the XVA desk will manage its risk accordingly,

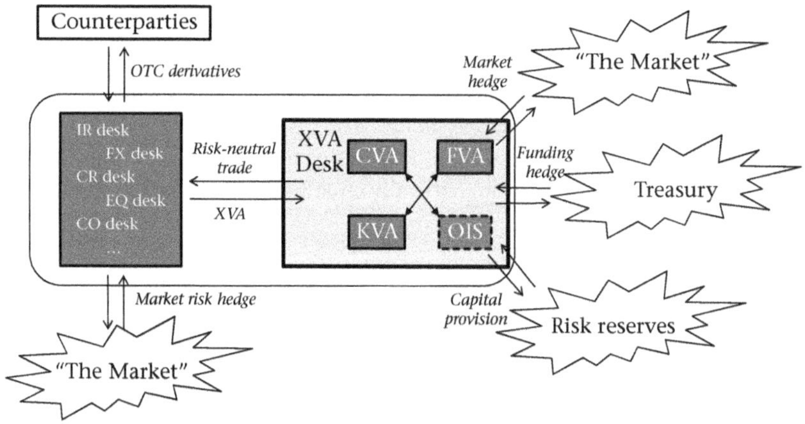

Figure 15.2 Illustration of an XVA desk in a trading organisation

distributing its risk allocation into the credit, funding, and capital sub-desks, and the hedging activities to its market, funding, and capital hedging sub-desks.

15.3.1 Actually, XVA desks generate a risk-neutral trade for the dealing desks

Quite interestingly, by setting up an XVA framework in an organisation, what we achieve is, precisely, the manufacture a risk-neutral Black–Scholes world for the dealing desks.

That is, with the CVA, FVA, and KVA charges, the XVA desk is going to deliver to the dealing desks a credit, funding, and capital insurance via the internal contingent credit, funding, and capital swaps (CCDS, CFS, and CKS). By doing this the dealing desk sees, precisely, that risk-neutral world they like so much: a world that is detached from credit events, funding events, or capital issues.

If a counterparty defaults, the CVA desk takes that hit. If our funding cost increases, the FVA desk takes that loss. If the cost of capital increases, the KVA desk absorbs that impact. Consequently, the dealing desks see that ideal world that the risk-neutral assumptions are based on.

In my experience, it is when the dealing desks understand this that they start liking the idea of an XVA desk; they become happy to pay the XVA charge as they now understand the benefits of it.

With this set-up, an institution creates centres of excellence for each source of risk. The CVA desk is the internal expert in credit, the FVA desk the internal expert in funding, the KVA the internal expert in capital management and, finally, the dealing desks are the experts in selling and hedging risk-neutral trades, which is what they know best how to do. In this way, everyone does what they know best and performance is optimised.

The OIS basis risk caveat: An additional caveat should be made. The new standard for "risk-free" rate is OIS. In the risk-neutral world, everything is based on this risk-free rate, so we need to manage that too. This is what the OIS desk does.

At present, each currency has a plurality of yield curves. Figure 15.3 shows different yield curves for the Euro as of November 2013. Before 2008, those curves were nearly identical, now they are not, especially in times of distressed markets. For example, the spread between the three-month USD Libor and the three-month treasury rate went up to 450 basis points in October 2008.

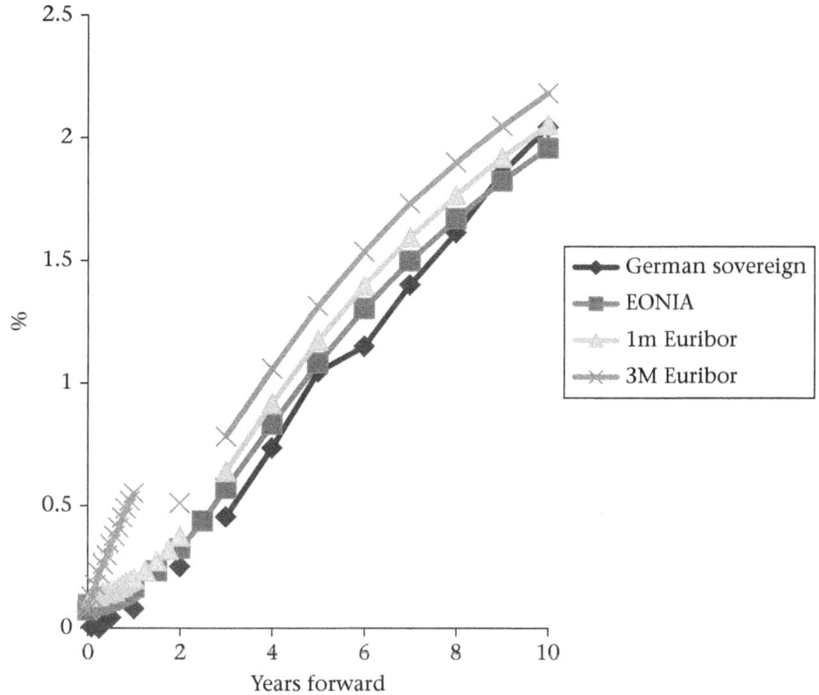

Figure 15.3 Illustration of euro yield curves as of November 2013
Source: Bloomberg.

Also, since 2008 the cross-currency basis risk can be important too. That is, if we price a forward using risk-neutral valuation with both OIS curves in each currency, we do not get the actual forward price traded in the market. So each currency pair has its own basis yield curve to price FX trades correctly.

In addition to all this, when a collateral agreement has FX optionality (e.g., when collateral can be posted in different currencies), then we face the "cheapest-to-deliver" problem. We have to model the currency in which posting collateral will be cheapest.

All this creates the OIS discounting pricing problem, which is highly technical and that has been widely discussed in recent literature. I recommend Kenyon and Stamm [52] for this.

FVA accounts for the change in value of a book of derivatives from the fact that a bank cannot fund itself with the OIS rate. This adjustment is most important for uncollateralised portfolios, as we have seen. In addition to this FVA, we need to manage this multi-curve pricing and collateral optionality issue. An OIS desk typically manages it, separating the direct funding curve problem from the more general market multi-curve one.[4] This can be done in two equivalent ways:

1. All the trading desks mark their positions using the OIS risk-free yield curve. Then, the OIS desk manages the basis and the cheapest-to-deliver risk.
2. All the trading desks mark their positions to Libor (old school style, as they all did historically), and then the OIS desk takes all the Libor to OIS risks and the cheapest-to-deliver risk, and manages it.

In the first of those two set-ups, the dealing desks will clearly see a risk-neutral world.

The OIS desk can typically sit in two places. Some institutions set it up inside the interest rate remit, as it is a very technical rates-related pricing and hedging problem and specialists tend to have an interest rate background. However, some other institutions place it under the XVA umbrella, as it is seen as another overall layer needed for all dealing desks, of any asset class, and also takes care of the cheapest-to-deliver collateral problem, which lies within the XVA mandate without any doubt. In this second way of looking at it, it is equivalent in many ways to the CVA, FVA, and KVA desks.

When done in this fashion, the XVA unit fully manufactures a risk-neutral portfolio for the dealing desks. That is why an OIS box appears in Figure 15.2.

15.3.2 XVA payments

So far we have always assumed that all XVA charges are paid upfront by the dealing desks. However, that does not need to be the case. XVA charges could be paid by the dealing desks as a running coupon.

This could be convenient for a swaps desk. In this way it can match better the XVA payments with the payments received from its clients. This is the case because they are, typically, going to receive income from their clients on a running coupon basis, and so it has a value to them to pay XVA as a running coupon too. However, an options desk may face the opposite situation.

However, this set-up can be somewhat more troublesome for the XVA desk. If paid upfront, the XVA desk will have from the beginning the pot of cash to allocate to the hedging, funding, and capital positions. This has a value to the XVA desk too.

This problem is equivalent to that of buying a car insurance and paying for it upfront or in monthly instalments. Always the insurance premium under an upfront payment is lower than through instalments, as the insurance company is pricing in its extra cost of managing belated payments.[5]

Equivalently, an XVA could potentially offer both possibilities to the dealing desks, with a slightly increased total XVA charge if paid via a running coupon to reflect the extra management and potential funding costs that the XVA desk may incur.

15.3.3 A grid of XVA charges

Each of the sub-XVA charges (CVA, FVA, and KVA) are influenced by many factors, of which two are most important and create some interesting interactions between them: the level of collateral and what we can do with that collateral.

At one pole we can have a fully uncollateralised facility that maximises counterparty credit risk and, hence, CVA and capital.[6] Also, it tends to have relatively high funding requirements as we will need to fund the collateral to be posted for the market-hedges of the trades.

At the other pole we have a centrally cleared facility. In this case CVA and KVA tend to be minimised, but FVA can easily be high because on top of having to fund the collateral of the market hedges, we need to fund the collateral posted to the clearing house.

Then we have a whole range of intermediate points driven by the terms of the collateral CSA agreement with the counterparty. If we take the most fundamental CSA for discussion,[7] then CVA and KVA tend to fall at an intermediate point between the uncollateralised and the cleared case. However, FVA is different. If rehypothication is allowed, funding requirements are minimised as all collateral received can be posted somewhere else as collateral, but if rehypothication is not allowed then, from an FVA standpoint, we are facing the same world as when the trades were unsecured.

All that is qualitatively illustrated in Figure 15.4. It must be noted that this discussion is rather general for illustrative purposes. Actual relative sub-XVA costs can vary very much depending on many factors like

Risk	Charge	Unsecured	Secured, no rehypothication	Secured, with rehypothication	CCP
Credit	CVA	H	M	M	L
Funding	FVA	H	H	L	M
Capital	KVA	H	M	M	L
Total	***XVA***	***⇒ This number dictates new trading incentives***			

H High cost M Medium cost L Low cost

Figure 15.4 Qualitative illustration of the XVA charges, subject to different trading conditions. Either totally unsecured (no collateralisation), secured via collateral agreements in which rehypothication may or may not be allowed, and over-secured via trade novation to a Central Counterparty (CCP)

hedging strategies, netting, funding levels, return on capital, etc., so the reader should not take these broad indications as final "rules". For example, we have assumed that market risk is nicely hedged, which may not be always the case. Typical cases that tend to create intense internal debate are CSA facilities with high thresholds, or with one-way thresholds. The impact on each charge can then be somewhat tricky to analyse as it depends on how close the price of the netting set is to the threshold levels, volatilities, and derivative sensitivities.

The main point to understand is that, in this XVA framework that tries to represent trading reality as close as possible, the value of a book of trades depends on many factors, both external and internal. The Black–Scholes pricing framework looks only at some (idealised) external ones. This novel XVA valuation procedure looks at all, both external and internal, factors.

Reshaping trading behaviour: Consequently to all this, one of the key points of this new XVA world is that it changes fundamentally trading patterns. In this environment, a dealing desk will look at a table like that illustrated in Figure 15.4 to design an optimal trading, hedging, collateral management, and counterparty relationship management strategy. Depending on the XVA charges of each option, combined with the counterparty's needs and demands, a dealing desk now has the visibility to decide what is the strategy that delivers the optimum value.

Also, it can perceive the marginal costs that its trading activities bring to the organisation, and consequently it can discuss optimal risk management strategies to maximise value. For example, if one book of trades has a high KVA charge, it can sit down with the XVA desk and study ways to minimise that charge with a limited impact on all other charges. This can include trade restructuring, new trade creation, trade unwinding, changing CSA agreements, etc. The XVA desk is the internal expert in credit, funding, and capital risk, and their interactions, so they are the ones that can provide the needed in-depth analysis to minimise the XVA charge; i.e., the trading associated costs.

It is very important to understand too that this XVA framework *must* also provide the incentives to reduce future costs in the organisation. This can be achieved by the XVA transferring cost benefits to the dealing desks when they manage to decrease XVA. If the trading operations are set up like this, traders will naturally find ways to minimise XVA as, in this way, they will book a profit.

As the reader can see now, this new world of XVA has the potential of changing profoundly trading behaviour. And as a matter of fact, this is precisely what we have been seeing in the market since 2008.

15.3.4 XVA desk mandate

Typically, an XVA desk can function under one of these mandates.

- **Insurance Model:** In this set-up, the XVA desk collects the XVA charge and puts it "aside" as a risk reserve, to cover future losses. Here, risks are not hedged as such, and the balance sheet has the full XVA P&L volatility.
- **Full Hedger:** In this set-up, the XVA desk is seen as a cost and volatility reduction desk. Here, an XVA desk aims to have a perfectly flat zero P&L every quarter.

  Given that that flat P&L may be impossible to achieve due to market hedging limitations, an XVA desk is going to have P&L swings. A good desk should then understand and control well that P&L volatility; a bad one is only going to see the hit after it has happened.

  As a result, senior management must always interpret correctly any large P&L fluctuation, and should not be fooled by a large profit in one quarter: it may be the product of luck, and not out of good XVA management.
- **Profit Center:** Here, the XVA desk, or some of its sub-desks, decide to run the credit and funding risks they carry,[8] and make money out of it. In that sense, they are a dealing desk like any other typical rates or FX desk, for example, with the only difference that their clients are only internal to the organisation.

  Perhaps in the future, if one day the XVA market is mature enough, these desks could offer their services externally to smaller institutions by selling contingent credit, funding, or even capital management swaps. There have been a few attempts, but at the time of this book going to press, we seem to be quite far away from that possibility.

  Going back to today's reality, one of the dangers of this set-up is that given that XVA can only be "marked-to-model", as there isn't any liquid market to mark it to, the XVA desk may have an incentive to over-price it, so that they can take away some margin from the dealing desks. Given the high model risk XVA models have, it is important to manage that risk correctly. I dedicate Chapter 16 to this topic.

All OTC derivative deals that an organisation has must go through the XVA desk. This gives the XVA function a massive responsibility, and a very special and integral view of the organisation; it is the centre point of all deals. Hence, in parallel to each of these models, the XVA desk is in a perfect position to carry out a number of central functions.

1. It is a natural place to manage the CSA collateral agreements. It is in a perfect place to evaluate the impact of different CSA arrangements to the different business units, negotiate CSA terms, etc.
2. The XVA desk sees all risks, so it can be the natural place where a firm can shape the overall position (e.g., short/long interest rates, FX rates, volatility, etc.) if needed.
3. It is also in a good position to minimise economic or regulatory capital needs, as it is facing both the capital calculation and the front end of the business.

15.4 A new era for risk management

Before the existence of this XVA framework, derivative dealing was done somewhat in the dark. It was carried out under the assumption that all risks were hedge-able, so trading institutions developed a very limited view of long-term risks. This is highlighted by the fact that, until very recently, when most professional spoke about "risk management", it was mostly referring to VaR, which has only a few days time horizon.

To complement and feed that idea, the risk management departments would manage risks by mostly putting *limits* to the front office trading activities: a VaR limit, an exposure limit, etc. This would create a very unhealthy relationship, as front office would perceive risk managers as some kind of policemen, only trying to inhibit business development. Understandably, this created a historically difficult relationship between those two units. I have worked with a number of institutions, both as a permanent employee and as a consultant, and have seen this pattern in every institution I have been to. Also, I have observed that, historically, the front office has tended to have the upper hand in this difficult relationship, as they have a history of creating very high profits that, really, hardly anyone would dare to challenge.

However, things changed profoundly as an effect of the 2008 banking critical point. In the 2007–9 period, banks lost an outstanding amount of the value that seemed to have been created over many years. Why? Because long-term risks had not been managed correctly.

Risk management had been mostly functioning via limit-setting techniques, but the cost of the risks that the trading activities were bringing on were not accounted for in the valuation of trades. This created an environment in which valuation was focused on the revenue coming from OTC derivatives and their market hedges, but not on the marginal costs that trading activity created, like credit, funding, and capital costs. This arguably created a pyramid scheme in which new deals were needed every year to earn revenue to cover costs from deals done in the previous years. This pyramid became obvious in 2008; we could even say that it exploded in 2008.

An XVA desk is punching at the core of all that. With this new XVA framework, risk management is not any more about setting up limits for trading; rather, it is about setting up a *cost to the risk* taken and leaving those that are experts in market behaviour, the trading and sales people, to decide what and how to trade. This new way of looking at risk management has opened a new era for it.

In this framework, the core of risk management circles around *putting a price to the risk* that trading activities generate. The more accurate that pricing is, the more competitive a trading house becomes. If it is priced too cheaply, it will run into trouble in the future; if priced too expensively, it will inhibit business development unnecessarily.

This is in contrast to the naive idea that the lower the XVA calculation is, the more competitive an institution is. The worst case scenario is that XVA doesn't reflect the true risks an organisation is facing in either direction. Then, obviously, within the accuracy constraints, the lower the costs (i.e., the lower XVA), the better for the institution.

However, this does not mean that limits can be completely forgotten, as it doesn't make sense that, for example, all credit risk is concentrated in only a few counterparties. However, a way to manage those limits could be, for example, by increasing the cost of XVA subject to how close or even how far out the risk is from the limit, as opposed to a blunt "yes" or "no" permit by risk management.

In other words, in the same way as this new XVA framework has changed trading behaviour, so also it changes very profoundly risk management. In this new world, risk management is not about policing around; rather it is about pricing risk and letting the business developers at the front line of the business, the "front office", who are the experts in market behaviour, decide on whether it is worthwhile going into a deal or not.

15.4.1 The difference between hedging and not hedging risk

As seen, an XVA desk has three fundamental ways to operate that are determined by the external environment it operates under.

In an insurance model, it doesn't hedge any risk. In a Full Hedger model, it aims at fully hedging all risks. Finally, in a Profit Center model, the organisation decides to run the XVA risks and try to make money out of them.

In the case of a hedging model, in either of the two versions, one of the main problems the XVA desk is facing is the market capacity to offer hedging instruments. For example, it is very common to not have any CDS depth whatsoever to multiple counterparties, so default events may not be hedge-able in those cases.

Which of those worlds we live in has strong implications for XVA measurement and XVA management strategy. For example, if we are facing a default risk hedge-able portfolio of trades with a counterparty, the Unexpected Losses coming from defaults will be small, and so KVA should be small. However, if we cannot hedge default events at all, we are not only exposed to average default scenarios, but also to severe ones, hence KVA will be relatively high.

Also, the models for each XVA version are going to be somewhat different. Under hedge-able conditions, we do not care about the expected cost of the risks we are taking, but only about the market price of hedging those risks. However, if we cannot hedge the risk, we still care, indeed, about the actual expected and unexpected losses coming from those risks.

In reality, most XVA desks are going to be somewhere in the middle of those two extreme hedging availability points.

Interestingly, I have seen through my consulting activities that those institutions that face an XVA world that is fairly hedge-able tend to see the XVA desk as a front office function, while those that can hardly hedge anything tend to set up that desk in the risk departments.

In any case, the role of the XVA managers, wherever they sit, is to find the right approach that delivers the optimum value for the institution, and subsequently for the institution's equity holders and creditors. This can be achieved by finding the best balance between the liquidity of hedging conditions, the cost of hedging, the cost of risk-reserving, the impact on the business, and the impact on risk levels.

And this is the difficulty and challenges that XVA desks face. In my opinion, it is one of the biggest challenges financial institutions have ever faced, from all fronts: business development, risk management, internal process optimisation, modelling methodologies, and systems development. Those houses that manage to do this best will have a clear competitive advantage going forward, and will deliver good stable financial institutions for the overall economy.

15.4.2 The path towards the optimal XVA set-up

An XVA desk with a full hedging and profit making functionality is, arguably, the most mature form of the XVA function. However, the optimal XVA set-up for a given organisation may not be the most developed one. That will depend on the size and needs of the institution, and on the market environment it faces. The different approaches to it can be seen in Figure 15.5.

1. In the most basic approach nothing is done regarding XVA. This is obviously suboptimal since the trading operation contains only a few trades.

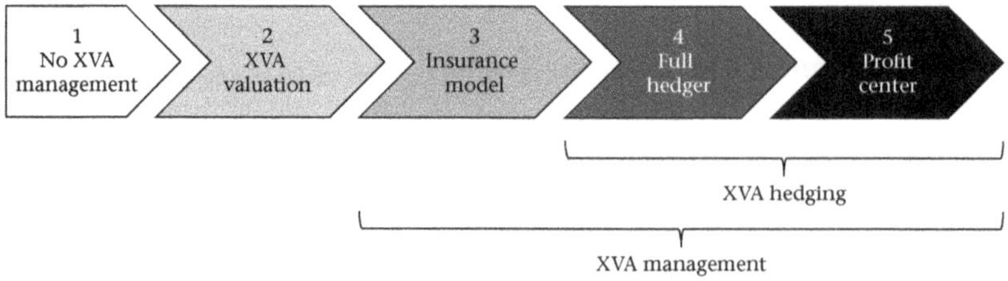

Figure 15.5 Qualitative illustration of the different stages of development in an XVA function

2. The next step forward is to build a system to measure XVA, so that trades can be valued correctly. In this way trading activities will reflect the future costs of trading, hence trading activity will be a close reflection of the true value that that activity brings to the organisation.
3. Further to this, an institution can collect the XVA charges in a risk reserve pot that will act as an *insurance* against future losses related to credit, funding, capital, etc.
4. A more developed XVA function will have an XVA hedging operation that will try to control as much as possible the P&L impact of those credit, funding, and capital related risks. In this set-up the organisation aims at making profits out of classical Black–Scholes risk-neutral derivative dealing, and so the XVA mandate is to hedge out all non-risk-neutral risks and have a zero flat P&L.
5. In the, arguably, most advanced approach, the organisation decides to run the non-risk-neutral risk in derivatives, and tries to make a profit out of them, as if the contingent credit, funding, capital, and (potentially) OIS swaps that the XVA desk sells internally were just another derivative from which to create value.

Which is the optimal point for an individual institution will depend on the purpose, environment, and size of it. For example, in the case of a tier-one investment bank, a hedging XVA function is needed; some banks have a Full Hedger model, some a Profit Center one. However, a fairly small hedge fund may decide to stop in an XVA valuation framework, being happy with being able to value the trades correctly. A large corporate with a medium sized trading operation, or a not-so-big financial institution, may find optimum value in an insurance model, where it can measure and accrue a reserve fund, so the trading operations do not cause any major hits in the mother company.

15.4.3 A massive technology challenge

We have seen that accurate XVA calculation is crucial to optimise the competitive advantage that a trading house can offer. Unfortunately, this is not enough; calculation *speed* is crucial too.

Those institutions that manage to develop an XVA technology platform that enables, ideally, quasi-instantaneous XVA valuations to sales people and traders, available on their screens, will be the winners in the space of the OTC derivative business. They will be the ones winning the deals and, most crucially, managing their risks efficiently.

We have seen in this book in great detail how complex these calculations can be. As a result, XVA desks can easily be the biggest technology challenge that financial institutions have ever seen. Intelligent investment in clever methodology and systems is one of the most important key success factors in this space, perhaps *the* most.

Also, given the complexities and all the interconnections this desk has with the whole organisation, senior leaders should not underestimate the important challenge that an XVA brings from a management point of view. Best practices are most important in this area too.

15.5 Conclusions

We have seen that XVA desks can offer an optimal set-up for trade valuation and risk management. XVA charges, which can be originally seen as price adjustments, should be seen in a mature trading operation as value generation instruments. In this set-up, XVA desks become central to trading activity and risk management.

Now, risk management is no longer about setting up limits or about allowing or forbidding trades, but instead about pricing future costs and risks correctly, and subsequently letting the front-office market experts decide on trading activities.

This creates a new world for traders and risk managers. Basically, XVA risk managers now create a bridge between an institution's equity holders and creditors and the front of the business. This is achieved by incorporating non-Black–Scholes risk-neutral costs to the trade valuation process, by facilitating the incorporation of trading marginal costs to the trading decision-making process and by managing the non-"risk-neutral" sources of uncertainty: credit, funding, and capital.

In this way, a trading house has the potential to maximise value. At least, in any case, to get closer to its maximum value generation capability than living in the naivity of the risk-neutral world.

Part IV | Further to XVA

16 Model Risk Management

In 2011, the Federal Reserve issued a letter on the topic of *Supervisory Guidance on Model Risk Management* [64] that established a new setting stone in the field. Up to the financial turmoil, model risk was all about checking the accuracy of a model, the so-called "model validation"; however, several model failures during the turbulent years highlighted the need for a broader approach to the problem: "model risk" is now seen as a source of risk that deserves complete focused attention.

Indeed, the activity of model management has evolved from understanding and checking the validity of a model, to understanding the impact that errors in models can have on an organisation, to managing that risk and, ultimately, to treating it as a source of economic capital like any other risk.

16.1 From model validation to model risk management

The Federal Reserve defined "model" quite nicely for us: "it is a quantitative method, system or approach that applies statistical, economic, financial or mathematical theories, techniques and assumptions to process input data into quantitative estimates". A less formal but handy definition could be "it is any process or numerical calculation that takes some inputs and delivers some numerical outputs, from which decisions are made".

When we are facing a model (or a set of models) in an organisation, there are three questions we need to tackle: (i) Is this model good? (ii) If this model goes wrong, what impact could it have on the organisation? (iii) How can we manage that risk?

- **Is this Model Good? Model Validation:** The first we need to realise is that all models have limitations, as they are by construction a simplified version of reality. Not only that, going beyond the surface of the question, what they really are is *a simplified mathematical interpretation of someone's view of reality.* We often find that what is important in a model for someone, isn't for someone else.

  A central question that we need to ask when we validate a model is: what are the limitations of the model? What can go wrong?

  Indeed, a model cannot be perfect, it cannot describe with total accuracy every feature that has happened and will happen in the future. In reality, the best we can hope for is that a model is *sound for purpose.* A model is not only a set of equations, it also contains a purpose, a scope in which it is intended to be applied. Then, a model is good for that purpose when any lack of accuracy delivered by the model is irrelevant for its purpose. This can easily be forgotten; we can easily be tempted to focus on minuscule details that can end up being irrelevant for the actual purpose of the model.

For example, a given model can be very good for pricing, because in pricing we care about expected (average) values and short-term moves that can be delta-hedged, but in risk management we care about the tails of the distribution of potential events, and so if a good pricing model does not mimic well the tails, it will not be good for risk management.

- **Model Impact:** If we try to narrow down this problem, very soon we need to understand the materiality and impact of the model. Models can have an impact on profit & loss calculations, risk management, economic capital, regulatory capital, research, stress and scenario testing, derivative pricing at inception, derivative pricing at balance sheet calculation, algorithmic trading, treasury, liquidity management, funding management, human resources, reputational risk, etc. The list is endless. A central question here is: what happens if something goes wrong?

  If we want to go beyond classical model validation into proper model risk management, we need (i) to create a map of all models in the organisation, (ii) to ascertain which departments or business functions use each of them, and how critical each model is for each of them and for the overall organisation, and (iii) to ascertain the impact on the organisation of that model failing.
- **Model Risk Management:** Once we have an understanding of the impact that a model failure could have, we need to manage that risk. This area must start with the correct governance, policies, and controls. A central question here is: does the organisation have the right framework to limit losses from model failures? It must be noted that the *correct* depth of these tasks and processes depends on the sophistication and size of the organisation, but it should always exist to some degree.

  Also, risk management and economic capital calculation should consider model risk. This can be quite a difficult task, as putting a monetary value to mistakes in models is far from trivial, but this does not mean that it should be left aside and forgotten. For example, we could study the probability that the assumptions of a model are broken (e.g., the probability that the FTSE 100 has a daily drop of more than 10%, if that makes the model break); or we could assess the economic impact on the organisation and, subsequently, impose an internal capital charge, within the KVA framework described in Chapter 14 for example, to those using that model to account for that risk.

As the reader may be able to see now, model risk is anything but trivial. We could write a whole book on the subject. However, to keep the size of this text under control, in this chapter we are only giving a general idea of the whole problem, to then focus on the first of the three questions, model validation, with a special focus on counterparty credit risk.

16.2 The fundamentals of model validation

Validating a model should be based on the following three golden pillars:

1. **Appropriateness:** Is the model appropriate for the job it is meant to do? For example, if it prices, does it price well? If it measures 99% VaR, does it measure it well?

   Importantly, there is a time component to this pillar that needs to be monitored. This comes typically from the fact that every model is going to be based on some assumptions that could become detached from reality as time progresses. For example, we could have an option pricing model that only works well for implied volatilities below a certain threshold, and so this model could break up in periods of market turbulence.

2. **Use:** Is the model used the way it is supposed to? This is key, as quite often a model is developed for one purpose, approved for it, but then it slowly drifts away in its use to areas for which it wasn't originally designed.
3. **Implementation:** Finally, does the actual implementation, typically in a piece of software or a spreadsheet, reflect accurately the original theoretical design? This is key too, as if a model implementation is not correct, the quality of the model output can be strongly compromised.

A proper model validation framework within a good model risk management function should consider these three pillars, and monitor them with sufficient frequency.

It is important to realise that a model is not only a set of equations. It is a set of equations, a calibration algorithm with its calibration frequency, and a set of data. We can have the same set of equations but calibrated in different ways, hence having in reality different models. Or calibrated to a set of data that contains lots of errors. A good model validation exercise should check both for the set of equations, how they are calibrated, and the quality of the data used for the calibration, in an integrated manner.

From a quantitative standpoint, the three areas that tend to be most affected by model validation in financial institutions are pricing, risk management, and capital calculations. Up to 2008, most emphasis was made on pricing, but a lot of effort is now put into the other two.

Pricing models are central in financial institutions, as many other functions rely on them in the organisation, ranging from derivative pricing at trade inception, profit & loss calculations, risk metric calculations,[1] stress testing, capital calculations, etc.

Regarding risk management and capital, the models used by both areas are often the same, as they share the same "philosophy" of trying to estimate potential future losses. Within those models, the ones that attract more quantitative focus are market risk, credit risk models, and operational risk models.

This book is centred around counterparty credit risk. However, in order to understand well the context and practicalities of assessing its model risk, we are also going to overview model risk for pricing and market risk management.

16.3 Checking pricing models

Lots of model risk groups started as pricing model validation teams. In the context of an investment bank, their role was (and still is, when checking pricing models) to check that the models used to price OTC derivatives are good enough.

When we validate a pricing model we need to look at two things. Firstly, we need to check that the price is correct and, secondly, that the "Greeks"[2] are also correct and complete.

16.3.1 Validating prices

Checking for the validity of a pricer for a liquid instrument is easiest, as what we have to do is compare the result of the pricer to the price given by the market. If that price is the same, the pricer is OK; otherwise, it needs to be revised. For this reason, getting a "vanilla" pricer right is not too difficult in general, as all we usually have to do is calibrate the pricer so that we get the correct answer out of it. In contrast, when the instrument is illiquid, things are not that simple because we do not have a reference market to look at. In these cases, the first thing we need to do is to make sure that the price does not allow for any arbitrage opportunities.

Secondly, institutions collaborate in consensus services (e.g., Totem) giving to each other risk-neutral prices of the same derivative, so they can assess if their pricing might contain errors.

Another good check for pricing is benchmark testing. In these tests, we are going to study the price and sensitivity differences that we get from alternative models; in other words, we should study the model choice impact. Any differences in results should be explained from the fundamental strengths and weakness of each model so that a decision regarding the optimality of the model under test can be made.

Having said that, building a pricer that gives the correct result has its difficulties, but what is more difficult is to build a pricer that is stable. By this we mean a pricer that is good under changing market conditions. This is a key feature that defines a "good" model.

This can be checked by stress-testing the pricing function. In this type of check, we stress the market factors to see at what stage the pricer starts to fail. For example, an interest rate pricer developed well in the past could easily fail to price well under the ultra-low interest rates that followed the 2008 market events. Every model is going to have a "breaking" point, beyond which the pricer is not good any more. Indeed, that breaking point is going to be different for an HJM than for a Libor model, for instance. Once the critical breaking points are detected, the model risk team should make sure that the pricer is never used beyond it, or if used because of short-term pressure, it should ensure that that risk is properly managed.

16.3.2 Validating sensitivities

Another check that needs to be done is sensitivity-testing. Typically, a pricing model is going to deliver both a price and sensitivities to the main market factors, so the OTC derivative can be hedged. If those sensitivities are not correct, the hedging positions are going to be subsequently incorrect, and the overall position (the OTC derivative plus its hedges) is going to "leak" P&L. This can be tested with hedging simulations in three ways.

1. **Hedging Simulations:** In these simulations, we are going to generate several random market scenario paths, price the derivative each day, for example, simulate the hedging positions a trader would put in place, and calculate the overall position P&L every day.

   We should observe two friction costs here. On the one hand, the bid/offer spread of the hedging positions is going to create an ongoing cost. On the other hand, the hedging strategy is going to be rebalanced periodically, in a non-perfect way, and this is going to deliver a P&L volatility. We should remove the first effect from the test, as that is not a model issue.[3] However, the second effect could be related to having the wrong price and sensitivities from the model under test. When this is the case, we are going to observe in the simulations two effects: a P&L "leak" and a P&L volatility.

   Regarding the leak, this could happen when the Greeks given by the model are not correct. If so, we are going to have a tendency to over or under-hedge and, as a result, the hedged position is not going to be completely hedged and will deliver a slow but continuous leakage of profits or losses.

   Regarding the volatility, even when the sensitivities are correct, we are going to have a P&L noise that comes from imperfections in the hedging strategy. These imperfections can arise from the fact that the derivative's price is sensitive to risk factors that are not being considered by the model. In theory, this noise should tend to average out to zero in the long run, but we should have a noise toleration policy; noise above the given threshold should be seen as too risky. These two model features are depicted in Figure 16.1.

   For example, let's say that we have an instrument very sensitive to rotations in a relevant forward curve (e.g., interest rates, commodites), but we price it and calculate sensitivities with a one-factor model that only shifts up and down the curve. Our hedging simulation may show no leak, but the P&L volatility is

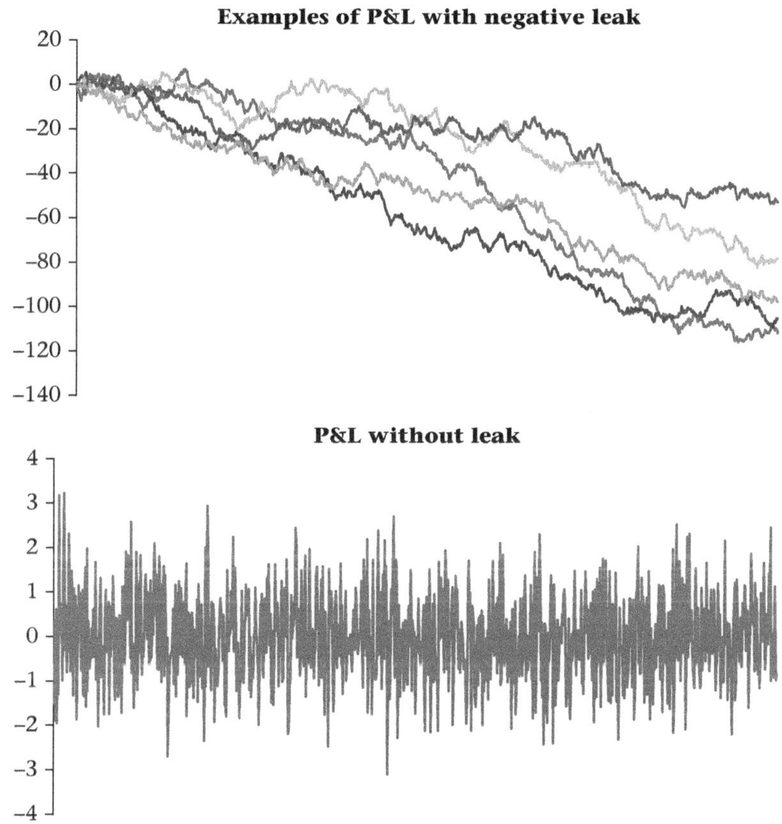

Figure 16.1 Illustration of hedging simulations with and without P&L leak

going to be higher than if we used a two-factor model because there is a risk factor that is not being hedged. In general, the more relevant market risk factors that a model is missing out, the higher the P&L volatility will be.

P&L volatility thresholds are quite subjective but, arguably, a good model should not deliver volatilities greater than 1–2 basis points of notional for vanilla instruments, or 20–30 basis points for exotic ones. Further to this, a model risk economic capital should be somehow positively related to this volatility, so that risk is managed and an incentive to design better models is created in the organisation.[4]

It must be noted that the scenarios used in this stochastic test do not need to be normally distributed. In fact, arguably, they should *not* be so, because they are intended to reproduce actual market variable behaviour, which does not follow normal distributions.

2. **Historical Backtesting:** It is a healthy important sanity check to study what would have been the behaviour in the past of the model under testing, with a particular focus on crisis periods. This can be done quite easily with the same framework designed for the hedging simulations, but imposing the realised path of the past as the scenario of market factors.

   Having said that, nice as it is to see that a model behaves well under the most relevant past market stress periods, good behaviour in this test does not imply that the model is good, as "the future will always be somehow different to the past". Other tests must be done too.

3. **Stress Model Testing:** Finally, it is also healthy to check under what conditions the hedging strategy breaks down and delivers either a P&L volatility beyond the acceptable parameters or a P&L leak. These tests should stress at least the most relevant market variables, market conditions, and model assumptions in the hedging simulations. Examples are implied volatilities for option pricers and simulated periods of high default rates for credit-related pricers.

16.3.3 CVA pricing model validation

The task of validating a pricing model is more difficult the more complex the OTC derivative is. The source of the problem does not only come from the general fact that the more complex something is, the more complicated it is to test it, but from the fact that complex derivatives tend to be also highly illiquid. If the derivative is super-exotic, the model validation team does not have a reference price to relate to and, so we then have to ask: what number can we validate it against?

This is the case with CVA, as it is the price of a super-exotic instrument: the Contingent Credit Default Swap (CCDS) we have discussed in Chapters 8 and 11. In fact, this instrument that is traded internally within banks is the most complex derivative ever created.[5] We are going to centre our discussion in this section on CVA as that is the focus of this book, but nearly everything said can be extrapolated to any exotic derivative.

The fundamental problem of CVA price model validation is that CVA cannot be marked-to-market; rather, it can only be marked-to-model.[6] As a consequence, we have the following situation, depicted in Figure 16.2: with the CVA pricing model we calculate the CVA price and the CVA sensitivities. Then, we are going to put in place CVA hedges using vanilla market instruments. When we calculate the P&L of the position some time later, we are going to calculate the CVA price with the model, and we are going to get the value of the hedging positions from the market. The difference between the P&L of those two sets of positions (the CVA and the hedges) is going to be the net P&L.

If the CVA model is utterly wrong, but *consistently* wrong with the sensitivities, the P&L from the CVA hedges are going to mimic well the changes in CVA price, and so we are going to see no P&L leak and very little P&L volatility. If so, the naive natural conclusion could be that the model is good.

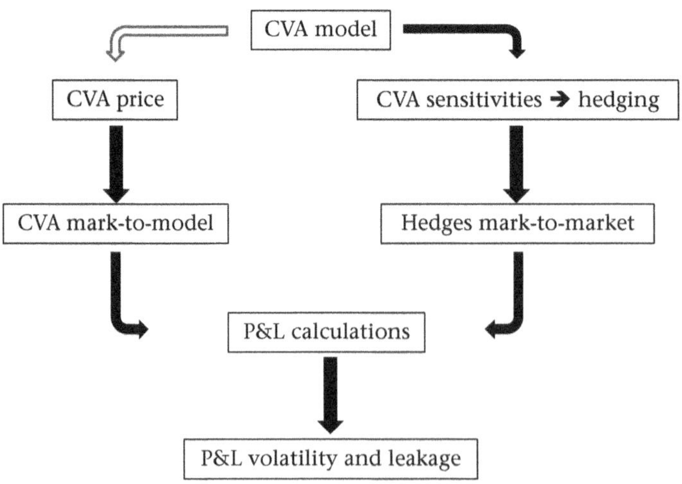

Figure 16.2 Illustration of the CVA model validation process

This problem can be clearly shown with an extreme illustrative example. Let's say that our (silly) CVA model delivers a price that is \$1m every Monday, \$2m every Tuesday, \$3m every Wednesday, etc. If we manage to build a hedge that mimics that, we are going to have no P&L leak and no P&L volatility whatsoever. Does this mean that our CVA model is good? Obviously not.

If we are a derivative dealer, when a derivative is nicely liquid and hedge-able, we are, really and only, in the business of hedging it, and so we do not really care where the market goes, or whether the market got this or that price correctly or not, because we can always buy and sell the instruments easily,[7] and so we only care about hedging. However, when we deal with illiquid securities, we do hold the underlying risk and, as such, if our pricing and hedging does not reflect the underlying *real* risks, we will see a divergence between the paper P&L and the *real* cash-flows we get from the derivative.

16.4 Checking risk models

The difference between pricing and risk model validation is often not 100% clear. Arguably, if a pricing model validation was done with full completeness, "perfectly", we may not need to validate risk models, as we could use pricing models for risk too. However, pricing models do not tend to model well the tails of the probability distributions, and because of that the models that financial institutions use to price and measure risk tend to be different.

The big difference between pricing and risk models is that the former tends to focus on the expectation, the average, of the distribution of future events; however, risk models focus on the *tails* of those distributions. This can make risk model development and validation a more difficult task than pricing, fundamentally because, arguably, trying to understand what could happen in the future "on average" seems easier than trying to understand what could be the 99th worst case scenario.

A key area of distinction is precision vs. conservatism. The goal of pricing models is to be as precise as possible; however, risk models need to be conservative by definition. For example, if we say that the price of something is going to be between 1 and 2, we could take the average 1.5 as our best estimate of the expected value. However, the point of risk is to know that, if we are measuring risk at the 90% confidence level, in only 1 out of 10 events are we going to be outside that risk metric. As a result, if we estimate that a given risk metric is between 10 and 12, then the risk metric we should take is 12, as it is the only way we can make sure that we are not going to be outside the risk metric more frequently than the definition of the risk metric indicates.

This simple distinction creates a major difference between the general philosophy of the way we develop and validate pricing vs risk models: pricing models must be precise on average, risk models must be conservative.

Further to this, I have been involved in a number of arguments around this distinction, some quants arguing that, using the example just explained, the best estimate for the risk metric is 11, its average, while other quants arguing that it should be 12. This mostly comes down to opinion, but at the end of the day it is not worth spending much time on these discussions, because in reality regulators demand financial institutions to be conservative in their risk models. As a result, 12 must be used in that example, regardless of our opinion.

Market and counterparty risk: Regarding OTC derivatives, there are two sets of risk models that get most of the attention these days: market risk and counterparty credit risk models. They are very different in nature, but sometimes confused, especially when CVA, which is the price of counterparty credit risk, comes onto the scene.

Our market risk managers try to manage the risk of losses that we may have if the markets move against us. For example, if we are long on an equity stock, market risk deals with the potential losses we could have on the value of our portfolio if that equity price drops. However, counterparty credit risk tries to manage the risk of losses coming from (i) a given counterparty defaulting and (ii) the book of trades with that counterparty being worth a positive number in our favour. As a result, following the same example, if we have all the exposure to that equity with one single counterparty, from counterparty risk we will be looking at scenarios in which the price of the stock is increasing.

As a result, from the exposure (e.g., the price of our book of derivatives) standpoint, market and counterparty risk look at the opposite sides of the distribution of values. Market risk looks at the negative side of it, while counterparty risk at the positive one, as shown in Figure 16.3. From a market risk point of view, the wider the tail of the distribution is on the left, the more risky the portfolio is, but from the counterparty risk standpoint, the wider it is on the right, the more risky the portfolio is.

Another difference is that market risk metrics typically measure potential losses at a high confidence level and short time scale. The most widely used metric is the 99% ten-day VaR.[8] The reason for using such a short time horizon is that, in the world of OTC derivatives, the market hedging strategies can be implemented within a few days, and so we are interested in short-term potential losses. Also, focus tends to be on the 99% confidence level because this level tends to be perceived as a "reasonable worst case".[9]

In contrast to this, counterparty risk tends to focus on much larger time horizons and lower confidence levels, the reason being that if we have a 20-year portfolio with a counterparty, this counterparty could default tomorrow, next year, or in ten years, and so we need to cover all those cases. Then, given these long time horizons, it does not make much sense to focus on the far end of the tails, as the more far out we are in time the higher the statistical uncertainty (e.g., the error) we have in those metrics. It is difficult to think that any model will be able to accurately measure the 99th percentile of the value of a portfolio in 20 years time. I have seen financial institutions using 90%, 95%, 97.5%, and, in some special cases, 99% for exposure management of counterparty risk.

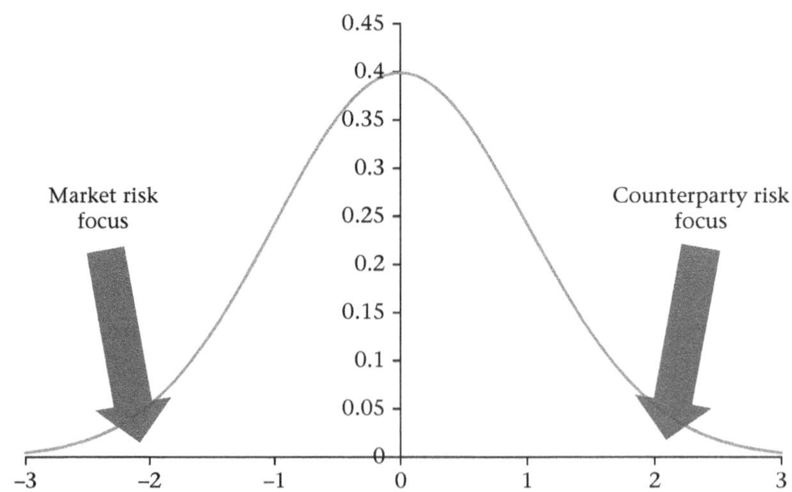

Figure 16.3 Illustration of the focus of both market and counterparty risk analytics in the future distribution of values for a given instrument or portfolio

The scope of risk models: From the model validation point of view, it is important to note that, in general, standard risk models are not expected to work in dislocated market conditions. In fact, arguably, standard risk models *should not* work in those markets. Those situations are expected to be covered by stress and scenario risk management, or by liquidity risk management. In fact, these risk functions could also be named "extreme market risk management".

This is especially the case for counterparty risk. In general, we should expect that market risk models are quite reactive to changing market conditions given the short-term nature of this risk type, typically ten days, but we should not expect counterparty risk models for exposure, that look at potential exposure years in the future, to account for a market crisis years before it happens.

Tests: There are two key tests that need to be used to validate risk models

1. **Historical Backtesting:** Nobody can see the future and, hence, there is no way we can know with certainty if, say, a 99% exposure risk metric will cover 99% of all future events. But what we can know is whether that metric has covered 99% of all events in the past. For that reason, this is one of *the* key model validation tests.

   Using VaR models as an illustrative example, the idea is that if we apply our 99% VaR model to the past, if the model is good we should only get around 1 in 100 days where the market loss is beyond the one-day VaR predicted the day before. If this is not the case, there is a chance that there is a problem with the model.

   However, we must note that the reverse argument is not true. The fact that a VaR model behaves well historically does not mean that the model is good for the future. Apparently, none of the risk models at Lehman Brother's before its default had any backtesting problem.
2. **Scenario and Stress Testing:** Similarly to pricing model validation, when we validate a risk model it is very important to understand what can make it break down.

   Every risk model is going to be based on a number of assumptions that could break at some point, under certain circumstances. What we are trying to understand with these scenario tests is what the level of stress is that can make the model's assumption break.

   This can be done via stress historical backtesting. In this test, we create artificially stressed historical data (e.g., increasing the volatility) and see at what level of stress the backtest indicates the model is failing.

   Another test can be running the model through unlikely but plausible scenarios (e.g., gradual but important USD devaluation with interest rates increases), trying to understand again the performance limits in the model.

   An effective model risk management function will be aware of the breaking points that a model has, so they can be monitored and managed if needed.

The most important tool to validate risk models is backtest. For that reason we are going to dedicate the whole of Chapter 17 to discussing the topic, with a special focus on counterparty risk models.

17 Backtesting Risk Models

One of the most important changes in the financial industry since the 2008 market events is the change in stance by governments, from a "loose" regulatory environment to a much more hands-on approach. In particular, national regulators have substantially increased their scrutiny over the models used by banks to calculate risk and capital. Also, the amount of capital that banks need to hold against their balance sheet has increased substantially and, hence, the cost–benefit balance of investing in good accurate models has shifted importantly towards better models.

This has driven a change in the way risk models are dealt with. In Chapter 16 we have seen the general model risk and model validation framework that has emerged from this change.

We finished that chapter indicating that, when we validate risk models, one of the most important tools we have is backtesting. In this chapter we are going to expand on that topic, explaining how it can be done both for market risk and counterparty risk models.

17.1 Market risk backtesting

In 1996, the Basel Committee set up very clear rules regarding backtesting of VaR models for IMA institutions [2]. This section explains that backtesting framework, as it is widely used by financial institutions at present.

The VaR capital charge that banks are currently subject to is based on the ten-day VaR.[1] However, in the regulatory framework, backtesting is done on the one-day VaR. This is because, as stated in reference [2], "significant changes in the portfolio composition relative to the initial positions are common at major trading institutions". As a result, "the backtesting framework ... involves the use of risk measurements calibrated to a one-day holding period".[2]

17.1.1 The backtesting methodology

From Basel's perspective, backtesting should be done at least quarterly using the most recent 12 months of data. This yields approximately 250 daily observations. For each of those 250 days, the backtesting procedure will compare the bank P&L with the one-day 99% VaR computed the day before. Each day for which the loss is greater than the VaR will create an "exception". The assessment of the quality of the VaR model will be based on the number of exceptions in the 12-month period under study.

The Basel Committee proposes three bands for the model:

Band	Meaning	Exceptions
Green	The model is fit for purpose.	0 to 4
Yellow	Potential problems with the model, but final conclusions are not definitive.	5 to 9
Red	Almost certainly, there is a fundamental problem with the model.	10 or more

An illustrative example of a VaR backtesting exercise is shown in Figure 17.1.

17.1.2 The probability equivalent of colour bands

The original definition of those bands is driven by the estimation of the probability that the model is right or wrong. A green model means that the probability that the model is right is 95%, a yellow model means that that probability is 4.99%, and a red band means that that probability is only 0.01%.[3] It must be noted that these definitions have important risk management implications; it is generally believed that a model that scores "Green" is good but, in reality, it still has a 5% chance of being wrong. Also, a model that scores "Red" still has a (small but non-zero) 0.01% chance of being good.

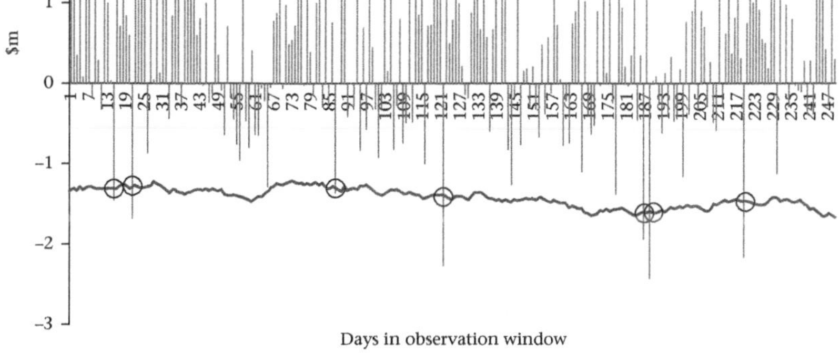

Figure 17.1 Illustrative example of a backtesting exercise for a VaR model. Each circle constitutes an exception

This is how those bands are calculated. Let's assume that we are studying a model that is known to be "perfect"; that is, that the model will measure the 99th percentile of the P&L distribution accurately. The idea here is that a perfect model will measure that 99th percentile well with in the limit with the number of backtesting days being infinite, but in our real case we have only 250 days. This granularity is going to have important implications.

Let's use the binomial distribution to compute the probability P of the number of exceptions (k) in a 12-month period that that model will give.[4] That probability is given by

$$P(k) = \binom{N}{k} p^k (1-p)^{N-k} \tag{17.1}$$

and is illustrated in Figure 17.2, top panel, with $N = 250$ and $p = 0.99$.

If we now draw a limit in the distribution of exceptions at the 95th and 99.99th percentiles, then the band limits are set at 4 and 9 exceptions.

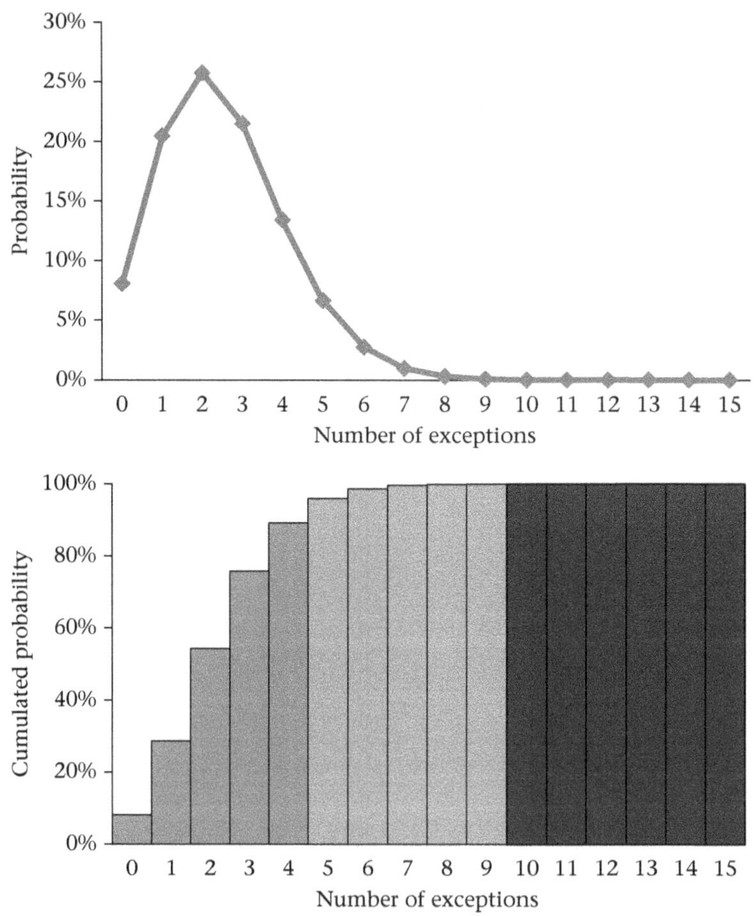

Figure 17.2 Probability distribution of exceptions, at 99% confidence, that a "perfect" model gives in a 12-month period

17.1.3 Consequences to banks

Under Basel, a bank's market risk capital charge is given by

$$\text{Market Risk Charge} = (3 + x + y) \cdot \text{MRM} \quad (17.2)$$

where x is given by the model performance, y is an add-on that national regulators can impose at their discretion, and the Market Risk Measure (MRM) was a ten-day VaR under Basel II, which is a ten-day-VaR plus stress-ten-day-VaR under Basel III and, at the time of this book going to press, is expected to change to an Expected Shortfall with varying time horizons.[5] Also, some regulators add an additional component called Risks-not-in-VaR (RniV), which accounts for the market risks which are not captured by the Market Risk model.

Regarding backtesting implications into the capital requirements, x is the number at stake. That number is given by the following table:

Num. exceptions	x
0–4	0.00
5	0.40
6	0.50
7	0.65
8	0.75
9	0.85
10+	1.00

After the large number of exceptions that all banks had in the 2008 financial crisis, reportedly some national regulators decided to remove the cap on x and increased it further as the number of exceptions went beyond ten.

Performance during the 2008 crisis: Risk Magazine: published in 2010 an interesting study of how VaR models performed during the 2008 crisis [53]. This study analysed ten of the most important global financial institutions. In 2008, six of these banks went to the red band (JP Morgan, Bear Stearns, Credit Suisse, Societe Generale, Deutsche Bank, and UBS), two stayed in the green band (Morgan Stanley and BNP Paribas), and two stayed in the green zone (Lehman Brothers and Goldman Sachs). Given that both Bearn Stearns and Lehman Brothers disappeared during 2008, the 12 months up to their collapse was considered for this study. Quite interestingly, Lehman Brothers remained in the green zone right until their bankruptcy.

This highlights one of the problems of market risk backtesting: it only looks backwards by construction, and so it does not test whether a model is ready for future events that have no historical precedents. Other limitations of this technique includes the fact that it does not consider market autocorrelation, even though it could perfectly exist in the market that is being studied.

This illustrates that backtesting is a most important test when judging the adequacy of a market risk model, though it must be taken as a part of a wider toolkit in an efficient model risk management framework. Most VaR models reported very few exceptions during the previous LTCM or dot-com crisis, but they broadly failed during 2008.

17.1.4 Market risk backtesting of CVA

Unfortunately, market risk backtesting has a limited value for CVA, for the reasons already explained in Section 16.3.3. Summarising, the problem is that CVA is a price that cannot be marked-to-market, because there isn't any liquid market for CCDSs.[6] Instead, it is marked-to-model. For this reason, as long as the Greek calculations that the model has are consistent with the CVA price, any daily backtest will appear good even when the model may be not that good.

An institution with a poor CVA model but that has consistent CVA pricing and Greeks may be misled by backtesting results. However, it will see the negative effects of it in the long run, when the institution has suffered a considerable number of defaults. If the CVA price has been inaccurate in the past, it will see how the CVA price and the CVA hedges are quite misaligned with the losses it actually suffered from those defaults.

As explained in Chapter 16, a way in which this can be managed is by performing realistic hedging simulations of the model. Also, the different sub-models in the CVA pricing model (i.e., the exposure calculation, default probability, and loss given default models) should be backtested historically. In this way we may be able to see potential misalignments between the credit risk actually taken by the institution in its portfolio of OTC derivatives and its credit price, CVA.

And that leads us quite nicely to the next section.

17.2 Counterparty risk backtesting

So far we have seen the problem of counterparty risk backtesting from a pricing and market risk standpoint. Now we are going to deal with this problem with the greatest depth, from the point of view of Counterparty Credit Risk (CCR) management.

This function typically uses models for two purposes:

1. To limit monitoring and general risk management of the counterparty risk embedded in the book of OTC derivatives.
2. To calculate the economic and regulatory capital related to counterparty risk.

Backtesting CCR models is the most difficult backtesting job we can have. This is due to two reasons. Firstly, the time horizon of CCR models is much longer than that of any other typical model. Pricing and market risk models look at a one-day, ten-day or, typically, upto a few weeks time horizon. However, in CCR models we are trying to estimate the value of a portfolio up to many years in the future. Even if we had all the data in the world, and all the computing power in the world, in order to backtest a five-year time horizon model prediction, for example, we will need 500 years of historical data to have only 100 independent points. We obviously do not have that data.[7]

Secondly, data can easily be scarce or meaningless. If we are backtesting the exposure of a given netting set, ideally we would need to have the value of that netting set, daily, from many years back, together with the value of every market parameter that affects that netting set. We usually do not have that data.

Furthermore, even if we had it, the composition of the netting set is going to have changed over time as trades mature and new trades are added to the netting set, adding another difficulty.

For these reasons, backtesting CCR models is a very difficult task. In fact, we could say that, in the case of CCR, the science of backtesting becomes the science of how to make the most out of limited data.

17.2.1 Splitting the problem into manageable sub-problems

CCR models have three well differentiated sub-models: default probability, loss given default, and exposure calculation models.

Regarding default probability and loss given default models, we saw in Chapter 7 that the models themselves are very simple due to the scarcity of data. For this reason, validating and backtesting these models tends to be a fairly simple task from a technical point of view. The validation of those models usually focusses on checking the appropriateness and conservatism of the many assumptions made in the models.

However, the story is quite different for exposure calculations. Those models can be quite sophisticated, and as a result their backtesting is quite convoluted.

For this reason, when a practitioner talks about backtesting of CCR models, nearly always he or she is referring to backtesting of the exposure models in the CCR calculation. We are going to focus on that problem from now on.

Exposure measurement backtesting: When we want to backtest CCR models, what we would ideally want is to backtest the exposures at netting set level, as it is at that level that a default crystallises into a loss. However, this is not usually possible in practice, because the composition of netting sets changes over time and, hence, comparing model outputs to realised netting set values cannot be done in a generalised manner.

The next step would be to try to backtest trade by trade. Again, this has the difficulty of trade maturity issues.

As a result, backtesting of the exposure side of CCR models tends to be split into two differentiated problems: validation of the pricing algorithms and backtesting of the RFE models. The former tends to use standard model validation techniques, but we need new backtesting methods for the latter.

There are two basic approaches to backtesting RFE models: via percentile envelopes or via a distance metric for the whole distribution function. Let's look at each of them in some more depth.

17.2.2 Backtesting via percentile envelopes

The easiest way to backtest an RFE model is using the percentile envelopes given by the RFE model. In this method we want to understand how often a realised time series stays within the percentile envelopes given by the model.

Let's say that we have a time series of a given risk factor x_{t_i} (typically, daily data) on which we want to test a given model. What we are going to do is choose a number of representative symmetric percentile pairs (e.g., 30–70%, 20–80%, 10–90%, 5–95%, 1–99%) and calculate how often the time series is outside of the envelopes. Then we compare that number to the number of points in the time series, calculate a percentage ratio and compare it to the expected one. If we do this several times, we can run some statistics from which we can give a score to the model. An example of this exercise is shown in Figure 17.3.

There are several ways we can create this score. Let's see one of them as an illustrative example.

Let's say we want to test an FX model. We want to test it against the exchange rates that we are most sensitive to (e.g., USDEUR, USDJPY, USDGBP, USDCHF, USDCAD, USDBRL). We start with one of these rates and get its past time series. We decide on a time period (δt) for which we can regard the time series behaviour as independent of[8] (e.g., 6 months). Then we pick a first time point (t_1) in the time series and draw the chosen percentile envelopes. Then we advance (δt) to t_2 and we draw the envelopes again. We proceed like this N times to t_N, until we have covered all the time series.

In each of these envelopes, we count how many days the time series lies outside of the envelope (the exceptions) and divide that number by the number of days that the envelope has. We do this for all

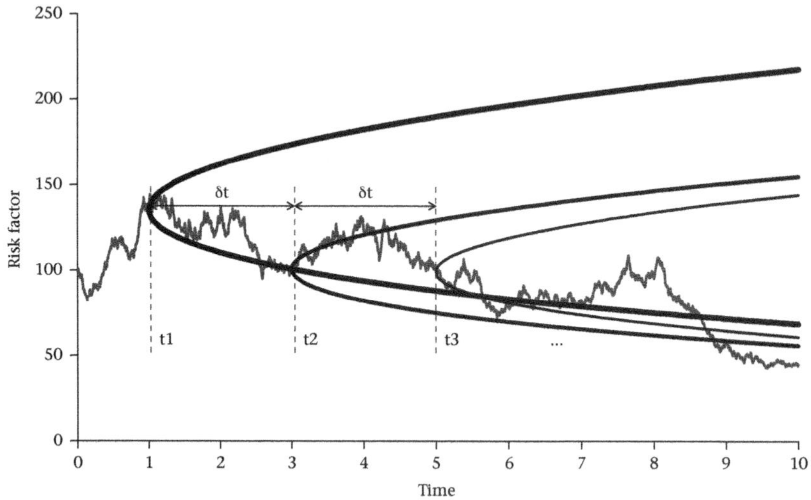

Figure 17.3 Illustration of backtesting methodology via percentile envelopes

envelopes. Then, we create an index (I) for this risk factor and percentile pair, which is the average of those coefficients.

This is illustrated in the following formula for a risk factor "$RF1$" and the percentile pair $x\% - (1-x)\%$.

$$I_{RF1}^{x\%-(1-x)\%} = \frac{\sum_{i=i}^{N} \frac{\text{Number of days outside of envelope}}{\text{Number of days the envelope has}}}{N} \tag{17.3}$$

Now, we are going to create a modified index ($\tilde{I}$) that is calculated by subtracting from I the expected percentage of exceptions I_E.[9]

$$\tilde{I}_{RF1}^{x\%-(1-x)\%} = I_{RF1}^{x\%-(1-x)\%} - I_{E}^{x\%-(1-x)\%} \tag{17.4}$$

In this way we are going to create an index $\tilde{I}$ per risk factor and percentile pair. Now we can build a table with all these indices, as follows

Risk factor/envelope	30–70%	10–90%	1–99%
RF1	2.1%	−0.4%	−2.5%
RF2	5.2%	2.0%	−4.5%
RF3	3.5%	−1.1%	−3.9%
...	...	...	...

It must be noted that the index $\tilde{I}$ is positive when the number of exceptions is greater than that expected, and vice versa.

A table like the one shown above can be quite a good tool to assess the quality of a model. For example, in that illustrative table it seems that the model tends to be aggressive for low percentiles as $\tilde{I}$ is positive in all of them in the 30–70% envelopes, but it seems to be conservative for high percentiles (the 1–99% envelopes).

Finally we can create an index score, per risk factor and per percentile envelope, by calculating a weighted average of each index $\tilde{I}$. The simplest version can have the same weight for all $\tilde{I}$, but we can also use a different weighting, so we are able to emphasise the effect from different parts of the distribution function,[10] or from different risk factors.[11] Finally, if wanted, we can create a final index score, blending all those weighted averages into one single final index.

In spite of that, it must be noted that in my experience the most valuable output of this study is a table such as that one illustrated above, as it provides, in one snapshot, a good balance between overall performance of a model and granular analysis.

Colour bands: One of the strengths of this backtesting methodology, its simplicity, is also one of its weaknesses, namely its lack of mathematical robustness.

In an ideal backtesting exercise, we would like to create colour bands as we have done for market risk. However, that does not seem to be possible here as a result of its lack of mathematical soundness. For example, there is a lack of independence in the calculation of the indices: typically, if a time series produces an exception some time far from the envelope starting point, it is quite likely that that exception continues for a long time; however, this effect is not so strong if the exception starts at the very beginning of the envelope.

Having said that, it is a very good methodology to provide a *sense* and an overview of how an exposure model performs. In fact, in many practical cases, it is good enough. It is simple to implement and to understand, two traits that are very valuable.

If needed, the backtesting methodology explained in Section 17.2.3 has the mathematical robustness to build, amongst other things, colour bands as done in the market risk case.

Calibration methodologies: It is easy to forget that a model is not only a set of equations, but also a calibration methodology and a calibration frequency. Our backtesting method needs to test all of that, reproducing the real calibration process as much as possible.

The calibration needs to be done "out-of-sample" if it is historically based. By this it is meant that if the model uses, say, a four-year historical calibration, in each creation of the envelopes we need to do a four-year historical calibration as of the day the envelopes start.

However, if the envelop creation frequency is higher than the real recalibration frequency, we need to adapt the backtesting recalibration accordingly. For example, if the backtest calculates new envelopes every month, but the real models are recalibrated every three months, we must recalibrate in the backtesting exercise every three months only.

Numerical envelopes: If the models under testing are simple enough, we can usually calculate the envelopes analytically. However, if they are complex, we many need to calculate them numerically with a Monte Carlo simulation per envelope.

Model risk on model validation: As said, this methodology is quite powerful for providing a good sense of how a model performs, but it is based on a number of quite subjective decisions. The way to compute the indices $\tilde{I}$ explained here is just one of many ways that could possibly be used. It is up to the backtester to decide which method is most appropriate.

This creates by itself a backtesting model risk that must be managed too. In certain environments it can be quite tempting to choose a backtesting method only because it results in a "pass" for the model. This degree of uncertainty needs to be understood and managed too.

17.2.3 Backtesting via distance metric of distribution functions

In this backtesting method we are going to compare the distribution of the risk factor given by the model over time with the distribution actually seen in the market. In other words, we want to check how the RFE model and the observed "real" process compare to each other, by comparing their distribution of changes in the risk factor at stake, for a give time step (the testing time horizon).

First of all, we are going to consider the realised path (a time series) of the risk factor to be tested.[12] That path is given by a collection of (typically daily) values x_{t_i}. We will set a time point in that time series where the backtest starts (t_{start}), and a time point where it ends (t_{end}). The backtest time window is then $T = t_{end} - t_{start}$. Then, if we pick a Δ time horizon over which we want to test our model (e.g., Δ = 1 month) we then proceed as follows. The reader can see in Figure 17.4 an illustration of this process.

1. The first time point of measurement is $t_1 = t_{start}$. At that point, we calculate the model risk factor distribution at a point $t_1 + \Delta$ subject to the realisation of x_{t_1}; this can be done analytically if possible, or numerically otherwise. We then take the realised value $x_{t_1+\Delta}$ of the time series at $t_1 + \Delta$ and observe where that value falls in the risk factor cumulative distribution function that was calculated previously. This yields a value F_1.[13]
2. We then move forward to $t_2 = t_1 + \delta$. We calculate the risk factor distribution at $t_2 + \Delta$ subject to realisation of x_{t_2}, and proceed as before: we observe where in the model distribution function $x_{t_2+\Delta}$ falls and obtain F_2 from it.
3. We repeat continuously the above until $t_i + \Delta$ reaches t_{end}.

The outcome of this exercise is a collection $\{F_i\}_{i=1}^N$ where N is the number of time steps taken.

The key point in this methodology is the following: in the case of a "perfect" model (i.e., if the empirical distribution from the time series is the same as the distribution that the model predicts), then $\{F_i\}_{i=1}^N$ will be uniformly distributed.

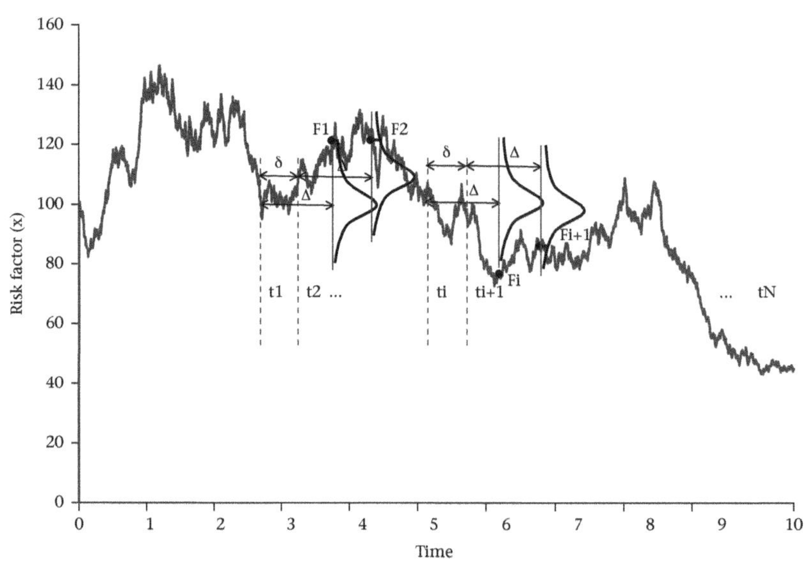

Figure 17.4 Illustration of backtesting methodology via distance metric of distribution functions

Now, we are going to define a distance metric D that measures the difference between the empirical (i.e., the "real" from the time series) and the model distributions. If that distance is zero, then the model is supposed to be "perfect".

There are a number of typical metrics for D. If we denote by F the theoretical cumulative distribution function given by the model and by F_e the empirical cumulative distribution function obtained from $\{F_i\}_{i=1}^{N}$,[14] then we can use, for example:

Anderson–Darling metric:

$$D_{AD} = \int_{\infty}^{-\infty} (F_e(x) - F(x))^2 \, w(F(x)) \, dF(x)$$
$$w(F) = \frac{1}{F(1-F)} \tag{17.5}$$

Cramer–von Mises metric:

$$D_{CM} = \int_{\infty}^{-\infty} (F_e(x) - F(x))^2 \, w(F(x)) \, dF(x)$$
$$w(F) = 1 \tag{17.6}$$

Kolmogorov–Smirnov metric:

$$D_{KS} = \sup_x |F_e(x) - F(x)| \tag{17.7}$$

Each metric will deliver a different measurement of D. Which of them is the most appropriate depends on how the model being backtested is actually used. It must be noted that this decision has some degree of subjectivity by the backtester.[15]

Having chosen a metric, we can compute now a value $\widetilde{D}$ that measures how different the model's distribution is compared to the empirical distribution from $\{F_i\}_{i=1}^{N}$.

Assessing D: The following questions arise now:

1. How large does $\widetilde{D}$ need to be to indicate that a model is bad? Or, equivalently, how close to zero must it be to indicate that our model is good?
2. N is a finite number, so $\widetilde{D}$ will never be exactly zero even if the model were perfect.[16] How can we assess the validity of $\widetilde{D}$?

In order to answer those two questions, we can proceed as follows. Let's construct an artificial time series using the model being tested, and then apply our above procedure to it, yielding a value D.[17] The constructed time series will follow the model perfectly by definition, but D will not be exactly zero. However, this deviation will only be due to "numerical noise". If we repeat this exercise a large number of times (M), we will obtain a collection $\{D_k\}_{k=1}^{M}$, *all of them compatible with a "perfect" model.* That collection of Ds will follow a certain

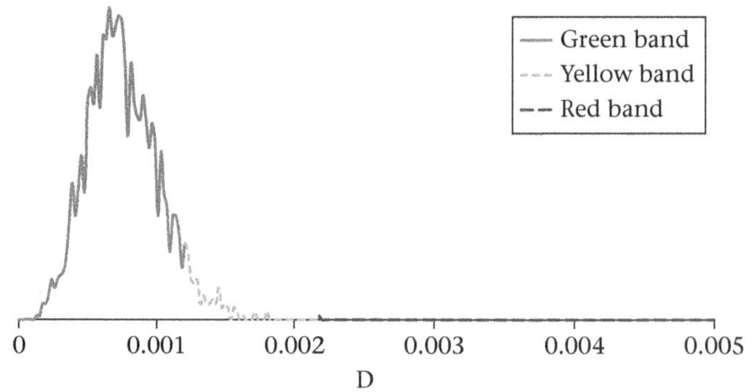

Figure 17.5 Illustrative example of the distribution of *D*s compatible with the model

probability distribution $\psi(D)$ that we can approximate numerically from $\{D_k\}_{k=1}^{M}$ by making M sufficiently large.

Now, having obtained $\psi(D)$, we can asses the validity of $\widetilde{D}$: if $\widetilde{D}$ falls in a range with high probability with respect to $\psi(D)$, then the model is likely to be accurate, and vice versa.[18]

The three bands

We are now in a position to extend the clear Basel framework established for market risk to the setting of counterparty risk. If we define D_y and D_r respectively as the 95th and 99.99th percentiles of $\psi(D)$, then we can define three bands for the model performance:

- Green band if $\widetilde{D} \in [0, D_y)$
- Yellow band if $\widetilde{D} \in [D_y, D_r)$
- Red band if $\widetilde{D} \in [D_r, \infty)$

This is illustrated in Figure 17.5 for a simple Geometric Brownian Motion model. With this three-band approach, a financial institution can easily score a model.

If interested, the reader can see an in-depth analysis of this methodology, as well as a number practical examples of how it can be used, in my paper published in the *Journal of Credit Risk* [71].

Scoring tables

When we assess a model, we want to do this for a number of representative risk factors and time horizons. Using the example from above, if we want to test an FX model, we should check it with a number of representative exchange rate pairs; we should choose those pairs that are most important to our book of derivatives.

Also, we have to select a number of time horizons Δ for the test. This should be driven by the materiality of the trades we have with those risk factors. For example, if 90% of our trades have a maturity of less than five years, it is in that period where we should focus our efforts. In this case typical values for Δ could be 1-day, 10-days, 1-month, 3-months, 1-year, 3-years, and 5-years.

With this information we can run the relevant tests on the representative risk factors, and build a table along the lines of:

Risk factor/delta	1-day	10-day	1-month	...
RF1	green	green	green	...
RF2	yellow	green	red	...
RF3	green	green	red	...
...	...	...	...	...

This table provides a very good snapshot of the quality of the model. Obviously, we are looking for lots of green and very little red.

In a good backtesting exercise, the analyst will go through every "yellow" and "red" score, and understand why it isn't green. Sometimes this will be because of data quality issues, sometimes because that particular test has some special issues, sometimes because the model is not good enough.

With all that extra information, that table will provide a most valuable piece of analysis regarding the quality of the model.

Further to this, we could build other blended scores per risk factor, per time horizon, per overall score, etc., but in my experience these blended numbers provide limited information because the granularity of the analysis melts away. A table of scores like the one shown presents most often the best trade-off between analysis depth and practicalities.

18 | Systems and Project Management

In this book we have dealt with the subject of counterparty and funding risk, and related topics. We have covered how to model it, and how to manage it.

One of the biggest problems of this type of risk is that the systems that we need to build for it are extremely complex. In fact, no doubt this is one of the biggest (if not the biggest) challenge that financial institutions have ever faced from a systems standpoint.

The effort that needs to be applied both to develop and maintain these systems is often underestimated. This is a mistake that I have seen over and over again. If we want to build a system that is capable of doing all the calculations that we need, and also solid enough so it can last a long time, we need to make sure that it is built well from the ground up. However, often, it is tempting to leave aside long-term quality for the benefit of short-term results. This does not mean that we must not develop anything until we understand everything fully, as if so we may never build anything at all. A balance must be reached here, always keeping in mind the following fundamental law.

Short Term Gain $\approx$ Long Term Pain

In this chapter we are going to see what are the basic options at hand regarding XVA systems, the most important elements of the system's architecture, and the key drivers of the decision process, implementation, and maintenance. Also, at the end, we'll discuss how to manage XVA quantitative projects to optimise efficiency.

18.1 The scale of the problem

In Chapter 3 we saw how the calculation of counterparty credit risk metrics can be split into three main steps:

1. Risk Factor Evolution (RFE)
2. Pricing
3. Risk Metric Calculation

From those steps, the very large majority of the computational effort is taken by pricing. I have measured this in a number of conditions, and that pricing step tends to take from 90% to in excess of 99%. The first RFE step takes something between less than 1% to up to around 10%. The computational effort of the third step, the risk metric calculation, is more or less negligible.

Limitless computational power: In order to illustrate the size of the problem, let's see for a second what we would do if computational power was not a constraint.

Large financial institutions can typically have a few million OTC derivatives on their books. For example, Lehman Brothers had reportedly 930,000 of them when it defaulted. For the sake of argument, let's say that we have a number D of one million of them.

CVA, for example, is a pricing metric. The typical level of precision that we want in OTC derivative prices is 1 basis point. The typical number of scenarios (N) that we need to use in order to achieve that pricing error in CVA ranges from 100,000 to a few million (see Section 3.11). Let's say that number is 1,000,000.

Ideally, in order to calculate the CVA "Greeks" by the simple method of re-running the calculation after a small shift of the relevant risk factor, the one most often used, we need at very least a resolution in the CVA price of 0.01 basis point. The pricing error expands in Monte Carlo simulations as the square root of the number of scenarios, which means that in order to calculate the Greeks correctly, we would need easily around 10,000,000,000 scenarios.

The expiry of the OTC derivatives ranges from a few weeks (e.g., FX derivatives) to up to 50 years (e.g., inflation derivatives). Let's say that the average expiry in our book of derivatives is ten years, so we capture well the risk from all upcoming payment dates. *Ideally* we would like to calculate the counterparty credit risk that we are exposed to every day from now to ten years. This is, approximately, 2,600 trading days. Let's call this number of time steps M.

So, in order to calculate one single set of counterparty credit risk metrics properly for our portfolio of OTC derivatives, we need to do the following number of calls to the derivative pricing functions: $D \times N \times M = 26,000,000,000,000,000,000$.

This is done to calculate one set of the risk metrics, which a well managed financial institution needs to do every day, at least. In addition, a number of subsequent calculations should be done. In order to calculate the CVA Greeks in the standard way, for example, we will need to repeat this calculation around, say, 100 times (being conservative).

Also, whenever a new derivative is transacted, or an existing trade is unwound, or when risk analysis is performed, we would need to re-run this calculation, partially this time for the netting set that is affected. For the sake of argument, let's say that we would want to do this calculation ten extra times each day because of this.

All this leads to the staggering number of calls to the pricing functions of $26,000,000,000,000,000,000,000$.

This calculation is, obviously, undoable.

All that financial institutions can hope for is to estimate counterparty risk metrics with the highest accuracy that is possible, given the computational constraints. Given that we cannot do what we *would like* to, let's see what we *can* do. Financial institutions implement the following solutions shortcuts so the calculation is somewhat doable.

Sensitivity calculations: We have said that in order to calculate XVA sensitivities, we'd need an accuracy of at least 0.01 basis point. This is needed when calculating the sensitivities via a brute-force approach; i.e., bumping the risk factor at stake and re-running the calculation. As already said, this extreme 0.01 bp resolution can be avoided in two different ways.

The optimal way to do sensitivity calculation is by implementing an Adjoint Algorithmic Differentiation technique. This method can compute as many sensitivities as needed with a maximum computational cost of four times the original XVA calculation [29]. The downside of it is that, being a very nice and straightforward method from a mathematical standpoint, its implementation into a commercial software, for the many sensitivities that are often needed, can be quite convoluted.

An alternative approach is to calculate the most important "Greeks" using the brute force approach *but* keeping the random numbers constant in each Monte Carlo run. In this way the sensitivity calculation becomes "blind" to the numerical noise and we get sensitivity numbers that have some stability.[1]

Farm computing: The largest financial institutions in the world have farms of a few hundred or a few thousand state-of-the-art processing units, available 24 hours a day, for these calculations. In spite of that, the reported number of scenarios that they use range between 1,000 and 10,000, and the number of time points between 25 and 100 [10]. More resolution than that is too expensive in general.

So, in this context, in order to calculate XVA metrics, we need to call each pricing function around 1,000,000 times in each calculation run.[2] Given that a large financial institution will have easily 1,000,000 derivatives, we are facing here around 1,000,000,000,000 pricing calls in each run.

The computational time of already optimised pricing functions ranges from approximately 1 millisecond for the simplest derivatives to several minutes for the complex ones.[3]

As a rough estimate, if we say that the average computing time is 10 milliseconds, and that we distribute the job between 200 CPUs, the estimated computing time would be 50,000,000 seconds, or 578 days.

This is still undoable.

Further measures: Given the outstanding amount of computational power we need, financial institutions need to implement further measures. They include:

- Constrain even more the number of scenarios and time points so the calculation can be done in a reasonable time, keeping in mind that, arguably, the lower acceptable limit is around 1,000 scenarios and around 20 time points. As a result of this, the quality of the calculation and subsequent XVA valuation and risk assessment decrease substantially.
- Do not attempt this calculation on the more sophisticated and exotic derivatives, as the computational effort of the pricing step is highest, sometimes completely prohibitive. Again, as a consequence, XVA valuation and risk management gets very negatively affected, as all we can do is obtain very approximated numbers for those sophisticated trades.

  Also, most importantly, regulatory capital increases substantially, as those trades cannot be processed through the best "advanced" risk models and regulatory capital becomes very high for them.[4] A consequence of this is that the "manufacturing" costs of exotic derivatives has gone up substantially, hence margins have decreased for derivative dealers and demand has decreased for those products.
- Increase further the number of processing units configured to do the calculation. However, there is a practical limit to this.
- Acquire very state-of-the-art processing units, so that the processing speed is as fast as the best available in the market.

18.2 What is and isn't required

If we want to build a good XVA system, first we need to understand what are the most important things we must get right and what we mustn't get wrong. Let's go through a list of them.

18.2.1 Dos

We must get right the following points.

Speed: As clearly seen, counterparty and funding risk systems need to price each OTC derivative around one million times each time we do a calculation. This comes from the typical 10,000 scenarios and around 100 time points in the Monte Carlo simulation that the best systems have.

Given that the vast majority of the computational effort is taken by the pricing step, any improvement there will have a substantial impact on the final computational capability and, subsequently, the quality of XVA valuation and risk management in financial institutions.

As a result of this outstanding need for computing power, anything that compromises calculation speed must be left aside or, at very least, justified very well with a strong business case.

Data management: Given the very large amount of data that these systems need to handle, and the speed at which it may be needed, we need large storage capacity, fast read/write technology for the storage media, and, if a global institution, worldwide networks with large bandwidths for the effective transmission of data.

Scalable systems: Based on experience, I can guarantee to the reader that, regardless of how big an XVA system is created today, one day it will need to grow, perhaps because the number of trades going through it has increased (e.g., a merger), because new calculations are required (e.g., new regulatory requirements), or because new methodologies are needed (e.g., multi- vs. single-yield curve risk sensitivities arise): the fact is that I have been facing this problem over and over again over past years.

As a result, it is crucially important that the systems are built so that it is easily scalable. By this is meant both from a hardware and software standpoint.

In the former case, typical systems run in a multi-CPU environment. The infrastructure must be built so that more CPUs can be added in easily, without having to change anything apart from the multi-CPU job distribution process, if at all.

In the latter case, the software architecture must be built so that everything is in modules, each taking a single responsibility in an isolated way. For example, a typical mistake seen is when a new pricer is added to a system that requires some RFE functionality that does not exist in the RFE module, that is added ad hoc to the pricer code at the beginning of it. If done like that, some time in the future another pricer will need the same RFE functionality, and so that code will have to be replicated, which we can guarantee will not be exactly the same. Also, if things are done in this way, maintenance becomes expensive and slow: any change done to the RFE will mean a change to the pricers to compensate for it. However, if *all* the RFE functionality is in the RFE module, and *all* the pricing functionality in the pricing module, *always*, none of these problems will ever arise.

It must be noted that this RFE/pricing is only an example, the point is that each code functionality must belong to different modules and *no exceptions* must be made.

Also, the interaction between the module inputs and outputs needs to be based on a flexible procedure (e.g., via object oriented programming) so that changes in the input/output requirements require minimum code updates.

Let's remember the key fundamental law:

$$\text{Short Term Gain} \approx \text{Long Term Pain}$$

Intra-day calculations: In most cases, an organisation will need to do fast intra-day calculations of counterparty risk metrics, for example, XVA prices that need to be calculated before a new trade is agreed with a client. When this is important, all the systems architecture needs to be designed to enable this feature, sometimes at the expense of the number of time buckets, the number of scenarios, or by limiting the amount of information needed for an intra-day run so that it is fast, for example.

Good sensitivities: It is also very important to be able to calculate good stable XVA sensitivities, otherwise hedging will be difficult and, inevitably, contain errors. We have seen two ways of achieving this.

Reactive to markets: Depending on what is most important to the organisation, the systems need to be sufficiently reactive to changing market conditions. For example, XVA desks tend to require prices very sensitive to the markets, and so these desks typically require very fast updates of market data and model calibration parameters. However, risk management metrics tend to be desired to be somewhat more stable in the face of swinging market conditions and so they do not require too sophisticated data update procedures.

Number of time steps: Ideally we want the exposure profile calculation to compute the exposure on the time points where the profiles peak. A typical set up for time steps is daily for one or two weeks, weekly up to a few months, fortnightly for a few months thereafter, monthly up to one or two years, quarterly up to five years, semi-annually up to 10 or 20 years, and annually up to the end of the simulation.

In the old times, before 2008, usually calculations were done up to around 20 years, but now regulators want to have all calculations up to the maturity of the last trade. Given that some inflation trades can go up to 50 years easily, we now need to simulate very far out into the future. Some banks run simulations up to 100 years forward, with five-year time steps toward the end.[5]

A degree of flexibility that an optimal XVA system should have is to provide the possibility of a cascade of dates in the calculation engine, considering the following hierarchy.

- **Default Profile Dates:** We want to report EPE, PFE, etc., profiles in a fixed collection of time points so that off-system downstream processes work swiftly, always with the same time points received from the XVA calculation.
- **Special Profile Dates:** We may want to calculate EPE, PFE, etc., profiles also at intermediate points (i.e., at time points in-between the default dates) so that special dates with relevant cash-flow can be accounted for. In this case, we may want the value reported on a given default date to be not the value calculated on that day, but to be the average or the maximum in that time bucket, depending on how conservative we want to be.
- **Special Pricing Dates:** Also, sometimes we may want to price some derivatives on some dates, even if risk profiles are not calculated on those dates. An example can be when the future price of the derivative depends on its past price.
- **Special RFE Dates:** Finally, sometimes we are going to have to price derivatives based on the value of some market risk factors in the past. For example, Asian options. In these cases, even if we do not price the derivative for all relevant RFE dates, we may want to simulate risk factor values for those days and store them, so they can be used by the pricers later in the simulation.

The default setting, the one most widely used, is that in which all the dates (i.e., RFE, pricing, profile calculation, and profile reporting) are the same, though it is a very good feature in a system to have flexibility to add special dates if needed.

It must be noted that each group of dates must be a subset of the one below in the hierarchy; otherwise the calculation cannot be done.

Good user interface: Institutions have to spend very significant amounts of cash, time, and effort in the development of XVA systems. Wouldn't we want the whole organisation to appreciate this effort, and use this system constantly? Let's not forget that, possibly, this is the only system in the organisation that has the capability to provide risk information many years forward in the future, so it has an unparalleled strategic value.

A mistake that is tempting to do is building a system that provides good quality information, but forgetting completely about how that information is displayed to the user in the organisation. Also, these systems have lots of input parameters to play with, but they could be hardly configurable by an end user in a *simple* way. Therefore a nice Graphic User Interface (GUI) is of utmost importance.

To put it in simple terms, if a risk manager or a trader receives the information in a fast, nice, colourful, and cool way, with attractive charts that deliver the information in a straight and clear manner, the user will easily become familiar with the calculation and will better understand the meaning of the information it provides.

In my experience, the importance of a good GUI can be easily underestimated.

Also, speed in that GUI is most important. We saw in Chapter 15 that one of the most important winning differentiator between financial institutions is the speed at which XVA analytics are provided to sales people, traders, and risk managers. A good GUI should deliver this speed.

Different calculation levels: We have seen that risk metrics can be calculated, in general, at four different levels: trade, netting set, counterparty, and portfolio levels. This is illustrated in Figure 18.1.

From a counterparty risk standpoint we do not have trades, we have netting sets. That is because, let's remember, in the case of a counterparty defaulting, all trades in a netting set are netted with each other for the liquidation of the portfolio. As a result, the CVA of a stand-alone trade has no meaning; what has meaning is the CVA or the incremental CVA of a netting set.

We can have a number of netting sets for a single counterparty, to reflect different geographies, asset classes, or for many other reasons. In any case, the CVA of a counterparty or portfolio is the sum of the CVAs of each netting set, *but* that is not the case with many other risk metrics.

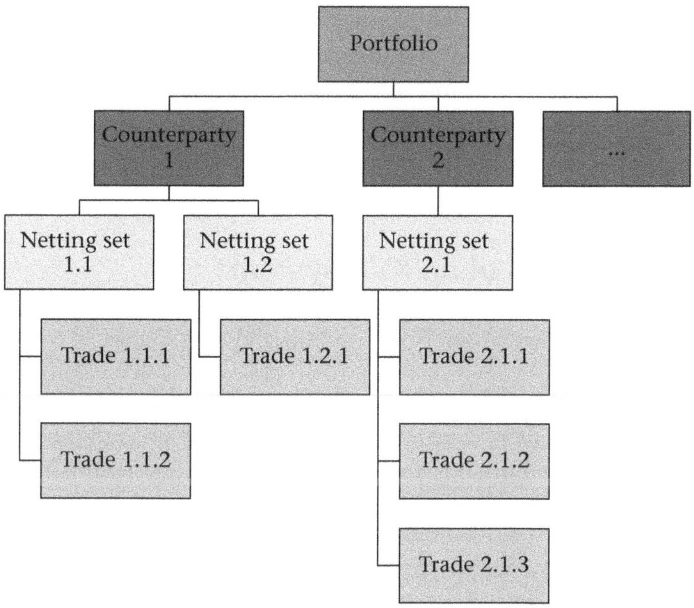

Figure 18.1 Illustration of the calculation hierarchy in an XVA system

For example, the PFE of a counterparty can be smaller than the sum of the PFEs of each netting set; or the maximum of the EPE profile of a counterparty can be smaller than the maximum of the EPE profiles of each netting set.[6]

Also, we have seen that metrics like FVA must be calculated at portfolio level to account for inter-netting-set funding benefits.

For these reasons, a good XVA system must be able to calculate all sorts of risk metrics at different calculation levels, as required by the final output. If a system does not have this functionality, typically calculating metrics at netting set level and, then, adding them up to come up with metrics at higher levels, we will be very often overestimating risk.

18.2.2 Don'ts

These are somewhat common mistakes to be avoided. precession within the numerical noise that exists in the whole calculation.

No computationally demanding methodologies: Given that one of the major problems we have is calculation time, any shortcuts that we can implement in the methodologies that accelerate the calculation is highly desirable, even at the expense of what may appear at first glance better precision in the calculation. This is, again, because the numerical noise that we are facing can be easily so high that we can sometimes allow ourselves to be a bit "blunt" in the methodology without any impact on the final result. A good quant will know when to be or not to be that "blunt".

An example of this could be implementing the not-so-sophisticated spline interpolation scheme for yield curves, as opposed to simple linear interpolation. They both will give the same ultimate XVA result in most cases, but one is much slower than the other.

No excessive job-breakdown: XVA calculations tend to be done in a multi-CPU farm environment. Experts in that field know very well that there is an optimal number of CPUs and a level of job-breakdown that achieves the lowest calculation time. Once that point is reached, adding more CPUs or breaking the jobs into smaller pieces not only do not decrease calculation time, but can even increase it. Finding the optimal point there is very important, and not an easy task. We need to understand well what is being calculated, to make sure that the calculation is being broken into pieces and put back together sensibly.

18.3 The basic architecture of an XVA system

Figure 18.2 illustrates a basic set-up of a counterparty and funding risk system.

1. **Data Input:** First of all, we need to collect all the data needed for the calculation. This can be typically split into four components: trade data, counterparty data, market data, and model calibration data. The process to generate this information needs to be run periodically, most often daily at least.
2. **Monte Carlo Engine:** We have already dedicated a large proportion of this book to how to design the Monte Carlo Engine. It is based on a number of model groups: RFE, Pricing, Collateral, and Right & Wrong Way Risk (R/WWR) models. As also said in this chapter, it is most important that each of those models is properly encapsulated, so that it does what it is supposed do, and no more. Otherwise maintenance and future development can become cumbersome.

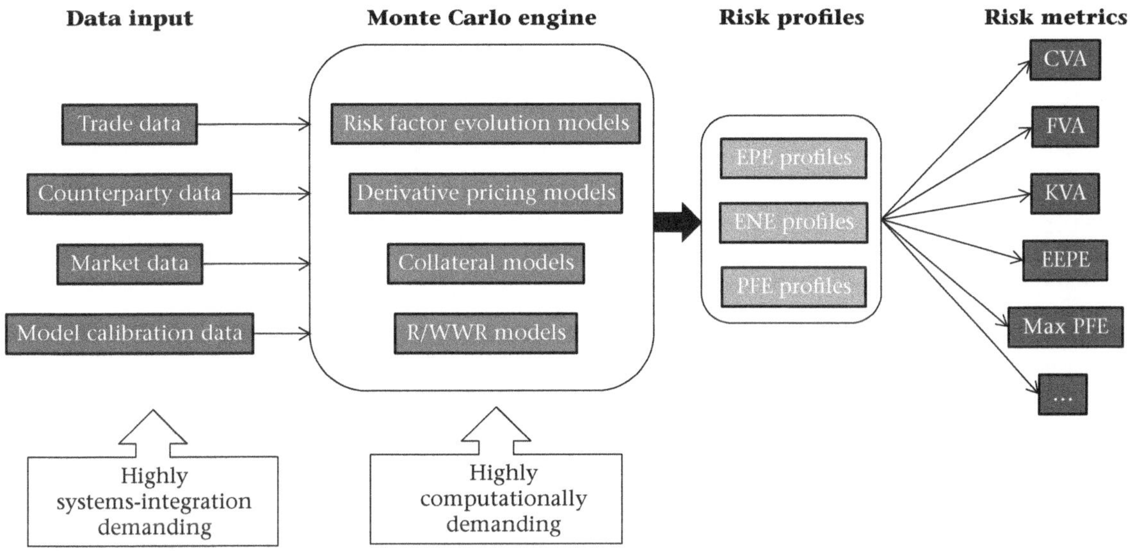

Figure 18.2 Illustration of the basic set up of an XVA system architecture

3. **Risk Profiles:** Once we have all the portfolio prices and collateral values from the models, we can calculate any desired risk metric in each desired time point, so that the system can calculate the risk profiles for each trade, netting set, counterparty, global portfolio, or a collection of them.
4. **Risk Metrics:** The final calculation is that of the risk metrics that are then used, like CVA, FVA, KVA, EEPE, Maxmium of PFE profile.

From those four steps, the two that are most tricky to implement are the first two. The Data Input process can be very demanding from a systems integration point of view, as well as data management. The Monte Carlo Engine can be very demanding from a computational standpoint. Let's look at each in some more depth.

18.3.1 Data input

Figure 18.3 illustrates in a generic way the process needed to generate the input data for an XVA calculation.

The starting point is collecting all the trades for the calculation. A financial institution should have only one trading system where everything is stored, but hardly anyone has that. In reality, XVA systems need to pull the trade information from a number of trade databases, to come up with an XVA unique Trade Data file.[7] To achieve this, we will need to build a "translating" process from each original trade database to the XVA repository. This can be quite a costly process to set up.

Once we know all the trades for the calculation, we must pull all the relevant information from each counterparty and netting set affected. The most relevant information includes collateral agreement details like existing collateral, eligible collateral, thresholds. With this information we can then build a Counterparty Data file.

With the information from the trade data and the counterparty data, we are going to pull all the market data (e.g., yield curves, FX rates, equity prices, commodity prices) that we need to price all derivatives and

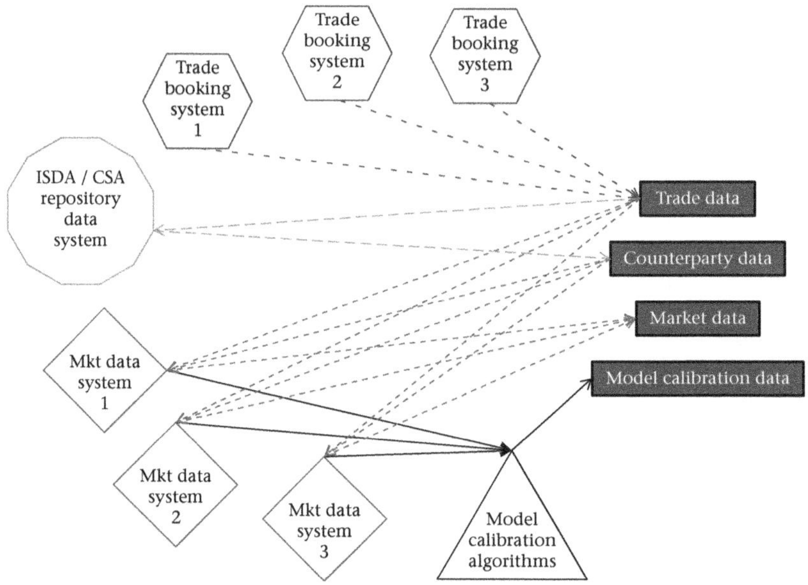

Figure 18.3 Overall illustration of the process needed to generate the input data for an XVA system

model collateral. This process will deliver a Market Data file with all the required information. This file should contain a snapshot of "today's" market.

Finally, we are going to stochastically evolve into the future many market risk factors, and for that we need the calibration of the models we are going to use. Typically these are volatilities, drifts, correlations, mean reversion levels, mean reversion speeds, jump intensities, etc. This process is typically going to deliver a Model Calibration file.

Timing: Quite easily this process can cause a bottle neck to the whole calculation. For example, in the case of a global bank, we may choose to wait for the last market to close (the US) before compiling all market data, so that all the data create a full snapshot of the markets at the close of a given day.

Unfortunately, a consequence of that is usually that we may not have enough time to run the whole XVA calculation before Asia's market opens, and hence we can only implement the newly updated system in the middle of a working day. This can lead to strange situations, like calculating a CVA price at a given time, going for a coffee, re-running the same calculation again and obtaining a different result, all because the system was updated while we went for our drink.

A way to minimise this impact, for example, can be to do three small updates, each when a group of markets close (e.g., Asia, Europe and the Middle East, Americas). The problem of this is that we will be running calculations with out-of-sync data. Another way to manage this is to run the calculation with "T+2" data (two days delayed); this avoids some issues, but obviously creates other ones.

There is no right or wrong solution to this problem of timing. It all depends in the priority of the needs the organisation has, as well as the system capability.

In any case, it can be appreciated how state-of-the-art data management, storage, and data network systems are very much needed here.

18.3.2 The Monte Carlo engine

The Monte Carlo engine is the core of the XVA system. We have discussed very extensively in this book how it works from a methodology point of view. In this section we are going to discuss it to some depth from a systems point of view.

Speed is critical in this engine. We have seen in the introductory section of this chapter how the scale of the computational problem we have is, simply, outrageous.

There are a number of technological techniques we can implement to manage this problem. They include:

1. **Parallel computing:** The most obvious technology improvement we can think of is throwing computing power at the problem. This can be achieved by splitting a full calculation job into independent sub-jobs, which are then distributed between different CPUs and computed in parallel. We have already mentioned this.

   This, being an obvious improvement, must be managed with care, as if we do not split the computing jobs intelligently, we are going to have problems. For example, if we want to integrate results, each part of the calculation must be based on exactly the same scenarios, and so they must be either shared by all CPUs, or calculated separately but identically by each of them. Another example is that the speed of a parallelised calculation has a lower bound, determined by the slowest sub-job. As a result, there is a point at which we do not improve speed no matter how many more CPUs we throw at the problem.

   The main idea to understand here is that parallel distribution of complex computations is a powerful technology, but a difficult science by itself, and as such it must be managed consciously.
2. **Vectorised languages:** Vectorised languages tend to be much faster than standard languages for the XVA's Monte Carlo calculations.[8] Tests that I have performed in this area have shown considerable improvements in computing times.

   I am far from being an IT guru, but I am told that this improvement comes from the fact that in a standard code for a Monte Carlo simulation, you are constantly creating loops inside loops. Each time a new instance of a loop is created or closed, memory needs to be allocated or deallocated. This is very time consuming. If we are doing the same calculation over and over again inside each loop, which is what a Monte Carlo simulation does, what we can do is allocate all the memory in one step (when we create the multidimensional variable), and then execute the calculations in each point of the variable in a more time-effective manner.

   The fact is that these type of languages seem to offer a very good optimisation tool for Monte Carlo simulations, so they should be considered, if possible, when building an XVA system.
3. **GPU Computing:** At the time of writing this book, I have been a number of times in conversations discussing XVA calculations with GPUs (Graphic Processing Units), as opposed to the standard CPUs. Simplifying things somehow, GPUs are like CPUs that are optimised to repeat the same operation over and over again, which is what we do in a Monte Carlo simulation. Reportedly, the speed improvements could be a few orders of magnitude.

   A number of Tier-1 financial institutions are implementing calculations in GPU farms. However, one of the main problems in this respect is that the Monte Carlo engine needs to be re-coded to enjoy the benefits, also that the GPU languages are still somewhat underdeveloped and that software and hardware maintenance is somehow costly. In spite of that, there have been a number of reported successful implementations.

   In any case, the key message here is that, if the reader is serious about building a state-of-the-art XVA system, GPU processing should be looked into, at least.

18.4 Save-and-use vs. on-the-fly calculation

One of the key decisions when we build a counterparty risk system is whether we implement a "save-and-use" approach or an "on-the-fly" architecture, as illustrated in Figure 18.4. This is so important that it deserves a section by itself in this chapter.

Basically, there are two ways we can set up an XVA system:

1. **Save-and-Use:** On the one hand, we can run a full portfolio calculation periodically, save all the results and, then, re-use them as needed. In this set-up, first we need to decide on the time steps for the calculation and on the number of scenarios. Then, after every portfolio run, we are going to save all the values of the risk factors *and* the prices of all derivatives in the portfolio in every scenario and time step. That is, for each risk factor and derivative we save a grid that contains the values of the risk factor and the derivative prices in the simulation. It is also quite useful to save a grid with the prices of each netting set, which is simply the sum of the pricing grids of the trades that it composed of.

   If we need to do an intra-day calculation adding a new trade, all we have to do is create its pricing grid by pricing the trade with the already saved relevant risk factors, add the new pricing grid to the netting set grid and, finally, recalculate the risk profiles and risk metrics.

   If we want to see the risk impact of removing a trade, all we have to do is remove that trade from the netting set, sum up prices per scenario and netting set, and recalculate the risk profiles or, alternatively, we can add the trade we want to remove to the netting set, but multiplying its pricing grid by -1, and then calculate the risk profiles and risk metrics as usual.

   Also, in some cases, we can estimate sensitivities by intelligently operating in the risk factor or pricing grids, without having to re-calculate everything.
2. **On-the-Fly:** On the other hand, we can have a system that recalculates everything necessary whenever we need a new calculation. We are going to do a full calculation daily and, then, any new netting set calculations are re-run when needed.

Each approach has positives and negatives. The *save-and-use* approach obviously optimises total computational effort, as we do not re-calculate things that we do not have to. However, on the flip side of it, we are quite stuck with the system: we cannot increase the number of scenarios if we'd like a high resolution calculation, or we cannot add new time buckets to the calculation. This can be an important limitation in

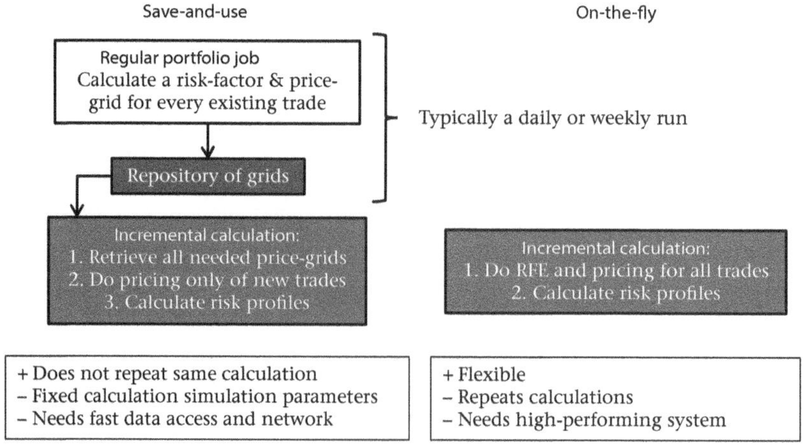

Figure 18.4 Illustration of the difference between save-and-use and on-the-fly architecture in XVA systems

some cases. Also, in an ideal system all the risk factors and pricing grids are calculated daily, but sometimes that is not possible; I know, for example, of organisations that do the full portfolio calculation weekly over the weekend and incremental runs daily.

The strengths of an *on-the-fly* system is that an analyst has a lot of flexibility in the calculation, as he or she is not constrained by pre-existing set-ups. For example, he may be interested in calculating risk profiles on some special dates, he may want to have a very accurate calculation that can be achieved by increasing the number of scenarios, he may want to study the impact of changing some parameters like volatilities, correlations, etc. All this is easily done in this set-up, as everything is calculated from the ground up every time. However, on the flip side, we need ultra-fast systems to be able to enjoy all this flexibility.

Technology wise, by contrast, in the save-and-use approach we are mainly going to need good and fast storage and networks systems, while in the on-the-fly approach we are also going to need super-fast processing systems.

I have worked extensively in both environments and each has its positives and negatives, but there isn't a general right or wrong approach in this respect. Which architecture is optimal depends on the aims of the organisation, budget, and available resources.

18.5 Internal development vs. third-party systems

Another central question that every organisation has to face when setting up an XVA system is whether to develop the system internally, or to buy an off-the-shelf third-party vendor system. Similarly to the core architecture of the system just described, there isn't a general right or wrong answer to this question, it is very specific to each organisation.

The positives of internal development is that given that we create things ourselves, we have full control over the methodologies and, in general, on the development process. The integration with existing systems should be best managed, as things are developed within them. However, on the negative side, given the complexity of an XVA system, these projects can be very political in an organisation, so internal development can become slow.

Regarding third-party systems, the positive is that things can be quite clean: you agree to a piece of development, a price, and you get what you pay for on time or, if not, penalties apply. This framework can be nice and simple to work with in that sense. The hardest piece of work in this architecture is the systems integration, the "piping", but getting the system up and running can be pretty fast. Also, we may leverage from existing past experience from other financial institutions that is embedded within the system we are buying.

On the flip side, in a third-party system we are stuck with what the vendor has; we may have some influence regarding future developments, but only to some extent. Also, the "piping" work that we need to do may be quite heavy, and upgrades to systems could be also project intense on our side. Finally, although we know what sales processes we want, may not really get what we thought we were getting.

I have worked a lot in both environments, and again there isn't any general winner. It all depends on the aims and the modus operandi of the institution.

18.6 Project management

In reality, when developing an XVA system, most of the time we invest on it is spent in making sure that things happen: building documents, chasing people, replying to emails, dealing with regulators, submissions to approval committees, etc. The list is endless. For this reason, good project management is crucial.

The first thing that needs to be said is that this topic tends to be neglected by technical professionals quite often that have a natural bias towards solving technical problems. This is why more and more firms are employing project management teams to help manage these projects efficiently and deal with the various teams involved.

The size and scale of XVA projects in financial institutions has increased substantially in the past few years. Before 2008, the interaction between front office and risk was somewhat limited. Often, they would have different systems that would replicate each other's work. Counterparty credit risk was seen as a secondary subject, and even within the risk organisation, different functions were sometimes replicating efforts. That is no longer the case. Front office is now strongly impacted on by counterparty risk calculations through CVA, the capital calculation, and by the trading limits set by risk. Also, front office now need a whole XVA valuation framework that affects quite strongly traditionally middle and back office functions. The risk department needs to be well aware of the credit calculations and hedging done by the front office, valuations need to include XVA, every department in the organisation is impacted on by regulatory requirements, etc.

Each organisation is different, with its culture and history, so we cannot build a detailed project management structure that suits perfectly all firms, but there are some common features that can be outlined for quantitative development projects.

18.6.1 RFE model development

When developing an RFE model, the following steps should be considered:

1. **Materiality:** The first thing that needs to be understood is the materiality of the project. This can be measured by the number of trades, number of netting sets, EPE or PFE impact, CVA impact, capital impact, etc. In fact, this analysis should be done before deciding the priority of a project precisely because this should be one of the main drivers of the decision. Other factors impacting on the priority of a project include regulatory requirements, senior management's view, complexity of a project and resources available.
2. **Trade Analysis:** We need to understand what kind of trades are affected by this RFE. Vanilla or exotic? Swap-like or option-like products? In this way we can assess, for example, to what extent we also need an implied volatility model, what dependency structures with other risk factors are needed to be modeled, etc.
3. **Computational Impact:** This is different to building an RFE model for around ten risk factors (e.g., a few special equities) than for a few thousand of them (e.g., all credit spread curves in the bank). If this is required for a few risk factors, we may be able to build, if needed, a very precise model, but for several thousand of risk factors we may have to use computational approximations and shortcuts; otherwise, the system may not be able to cope with the calculation.
4. **Risk Factor Analysis:** It is very important to analyse the risk factor data. We need to look at how smooth its evolution is; does it show jumps or spikes? What is its typical volatility, skew, and kurtosis? Are changes absolute or proportional in magnitude (i.e., normal or log-normal)? What is the dependency behaviour with other risk factors? If we are modelling a curve, what is the dependency behaviour within the curve? Can we model it with a few principal components? This, being always important, is central for RFE models that lead to risk management and regulatory capital calculations.

5. **Model Design:** With all this information, we can design a model for the risk factor. We need to decide what type of model is suitable and consider different alternatives. A model that is flexible and able to be enhanced in the future, should the needs of the institution change, could save the bank significant time and resources. Documenting alternative models that were considered but not chosen is essential; this could be a request by regulators, internal audit, model validation as well as help to educate future members of the team.
6. **Prototype Implementation:** The first thing that we need to do is build the model in a prototype environment. In my experience, something as simple as spread sheets can be a most appropriate tool for this. The reason is that you can *see* the numbers being created, so tracking down errors is easiest, and the graphic interface, the plots, is very good and easy to use. The price that you have to pay is that the programming language is quite limiting, but in my personal experience it is worth the effort in this prototype stage. However, there are many other good alternatives to this to suit different tastes.
7. **Prototype Calibration:** We have already mentioned that a model is not only a set of equations; it also comprises their calibration methodology. This methodology needs to be implemented too in a prototype environment to avoid surprises further down the line.
8. **Testing:** Every model needs to be tested. Model validation will do an official independent testing, but the developer should also do a thorough testing of it, trying to replicate what model validation will do. This can include backtesting against realised past values. Chapter 17 explained in detail the process of backtesting so we will not elaborate further here.
9. **Model Benchmark:** Also, it is a good sanity check to compare the results of the model with those obtained by other alternative models, especially if there are other for the same risk factor in the organisation, or if it challenges the status quo. When that is the case, this is often required by model validation, audit, or regulators.
10. **Design Cycle:** Obviously, the previous steps are not done in isolation. In practice, there will be a number of iterations of the model at design stage until it passes the testing requirements and how it compares to other models is well understood. Once it passes all the testing requirements, we can proceed to the next stage.
11. **Development in UAT:** Now we need to develop the model in the actual production system where it will be finally used. Obviously, it needs to be done in a User Acceptance Testing (UAT) environment.
12. **Testing in UAT:** Once developed, it needs to be tested very thoroughly, challenging all the possible inputs to the model, and comparing results with the prototype version of the model. In this case, it is most useful if the architecture of the prototype version and the UAT version are the same; in this way, it is quite easy to track down differences in output and find errors.
13. **Organisation Impact Test:** Often, when a new RFE model is developed, there are no trades that may be using another version of that RFE in the Monte Carlo engine. When this is so, there is no "before" scenario in it to compare the new RFE against. However, if there are already pricers available that will be using this risk factor, then the risk of the portfolio should be run with and without the new risk factor model, and an impact analysis should be done. This is therefore a necessary step only in cases where a new RFE model adds a new risk factor to an existing trade type.

    Examples include a volatility RFE which will impact on equity options that were previously modelled using simulated equity prices but constant volatilities, or an FX RFE that will impact on an interest rate swap in a different currency to the institution's base currency.
14. **Go-live:** Finally, the RFE will go live. It should be in "watch" mode for at least one week, in order to quickly detect any errors.

18.6.2 Pricing model development

When developing a pricing model, the first rule that must be always preserved is that it must be completely split from the RFE model. The pricer must get a set of risk factor values and provide a price for the trade without modifying the risk factors. If these two functions (RFE and pricing) are not well separated and encapsulated in the code, I can guarantee that it will create an overhead of resources in the future.

The following steps should be considered when designing a pricing model:

1. **Materiality:** Similarly to RFE models, before we launch the project, we need to understand the materiality of the pricer we want to build. This can be assessed by the number of trades, number of netting sets, EPE or PFE impact, CVA impact, capital impact, etc. It is a good idea to use a number of these metrics, as it is quite usual that certain trades are, for example, traded frequently, but have a limited impact on capital, CVA, or other exposure metrics due to netting effects, or because notionals tend to be small.
2. **Computational Impact:** Again, sometimes we will need to build pricers for trades that are rare but very important because they have huge notionals, and other times for trades that are very frequent but with small notionals. In each case the computational impact is different; we should take this into account. If, for example, the number of trades is small but the trades are large in size, we may decide to develop a slow pricer that is very precise, though that cannot apply in the opposite case.
3. **Model Design:** Always, when we build a pricer for an XVA system, the organisation already has a pricer for its valuation and hedging. In principle, this should be the starting point for the pricer we want to build.

   As said, a key difference between this existing method and the one we need in our XVA system is that, now, we need to call that pricer around 1,000,000 times in each calculation run, so our pricers need to be ultra fast.

   If the existing methodology is fast enough for our purposes, there is no need to reinvent the wheel and we should use that methodology; that is rarely the case, though. If it is not fast enough, we must simplify it so that, at the end, the exposure profiles are not affected, or affected only in a limited way.
4. **Prototype Implementation:** Once we have decided which model to use, or the set of models to test, we need to build the pricer in a prototype environment where we can compare different model caveats and perform tests.
5. **Speed Benchmarking:** As already mentioned several times, computational speed is key in XVA analytics. For this reason we want to have an idea of how fast or slow the new pricer is. In order to do this, we should compare the speed of the new pricer to other pricers that already exist in the counterparty risk system and that are frequently used. A good benchmark could be a ten-year interest rate swap or a Black–Scholes option pricer. Note that these benchmarks must be all done under the same computational conditions.
6. **Impact on Computing Effort:** With the previous measurement, and with the number of trades that will be calling this new pricer, we will be able to estimate the impact on the overall computing time.
7. **Pricer Testing:** In the prototype environment we should be able to compare the output of the new pricing methodology to be used in the XVA system to the pricer already existing in the organisation for standard valuation purposes. We should be able to understand what are the differences, when they occur, estimate how they may affect the final output, etc.
8. **Design Cycle:** In this case as well, there may be a design cycle by which different caveats for the pricer are considered until the final decision is taken.[9]
9. **Development in UAT:** Once the decision is taken, the pricer should be developed for the production system.

10. **Testing in UAT:** Finally, the pricer needs to be tested for the production system. At this stage it will be tested in isolation and compared with the prototype implementation. As a result, the closer the code architecture of both implementations is, the easier the comparison will be. It is important to do checks for a very wide range of input combinations, focusing on special cases such as that inputs are equal to zero, correlations are equal to 1, etc.
11. **Organisation Impact Test:** Finally, the whole book of trades will be run with and without the new pricer and an impact analysis will be done, seeing what netting sets get mostly affected, by how much, etc. Any large change needs to be well understood.
12. **Go-live:** When all tests have been passed, we are ready to go live.

18.6.3 Beyond RFE and pricing models

As we can see now, the development of models for XVA systems is anything but simple. This is a consequence of both the complexity of the calculation, the systems, and the wide range of interactions with several parts of the financial institution.

All the steps described here need to be considered when developing a model. In my experience, if one or several steps are skipped, it will most likely backfire by necessitating the having to come back and make changes after a lot of work has been done, or by having a system that lacks robustness and, hence, needing a lot of maintenance.

Based on my experience again, a key success element is the close interaction of the model designer with the system developers. The closer that interaction is the better all projects will flow, both in terms of execution time and quality of the final product.

Documentation: One part of a project execution that has not been been mentioned yet, but that deserves a comment at the very least, is the submission of documentation, for several different purposes. In practice, when working in a financial institution, that can take a significant amount of time. Several layers of documentation may need to be prepared, depending on the scope of the project and on the firm's culture and size. Sometimes it needs to be very technical, sometimes at a high level; it may also be required for a different purpose: for senior management, for regulators, for model validation, for IT developers, for technical users. The key success element here is to understand how the audience thinks, and use their language in the documentation.

Regarding submission for approvals, there are usually three levels: model validation revision, internal audit approval, and regulatory approval. They may be needed to a small and large extent depending on the final use of the model, the internal policies, and the standpoint of the regulator.

Another typical layer of documentation is the specification documents for systems or IT developers. Good quality documentation is key here; it is very common that a project gets delayed because of lack of proper communication between different parties. One would expect that internal development would be more efficient than through a third-party vendor system as you can have more control over the whole process. In my experience, the contrary can be true too. When dealing with a third-party vendor the specification documents constitute a contract in practice, and so both parties have a clear short-term incentive to avoid misunderstandings. The best way to ensure that communication does not have any misunderstanding is (i) the methodology team writes a specification document; (ii) the systems or IT team rewrite what they have understood of the specification document, in their own language; and (iii) the project only starts when the methodology team agrees to every word of the document they receive. This may seem an overhead of work, but in my experience it saves indeed a lot of time in the long run.

A final layer of documentation is user documentation. This must be very simple, with a "quick start guide", and it must use the language of the users.

In any case, this overhead of work can be very time consuming but it is very important, as we all want to have our models nicely approved, delivered on time, within budget, and with a high degree of user acceptance. The key to success here is to work *with* the audience, to speak their language.

Data quality: Another point that needs to be highlighted is the importance of good data quality of the model inputs. There is a very large range of data that is required for a model to be able to provide accurate results: trade data, collateral data, market data, counterparty static data, legal agreement data. Thorough data checks need to be performed on a regular basis in order to ensure all data is accurate. Even the most sophisticated model will not be useful without correct input parameters and therefore it is essential to invest in a robust data quality process.

A practical approach: As the reader can see, in reality the majority of the time spent in an XVA analytics development project is spent on non-glamorous tasks. In practice, tasks like measuring materiality, improving computational time, building documentation, communicating with the several parties involved in the whole process, take most of the time.

Without managing them effectively, the project will not go very far.

19 Central Clearing and the Future of Derivatives

We have seen in this book that the financial industry in general, and the market of derivatives, is changing profoundly. This process should be welcome as, if managed well, it can create a very solid banking sector, which is one of the most important pillars of modern societies. However, as in every transformation, it must be handled with care too, to avoid creating the seeds for other problems in the future.

One of the most important consequences of the 2008 events is that the G20 governments decided to push very strongly for central clearing in the derivatives market. In their 2009 Pittsburgh summit it was stated that "all standardised OTC derivative contracts should be traded on exchanges or electronic trading platforms, where appropriate, and cleared through central counterparties by end-2012 at the latest. OTC derivative contracts should be reported to trade repositories. Non-centrally cleared contracts should be subject to higher capital requirements". Perhaps the implementation of this mandate is taking longer than originally expected given the complexity of the task, but the agenda persists and is intended to remain for the foreseeable future.

In parallel, another most important consequence of the 2008 events is the end of a 35-year-long macroeconomic credit cycle. This is also having a major impact on the financial industry.

In this final chapter, we are going to analyse what is the future of the financial sector, with a special focus on the business of OTC derivatives, central clearing, and the economic environment banks are most likely to operate under.

19.1 Central counterparties

As said, the 2008 market events generated in policy-makers and regulators a strong view that the over-the-counter derivative market should be steered towards clearing as many trades as possible through central counterparties (CCPs). The reason behind this was very well illustrated by the Lehman Brother's default: its exposures via bilateral agreement caused havoc in the financial system, while the losses in the trades it had cleared with CCPs were managed relatively easily.

This idea of central clearing may seem to reduce risk at first glance, but in reality it goes deeper than that. Instead, what it does is transform counterparty risk in form and shape. It reduces some risks, but creates other ones. In this section we are going to review how CCPs operate, their role, how to calculate CCP exposures, and what the implications to the financial industry are.

19.1.1 Risk transformation through central counterparties

The idea of clearing is centred around the concept of *novation*. Let's say that two institutions agree to enter into an OTC derivative contract. When this trade is cleared, a third party (the CCP) comes onto the scene by intermediating between the counterparties. When that happens, the CCP becomes the counterparty for each of the institutions. As a result, the counterparty risk that each institution originally had with each other is transferred to the CCP as the new counterparty that each side of the deal is seeing. This is illustrated in Figure 19.1.

Each of the institutions that can clear directly through a CCP are called *members*. CCPs change quite deeply the bilateral connections in the market that arise from derivative trading. This is illustrated in Figure 19.2. It can be seen how the network of interconnections between counterparties becomes much cleaner when a CCP comes onto the stage.

It must be noted that, given the structure of the CCP, it carries no market risk at all, as every derivative has its long and short position with two members.

For an institution to become a member of a CCP it must meet certain criteria, that typically can only be met by tier-1 or some tier-2 investment banks. This set-up may seem to leave out of clearing an important part of the derivatives markets (e.g., smaller banks, asset managers, hedge funds, corporates), but this limitation is solved by the clearing brokerage service that CCP members can offer. In this set-up, a non-member can clear a trade through a CCP via a member, as illustrated in Figure 19.3.

Most often CCP members will offer a clearing service to their clients, for which they may charge a fee.

CCPs as risk reshapers: At first glance, CCPs bring a number of obvious benefits:

- **Reduction of Counterparty Risk:** CCPs should reduce counterparty risk in two ways. Firstly, if they are managed correctly, in a conservative way, their default probability should be smaller than those of commercial banks. We are going to see in Section 19.1.2 how this low default probability is achieved.

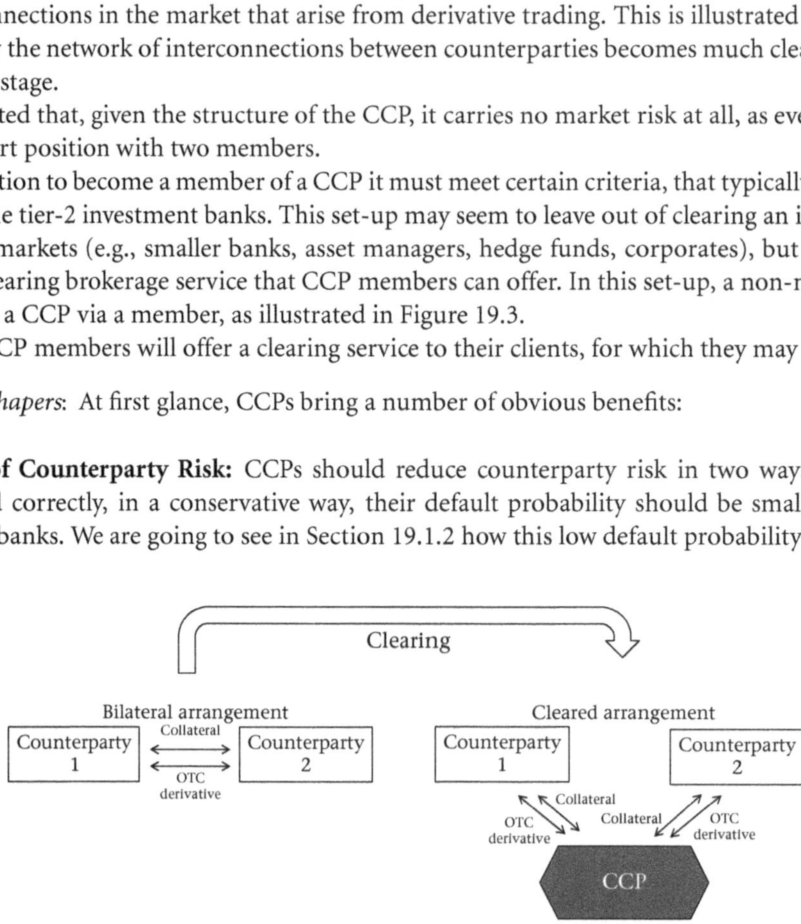

Figure 19.1 Illustration of the concept of novation that takes place when a derivative is centrally cleared

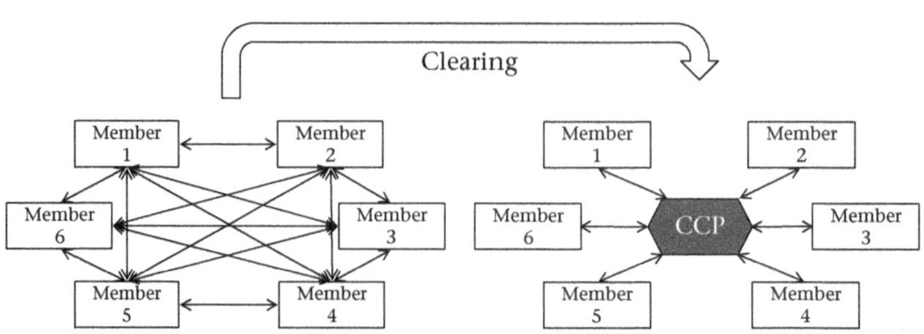

Figure 19.2 Illustration of counterparty risk interconnections with and without central clearing

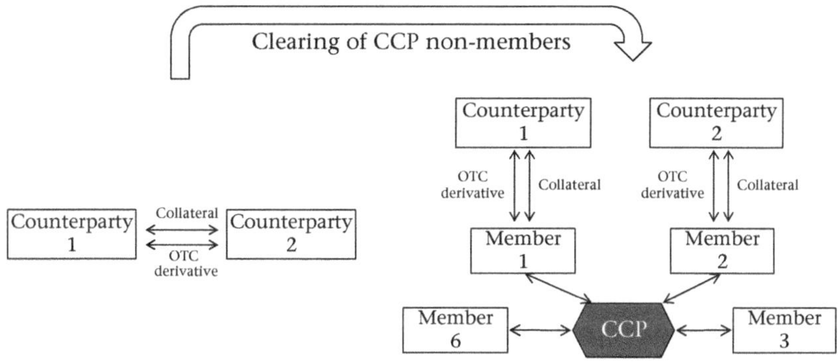

Figure 19.3 Illustration of the clearing arrangement with CCP non-members

Secondly, the CCP can theoretically enjoy the benefits of *multilateral* netting, as opposed to *bilateral* netting, which is what we have seen so far in the book. Let's say that three banks have interest rates swaps in place so that they completely net each other off in a triangular way. If all swaps are arranged as bilateral trades, each bank will have two swaps with each of the other two banks, which don't net each other off completely. However, if cleared through the same CCP, the CCP can enjoy the benefit of the triangular netting, hence reducing the total counterparty risk exposure that the overall system has.

- **Barrier to Counterparty Risk Domino Effect:** One of the problems that the global financial system faced in 2008 was that the network of connections that banks had with each other propagated defaults (or near defaults) very quickly across the financial industry. If one institution defaulted, all other institutions that were waiting a payment from the defaulted institution became at risk of defaulting. Subsequently the ones expecting payments from the second-layer institutions at risk, also became at risk, etc. This domino effect brought the interbank market to a near freeze.

  Central clearing of derivatives should reduce this risk, as the CCPs will act as shock absorbers in the event of one of its member's defaulting, hence reducing the impact of a default to the financial system.
- **Enhanced Market Information:** Another significant concern of the industry in 2008 was that, if one counterparty defaulted, the market did not know what was each institution's exposure to that counterparty. This phenomenon is sometimes called *asymmetry of information.* Also, regulators were unable to understand where the risks were lying because there was no central repository of derivatives data. CCPs help in this regard as they are centralised points of trading and, thus, trade information can be managed naturally.
- **Orderly Default Procedure:** In the event that one CCP member defaults, the CCP will be in a position to reallocate to the surviving members, close out, or hedge the open positions left by the defaulted member. In fact, CCPs have clear rules and procedures for this, typically via an auction process.

However, central clearing creates some risk:

- **Potential Increase of Exposure:** Duffie and Zhu published an interesting piece of work [35] in which they show that "adding a CCP for a class of derivatives... reduces netting efficiency, leading to an increase in average exposure to counterparty default. Clearing two or more different classes of derivatives in separate CCPs always increases counterparty exposure relative to clearing the combined set of derivatives in a single CCP".

The theoretical reduction in exposure achieved via multilateral netting may only be achieved when the CCP space is highly concentrated (i.e., very few CCPs) and when they clear a wide range of derivative types.

In other words, this negative effect of increased total exposure can only disappear if (i) CCPs can clear all or most trades in all asset classes (quiet difficult if not impossible) and (ii) if there are very few CCPs, which leads us to the next point.

- **Concentration Risk:** One of the basic principles of managing risk is diversification. However, a clearing house increases concentration risk in the industry. A CCP is considered unlikely to default; however, if it defaults we will definitely be seeing a financial catastrophe.
- **Decreased Incentives for Risk Management best Practices:** By clearing all trades to a CCP, effectively an institution is delegating the problem of counterparty risk to the clearing house. Consequently, the incentive it has to understand and manage that risk strongly diminishes and, hence, those institutions that are worst at managing risk receive a relative competitive advantage. This, in addition to a moral hazard, this can create an overall financial industry with lower risk management standards.

It is often said that CCPs reduce systemic risk. Here, systemic risk refers to the domino effect and the asymmetry of information that can amplify credit problems in the financial system, as we saw in 2008 when the whole financial industry came to a near-halt. In the event of a large bank defaulting, a CCP will act as a shock absorber so that the negative impact will be less severe to the financial system. In that sense, it does reduce systemic risk, as it reduces the probability of a system halt. *However*, if for whatever reason a CCP is not able to absorb one of the shocks it might receive, or if it faces an internal problem that constrains its ability to act, the impact to the financial system will be unparalleled.

Expressed in quantitative terms, a central clearing arrangement creates tail risk. It creates events that are highly unlikely (a CCP defaulting), but that will have an unimaginable impact on the economy should they happen.

This is why it is a deep mistake to think that central clearing *reduces* counterparty risk. What it does is to *change its shape.*

19.1.2 CCP structure and implications

Let's move on and understand a bit more about how CCPs operate.

The loss waterfall: What happens in a CCP when a member defaults can be quite complicated, but by simplifying things a bit it can be seen as having a cascade of layers of shock abortion:

1. **Defaulted Member's Margin:** We have already seen in Chapter 4 the concept of independent amount and collateral posting. When dealing with a CCP, those things are usually called *initial margin* and *variation margin.* A member of a CCP will always have an initial margin to post that should cover for the gap risk it creates in the CCP. Also, the CCP and the member will exchange a variation margin as the portfolio value changes, to ensure it is always sufficiently collateralised. This will basically follow the same method as a CSA with zero thresholds and daily remargining.
2. **Defaulted Member's Reserve Fund Contributions:** For a financial institution to become a member of the CCP, it needs to contribute to the reserve fund. The margin that each member posts will account for losses in the event of their default up to a certain confidence level, typically 99%.[1] When stress market conditions result in default losses above the set confidence level, further losses will be covered by the defaulted member's contributions to the reserve fund.

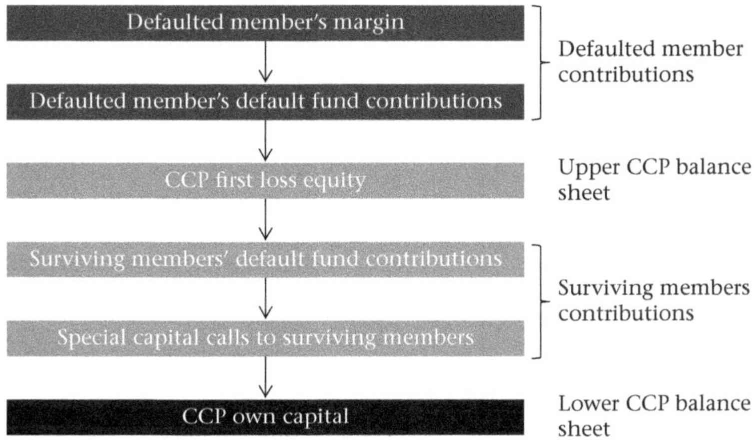

Figure 19.4 Illustration of the cascade of losses in a CCP when a member defaults

3. **CCP First Loss Equity:** If the defaulted member's contributions are not enough, then the CCP will use some of its equity.
4. **Surviving Members' Reserve Fund Contributions:** If the sum of the above is not enough, then the CCP will start pulling resources from the remainder of the reserve fund. At this point the CCP starts mutualising losses, as even the surviving members that never interacted with the defaulted entity will start paying for the default losses. This can be seen, in fact, as an insurance policy that each member takes against being massively hit by a default.
5. **Special Capital Calls:** If the reserve fund is exhausted, the CCP could make additional capital calls to its surviving members.
6. **CCP Capital:** Like any other financial institution, a CCP will have its own capital that should be calculated as directed by internal policies and regulators.

This cascade of loss absorption should make a clearing house a default-remote entity. However, it must always be remembered that default-remote does not mean "impossible" to default; a widespread thought that large banks could not fail was one of the causes of the financial crisis in 2008. In fact, Basel III recognises this by assigning a risk weight of 2% to trades that are cleared through a central counterparty, which is basically considering a CCP as a super-AAA entity, as can be implied from Figure 19.5.

Level of conservativeness: A CCP must find a balance between the level of collateral and reserve fund it collects, and the funding cost that it causes to its members.

On the one hand, if the level of financial buffer it holds is too high, it could discourage its members to clear their trades through the CCP via the opportunity cost of the collateral posted and the reserve fund contributions by the member. However, on the other hand, if that buffer is not sufficient, it will not be able to absorb potential future losses. A CCP and the CCP's regulatory framework must find the right balance between these two extremes. This is not an easy task.

Also, it must be considered that the more assets the CCP absorbs from the system as collateral, the safer the CCP would appear to be, but if taken to an extreme it could absorb too much liquidity and, actually, cause a liquidity crisis in the financial system. For this reason, it is important that CCPs are run so that in turbulent

Rating	PD	RW
AAA	0.03%	22.92%
AAA	0.03%	22.92%
A	0.06%	32.81%
BBB	0.22%	62.09%
BB	1.10%	113.04%
B	5.58%	164.59%
CCC	28.23%	240.38%

Loss Given Default:	40%	
Maturity:		5 yrs

Figure 19.5 Typical default probability and risk weight (RW) for capital calculation, assuming loss-given-default of 40% and a portfolio maturity of five years, with a regulatory PD floor of 0.03%

times the temptation is avoided of asking for too much extra margin to preserve their safety, as by doing so liquidity will be removed out of the system when it is most needed.

Margins for a member should be calculated to cover the gap risk of the CCP. Typically, a 99% confidence level and a five-day liquidity horizon can be chosen. In CSA terminology, this means an MPR of five days, as members are supposed to be large institutions whose default will be noticed immediately. However, these five days should be increased if there are any liquidity concerns in the member's portfolio of trades or collateral. This calculation should be done with market parameters assuming the default of the member (e.g., stressed volatilities).

The financial resources the CCP has should be sufficient to withstand, at the very least, the failure of its largest member, though it is advisable to consider the case of two or more firms defaulting in a short period of time. Indeed, Basel's recommendation is that a CCP should maintain enough resources to absorb the failure of its two largest members in extreme but plausible conditions [13].

The CCP's, resources should be able to cover for the losses from the defaulted members and enable normal operations with the surviving members. The reserve fund is used when we are already in a, typically, one in a hundred scenario,[2] and so it should be calculated via stress scenario techniques, where all market variables, including volatilities, correlations, and liquidity, are stressed to extreme values. Another technique to calculate the reserve funds needed is via credit portfolio theory (see Chapter 7) with a confidence level of a super AAA entity, as considered by Basel III.

Collateral segregation and rehypothication: A CCP will typically accept collateral in the form of cash and high-quality securities, like AAA rated government bonds. As a result, it will have to account for the riskiness of the collateral by simulating it in a collateral algorithm. If that is not possible, then a haircut should be applied, but we must remember the inaccuracy that this produces in the risk calculations mentioned in Chapter 4.

For a CCP to be a rock-solid shock-absorber entity, it must be able to withstand very large market shocks in a way that, most importantly, does not transmit the financial distress to other institutions. This creates another balancing problem to CCPs.

On the one hand, a CCP should ideally keep in-house all the financial resources it holds.[3] By doing this it will remain totally independent of external financial institutions and increase its capacity as a shock-absorber. However, doing this will be very expensive in terms of opportunity cost, and subsequently be expensive for the clearing members to the extent that it can become uneconomical for them to clear trades. Also, this strategy can cause unwanted liquidity constraints in the market.

On the other hand, it could reinvest most of its resources so it becomes cheaper to run, even if at the expense of decreasing its capability to absorb financial distress.

A fine balance between these two poles must be reached. As said, Basel recommends that a CCP should hold enough resources to withstand the failure of its two largest members.

Type of products: One of the prerequisites to clear a product is that it must be standardised. This should not be a problem with a number of vanilla swaps or options, where there is market consensus as to how they are structured.

However, one of the key elements of the over-the-counter derivatives market is that they can be tailored to the need of the client. This has been, in fact, a key component of the growth and success of that market.

The demand for tailor-made structured and exotic trades is there because those trades fulfil an important hedging and risk management role to the individual users and the overall economy. They are excellent risk transferring and management products, if dealt with correctly. Consequently, they are intrinsically good. However, bilateral trades should be obviously priced at a premium compared to a theoretical equivalent one that had been cleared as a result of the extra risk they carry. This was depicted in Figure 15.4.

How much exposure is reduced with a CCP? We have said that, in principle, a CCP should reduce the overall exposure in the market via multilateral netting. However, an in-depth analysis of this indicates that the benefits may not be straightforward to achieve.

For example, let's say that an institution has traded a portfolio of swaps with an exposure of $10 and a book of FX trades with an exposure of −$8, all under the same netting agreement with a counterparty, so that the overall exposure under bilateral conditions is $2. If these swaps are cleared, they may be subject to multilateral netting in the CCP, but from the institutions standpoint it leaves an exposure of $8 in the FX book, hence increasing the bilateral exposure.

As already said, Duffie and Zhu expanded this argument into a theoretical model indicating that multilateral netting may not be as achievable as may appear at first glance [35].

As a result, to really benefit from one of the main advantages of CCPs, multilateral netting, we also increase its biggest problem: concentration risk.

Concentration risk: We have touched on this already, but it is so important that we should emphasise it. The current CCP environment has around 30 CCPs, but only a handful of them dominate the market.[4] From the exposure reduction point of view, this high concentration is good, as said. However, having only, say, five dominant CCPs in the world is equivalent to having five power plants to produce the majority of the electricity in the world; it feels very far from a low risk strategy.

19.1.3 Calculation of exposures

Let's see how to calculate exposures from both relevant points of view: from the CCP and from the member's standpoint.

From a CCP standpoint: A CCP should first calculate the exposure profile up to the maturity of the portfolio it has with the member. Its main concern is from a risk management standpoint, as opposed to pricing, so it should consider either PFE or CESF risk metrics at a high confidence level. Basel suggests 95–99% as the confidence level [58]. Real-world calibration should be used. Also, the risk metric should ideally account for tail risk, so CESF is better than PFE. The initial margin could be the maximum of the risk profile over the life of the portfolio. This is illustrated in Figure 19.6.

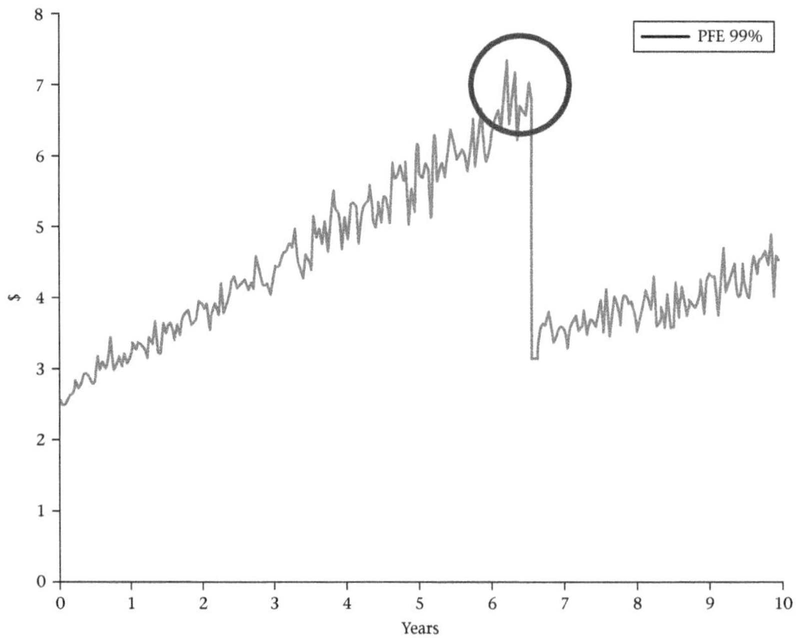

Figure 19.6 Illustration of an Initial Margin calculation

It must be noted that the exposure profile should be calculated as the exposure *subject* to default. We should expect that when a member defaults there will be some degree of market distress, especially if the member is a SIFI.[5] This should be reflected in the calculation. Also, right/wrong-way risk must be taken into account to consider dependencies between the value of the book of trades and the potential default of the member;[6] we have dedicated the whole of Chapter 10 to this, and we show that this effect can both increase or decrease the exposure. It is important to consider both sides of the effect, as otherwise the initial margin charged will not be reflecting the true economic risks.

Based on the example of Figure 19.6, one could argue that a CCP does not need to charge $7 of initial margin (the profile peak) based on a potential default in six years; it could charge $2.5, which is the gap risk "today". In this regard, the described methodology of charging for the peak exposure during the life of the trade can be seen as too conservative. As an alternative, a CCP could calculate its initial margin periodically (e.g., yearly), and change it *dynamically* only for the peak of the profile during the relevant period (e.g., first year). This, in many cases, will result in a lower margin requirement and will therefore make the CCP appear more competitive. However, using this methodology the CCP may have to increase the initial margin requirement when a member is going through credit problems, hence contributing to the problem itself.

This creates an important dilemma for the CCP and the regulators: CCPs operate as companies for profit. That set-up optimises performance in many ways, but a CCP may be tempted to have an aggressive initial margin policy (e.g., charge $2.5 in the example) to capture more business, potentially endangering its long term viability and the stability of the financial system. CCPs and regulators must deal with this matter with care.

Regarding variation margin, this should be calculated daily, if not intra-daily. The portfolio of derivatives should be priced and the variation margin should be the amount that makes the value of the facility (i.e., book of trades plus accumulated variation margin) zero. The initial margin should be outside of this calculation, as it is an amount posted separately, to cover for the gap risk in the event of a member default.

From a member standpoint: In many cases, a derivatives dealer is over-collateralised with its clients (hedge funds, corporates, fund managers, etc.), as it is typically a credit strong institution compared to its clients[7] and, hence, it can demand an initial margin (or independent amount) as an extra safety cushion. However, in the case of CCPs, a derivatives dealer (the CCP member) will be under-collateralised. As a result, it has both the initial margin and its own gap risk at risk should the CCP default. This in addition to its contributions to the default fund.

To manage the credit risk the member is exposed to, it can treat the CCP as a counterparty, with a CSA with daily margining and always independent amount in favour of the counterparty (the CCP). However, it has to consider a few special features.

- We have seen that when calculating the exposure to a counterparty, we must remember that it is *subject* to default. As a result, a CCP may reduce counterparty risk because they are very unlikely to default; however, their exposure to default can be very high. Indeed, if a CCP defaults, we can be sure that the stress in the market will be unparalleled, and hence any gap risk calculation must take that into account with very stressed market volatilities, correlations, and other parameters.
- Also, in this case, we know that wrong-way risk will be a major risk component too, as a default of a CCP will most likely put at risk of default many other financial institutions.
- Finally, it will be important to control the risk to a CCP via stress and scenario testing, given that we know the potentially very large impact of a CCP defaulting in the market.

If the CCP made dynamic initial margin calls, the replication of those calls is somewhat tricky to achieve. This problem was discussed in Section 13.3.

19.2 The banking environment

As a result of the described governmental push, it is clear that the future of the world of derivatives concerns having a substantial amount of them through central clearing. This is being provoked by policy-makers with a blend of economic incentives (e.g., the risk weight of exposures with CCPs is only 2% for regulatory capital) and coercive measures (e.g., mandatory clearing).

In order to understand the future of banking and of OTC derivatives, we must analyse things in the broader context in which they operate.

The end of the credit cycle: The Western economies and the banking industry have suffered a number of crises in the past decades. However, the 2008 crises was different. What made it different was the ultra-low level of the interest rates.

Up to 2007, for decades, governments would decrease interest rates whenever an economic recession was on the way, via their central banks. By doing that more money gets into the economy via the money multiplier mechanism that banks provide (see Section 1.2) and the economy gets then activated. The vehicle for this provision of economic stimulus is the banks via the credit provision they deliver. As a result, banks have enjoyed for decades an environment with a constantly increasing monetary base (i.e., an ever increasing market size for financial services) and a consequent constant expansion of their balance sheet.

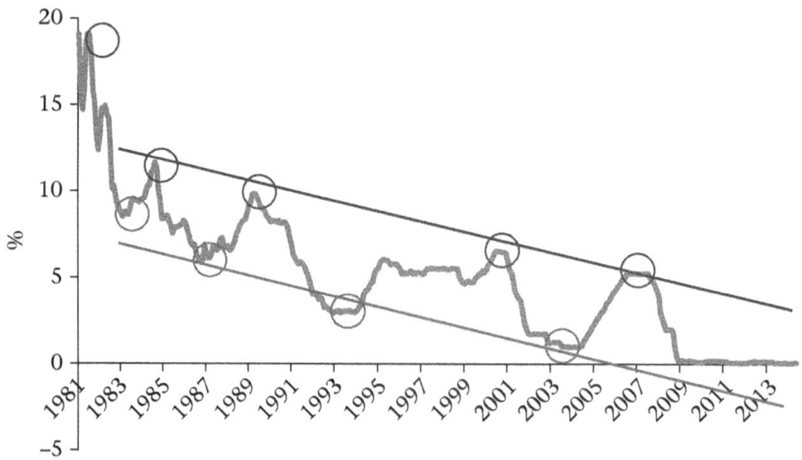

Figure 19.7 Time series of the US Effective Federal Funds Rate
Source: Federal Reserve Bank of St. Louis.

Given that banks were, basically, operating with this ongoing external impulse, the returns that the financial industry has been generating in the past few decades has been phenomenal, with only a few "hiccups" from time to time. Basically banks were the centre, the vehicle, of the Western governments' economy reflating machinery.

These so-called "business cycles" have been quite obvious in the past few decades: every few years, typically around five to ten years, governments see a crisis on the horizon, interest rates are decreased, the economy gets reactivated within a couple of years, then the rates are increased again to control inflation, and off we go with the next cycle a few years later.

However, there is a very important point to be made: the point of high interest rates in each cycle has always been lower than in the previous one. This can be clearly seen in Figure 19.7. It seems that, as interest rates are increased to avoid over-exciting the economy and to constrain inflationary pressure, there is an interest rate point that, when reached, the economy gets "choked" and central banks need to lower rates again to reactivate economic activity, to provide some fresh air. And this is the crucial point: that choking point has been lower in every cycle.

Obviously, this way of managing economic crisis works only until the fuel (interest rates) is exhausted, which is the point reached in 2008. That is why that crisis was different to any other one lived through by most of us in the past: the standard technique used by governments, via monetary policy, to manage recessionary scenarios, ran out of fuel. As a result, central banks had to come up with Quantitative Easing (QE) and other "unorthodox" measures. Governments (i.e., politicians) have been spoiled over decades into thinking that monetary policy can solve every crisis,[8] but such policy is effective only until we reach zero interest rates.

Implications: In any case, leaving aside economic policy matters that are beyond the scope of this book, the implications of this environment for the financial industry are twofold:

1. The banks are only one of several parties involved in the build-up to the 2008 crisis, not the cause of it.
2. The financial industry has to change dramatically. By this it is not meant "it would be good if it changes", it means that "it will change". In fact, it is already changing.[9]

A future of high uncertainty: It may not be possible to foresee the future but, in my view, we can be pretty sure that the future is highly unstable. This is so because common sense dictates that "unorthodox" measures tend to lead to "unorthodox" outcomes.

At the time of this book going to press, there is an intense debate about whether, when, and how some Western central banks will tighten monetary policy; i.e., increase interest rates, withdraw quantitative easing, etc. Given that the majority of the economic stimulus in the post-2008 recessive period has been monetary based, we should expect a new "choking" point like the ones we have seen in the past.

Trying to guess how that "choking" point will crystallise, and how governments and central banks will react to it, seems mission impossible, but there seems to be some degree of consensus between analysts that we may be facing a future of either high inflation or deflation. All this analysis happens while central banks are doing their best at trying to keep a low inflationary environment, but it seems that their room for error is becoming increasingly narrower, to the extent that some analysts believe it is not possible to hit the target of low inflation and good economic growth for very long [66].

In other words, we don't know where we are heading, but the chances that we are heading for a highly uncertain economic world are substantial. And this is precisely what "risk" is.

19.3 The future

Now that we understand the push that OTC derivatives are having towards central clearing, and the environment banks are going to operate under in the future, let's discuss what may be ahead of us.

Simple OTC derivatives will dominate the market: Regarding bilateral OTC derivatives, the regulatory environment has made exotic derivatives very expensive to trade from a capital standpoint. Arguably, this is good, as measuring the risk of those trades requires repricing it thousands or millions of times on an ongoing basis, which is not readily possible given the current technology. As a result, given that we cannot measure their risk well, we'd better assume they are very risky. This creates a strong shift in the derivatives market towards vanilla trades that can be better risk-managed.

In addition, this shift is further emphasised by the fact that those vanilla trades will tend to go away from bilateral agreements and move into central counterparties, hence decreasing further their regulatory capital cost.

All this together makes a clear business case in favour of simple OTC derivatives, unless new technology appears that enables proper risk management of exotic trades. This is the only event that could potentially shift this balance of vanilla vs. exotic trading.[10]

Risk management will be crucial: Given that we seem to be heading towards a highly uncertain (i.e., highly risky) economic environment, those institutions that have a solid risk management function and culture should benefit from this; in principle.

The term "in principle" is added because, in my view, one of the negative implications of the strong intervention that governments are having in the risk management practices of financial institutions is that, in reality, they (the institutions) have now a decreased incentive to do a better job of risk-managing their books. For example, counterparty credit risk management is now being delegated to the clearing houses and, hence, the return on investment in risk systems and process decreases substantially as more trades are cleared.[11]

Potential credit dislocations may crystallise: Another negative effect of the push toward clearing is the creation of gaps for market dislocations. Given that banks have had a long history of always finding and filling these gaps, one should think that the same should happen again.

A clear example of this could be seen in the European sovereign market. For years, a Greek or Spanish government bond would qualify similarly to a German bond from a regulatory standpoint. Given that its capital cost was effectively the same, European banks loaded themselves with European periphery bonds because their return on capital was relatively high. As a result European periphery countries could borrow money cheaper than their economic fundamentals indicated. The sovereign bond crisis that we saw in 2011 was the rebalancing of those market dislocations, and in my view this is also central to the overall excessive credit risk taken by individuals of those countries in the 2000–8 period.

A similar effect could happen in the OTC derivative markets with central counterparties. The capital cost that has been assigned to them by Basel III is given by a risk weight of only 2%. What are the implications of that number?

If we look at Figure 19.5, by giving a 2% risk weight to a clearing house we are effectively saying that it has a default probability *much* lower that a AAA entity.[12] In other words, that the US, German, or Japan governments are considerably more likely to default than a CCP. I think this defeats common sense and, as a result, we will easily end up with CCPs absorbing more credit risk than their economic fundamentals dictates, with the potential subsequent market dislocations.

Further to this, it must be noted that this problem in the CCP world is perhaps only the most obvious example of those potential market dislocations, but they could happen in many trading areas.[13]

I think this is a real risk we are facing, with a clear example in trading activity being pushed towards CCPs well beyond what the economic fundamentals seem to dictate.

High regulatory risk will remain: Given that governments and central banks have become the lenders and equity holders of last resort, at any cost, for financial institutions, they now feel they can dictate how banks manage their risk. It must be said, in principle this makes sense. This agenda is being implemented to a high extent via regulatory capital.

A side effect of this environment is that regulatory risk has become a major business risk that banks and trading houses face right now. This is because nobody knows how regulations will look like in only a couple of years.

A good example of that is this very book. I have had to revise the chapter on regulation several times, and at the end I decided to leave it somehow "loose", as any clear specifics in that field at the time of this book going to press will likely have changed by the time a reader goes through them, potentially a numbers of years later.

If this is the case for a "simple" book, the reader can imagine how difficult it is to manage this regulatory risk in a financial institution. This environment of high uncertainty inhibits research and market innovation in financial institutions, which is one of the most important drivers of economic wealth creation in Western societies.

The "law of one price" will remain dead: One of the most important concepts that this book puts forward is that the "law of one price" for derivatives does not hold; that is, that the same derivative can have more than one "correct" price, depending on a number of circumstances. This was explained in Section 12.5. We should expect this to remain unchanged for the foreseeable future.

Before 2008, we lived in a world in which pricing arbitrage could be done quite cheaply, and so we lived in a world very close to that described by the Black–Scholes risk-neutral pricing framework, in which if the price of a derivative diverted a fairly small amount from its risk-neutral price, arbitrageurs would make free money out of it. Consequently, the price of derivatives remained very close to that no-arbitrage price.

Things have changed, and it appears will keep on changing for some time. This is very well corroborated by the following anecdotal evidence. Some time before this book was going to press, I was phoned by a journalist from *Risk Magazine*. The journalist was writing a piece on the consequences of the withdrawal of several basis-arbitrage hedge funds from the market, and wanted to hear my opinion on the matter. A key point that the journalist was transmitting was that "several hedge funds that have been making money arbitraging the basis between credit indices and its constituents[14] are getting out of that market, because of the increasing margin requirements they are facing, that make those arbitrage strategies uneconomical now".

In other words, the cost of trading has increased, sometimes substantially. Consequently, the price bracket in derivatives in which arbitrage strategies cannot be exercised has become quite wide and, therefore, we live in a world in which the same derivative could have different prices depending on the trading environment it operates in, the most obvious sources of differentiation being those explained in this book: credit, funding, and capital requirements.

Nothing suggests that should change any time soon. In fact, if anything, the contrary.

A great opportunity for a positive change in the financial industry: In spite of everything said in this section, we should also see the positive side of these changes as opportunities. The 2008 events sent an X-ray into the financial system, showing its weakness and, let's say it too, strengths. With the exception of populist, political, and selfish corporate decisions, all parties in the financial industry community are generally doing their best to build a more robust financial system.

Banks have realised that several years of earnings can be lost in only a few months if the long-term risk carried on their books is not well understood and properly managed. I have noticed a shift in mentality in financial institutions towards a more risk-conscious approach. This is good.

Regulators have also realised that they need to understand in more depth the details of the world they regulate. I have also seen a positive shift in their approach to their task.

The shape and form of the financial industry in the future is unknown, but what is clear is that it is changing very deeply. We, finance professionals, have in front of us the opportunity to build a financial system for ourselves, our children, and grandchildren that is solid and robust. Everyone will benefit from that. Banks and financial institutions will achieve more sustainable business models, finance professionals will be able to work in a more constructive and sensible environment, clients will benefit from solid service providers and better products, and the taxpayer will (hopefully) not have to fund bail outs anymore.

In my view, finance professionals should accept the new world we are entering into, as opposed to fighting it. We must stop moaning and complaining about the regulations; rather, we must accept them. However, this does not mean that we must not be critical about them, and we should express our concerns in the right forums.

Overall, we are witness to the dawn of a new era for financial institutions. We should make the most out of it. In the same way as the 2008 crisis may have been a once-in-a-life-time crisis, so it created a once-in-a-life-time opportunity for us.

19.4 What will make the financial industry stable and safe?

It is true that financial institutions and finance professionals have become more aware of the importance of risk management. This is good because, as explained in Chapter 1, economic risk measurement, risk allocation, and risk distribution are at the very core of the business of finance. Also, regulators are becoming better at understanding the details of the often difficult financial environment they regulate. This is all good news.

However, a large push of this change is being motivated by increasing regulatory capital requirements. This, being arguably a good tool, is limiting in some important ways.

Fairly recently I saw again the famous movie *Titanic*. We can learn a good lesson from the unfortunate events that the film narrates.

One could think that the reason why so many people died in that unfortunate accident is because there weren't enough life boats for all the passengers. However, we must realise that the heart of the problem was the risk that the captain decided to take by cruising too fast where there had been iceberg warnings. Once the accident happens, of course you want to have enough life boats for everyone, but what makes sea navigation safe is, mostly, having people in charge of it that understand well the risks they are taking and that minimise the probability of an accident happening.

Capital is for a bank what emergency boats are for a cruiser: a safety cushion when everything else has failed. Therefore, what is going to make the financial industry safe and stable is not (only) having more capital, but being managed with a clear sense of risk awareness, all over the short, medium and long term. Anything else will prove, in my view, fruitless in the long run. Thinking that having more capital in banks means having a more solid financial system is like thinking that having more life boats means having a more secure naval transportation industry, or that having more airbags will make car transportation safer.

Because of this, it is important that all parties in the financial industry, finance professionals and regulators, focus their efforts on increasing the culture of risk management in banks, as opposed to having more capital as such, sometimes in quite an unsensible and non-risk-sensitive manner.

Part V | Appendices

Appendix A
The Money Multiplier

In order to understand better the role of banks in the economy, we must understand some basics of monetary policy in modern economies: the money multiplier. This can be best understood with an example.

We start with a fictional economy with no money. Then the government creates a central bank, prints \$100, and gives it to someone (for some service that has been provided to the government, for example). This person will go and deposit this \$100 in a bank. We have seen that this bank can lend out some of those \$100; let's say that the government lets the bank lend 90% of the money it holds (i.e., the reserves ratio is 10%). Now this bank lends out \$90, and then the person (or people) receiving those loans deposit that money into this or another bank. From those new \$90, banks must hold in reserve 10% (\$9) and the rest (\$81) can be lent out. Then another cycle starts and from those \$81, \$8.1 are held by banks as reserves and \$72.9 are lent out. This can go on and on until the money held by the banks as reserves is the original \$100, and then the money the economy has is somewhere close but below \$1,000. This is illustrated in Figure A.1.

With this simplistic example, the reader can see how banks, by having a reserve ratio lower than 100% do, actually, create money.

Reserve ratio:	10%			
Cycle	Deposits	Lent out	Reserves	Cumulated deposits
1	100	90	10	100
2	90	81	9	190
3	81	73	8	271
4	73	66	7	344
5	66	59	7	410
6	59	53	6	469
7	53	48	5	522
8	48	43	5	570
9	43	39	4	613
10	39	35	4	651
11	35	31	3	686
12	31	28	3	718
13	28	25	3	746
14	25	23	3	771
15	23	21	2	794
16	21	19	2	815
17	19	17	2	833
18	17	15	2	850
19	15	14	2	865
20	14	12	1	878

Figure A.1 Illustration of money creation through the banking credit system

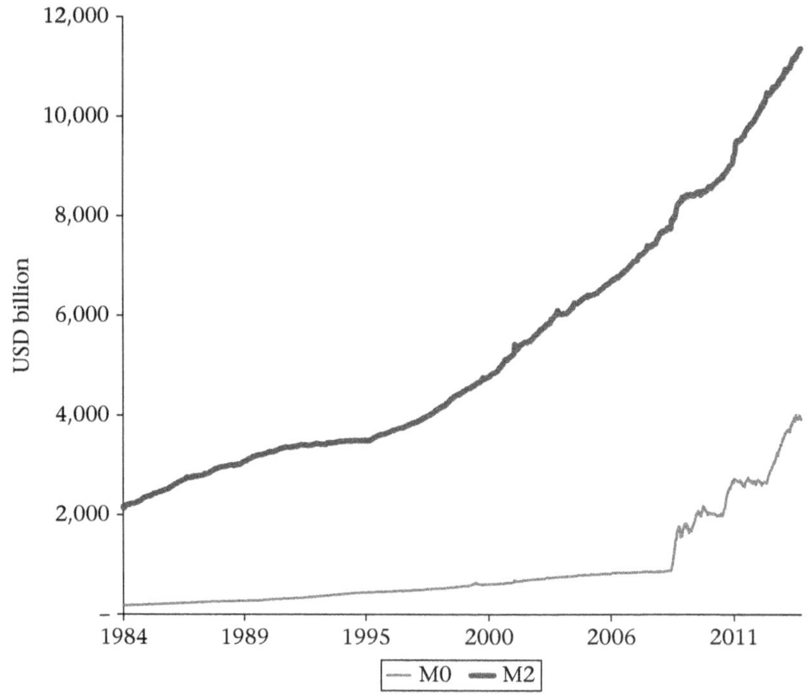

Figure A.2 Time series of the Federal Reserve monetary base (M0) and M2 metrics
Source: Federal Reserve Bank of St Louis.

There are two broad metrics of money: central bank money ($100 in our example) and commercial bank money ($1,000 in our example). In practice, things are more complicated than this and there are a number of money metrics: M0, M1, M2, M3. Usually, M0 is the central bank money, and M1, M2, and M3 reflect different stages of the money creation process.[1] For example, in the case of the US Federal Reserve, they call central bank money the monetary base, and then they use M1 for the basic currency plus current account balances, and M2 for M1 plus other instruments that can be converted quickly into M1. In practice, M2 is the money roughly held by households, the one that really matters most in many cases. In Figure A.2 the reader can see how these metrics have evolved over time. The start of the intervention of the Fed in the money supply in 2009 with the quantitative easing programmes can be clearly appreciated; this is the modern way of printing money. It had to do that to keep M2 growth at a steady level, because the creation of money provided by the banks became locked by the excessive credit risk they had.

The main point to understand is that banks, through the credit cycle, create money. This creation of money is key to the economy, and if it breaks the whole economy can collapse. This is the reason behind the rescue of the banking system in the aftermath of the 2008 crisis. Without healthy banks, a modern economy cannot function.

Appendix B
Overestimation of the Exposure Metric under the Adding Rule

We are going to see in this section how the adding rule is correct for EPE and ENE, but how it overestimates exposures for PFE, CESF, and EEPE.

B.1 EPE and ENE

Let's say we have two netting sets. We are calculating exposures in a Monte Carlo simulation with N number of scenarios. For a given time point in the simulation, the EPE of each netting set is

$$EPE_1 = \frac{\sum_{i=1}^{N} V_{1,i}^{+}}{N}$$
$$EPE_2 = \frac{\sum_{i=1}^{N} V_{2,i}^{+}}{N} \tag{B.1}$$

where $V_{1,i}$ and $V_{2,i}$ are the prices of each netting set for scenario i and $(\cdot)^{+} = \max(\cdot, 0)$. The EPE of both netting sets is going to be

$$\begin{aligned} EPE_{\text{portfolio}} &= \frac{\sum_{i=1}^{N} (V_{1,i}^{+} + V_{2,i}^{+})}{N} \\ &= \frac{\sum_{i=1}^{N} V_{1,i}^{+}}{N} + \frac{\sum_{i=1}^{N} V_{2,i}^{+}}{N} \\ &= EPE_1 + EPE_2 \end{aligned} \tag{B.2}$$

This argument can be extended to several netting sets easily. It shows that the EPE of a number of netting sets is the sum of the EPE of each netting set. An equivalent argument can be easily constructed for ENE.

B.2 EEPE

However, things are going to change when we consider the Effective Expected Positive Exposure for regulatory capital. This can be easily seen with an example.

Let's say we have two netting sets with an EPE profile each as EPE_1 and EPE_2 as shown in Figure B.1. The correct EEPE of the portfolio is shown in $EEPE_{12}$; this was calculated by adding EPE_1 and EPE_2, and then by "effectivising" the result. That $EEPE_{12}$ is different to $EEPE_1 + EEPE_2$, which was calculated by "effectivising" first each EPE_1 and EPE_2, and then adding them up. It can be shown that $EEPE_{12} \leq EEPE_1 + EEPE_2$ for any EPE_1 and EPE_2 profiles.

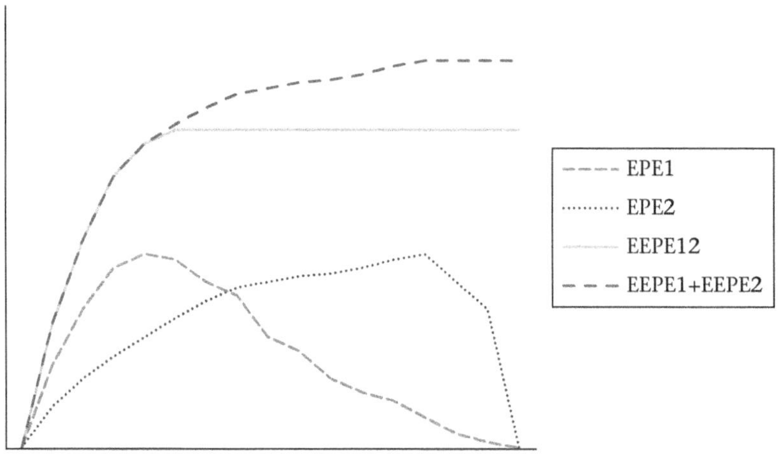

Figure B.1 Example showing how the adding rule overestimates exposure in the regulatory EEPE

B.3 PFE

The example given in Section 3.4 with the "maximum I can be owed" as the exposure risk metric is a good example for a VaR-like metric such as PFE that is overestimated under the adding rule.

The adding rule can over or underestimate the PFE. Perhaps it is easiest to see this with examples.

Let's consider a PFE calculation using a Monte Carlo simulation of two nettings sets as shown in Figure B.2. The example on the top shows how the sum of the PFEs of both netting sets can be lower than the PFE of the aggregated portfolio. The example on the bottom shows the opposite example, how the sum of the PFEs of both netting sets can be higher than the PFE of the aggregated portfolio.

As shown in those examples, the adding rule can either over or underestimate PFE, but it must be noted that in most practical cases it overestimates it.

B.4 CESF

We may expect that CESF should behave as a coherent risk metric when applied over a number of netting sets, but that is not the case if we floor it at zero, as tends to happen when CESF is used in commercial environments.

Figure B.2, at the top, shows an examples of CESF being underestimated by the adding rule, and at the bottom another example where it is overestimated.

Example of adding rule that underestimates PFE and CESF					
	Prices ($)		Exposures ($)		
	Netting set 1	Netting set 2	Netting set 1	Netting set 2	Aggregated netting sets
Scenario 1	20	8	20	8	28
Scenario 2	−1	10	0	10	10
Scenario 3	−2	20	0	20	20
Scenario 4	−3	7	0	7	7
Scenario 5	−4	5	0	5	5
Scenario 6	−5	5	0	5	5
Scenario 7	−6	−5	0	0	0
Scenario 8	−7	6	0	6	6
Scenario 9	−8	−7	0	0	0
Scenario 10	−9	2	0	2	2
Scenario 11	−10	1	0	1	1

Confidence level:	70%	
	PFE	CESF
Netting set 1	−3	5.7
Netting set 2	7	12.7
Nettng set 1 + 2 (added risk)	4	18.3
Netting set 1 + 2 (aggregated risk)	7	19.3

Example of adding rule that overestimates PFE and CESF					
	Prices ($)		Exposures ($)		
	Netting set 1	Netting set 2	Netting set 1	Netting set 2	Aggregated netting sets
Scenario 1	10	−4	10	0	10
Scenario 2	9	−1	9	0	9
Scenario 3	8	1	8	1	9
Scenario 4	7	7	7	7	14
Scenario 5	6	8	6	8	14
Scenario 6	−3	5	0	5	5
Scenario 7	−4	11	0	11	11
Scenario 8	−5	6	0	6	6
Scenario 9	−6	9	0	9	9
Scenario 10	−7	2	0	2	2
Scenario 11	−8	1	0	1	1

Confidence Level:	70%	
	PFE	CESF
Netting set 1	7	9.0
Netting set 2	7	9.3
Nettng set 1 + 2 (added risk)	14	18.3
Netting set 1 + 2 (aggregated risk)	10	13.0

Figure B.2 Example of the adding rule overestimating and underestimating PFE and CESF

CESF becomes a non-coherent risk metric when the PFE value corresponding to the confidence level we are considering is negative. When this happens the flooring is going to alter the exposure values at the tails, so that the averge of them (the CESF) can lose its coherence. However, when the PFE is a positive value (most cases), then the CESF is coherent.

Appendix C
Calculation of Exposure Contributions

Let's have a portfolio (often a netting set) with N trades, each referred to as i. We have an exposure metric at the future time point t of $E_{Port,t}$.[1] We are looking for the contribution of each of those trades to the overall exposure $E_{i,t}$, where

$$E_{Port,t} = \sum_i E_{i,t} \tag{C.1}$$

Contribution via notional deltas (the Euler Algorithm): For simplicity of notation, let's remove the time index in the algorithm without any loss of generalisation:

$$E_{Port} = \sum_i E_i \tag{C.2}$$

A nice property of the contribution metric E_i must be that if we put the notional of the trade N_i to zero that contribution is zero, if we double the notional that contribution doubles, etc. In other words, what we are saying here is that the exposure is a homogeneous function of degree one to each trade contribution. Hence, if we apply the Euler's Homogeneous Function Theorem,

$$E_{Port} = \sum_i N_i \frac{\partial E_{Port}}{\partial N_i} \tag{C.3}$$

That is,

$$E_i = N_i \frac{\partial E_{Port}}{\partial N_i} \tag{C.4}$$

Each of those derivatives is the "notional delta" to which we can give a Greek letter following the tradition on sensitivity naming. Let's call it Nu ($\nu_i = \frac{\partial E_{Port}}{\partial N_i}$), and so

$$E_i = N_i \nu_i \tag{C.5}$$

or

$$E_{Port} = \sum_i N_i \nu_i \tag{C.6}$$

A numerical estimate for Nu is

$$\nu_i = \frac{E_{Port}(N_i + \epsilon N_i) - E_{Port}(N_i)}{\epsilon N_i} \tag{C.7}$$

Typically, to do this numerical derivative, we are going to "bump" the notional by a small quantity "α" (e.g., $\alpha = 1.01$). So, if we call $\alpha = 1 + \epsilon$, then

$$\nu_i = \frac{E_{Port}(\alpha\, N_i) - E_{Port}(N_i)}{(\alpha - 1)N_i} \tag{C.8}$$

or, introducing this into Equation C.5,

$$E_i = \frac{E_{Port}(\alpha\, N_i) - E_{Port}(N_i)}{\alpha - 1} \tag{C.9}$$

Calculating numerically these trade contributions to the overall exposure is quite an easy task if we have in memory (of the exposure calculation system) the price scenarios of each trade, each in a price "grid". If that is the case, all we have to do is multiply each grid by α, recalculate the portfolio exposure ($E_{Port}(\alpha\, N_i)$), and then calculate Equation C.9 for each trade quite easily.

If we do not have the price grids in memory, or if we don't have access to them for whatever reason, we will have to do a full new Monte Carlo simulation for each calculation of $E_{Port}(\alpha\, N_i)$. If we cannot keep the same random numbers in it, ν_i is going to have the numerical noise of the simulation, hence α will need to be a relatively large number (e.g., 1.05 or 1.1, depending on the number of scenarios in the simulation). Obviously, this will decrease the quality of the measurement. Also, an alternative faster method could be implementing an Algorithmic Adjoint Differentiation (AAD) method for this derivative.

Needless to say, in the former case (price grids in memory) this calculation is going to be very simple and ultra-fast.

Contribution via expectations: Let's make for a second that, in order to calculate the exposure of our portfolio, we are going to run N_E full Monte Carlo simulations, each referred to as "k", and each delivering an exposure $E_{Port,k}$, so that

$$E_{Port} = \frac{\sum_k^{N_E} E_{Port,k}}{N_E} \tag{C.10}$$

In particular, if the exposure metric comes from an exposure profile, we can do that for each time point, so that

$$E_{Port,t} = \frac{\sum_k^{N_E} E_{Port,t,k}}{N_E} \tag{C.11}$$

Let's make a trivial statement now: the portfolio exposure is going to be the price of the portfolio when that price is the exposure, and that value of the portfolio is going to be the sum of the values of each trade. That is, if we have N trades, each referred to with an index "i",

$$E_{Port,t} = \frac{\sum_k^{N_E} \sum_i^{N} P_{i,t,k} | P_{Port,t} = E_{Port,t}}{N_E} \tag{C.12}$$

Now, we can swap those two sums, and put the N_E inside the sum in the number of trades (i),

$$E_{Port,t} = \sum_i^N \frac{\sum_k^{N_E} P_{i,t,k} | P_{Port,t} = E_{Port,t}}{N_E} \tag{C.13}$$

Each term inside the sum in "i" is the expected value of the price of trade (i) when the price of the portfolio is the exposure,

$$\frac{\sum_k^{N_E} P_{i,t,k}|P_{Port,t} = E_{Port,t}}{N_E} = \mathbb{E}(P_{i,t}|P_{Port,t} = E_{Port,t}) \tag{C.14}$$

and, as a result,

$$E_{Port,t} = \sum_i^N \mathbb{E}(P_{i,t}|P_{Port,t} = E_{Port,t}) \tag{C.15}$$

In other words, if $E_{Port,t} = \sum_i^N E_{i,t}$, the contribution of each trade to the exposure ($E_{i,t}$) can be given by

$$E_{i,t} = \mathbb{E}(P_{i,t}|P_{Port,t} = E_{Port,t}) \tag{C.16}$$

In order to calculate these contributions $E_{i,t}$ we need to run the Monte Carlo simulations where we calculate the exposure lots of times (i.e., make N_E large enough), and then calculate the average of the prices of each trade in the scenario where the price of the portfolio equals the exposure.[2] However, this could be undoable in many cases for reasons of computational time limitations.

In practice, we can estimate it in two ways:

- We do only one simulation ($N_E = 1$) and we say that $\mathbb{E}(P_{i,t}|P_{Port,t} = E_{Port,t})$ is the value $P_{i,t}$ in the one simulation that we have. That is like saying that the best estimate of an average when we only have one sample is the value of that sample itself.
- Alternatively, we also leave $N_E = 1$ but we can get a bracket of scenarios around that one in which $P_{Port,t} = E_{Port,t}$, and take the average of those portfolio prices. For example, if we run our Monte Carlo simulation with 10,000 scenarios, we take the 100 scenarios with a portfolio price closest to the exposure, and take the average of those 100 scenarios as a proxy for the expectation.[3]

The difference between both contributions: We have seen two approaches for the contribution of each trade to the portfolio exposure. A natural question that may follow is whether they are the same or not.

If we call $p_{i,t} = \frac{P_{i,t}}{N_i}$ as the price per unit of notional of trade i, both methodologies are going to lead to the same result when

$$\frac{\partial E_{Port,t}}{\partial N_i} = \mathbb{E}(p_{i,t}|P_{Port,t} = E_{Port,t}) \tag{C.17}$$

for every trade. I understand that, generally speaking, Equation C.17 is not going to hold, hence each methodology may lead to a different distribution of exposures amongst the portfolio trades.

Acknowledgements

I would like to thank Pilar Barrios from AFI for useful discussions on this topic.

Appendix D
Coherent Risk Metrics

Let's say that we have a portfolio X, or a number of them X_1, X_2, etc., and a real number, the risk metric, that measures their risk, $\varrho(X)$. This risk metric is said to be "coherent" if

1. **Normalised:** The risk of having nothing is zero.

$$\varrho(0) = 0 \tag{D.1}$$

2. **Monotonicity:** If one portfolio is always smaller in value than another one, the risk of the first one is always lower than that of the second one.

$$\text{Value}(X_1) \leq \text{Value}(X_2) \Longrightarrow \varrho(X_1) \leq \varrho(X_2) \tag{D.2}$$

3. **Sub-additivity:** The risk of a portfolio is smaller or equal to the sum of the risk of its parts.

$$\varrho(X_1 + X_2) \leq \varrho(X_1) + \varrho(X_2) \tag{D.3}$$

4. **Positive Homogeneity:** If we increase the size of a portfolio, the risk increases proportionally to it.

$$\varrho(\alpha X) = \alpha\, \varrho(X),\ \alpha \in \mathbb{R},\ \text{for } \alpha \geq 0 \tag{D.4}$$

5. **Translation Invariance:** If a proportion of a portfolio is R, a riskless sub-portfolio, with return r, then the risk decreases by r.

$$\varrho(X + R) = \varrho(X) - r \tag{D.5}$$

In other words, adding cash to a portfolio only decreases the risk.

Appendix E
The Market-Credit Link in the Merton Model Approach for DWR

Further to Section 10.2, we want to see how to create a dependency structure between the X and the Y variables in the Merton model approach for DWR.

There are two versions of this in the literature: Cespedes *et al.* and D. Rosen & D. Saunders [32, 69] link the market variable X and the default latent variable Y with a joint normal distribution function with a given correlation r. Cesari *et al.* [31] state that $X \equiv Y$. In the former case, the dependency structure between the market factor X and the latent variable Y is a bivariate normal distribution with correlation $\beta = r \cdot \rho$. In the latter case that dependency structure also follows a bivariate normal distribution but with a correlation $\beta = \rho$.

Given the Merton theoretical framework, we can proceed as follows to calculate the scenario weights $w_{t,i}$. At a given time point t, scenario i will have a value for the exposure $V_{t,i}$, from which we can calculate its corresponding $X_{t,i}$ using Equation 10.5. Then, we either generate a corresponding $Z_{t,i}$ using the bi-normal distribution function with correlation r, or we simply state that $Z_{t,i} = X_{t,i}$. Once we have $Z_{t,i}$, we calculate the default probability in this given scenario and time point using Equation 10.4. The weight for that scenario and time step is $w_{t,i} = PD(Z_{t,i})$. If we proceed like this for every scenario and time step, we can attach a weight to each of them, hence transforming $\Psi(V)$ into $\Psi'(V)$.

The reader should note that the versions of this methodology shown here are equivalent. We have indicated that the former version can be reduced to a single bivariate normal distribution with a correlation $\beta = r \cdot \rho$. Since both r and ρ are non-observable variables, what really matters is β (which is also an unobservable variable). As a result, both versions are the same with the only difference that one of them decomposes the β into two further parameters.

This modelling framework has been used in the literature to give estimates of the α parameter used in the Basel Committee framework for capital calculation, giving values for α that range from 0.89 to 1.27 [32].

Appendix F
Stressed Scenario DWR Model

The Stressed Scenario Model (Section 10.2) is based on three key points.

Firstly, following Turlakov [76] we need to postulate what will be the impact on the markets of the counterparty's sovereign default (e.g., if the Korean government defaults on its debt, the KRWUSD exhange rate drops by 30%). We then calculate the EPE profile of the book of trades under consideration with that stressed market scenario as a starting point. If the portfolio contains WWR, this new stressed EPE will be higher than the standard one.

Secondly, "since the major market dislocation is given by the situation of the sovereign defaulting as well [as the counterparty]"[76], the actual EPE of the portofolio will be given by a combination of those two stressed and unstressed EPE profiles, with the default probability of the sovereign defaulting conditional on the counterparty having defaulted as the weight between them:

$$EPE_{DWR} = P(sov|cpty)EPE_{stress} + (1 - P(sov|cpty))EPE \tag{F.1}$$

Thirdly, we say that the default probability of the sovereign conditional on the counterparty having defaulted is λ times the sovereign default probability: $P(sov|cpty) = \lambda P(sov)$.

All this, together with some simple smooth interpolation assumptions, leads to a DWR expected exposure profile given by

$$EPE_{DWR} = EPE + \lambda P(sov)\,(EPE_{stress} - EPE)\left(1 - \tanh\left(\frac{P(sov)}{P_{thres}}\right)\right), \tag{F.2}$$

where P_{thres} is "a near default or half-life threshold marking the crossover between the two extremes".

Appendix G
The Merton Model Equity–Credit Dependency

Merton, Black and Scholes proposed in the early 1970s a very simple but effective model that links the equity value with the credit standing of a company [55, 22]. In that model, the company's assets (A) are supposed to follow a normal diffusion process. The firm has an amount of debt (D), seen as a zero-coupon bond, that matures at the time point T. In this context, the value of the equity at time T will be

$$E_T = \max(A_T - D, 0) \tag{G.1}$$

Given that the assets A follow a normal diffusion process, the current equity value is that of an option under the Black–Scholes framework, where the strike is D:

$$\begin{aligned} E_0 &= A_0 N(d_1) - D e^{-rT} N(d_2) \\ d_1 &= \frac{\ln \frac{A_0 e^{rT}}{D}}{\sigma_A T} + 0.5 \sigma_A \sqrt{T} \\ d_2 &= d_1 - \sigma_A \sqrt{T} \end{aligned} \tag{G.2}$$

Where σ_A is the assets' volatility, and r is the assets' expected return. Further to this, it can be shown that the equity volatility and the default probability are given by [48]

$$\sigma_E = \frac{\sigma_A N(d_1)}{N(d_1) - L N(d_2)} \tag{G.3}$$

$$PD = N(-d_2) \tag{G.4}$$

As a result, for a given value of σ_A and r, a time horizon T and a debt level D, we can obtain the functional dependency between the equity value E_0 and the probability of default PD from Equations G.2 and G.4.

Figures G.1 and G.2 show this dependency form and the equity implied volatility term structure for the particular case of $\sigma_A = 20\%$, $r = 10\%$, and $D = 50$.

We cannot obtain a functional form for the equity–credit dependency from Equations G.2 and G.4, but we can at least see how it fits to a number of basic functions we have used for $g(x)$ in Equation 10.6. In particular, if we try an exponential, power, and logarithmic fit, we can estimate the quality of the fit using the typical least-squared R^2. The results are shown in the following table for a range of reasonable asset volatilities σ_A[1] (the value of the asset expected return r was seen to have very small impact):

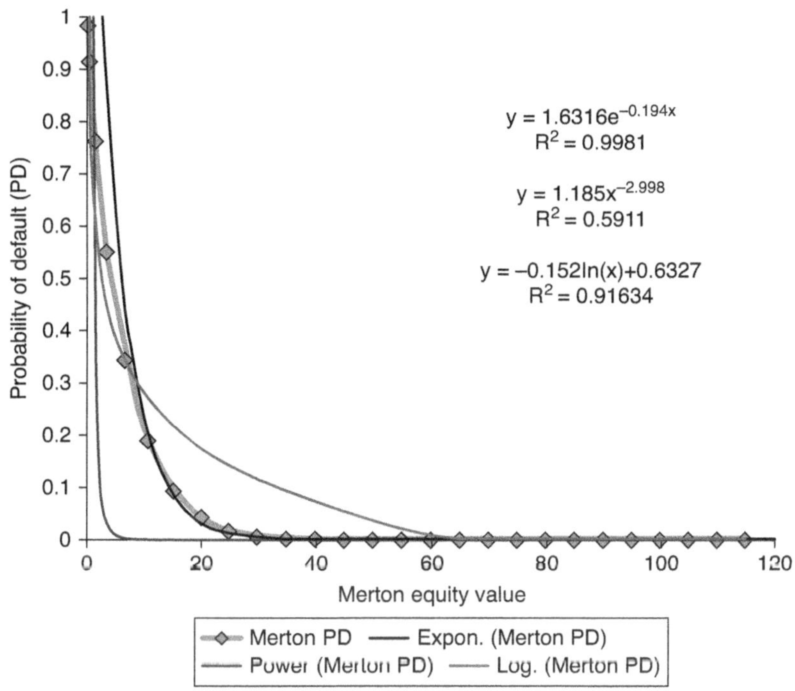

Figure G.1 Dependency structure implied by the Merton model between equity prices and default probabilities, together with exponential, power, and logarithmic fits ($\sigma_A = 20\%,\ r = 10\%,\ D = 50$)

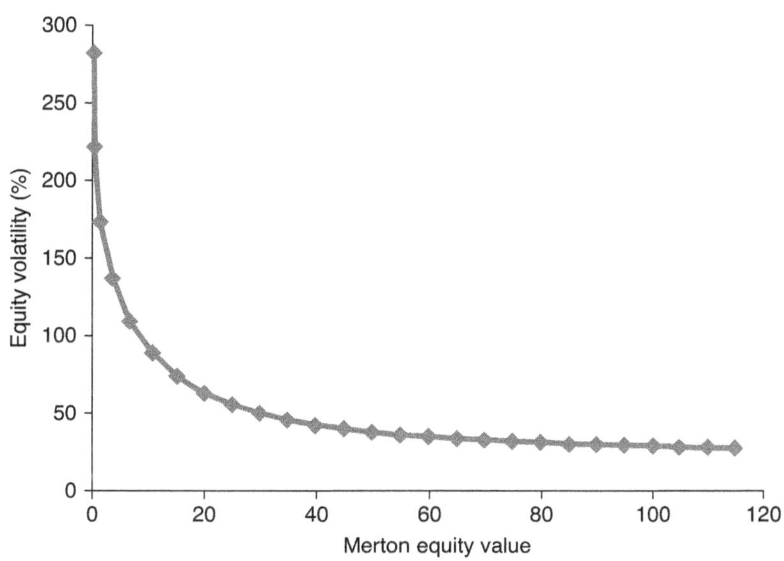

Figure G.2 Volatility term structure implied by the Merton model ($\sigma_A = 20\%,\ r = 10\%,\ D = 50$)

	$\sigma_A = 5\%$	$\sigma_A = 10\%$	$\sigma_A = 20\%$	$\sigma_A = 40\%$	$\sigma_A = 60\%$
Exponential R^2	0.990	0.993	0.998	0.999	0.996
Power R^2	0.201	0.361	0.591	0.798	0.882
Logarithmic R^2	0.693	0.837	0.916	0.968	0.992

It can be seen how the functional form between the equity price and the default probability in a Merton model seems to be very close to an exponential function, at least in this tested case. A logarithmic function fits the data well only for high asset volatility values and a power fit seems to be the worst fit.

Appendix H
Right and Wrong-Way Risk in Equity Options

We have seen in Chapter 10 that a typical example of DWR happens when a derivatives dealer sells an equity option to a counterparty on a stock that is strongly linked to the counterparty's own stock.

In this section we shall study an example where a put option delivers wrong-way risk, but its complementary call option delivers right-way risk; all in the uncollateralised case. When collateralised, we shall see how the profiles change importantly from a call to a put because of the changes in the profile of the option delta $\Delta(x)$.

Long put option: Suppose that we buy a five year at-the-money put option to Bank of America, with JP Morgan as the reference entity, and we use the power function that we have for Bank of America [75, 72], $g(x) = 0.44749\,x^{-1.2216}$, where x is the stock price of Bank of America. Figures H.1 and H.2 show the impact of this DWR on this trade for the uncollateralised and collateralised cases respectively.

In the uncollateralised case (Figure H.1) we can see WWR: the exposure metrics increase when DWR is considered. This is the case because when the counterparty default probability is high, the option tends to be in-the-money given the high correlation between JP Morgan and Bank of America stocks.[1] As a result,

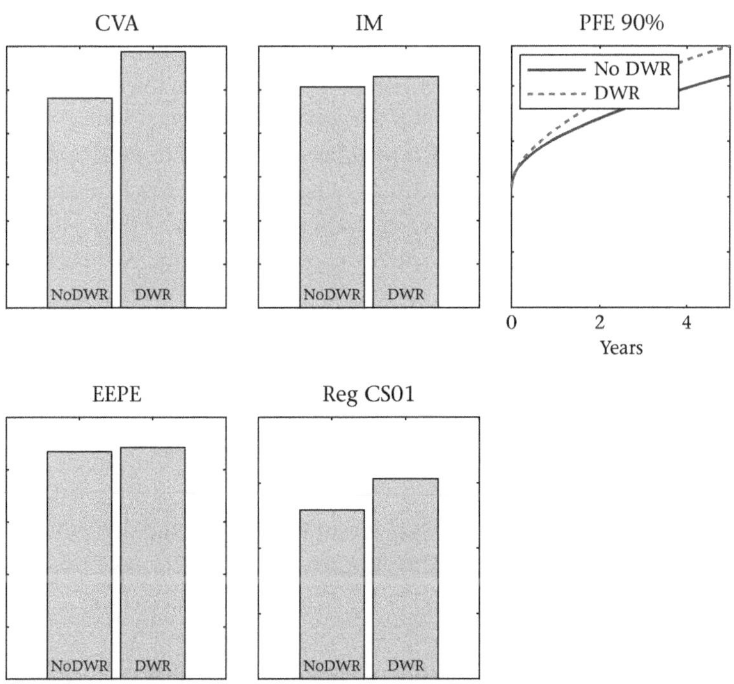

Figure H.1 Impact of DWR modelling on counterparty credit risk metrics on an uncollateralised long put option. The left bar is without DWR modelling, the right bar with DWR modelling

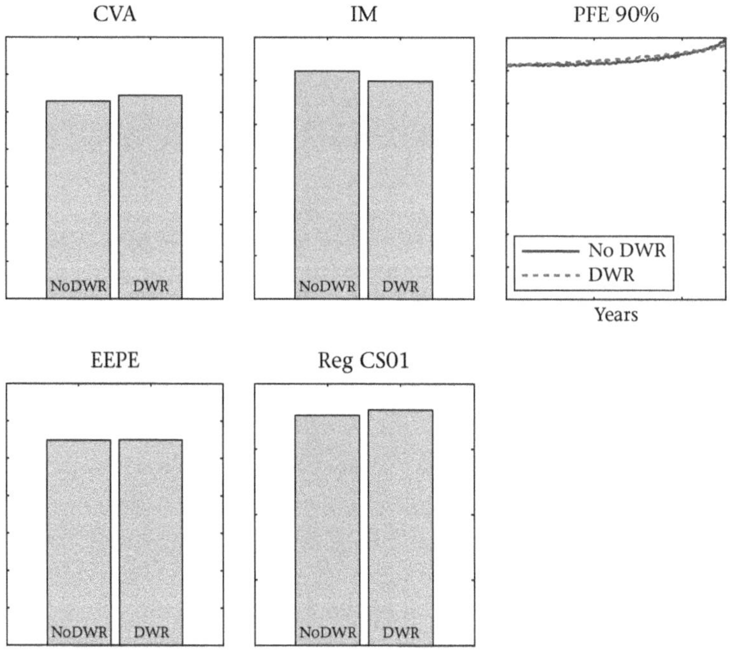

Figure H.2 Impact of DWR modelling on counterparty credit risk metrics in a collateralised long put option. The left bar is without DWR modelling, the right bar with DWR modelling

CVA, IM, the PFE-90%, and the CVA's regulatory CS01 increase clearly when DWR is considered. EEPE also increases, but less as it is only calculated in the first year of the trade, when the DWR has not yet had sufficient time to kick in.

On the other hand, the collateralised case shows very little sensitivity to DWR effects. This is due to two interacting effects here; a higher weight w as the equity value decreases, and a smaller δP as the equity value decreases (due to the geometric diffusion nature of x), seem to cancel each other out.

In fact, though small in magnitude, we see an interesting effect here: the balance between $\delta(x)$, $g(x)$, and the geometric nature of δP deliver a small WWR up to four years, while it then tends to disappear in the fifth year.[2]

Short put option: If we now short the same put option, the collateralised risk metrics that we obtain are shown in Figure H.3.[3] It can be seen how those metrics are very similar to the long put option case. As already indicated, this is due to the near-symmetry of Equation 10.15 for long/short transformations.

Long call option: We now discuss the complementary example: a call instead of a put option, with everything else the same. The results when we are long on this trade can be seen in Figures H.4 and H.5.

The uncollateralised case (Figure H.4) shows a strong right-way risk behaviour. This is because the paths in the MC simulation that carry highest weight are those where the Bank of America stock prices are low, but in those cases the option will tend to be out-of-the-money, and so the exposure weighted by the counterparty default probability is lower than when the weighting is not considered. The impact is very strong in this case: a reduction of nearly 50% in CVA and IM, a very substantial decrease of the exposure profile and a decrease

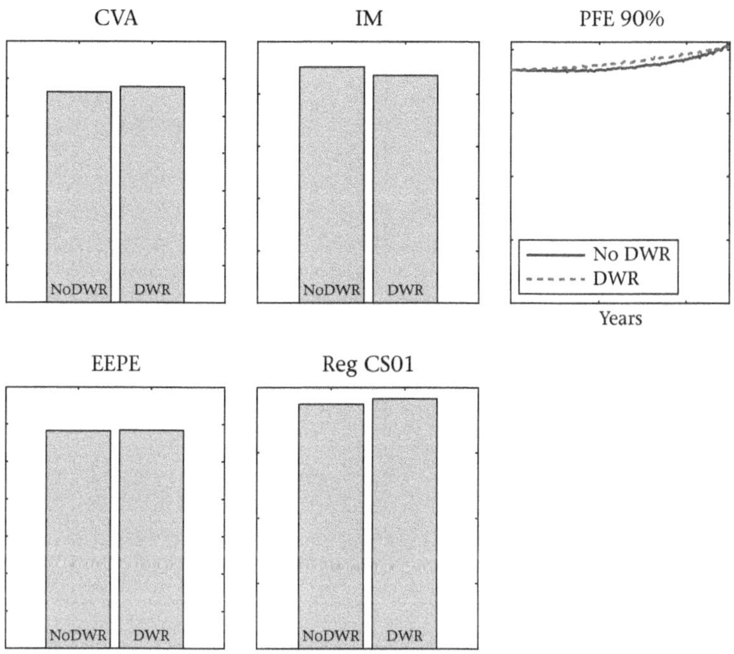

Figure H.3 Impact of DWR modelling on counterparty credit risk metrics in a collateralised short put option. The left bar is without DWR modelling, the right bar with DWR modelling

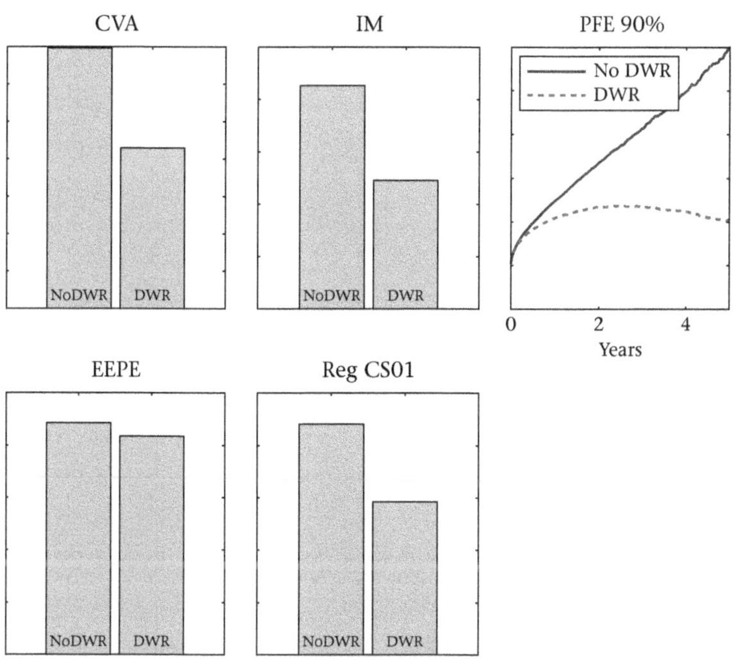

Figure H.4 Impact of DWR modelling on counterparty credit risk metrics in a uncollateralised long call option. The left bar is without DWR modelling, the right bar with DWR modelling

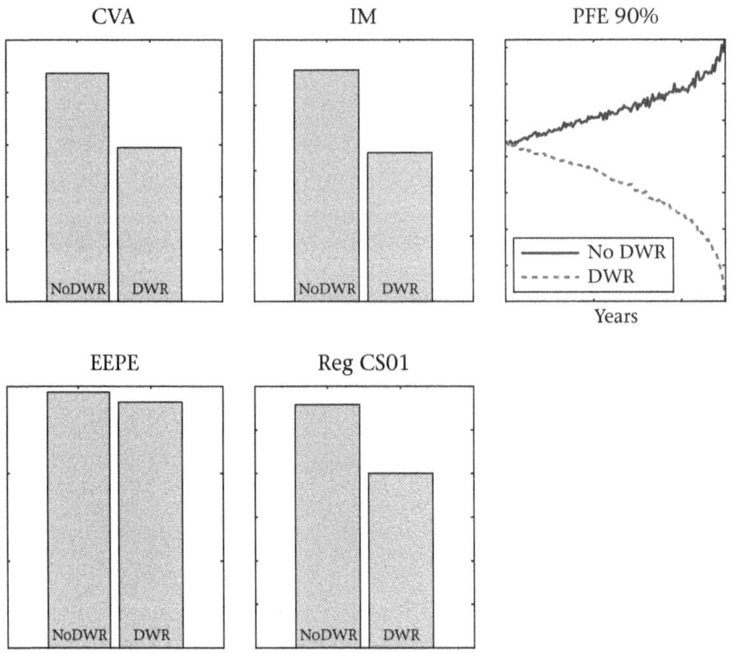

Figure H.5 Impact of DWR modelling on counterparty credit risk metrics in a collateralised long call option. The left bar is without DWR modelling, the right bar with DWR modelling

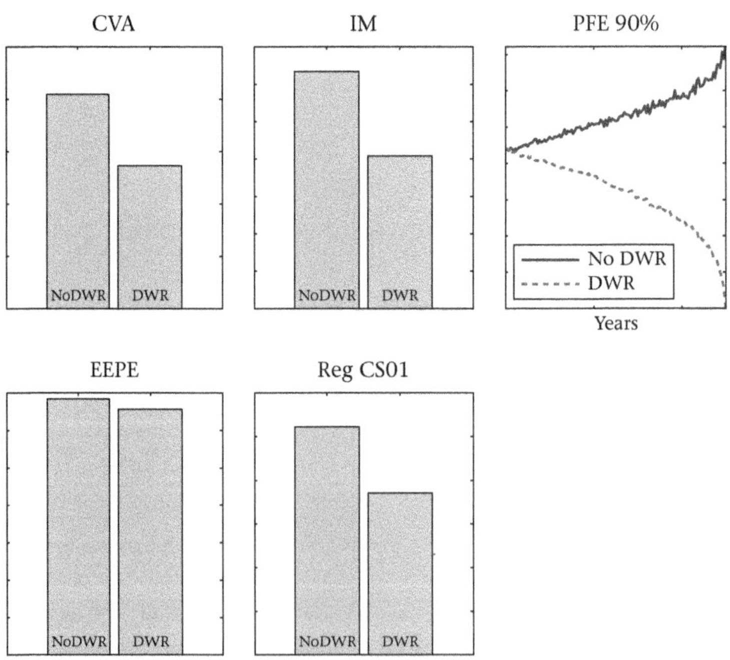

Figure H.6 Impact of DWR modelling on counterparty credit risk metrics in a collateralised short call option. The left bar is without DWR modelling, the right bar with DWR modelling

of around 10% of CCR capital and of around 40% of CVA capital. We would like to remind the reader that these measurements are completely realistic, as they are calibrated to real market data[4].

In the collateralised case (Figure H.5) the DWR effect is very strong too, as the MC paths that carry high weight w (when the stock prices are low) have a small delta. So the ten-day changes in the option price are very small when w is big. As a result we can see a right-way risk that nearly halves the CVA and IM, decreases the exposure profile quite dramatically, reduces CCR capital by about 10%, and CVA capital by about 35%.

Short call option

Suppose now that we short that call option. The collateralised risk metrics that we obtain are shown in Figure H.6. Again, a remarkable effect is observed. The credit metrics are very similar to the long call option, again because of the near-symmetry of Equation 10.15 for long/short transformations.

Appendix I
A Full XVA Valuation Framework

We are going to introduce the idea of XVA in two steps. First considering CVA pricing from a risk-neutral standpoint, and then introducing a derivative valuation through a full XVA framework.

These pricing and valuation frameworks are based on the fundamental theorem of asset pricing that states that the fair value of a financial product "today" is the expectation of the present value (PV) of its future cash flows.

$$P_0 = \mathbb{E}\left(\sum_i PV(\text{future cash flow}_i)\right) \tag{I.1}$$

We assume that there exists a "risk-free" interest rate between the time points u and $u+du$ (r_u), so that the present value of a generic future cash flow at t (X_t) is given by

$$PV_0 = e^{-\int_0^t r_u\,du} X_t \tag{I.2}$$

In other words, $DF_{0,t} = e^{-\int_0^t r_u\,du}$ is the riskless discount factor.

If we are trying to value a derivative that is going to have a future cash flow $X_t = x_t\,dt$ between t and $t+dt$, then,

$$\sum_i PV(\text{future cash flow}_i) = \int_0^T e^{-\int_0^t r_u\,du} x_t\,dt \tag{I.3}$$

where T is the maturity of the derivative. Consequently,

$$P_0 = \mathbb{E}\left(\int_0^T e^{-\int_0^t r_u\,du} x_t\,dt\right) \tag{I.4}$$

Given that so far we live in the risk-neutral world, this price should be the same as that obtained by the Black–Scholes model. That model equates the price of a derivative (a set of future cash flows contingent on some external risk factors like, typically, interest rates, FX prices, etc.) to the price of hedging its risk out and producing in this way a risk-less portfolio. In that context, the price of a derivative and its evolution is given by Equations 13.1 and 13.2.

I.1 Risk-neutral pricing with counterparty risk

A financial derivative is a contract between two entities, the "counterparties", to exchange a number of cashflows up to the maturity date. During this time, one or both of these counterparties may default.

The classic "risk-neutral" pricing theory does not contemplate that any market player can default. In order to incorporate this, let's say that

- Any counterparty of the derivative can buy credit protection insurance on the other counterparty defaulting, typically in the form of a Credit Default Swap (CDS).
- That these CDS contracts have unlimited liquidity and no transaction costs.
- That the external entity selling the CDS cannot default.

Let's calculate the expectation of the present value of future cash flows in this world.

The expectation of a generic quantity Z in the future can be obtained by summing the product of the value of Z in each possible event by the probability of each event happening. In other words,

$$\mathbb{E}(Z) = \sum_i \mathcal{P}_i Z_i \tag{I.5}$$

where $\mathcal{P}_i$ is the probability of event i, and Z_i is the value of Z if event i takes place.

If we have a bilateral derivative contract with a counterparty, there are four events that may happen in the future interval from t to $t+dt$, subject to both counterparties having survived up to the time point t:

1. That both counterparties are survived at $t+dt$.
2. That we survive up to $t+dt$, but our counterparty defaults during the interval $(t, t+dt)$.
3. That we default during the interval $(t, t+dt)$, but our counterparty survives up to $t+dt$.
4. That both counterparties default during the interval $(t, t+dt)$.

Let's say that there is a "default intensity" λ so that the default probability of an entity in the interval $t+dt$ is given by $\lambda_t\, dt$. It can be shown how, in this framework, the survival probability of that entity up to the time point t, subject to being "alive" at $t=0$, is given by

$$S_{0,t} = e^{\int_0^t \lambda_u du} \tag{I.6}$$

A snapshot of the four possible events we are facing, with their probabilities $(\mathcal{P}_i)$[1] and the cash flows that would occur in each of them, is shown in the following table

Event	$\mathcal{P}_i$ in $(t, t+dt)$	Cash flow
1	$S^{our}_{t,t+dt}\, S^{cpty}_{t,t+dt}$	$x_t \cdot dt$
2	$S^{our}_{t,t+dt}\, \lambda^{cpty}_t\, dt$	$-(1 - RR^{cpty}_t)\, P^+_t$
3	$\lambda^{our}_t\, dt\, S^{cpty}_{t,t+dt}$	$-(1 - RR^{our}_t)\, P^-_t$
4	$\lambda^{our}_t\, \lambda^{cpty}_t\, dt$	$(RR^{cpty}_t - RR^{our}_t)\, P_t$

where $x_t\, dt$ is the cash flow that takes place in the derivative in the interval $(t, t+dt)$ if no default happens, P_t is the price of the derivative at time t,[2] $P^+_t = \max(P_t, 0)$, $P^-_t = \min(P_t, 0)$, and RR represents the recovery rate obtained by the surviving party when a default occurs.[3]

If we say that the survival probability in an infinitesimal time step $S_{t,t+dt} \simeq 1$, and that both counterparties, joint default probability is nearly zero $(\lambda^{our}_t \lambda^{cpty}_t\, dt \simeq 0)$, and noting also that the probability of all these events must be multiplied by the probability of both counterparties having survived at t

$$S^{our}_{0,t}\, S^{cpty}_{0,t} = e^{-\int_0^t (\lambda^{our}_u + \lambda^{cpty}_u) du} \tag{I.7}$$

then the price of the derivative that accounts for counterparty risk is given by

$$P_0^{CptyRisk} = \mathbb{E}\left(\int_0^T e^{-\int_0^t (r_u+\lambda_u^{our}+\lambda_u^{cpty})\,du}\, x_t\, dt\right) \tag{I.8}$$

$$-\mathbb{E}\left(-\int_0^T e^{-\int_0^t (r_u+\lambda_u^{our}+\lambda_u^{cpty})\,du}\, \lambda_t^{cpty}\,(1-RR_t^{cpty})\, P_t^+\, dt\right) \tag{I.9}$$

$$-\mathbb{E}\left(-\int_0^T e^{-\int_0^t (r_u+\lambda_u^{our}+\lambda_u^{cpty})\,du}\, \lambda_t^{our}\,(1-RR_t^{our})\, P_t^-\, dt\right) \tag{I.10}$$

where we have the sum across all possible time points in t.[4]

We have basically assumed that event 4 in the table above has a negligible probability. If the correlation between our default event and our counterparty's is relevant, we cannot ignore that term. In the extreme case in which that correlation is close to one,[5] then events 2 and 3 can become negligible, and it is event 4 which is the one that is most important.

Coming back to the standard case (negligible event 4), if we say now that $DF_{0,t}^* = e^{-\int_0^t (r_u+\lambda_u^{our}+\lambda_u^{cpty})\,du}$ is the risky discount factor and that the recovery rates are constant over time, then

$$P_0^{CptyRisk} = \mathbb{E}\left(\int_0^T DF_{0,t}^*\, x_t\, dt\right) \tag{I.11}$$

$$-\mathbb{E}\left((1-RR^{cpty})\int_0^T DF_{0,t}^*\, \lambda_t^{cpty}\, P_t^+\, dt\right) \tag{I.12}$$

$$-\mathbb{E}\left((1-RR^{our})\int_0^T DF_{0,t}^*\, \lambda_t^{our}\, P_t^-\, dt\right) \tag{I.13}$$

Furthermore, let's assume now that the discount factors are independent of x_t and P_t and that default events are independent of x_t and P_t (i.e., that there is no right or wrong-way risk). Then,

$$P_0^{CptyRisk} = \int_0^T DF_{0,t}^*\, \mathbb{E}(x_t)\, dt \tag{I.14}$$

$$-(1-RR^{cpty})\int_0^T DF_{0,t}^*\, \lambda_t^{cpty}\, \mathbb{E}(P_t^+)dt \tag{I.15}$$

$$-(1-RR^{our})\int_0^T DF_{0,t}^*\, \lambda_t^{our}\, \mathbb{E}(P_t^-)dt \tag{I.16}$$

If now we define the Expected Positive Exposure as $EPE_t = \mathbb{E}(P_t^+)$ and the Expected Negative Exposure as $ENE_t = \mathbb{E}(P_t^-)$, then

$$P_0^{CptyRisk} = \int_0^T DF_{0,t}^*\, \mathbb{E}(x_t)\, dt \tag{I.17}$$

$$-(1-RR^{cpty})\int_0^T DF^*_{0,t}\,\lambda_t^{cpty}\,EPE_t\,dt \tag{I.18}$$

$$-(1-RR^{our})\int_0^T DF^*_{0,t}\,\lambda_t^{our}\,ENE_t\,dt \tag{I.19}$$

The first term (Equation I.17) is the "classic" risk-neutral valuation under the risky discounting measure, the second term (Equation I.18) is the assets side of CVA, sometimes called just "CVA", and the third term (Equation I.19) is the liability side of CVA, sometimes referred to as "DVA".

$$CVA_{asset,0} = (1-RR^{cpty})\int_0^T DF^*_{0,t}\,\lambda_t^{cpty}\,EPE_t\,dt \tag{I.20}$$

$$CVA_{liab,0} = (1-RR^{our})\int_0^T DF^*_{0,t}\,\lambda_t^{our}\,ENE_t\,dt \tag{I.21}$$

Therefore,

$$P_0^{CptyRisk} = P_0^* - CVA_0 \tag{I.22}$$

$$CVA_0 = CVA_{asset,0} + CVA_{liab} \tag{I.23}$$

If s_t is the credit spread of the CDS of a given entity, it is quite common to say that $s_t \simeq (1-RR)\,\lambda_t$. Then, in this context,

$$CVA_{asset,0} \simeq \int_0^T DF^*_{0,t}\,s_t^{cpty}\,EPE_t\,dt \tag{I.24}$$

$$CVA_{liab,0} \simeq \int_0^T DF^*_{0,t}\,s_t^{our}\,ENE_t\,dt \tag{I.25}$$

And, finally, if s_t is a fairly constant number, and we define

$$\widehat{EPE_0^*} = \int_0^T DF^*_{0,t}\,EPE_t\,dt \tag{I.26}$$

$$\widehat{ENE_0^*} = \int_0^T DF^*_{0,t}\,ENE_t\,dt \tag{I.27}$$

then,

$$CVA_{asset,0} \simeq \widehat{EPE_0^*}\cdot s^{cpty} \tag{I.28}$$

$$CVA_{liab,0} \simeq \widehat{ENE_0^*}\cdot s^{our} \tag{I.29}$$

Sometimes it is also common practice to neglect the "riskiness" of the discount factors. This is a good approximation when both counterparties are entities with good credit standing, and when the book of trades between them doesn't mature too far in time (i.e., when T is not too big). In these cases,

$$CVA_{asset,0} \simeq s^{cpty} \cdot \int_0^T DF_{0,t}\, EPE_t\, dt \tag{I.30}$$

$$CVA_{liab,0} \simeq s^{our} \cdot \int_0^T DF_{0,t}\, ENE_t\, dt \tag{I.31}$$

or

$$CVA_{asset,0} \simeq \widehat{EPE_0} \cdot s^{cpty} \tag{I.32}$$

$$CVA_{liab,0} \simeq \widehat{ENE_0} \cdot s^{our} \tag{I.33}$$

I.2 Derivative valuation with counterparty, funding, and capital risk

Now, we want to somehow formalise the idea of *value to me* introduced in Chapter 12 and expanded subsequently.

The pricing framework just seen provides a risk-neutral price with counterparty risk. However, as explained throughout the book, this is different to the value of a derivative (Section 12.5.1). The *price* of a derivative tries to capture how much two generic institutions should trade the derivative for, with limited consideration of the specific environment they operate in. In contrast, the *value* of a derivative tries to capture that specific environment. In particulari, the *value to me* (VtM) is given by

$$VtM = P_{sale} - P_{manufacturing} \tag{I.34}$$

where P_{sale} is the expectation of the present value of the future cash flows in the deal with the counterparty, and $P_{manufacturing}$ is the expectation of the present value of the future cash flows in the activities we need to do to "synthetically manufacture" the trade. These activities are going to be managing the effects of market, counterparty, funding, and capital risk. This can be done by actually hedging risk out in the trading markets, when possible, or by accruing a risk reserve for that risk when not possible.

The selling price

If we are a dealer and we want to sell a derivative to a client, following the Black–Scholes thinking process we start our valuation saying that there are a collection of financial positions, which we can set against the markets, and which carry the same but symmetrical market risk as did the original one that we want to sell to the client. Those trades are the so-called *hedging* positions.

Let's simplify the language and say that one single position hedges the derivative. That hedging position is going to have a cash flow $x_t\, dt$ in the time interval $(t, t+dt)$.

Typically, a derivatives dealer is going to put a spread on top of that hedging cash flow, from where the profit is made. In this way, the cash flows in the derivative sold to the client are given by $(x_t + \delta_t)\, dt$. Therefore,

$$P_{sale} = \mathbb{E}\left(\int_0^T DF^*_{0,t}\, (x_t + \delta_t)\, dt \right) \tag{I.35}$$

The manufacturing price

On the manufacturing side of the equation, we have four components:

$$P_{manufacturing} = P_{MarketRisk} + P_{CounterpartyRisk} + P_{FundingRisk} + P_{CapitalRisk} \tag{I.36}$$

Let's get into each of these terms.

- **Market Risk:** We have said that the cash flows in the hedging position are going to be $x_t\,dt$ in the time interval $(t, t+dt)$. Hence,

$$P_{MarketRisk} = \mathbb{E}\left(\int_0^T DF^*_{0,t}\, x_t\, dt\right) \tag{I.37}$$

  Strictly speaking, the discount factors in Equations I.35 and I.37 are going to be different, as the counterparties in the bilateral and hedging positions are not going to be the same. However, that refinement results in a second-order adjustment that we are going to ignore for now.
- **Counterparty Risk:** We have seen that CVA represents the cost of hedging out counterparty risk. The asset side of CVA can be hedged by buying a series of CDSs in the market, so that

$$CVA_{asset} \simeq \widehat{EPE^*_0} \cdot s^{CDS,cpty} \tag{I.38}$$

  However, the liability side of CVA is a different story. We saw in Chapter 8 that it represents the cost that we would incur to hedge our own default. The way our counterparty can do that is by buying a CDS on us, hence paying our credit spread ($s^{CDS,our}$) for that credit insurance. However, that is totally irrelevant to us, as that is not a cost that we have. The cost that we have to hedge out our own default is *borrowing* the cash we need to pay in the future, and putting it aside so that we can use it as time progresses. The cost of doing that self-hedge is given by our funding spread, which is the credit spread (s^{our}) plus a liquidity spread (l^{our}).[6] As a result, our cost of hedging our own default is given by

$$CVA_{liab} = \widehat{ENE^*_0} \cdot (s^{CDS,our} + l^{our}) \tag{I.39}$$

  Putting all this together,

$$P_{CounterpartyRisk} = \widehat{EPE^*_0} \cdot s^{CDS,cpty} \tag{I.40}$$
$$+ \widehat{ENE^*_0} \cdot s^{CDS,our} \tag{I.41}$$
$$+ \widehat{ENE^*_0} \cdot l^{our} \tag{I.42}$$

  Equation I.40 leads to the asset side of CVA, Equation I.41 to the liability side of CVA, and Equation I.42 to a Liquidity Value Adjustment (LVA).

$$CVA_{asset} = \widehat{EPE^*_0} \cdot s^{CDS,cpty} \tag{I.43}$$
$$CVA_{liab} = \widehat{ENE^*_0} \cdot s^{CDS,our} \tag{I.44}$$
$$LVA = \widehat{ENE^*_0} \cdot l^{our} \tag{I.45}$$

LVA: This last LVA term could be seen as a funding risk term, as it is a cost that is attached to the liquidity-funding premium. This number reflects the fact that the bond market has a different liquidity environment to that of the CDS market. Basically, two institutions can agree on a credit insurance contract just by signing the respective CDS document, but if one wants to buy or sell an actual bond with that same credit risk, that bond needs to be found somewhere, and there is an actual limited availability of them. In other words, they are not infinite in the real life, as the Black–Scholes model assumes. Hence LVA is an adjustment that we must do to the risk-neutral value of a portfolio of trades to account for the real liquidity constrains that we face in the funding and credit market.

- **Funding Risk:** In addition to the liquidy-funding risk that we have just seen, there are two other sources of funding risk to be considered.

CollVA: Firstly, we are going to have to fund the net collateral that we have to post (and receive) from all our trading positions. If s_t^{borrow} and s_t^{lend} are the spread over the risk-free rate at which we can borrow and lend unsecured cash, then, following the same idea of the CVA derivation, the Collateral Cost Ajustment ($CollCA$) and Collateral Benefit Adjustment ($CollBA$) are

$$CollCA_0 = \int_0^T EPE_t^{collateral} \cdot DF_t^* \cdot s_t^{borrow}\, dt \tag{I.46}$$

$$CollBA_0 = \int_0^T ENE_t^{collateral} \cdot DF_t^* \cdot s_t^{lend}\, dt \tag{I.47}$$

where $EPE_t^{collateral}$ and $ENE_t^{collateral}$ represent the expected positive and negative exposure of the net collateral needs. Then,

$$CollVA = CollCA + CollBA \tag{I.48}$$

HVA: Secondly, we are going to have an additional funding adjustment from the difference in cash needs from the trade that we have with a counterparty and the trade that we buy in the market to hedge its market risk. For example, we may hedge a swap with annual coupons sold to a client with a swap with quarterly coupons bought in the market. If $(x_t + h_t)\, dt$ represents the cashflows in the hedging trade, where x_t would be the cash flows from the perfect hedging trade, then we need to fund the extra h_t if we need to borrow it, or we can lend it out too if we have an excess of it. This means that we are going to have two new adjustments: Hedging Cost Adjustment (HCA) and Hedging Benefit Adjustment (HBA) that, following again the ideas previously expressed, are

$$HCA_0 = \int_0^T EPE_t^h \cdot DF_t^* \cdot s_t^{borrow}\, dt \tag{I.49}$$

$$HBA_0 = \int_0^T ENE_t^h \cdot DF_t^* \cdot s_t^{lend}\, dt \tag{I.50}$$

where EPE_t^h and ENE_t^h represent the expected positive and negative exposure of the extra hedging cash needs. Then,

$$HVA = HCA + HBA \tag{I.51}$$

FVA: Given that we have seen that there are three sources of funding risk, funding-liquidity (LVA), collateral funding (CollVA), and extra hedging funding (HVA), we can put all this together into one term to simplify things somewhat:

$$FVA = CollVA + LVA + HVA \tag{I.52}$$

- **Capital Risk:** We saw in Chapter 14 that capital does represent a real cost for an organisation. This is definitely the case in regulated financial institutions as they need to do a capital allocation in their balance sheet as dictated by their regulators, but it could also be the case in unregulated organisations if they want to build a risk reserve against unexpected losses. In this context, following again the thinking process shown before, we can see KVA as

$$KVA_0 = \int_0^T EK_t \cdot DF_t^* \cdot r_{c,t} \cdot dt \tag{I.53}$$

where EK_t is the expected capital at time t and r_c is the rate of cost of funding that the institution has. We saw in Chapter 14 that a good candidate for this r_c is the Weighted Average Cost of Capital (WACC).

Putting all this together, the manufacturing cost of a book of derivatives is going to be given by

$$P_{manufacturing} = \mathbb{E}\left(\int_0^T DF_{0,t}^* x_t \, dt\right) + CVA + FVA + KVA. \tag{I.54}$$

Funding double-counting: We saw in Section 12.8 that in order to avoid funding double-counting, or seen from another angle, in order to reflect our actual act of managing our own default, we may want to make $CVA_{liab} = 0$ and $LVA = 0$.

The value to me: Putting together Equations I.34, I.35, and I.54, the *value to me* of a derivative is given by

$$VtM = Profit_{RiskNeutral} - CVA - FVA - KVA \tag{I.55}$$

where

$$Profit_{RiskNeutral} = \int_0^T DF_{0,t}^* \mathbb{E}(\delta_t) \, dt \tag{I.56}$$

The break-even point: For a trade to be economical for a dealer, the *VtM* must be positive. As a result, the spread δ_t needs to be such that

$$Profit_{RiskNeutral} > XVA \tag{I.57}$$

where $XVA = CVA + FVA + KVA$.

From a derivatives user standpoint, *VtM* is typically going to be a negative number. It needs to be small enough so that this *VtM* cost is meaningfully related to the real risks it hedges.

Relation to the Black–Scholes risk-neutral world: In the classic Black–Scholes risk-neutral theoretical world,

- $XVA = 0$, as there is no default, funding, or capital risk.
- $\delta_t = 0$, as we are looking for the "fair" price.
- $Profit_{RiskNeutral} = 0$, due to the Law of One Price.

Consequently, $VtM = 0$ in that framework.

Notes

1 The Banking Industry, OTC Derivatives and the New XVA Challenge

1. Securitising in this context means that the customers give the house as "collateral" for the loan, so that if they cannot pay the loan the bank can reposses the house. These secured loans are, thus, less risky for the bank than unsecured ones, so the bank is willing to charge a relatively lower interest for it.
2. Money is not a static thing in the sense that its value changes over time. For example, if I can obtain a 5% rate if I deposit my money in a bank, then \$95 today will be worth around \$100 in 1 year and, for the same reason, \$100 in 1 year are worth \$95 today. As a result, the present value of future payments that I have changes as interest rates fluctuate. We will expand much more on this concept throughout the book.
3. Roughly, if we give \$1 to 100 customers to pay back in the near future, and we expect that, on average, two of them will not pay back, the value of those loans is \$98. However, if something happens, like an economic recession that we did not foresee, and 10 out of those 100 customers are not able to pay back the loans, then their value needs to be marked down to \$90 and we will see an \$8 loss on our balance sheet.
4. Not the bank's equity itself, but equity from another company.
5. Number invented for illustrative purposes.
6. Some readers may be surprised by this, but these things do happen as some of these derivatives can be very sophisticated and, sometimes, senior management has not paid enough attention to them.
7. It must be noted that, given the certain flexibility there is here, the industry is trying to define eligible products for each book that minimise uncertainty.
8. For example, let's say that the bank's balance sheet is five times the equity. Then a 20% increase in the size of value of the assets will double the equity size and, also, a 20% drop in the value of the assets will dilute all the equity. However, let's say that the balance sheet is 100 times the equity; in that case a 20% increase in the value of the assets will multiply the value of the equity by 20, but a small decrease of only 1% in the value of the assets will eat all the equity out and the bank will have to close down. This example shows how high leverage means high potential return for the bank as a business, but also means high risk for itself and for the economy. Hence a central question here is how much is high or low leverage? This topic is constantly being addressed by regulators and the financial industry.
9. For example, a reserve ratio is not imposed by the government in the UK or in Sweden, it is 1% in the eurozone, 2.5% in Switzerland, 4% in Russia, 9% in Israel, in the US it can be none, 3% or 10% depending on the account size, etc [1].
10. Another way to look at this could be by comparing the financial industry to the real estate industry. An investment services house is like a construction company in the sense that they buy, build and sell stuff, but a financial services company is like a real estate agent: they provide management and trading of houses and, as such, their business is (in principle) unaffected by changes in the property prices. Real estate agents are of course affected by the prices in the sense that when prices go up, it usually means that activity increases, so they tend to carry more business, but this is an indirect connection. Similarly,

financial service providers have more business in growing economies, but the nature of their business is, at first order, "market neutral".

11. Climbing mountains above 8,000 metres.
12. A call option on the underlying X with a strike K is a contract that pays to us, on a given date (T), the difference between those two prices when it is in our favour, but nothing happens if it is against us, multiplied by a notional N. That is, it pays $N \cdot \max(X_T - K, 0)$.
13. Market risk arises from the change in price of a financial derivative as a result of changes in the underlying risk factors it depends on; e.g., interest rates, FX rates, etc.
14. Also known as "Black–Scholes" theory.

2 The Roots of Counterparty Credit Risk

1. There are two typical places where this confusion arises. One is CVA, the other one is IRC. As we are going to see, CVA is the market price of counterparty credit risk. As such, CVA has market risk embedded in it, as the price of that risk fluctuates as, for example, credit spreads change. However, two very different things are the default risk in a book of trades, and the changes in the price of hedging out that risk (its market risk). The Incremental Risk Charge (IRC) imposed by the Basel Committee also creates confusion as that charge tries to measure how much my book of trades can change in value (hence, it is a market risk) when credit conditions deteriorate in the market place. IRC is a market risk charge. We will expand on these concepts much more during subsequent parts of this book.
2. As a first proxy, we can say that this yield curve is the difference between the interbank curves of both yield curves of each currency. This proxy was very good up to 2008, but it has caused important miss-pricing since then.
3. Interestingly, the ISDA and BIS data indicate that the financial system may have been, in aggregate, overcollateralised in 2011.
4. ISDA Margin Survey 2014.
5. It must be noted that if a framework along the lines of the example is stated in the CSA, it may create difficulties for a counterparty precisely when its credit rating gets downgraded, similarly to break clauses. This could create liquidity constraints to the counterparty and should be managed appropriately.
6. Repo for bonds, stock lending for equities, or even a cross-currency swap for FX.

3 Exposure Measurement for Uncollateralised Portfolios

1. For now, we assume that we need only one yield curve per currency.
2. See Chapter 17 for details on backtesting.
3. This applies not only to yield curves, but to any kind of forward looking curve, like credit spreads, commodities, etc.
4. We are choosing three parameters as an illustrative example. In principle, the more parameters the more accurate the analytical function will be compared to the actual yield curve.
5. A quantity that we add to a basic interest rate to come up with the rate that we actually want.
6. The generic term often used for equity borrowing and lending, due to its similarities to the bond repo market.

7. Let's say that we model an index as an individual GBM process, and its constituents also with individual GBM processes. Dependency is modelled with a correlation matrix between all the Brownian numbers that drive all GBM processes. If in our portfolio we are long on the stocks that form the index and short on the index, the value of the portfolio in the future will be positive in some scenarios, and negative in some others, since the positions are not correlated correctly and hence *the exposure will be considerably higher than the basis risk we observe in the data.*
8. Typically via Cholesky or Spectral decomposition.
9. Injected via very low interest rates and the money that multiplier banks provide; see Section 1.2.
10. See Appendix E.
11. See Chapter 10.
12. We would need a liquid market of standard and digital CDSs.
13. This is the effect that is often mistaken by a mean reverting process in the hazard rate.
14. As with equities, the correlation matrix may be too large, as we will typically have from a few hundred to a few thousand credit spreads to model.
15. CDS obligors that share the same economic environment, for example from the same country or industry sector, tend to move in parallel.
16. See the Empirical Analysis approach.
17. The spread over the "risk-free" rate needed to price the bond at par.
18. This spread is due to differences in the markets these products trade in. One important reason is liquidity in the cash market versus the derivative market. A bond is a physical product with a specific size available whilst CDSs are synthetic products which can be created, in principle, by any two institutions willing to do so.
19. Sorry, a bit morbid, but it is what it is.
20. E.g., the effort grows with n^3 for Choleski decomposition.
21. As mentioned, each scenario is a possible state of the world in the future. All trades need to be priced with the same state of the world before netting.
22. We say "roughly" because overhead calculations and distributed computing will tend to deviate it from a linear relationship.
23. Reportedly, Lehman Brother's portfolio of OTC derivatives had 930,000 of them.
24. Reportedly this is the maximum number of scenarios any institution has in its Monte Carlo simulations. In fact, many report less than that, but never lower than 1,000.
25. Using the Aggregation rule.
26. Interestingly this applies even when CVA cannot be arbitraged.
27. A very clear example is when modelling the credit spreads. For decades it has been thought that credit spreads were mean reverting, while if you look into the data you do not see any mean reversion at all [73].
28. In this trade we have settlement risk coming from the fee, but that risk is usually managed separately from counterparty risk.
29. These models are obviously extremely useful and are standard market practice. Black–Scholes–Merton made a significant contribution to the financial industry and to the world economy with their work, but it should be highlighted that the lack of precision in the distribution functions can potentially lead to miss-pricing and miss-risk-management. In fact, there are hedge funds that arbitrage this limitation. This issue is particularly relevant in risk-management, as the lack of precision is most severe in the tails of the distribution functions.
30. E.g., as already said computational effort goes with n^3 for Choleski decomposition methods.

4 Exposure Measurement for Collateralised Portfolios

1. That is, we post collateral when the value of the netting set is below −\$5m, and we receive collateral when the MtM of the portfolio is above +\$1m. The difference in the size of threshold implies that we are perceived as having a stronger credit quality than the counterparty.
2. If a USD bond, in USD; if EUR cash, in EUR; etc.
3. It simulates the value of the risky non-cash collateral as per the simulation models that we have. For example, if we have equity as collateral, and we model it with the typical SDE $dS = S\mu\, dt + S\sigma\, dW$, it assigns a new value to S_i with S_{i-1} as the starting point and a $\Delta t = t_i - t_{i-1}$. We can also refer to this as the state of the collateral at t_i given the filtration $\mathcal{F}_{i-1}$.
4. As said, daily is becoming increasingly popular.
5. That makes sense for pricing, for example, where we are interested in average values, but it is not best practice for risk management, where we are interested in tail events. In risk management the market standard is to use the full margining frequency.
6. Products with a $\Delta = 1$ to its underlying. Forwards are delta-1 products, options aren't.

5 Exposure Allocation

1. We have not discussed yet how to calculate these single number exposure metrics. Any reader not familiar with these concepts should just assume they are one single number that measures counterparty risk.
2. See Appendix C.
3. See Appendix C.
4. When doing this, the sum of the contributions E_i of each trade may not be equal to the overall portfolio exposure. Hence a dilation factor should be applied to the contributions so that $E_{Port} = \sum_i E_i$.
5. Especially in the early days, when these concepts of netting and risk where fairly new to a large part of the financial community.
6. Consider the example previously mentioned of a netting set composed of two trades, being nearly identical except that we are long on one and short on the other one: let's say that the individual exposure of trade 1 is \$10, trade 2 is \$9, and the exposure of both trades in a netting agreement is \$1. With this allocation technique, trade 1 "contributes" with \$0.53 of exposure and trade 2 with \$0.47; both numbers are positive even though they offset the risk of each other quite strongly.
7. One of the largest incentives to investments is uncertainty of future costs. CVA is usually charged upfront, so dealing desks can completely forget about counterparty risk once it is paid.
8. The first year average of the non-decreasing EPE profile. See Chapter 9 for details.
9. The risk metric that is quite common is the maximum of the PFE profile, but let's analyse it here for EPE instead so we can relate it to the results from the EEPE analysis. These results can be expanded to any risk metric based on the maximum value of a profile.

6 Proxies for Exposure Measurement

1. Let's remember that we need to price each trade around 1,000,000 times.
2. By ideal CSA we mean daily frequency and zero thresholds, initial margin, minimum transfer amount, and rounding.

3. This is equivalent to multiplying each $\Delta V_{i,t_j}$ by that quantity.
4. This reflects losses coming from changes in the value of the institution's balance sheet as a result of changes in the market variables like interest rates and FX rates.
5. Or the desired MPR.
6. μ and σ are the drift and volatility of the underlying S.
7. We can also manipulate the drift of the underlying RFE by changing the interest rate in the Black–Scholes option pricer, but then we are also changing the discount factor, so we must do this with care.
8. All short or long.
9. See Section 3.4.
10. In general, volatilities will decrease as trades roll-over, but it does not need to be necessarily the case due to netting effects. We may need to do a trade analysis first to then come up with an estimation of the volatility profile.

7 Default Probability, Loss Given Default, and Credit Portfolio Models

1. This is for OTC derivatives. For loans it is Exposure + Accrued Interests + CCF x Undrawn.
2. Strictly speaking, the CDS payment is triggered if a "credit event" takes place, which does not need to be a technical default. These credit events are very extensively defined with long legal documents. In this text we are going to refer to these credit events as "defaults" in general, without going into legal details.
3. 1 bps = 0.01%.
4. This is a high level outline of the CDS market. There are many other features to be considered, like upfront payment, credit seniority, etc.
5. This spread described here is the so-called "par" credit spread: the CDS coupon, as a percentage of notional, that makes the value of the CDS zero at inception. The CDS market has evolved recently, and CDSs with upfront payments and an adjusted running coupon are now common. However, an equivalent par spread can always be calculated.
6. Strictly speaking, s is not a price, but a running coupon. However, practitioners usually refer to it as a price because it mostly determines the value of a CDS contract. This is the same way in which an implied volatility highly determines the value of an option and, hence, option experts talk about a "10% volatility at-the-money option" to refer to its price too.
7. This is usually done with numerical techniques, as this inversion may not be possible analytically.
8. Fixed by the market, the traded credit spread value.
9. Also known as a "binary" CDS.
10. There were some attempts to use stochastic LGD models to price CDOs at the peak of the 2008 prices, as the traded prices went to levels so unreasonable that standard CDO pricing techniques, with constant LGD, were giving unreasonable results. However, these attempts never really took off as standard in the industry.
11. In particular, it is compulsory in regulatory capital models.
12. Through-the-cycle default probability for BB bonds is around 1% in many classifications of credit ratings.
13. As data indicated that we were at the bottom of a credit cycle, the point-in-time PD was lower than the through-the-cycle PD, suggesting that default rates were due to increase "soon", as assessed by a number of experts.
14. Perhaps important to emphasise is a clear distinction between the probability of default and the default rates. The probability of default is a number, assigned to a group of institutions, that estimates how many

of them will have defaulted within the next year (in percentage). The default rate is the realised number of defaults we have seen in the market, for a given time period.

15. In this example, it is 12: three regions multiplied by four sectors.
16. This is often referred to as "correlation structure" too, even though they are not the same; we can have very different dependency structures with the same correlation factor.
17. A Merton-like model, described in detail later in the chapter.
18. Adjusted for non-rated corporates. D is defaulted. It considers that once in a D, a company does not leave that state.
19. It must be said that some people claim the opposite, i.e., that the credit quality at origination is an LGD important driver. That could explain the proximity between observed LGDs for secured and unsecured transactions. Banks usually lend unsecured to investment grade companies and secured to sub-investment grade. To my knowledge, there has not been a specific paper on this topic, but possibly there will be something coming in the future.
20. I.e., in years of recession.
21. Some people seem to argue that the relation is not between year of default but year of recovery, i.e., if most of your cash flow is recovered in a downturn year you recover less than if it is collected in a good year.
22. As said, we'd need two liquid credit products with the given counterparty to calibrate LGD to the market. We practically never have that.
23. The one used to calculate the CVA-VaR regulatory capital charge, to be discussed in detail in Chapter 9.
24. As we will see in Chapter 10.
25. Interestingly, one could argue the same for pricing when there isn't a liquid CDS for the counterparty, as in this case we cannot hedge default events. However, the standard in the industry is to calibrate CVA to market-implied credit spreads *always*.
26. The risk coming from events that have low probability but high impact, such as, for example, when many of our counterparties default at the same time.
27. The regulators, version of Economic Capital.
28. A portfolio of an infinite number of infinitesimal positions, as opposed to a limited number of real positions.

8 Pricing Counterparty Credit Risk

1. By CVA related we mean CVA paper losses in the balance sheet.
2. For simplicity, we are going to assume zero risk-free interest rates.
3. This is the "average" positive exposure. An average does not make much sense when there is only one possible event, but this argument will be extended if this game is played lots of times, or if this trade is in a large book of trades.
4. The term's structure of credit spreads is assumed to be flat, for simplicity.
5. We are assuming here that the CDS spread is the same as the spread over government risk-free bonds that a bank needs to pay to fund itself (i.e., that there is no credit spread basis risk), and that there are not problems in finding any amount of funding at all. We will break these assumptions later, but let's start like this for illustration purposes.
6. In fact, leveraging is at the core of the modern economic system, as the money multiplier mechanism created by banks is what makes the credit cycle function.

7. Reminder: $EPE_t = \int_{-\infty}^{\infty} P^+ \Psi_t(P) dV$, $ENE_t = \int_{-\infty}^{\infty} P^- \Psi_t(P) dV$, $(\cdot)^+ = \max(\cdot, 0)$, $(\cdot)^- = \min(\cdot, 0)$, $MtM_t = EPE_t + ENE_t$, $MtM_t = \mathbb{E}(P_t)$.
8. By marginal is meant that the counterparty has survived up to that u and defaults in the infinitesimal period du after u.
9. Often it is only studied in its wrong-way-risk version, as it is the negative side of this effect, but I will show in Chapter 10 how the positive side of it (right-way-risk) is as important as its negative side for pricing, risk allocation, and risk management.
10. Which, at the end of the day, is the same: a dealing desk is going to charge as much as it can within the competitive brackets, and will try to have as few costs as possible, like any other business.
11. Or any agreed set of days.
12. Strictly speaking, the ISDA documents do not state that it *must* be considered, but that it *may*. Unfortunately this leaves room for interpretation.
13. The point on the left in Figure 8.3.
14. As the defaulted one does not exist any more, see [25].
15. What we are doing here is a Taylor expansion of s in λ. That expansion is good only for small values of λ.
16. In fact, any trades that cannot be treated properly in a bank's Monte Carlo counterparty risk system must be taken out of the calculation for regulatory capital, and then capital for these trades are added on top. This is quite punitive for the bank because (i) any netting effects within the netting set is lost and (ii) the capital charge applied to that exotic trade is high.

9 Regulatory Capital

1. Banco Bilbao Vizcaya Argentaria, Bank of America, Bank of China, Bank of New York Mellon, Banque Populaire CE, Barclays, BNP Paribas, Citigroup, Commerzbank, Credit Suisse, Credit Agricole, Deutsche Bank, Dexia Group, Goldman Sachs, HSBC, ICBC, ING Bank, JP Morgan Chase, Lloyds Banking Group, Mitsubishi UFJ FG, Mizuho FG, Morgan Stanley, Nordea, Royal Bank of Scotland, Santander, Societe Generale, Standard Chartered, State Street, Sumitomo Mitsui, UBS, Unicredit Group, Wells Fargo.
2. In particular, the Leverage Ratio is the "average of the monthly leverage ratio over the quarter based on the definitions of capital and total exposure"[59].
3. With notional exchange.
4. €8 billion of average month-end notional in June, July, and August, tested annually.
5. Plus remargining period.
6. Possibly to be replaced by an Expected Shortfall (ES) metric.
7. Reportedly, some banks had an $x > 1$ at the hype of the 2008 crisis, even though the Basel accord doesn't contemplate it.
8. The average of the tail in the probability distribution, at the given confidence level.
9. See Appendix D.
10. When this is so, the model is deemed "not fit for purpose" and must be changed under the present rules. See Section 17.1.
11. Also called Comprehensive Risk Measure (CRM).
12. Strictly speaking, RWA will be taken from the maximum of (i) average $\text{VaR}_{99.9\%,1yr}$, calculated weekly at least, over the last 12 weeks, and (ii) the most recent $\text{VaR}_{99.9\%,1yr}$.

13. By this it is meant that it is the charge that seems to have more "bells and whistles" in its calculation, but for the underlying models to come up with a VaR, IRC, etc., charge can be as complex as the ones used for CCR.
14. See Chapter 10.
15. Formerly known as the Non-Internal Models Method (NIMM).
16. By "margin" is meant the Variation Margin.
17. Margin Period of Risk, often 10 days.
18. E.g., derivatives dependent on the difference between two risk factors.
19. Or up to maturity date, if it is smaller than one year.
20. We are including EPE_{reg} in this list of definitions to avoid confusion in the reader should he or she read Basel documentation. However, this EPE_{reg} is not used for the capital calculation.
21. The ASRF model assumes an infinitely small number of counterparties as opposed to a limited number, but the risk of the latter is greater than the theoretical risk of the former.
22. For example, if "through-the-cycle" PD for BB companies is 1%, in economically good years only, say, 0.8% may default, but in bad years we could have a, say, 1.5% default rate.
23. In this model, it is assumed that the LGD is independent of the PD. Also, that the LGD is always the same constant number.
24. The calculation uses the ASRF model and the correlation function explained later in this section.
25. Exceptions: For residential mortgages, $\rho^2 = 0.15$. For qualifying revolver retail exposures $\rho^2 = 0.04$. For other retail $\rho^2(PD) = 0.03\frac{1-e^{-35PD}}{1-e^{-35}} + 0.16\left(1 - \frac{1-e^{-35PD}}{1-e^{-35}}\right)$. $Adj(S)$ is zero for banks and sovereigns.
26. Not for governments.
27. Data in this regard is very limited, as very few companies default directly from an investment grade (say, AA). Most defaults happen after a gradual deterioration of the credit quality of the name, and so data analysis can be somewhat troublesome.
28. As opposed to the one that delivers the highest EaD per counterparty or per netting set.
29. See reference [59], page 40, for details on this.
30. This multiplication can create a power effect in the MPR: if, for a given netting set, the original MPR was ten days and there is a dispute that goes beyond ten days, then MPR gets set to 20 days. Then, if there is another dispute that goes beyond 20 days, MPR gets adjusted to 40 days, etc.
31. With an additional discounting correction for non-IMM institutions.
32. This LGD is market implied, which is different to the LGD used in the IRB approach for the CCR capital calculation (Section 9.2.4), computed with either internal models or rating agencies, that is historically calibrated.
33. Reminder: $(\bullet)^+ \equiv \max(\bullet, 0)$.
34. The marginal survival probability S_i^{marg} between two time points t_{i-1} and t_i is defined as the survival probability between t_{i-1} and t_i subject to survival at t_{i-1}. If the survival probability at each point is given by S_i, then $S_i^{marg} = S_{i-1} - S_i$. If $\overline{\lambda}_i$ is the cumulated default intensity at t_i then, by definition, $S_i = \exp\left(-\overline{\lambda}_i \cdot t_i\right)$. A commonly used approximation is to say that $\overline{\lambda}_i \simeq s_i/LGD$, where s_i is the credit spread at t_i. Hence Equation 9.33 for S_i^{marg}. This is then floored at zero as this calculation is only an approximation and it could deliver a negative marginal survival probability, which would be senseless.
35. The reader may have noted that we say "EE_i is the regulatory Expected Exposure". This means that the Expected Exposure profiles *must* be the same in the CCR (see Section 9.2.4) than in this CVA-VaR calculation. This has created some challenges in banks, as Expected Exposure profiles tend to be calculated using

market-implied calibrations for the purpose of CVA pricing, but historical calibration for the purposes of risk management and CCR capital calculation.

36. This definition of *eligible* CVA hedges for regulatory capital calculation purposes created some friction in the industry, as CVA is also sensitive to non-credit risk factors like interest rates or FX rates. To minimise CVA volatility, banks put in place hedges in these risk factors but the regulatory capital charge does not recognise them.

10 Right and Wrong Way Risk

1. Furthermore, this is often referred to as "market-credit" *correlation*, but the reader should bear in mind that is a language simplification, as correlation is only one basic measure of dependency. In general, we are interested in the dependency structure, which will have a correlation factor reflecting the linear interdependency of the factors at stake, but that can be oversimplified if we refer to it only as a correlation effect. We are going to see later how this oversimplification can lead to exposure miss-calculations.
2. The reader can find the basics of CDS contracts in Section 7.1.
3. In fact, the Basel Committee recognises this through its CCR capital charge: in such cases the models must be set up so that "EAD equals the value of the transaction under the assumption of jump-to-default" [59].
4. Let's say that we have a cross-currency swap with an emerging market (EM) government that is fully and symmetrically collateralised. Because of that, the only credit risk that we have is the close-out risk. The key special feature of this type of trade is that, as data shows (Asian crisis, Russia, Argentina, etc.), there tends to be a big devaluation jump immediately *after* default. For this reason, if we are long on the EM currency in the defaulted trade, for example, our naked market hedges are short on that currency, hence those hedges should provide a positive profit after default, and so the real credit risk is quite small. If we are short on the EM currency in the trade, the opposite happens. This is especially important in collateralised facilities as in those cases we are highly sensitive to short-term market moves. This phenomenon is characteristic of FX transactions with emerging markets; it does not appear in any other asset class or counterparties. The key element here is that the counterparty is so important that its default triggers a jump in the FX rate *after* default.
5. The authors deem that by "market values" the same is meant as what we call here "exposures".
6. By RFE models is meant all the models of market factors (e.g., interest rates, FX rates, equity prices, commodity prices, implied volatilities, credit) that drive the exposure metrics.
7. The Girsanov Theorem.
8. Per MC engine time step.
9. $V_{t,i} = (P_{t,i})^+$, where $P_{t,i}$ is the price of the portfolio of trades at the MC time point t and scenario i.
10. For example, suppose that we are trying to measure WWR in a counterparty with an annual default probability of 1%. If our MC simulation is calculating the default probability over a time step of one week, the default probability over that period will be approximately 0.02%. This means that, on average, we will have to generate 5,000 default simulations to obtain one single default event. As a result, the number of simulations $N \cdot M$ will explode. This is clearly suboptimal. The second version proposed, in which default events are simulated conditionally on a set of values for the market factor, should improve this situation compared to the first version, though it will also be too computationally demanding in most cases.
11. For CVA, we calculate unidirectional CVA. For initial margin, the maximum of the PFE profile at 99% confidence. We use the PFE profile at 90% confidence for exposure management, and for regulatory

capital, both the EEPE and the regulatory CS01. We model collateral with an ideal CSA: daily margining, zero threshold, zero minimum transfer ammount, zero rounding, etc., and an MPR period of ten days.

12. As of the first quarter of 2013.
13. See Figure 10.3.
14. A balance between $g(x)$ and the geometric nature of δP.
15. Because if we are long a receiver swap, we are effectively short a payer swap.
16. Appendix H.
17. To gain some intuition about why this happens, let's say that WTI volatility is very low, nearly zero. In that case, the CVA prices will be very similar with or without a DWR framework because the WTI scenarios in an MC simulation will be all concentrated around the starting WTI price and, then, the weightings w_i in all scenarios will be nearly the same; hence it is almost like having no DWR effect. We can see this in Figure 10.12: CVA price with and without DWR modelling converge for small volatilities. As the volatility increases, the way the CVA price changes will be different with or without DWR effect, as the DWR effect will provoke a spread of the weightings w_i. This spread will be higher as the volatility increases. Hence, the vega is quite different with or without DWR effects.
18. Being a bit more technical, if the price of the trade (or portfolio of trades) is given by $P = f(x)$, the MC simulation that calculates credit metrics will evaluate the trade in every scenario using that function and, then, when calculating risk metrics like EPE or PFE, it will weigh each scenario by $w = g(x)$. Since $g(x)$ will generally be a monotonic function, the case for right or wrong-way risk is quite straightforward when $f(x)$ is also monotonic. The strength of the DWR will be determined by $g(x)$ and typically the volatility of the market factor x too, as the higher volatility the more likely that the market factor x will reach points of very high or very low default probability.
19. For the standard CSA used in the examples, with ten days of close out risk.
20. See Appendix H.
21. Perhaps with the special exception of collateralised FX trades with sovereign emerging markets, where the default itself can trigger a jump in the underlying market and, hence, a scenario-based approach may be needed as explained.

11 CVA Desk, a Bilateral Dance

1. Although we have seen that an equivalent running premium can be calculated too.
2. The equivalent of the CVA hedges that a CVA puts in place.
3. A digital CDS pays the full notional if a default of the CDS obligor occurs.
4. Importantly, this is in addition to the credit spreads of the counterparties in a netting set, since if the book of trades contains credit derivatives, both $\widehat{EPE}_t$, and $\widehat{ENE}_t$ will be sensitive to their underlying credit spreads.
5. Via gamma or cross-gamma effects.
6. By a "liquid counterparty" is meant a firm whose CDS trades quite frequently, with low bid/offer spreads and good availability of tenors.
7. Plus other hedges and operational costs.
8. Daily margining, zero threshold, zero MTA, etc.
9. Or the Loss Given Default $LGD = 1 - RR$.
10. Or very close to it.

11. Strictly speaking, due to *joint* default probability effects, the probability of a number of counterparties defaulting in a given time period is lower than the sum of each individual probability. However, this portfolio effect is ignored when pricing default risk as we are interested in each netting set as a stand-alone entity for pricing and default hedging purposes. This joint default effect could be taken care of by the capital calculation and KVA if needed.
12. We are going to repeat a few ideas already mentioned, for the benefit of those reading only this CVA chapter.
13. Meaning that the capital is higher, often notably higher, than the true economic risk would indicate, should that analysis be done.
14. Effective Expected Positive Exposure.
15. It must be the same EPE profile used in the CCR calculation.
16. That is why it is a market risk charge: it is a charge on the *volatility* of the price of counterparty risk, not on the counterparty risk as such. We could have massive CVA, hedged, so that the CVA charge is very small, or we could have small CVA, not hedged, that could give very high CVA charge.
17. Sometimes this argument is criticised by saying that XYZ could only do that with a few trades, as if it did it across the board it would be killing all its business. In my view, if XYZ decides to take advantage of those events to close its business, so be it; it will book a profit compared to it having tried tried to close it on the previous Friday.

12 FVA Desk, the Effect of Funding

1. We are implicitly saying that AAA is the best proxy for a so-called "default-free" counterparty.
2. If the counterparty defaults.
3. If we default. This is a negative number.
4. We'll discuss later what this risk-free rate is. Let's say for now that it exists, and it is the rate at which a "non-defaultable" organisation can borrow unsecured cash.
5. OIS stands for Overnight Index Swap. It is a swap whose floating side is the average of the interbank overnight lending rate.
6. The more concentrated a market is in only a few sellers or buyers, the more power those players will have to influence the price.
7. With a "risk-free" discounting curve.
8. We are not going to use any formulas for P_{sale}, for now, because we want to highlight that, if we are to run a business in a realistic manner, we need to realise that this price is agreed by people, and people are indeed driven by non-rational thinking. This may come as a surprise to many readers, that have a strong quantitative background and tend to think that economic decisions are driven by rational numbers; however, this is not true. This is very nicely explained by the Nobel price winner in economics Daniel Kahneman in his book *Thinking, Fast and Slow* [49].
9. Later in the book we will introduce also the cost of capital and other costs. Let's leave those aside for now, to avoid further complications.
10. Often we are going to have to borrow cash, but it could happen that the trade creates a funding benefit so we can lend cash instead, or borrow less.
11. See Section 11.10.
12. As far as hedging is possible given the market's restrictions.

13. Also, as far as hedging is possible given the market's restrictions.
14. By "portfolio" we mean all the positions that the organisation has.
15. A "funding set" is a portfolio of financial instruments that an institution decides to manage so that there are cross-instrument funding benefits within the funding set, but not outside of it. For example, a typical funding set is the book of derivatives.
16. In a frictionless market.
17. Or $CVA_{liab} + LVA$.
18. Provided the market is liquid.

13 Calculating and Managing FVA

1. To be more precise, these are the unsecured forward short spreads.
2. FVA being a portfolio calculation, the riskiness of DF^* comes from the survival probability of ourselves and all counterparties. Strictly speaking, in the calculation of the $\mathbb{E}(\cdot)$ operator in Appendix I.2, we need to account for all the cases in which counterparties survive and default, with a joint probability distribution function, and considering all possible survival cases in a Monte Carlo simulation. In practice this strictly correct portfolio FVA calculation is undoable in most cases, with portfolios of many counterparties, so DF^* can be relaxed to generically averaged survival probabilities. Sometimes this is relaxed all in all by disregarding the risky side of it: $DF^* \simeq DF$.
3. By this is meant cashflows like option premiums, coupon payments, not the collateral calls.
4. One grid is each a collection of 1,000,000 values, coming from the 100 time steps × 10,000 scenarios.
5. That is, i ranges from 1 to 10,000, and j from 0 to 100 in our example.
6. Under the Black–Scholes risk-neutral pricing framework as a proxy.
7. It must be noted that, if we prefer, we could sum up P from each netting set, as the result is going to be the same as summing up all individual trades.
8. As a reminder, let's illustrate the source of this funding risk with the following example. Let's imagine we are a derivatives dealer and sell an option to a client for, say, \$1. After we do that sale, we are going to set a symmetric hedging position in an exchange; we are going to buy the same option, from an exchange, at, say \$0.9. In this deal, we make \$0.1. If we imagine now that both the bilateral agreement with the client and with the exchange operates on an uncollateralised basis, for illustration purposes, then what we are going to do is transfer \$0.9 from the payment we receive from the client to the exchange, and the other \$0.1 is going to stay in our pockets. As a result, we are going to have a funding benefit in this example: we can use that \$0.1 to reduce overall funding needs. Another example takes place if we hedge a swap with another swap that has the same tenor but different payment frequency; in this case the swap payments are not going to match each other, hence creating funding risk.
9. Here we are assuming that, quite nicely, $IM^{hedge} \simeq \alpha\, P_t$. If this is not a good proxy for the initial margin, the equations become a bit more complicated, but the general idea remains unchanged.
10. Only cash collateral for variation margin, all in the same currency, daily margining, fully collateralised, etc.
11. Another way of seeing this is that if the institution decides to lend cash out, above the risk-free rate, it will then be taking credit risk, which would need to be accounted for, typically by discounting those loans at a risky discount factor.
12. But not completely, as an initial margin can still be posted with highly rated bonds.
13. Strictly speaking, there could still be some residual interest rate risk, equity-repo risk, or dividend risk.

14. This example illustrates that the haircut method can overestimate risk: it will require more collateral than is actually needed.
15. The simulation of the collateral needs to be done with the appropriate dependency structure with all other risk factors that affect the risk-neutral price of the trades in the netting set.
16. This includes the so-called "cash equivalents", like US government debt securities.
17. The theorists will oppose this very strongly, and indeed they will claim that this type of behaviour introduces a bias in the market that creates, eventually, arbitrage opportunities. "That is the case because the changes in the credit spread of a financial institution, and subsequently in the funding rate, already takes this balance sheet credit quality issue into account, and so introducing that extra incentive creates a distortion in the market", they would say. This highlights both the strength and weakness of the FVA framework. What that tier-1 bank is effectively doing is saying that the market sensitivity to the credit quality of my balance sheet is not correct, and so it decides to amend it accordingly. The problem and the strength of FVA is that it is not a number driven by finance fundamentals, but by market experience, and so nearly anything is valid with it. And this is precisely why theorists oppose it.

14 KVA Desk, Capital Management, and RAROC

1. It must be noted that, strictly speaking, the calculation of a single product value may not consider the correlation effects that are considered in the portfolio economic capital model, so a correction for this may be implemented too.
2. This was a historical mistake in financial institutions. Since bonuses were based on absolute profits in many cases, trading units had an actual incentive to place risky positions: a lot to win if things go well, but nothing to lose (as the bank's capital was absorbing the losses) if things go bad.
3. And in the unlikely event that the coin falls on its side, the toss is void and we repeat it.
4. The cash we need to have at the beginning of the game to ensure we will not go to jail.
5. The reader can also consult Green *et al.* [40].
6. The reader is referred to Section 12.5.1 for a discussion of the difference between price and value.
7. I am is not excusing bank managers with this. In fact, quite the contrary. I am only describing what I see.
8. As far as the economic capital model is a an accurate model.
9. Having said that, also the industry is clearly gearing up momentum in this direction. The author hopes this chapter helps in that respect.
10. Due to different netting effects, for example.
11. It would make this chapter too long, and would extend beyond its scope.
12. At the time of this book going to press. This may change soon to an expected shortfall at the 97.5% confidence level, and with varying time horizons. See Chapter 9.
13. Or any other market risk metric in a similar way, like expected shortfall.
14. If we want to go finer, we can put an idiosyncratic component on top, but it will be difficult to notice any difference in the KVA value.
15. An alternative model could be using a typical Black-Karasinsky model for the spread. We can model the spread directly, and it will substantially deliver the same results as if we model the hazard rate of the counterparty.
16. That is, its price is roughly zero.
17. That is, it has a positive value in our favour.

18. A very expensive alternative is to do this calculation both in an advanced and non-advanced framework, and say that KVA_{exit} is somwhere in the middle of those two. However, this seems quite impractical, as this means that the bank will have to implement more than one regulatory capital model.
19. The dealing desks manage only the market risk.

15 XVA Desks: A New Era for Risk Management

1. The Market Risk component of KVA was noticeably higher than the rest, but that is because it is assumed that the swap is not market-risk hedged, often a non-realist scenario.
2. Needless to say, things are not as clean as that. There is a self-feeding loop so that if costs increase across the board, prices tend to go up and demand decreases, and vice versa, creating a market-pricing feedback loop. However, the point is to understand that prices are not given by a Black–Scholes equation, but mainly by the reality of costs and benefits, offer and demand, to which the Black–Scholes world only adapts *as closely as its limiting assumptions permit.*
3. See Chapter 19 for a more complete view of the controversial topic of bonuses.
4. Originally these two problems were mixed up, as we can see that our funding curve is another yield curve. However, it is better to split it up, as it is the market standard now.
5. Plus the value to the customer of not having to may too much upfront; but that is another problem.
6. From its default-risk capital charge.
7. Daily margining, zero threshold, zero minimum transfer amount, only cash as collateral in the correct currency, no initial margin, etc.
8. And, potentially, OIS risk.

16 Model Risk Management

1. Even if risk models are different to pricing models, they often use pricing models to reprice derivatives.
2. Typically, first and second order derivatives of the price with respect to the market factors.
3. Unless the model accounts for the bid/offer spread, as opposed to pricing to mid-market, which is usually the case.
4. When a model goes live, its inherent P&L will be seen in the actual accounting P&L, so putting a model-risk capital charge on it could be double-counting market risk capital. The model risk capital should account for the risk that models fail and for the volatility that they may create without double-counting it in other parts of the capital calculation.
5. Anyone disagreeing with this, please think of another derivative that is more complex, and now calculate CVA on it. This CVA calculation will be much more complex than the derivative pricing itself, however complicated that was.
6. By "mark-to-market" is meant calculating the price of the derivative as inferred from the market. When there is no market for the derivative, then a model calculates what that price would be under no-arbitrage conditions. However, all that is based on theoretical conditions as there isn't precisely any market where arbitrage may be exercised or tested.
7. Leaving aside for now liquidity stress scenarios.
8. Although this may change to 97.5% Expected Shortfall (ES) following the potential capital changes explained in Chapter 9.

9. It is important to note that this is not really the "worst" case, as sometimes naively thought; in fact, we should expect that, every year, around two or three days market losses will be above the 99% VaR. Alternatively, a 97.5% Expected Shortfall is used because it delivers a similar level of risk to 99% VaR.

17 Backtesting Risk Models

1. At the time of this book going to press, the industry is expecting a change to an Expected Shortfall metric. See Section 9.2.2.
2. However, the Basel Committee expresses concerns that "the overall one-day trading outcome is not a suitable point of comparison, because it reflects the effects of intra-day trading, possibly including fee income that is booked in connection with the sale of new products". Given this difficulty in dealing with this intra-day trading and fee income, it is left to the national regulator to manage this issue as found appropriate.
3. In fact, the Basel Committee was more refined than this. It considered both the probability that an accurate model appears as inaccurate and vice versa, and came up with those 95% and 99.99% as the most appropriate limits for the bands.
4. This implies that, by construction, the backtesting methodology does not account for autocorrelation in the market. This is a limitation of this method.
5. See Section 9.2.2
6. Reminder: a Contingent Credit Default Swap (CCDS) is the credit derivative traded internally in financial institutions, whose price is CVA.
7. Furthermore, even if we had the data, we can easily say that the dynamics of the markets more than a century ago were quite different to present day ones, hence backtests going that far back would have quite a limited value.
8. I.e., zero autocorrelation.
9. For example, in the case of 20–80% envelopes this number is $I_E = 40\%$. In the case of 10–90% envelopes this number is $I_E = 20\%$.
10. For example, $\frac{1}{x(1-x)}$ will give more weight to the tails of the probability distribution.
11. For example, a weight along the lines of $\frac{\text{Number of trades sensitive to the currency}}{\text{Total number of trades}}$ for an FX model test will give focus to those currencies that are more important to the portfolio.
12. See Kenyon [50].
13. For the sake of clarity, the reader should note that $F_i \in (0,1)\,\forall i$.
14. For a time horizon Δ.
15. For example, in risk management we are most interested in the quality of the models in the tails of the distribution, so we may want to use the Anderson–Darling metric. In capital calculations or CVA pricing we are interested in the whole of the distribution function, so we may want to use Cramer–von Mises. If we are happy with small general deviations, but never want large deviations, then we may want to use Kolmogorov–Smirnov.
16. Zero is attained in the limit: $\lim_{N\to\infty} D = 0$.
17. That artificial time series must have exactly the same time data as the empirical collection of values x_{t_i}.
18. Strictly speaking, what we can say is that if $\widetilde{D}$ falls in a range with high probability in $\psi(D)$, then the model is compatible with a "perfect" model with high probability.

18 Systems and Project Management

1. It is important to note that we are not getting rid of the numerical noise, we just choose to become blind to it.
2. 10,000 scenarios by 100 time points.
3. Obviously, these numbers depend on the actual system. We should take them as general guidelines.
4. Regulatory capital for those sophisticated trades needs to be processed via "standard rules" that are very capital punitive.
5. Sometimes we have to wonder at what is the real meaning and accuracy of a prediction so far away in the future.
6. As a result, the Basel approach to add capital per netting set is unnecessarily conservative and creates uneconomic incentives.
7. In this section we are going to say "file" here in a generic way. It could obviously be a set of files, databases, etc.
8. By a vectorised language is meant one in which a variable can be a vector, matrix, hyper-matrix, etc., and where operations with them can be handled with one single command in the code. Matlab is an example of this.
9. In my experience this iterative cycle is very frequent and important in RFE models, though it tends to be much simpler for pricers, as we already have an existing pricing function that we are trying to match.

19 Central Clearing and the Future of Derivatives

1. The Basel Committee states that the confidence level should be at least 95% [58].
2. If margins are calculated with a 99% confidence level.
3. I.e., no rehypothication, no investments, all collateral in segregated accounts, etc.
4. Notably LCH.Clearnet, CME, ICE, Eurex, and DTCC [68].
5. Systematically Important Financial Institution.
6. Sometimes it is thought that stressing market conditions is equivalent to wrong-way risk. That is not correct, as is explained in Chapter 10.
7. At least this is how they were, and how they are supposed to be.
8. Arguably because monetary policy typically takes around two years to have an effect, while other deeper productivity enhancing measures can take much longer. Western governments live in four-year democratic cyles and, consequently, policy-makers do not tend to apply unpopular measures whose positive effects can only be felt after the next election.
9. This is inevitable because, up to now, banks could generate more profits out of sizing up their business in parallel to the real-economy monetary boost, though this may not be as easily possible any more given that the facilitator of that link between the banking business and the real economy was the provision of credit, which has now exhausted its current cycle.
10. It must be noted that it will be very good for the overall economy if this happens. Exotic trades are ideal instruments for final derivative users (e.g., corporates, pension funds) to have risk hedging products tailored to their needs. A key role of derivatives dealers is to facilitate that risk hedging environment so that everyone benefits from it.
11. The last few years has witnessed an important increase in the budgets and headcount of the risk management function in financial institutions. However, we must not get mislead here: most of this increased

effort has been focused at coping with the overwhelming increased regulatory requirements, not at truly enhancing the internal risk management function. Hence this increased effort will decrease the risk of banks only as long as the regulatory requirements match the true risks an institution has, which is far from well in most or all cases.

12. It must be noted that it could also mean that the LGD is very high. However, to obtain a RW of 2% with a PD of 0.03% (the regulatory floor) and a maturity of five years for example, we need an LGD of 3%, which is *very* unrealistic. This is especially the case if we realise that a CCP default will create, quite frankly, a super-crisis, so assuming such a high LGD seems very unrealistic.
13. There seems to be a general tendency with some regulators to try to standardise as much as possible capital calculations. This is because, so it is said by those regulators, it doesn't feel right that two similar banks have different regulatory capital in the same book of trades. This is a result of the degree of flexibility that regulatory frameworks offer and the different historical datasets that each bank may have. The solution that some are pushing for is to simplify and standardise the regulatory capital calculation. This will no doubt make regulatory capital calculation more stable across different institutions. However, a negative consequence of moving in that direction is that capital calculation will be less sensitive to the true risks a bank has, hence providing the incentives to steer trading activity into being detached from its economic fundamentals, and hence creating the seeds for future market dislocations.
14. E.g., selling protection on the index and buying protection on its individual constituents, to cash in the index misprice.

A The Money Multiplier

1. We say "usually" because different central banks define each M in a different way.

C Calculation of Exposure Contributions

1. This can be any exposure metric: an EPE profile, a PFE profile, a regulatory EEE profile, or any other metric coming from them where the time component disappears: CVA, peak PFE, EEPE, etc.
2. In practice, we get the price in the scenario with a portfolio price closest to the exposure, or we get the scenario with the price immediately below and above the exposure and do an interpolation between them.
3. When doing this, the sum of the contributions E_i of each trade may not be equal to the overall portfolio exposure. Hence a dilation factor should be applied to the contributions so that $E_{Port} = \sum_i^N E_i$.

G The Merton Model Equity–Credit Dependency

1. It must be empathise the difference between the asset volatility σ_A, a model convenience, to the equity volatility σ_E, an observable. The "reasonable" range for σ_A was estimated from a range of reasonably wide values for σ_E (between 10% and 100%) in the case in which $A_0 = 2\,D$.

H Right and Wrong-Way Risk in Equity Options

1. Historical correlation of 78%.
2. The calculations shown in Figure H.2 were done with 500,000 scenarios to minimise the noise.
3. Uncollateralised short options have zero credit risk, so there is no need for that graph.
4. As of January 2013.

I A Full XVA Valuation Framework

1. Remembering that these $\mathcal{P}_i$ are subject to both counterparties having survived up to time t.
2. Strictly speaking, P_t should be the replacement value of an equivalent derivative should a default occur. That replacement trade would be with a counterparty with equivalent credit quality of the defaulted entity. This leads to two problems: firstly, what "credit quality" should we use? One second before the company defaults? One year before? This is not clear. Secondly, this creates a mathematical recursive loop, as P_t should contain also a counterparty risk adjustment. It is market practice to ignore this refinement in the calculation because it is very difficult to solve and, importantly, it hardly makes any difference in most practical cases.
3. It should be noted that both cash flows in terms 2 and 3 must have a negative sign. In the case of 2, this is because it is a loss that we could incur. In the case of 3, this is because it is a net gain, but P_t^- is a negative number, and so it needs a negative sign to counteract it.
4. Integrated in continuous time.
5. E.g., our counterparty is one of our sister companies in another country, of which we own a large part of the stock, but not all.
6. Strictly speaking, that cost is given by the full funding rate, but we can discount the risk-free rate from it as, in principle, we can deposit those funds into a quasi-non-defaultable entity, like the central bank, or invest them in government bonds that should return the risk-free rate back to us. So the net cost is the funding spread.

Bibliography

[1] Wikipedia, Reserve Requirement.

[2] *Supervisory framework for the use of "backtesting" in conjunction with the internal models approach to market risk captial requirements*, tech. rep., Basel Committee of Banking Supervision, 1996.

[3] *Determinants of recovery rates on defaulted bonds and loans for North American corporate issuers*, tech. rep., Moody's Investors Service, 2004.

[4] *An explanatory note on the Basel II irb risk weight functions*, tech. rep., Basel Committee of Banking Supervision, 2005.

[5] *International convergence of capital measurement and capital standards*, tech. rep., Bank for International Settlements, 2006.

[6] *Guidelines for computing capital for incremental risk in the trading book*, tech. rep., Bank for International Settlements, 2009.

[7] *Isda close out amount protocol*, tech. rep., International Swaps and Derivatives Association, 2009.

[8] *Revision to the Basel II market risk framework*, tech. rep., Bank for International Settlements, 2009.

[9] *Market review of OTC derivative bilateral collateralization practices*, tech. rep., International Swaps and Derivatives Association, 2010.

[10] *Reflecting the fair value of financial instruments, a survey*, tech. rep., Ernst & Young, 2010.

[11] *High yield default and recovery rate volatility in recession and recovery*, tech. rep., Fitch Ratings, 2011.

[12] *CVA capital charges: a comparative analysis*, tech. rep., Solum Financial Partners, 2012.

[13] *Principles for financial market infrastructures*, Committee on Payments and Settlement Systems, Bank for International Settlements. April 2012.

[14] *Counterparty risk and CVA survey*, tech. rep., Solum Financial Partners and Deloitte, 2013.

[15] *Fundamental review of the trading book: a revised market risk framework*, Basel Committee on Banking Supervision, Bank for International Settlements. October 2013.

[16] E. Altman, *Current conditions in the distressed and high yield bond and bank loan markets and outlook*, in RJ Chambers Memorial Lecture, Sydney, 2006.

[17] E. Altman, A. Resti, and A. Sironi, *Default recovery rates in credit risk modelling: a review of the literature and empirical evidence*. 2003.

[18] E. I. Altman, B. Brady, A. Resti, and A. Sironi, The link between default and recovery rates: theory, empirical evidence and implications, *Journal of Business*, 78 (2005).

[19] T. Baer, A. Mehta, and H. Samandari, *The use of economic capital in performance management for banks: a perspective*. McKinsey & Company, January 2011.

[20] L. Becker and M. Cameron, No CVA exemptions in Basel III rules, *Risk Magazine* (2013).

[21] N. Benjamin, A. Cathcart, and K. Ryan, *Low default portfolios: a proposal for conservative estimation of default probabilities*. 2006.

[22] F. Black and M. Scholes, The pricing of options and corporate liabilities, *Journal of Political Economy* (1973).

[23] C. Bluhm, L. Overbeck, and C. Wagner, *An introduction to credit risk modeling*, Chapman and Hall.

[24] D. Brigo and M. Masetti, *A formula for interest rate swaps valuation under counterparty risk in presence of netting agreements*. www.damianobrigo.it, 2005.

[25] D. Brigo and M. Morini, Close-out convention tensions, *Risk* (2011).

[26] C. Burgard and M. Kjaer, *Generalised CVA with funding and collateral via semi-replication*. December 2012.

[27] M. Cameron, Osfi copies us CVA charge to protect canadian banks, *Risk Magazine* (2013).

[28] M. Cameron, The black art of FVA, part ii, *Risk Magazine* (2014).

[29] L. Caprioti and J. Lee, Adjoint credit risk management, *Risk Magazine* (2014).

[30] L. Carver, Deutsche bank loses eur 94 million on CVA mismatch, *Risk Magazine* (2013).
[31] G. Cesari, J. Aquilina, N. Carpillon, Z. Filipoviċ, G. Lee, and I. Manda, *Modelling, pricing and hedging counterparty credit exposure*, Springer, first edn, 2009.
[32] J. C. G. Cespedes, J. A. de Juan Herrero, D. Rosen, and D. Sounders, Effective modeling of wrong way risk, counterparty credit risk capital, and alpha in Basel II, *The Journal of Risk Model Validation*, 4 (2010), pp. 71–98.
[33] M. Choudhry, *The Principles of Banking*, Willey Finance, first edn, 2012.
[34] K. Chourdakis, E. Epperlein, M. Jeannin, and J. McEwen, *A cross-section across CVA*, tech. rep., Nomura, 2013.
[35] D. Duffie and H. Zhu, *Does a central clearing counterparty reduce counterparty risk?* March 2010.
[36] J. Frye, Collateral damage, *Credit Risk* (2000).
[37] J. Frye, A false sense of security, *Risk* (2003).
[38] M. Fujii, Y. Shimadaz, and A. Takahashi, *A note on construction of multiple swap curves with and without collateral.* www.ssrn.com, 2009.
[39] M. Gibson, *Measuring counterparty credit exposure to a margined counterparty*, tech. rep., Federal Reserve Board, Washington, D.C., 2005.
[40] A. Green, C. Kenyon, and C. Dennis, *KVA: Capital valuation adjustment.* February 2004.
[41] Y.-T. Hu and W. Perraudin, *The dependence of recovery rates and defaults.* 2002.
[42] J. Hull and A. White, CVA and wrong way risk, *Financial Analysis Journal*, 68 (2012), pp. 58–69.
[43] J. Hull and A. White, The FVA debate, *Risk*, 25 (2012).
[44] J. Hull and A. White, *Collateral and credit issues in derivatives pricing.* Jan 2013.
[45] F. Iacono, *Quantifying right-way and wrong-way risk*, Riverside Risk Advisors, 1 (2011).
[46] N. Iqbal and S. A. Ali, *Estimation of probability of defaults (pd) for low default portfolios: an actuarial approach.* http://www.ermsymposium.org.
[47] C. James, *Raroc based capital budgeting and performance evaluation: a case study of bank capital allocation.* The Wharton School, University of Pennsylvania, October 1996.
[48] E. P. Jones, S. P. Mason, and E. Rosenfeld, Contingent claims analysis of corporte capital structure: an empirical investigation, *Journal of Finance*, 39 (1984).
[49] D. Kahneman, *Thinking, fast and slow*, Penguin Books, 2011.
[50] C. Kenyon, *Model risk in risk factor evolution*, in Confererence: Measuring and Controlling Model Risk, London, 2011.
[51] C. Kenyon and A. Green, Pricing CDSS' capital relief, *Risk Magazine* (2013).
[52] C. Kenyon and R. Stamm, *Discounting, Libor, CVA and Funding*, Palgrave Macmillan, 2012.
[53] C. Lazaregue-Bazard, Exceptions to the rule, *Risk Magazine* (2010).
[54] J. Lee, *Credit value adjustment (CVA).* Presentation, Citi Global Markets. June 2010.
[55] R. C. Merton, On the pricing of corporate debt: the risk structure of interest rates, *Journal of Finance*, 3 (1974).
[56] T. Newton, Europe edges towards three-pronged CVA exemption, *Risk Magazine* (2013).
[57] S. Noh, Lesson from Lehman Brothers for hedge fund managers: the effect of a bankruptcy filing on the value of the debtor's derivative book, *The Hedge Fund Law Report*, 5 (2012).
[58] B. C. of Banking Supervision, *Recomendations for central counterparties*, tech. rep., Bank for International Settlements, 2004.
[59] B. C. of Banking Supervision, *Bassel III: A global regulatory framework for more resilient banks and banking system*, tech. rep., Bank for International Settlements, 2011.
[60] B. C. of Banking Supervision, *Margin requirements for non-centrally cleared derivatives*, tech. rep., Bank for International Settlements, 2013.
[61] B. C. of Banking Supervision, *The standardised approach for measuring counterparty credit risk exposures*, tech. rep., Bank for International Settlements, 2014.
[62] S. Ou, D. Chiu, and A. Metz, *Corporate default and recovery rates, 1920–2010*, tech. rep., Moody's, 2011.
[63] A. Pallavicini, D. Perini, and D. Brigo, *Funding value adjustment: a consistent framework including CVA, DVA, collateral, netting rules and re-hypothication.* December 2012.
[64] P. Parkinson, *Supervisory guidance on model risk management*, tech. rep., Federal Reserve, 2011. Document SR11-7.

[65] V. Peterbarg, Funding beyond discounting: collateral agreements and derivatives pricing, *Risk* (2010).
[66] J. Pimbley, *Monetary policy risk? deflation!* www.garp.org, June 2014. Maxwell Consulting, LLC.
[67] M. Pykhtin and D. Rosen, *Pricing counterparty risk at the trade level and CVA allocations*, Finance and Economics Discussions Series (2009). Division of Research and Statistics and Monetary Affairs. Federal Reserve Board, Washingtong DC.
[68] J. Quarry, B. Wilkinson, T. Pittaway, and J. Cheah, *OTC derivatives clearing*, tech. rep., Oliver Wyman (2012).
[69] D. Rosen and D. Saunders, CVA the wrong way, *Journal of Risk Management in Financial Institutions*, 5 (2012), pp. 152–272.
[70] I. Ruiz, *Technical note: on wrong way risk.* www.iruizconsulting.com, February 2012.
[71] I. Ruiz, Backtesting counterparty risk: how good is your model?, *Journal of Credit Risk* (2014).
[72] I. Ruiz, P. D. Boca, and R. Pachón, Optimal right and wroing way risk, *Financial Analysts Journal* (2014).
[73] I. Ruiz and P. del Boca, Modelling credit spreads for counterparty risk: mean-reversion is not needed, *Intelligence Risk*, 2 (2012).
[74] I. Ruiz and R. Pachón, *Advanced counterparty risk and CVA via stochastic volatility* (2012).
[75] I. Ruiz, R. Pachón, and P. del Boca, *Optimal right and wrong way risk.* www.iruizconsulting.com, April 2013.
[76] M. Turlakov, Wrong-way risk, credit and funding, *Risk Magazine*, 1 (2013).
[77] F. Vrins and J. Gregory, Getting CVA up and running, *Risk* (2011).
[78] J. Zhang, *How useful are economic capital and regulatory capital as risk measures: an empirical assessment and implications.* IACPM, 2011. Moody's Analytics.

Index

Printed and bound by CPI Group (UK) Ltd, Croydon, CR0 4YY